Illustrator® CS4 Bible

Illustrator® CS4 Bible

Ted Alspach

WILEY

Wiley Publishing, Inc.

Illustrator® CS4 Bible

Published by
Wiley Publishing, Inc.
10475 Crosspoint Boulevard
Indianapolis, IN 46256
www.wiley.com

Copyright © 2009 by Wiley Publishing, Inc., Indianapolis, Indiana

Published by Wiley Publishing, Inc., Indianapolis, Indiana

Published simultaneously in Canada

ISBN: 978-0-470-34519-1

Manufactured in the United States of America

10 9 8 7 6 5 4 3 2 1

For general information on our other products and services or to obtain technical support, please contact our Customer Care Department within the U.S. at (800) 762-2974, outside the U.S. at (317) 572-3993 or fax (317) 572-4002.

Library of Congress Control Number: 2008939706

Trademarks: Wiley, the Wiley logo, and related trade dress are trademarks or registered trademarks of John Wiley & Sons, Inc., in the United States and other countries, and may not be used without written permission. Adobe and Illustrator are registered trademarks of Adobe Systems Incorporated in the United States and/or other countries. All other trademarks are the property of their respective owners. Wiley Publishing, Inc. is not associated with any product or vendor mentioned in this book.

Wiley also publishes its books in a variety of electronic formats. Some content that appears in print may not be available in electronic books.

About the Author

Ted Alspach is the author of more than 30 books on desktop publishing and graphics as well as hundreds of articles and reviews on related topics, including the *Illustrator Bible* series and the *Illustrator For Dummies* series. Ted was the Group Product Manager for Illustrator and the Creative Suite at Adobe Systems for more than seven years. Ted also runs Bézier Games (`http://games.bezier.com`), a board game publishing company, and has designed more than a dozen games and expansions for popular games, including *Rapscallion*, *Seismic* (Atlas Games), *Start Player*, and *Ultimate Werewolf*.

Acknowledgments

Thanks to everyone at Wiley who put in the time and effort to produce another great edition of this book!

Credits

Senior Acquisitions Editor
Stephanie McComb

Project Editor
Christopher Stolle

Technical Editor
Dennis R. Cohen

Copy Editor
Kim Heusel

Editorial Manager
Robyn Siesky

Business Manager
Amy Knies

Senior Marketing Manager
Sandy Smith

Vice President and Executive Group Publisher
Richard Swadley

Vice President and Executive Publisher
Barry Pruett

Project Coordinator
Kristie Rees

Graphics and Production Specialists
Stacie Brooks
Carrie A. Cesavice
Andrea Hornberger
Jennifer Mayberry

Quality Control Technician
Laura Albert

Proofreading
Christine Sabooni

Indexing
Christine Spina Karpeles

Preface

You're holding in your hands the biggest, most thorough, and most helpful guide to Adobe Illustrator you'll find anywhere.

The Illustrator CS4 Bible is the book I wrote because I couldn't find the book I wanted about Adobe Illustrator. Now I have it, and believe it or not, I'm constantly using my own book as a reference. I'd love to tell the world, "Sure, I know that," without putting them on hold while I search the index for the Reset Tracking to 0 shortcut for a Mac (⌘+Shift+X, by the way). There's just too much about Illustrator for any one person to keep in his or her head at one time; now, this latest edition of this book gathers all the Illustrator information you can't remember and makes it more available and easier to follow than the plot twists on your favorite soap opera.

If you're at your local bookstore looking at the different Illustrator books, don't just pick this one because it weighs the most (sorry about that . . . I get more thank-you letters from chiropractors who've stayed in business because of this monstrosity) or because it works great as a booster seat for your two-year-old nephew. Instead, take a look-see through these pages, which are stuffed to overflowing with in-depth Illustrator information that you just won't find anywhere else.

What's New in This Edition

Illustrator CS4 has added a variety of new features and has revamped some of the old standby tools. In this edition, you find complete coverage of the new functions and features as well as extensive explanations on how these new features work. For a complete listing of new features and enhancements, see Chapter 1.

Is This the Illustrator Book for You?

I've been to bookstores and seen the other Illustrator books out there. Some of them are quite good. Some of them are fairly awful. But none of them can match the *Illustrator CS4 Bible* for thoroughness, usefulness, or completeness. I've left no vector-based stone unturned.

Here are more reasons why the *Illustrator CS4 Bible* is the best overall book on Illustrator:

- **The most complete coverage of Illustrator:** This book isn't big because I wanted to hog all the retail book space for myself (of course, that's not a bad idea), but it's because I tried to include every possible thing you'd ever want to know about Illustrator. From learning the basics of drawing to creating outstanding special effects with vectors and rasters, it's all here.

- **Fun, original, different artwork to illustrate the techniques and capabilities of Illustrator:** When I say different, I'm not talking about performance art. Instead, I mean that each technique is created with a different piece of artwork. Some of it is simple, and some of it is complex — with each piece showing not only a particular feature but also other Illustrator capabilities.

- **Clean artwork without those annoying jaggies:** This is vector software. When you think of vectors, you probably think of smooth, flowing paths that don't look like someone filled in a bunch of squares on a sheet of graph paper. So, instead of using screenshots for paths shown in this book, each path was painstakingly drawn in Illustrator. I think you'll appreciate the difference.

- **Top-notch technical prowess:** Again, the *Illustrator CS4 Bible* has gotten the best possible people to do a technical review of the book. Previous editions were technically reviewed by Eric Gibson, the lead technical support engineer for Illustrator; Andrei Herasimchuk, who designed and implemented the Illustrator interface; and Sandra Alves, a user interface designer for Adobe Photoshop. This current edition has been technically reviewed by Dennis R. Cohen, technical editor of the last four editions of the *Illustrator Bible* as well as a contributor to and technical reviewer of numerous Illustrator and Photoshop titles.

- **Perfect for teaching:** If you know Illustrator inside and out, you'll find that the *Illustrator CS4 Bible* is the best teaching tool available for Illustrator, with examples and explanations that perfectly complement a teaching environment. Many computer-training companies teaching Illustrator use this book, as do schools and universities.

- **Real-world examples and advice:** Illustrator doesn't exist in a vacuum. Instead, it's often used in conjunction with other programs and in a variety of different environments and situations. Some people use Illustrator to create logos, others create full-page advertisements, and still others create entire billboards with Illustrator. Throughout this book, I present various real-world situations and examples that add to your understanding of each topic.

You don't need to be an artist or a computer geek to learn Illustrator with this book. No matter what your level of Illustrator experience is, you can undoubtedly find new things to try and will learn more about Illustrator along the way.

How to Get the Most Out of This Book

You may want to be aware of a few matters before you dive too deeply into the mysteries of vector-based graphics, Adobe-style:

- **Versions:** When you see the word *Illustrator,* it refers to all versions of Illustrator. When I stick a number after the word Illustrator, it's relevant to that version only. When Adobe releases the next major upgrade, look for a new version of this book to help you through it.

- **Menu and keyboard commands:** To indicate that you need to choose a command from a menu, I write something like MenuName ⇨ Command — for example, File ⇨ Save. If a command is nested in a submenu, it's presented as MenuName ⇨ Submenu ⇨ Command, as in Effect ⇨ Distort & Transform ⇨ Roughen. If a command has a keyboard command, I mention that for both Mac and Windows versions. For example, Save is Command+S on a Mac, which I'll present as ⌘+S. ⌘ corresponds to the ⌘ symbol on the Mac keyboard. The other Mac keys are spelled out — Option, Shift, Tab, and so forth. Save is Ctrl+S for Windows (Ctrl corresponds to the Ctrl key on the Windows keyboard). So, both platforms are specified by saying, "To save a document, press Ctrl+S (⌘+S)." The Windows convention is stated first and the Mac convention follows in parentheses. There are some other minor differences in things like menus, dropdown lists (popup menus), and so on, between the Windows and Mac versions, but you won't have any problem identifying these elements, no matter what you call them.

- **This is not a novel:** As much as I'd like you to discover plot intricacies, subtle characterizations, and moral fabric woven into the story, none of those things exist in this book. You can use this book in two ways:

  - Look up what interests you in the Contents or the Index and then refer to that section. Rinse and repeat as necessary.

  - Slowly, calmly work your way through the entire book, trying out examples (the funky steps that are almost everywhere) and techniques as you run across them. The book is designed to be read this way, with each chapter building on the previous chapter.

- **Mac and Windows versions used when writing this book:** I shuffled between a Mac and a Windows computer when writing this book: The Mac uses OS X 10.5 Leopard, while the Windows computer uses XP SP2. Few items, if any, should be different on Vista, Tiger, and other operating systems supported by Illustrator CS4, but there could be a few minor differences between the platforms.

What's a Computer Book without Icons?

Nonexistent, for the most part. I've included several icons throughout this edition that may make reading this book a little more enjoyable and helpful:

CAUTION Danger, Will Robinson!!! Caution icons let you know about all the nasty things that can happen and how to avoid them.

CROSS-REF These icons point you to other places in the book where you can find more information on a given topic.

NEW FEATURE These icons indicate what's new in Illustrator CS4. Kind of like finding a prize in your cereal box.

NOTE This icon notes interesting tidbits. It's sort of like having Cliff from *Cheers* rambling on about something every few pages — interesting but not essential. Just something I thought you might want to know.

TIP These icons indicate some sort of power-user secret that you absolutely need to know to be able to illustrate with the big kids.

What's Inside the Book

Here's a brief rundown on what to expect in this *Illustrator CS4 Bible*:

- **Part I: Illustrator Basics:** This section introduces the new features you find in Illustrator CS4. It also points out all the funky elements of the cool Illustrator interface and how to work with documents. It also covers the basics of drawing, painting, and working with objects. You learn how to color things, how to uncolor things, and how to delete those things when you don't like their colors.

- **Part II: Putting Illustrator to Work:** This section puts you to work by learning about type and how to fine-tune those paths and objects you drew in Part I. It also gives you a chance to bend and distort paths. Part II also contains a healthy dose of the hard stuff — such as compound paths, masks, blends, patterns, and type.

- **Part III: Mastering Illustrator:** This is the section that contains the nitty-gritty — and I don't mean the dirt band. Hot topics such as using Illustrator styles, effects, and techniques for creating fantastic graphics are presented. I even show you how to customize Illustrator to work better and faster.

- **Part IV: Getting Art Out of Illustrator:** This section describes the ways to get stuff out of Illustrator. Artwork can go to the print world, or on an all-expenses-paid trip to the Web, or into all the other great Adobe Creative Suite applications.

- **Appendix:** The appendix contains information on Illustrator CS4 shortcuts.

Contents at a Glance

Contents

Contents

Contents

Contents

Contents

Contents

Contents

Contents

Contents

Part I

Illustrator Basics

Chapter 1

What's New in Illustrator CS4?

I t's always exciting to see what's new in new versions of your favorite software. Longtime Adobe Illustrator fans certainly have a great interest in learning about the new features in Illustrator CS4, but those changes aren't of interest only to people who've used Illustrator extensively in the past. New users and people who currently use other products instead of Illustrator also want to know if this new version adds must-have features.

In this chapter, I introduce several features that have been added to Illustrator CS4 as well as some changes that make existing features easier to use or simply more powerful. Fortunately, Illustrator CS4 maintains a strong connection with the past so that you don't have to relearn much at all. Still, many of the changes that have been made are important ones that you'll find useful and fun. Let's dig in!

Multiple Artboards

For 13 versions (give or take a few depending on what you consider a version), Illustrator has supported a grand total of one page. Yes, there are clever workarounds (page tiling, resetting ruler origins, etc.) and even a plug-in from a third party that cleverly automates layers to simulate multiple pages, but the reality is that Illustrator was always a single-page application. That is until version CS4. In Illustrator CS4, you finally get multiple pages.

In order to prevent confusion with Adobe's awesome page-layout application, Adobe InDesign, the powers that be at Adobe have decided to call these new multiple pages *multiple Artboards*. Technically, Adobe is totally right in doing so here because Illustrator has always had the Artboard metaphor, not a page metaphor. And I'm going to call them multiple Artboards because everyone I know at Adobe who works on Illustrator will yell at me if I don't, but we know the truth: They're multiple pages.

If you're used to a page-layout application, you'll be thinking about heading right over to the Pages panel to check it out. But, of course, because they aren't *pages,* there's no such beast. In fact, there's no Artboards panel either. No, what Adobe has done is to give you an Artboard tool, which puts Illustrator into Artboard mode, as shown in Figure 1.1.

Multiple Artboards are shown in Artboard mode as regular rectangles on a darkened background.

Figure 1.1 actually has three *overlapping* Artboards; when you print pages 1–3 of this document, each Artboard is on a new page. Neat!

CROSS-REF   For more on multiple Artboards, see Chapter 3.

Welcome to the New and Improved Appearance Panel

Ever since Illustrator 9, the Appearance panel redefined how Illustrator was used, turning a powerful vector-illustration application into the powerhouse it is today. Several versions later, Adobe added all sorts of great extras to the Appearance panel, which is shown in Figure 1.2. Enhancements include hiding and showing effects, quick access to stroke/fill/transparency attributes, and one-click access to applied effects. It's all polish, but it's the super-shiny kind.

FIGURE 1.2

The updated Appearance panel has links and eyeballs.

In addition, the Graphic Styles panel icons are now much more representative of the actual style than in previous editions, which makes the thumbnails much more useful than before.

Dropdowns (and Popups) Aplenty

Those handy little dropdown lists (popup menus) you saw on the Appearance panel are in the Control panel too, and they're just as handy there as they are in the Appearance panel. Figure 1.3 shows how you can quickly access graphic styles from the Control panel.

FIGURE 1.3

You can choose styles from the Control panel with the ever-present dropdown lists (popup menus).

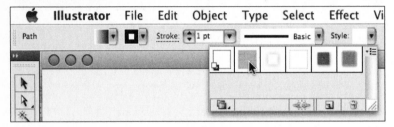

Align Points Like They're Objects

You can quickly align points by using the Align panel buttons (which are usually present on the Control panel too). Simply use the Direct Selection tool to select a series of points and then use an Align button to align or distribute the points quickly and accurately.

 **For more on using the various selection tools, see Chapter 6.**

Smart Guides That Are Really Smart

Smart Guides used to be weak little guys, lining up to various objects and paths and such as necessary but never really helping as much as they thought they were. CS4 Smart Guides, as shown in Figure 1.4, live up to their name by providing alignments that are intelligent and incredibly helpful.

FIGURE 1.4

Dragging this ellipse around with Smart Guides on shows alignments to everything else in the document.

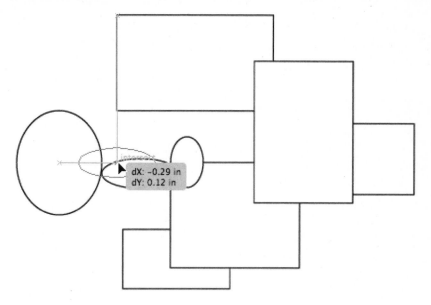

The Blob Brush Tool

Ever wish you could just drag a brush around the screen and bunch all the artwork under it into a single object? Well, that's what the Blob Brush tool does for you. Figure 1.5 shows what happened to Figure 1.4 when I dragged the Blob Brush tool through those paths.

FIGURE 1.5

Paths from Figure 1.4 have been Blob-brushed into one big path (with a little rectangle left over).

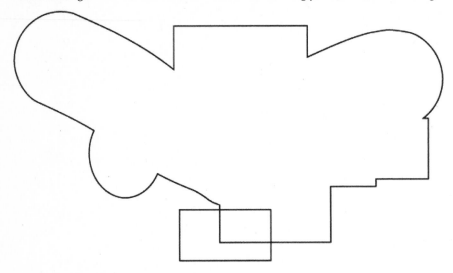

Color Separations Preview

If you've ever schlepped your Illustrator documents over to Photoshop just to see how they were going to separate, you'll absolutely love the new Separations Preview panel. It shows you not just CMYK separations but also spot color separations. Figure 1.6 shows the Separations Preview panel.

FIGURE 1.6

The new Separations Preview panel

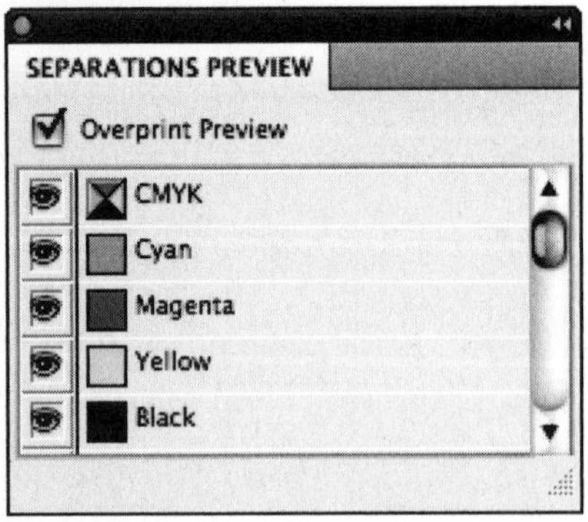

Color Blindness Preview

When doing color work, this handy new feature allows you to see what your document looks like to anyone who is color-blind. These options are available in the View Menu (View ➪ Proof Setup ➪ Color blindness — Protanopia-type and View ➪ Proof Setup ➪ Color blindness — Deuteranopia-type).

Gradient Enhancements

Gradients have been given a few notable enhancements, specifically the ability to apply opacity to a gradient stop and to edit gradients live directly on an object, as shown in Figure 1.7.

FIGURE 1.7

You can edit gradients directly on the Artboard.

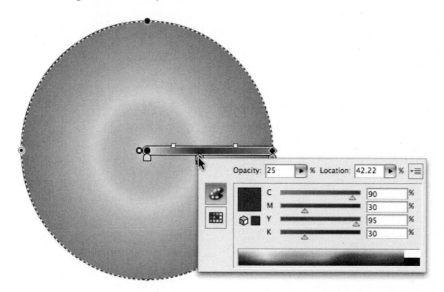

No More Filter Menu!

A relic from the early 1990s, the Filter menu has finally been removed from Illustrator. No longer will I have to patiently explain the difference between effects and filters and why you should never use filters, and if that's the case, why does the menu exist? This simplifies Illustrator tremendously and forces laggards (you know who you are) to finally start experiencing the wonders of effects.

Summary

Illustrator CS4 has some major changes and several minor ones compared to earlier versions. This chapter introduced several of the new features in order to give you a bit of the flavor of the new version. You learned that:

- Multiple Artboards are Illustrator's version of multiple pages.
- The Appearance panel has been given a facelift to allow for hiding and showing effects.
- Links and dropdowns are now part of the Control and Appearance panels, allowing for quick access to a number of features.
- Smart Guides are now super smart, with the ability to help you align to anything else in your document.
- Color separations can now be viewed directly inside Illustrator thanks to the new Separations Preview panel.
- Gradients can have transparency applied to gradient stops.
- The Filter menu is gone — and good riddance!

Chapter 2

Understanding Illustrator's Desktop

Not too long ago, commercial artists and illustrators worked by hand, not on computers. You might find it hard to believe, but they spent hours and hours with T-squares, rulers, French curves, and type galleys from their local typesetters.

Now, of course, most artists and artist wannabes spend hours and hours with their computers, mice, digitizing tablets, monitors, and on-screen type that they set themselves. A few traditional artists are still out there, but more and more make the transition to the digital world every day.

After that transition, computer artists usually come face-to-face with Illustrator, the industry-standard, graphics-creation software for both print and the Web. The following is a typical example of how people get to know Illustrator.

IN THIS CHAPTER

Launching and using Illustrator

Using shortcut keys

Working with Illustrator's interface

Moving around in Illustrator

Using Outline and Preview modes

Understanding the Edit functions

Picasso Meets Illustrator: Getting Started

Illustrator arrives, and the enthusiastic artist-to-be — I'll call him Picasso — opens the box, pops in the DVD, and installs the product. A few minutes later, Picasso launches Illustrator, opens a new file, and is faced with a clean, brand-new, empty document. A world of possibilities awaits — just a few mouse clicks away. But Picasso is a little intimidated by all that white space, just as many budding young writers wince at a new word-processing document with the lone insertion point blinking away.

So, Picasso decides he'll play with the software before designing anything for real. He chooses the Rectangle tool first, clicks, drags, and voilà! A rectangle appears on the screen! His confidence soars. He may try the other shape tools next, but sooner or later, Picasso starts playing with some of the software's other features. Eventually, he eyes the soon-to-be-dreaded Pen tool. And thus starts his downward spiral into terror.

Confusion ensues. Hours of staring at an Illustrator document and wondering "Why?" take up the majority of his time. Picasso doesn't really understand fills and strokes, he doesn't understand stacking order and layers, and he certainly doesn't understand Bézier curves.

Picasso goes through the tutorial three times, but whenever he strays one iota from the set-in-stone printed steps, nothing works. Picasso becomes convinced that the Pen tool is Satan's pitchfork in disguise. Patterns make about as much sense as differential equations. Then, he encounters things such as effects that can be edited later (huh?), miter limits for strokes (yeah, right!), and the difference between targeting a group or all the objects in that group (huh? again). All are subjects that seem quite foreign and impossible to understand.

Picasso had never used or seen software as different as Illustrator.

Ah, but you have an advantage over Picasso. You have this book. The following sections in this chapter take you through the interface and common editing commands that help you construct better illustrations. The other areas focused on are the basic Illustrator functions, from setting up a new document to understanding exactly what paths are and how Illustrator uses them.

CROSS-REF   **Don't worry if you don't already know what the Pen tool is — you learn lots more about each of the drawing tools in Chapter 4.**

Getting started with Illustrator

The first step in getting started is to install the software, which is slightly different depending on whether you use a Mac or a Windows computer. After the software is installed, you can launch Illustrator in one of the following ways:

- Double-click Illustrator's application icon.
- Double-click an Illustrator document, which automatically launches Illustrator.
- In Windows, choose Start ➪ Programs ➪ Adobe Illustrator.

Quitting Illustrator

Now that you know how to open the program, it's time to learn how to close it. You can end your Illustrator session at any time by choosing File ➪ Exit (or Illustrator ➪ Quit). This action closes the current document and exits the application. If you've not previously saved your document, Illustrator prompts you to do so before exiting the application. Of course, you can also choose to not save your changes. But be prepared for the consequences.

You can also close Illustrator in one of these ways:

■ **Mac OS X:** Click and hold the Illustrator icon in the Dock and then click Quit or Ctrl+click the Dock icon and then click Quit. You also have the option of pressing Ctrl, clicking the Illustrator icon in the Dock, and then choosing Quit or pressing ⌘+Q.

■ **Windows:** Right-click Illustrator's taskbar icon and then choose Close or press Alt+F4 and then choose Close from the popup menu. You can also close Illustrator by right-clicking the taskbar icon and choosing Close from the popup menu or by pressing Ctrl+Q.

Working with Illustrator's Interface

Understanding the interface is the first step in learning Illustrator. Adobe has kept its products looking consistent so that using all its programs together is easy. The tools, panels, and menus are pretty similar when using Illustrator, Photoshop, and InDesign.

Illustrator's interface offers many elements that let you work in optimum productivity. After you understand the interface, the creation process is much easier. When looking at Illustrator, you find the following:

■ **Document window:** The document window appears when you open an existing document or start a new document.

■ **Tools panel:** The Tools panel houses the tools you need to create amazing artwork. The tools are set as icons that represent what the tool looks like.

■ **Panels:** Panels allow you to choose options such as colors, line width, styles, etc. You can move panels around (floating) to any location, and you can also close or open panels as needed. Panels can be somewhat permanently docked together. If panels are docked together, changing the size of one panel tends to increase the size of one or more of the other panels.

■ **Control panel:** The Control panel is a special panel that normally appears just below the menu bar. This panel allows you to quickly choose applicable settings to the currently selected tool.

■ **Menu:** The main menu is across the top of the window in Windows and across the top of the main monitor on a Mac. The main menu allows you to access many of Illustrator's powerful commands. Illustrator also makes use of popup context menus that appear when you right-click (Ctrl+click) many objects.

■ **Zoom control:** The zoom control provides a quick method of zooming in or out in the document window so that you can see fine details or the entire drawing.

- **Status bar:** The status bar typically shows you what tool is currently being used. You can also choose from several different status bar options if you prefer to see other information, such as the current date and time, the number of undo levels that are available, the color profile that's being used, or the status of shared documents.

- **Artboard:** The Artboard is the part of the document window that contains the art you want to print. It's typically shown as a thin black rectangle.

Working in the document window

The document window, as shown in Figure 2.1, is where you perform all your work. It contains two main elements: the Artboard and the Pasteboard.

TIP You can move the printable area represented by the dashed lines using the Print Tiling tool (one of the two optional modes of the Hand tool). The Print Tiling tool is covered later in this chapter.

Illustrator windows act like windows in most other programs. You use the title bar at the top of the window to move the window around your screen. On the title bar is the name of the document. If you've not yet saved your document, the name of the document is Untitled-1, with the number changing for each new document you create. (Hint: Save it as soon as you create it!) Next to the title of the document is the current viewing percentage relative to actual size.

NOTE If you've not maximized the document window, the document's name appears in the document window's title bar rather than in Illustrator's title bar in Windows. This extra document window title bar reduces the size of your workspace, so you may want to maximize the document window in order to gain a little more room to work on your document.

TIP If you're using a Mac, after you save a document, you can ⌘+click the document name in the title bar to see a full path to its location.

The scroll bars let you see what is above and below or right and left of the current viewing area. I discuss scroll bars later in this chapter.

Three vital buttons help you close, minimize, and maximize the various windows you open in Illustrator. You find these buttons in the upper-left corner on a Mac and in the upper-right corner in Windows. In Windows, you also find a second set of these buttons — the upper set controls the entire Illustrator window, while the lower set controls the document window.

In addition to these buttons, Illustrator offers three options that help you quickly access your files. The Cascade, Tile, and Arrange Icons commands are all accessible via the Window menu:

- **Cascade:** When you have multiple files open, this command lines up all the title bars in a staggered (stairstep) arrangement going down and to the right.

- **Tile:** With multiple files open, this command tiles the windows next to one another to fill the application window.

- **Arrange Icons:** This command arranges your open files into neat rows.

FIGURE 2.1

The document window contains the page surrounded by the Artboard.

Control panel

Tools panel   Menu   Floating panels

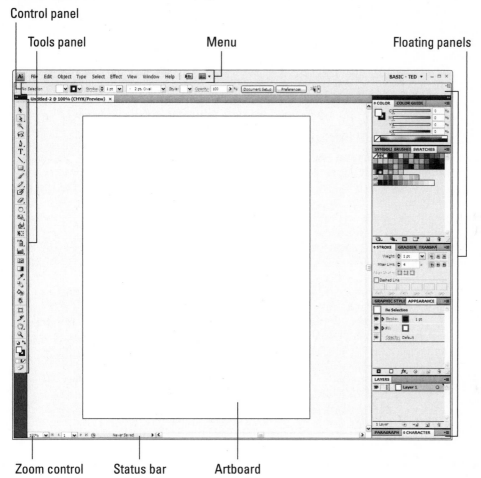

Zoom control   Status bar   Artboard

Understanding the Artboard

The Artboard is the area of your document that prints. The area of the Artboard doesn't have to be the same as the printed document. The Artboard is designated by black lines that form a rectangle in the document window and shows the largest area in which you can print. To set the size for the Artboard, click the Artboard tool, which allows you to change the size of the Artboard by dragging handles just as you would with the Bounding Box (where you also drag the handles to resize length and width of a selection). If you don't want to see the Artboard (perhaps because you're working on a large document that won't entirely fit on the Artboard), choose View ⇨ Hide Artboard. To show the Artboard again, choose View ⇨ Show Artboard. Hiding the Artboard doesn't impact your art. It remains in view when the Artboard is hidden.

 **To change the printing page size, use the Media options in the Print dialog box. To access the Print dialog box, choose File ⇨ Print.**

If you're placing your Illustrator files into another application, such as Photoshop or InDesign, the size of the Artboard limits the size of your artwork; anything extending outside the Artboard doesn't appear in other applications.

Getting to know the work area

When using Illustrator, the worst thing that can happen is for you to lose an illustration on which you're working. "Where'd it all go?" you cry. This can happen very easily in Illustrator. Just click a few times on the gray parts of the scroll bars at the bottom of the document window. Each time you click, you move about half the width (or height) of your window, and a few clicks later, your page and everything on it is no longer in front of you. Instead, you see the work area's scratch area, usually a vast expanse of white nothingness.

The work area measures 227.5 × 227.5 inches, which works out to about 360 square feet of drawing space. At actual size, you see only a very small section of the Artboard. A little letter-size document looks extremely tiny on a work area this big. If you get lost in the work area, a quick way back is to choose View ⇨ Actual Size. This puts your page in the center of the window, with a 100% view, at which time you can see at least part of your drawing. To see the whole page quickly, choose View ⇨ Fit in Window, which resizes the view down to where you can see the entire page.

 **Although the View ⇨ Actual Size and View ⇨ Fit in Window commands may seem to do the same thing, look closely and you'll see a subtle difference between the two. The View ⇨ Fit in Window command always shows the entire Artboard — which, depending on your monitor's resolution setting, may not be the same as the 100% view produced by the View ⇨ Actual Size command.**

This discussion assumes, of course, that you've actually drawn artwork on the Artboard. If you've drawn your artwork way off to the side of the work area, away from the Artboard, you may have more difficulty finding your drawing. At this point, you probably want to choose View ⇨ Fit All in Window, which takes you directly to all the art in your document.

Using the Print Tiling tool

The Print Tiling tool, which you access via the Hand tool (which I discuss later in this chapter), changes how much of your document prints. It does this by moving the printable area of the document without moving any of the printable objects in the document. Clicking and dragging the lower-left corner of the page relocates the printable area of the page to the place where you release the mouse button.

> **TIP** Double-clicking the Print Tiling tool slot resets the printable-area dotted line to its original position on the page.

The Print Tiling tool is useful when your document is larger than the biggest image area that your printer can print. The tool allows you to *tile* several pages to create one large page out of several sheets of paper. *Tiling* is the process by which an image is assembled by using several pieces of paper arranged in a grid formation. A portion of the image prints on each page, and when you fit the pages together, you can view the image in its entirety. Tiling is good only for rough prints because you typically need to manually trim about a quarter-inch around the edge of each sheet of paper; most printers don't print to the edge of the paper.

> **CROSS-REF** For more on printing, see Chapter 18.

Working with the Tools panel

The Tools panel, as shown in Figure 2.2, contains all the tools that you use to draw objects in your documents. The Tools panel normally appears as a panel on the left edge of the document window. To close the Tools panel, you can either click the x (the little circle on a Mac) at the top of the Tools panel or choose Window ➪ Tools. You make the Tools panel visible by placing a check mark next to the Window menu's Tools menu item. You hide the Tools panel by clicking the checkmarked item so that no check mark appears next to the Tools menu item.

If you drag the Tools panel to the right of its sticky panel location, it becomes a floating panel. To turn it back into a panel, drag it to the left edge of the document.

> **TIP** You can quickly swap between single- and double-column views of the Tools panel by clicking the arrows just above the top of the Tools panel.

> **TIP** To toggle the display of all panels, not just the Tools panel, press Tab. Each time you press Tab, the panels either hide or are redisplayed — depending on their current state. This won't work if you're using the Type tool with an active insertion point, of course.

> **TIP** You can show and hide all the panels except the Tools panel by pressing Shift+Tab (again, don't try this when you're using the Type tool with an active insertion point).

To choose a tool, click the tool you want to use in its slot within the Tools panel and then release the mouse button. This highlights it on the Tools panel. You can also choose tools by pressing a key on the keyboard. For example, pressing P selects the Pen tool. You can deactivate a tool only by selecting another one.

> **CROSS-REF** Appendix A lists all the shortcut keys for selecting each of the tools.

Many tools have additional popup tools, which are tools that appear only when you click and hold the mouse on the default tool. Illustrator denotes the default tools that have popup tools with a little triangle in the lower-right corner of the tool. To choose a popup tool, click and hold a tool with a triangle until the popup tools appear and then drag to the popup tool you want. The new popup tool replaces the default tool in that tool slot and stays there until you choose another tool from that tool slot.

> **TIP** **You can browse through the popup tools by pressing Alt (Option) while clicking a tool. Each click displays the next tool.**

> **TIP** **You can customize the tool shortcuts under the Keyboard Shortcuts dialog box found under the Edit menu. In this dialog box, simply choose the tool you want to change and then type the new shortcut letter, number, or symbol. You can also do this in Adobe Photoshop and Adobe InDesign.**

Any tool with a popup option also has a tearoff tab on the right side. You can make the flyout a free-floating panel by clicking this tearoff tab. Use this feature if you find that you're constantly switching between tools in that tearoff. Then, you won't have to click+hold and drag to the next tool.

Viewing the Tool Tips

What if you forget the function of a specific tool or you can't tell the difference between the various tools in Illustrator? No problem! Illustrator comes equipped with a handy Tool Tips feature that identifies tools quickly and easily. When you have Tool Tips activated (and it is by default), you simply move your cursor over the element you want to identify, and a yellow text box pops up and tells you its name. For example, when you place your cursor over the Type tool, a box appears with the words Type Tool (T). The letter within the parentheses indicates the keyboard shortcut for the tool. In this example, if you press T, you activate the Type tool without clicking it. Illustrator provides Tool Tips for every tool in the Tools panel as well as for the panel controls.

If you find the Tool Tips annoying or if you know the tips well enough not to need the Tool Tips, you can disable them in the General screen of the Preferences dialog box. To open the Preferences dialog box, simply choose Edit (Illustrator) ⇨ Preferences ⇨ General and then deselect the Show Tool Tips option.

Using the panels

Panels are small windows that are similar to dialog boxes. Panels can float or be docked. To make the following discussion a little more readable, I'll refer to both as panels; they're mostly interchangeable terms when discussing how they work and the contents of each of them, but differences are noted below.

FIGURE 2.2

The Tools panel holds all the tools you need to draw in Illustrator. The Tools panel on the left is the single-column version that you see by default in Illustrator, while the one on the right is the double-column version.

Panels allow you to control virtually every aspect of the Illustrator drawing environment. Illustrator has 34 standard panels and an unlimited number of library panels (for swatches, symbols, brushes, styles, and more), all of which can remain open while you work on your document panel. Technically speaking, a panel is a *modeless* window. The big difference between a modeless window and a dialog box is that you don't have to close the modeless window to perform other tasks. Therefore, you can work with the features on one panel without having to close another panel.

Unlike windows, panels are never really active. Instead, the one you're working in is in the front. If the panel has editable text fields, Illustrator highlights the active one or makes the text cursor blink. To bring a panel to the forefront — that is, bring it into focus — simply click in it anywhere.

Panels are like regular windows in many ways. Each panel has a title bar that you can click and drag to move it. The title bar also has buttons for minimizing a regular panel or zooming (back to regular size) a minimized one and closing the panel. Each panel also has a tab with the name of the panel within it.

NOTE You can use the title tab to toggle between the minimized state (showing only the title tab) and the maximized state (showing the entire panel) by double-clicking the title tab.

Occasionally, a panel has a handle on the lower-right corner that looks like a triangle made up of dots, as seen in Figure 2.3. You can use this handle for changing the panel's size by clicking and dragging the corner containing the handle.

TIP For some panels (such as the Color panel), a double-arrow icon appears to the left of the title name. Clicking this icon toggles the panel size among several different sizes.

FIGURE 2.3

You can resize a panel that has a dotted triangle in its lower-right corner.

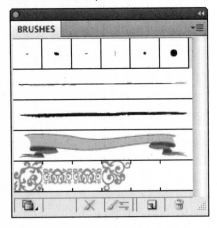

Linking together and tearing apart panels

You can place panels together in different combinations by *tabbing* and *docking* them. Tabbing stacks the tabs for several panels into a single panel. Docking aligns the panels without stacking them into the same space.

Each panel (except for the Tools panel) has a tab on it. Clicking the tab of a panel brings it to the front. Dragging a tab from one panel to another moves that panel into another panel. Dragging a tab out of a panel makes the panel separate from the previous panel. Figure 2.4 includes a set of panels that have been tabbed together. When you create a set of panels like this, it stays grouped together even if you quit Illustrator and relaunch.

If you drag a floating panel to the right side of the screen, it becomes a docked panel. If you drag a docked panel into the document window, it becomes a floating panel.

 By default, Illustrator tabs certain panels together. You can drag them apart and then tab others together to suit your method of working.

 To restore the default panel layout, choose Window ⇨ Workspace ⇨ Default.

You can dock panels together by dragging the tab of one panel to the bottom of another panel. When the bottom of the other panel darkens, releasing the mouse button docks the moved panel to the bottom of the other one. Then, when you move the other panel, the docked panel moves with it. To separate a panel from the others, click and drag the tab away from the original panel.

FIGURE 2.4

This panel contains a number of panels tabbed together.

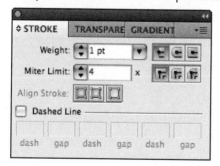

Working with panels

Panels are even more useful when you can reveal and hide them to suit your needs. Under the Window menu, you can choose which panels show and which ones hide. Simply click the check box next to a panel to show it, and deselect the check box next to the panel to hide it. Some panels use a keyboard shortcut to access them, and others are accessed through the Window menu. To see the shortcuts, look to the right of the panel name. Under the Window menu, you can see what panels are visible by the check mark next to them.

The panels are discussed throughout this book in various chapters. Here are some of the available panels:

- **Actions:** Use this panel to record a sequence of events to play at any time.
- **Align:** This panel lets you align objects (Shift+F7).
- **Appearance:** Use this panel to check the attributes of a selected object (Shift+F6).
- **Attributes:** Use this panel to view the overprinting and any URLs associated with the selected object (Ctrl+F11/⌘+F11).
- **Brushes:** Use this panel to choose a brush type (F5).
- **Color:** This panel lets you apply color to your illustrations (F6).
- **Color Guide:** This panel lets you access the Live Color feature (Shift+F3).
- **Control:** This is the panel along the top edge of the document window.
- **Document Info:** This panel shows information about the document, such as color mode, Artboard dimensions, and other options.
- **Flattener Preview:** Use this to see certain areas of flattened artwork. You can also adjust the Flattener options here.
- **Gradient:** This panel is used for changing and applying gradients (Ctrl+F9/⌘+F9).
- **Graphic Styles:** This panel lists the default graphic styles and lets you save graphic styles (Shift+F5).
- **Info:** This panel displays information on the selected object. It's used for measuring objects or distance (F8), among other things.
- **Layers:** This panel lets you put objects on different layers for easier organization (F7).
- **Links:** This lists the placed objects that are linked to the document.
- **Magic Wand:** Use this to adjust the settings for the Magic Wand tool.
- **Navigator:** Use this to quickly move around a large document.
- **Pathfinder:** Use this to combine, split, divide, and do more to multiple paths (Shift+Ctrl+F9/Shift+⌘+F9).
- **Separations Preview:** Use this to view the individual printing plates in your document.
- **Stroke:** This panel lets you adjust the width and style of the stroke (Ctrl+F10/⌘+F10).
- **SVG Interactivity:** Use this panel to set options for Scalable Vector Graphics.
- **Swatches:** This panel houses preset colors, gradients, and patterns.

- **Symbols:** This panel houses preset symbols and lets you define new symbols (Shift+Ctrl+F11/Shift+⌘+F11).

- **Tools:** This panel contains all of Illustrator's tools.

- **Transform:** This panel lets you move, scale, and apply other transformations (Shift+F8).

- **Transparency:** Use this panel to adjust the opacity of objects (Shift+Ctrl+F10/Shift+⌘+F10).

- **Type:** Use this panel to adjust a variety of type options, including:
  - Character (Ctrl+T/⌘+T)
  - Character styles
  - Glyphs
  - OpenType (Alt+Shift+Ctrl+T/Option+Shift+⌘+T)
  - Paragraph (Alt+Ctrl+T/Option+⌘+T)
  - Paragraph styles
  - Tabs (Shift+Ctrl+T/Shift+⌘+T)

- **Variables:** This panel is used to set the options for data-driven graphics.

Using Illustrator's menus

Although Adobe places more emphasis on Illustrator's panels and other elements, such as its Tools panel, you still find many important and useful features in Illustrator's menus.

Some general rules apply to Illustrator menus:

- To choose a menu item, pull down the menu, choose the menu item you want, and then release or click the mouse button. If the cursor is not on that item but is still highlighted, the command can't take effect.

- Whenever an ellipsis appears (three little dots that look like this …), choosing that menu item displays a dialog box where you must verify the current information by clicking OK or by typing more information and then clicking OK. If the option has no ellipsis, the action you choose occurs immediately.

- When you see a key command listed on the right side of the menu, you can press that key instead of using the mouse to pull down a menu. Using key commands for menu items works just like clicking the menu bar to choose that item.

- If you see a little triangle next to a menu item, it means the menu possesses a submenu. You can choose items in the submenu by scrolling over to the menu and then scrolling up or down to choose the menu item needed. Submenus usually appear on the right side of the menu, but due to space limitations on your monitor, submenus may appear on the left side for certain menus.

Panel menus

Not only does the main document window have menus, but panels have menus too. You can find a variety of features and options to meet your creative needs. To open these menus, simply find and click the triangle located in the top-right corner of most panels. Figure 2.5 gives an example of the options you have available when you access the Swatches panel's menu. These options and features change with each panel.

FIGURE 2.5

You can find a multitude of options by accessing a panel's menu.

Context-sensitive menus

Illustrator provides context-sensitive menus that appear right under your cursor as you work. Right-click (Ctrl+click) anywhere in a document window to open a context-sensitive menu. These menus contain commands that relate to the type of work you're doing and the specific tool you have. Figure 2.6 shows a context-sensitive menu that opens in a document when a rectangle shape is created and selected. This menu looks different if another object is selected.

NOTE Context menus in Illustrator tend to be less useful than other programs that rely heavily on contextual menus to accomplish tasks. There are very few commands that only appear in the context-sensitive menus, such as Isolate selected group and Send to current layer. Don't fall into the trap of right-clicking to see what you can do; Illustrator relies much more heavily on panels, tools, and the menu bar options (as well as numerous keyboard shortcuts) than it ever does on context menus.

FIGURE 2.6

When you right-click in the document window, Illustrator reveals a context-sensitive menu.

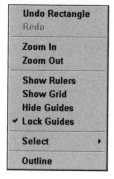

Typing keyboard commands

Keyboard commands are shortcuts for common activities that you perform in Illustrator. These shortcuts typically use the Ctrl (⌘) key in combination with other keys. Some menu items don't have keyboard commands; usually, you have to choose those items from a menu.

Keyboard commands are as important to an Illustrator artist as the mouse is; with a little practice, you can learn them quickly. Besides, many of the default keyboard commands are the same from program to program, which makes you an instant expert in software that you haven't used yet! Good examples of this are the Cut/Copy/Paste, Select All, and Save commands:

- **Cut/Copy/Paste:** You activate these by pressing Ctrl+X (⌘+X), Ctrl+C (⌘+C), and Ctrl+V (⌘+V), respectively.
- **Select All:** You can select everything in a document by pressing Ctrl+A (⌘+A).
- **Save:** You can quickly save your work by pressing Ctrl+S (⌘+S).

Using the status bar

The status bar, located on the lower left of your document window, has a Zoom popup list and a button that displays useful and otherwise difficult-to-find information. To change the item shown in the status bar, click the triangle to the right of Show and then choose a different item. Although the default for this button displays the tool that you're currently using, you can change the information to display one of the following instead:

- **Version Cue Status:** Choose this to see the Version Cue information for shared files. This option is available only if you have Adobe Creative Suite installed.
- **Current Tool:** Choose this to show the selected tool's name.
- **Date and Time:** Use this to show the current date and time.
- **Number of Undos:** This is a handy option that shows the number of queued undos and redos.
- **Document Color Profile:** This shows the current Color Profile.

Mousing around in Illustrator

Illustrator requires the use of a mouse for selecting items, pulling down menus, moving objects, and clicking buttons. Learning to use the mouse efficiently requires patience, practice, and persistence.

You use the mouse to perform five basic functions in Illustrator:

- **Pointing:** Move the cursor around the screen by moving the mouse around your mouse pad.
- **Clicking:** Press and release the left mouse button (or the only button on some Mac mice) in one step. You click to select points, paths, and objects and to make windows active.
- **Dragging:** Press the mouse button and keep it pressed while you move the mouse. You drag the cursor to choose items from menus, select contiguous characters of text, move objects, and create marquees (dotted rectangles used for zooming the view).
- **Double-clicking:** Quickly press and release the mouse button twice in the same location. You double-click to select a word of text, highlight a text field with a value in it, access a dialog box for a tool, and run Illustrator (by double-clicking its icon).
- **Right-clicking (Ctrl+clicking):** This displays a context-sensitive menu when you click the right mouse button (or Ctrl+click on a Mac).

The cursor is the little icon (usually an arrow) that moves in the same direction as the mouse. In Illustrator, the cursor often takes the form of the tool that you're using. When the computer is busy, an hourglass (Windows) or a spiraling circle (Mac) takes its place.

Navigating Around Your Document

Being able to move through a document easily is a key skill in Illustrator. Rarely can you fit an entire illustration in the document window at a sufficient magnification to see much of the image's detail. Usually, you're zooming in, zooming out, or moving off to the side, above, or below to focus on certain areas of the document.

Understanding the Zoom tool

The most basic navigational concept in Illustrator is the ability to zoom to different magnification levels. Illustrator's magnification levels work like a magnifying glass. In the real world, you use a magnifying glass to see details that aren't readily visible without it. In the Illustrator world, you use the different magnification levels to see details that aren't readily visible at the 100% view.

Changing the magnification levels of Illustrator doesn't affect the illustration. If you zoom in to 400% and print, the illustration still prints at the size it would if the view were 100% (you can adjust the printing size in the Print dialog box). It doesn't print four times as large. Figure 2.7 shows the same Illustrator document at 100% and 400% magnification.

In Illustrator, 100% magnification means that the artwork you see on the screen has the same physical dimensions when it prints. If you place a printout next to the on-screen image at 100% magnification, it appears at about the same size, depending on your monitor resolution (the higher the resolution, the smaller the document looks on-screen). Over time, monitor pixels per inch have increased from the standard 72 pixels per inch (ppi) of 1990s models to today's 96 ppi to 120 ppi versions, so if you have a flat-screen monitor, the on-screen version looks noticeably smaller than the printed version.

TIP For those of you who plan to use Illustrator with Photoshop, remember that in Photoshop, the 100% view is different. In Photoshop, each pixel on-screen is equal to 1 pixel in the image. Unless the ppi of the image matches that of the screen (and it would if Web graphics were being designed), the 100% view tends to be larger than the printed dimensions of the image when you're using Photoshop.

Using the Zoom tool

Perhaps the easiest way to control the magnification of your artwork is with the Zoom tool. This tool (which is located in the right column of the Tools panel) can magnify a certain area of artwork and then return to the standard view.

FIGURE 2.7

An Illustrator document at 100% (top) and 400% (bottom) magnifications

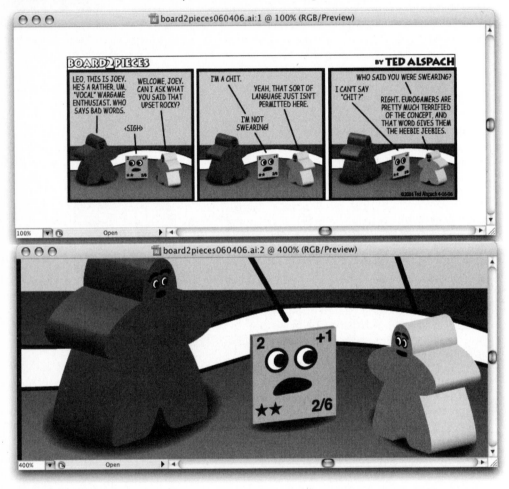

To use the Zoom tool to magnify an area, choose it from the Tools panel by clicking it once. The Zoom cursor takes the place of the Arrow cursor (or whatever tool was previously selected). It looks like a magnifying glass with a plus sign in it. Clicking any spot in the illustration enlarges the illustration to the next magnification level, with the place you clicked centered on your screen. The highest magnification level is 6400% — which, as all you math aficionados know, is 64 times (not 6,400 times!) bigger than the original. Where you click with the Zoom tool is very important:

- **Clicking the center of the window** enlarges the illustration to the next magnification level.

- **Clicking the edges (top, bottom, left, or right) of the window** makes the edges that you didn't click (and possibly some or all of your artwork) disappear as the magnification increases.

- **Clicking the upper-right corner** hides mostly the lower-left edges and so forth.

If you're interested in seeing a particular part of the document close up, click that part at each magnification level to ensure that it remains in the window.

If you zoom in too far, you can use the Zoom tool while pressing Alt (Option) to zoom out (you see a minus sign in the middle of the magnifying glass to indicate this). Clicking with the Zoom tool while pressing Alt (Option) reduces the magnification level to the next-lowest level. You can zoom out to 3.13% ($^1/_{32}$ actual size). Releasing Alt (Option) causes the Zoom tool to zoom in instead of out.

When you use the Zoom tool, you magnify everything in the document, not just the illustration. You magnify all paths, objects, the Artboard, and the Page Setup boundaries equally. However, the way certain objects appear (the thickness of path selections, points, handles, gridlines, guides, and Illustrator user interface components, such as panels and windows) doesn't change when you zoom in.

If you need to zoom in to see a specific area in the document window, use the Zoom tool to draw a marquee by clicking and dragging diagonally around the objects that you want to magnify. The area thus magnifies as much as possible so that everything inside the box just fits in the window that you have open. If you drag a marquee box as you press and hold Alt (Option), you do the same thing as if you had just clicked to zoom out.

> **TIP** To move a zoom marquee around while you're drawing it, press and hold the spacebar after you begin drawing the marquee but before you release the mouse button. When you release the spacebar, you can continue to change the size of the marquee by dragging.

Other zooming techniques

You also can zoom in and out by using commands in the View menu. Choose View ➪ Zoom In to zoom in one level at a time until the magnification level is 6400%. The Zoom In menu item zooms from the center of the current window view. Choose View ➪ Zoom Out to zoom out one level at a time until the magnification level is 3.13%.

Although Illustrator can zoom to any level, it uses 23 default zoom levels when you click the Zoom tool or when you access the Zoom In and Zoom Out menu items (or their respective keyboard commands). Table 2.1 lists each of the default Zoom In and Zoom Out default levels.

> **TIP** You can quickly zoom in or out using the scroll wheel on your mouse. Press Alt (Option) and then rotate the wheel to zoom in and out.

TABLE 2.1

Zoom In and Zoom Out Default Levels

Zoom Out	Ratio	Zoom In	Ratio
100%	1:1	100%	1:1
66.67%	2:3	150%	3:2
50%	1:2	200%	2:1
33.33%	1:3	300%	3:1
25%	1:4	400%	4:1
16.67%	1:6	600%	6:1
12.5%	1:8	800%	8:1
8.33%	1:12	1200%	12:1
6.25%	1:16	1600%	16:1
4.17%	1:24	2400%	24:1
3.13%	1:32	3200%	32:1
		4800%	48:1
		6400%	64:1

Zooming to Actual Size

You can use different methods to automatically zoom to 100% view. The first method is to double-click the Zoom tool in the Tools panel. This action changes the view to 100% instantly. Your other choices are as follows:

- **Using the Zoom feature in the status bar:** To do this, simply click the dropdown arrow in the left corner of the status bar and then choose 100% or type **100** in the field there.

- **Using the View menu:** This is the best way to zoom to 100% magnification because it not only changes the image size to 100%, but it also centers the page in the document window. Simply choose View ⇨ Actual Size.

Zooming to Fit in Window size

Fit in Window instantly changes the magnification level of the document so that the entire Artboard (not necessarily the artwork, if it isn't located on the page) fits in the window and is centered in it. You can choose from two different methods to change the document view to the Fit in Window size:

- **Use the View menu:** One way to automatically change to the Fit in Window view is to choose View ⇨ Fit in Window.

- **Use the Hand tool slot:** Simply double-click the Hand tool.

 You can quickly go to 3.13% by pressing Ctrl (⌘) and then double-clicking the Zoom tool in the Tools panel.

Zooming to a specific magnification

If you want to view a document at a specific zoom level, double-click the view area at the bottom-left corner of the active document window, type the magnification you want to zoom to, and then press Enter or Return.

NOTE When you specify a magnification, you don't change the document. Rather, you change how you view the document. For this reason, you can never undo any type of magnification-level change. Choosing Edit ⇨ Undo after zooming undoes the last change you made to the document before you changed the magnification level, not the magnification-level change.

Zooming with the Navigator panel

Of course, being able to zoom in very closely to your artwork does have a pitfall. The more you zoom in on an illustration, the less of that illustration you see at one time. The Navigator panel (shown in Figure 2.8), which you access by choosing Window ⇨ Navigator, helps you out by letting you see the entire illustration as well as the portion into which you've zoomed (indicated by a red viewing rectangle). You have several options within the Navigator panel for changing your view:

FIGURE 2.8

The Navigator panel shows a snapshot of the document.

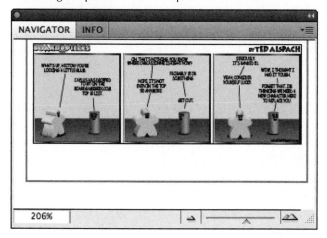

- **The red rectangle:** You can stay zoomed in and move easily to another section by dragging the red rectangle (which actually scrolls), located in the center of the Navigator, to another area.

- **The popup menu:** You access this menu by clicking the triangle located on the upper-right corner of the panel. The Navigator panel's popup menu includes a View Artboard Only option. This option sets the thumbnail in the Navigator panel to show only the extent of the Artboard. If this option isn't set, the thumbnail shows all objects included in the document.

- **The magnification level box:** You can type an exact magnification level in the box in the lower-left corner of the Navigator panel.

- **The slider:** Located at the bottom of the Navigator panel is a slider that gives you yet another way to zoom in and out by dragging the slider to the left or right.

- **The Zoom In and Zoom Out tools:** The Zoom In and Zoom Out tools look like little triangles and big triangles on either side of the slider triangle. You can zoom in and out a preset amount (using the same amounts used by the Zoom In and Zoom Out tools and menu items) by pressing the Zoom In or Zoom Out icons.

CAUTION   The Navigator panel can slow down Illustrator if your artwork contains many patterns, gradients, and gradient mesh objects. To avoid this slowdown, you can close the Navigator panel by choosing Window ⇨ Navigator.

Using the scroll bars to view your document

Sometimes, after you zoom in to a high magnification, part of the drawing that you want to see is outside the window area. Instead of zooming in and out repeatedly, you can use the scroll bars on the right side and bottom edges of the document window to move around inside the document. The right scroll bar controls where you are vertically in the document window. The bottom scroll bar controls where you are horizontally in the document window.

The scroll bars contain three elements: up and down arrows, a gray area (or bar), and a *thumb*, also called the *elevator box*, which is a gray square (in Windows) or a blue oval (on a Mac) that rides along the scroll bar. The gray area of the right scroll bar is proportionate to the vertical size of the work area (the space around the Artboard). If the little elevator box is at the top of the scroll bar, you're viewing the top edge of the work area. If it's centered, you're viewing the vertical center of the work area. The techniques are as follows:

- **Using the up and down arrows:** When you click the up arrow, you display what is above the window's boundaries by pushing everything in the window down in little increments. Clicking the down arrow displays what is below the window's boundaries by pushing the document up in little increments.

- **Using the thumbs:** Dragging the thumb up displays what is above the window's boundaries proportionately by whatever distance you drag it. Dragging the thumb down displays what is below the window's boundaries proportionately by whatever distance you drag it.

■ **Using the gray bar:** Clicking the gray bar above the thumb and between the arrows displays what is above the window's boundaries in big chunks. Clicking the gray bar below the thumb and between the arrows displays what is below the window's boundaries in big chunks.

CAUTION Be careful not to drag too far or you preview beyond the top of the Artboard.

NOTE On a Mac, if you want to specify how far Illustrator scrolls when you click the gray bar, you can set this in the System Preferences. Also on a Mac, the default is for the up and down arrows to be together. You can change this in your system's General preferences to place the scroll bars together or at the top and bottom.

Scrolling with the Hand tool

The Hand tool improves on the scroll bars. The Hand tool — which looks like a hand — is located at the bottom of the first column of the Tools panel, just above the color options.

Instead of being limited to only horizontal and vertical movements, you can use the Hand tool to scroll in any direction, including diagonally. The Hand tool is especially useful for finding your way around a document when you're viewing it at a high magnification level. The higher the magnification level, the more you're likely to use the Hand tool.

TIP To quickly access the Hand tool, press H or press and hold the spacebar. Clicking and dragging the page moves the document around inside the document window while the spacebar is pressed. If you release the spacebar, you return to the previous tool. This works for all tools, but the Type tool works a little differently. If you're currently using the Type tool in a text area, press Ctrl+spacebar (⌘+spacebar) to access the Zoom tool, and release Ctrl (⌘) while keeping the spacebar pressed to gain access to the Hand tool.

When you click in the document, be sure to click the side that you want to see. Clicking at the top of the document and then dragging down allows you to scroll down through almost an entire document at a height of one window. Clicking in the center and then dragging allows you to scroll through only half a window's size at a time.

The best thing about the Hand tool is that it works live. As you drag, the document moves under the Hand. If you don't like where it's going, you can drag it back, still live. The second best thing is that accessing it requires only one keystroke: either pressing H or pressing and holding the spacebar.

NOTE You can't use Undo to reverse scrolling that you've done with the scroll bars or the Hand tool.

Scrolling with the Navigator panel

Use the red rectangle in the Navigator panel to quickly scroll to another location within a document. Clicking and dragging within the red rectangle moves the viewing area around live, whereas clicking outside the rectangle snaps the view to a new location.

 **TIP** You can change the red rectangle to another color by choosing Panel Options from the Navigator panel's popup menu.

Opening a new window

So, now you've learned how to zoom and pan around the document window, and you probably have many different sections of your artwork that you want to focus on. Illustrator lets you create a number of windows for the current artwork by choosing Window ➪ New Window.

This option creates a new window that's the same size as the current window. You can then zoom and pan within this new window while maintaining the previous window. You can place these windows side by side to see the artwork from two unique perspectives. Illustrator gives each new window a different reference number, which appears in the title bar.

Using Illustrator's Modes

Illustrator offers several options when it comes to how you view your illustrations. This section explains how to discover these views as well as create and customize your own views.

Working in Outline mode versus Preview mode

In the old days, everyone worked in Outline mode (originally called Artwork mode). In Outline mode, you see only the guts of the artwork — the paths without the fills and strokes applied, as shown in Figure 2.9. To see what the illustration looked like with the fills and strokes applied, you had to switch to Preview mode. Usually, the preview was not quite what you had in mind, but to make changes, you had to switch back to Outline, then to Preview again to check, and so forth. Many users of Illustrator from that time refer to it as the golden age — with not a little trace of sarcasm.

Today, Illustrator allows you to edit your work in both Outline and Preview modes. You can also print a document from either mode. Saving the document while you're in Outline mode doesn't affect anything in the document, but the next time you open it, it displays in Outline mode. The same thing applies to Preview mode: Whatever mode you're in is saved with the artwork.

You can't undo a Preview or Outline mode change (for example, going from Preview to Outline). If you make a Preview or Outline mode change and then close your document, Illustrator asks you if you want to save changes, which in this case refers only to the view change. The current view mode is always displayed in the title bar next to the document name.

FIGURE 2.9

Artwork shown in Outline mode

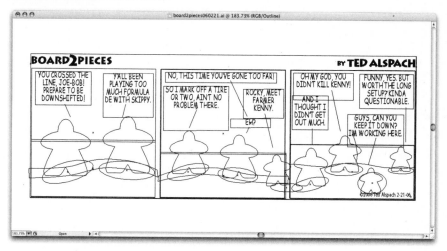

Understanding Outline mode

You may find working with a drawing in Outline mode significantly faster than working with it in Preview mode. In more complex drawings, the difference between Outline mode and Preview mode is significant, especially if you're working on a very slow computer. This is even more noticeable when the artwork contains gradients, patterns, placed artwork, and blends. Outline mode is much closer to what the printer sees — as paths. *Paths* define the edges of the objects with which you're working.

CROSS-REF For more on paths, see Chapter 4. For more on selecting and editing paths, see Chapter 6.

Getting used to Outline mode can take some time. Eventually, your brain can learn to know what the drawing looks like from seeing just the outlines, which show all the paths. The one big advantage of Outline mode is that you can see every *path* (a single entity in your drawing made up of one or more straight or curved lines) that isn't directly overlapping another path. In Preview mode, many paths can be hidden. In Outline mode, invisible masks are normally visible as paths, and you can select paths that were hidden by the fills of other objects. To select paths in Outline mode, you must click the paths directly or draw a marquee across or around them.

To change the current document to Outline mode, choose View ➪ Outline. In Outline mode, the illustration disappears and is replaced on-screen by outlines of all the paths. Text that has yet to be converted into outlines looks fine (*not* outlines, because it isn't paths — it's text), although it's always black.

NOTE You can change how a placed image displays in Outline mode by selecting or deselecting the Show Images in Outline Mode option in the Document Setup dialog box. To display the Document Setup dialog box, choose File ⇨ Document Setup. A placed image displays as a box if you click the Show Images in Outline Mode check box. If you leave this check box deselected, the image displays only in black and white and is surrounded by a box.

Understanding Preview mode

In Preview mode, you can see which objects overlap, which objects are in front and in back, where gradations begin and end, and how patterns are set up. In other words, the document looks just the way it will look when you print it.

NOTE In Preview mode, the color you see on-screen only marginally represents the actual output because of the differences between the way computer monitors work (red, green, and blue colors — the more of each color, the brighter each pixel appears) and the way printing works (cyan, magenta, yellow, and black colors — the more of each color, the darker each area appears). Monitor manufacturers make a number of calibration tools that decrease the difference between what you see on a monitor and the actual output. You can also use software solutions. One software solution, CIE calibration, is built in to Adobe Illustrator (choose Edit ⇨ Color Settings). Mac users can use ColorSync.

Choosing View ⇨ Preview changes the view to Preview mode.

The biggest disadvantage of Preview mode is that Illustrator begins to draw and fill in the various parts of your image, which can take some time, especially if your computer is slow. When you change the image, the screen redraws. You can stop screen redraw by pressing Ctrl+Y (⌘+Y) at any time.

Another disadvantage of Preview mode is being unable to select the path you want to change in the image. Sometimes, so much stuff appears on your screen that you don't know what to click! This problem can become more complicated when you include fills in the mix because the strokes on those paths are also visible. Instead of selecting a path by clicking it, you can select entire paths by clicking the insides of those paths in a filled area.

Understanding Overprint Preview mode

Drawing in Illustrator often results in one or more objects overlapping each other, meaning that the colors of these objects also overlap. When you print these objects, the top color blocks, or *knocks out*, anything below it. The advantage of using this feature is that your illustration becomes cheaper and easier for a printer to generate. To see how your overprint will look after you've set the Overprint feature, you can view it in Overprint Preview mode by choosing View ⇨ Overprint Preview.

Understanding Pixel Preview mode

Because most Web page graphics are pixel-based, Pixel Preview mode is specifically intended for graphics that designers want to place on Web pages. This mode lets you view images before converting them to a Web graphics format. Choose View ➪ Pixel Preview, and Illustrator places a check mark next to the Pixel Preview option and then shows a raster form of your image. Figure 2.10 shows what you would see in Pixel Preview mode. In the figure, the artwork is zoomed to 400% to more clearly show the effect of Pixel Preview mode.

CROSS-REF For more on color and overprinting, see Chapters 7 and 18. For more on creating Web graphics, see Chapter 19.

FIGURE 2.10

With Illustrator's Pixel Preview option, you can view an image in Pixel Preview mode.

Using and creating custom views

Illustrator has a special feature called custom views that allows you to save special views of an illustration. Custom views contain view information, including magnification, location, and whether the illustration is in Outline mode or Preview mode. If you have various layers or layer sets in Preview mode and others in Outline mode (layers in Preview mode are indicated by regular eyeballs to the left of their names in the Layers panel, while layers in Outline mode show an outlined eyeball), custom views can also save that information. Custom views, however, don't record whether templates, rulers, page tiling, edges, or guides are shown or hidden.

If you find yourself continually going to a certain part of a document, zooming in or out, and changing back and forth between the Preview and Outline modes, that document is a prime candidate for creating custom views. Custom views are helpful for showing clients artwork that you created in Illustrator. Instead of fumbling around in the client's presence, you can, for example, show the detail in a logo instantly if you've preset the zoom factor and position and have saved the image in a custom view.

To create a new view, set up the document in the way that you want to save the view. Then, choose View➪New View, and name the view in the New View dialog box. Each new view name appears at the bottom of the View menu. No default keyboard shortcuts exist for these views, but you can create your own shortcuts by using the Keyboard Shortcuts dialog box, available under the Edit menu. You can create up to 25 custom views. Custom views are saved with a document as long as you save it using the Illustrator format.

Using screen modes

So, you've been working on an illustration for an important client (actually, they all are important), and the client scheduled an appointment to see your progress, but the best part of the work is hidden behind the panels and the Tools panel. You can turn off the panels and the Tools panel or you can switch between the different screen modes.

Illustrator uses three screen modes represented by the three buttons at the bottom of the Tools panel. They are Standard Screen Mode, Full Screen Mode with Menu Bar, and Full Screen Mode. In addition to clicking the screen mode buttons in the Tools panel, you can also press F to switch between the three modes.

Using the Edit Commands

In most programs, including Illustrator, many basic functions of the Edit menu work the same way. If you've used the Edit menu in Photoshop or Microsoft Word, for example, you should have no trouble using the same functions in Illustrator because the menu options are located in the same place in each program, as shown in Figure 2.11.

FIGURE 2.11

The various commands under the Edit menu help you to quickly cut, copy, and paste objects from place to place as well as help you undo and redo previously applied commands.

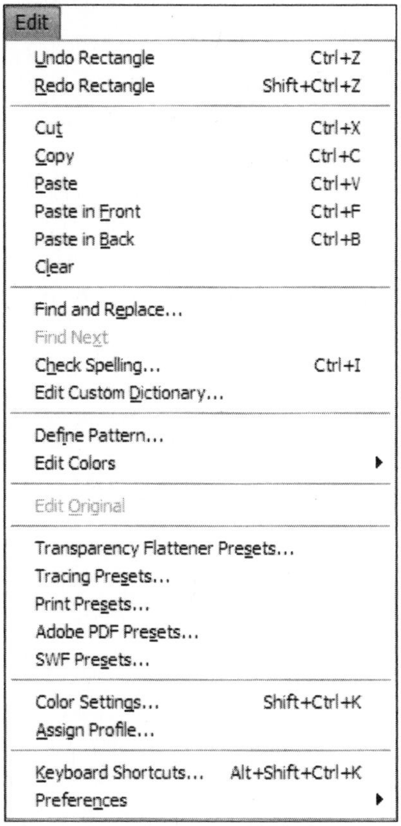

Edit	
Undo Rectangle	Ctrl+Z
Redo Rectangle	Shift+Ctrl+Z
Cut	Ctrl+X
Copy	Ctrl+C
Paste	Ctrl+V
Paste in Front	Ctrl+F
Paste in Back	Ctrl+B
Clear	
Find and Replace...	
Find Next	
Check Spelling...	Ctrl+I
Edit Custom Dictionary...	
Define Pattern...	
Edit Colors	▶
Edit Original	
Transparency Flattener Presets...	
Tracing Presets...	
Print Presets...	
Adobe PDF Presets...	
SWF Presets...	
Color Settings...	Shift+Ctrl+K
Assign Profile...	
Keyboard Shortcuts...	Alt+Shift+Ctrl+K
Preferences	▶

Using the Clear command

The most simplistic Edit command is Clear. In Illustrator, it works almost exactly like Backspace (Delete). When something is selected, choosing Clear eliminates what is selected.

You're probably asking yourself, "If Backspace (Delete) does the same thing, why do we need Clear?" or "Why didn't they just call the Clear command Backspace (Delete)?" Ah, the makers of Illustrator are a step ahead of you in this respect. Note that I said "almost" the same way; there's a subtle yet important difference in what the Clear command does and what Backspace (Delete) does, due to Illustrator's abundant use of panels.

If you're working on a panel and have just typed a value in an editable text field, Backspace (Delete) deletes the last character typed. If you tabbed down or up to an editable text field and highlighted text or if you dragged across text in an editable text field and highlighted text, then Backspace (Delete) deletes the highlighted characters. In all three situations, the Clear command deletes anything that's selected in the document.

Cutting, copying, and pasting

The Cut, Copy, and Paste commands in Illustrator are very handy. Copying and cutting selected objects places them on the Clipboard, which is a temporary holding place for objects that have been cut or copied. After you place an object on the Clipboard, you can paste it in the center of the same document, the same location as the cut or copied object, or another document, such as Illustrator, InDesign, or Photoshop.

Choosing Cut from the Edit menu deletes the selected objects and copies them to the Clipboard, where they're stored until you cut or copy another object or until you shut down or restart your computer. Quitting Illustrator doesn't remove objects from the Clipboard.

Choosing Copy from the Edit menu works like Cut, but it doesn't delete the selected objects. Instead, it just copies them to the Clipboard, at which time you can choose Paste and slap another copy into your document.

Choosing Paste from the Edit menu places any objects on the Clipboard into the center of the document window. Paste is not available if nothing is on the Clipboard.

 **Alternatively, you can use the Paste in Front and Paste in Back options to position the object you're pasting relative to other objects.**

Now, here's the really cool part: Just because you've pasted the object somewhere doesn't mean it isn't on the Clipboard anymore. It is! You can paste again and again — and keep on pasting until you get bored or until your page is an indecipherable mess, whichever comes first. The most important rule to remember about Cut, Copy, and Paste is that whatever is currently on the Clipboard is replaced by anything that subsequently gets cut or copied to the Clipboard.

Cut, Copy, and Paste also work with text that you type in a document. Using the type tools, you can select type, cut or copy it, and then paste it. When you're pasting type, it goes wherever your blinking text cursor is located. If you have type selected (highlighted) and you choose Paste, the type that was selected is replaced by whatever you had on the Clipboard.

You can cut or copy as much or as little of an illustration as you choose; you're limited only by your hard drive space (which is used only if you run out of RAM).

TIP **If you ever get a message saying you can't cut or copy because you're out of hard drive space, it's time to start deleting stuff from your hard drive. Or simply get a bigger hard drive.**

Thanks to the Adobe PostScript capability on the Clipboard, Illustrator can copy paths to other Adobe software, including InDesign and Photoshop. Paths created in those packages (with the exception of InDesign) can be pasted into Illustrator. With Photoshop, you have the option of pasting your Clipboard contents as rasterized pixels instead of as paths.

You have the ability to drag Illustrator artwork from an Illustrator document right into a Photoshop document. In addition, because Adobe lets you move things in both directions, you can drag a Photoshop selection from any Photoshop document right into an Illustrator document.

Undoing and redoing

You can keep undoing in Illustrator until you run out of either computer memory or patience. After you undo a bunch of times, you can redo by choosing Redo a bunch of times, which is found right below Undo in the Edit menu. And guess what? You can redo everything you've undone. So, if you undo 20 times, you can then immediately redo 20 times, and your art looks just like it did before you started undoing.

Choosing Undo from the Edit menu undoes the last activity that was performed in the document. Successive undos undo more and more activities, until the document is at the point where it was opened or created or you've run out of memory.

Choosing Redo from the Edit menu redoes the last undo. You can continue to redo undos until you're back to the point where you started undoing or you perform another activity, at which time you can no longer redo any previous undos. You have to undo the last thing you did and then actually do everything again. In other words, all the steps that you undid are gone. It's fine to use the Undo feature to go back and check out what you did, but after you've used multiple undos, don't do anything if you want to redo back to where you started undoing from. Got that?

Summary

In this chapter, you learned the following:

- Illustrator may seem difficult to learn at first, but with this book and a bit of dedication, you can master it.
- Illustrator has many keyboard shortcuts that increase productivity.
- Adobe has kept the interface similar across its products.
- The document window, Tools panel, panels, menus, and status bar look the same in many Adobe applications.
- You can view Illustrator documents at virtually any magnification level without actually changing them.

- Use the Hand tool to scroll around your document.
- Illustrator's Outline mode lets you see paths without their strokes and fills.
- Cut, Copy, Paste, Undo, and Redo are under the Edit menu.
- Illustrator provides virtually unlimited undos and redos.

Chapter 3

Working with Illustrator Documents

When you create an illustration in Illustrator, you're actually creating a document that you can place on the Web, send to a printer, or simply save on your computer. This chapter covers how to set up and change a document, how to open and save files, and how to export and place files. You also find out the difference between pixel-based documents and vector-based documents.

Setting Up a New Document

When you first load Illustrator, you see the Illustrator Welcome Screen, as shown in Figure 3.1, which allows you to choose to create a new document from scratch or from an existing Illustrator template. Alternatively, you can choose to open an existing document so that you can do some additional work with that document.

> **NOTE** The Illustrator Welcome Screen lists recently opened files, allowing you to open them directly with a single click on the name of the file and also allowing new documents to be quickly created from the list of document profiles on the right.

If you have Illustrator already up and running without the Welcome Screen showing, you can create a new document by choosing File ➪ New or by pressing Ctrl+N (⌘+N). This new document now becomes the active document. An *active document* means that the document is in front of any other documents.

FIGURE 3.1

Illustrator's Welcome Screen allows you to create a new document or open an existing one.

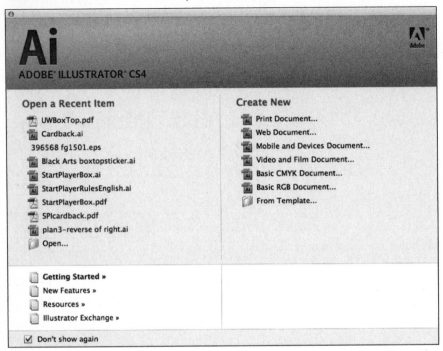

The New Document dialog box, as shown in Figure 3.2, offers several settings you can set before you start working on a new document:

- **Name:** You can type a name for your new document.

- **New Document Profile:** This is a named set of all the settings in this box. By choosing a different named set, all the values below will update.

- **Number of Artboards:** The first field lets you set how many Artboards will appear initially when you create your document. The buttons to the right of this field control how the Artboards are positioned relative to each other.

- **Size:** This allows you to choose standard preset dimensions, such as Letter or Legal, for your document.

- **Width and Height:** Instead of selecting a preset size, you can specify exact dimensions in the Width and Height text fields.

- **Units:** You can select the units you prefer to work in. Most artists choose points, but some prefer working in picas, inches, millimeters, centimeters, or pixels.

■ **Orientation:** You can choose the orientation of the page. The orientation options are portrait (meant to be viewed vertically) and landscape (meant to be viewed horizontally).

■ **Bleed:** This controls the bleed settings for the document (how far outside the edges of the defined document artwork will print).

■ **Color Mode:** You can choose from the CMYK and RGB color modes.

CROSS-REF For more on CMYK and RGB, see Chapter 7.

■ **Raster Effects:** This is the resolution that raster-based effects (like drop shadows) will use. Print documents should have at least 150 (although 300 is preferred), while Web-based documents should use 72.

■ **Preview Mode:** You can choose to automatically preview your document in Pixel Preview mode (showing pixels at 100% or closer) or Overprint Preview mode (showing the results of objects set to Overprint).

FIGURE 3.2

Use the New Document dialog box to choose the basic settings for a new document.

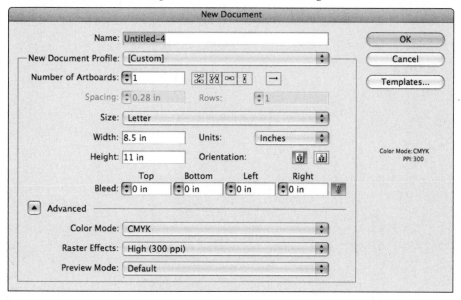

The document window initially appears at Fit in Window size. In the title bar at the top of the window, you see Untitled-1 (or another number, depending on how many new documents you have started during this particular session of Illustrator) and the percentage zoom the document is displayed at. As soon as you save the document, the title bar contains the name of the document.

You can't change the way that some of the panels or presets appear when you first start Illustrator. For example, the Selection tool is always selected in the Tools panel. Another unchangeable item is the initial paint style with which you begin drawing: a fill of White and a stroke of 1-point Black. The character attributes are always the same: 12-point Myriad Roman, auto leading, flush-left alignment.

Modifying the Setup of a Document

After you create a document, you need to go to the Document Setup dialog box (shown in Figure 3.3) to change almost anything about the document structure and how you work with that document by choosing File ➪ Document Setup.

FIGURE 3.3

The Document Setup dialog box provides options for controlling your document's settings.

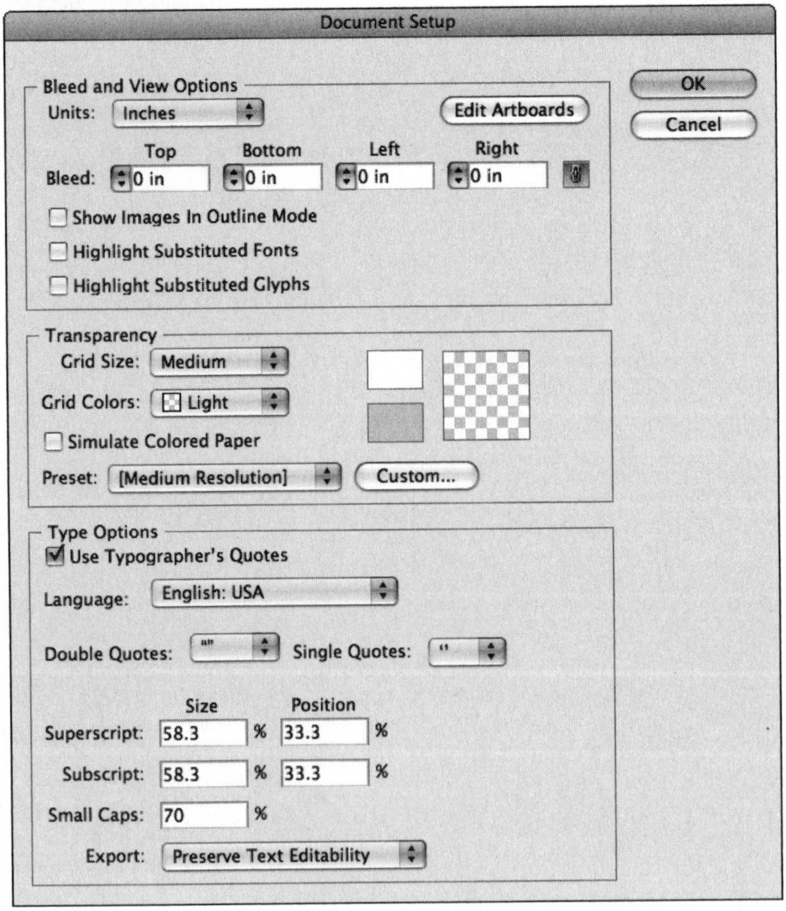

At the top of this dialog box is a list box (a popup menu on the Mac) that includes sections of options for Bleed and View, Transparency, and Type.

NEW FEATURE Document Setup no longer contains Artboard options. Instead, you need to either click Edit Artboards in the Document Setup dialog box or select the Artboard tool from the Tools panel.

Adjusting the Bleed and View Options

At the top of the Document Setup dialog box is a section called Bleed and View Options, although it could just as easily have been called miscellaneous options we didn't know where else to put. This section contains the following settings:

- **Units:** This sets the unit of measurement for this document. All basic measurements that are displayed in Illustrator use this setting for the current document.

- **Edit Artboards:** This button is a little unusual. It simulates choosing the Artboard tool. It's most likely here for those of us who instinctively press Ctrl+Alt+N (⌘+Option+N) to change the Artboard size and then remember that the Artboard options aren't here anymore.

NEW FEATURE To quickly access the Artboard tool (and thus the Control panel options to let you quickly change the page), press Shift+O, which selects the Artboard tool and throws you instantly into Artboard mode so you can access the Control panel.

- **Bleed:** This sets the amount of outside gutter around the edge of the printed page (or PDF) that appears. It's useful for projects where backgrounds and artwork extend off the edges of the page.

- **Show Images In Outline Mode:** Instead of seeing the glorious detail in your placed images, selecting this option puts a very neat late-1980s box frame in its place, as shown in Figure 3.4.

- **Highlight Substituted Fonts:** When a font isn't available, Illustrator substitutes another font for it. This highlights those substituted fonts.

- **Highlight Substituted Glyphs:** When a glyph isn't available, Illustrator substitutes another character or a space for it. Selecting this option highlights those temporarily changed characters.

Working with Transparency options

Transparency options refer to making a transparent background screen. Many users like to use a transparent grid to see the opacity of their objects. On a white background, the opacity isn't easy to see. Just as in Photoshop, you can see a checkered grid that shows the opacity of the objects in front. The Flattener settings let you pick a resolution for the object when you change it to a rasterized (pixel) object when it's flattened — that is, converted into a single layer with all overlapping objects combined. The Transparency options are also found in the Document Setup dialog box.

- **Grid Size:** This list box (popup menu) lets you can change your grid size to small, medium, or large.

- **Grid Colors:** You can customize your own grid colors.

- **Simulate Colored Paper:** Selecting this check box makes the Artboard color match the grid color you've chosen.

- **Preset:** Select a preset (high, medium, or low resolution) from the Preset list box (popup menu) or choose a Custom setting.

Selecting the Show images In Outline Mode option changes placed images from their original full-detailed glory (left) to a box frame (right).

Changing Type options

In the Document Setup dialog box, you can also change these Type options:

- **Use Typographer's Quotes:** Select this option to use smart (curved) quotes rather than the dumb (straight) ones.

- **Language:** Choose a desired language from the menu. You can choose from a variety of languages, including English, French, Finnish, but you must have the language set up on your system to be able to use that language.

- **Double Quotes:** Choose the style from the dropdown list (popup menu). You have a variety of quotes to choose from. Some users like the curved quotes rather than the straight ones.

- **Single Quotes:** Choose the style from the dropdown list (popup menu). The choices of single quotes are the same as the double quotes.

- **Superscript, Subscript, and Small Caps:** Choose the Size and Position for Superscripts, Subscripts, and Small Caps as a percentage of the original size.

- **Export:** In this list box (popup menu), choose from Preserve Text Editability and Preserve Text Appearance. In this case, you can either choose to be able to edit the text (but it may not look like you intended) or let the text look like it should (but make it so you can't edit it).

Artboards

In Illustrator, the Artboard defines the maximum drawing area that you can print. The Artboard is useful as a guide to where objects on a page belong. The maximum printable size is 227 × 227 inches or 358 square feet (provided that you can find a printer to print that big). You can define any number of Artboards, each can be any size, and when it comes time to print, you can print them independently or any combination of them.

Commercial printers print colored artwork using separate plates for each of the different primary colors (typically, they use four different plates). An application such as Illustrator can break down color images into the *separations* that are used to create these plates. *Crop marks* are lines that are printed as an aid to determining where to trim (or crop) the printed page when the document is printed on oversized paper.

Illustrator's separation setup ignores the Artboard and places crop marks around the entire image-able area. The *imageable area* is only the area where artwork exists. It may be within the Artboard, but it also may extend onto the Pasteboard. When you export an illustration to another program, such as QuarkXPress or InDesign, the Artboard is ignored entirely.

Choosing the Artboard measurement units

You can view a document in points, picas, inches, centimeters, millimeters, or pixels. The measurement units affect the numbers on the rulers and the locations of the hash marks on those same rulers. The measurement system also changes the way measurements display in the Info panel and in all dialog boxes where you type a measurement other than a percentage.

You change the measurement system in one of three ways:

- **Using the Preferences dialog box:** Use this method if you want to change all documents. To do so, choose Edit (Illustrator) ⇨ Preferences ⇨ Units & Display Performance.

- **Press Ctrl+Alt+Shift+U (⌘+Option+Shift+U):** This cycles through all the available units in your active document.
- **Using the Document Setup dialog box:** Use this method for the currently active document. You open this dialog box by choosing File ⇨ Document Setup.

The Artboard tool

The Artboard tool allows you to change existing Artboards and create new Artboards. The Artboard tool is in the lower half of the Tools panel, as shown in Figure 3.5.

As soon as you select the Artboard tool, the screen changes, making everything outside the Artboard area darkened and putting a big dashed line around the Artboard. The Control panel also changes, displaying the options shown in Figure 3.6.

FIGURE 3.5

The Artboard tool is found in the lower section of the Tools panel.

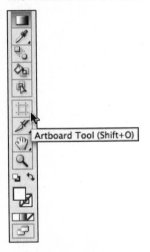

FIGURE 3.6

Choosing the Artboard tool results in a different set of options in the Control panel.

From this view of the Control panel, you can quickly change to preset page sizes (left side) and type specific dimensions for your existing Artboard. You can also quickly add a new Artboard by clicking the New Artboard button.

But what's great about this tool is that you can now modify an existing Artboard or create new ones with the tool. Just click and drag outside of the existing Artboard to create a new Artboard. Click once on any existing Artboard to select it and then grab one of its handles to modify it.

Changing the Artboard size using the Control panel

Choose the size of the Artboard by selecting one of the following preset sizes in the Size dropdown list (popup menu) on the left edge of the Control panel, as shown in Figure 3.7:

FIGURE 3.7

The crazy number of options in the Size list

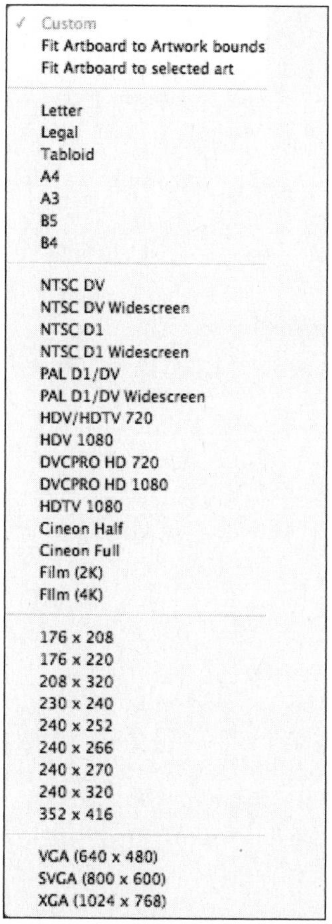

```
✓  Custom
   Fit Artboard to Artwork bounds
   Fit Artboard to selected art

   Letter
   Legal
   Tabloid
   A4
   A3
   B5
   B4

   NTSC DV
   NTSC DV Widescreen
   NTSC D1
   NTSC D1 Widescreen
   PAL D1/DV
   PAL D1/DV Widescreen
   HDV/HDTV 720
   HDV 1080
   DVCPRO HD 720
   DVCPRO HD 1080
   HDTV 1080
   Cineon Half
   Cineon Full
   Film (2K)
   Film (4K)

   176 x 208
   176 x 220
   208 x 320
   230 x 240
   240 x 252
   240 x 266
   240 x 270
   240 x 320
   352 x 416

   VGA (640 x 480)
   SVGA (800 x 600)
   XGA (1024 x 768)
```

- **Custom:** Any size you type into the Width and Height fields of the Document Setup dialog box automatically changes the Size dropdown (popup) to Custom.

- **Fit Artboard to Artwork bounds:** Choosing this option instantly changes the size of the Artboard to the size of all the artwork in your document.

- **Fit Artboard to selected art:** Choosing this option instantly changes the size of the Artboard to the size of all the artwork you currently have selected.

- **Letter:** 8.5 × 11 inches

- **Legal:** 8.5 × 14 inches

- **Tabloid:** 11 × 17 inches

- **A4:** 8.268 × 11.693 inches (21 × 29.7 centimeters)

- **A3:** 11.693 × 16.535 inches (29.7 × 42 centimeters)

- **B5:** 7.165 × 10 inches (18.2 × 25.4 centimeters)

- **B4:** 10.118 × 14.331 inches (55.7 × 36.4 centimeters)

NOTE A4, A3, B5, and B4 are paper sizes used outside the United States.

- **NTSC and so on:** The options in this section change the Artboard to the size (in pixels) of these video-centric choices.

- **176 × 208 and so on:** Makes your Artboard 176 × 208 pixels or the dimension you choose in this section

- **VGA and so on:** Makes your Artboard the appropriate screen size

Setting the Artboard orientation using the Control panel

You define the orientation of your Artboard by choosing one of the two Orientation pages. On the left is Portrait orientation, and on the right is Landscape orientation:

- **Portrait orientation:** You use this when the document is taller than it is wide. You can also think of portrait orientation as the vertical view.

- **Landscape orientation:** You use this when the document is wider than it is tall. You can also think of landscape orientation as the horizontal view.

The Artboard Options dialog box

Clicking the Artboard Options button displays the Artboard Options dialog box, as shown in Figure 3.8. This dialog box is really useful if you don't have the Control panel displayed, but I'm sure you do, so the Artboard Options dialog box becomes much, much less useful. In fact, the only thing you can change here that you can't change in the Control panel is the Fade option (in the oddly named Global section). If you have a pre-Intel processor Mac, you might want to deselect this option with complex documents, but otherwise, you can safely ignore these options.

FIGURE 3.8

The Artboard Options dialog box

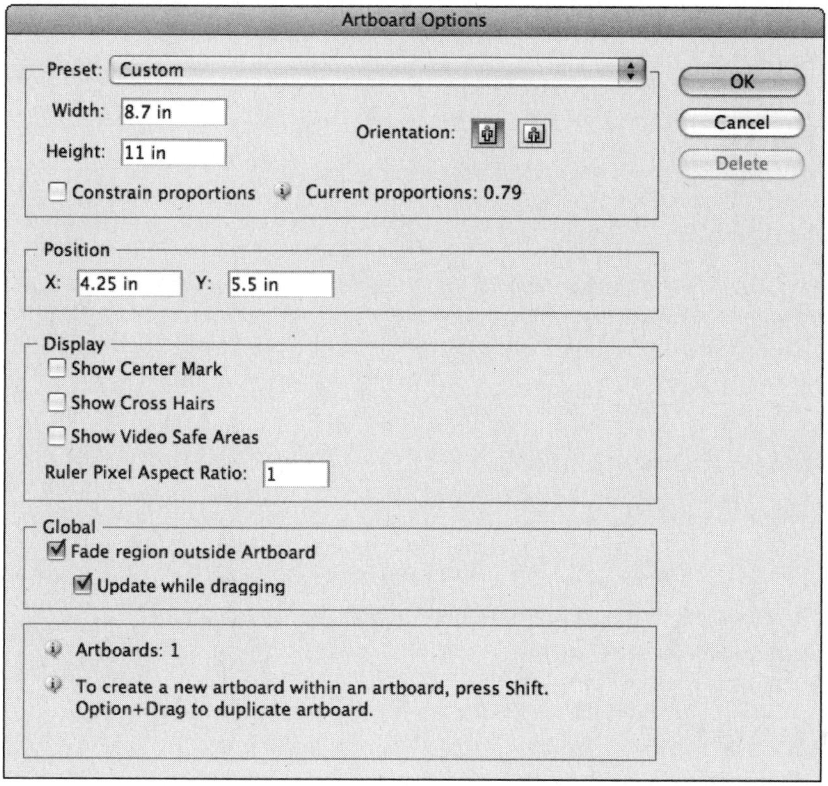

Artboard Options		
Preset: Custom		OK
Width: 8.7 in	Orientation:	Cancel
Height: 11 in		Delete
☐ Constrain proportions Current proportions: 0.79		

Position
X: 4.25 in   Y: 5.5 in

Display
☐ Show Center Mark
☐ Show Cross Hairs
☐ Show Video Safe Areas
Ruler Pixel Aspect Ratio: 1

Global
☑ Fade region outside Artboard
   ☑ Update while dragging

Artboards: 1

To create a new artboard within an artboard, press Shift.
Option+Drag to duplicate artboard.

Opening and Closing Illustrator Files

You can open many types of files in Illustrator. To open a file, choose File ⇨ Open or press Ctrl+O (⌘+O) to display the Open dialog box. Find the file you want to open, and double-click it to open it into a document window on the screen.

To close the active Illustrator file, choose File ⇨ Close or press Ctrl+W (⌘+W). The active document is the one that's in front of all other documents. Closing an Illustrator document doesn't close Illustrator; it continues running until you choose File ⇨ Exit (Illustrator ⇨ Quit Illustrator).

If you saved the file prior to closing it, the file just disappears. If you've modified the file since the last time you saved it, a message box appears asking whether you want to save changes before closing. If you've not saved the file at all, the Save As dialog box opens so that you can name the file and choose a location for it. If you click Don't Save (or press D while the message box is showing), then any changes that you made to the document since you last saved it (or if you've never saved it, all the changes you made since you created it) are lost. Clicking Cancel or pressing Esc takes you back to the drawing, where you can continue to work on it.

Saving Files

Saving and backing up Illustrator documents are some of the most important Illustrator tasks you can perform.

To save a file, choose File ⇨ Save or press Ctrl+S (⌘+S). If you've previously saved the file, updating the existing file with the changes that you've made takes just a fraction of a second. If you've not yet saved the file, the Save As dialog box similar to the one shown in Figure 3.9 opens. Illustrator files are best saved as AI files (with the .ai extension) because this is the native Illustrator format, which preserves all Illustrator-specific information.

When saving files, remember these tips and tricks:

- **Decide where to save the file:** Ensure that the name of the folder where you want to save the file is displayed above the file list window. Saving your working files in a location other than the Illustrator folder is a good habit. Otherwise, you can have trouble figuring out which files are yours, which files are tutorial files, etc.

- **Name the file something distinctive:** If you look for a file six months from now, you may not recognize it. Avoid using Untitled-1, Untitled-2, etc. Such names are nondescriptive, and you can too easily replace the file at a later date with a file of the same name. For the same reasons, don't use Document 1, Document 2, etc.

Here are your formatting choices for saving an Illustrator file:

- **Adobe Illustrator Document:** For use when passing between users who have Adobe Illustrator.

- **Illustrator EPS (eps):** For use when sending or passing files between users who may not have Illustrator but can place or open the files in another program, such as InDesign or Photoshop.

- **Illustrator Template (ait):** For use in creating templates that you can use as guides for future drawings

- **Adobe PDF (pdf):** For use in sending the file to anyone who has or can download Adobe Reader or Acrobat Standard or Professional

- **SVG Compressed (svgz):** For use when creating a Web page. This option generally produces smaller files than the uncompressed SVG format.

■ **SVG (svg):** For use when creating a Web page. SVG stands for Scalable Vector Graphics and is an XML-based format that can produce much smaller file sizes than the typical bit-map formats, such as JPEG and TIF.

The Save As dialog box allows you to save your document in several different formats.

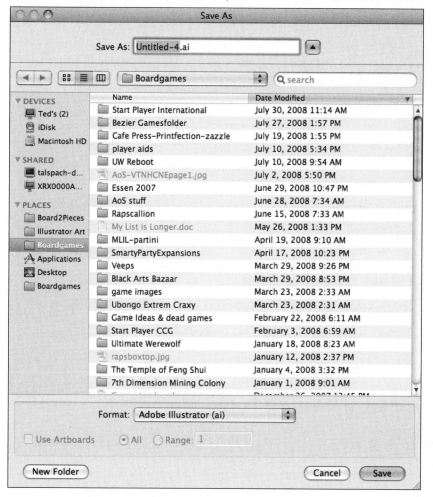

When Should I Save?

You really can't save too often. Whenever I put off saving for just a few minutes, that's when the application aborts or unexpectedly quits. Depending on your work habits, you may need to save more frequently than other people do. Here are some golden rules about when to save:

- **Save as soon as you create a new file.** Get it out of the way. The toughest part of saving is deciding how and where you're going to save the file and naming it. If you get those things out of the way in the beginning, pressing Ctrl+S (⌘+S) later is fairly painless.

- **Save before you print.** It's just a good idea in case your program quits when you print.

- **Save before you switch to another application.** This is another good idea in case you forget that you still have the application running or another application forces you to restart, such as when you're loading new programs.

- **Save right after you do something that you never want to have to do again.** For example, you want to save after getting the kerning just right on a logo or matching all the colors in your gradients so that they meet seamlessly.

- **Save after you use an Effect command that takes more than a few seconds to complete.**

- **Save before you create a new document or go to another document.**

- **Save at least every 15 minutes.** This is just a good, basic rule; that way, you're sure to have the latest version in case of a power outage that can shut your system down immediately.

Using the Save As command

You activate the Save As command by choosing File ➪ Save As or by pressing Shift+Ctrl+S (⌘+Shift+S). By using this command, you can save multiple versions of the document at different stages of progress. If you choose Save As and don't rename the file or change the save location, Illustrator prompts you to replace the existing file. If you choose Replace, Illustrator erases the file that you saved before and replaces it with the new file that you're saving.

Understanding the Save a Copy command

The Save a Copy command that you activate by choosing File ➪ Save a Copy or by pressing Ctrl+Alt+S (⌘+Option+S) saves a copy of your document at its current state (with copy appended to the filename) without affecting your document or its name. The next time you press Ctrl+S (⌘+S), Illustrator saves your changes to the original and the copy isn't affected by any of your changes.

Reverting to the last saved version

Choosing File ➪ Revert is an option that automatically closes the document and opens the last saved version of it. This option is grayed out if you've not yet saved the file. When you select it, a dialog box appears asking you to confirm that you actually do want to revert to the last saved version of the document.

 **You can't undo a Revert action, and you can't redo anything you've done up to that point with the document.**

Saving for Web & Devices option

Saving an Illustrator file for the Web is an easy step that ensures Illustrator properly saves your file for Web usage. This option allows you to choose various settings, such as the amount of compression that's applied to your document in order to reduce the file size so that your Web pages load faster. Choose File ➪ Save for Web & Devices or press Alt+Shift+Ctrl+S (⌘+Shift+Option+S) to access the Save for Web & Devices dialog box, as shown in Figure 3.10.

FIGURE 3.10

The Save for Web & Devices dialog box allows you to save your document in a format suited for use on the Web.

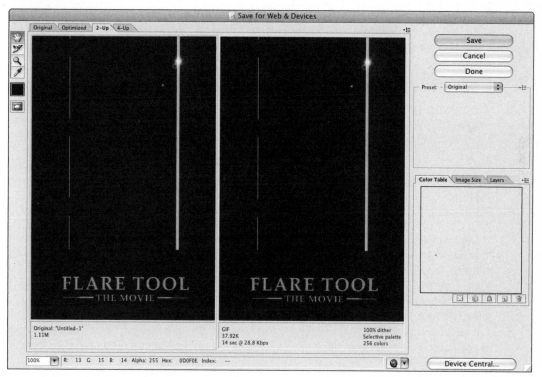

The tabs you see in the Save for Web & Devices dialog box are Original, Optimized, 2-Up, and 4-Up. The first tab, Original, shows the file in its original state. The second tab, Optimized, shows the file in the optimized settings you chose at the right of the Save for Web & Devices dialog box. The third and fourth tabs, 2-Up and 4-Up, respectively, show the figure in the original state along with one or three of the other default options so you can decide which option best suits your needs.

 **For more on the Save for Web & Devices dialog box, see Chapter 19.**

Understanding file types and options

You can save and export Illustrator files in several ways. Actually, you can save in and export them to many different formats using the File ⇨ Save As and File ⇨ Export commands.

Saving an Illustrator file with the wrong options can dramatically affect whether you can place or open that file in other software as well as what features Illustrator includes with the file when Illustrator reopens it. Saving a document as an older version of Illustrator may alter the document if the older version is missing features you used in your document.

As a rule, unless you're going to take your Illustrator document into another program, you can save it as an Adobe Illustrator (.ai) file without any problems. This keeps the file size down and makes saving and opening the file much quicker.

Using Illustrator's compatibility options

Most software packages are forward-compatible for one major version, but Illustrator is novel in that you can open an Illustrator 1.1 file in the CS4 version of the software, even though many years have passed between those product versions.

If necessary, you can also export an Illustrator document to certain older Illustrator formats using the Illustrator Options dialog box. To open this dialog box, select File ⇨ Save As and then choose Illustrator from the Save as type list box. In the options dialog box, you can choose the version of Illustrator to save as.

The only real reason to save illustrations in older versions of Illustrator is to exchange files with Illustrator users who haven't upgraded from an old version. This is pretty much always a bad idea, as saving as a legacy version may remove useful information from your Illustrator file. Within a few months after the release of Illustrator, most users will be upgrading. If they aren't, they probably don't understand the new features and usefulness of the latest version (or in the case of many printers/service providers, they just don't want to deal with the hassle of upgrading). Regardless of why people aren't upgrading, it's going to cause compatibility issues for you, so encourage them to upgrade as soon as possible. If they're truly serious about using Illustrator, they need to be using the most current version. I won't deal with printers who aren't on the most current version of Illustrator because they tend to be technically incompetent when it comes to working with my files correctly, which almost always results in printer-specific errors. The following list provides information about saving files in each version:

- **Illustrator CS3:** Saves the file with all Illustrator CS3-compatible features intact
- **Illustrator CS2:** Saves the file with all Illustrator CS2-compatible features intact
- **Illustrator CS:** Saves the file with all Illustrator CS-compatible features intact
- **Illustrator 10:** Saves the file with transparency, color profiles, and embedded fonts
- **Illustrator 9:** Saves the file with transparency and color profiles
- **Illustrator 8:** Saves the file in a cross-platform (Mac and Windows) Illustrator 8 format. Illustrator 8 added support for EMF file format and drag-and-drop to Microsoft Office products (Windows), Japanese format FreeHand files, and DXF file formats.
- **Illustrator 3:** Saves the file in the Illustrator 3 format. In fact, you can use the Illustrator 3 format for lots of cheating — doing things that Illustrator normally doesn't allow you to do (like opening up a file in Illustrator 3, 4, 5, 5.5, 6, or 7). For example, technically, you can't place gradients or masks into patterns. But if you save a gradient as an Illustrator 3 file and reopen it in Illustrator 7, the gradient becomes a blend, which you can use in a pattern (although Illustrator's Expand feature is quicker for this sort of thing).
- **Japanese Illustrator 3:** Saves the file in the Japanese Illustrator 3 format, which preserves the Japanese type options.

Saving as Illustrator EPS

If you do have to place your Illustrator document in a non-Adobe program, such as QuarkXPress, you may want to save the file as Illustrator EPS (Encapsulated PostScript). First, choose File ➪ Save As to display the Save As dialog box. Then, select the Illustrator EPS option in the Save as type list box (Format popup menu), name the file, and click Save to open the EPS Options dialog box, as shown in Figure 3.11.

The following Preview options affect the way that other software programs see Illustrator files when you save them as Illustrator EPS files:

- **None:** This option lets most software programs recognize the Illustrator document as an EPS file, but instead of viewing it in their software, you see a box with an X in it. Usually, this box is the same size as the illustration and includes any stray anchor points or control handles. The file prints fine from other software.
- **TIFF (Black & White):** This option saves the file with a preview for Windows systems. Page-layout or other software programs for PCs that can import EPS files can preview illustrations that you save with this option.
- **TIFF (8-bit Color):** This option saves the file with a color preview for Windows systems. Page-layout and other software programs display this file in 8-bit color (256 colors) when you place it in a document. An Illustrator file that you save with a color preview takes up more file space than a file saved with any other option.

FIGURE 3.11

The EPS Options dialog box allows you to specify how EPS files are saved.

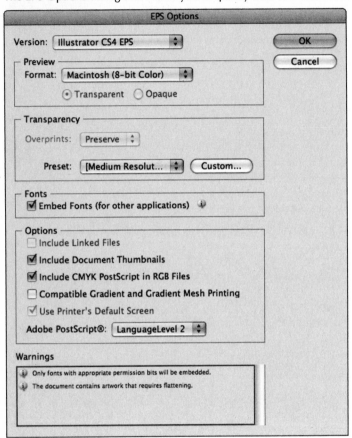

NOTE Two additional preview options are available on a Mac. Macintosh (8-bit color) maps to a selected 256-color panel. In Macintosh (Black & White), anything at 50% or higher intensity maps to black, while everything else maps to white.

In addition to the Preview options, you can choose from several other options that affect how the EPS file is saved:

- **Transparency:** You can Preserve or Discard Overprints. Overprinting allows underlying colors to appear through transparent areas of the drawing.

- **Fonts:** Choose to embed the fonts with the file (although this makes the file larger) so you don't have to worry about font substitution if someone else doesn't have your font.

- **Options:** These let you include linked files to ensure that any necessary files are included. Click the following check boxes to ensure you gain the best results when saving as an EPS:

  - **Include Document Thumbnails:** Allows someone to determine the file contents without opening the file

  - **Include CMYK PostScript in RGB Files:** Allows for more accurate color printing

  - **Compatible Gradient and Gradient Mesh Printing:** Allows older (10+ years) printers to do a better job of printing gradients, but decreases the quality of gradients in most printers

  - **Adobe PostScript®:** Allows for compatibility with applications that don't support newer PostScript versions (you can choose from Level 2 or Level 3 here)

 The Mac version also provides a Use Printer's Default Screen check box. It instructs Illustrator to use any default screen defined in the printer's PPD file.

Saving files as Adobe PDF

One reason for saving a file in Illustrator as PDF (Portable Document Format) is because anyone can load Adobe Reader for free and view the file. But the better reason is that all applications you will probably ever deal with can open, view, and place PDF files. To save your document in PDF, first choose File ⇨ Save As and select Adobe PDF in the Save as type list box (Format popup menu). Click Save to display the Save Adobe PDF dialog box, as shown in Figure 3.12.

This dialog box includes seven areas that you can use to set options. You select the settings by choosing from the list on the left side of the dialog box. The following lists the areas and their options:

- **General:** Under this category, you can set the Compatibility ranging from Acrobat 7 (PDF 1.6) to Acrobat 4 (PDF 1.3). If a user has an older version of Acrobat, you may need to save with backward-compatibility so the user can read the file. Depending on the PDF version you select, the following options may also be available:

  - **Preserve Illustrator Editing Capabilities:** Saves all Illustrator data in the PDF file so that you can reopen and edit the PDF file in Illustrator

  - **Embed Page Thumbnails:** Includes a thumbnail image that appears in the Open or Place dialog boxes

  - **Optimize for Fast Web View:** Creates a file that can be viewed more quickly in a Web browser

  - **View PDF after Saving:** Opens the document in your PDF viewing application after it's saved

  - **Create Acrobat Layers from Top-Level Layers:** Creates layers in the PDF file (useful for multilanguage versions of your file, for example)

  - **Create Multi-page PDF from Page Tiles:** Combines all pages of your document into a multipage PDF file

FIGURE 3.12

The Save Adobe PDF dialog box provides many options for controlling how PDF files are saved.

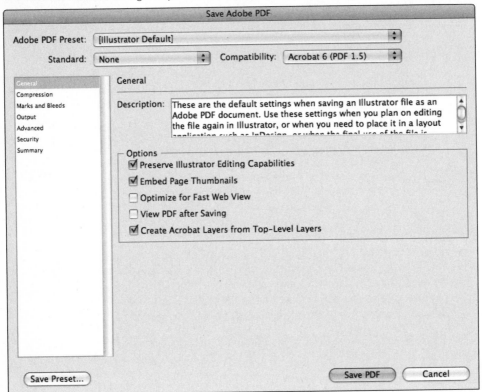

- **Compression:** In this area, you can change compression settings for Color Bitmap Images, Grayscale Bitmap Images, and Monochrome Bitmap Images. You also have a check box that determines whether to compress text and line art. This makes for a smaller file for e-mailing or uploading files to other users. These image types offer similar options, but you can choose different compression settings for each of them. These options are available:

  - **Downsampling:** Reduces the file size by reducing the number of pixels in the image

  - **Compression type:** Allows you to choose from no compression, JPEG, JPEG2000, and ZIP compression. You may need to experiment with the various options to see which type of compression produces optimal results for your particular document.

■ **Image Quality:** Allows you to choose the level of quality for JPEG and JPEG2000 image files. Lower-quality files are smaller but may not result in quite the appearance you want.

■ **Marks & Bleeds:** In this area, you set the Printer's Marks — lines printed outside the image area that show how to trim the drawings once you get them back from the printer or how to register the multiple color pages — Printer Mark Type, Trim Mark Weight, and how far to offset it from the artwork. The Bleeds for the top, bottom, left, and right of the page are set here. Bleeds are used to print images slightly oversize so that white edges won't appear once the images are trimmed.

■ **Output:** You use this category to specify how colors are converted between the RGB and CMYK color profiles when the file is saved. RGB is typically used for on-screen display, while CMYK is generally considered a more accurate profile for printed documents.

■ **Advanced:** The Advanced PDF settings are Fonts and Overprint and Transparency Flattener Options. Use these options to embed fonts for use in other applications and to set your transparency and overprinting abilities in other applications (if you're saving the file in PDF version 1.3). The transparency and overprinting options control the way underlying colors appear through transparent areas of the drawing.

■ **Security:** Under this area, you set whether the document requires a password for a user to open it and whether the password restricts editing. You also set the Security Permissions and the Acrobat Permissions (printing allowed, changes allowed, copying of text, images, or other content and enabling text access of screen-reader devices for the visually impaired).

■ **Summary:** In this area, you can see all the other options that Illustrator saves with the file.

> **TIP** You can save all the options under the Adobe PDF dialog box as presets by clicking Save Preset. This makes it easier for you to reuse the same settings in the future.

Saving files in SVG

Scalable Vector Graphics, or SVG, is a *vector-based* image format based on XML (eXtensible Markup Language), and it's one of the formats supported by Illustrator. Vector-based formats often have smaller file sizes than do bitmap image formats, so utilizing vector-based images for the Web can offer some important advantages in keeping Web page load times to a minimum. Figure 3.13 shows the SVG Options dialog box.

To save Illustrator documents in SVG format, choose File ➪ Save As to display the Save As dialog box. In the Save As dialog box, choose SVG from the Save as type list box (Format popup menu). You can also choose the compressed SVG option to create an even smaller file.

FIGURE 3.13

The SVG Options dialog box allows you to create vector-based images for the Web.

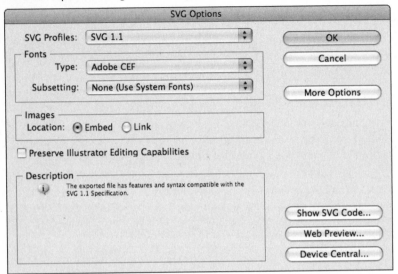

These are the SVG options:

- **Profiles:** This option allows you to specify the Document Type Definition level for your XML file. Older browsers may not support all features of newer DTD levels, but you generally want to choose SVG 1.1 for maximum flexibility.

- **Fonts Type and Subsetting:** These options allows you to specify the type of fonts to embed and to choose which characters are included — such as the characters that are actually used rather than the entire font set. You can choose None, Only Glyphs used, Common English, Common English and Glyphs used, Common Roman, Common Roman and Glyphs used, and All Glyphs.

- **Images Location (Embed or Link):** If you choose Embed, the file size is larger because it includes the placed image as part of the file. If you choose Link, it looks for the file on the system and accesses it that way (smaller file size).

- **Preserve Illustrator Editing Capabilities:** This option lets you choose to keep the editing capabilities in Illustrator. That way, you can use Illustrator to do any edits on the file.

CROSS-REF The more advanced options are the CSS Properties, Decimal Places, Encoding, Optimize for Adobe SVG Viewer, Include Extended Syntax for Variable Data, and Include Slicing Data. These options are covered in depth in Chapter 19.

Using the Export Command

Adobe Illustrator allows you to export to several file formats. Most of the export formats are bitmap formats, such as TIFF and JPEG. You can also export in PDF so that you can read Illustrator documents with Adobe Reader. When you choose the Export option, these formats are available:

- **AutoCAD Drawing (dwg):** This is the standard format for vector drawings created in AutoCAD.

- **AutoCAD Interchange File (dxf):** This is the tagged data of the information in an AutoCAD file.

- **BMP (bmp):** This is the standard Windows format. In BMP format, you choose the color model, Resolution, Anti-alias (jaggy edges), File format, Depth (number of colors or gray), and Compression.

- **Enhanced Metafile (emf):** Windows users use this format for exporting vector data.

- **JPEG (jpg):** You use this format mainly to show photographs on the Web.

- **Macintosh PICT (pct):** You use this format with Macintosh graphics and page-layout programs for transferring files.

- **SWF:** Adobe Flash uses this format for animated Web graphics.

CROSS-REF For more on the various options in the SWF Options dialog box, see Chapter 19.

- **PCX (pcx):** This is an older bitmap format that's not used very often because better options, such as JPEG, exist.

- **Photoshop (psd):** You use this format for taking the file into Photoshop by saving it as a raster image in the Photoshop format.

- **Pixar (pxr):** This is an older format developed by Pixar.

- **PNG (png):** This is the alternative to GIF and JPEG. Use this for lossless compression. However, not all older Web browsers support PNG.

- **Targa (tga):** You use this format for systems that use the Truevision video board.

- **Text Format (txt):** Use this format to export text into a plain text format.

- **TIFF (tif):** You use this format to move files between different programs and different computer platforms.

- **Windows Metafile (wmf):** You mainly use this on Windows applications for 16-bit color. WMF is supported by most Windows layout and drawing applications.

When you choose a format type, a specific dialog box that relates to that particular format appears. For example, Figure 3.14 shows the SWF Options dialog box that opens when you export an Illustrator document as an SWF file.

FIGURE 3.14

The SWF Options dialog box allows you to specify options for saving in the Flash format.

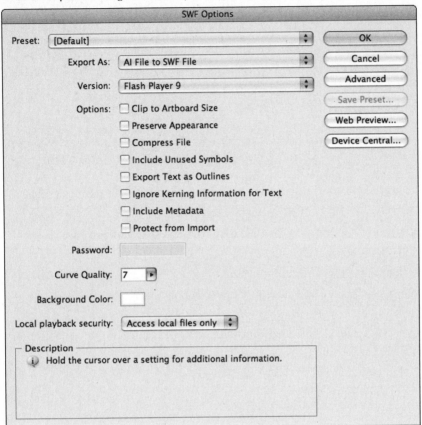

Placing Art

It's not necessary to create your entire Illustrator document from scratch if you already have some existing artwork that you want to use. You can use most types of image files in an Illustrator document, including both bitmap and vector-based images.

To place files into an Illustrator document, follow these steps:

1. **Choose File ⇨ Place.** The Place dialog box, as shown in Figure 3.15, opens.
2. **Navigate to the folder containing the file.** You can click the dropdown arrows on the popup menu to navigate to your file.

3. **Select the files that you want to place.** Only files that you can place appear in the file window. Because you can also place text files, be sure that the file you've selected is indeed an image document.

The Place dialog box allows you to choose image files to add to your Illustrator document.

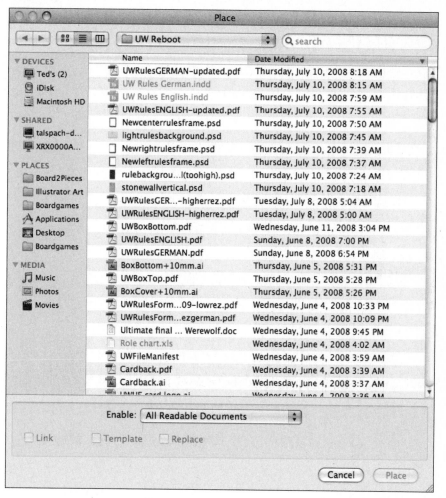

4. **Choose how you want to place the art. You have three options:**

   ■ **Link:** Normally, the option is unselected. Illustrator places the art within the Illustrator file. You generally don't want to select this option because it prevents the two files from being separated; if you have one but not the other, you're out of luck. However, there are several good reasons to link the file. First, placed art can be huge and may make your Illustrator file too large. Second, if you need to make changes to a placed art file included in an Illustrator file that you've saved with a preview, you must replace the placed art in the preview file with the new version. Preview shows the actual placed image and Outline shows a box with an X through it. If you link the placed art instead of including it, the art is automatically updated when you make changes. And, finally, you can share placed art that you've linked across multiple files. For example, you can place a business letterhead or logo in all your company files.

   ■ **Template:** The template option makes your placed file a template. When you make a placed file a template, it automatically locks in on a template layer in the Layers panel and dims the image so that you can use it to trace over.

   ■ **Replace:** You may want to replace placed art with new versions or completely different artwork. Illustrator has made this process painless. If you select placed artwork, a dialog box appears asking if you want to replace current artwork or place new artwork, not changing the selected artwork. Use this to keep a certain size or transformation that you used in another placed image. Simply select Replace, and the selected image replaces the existing one, transformation and all.

5. **Click Place at the bottom of the Place dialog box.** After you place art into Illustrator, you can transform it (move, scale, rotate, reflect, and shear it) in any way.

> **TIP**
>
> The really cool part about changing placed art this way is that if you've placed transformed artwork, the artwork you exchange with it via the Place command has the exact same transformation attributes. For example, if you scale down placed artwork to 50% and rotate it 45°, artwork that you exchange also scales down 50% and rotates 45°.

> **CAUTION**
>
> Be careful when importing artwork other than EPS images into Illustrator because TIFF and most other bitmap formats increase the size of your document dramatically.

Placing Photoshop Art in Illustrator: Understanding Vectors and Pixels

The main use of the Place command is to import raster-based images into Illustrator. These can be photographic images used within your design or images that you can trace, but this raises a critical question, the answer to which will help you understand how images created with a paint program like Photoshop differ from Illustrator: What is the difference between raster and vector images?

In its original version, Illustrator was a pure vector piece of software. But since Version 8, the border has been crossed, and Illustrator is just this side of the pixel border. What does this mean? It means that you can do things to pixels in Illustrator that you can't do in Photoshop. (Ah, now I've got your attention!) For example, you can use Photoshop filters in Illustrator, but you can't apply these filters to vector images. Because Photoshop filters work only on pixel-based images, you can rasterize — that is, convert your paths into a pixel-based image — or simply use the Effect menu to get some amazing effects.

CROSS-REF For more on the Effect menu see Chapter 15.

You can move between Photoshop and Illustrator in one of three ways:

- Place the raster image using the File ➪ Place menu.
- Use the Clipboard to transfer images.
- Drag and drop your art between the two programs.

But before you get into the ins and outs of moving Photoshop art to Illustrator, and vice versa, you need to understand the difference between vectors and pixels.

The essence of Illustrator is the ability to manipulate outlines. When you think vectors, think Illustrator's paths. Illustrator's paths consist of *outlines*, which you can resize and transform into any imaginable shape and fill with various colors and gradients. You can stretch vector-based images, and they won't look any worse — unless you scale blends and gradients too large. This means that when you create a curve in Illustrator, it's really a curve — not a jagged mass of pixels.

When you think pixels, think Photoshop's little teeny-tiny squares of color — squares that don't ever change position and that you don't add to or subtract from. The only characteristic you change about pixels is their color. Pixels can only be square, and they take up space. Pixels exist on an immobile grid. Enlarging a pixel-based image results in giant, ugly squares of color.

Placing raster images

Even with its pixel capabilities, Illustrator is no Photoshop. There are tools and features in Photoshop that are invaluable for adjusting pixel-based artwork. Adobe recognizes this, so it has provided several methods for moving pixels to Photoshop from Illustrator and from Photoshop to Illustrator.

The most rudimentary way, which has existed for several versions of both software packages, is to save art in a format the other program can read and then to open or place the art in the other program. To place Illustrator art into Photoshop, save the art in Illustrator format and then open the art in Photoshop. To place Photoshop art into Illustrator, save in Photoshop as a format that Illustrator can read, such as TIFF, and then in Illustrator, choose File ➪ Place and select the file.

Using the Clipboard

The next way is through Adobe's wonderful PostScript on the Clipboard process, which allows for transferring artwork between Adobe software programs by simply copying in one program and pasting in another. To place Illustrator art in Photoshop, copy the art in Illustrator, switch to Photoshop, and paste the art into any open document. To place Photoshop art in Illustrator, copy the art in Photoshop, switch to Illustrator, and paste the art into an open document. This process works best for smaller files.

Dragging and dropping

The easiest way to move art between these programs is to drag it from one program to the other. To drag art from Illustrator to Photoshop, select the art in Illustrator and then drag it out of the Illustrator window into a Photoshop window. To drag art from Photoshop to Illustrator, select the art in Photoshop and then drag it out of the Photoshop window into an Illustrator window.

TIP You must have a window from the drag-to application open when you start dragging for drag-and-drop to work between programs. If the window is hidden behind other windows, drag to the destination application's taskbar button, pause while the window is displayed, and then drop into the destination window.

Running Mac OS X 10.3 (Panther) or later, press F9 to invoke Exposé and tile all the windows of all running applications. Select the one containing the item you want to drag, select the item in that window, and start the drag. While keeping the mouse button down, press F9 again and continue the drag to the window where you want to drop your selection.

To place paths from Photoshop into Illustrator, select the paths in Photoshop with the Path Selection tool, copy the paths, and then paste them into Illustrator.

Working with Document and File Information

All files have information that's recorded when you save a file. You can see most of the information about a file by looking at the Document Info panel, as shown in Figure 3.16. You can use this information to see the graphic styles, patterns, gradients, custom colors, fonts, and placed art. Knowing what the file consists of when saving it or choosing an option to save or export is helpful. Another option is to save the document information as its own file.

Document Info and File Info are two different things. Document Info is a panel found under the Window menu. File Info is found under the File menu, and you can make additions to the information.

FIGURE 3.16

The Document Info panel shows a variety of details about the active document.

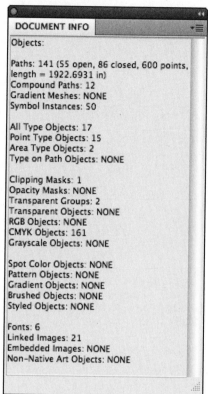

```
DOCUMENT INFO                          ▾≡
Objects:

Paths: 141 (55 open, 86 closed, 600 points,
length = 1922.6931 in)
Compound Paths: 12
Gradient Meshes: NONE
Symbol Instances: 50

All Type Objects: 17
Point Type Objects: 15
Area Type Objects: 2
Type on Path Objects: NONE

Clipping Masks: 1
Opacity Masks: NONE
Transparent Groups: 2
Transparent Objects: NONE
RGB Objects: NONE
CMYK Objects: 161
Grayscale Objects: NONE

Spot Color Objects: NONE
Pattern Objects: NONE
Gradient Objects: NONE
Brushed Objects: NONE
Styled Objects: NONE

Fonts: 6
Linked Images: 21
Embedded Images: NONE
Non-Native Art Objects: NONE
```

Looking at document information

You find general file information in the Document Info panel. You can use the Document Info feature in any document by choosing Window ➪ Document Info. The Document Info panel offers a number of different types of information that you can access through the panel's menu:

- **Document:** Lists the Color Mode, Color Profile, Ruler Units, Artboard Dimensions, Show Images in Outline mode (off or on), Highlight Substituted Fonts (off or on), Highlight Substituted Glyphs (off or on), Preserve Text Editability, and Simulate Colored Paper (off or on)

- **Objects:** Lists the Paths, Compound Paths, Gradient Meshes, Symbol Instances, All Type Objects, Individual Type Objects, Area Type Objects, Type on Path Objects, Clipping Masks, Opacity Masks, Transparent Groups, Transparent Objects, RGB Objects, CMYK Objects, Grayscale Objects, Spot Color Objects, Pattern Objects, Gradient Objects, Brushed Objects, Styled Objects, Fonts, Linked Images, Embedded Images, and Non-Native Art Objects

- **Graphic Styles:** Lists the graphic styles used by name

- **Brushes:** Lists the brushes used by name

- **Spot Color Objects:** Lists any objects that have a spot color applied by name

- **Pattern Objects:** Lists any objects with a pattern by name

- **Gradient Objects:** Lists any objects with a gradient by name

- **Fonts:** Lists all fonts used

- **Linked Images:** Lists any images that are linked by Location, Name, Type, Bits per Pixel, Channels, Size, Dimensions, and Resolution

- **Embedded Images:** Lists any images that are embedded by Type, Bits per Pixel, Channels, Size, Dimensions, and Resolution

- **Font Details:** Lists more information, such as PostScript name, Language, and Font type

 If you select the Selection Only option in the Document Info panel menu, the panel contains only information about the document's selected objects.

Saving document information

The last option in the Document Info panel's menu is the Save option. You select this option to save the information in a text file that you can view in any text editor. This method of viewing the document information offers the advantage of being able to see all the various pieces of information at once without needing to select different menu options.

Finding file information

In addition to the document information, you can also view (and modify) the information about the file. To access File Info, choose File ➪ File Info. The File Info dialog box (which is unnamed except for the name you used to save the Illustrator document) has several areas of information (although they're not all relevant for every file). You can use this dialog box to type the information you want to be saved with the file, such as the name of the author and a copyright notice.

Summary

Understanding Illustrator's documents is one of the basic yet most important areas of Illustrator. The main thing to keep in mind is to save and save often. This chapter covered the following topics:

- Choose File ⇨ New to set up a new document with Artboard dimensions and units.

- You can change the document setup at any time by accessing the Document Setup dialog box. Access this box quickly by choosing File ⇨ Document Setup.

- You can modify the existing Artboard and add new ones using the Artboard tool.

- You can add a variety of files to an Illustrator document with the Place command.

- Illustrator files are best saved as AI files.

- You can also export Illustrator files into a variety of formats. If you want to retain editing capabilities, save a version as an Illustrator file too.

- Document Info and File Info are two different things. The Document Info is a panel found under the Window menu. The File Info is found under the File menu, and you can make additions to this information.

Chapter 4

Understanding Drawing and Painting Techniques

I n this chapter, you learn about paths, which are the basic lines that make up the various objects. This chapter also covers using Illustrator's drawing tools, including the Pen, Pencil, and Paintbrush tools, to create these paths. And I talk about the techniques behind many cool effects that you can create by using these tools.

Working with Paths

The most basic element in Illustrator is a path. A *path* is what Illustrator calls the black line segment that appears when you draw a line. When you select a path, its anchor points appear. A path must have at least two *anchor points*, which appear as small squares along the path and control which way the path goes. Paths look different in Preview and Outline modes. In Preview mode, you actually see the line weight, dashed style, color, and any effects applied to that line. In Outline mode, you simply see a thin line. Without two anchor points, you can't draw a path like the one shown in Figure 4.1. Conceptually, there's no limit to the number of anchor points or segments that you can have in any one path. Depending on the type of anchor points that are on either end of a line segment, you can make a segment straight or curved. A single anchor point never prints anything.

CROSS-REF For more on Preview and Outline modes, see Chapter 2. For more on selecting paths, see Chapter 6.

IN THIS CHAPTER

Working with paths

Understanding anchor points and control handles

Drawing paths with the Pencil and Pen tools

Using the line tools

Using the Paintbrush tool

Working with other brushes

FIGURE 4.1

This path consists of two anchor points.

Understanding types of paths

Now that you know what a path is, you should understand the three major types of paths:

- **Open paths:** Two distinct endpoints, with any number of anchor points in between. An example of this is a simple line that you draw with the Pencil tool.

- **Closed paths:** Continuous paths, with no endpoints and no start or end — a closed path just continues around and around. An example of this is a shape that you create with one of Illustrator's shape tools, such as a rectangle or a circle.

- **Compound paths:** Two or more open or closed paths.

CROSS-REF For more on creating shapes in Illustrator, see Chapter 5. For more on compound paths, see Chapter 12.

Understanding anchor points

As stated earlier, paths consist of a series of points and the line segments between these points. These points are commonly called anchor points because they anchor the path; paths always pass through or end at anchor points. Anchor points are automatically created as part of a path; no path can exist without anchor points to define it.

Anchor points consist of control handles and control handle lines. *Control handles*, which appear as small squares along the path, determine how sharply or gradually the curve bends at each anchor point. Control handle lines run on a tangent along the path and are attached to the path by the control handle. They determine the direction of the curved path. The next section discusses control handles and control handle lines in more detail. Anchor points, control handles, and control handle lines don't appear on the printed output of your artwork. In fact, they appear only in Illustrator and Photoshop, never on artwork imported into other applications.

There are two classes of anchor points:

- **Smooth:** These anchor points have a curved path flowing smoothly through them. Most of the time, you don't know where a smooth point is until you select a path. Smooth points keep the path from changing direction abruptly. Every smooth point has two linked control handles.

- **Corner:** In this class of anchor points, the path changes direction noticeably at those specific points. There are three different corner points:

  - **Straight:** These are anchor points where two straight line segments meet at a distinct angle. There are no control handles on this type of anchor point.

  - **Curved:** These are points where two curved line segments meet and abruptly change direction. Each curved corner point has two independent control handles. Each handle controls a curve, and you can change only one side if you want.

  - **Combination:** These are the meeting places for straight and curved line segments. A combination corner point has one independent control handle. The one control handle controls the curve.

Figure 4.2 shows the different types of anchor points in Illustrator.

Understanding control handles and control handle lines

If an anchor point has a control handle coming out of it, the next segment is curved. No control handle, no curve. Couldn't be simpler.

As stated before, control handles are connected to anchor points with control handle lines. Figure 4.3 shows what happens when an anchor point with no control handle and an anchor point with a control handle are connected to another anchor point. Figure 4.4 shows the anchor points, control handles, and the control handle lines on a path.

FIGURE 4.2

Illustrator has several types of anchor points.

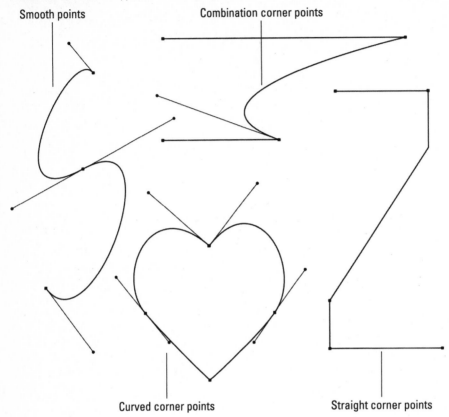

Smooth points

Combination corner points

Curved corner points

Straight corner points

FIGURE 4.3

An anchor point without a control handle and an anchor point with a control handle are connected to new anchor points, resulting in a straight line segment and a curved line segment.

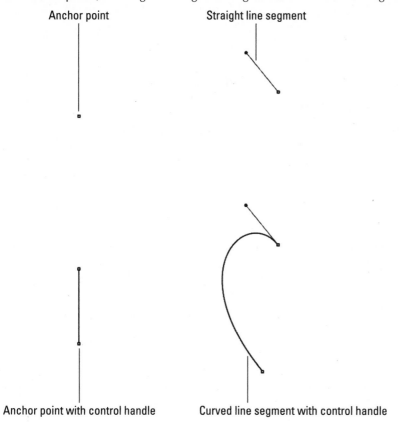

Anchor point

Straight line segment

Anchor point with control handle

Curved line segment with control handle

FIGURE 4.4

Anchor points, control handles, and control handle lines along a path

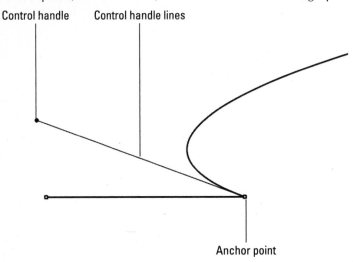

The basic concept to remember about control handles is that they act as magnets by pulling the curve toward them. This presents an interesting problem because each curved line segment usually has two control handles. Just as you might suspect, the control handle exerts the greatest amount of force on the half of the curved segment nearest to it. If there's only one control handle, the segment curves more on the side of the segment with the control handle than on the side with no control handle.

The greater the distance between a control handle and its corresponding anchor point, the farther the curve (on that end of the curve segment) pulls away from an imaginary straight segment between the two points. If the control handles on either end of the segment are on different sides of the curved segment, the curved segment takes on a reversed S shape, as shown in Figure 4.5. If the control handles on the ends of the curved segment are on the same side, the curve takes on a U shape.

Regardless of whether the anchor point is a smooth point, a curved corner point, or a combination corner point, control handle lines coming out of an anchor point are always tangent to the curved segment where it touches the anchor point. Tangent refers to the touching of the control handle line to the curved segment as it crosses the anchor point, as shown in Figure 4.6.

TIP To adjust the curves without moving the control handles, click the curve and then drag it. Keep in mind that you're changing both control handles at once, which can make adjusting the curve hard to control.

FIGURE 4.5

Control handles pull the line segment away from the straight line that would normally exist between them. The bottom path is a reversed S shape because the control handles are pulling in opposite directions.

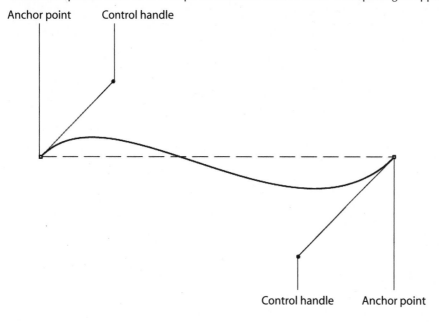

FIGURE 4.6

Control handle lines run tangent to the path where the path meets the anchor point.

A Little History on Bézier Curves

If you don't know much about geometry (or maybe don't remember much — it was back in high school, after all), you may find the very concept of creating curves by using math frightening. But most of the curve creation in Illustrator takes place behind the scenes when you use a drawing tool, such as the Pen tool.

PostScript curves are based on Bézier curves (pronounced bez-ee-ay), which were created by Pierre Bézier as a way of controlling mechanical cutting devices, commonly known as Numerical Control. Bézier worked for Renault (the car manufacturer) in France, and his mission was to streamline the process by which machines were controlled.

A mathematician and engineer, Bézier developed a method for creating curves using four points for every curved segment. He placed two points at either end of the segment — in Illustrator, these correspond to the anchor points — and made two points float around the curve segment to control the curve's shape; these are control handles in Illustrator. Using these four points, you can create any curve; using multiple sets of these curves, you can create any possible shape. John Warnock and Chuck Geschke of Adobe decided that Bézier curves were the best method for creating curves in a page description language (PostScript), and suddenly, those curves became a fundamental part of high-end graphic design.

Bézier curves are anything but intuitive, and in fact, they represent the most significant stumbling block for beginners learning Illustrator. After you master the concept and use of these curves, everything about Illustrator suddenly becomes easier and friendlier. Don't try to ignore them because they won't go away. You'll find it easier in the long run to try to understand how they work.

Understanding how fills and strokes relate to paths

If paths are the basic concept behind Illustrator, you may be wondering where the colors and patterns fit in. You apply all colors and patterns to Illustrator paths using *fills* and *strokes*. Basically, a fill is a color or pattern that appears within a path, and a stroke is a special style that you apply along a path.

CROSS-REF For more on applying available fills and strokes to shapes, see Chapter 5. For more on creating custom fills and strokes, see Chapter 10.

You should remember from Chapter 2 that when you work in Illustrator in Outline mode (View➪ Outline), only paths are visible. In Preview mode (View➪ Preview), fills and strokes applied to paths are visible. Unless a path is selected in Preview mode, that path (anchor points and line segments) isn't visible. You can toggle between Outline mode and Preview mode by pressing Ctrl+Y (⌘+Y). Figure 4.7 shows closed paths with different fills in both Outline mode and Preview mode.

FIGURE 4.7

Closed paths with different fills: The top row shows how they appear in Outline mode, while the bottom row shows what they look like in Preview mode.

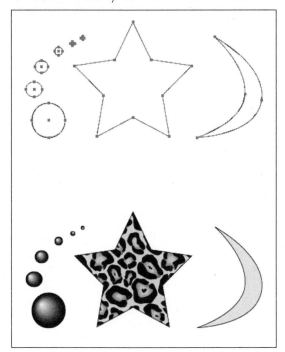

You can also fill open paths. The fill goes straight across the two endpoints of the path to enclose the object. Figure 4.8 displays different types of filled open paths. Filling an open path is usually not desirable, although in some circumstances, doing so may be necessary. Because the fill goes from the endpoints of the path, if you have an irregular-shaped path, the fill can look strange. If you're looking to create a cool pair of sunglasses, use a filled path for an unusual look.

CAUTION A straight line with a fill can cause problems when you go to print. In PostScript, when you specify a fill but only have two dimensions to an object (a straight line), it prints (rasterizes) at 1 device pixel. At 100% on-screen, the filled line looks exactly like a 1-point stroked line (72 dpi = 1 device pixel = $1/72$ inch and 1 point = $1/72$ inch). When you zoom in to 200%, the stroked line scales by 200%, but the filled line stays the same (1 device pixel or $1/72$ inch). When you print this line to a typical laser printer, 1 device pixel is as tiny as $1/300$ or $1/600$ inch. By the time you print to a typical imagesetter printer, 1 device pixel becomes $1/2570$ inch, making it too small to be visible in most situations. The key to fixing it is to ensure that any paths you don't want filled have a fill of None before sending the document to print.

FIGURE 4.8

Open paths with different fills: The top row shows how they appear in Outline mode, while the bottom row shows how they appear in Preview mode.

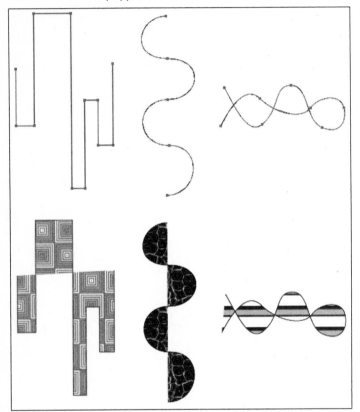

Besides filling paths, you can also stroke paths with a tint of any color or a pattern. These strokes can be any weight (thickness), and the width of the stroke is equally distributed over each side of the path. Open paths have ends on the strokes; these ends can be cropped, rounded, or extended past the end of the stroke by half the width of the stroke. Several different paths with strokes are shown in Figure 4.9.

CROSS-REF For more on printing, see Chapter 18. For more on stroke weight, color, and attributes, see Chapter 5.

A single point is also considered a path; however, single points in Illustrator have no printable qualities. This isn't readily noticeable because you can assign a fill or stroke color to a single point, although you can't see it in Preview mode or when you print it. When the document is color-separated, it causes a separation of the color to print, even if nothing else on that page uses that same color, and the separation appears blank.

TIP If you think that you may have individual anchor points floating around your illustration, you should select all of them at once by choosing Select ➪ Object ➪ Stray Points and then delete them.

FIGURE 4.9

Various paths with different strokes applied to them

Fills and strokes in Illustrator can be colors (including an opaque white), which knocks out any color underneath. Fills and strokes can also be transparent. Transparency in Illustrator is commonly referred to as a fill, a stroke, or None.

CROSS-REF For more on color separations, see Chapter 18. For more on transparency, see Chapter 7.

Drawing Paths with Illustrator Tools

The most effective (and challenging) way to create paths is to draw them with one of the drawing tools. The Pen, Pencil, and Paintbrush tools are the most common drawing instruments, but Illustrator also has a Brushes panel, including three key brushes — the Art Brush, the Scatter Brush, and the Pattern Brush. If you're looking for the Calligraphic option, you find it as a brush option that you can choose in the Brushes panel. The Smooth tool and the Path Eraser tool are two other helpful tools. They're located in the Pencil tool's popup menu. These two tools cut editing time drastically by letting you clean up lines and fix errors with the stroke of a brush.

Of the three main tools used to draw paths in Illustrator, the Pen is the most difficult to use, but it often yields the best results. The Pencil is by far the easiest but requires some editing to smooth the bumpy lines. The Paintbrush tool combined with a tablet can create some amazing hand-drawn looks in your art.

Each tool has its place, and you use all three to achieve the most productivity. So, practice using all the tools to find which one works best for whatever you may want to achieve. Figure 4.10 shows an illustration created using several different tools.

Using the Pencil tool

When you want to draw rough edges or realistic illustrations that don't look computery — for example, a map drawing with beautiful bumpy edges — the Pencil tool is the one to use. The Pencil tool is housed in the Tools panel with the tools that edit it — the Smooth and Path Eraser tools — and draws a free-form stroked path wherever you click and drag the cursor. However, instead of creating a closed path that's a certain width, the result is a single path that approximately follows the route you take with the cursor. The Pencil tool has the unique capability to make the lines you draw look … well … good.

Actually, part of the Pencil tool's charm is also its biggest drawback. Unlike the Pen tool — which creates precise, super-smooth lines but is difficult to control — the Pencil tool is much easier to use, but it draws lines that are far from perfect. This is because the Pencil tool creates only smooth points and corner anchor points. When you select the Pencil tool's anchor point, two control handles appear. If you remember the earlier discussion on anchor points, you know this means that you can neither draw a smooth anchor point — although at first glance, you may think you can — nor a straight corner point with the Pencil tool. This makes the construction of precise objects nearly impossible.

Before you use the Pencil tool for the first time, you should change the paint style attributes to a fill of None and a stroke of 1-point Black. Having a fill other than None while drawing with the Pencil tool often results in bizarre-looking shapes. To choose these settings, begin in the color section near the bottom of the Illustrator Tools panel. Click the Fill square and then click the None (red slash) box to ensure the fill is None. Select the stroke (outlined rectangle) and then choose Black to ensure the stroke has a black stroke. Choose Window ➪ Stroke to display the Stroke panel and then choose 1 point from the Weight dropdown list (popup menu).

FIGURE 4.10

In this illustration, the various objects were created using several tools.

To use the Pencil tool, follow these steps:

1. **Double-click the Pencil tool.** The Pencil tool is the tenth tool down in the Tools panel and is housed with the Smooth tool and the Path Eraser tool (which are discussed later in this chapter), which help smooth and edit Pencil tool paths. The Pencil tool, obviously, has a pencil for its icon. Double-clicking this icon opens the Pencil Tool Preferences dialog box, as shown in Figure 4.11.

2. **Adjust the options in the Pencil Tool Preferences dialog box. The options are as follows:**

   ■ **Fidelity:** The Fidelity setting controls how far (measured in pixels) curves may stray from the original dotted line that appears as you draw with the mouse. A low fidelity value results in sharper angles; a high fidelity value results in smoother curves. The lowest Fidelity number is .5 pixels, the highest is 20 pixels, and the default is 2.5 pixels.

NOTE As stated previously, although you think you can create them at first glance, you can't create smooth anchor points. You may find this especially deceiving when you set Fidelity to a high number so that all the anchor points look like they're smooth points. This isn't the case. In fact, most anchor points created with the Pencil tool — with the exception of endpoints — are curved corner points, which are anchor points with two independent control handles shooting out.

FIGURE 4.11

In the Pencil Tool Preferences dialog box, you can change the fidelity and smoothness for the Pencil tool.

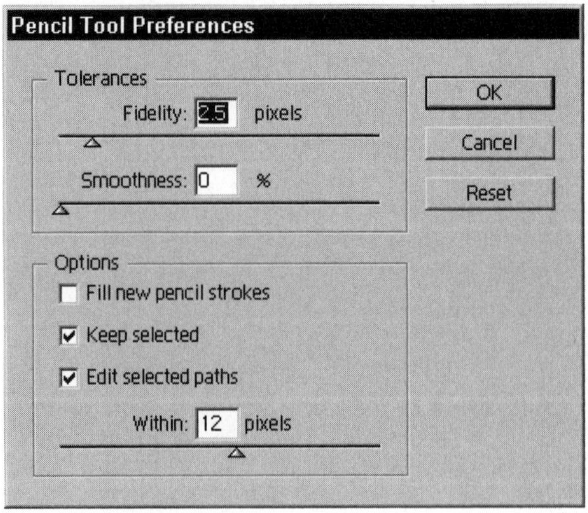

- **Smoothness:** Measured as a percentage, the Smoothness value determines how well the Pencil controls the bumpiness or irregularity of the line. A low Smoothness value results in a coarse, angular path, while a high Smoothness value results in a much smoother path with fewer anchor points.

- **Fill new pencil strokes:** Applies a fill to new pencil strokes when clicked and applies no fill when deselected.

- **Keep selected:** This option keeps the last path you drew selected in case you want to edit or do any changes right after drawing the path.

- **Edit selected paths:** If you click this check box, you can edit the path with the Pencil tool. If you don't click this check box or if you deselect it, you can still edit, but you have to use the selection tools.

- **Within pixels:** This value sets how close your drawing has to match the existing path to be editable; this works only when you click the Edit selected paths check box.

3. **Click OK.** Illustrator applies your preferences when you start using the Pencil tool.

4. **Begin dragging the mouse.** The Pencil tool resembles a little pencil when you're drawing. As you drag, a series of dots follows the cursor. These dots show the approximate location of the path you've drawn. The location of a path drawn with the Pencil tool is directly relevant to the speed and the direction in which the cursor moves.

TIP Pressing Caps Lock (engaging it) changes the cursor from the Pencil shape to crosshairs. The line of points comes from the dot in the center of the crosshairs. Use the crosshairs if you want to see exactly the point from which the drawing starts. You can set your cursors to always be crosshairs just by opening the Preferences dialog box (by pressing Ctrl+K [⌘+K]) and then clicking the Use Precise Cursors check box. When this option is selected, Caps Lock changes the cursor back to the regular tool.

5. **Release the mouse button.** The path of dots is transformed into a path with anchor points, all having control handle lines and control handles shooting off from them. The faster you draw with the Pencil tool, the fewer points that are created; the slower you draw, the more points that are used to define the path.

TIP You can repeat the item you just drew quickly and easily. Using the Selection tool, click the object you drew and then press Alt (Option). Next, drag the item elsewhere on the Artboard to make a copy of the original object. For more on the selection tools, see Chapter 6.

TIP Using the Smooth tool, you can instantly transform a swooping, uneven, jagged line that looks terrible as you draw into a beautifully curved piece of artwork reminiscent of lines drawn traditionally with a French curve.

How the Fidelity and Smoothness Options Affect a Line

Because drawing good-looking paths with the Pencil tool and a mouse is just a tad difficult and frustrating, Illustrator provides a way to determine how rough or smooth your path will be before you draw it.

Normally, paths that appear from the dotted lines created with the Pencil tool are fairly similar to those dotted lines in direction and curves and such. When lines are being drawn, though, human error can cause all sorts of little bumps to appear, making the path look lumpy. In some cases, as in map creation, lumpy is good. More often than not, though, lumpy is an undesirable state for your illustrations.

The smoothness — or jaggedness — of the resulting paths drawn with the Pencil tool depends on the Fidelity and Smoothness options in the Pencil Tool Preferences dialog box, which determines how jagged or smooth each section appears, from the dotted line to the path. As stated before, a low Fidelity value results in sharper angles and a high Fidelity value results in smoother curves, while a low Smoothness value results in a coarse, angular path and a high Smoothness value results in a much smoother path with fewer anchor points.

At a Fidelity setting of .5, paths appear jagged and rough. Also, many more anchor points are present, although there are still no straight corner points. A setting of .5 is great for creating some photorealistic illustrations of complex, detailed objects, such as tree leaves and textures. When the setting is this low, the resulting path follows the dotted line as closely as possible.

When the Fidelity option is set to 20, paths created with the Pencil tool appear extremely smooth. Illustrator uses the smallest number of anchor points, and the curve of the line appears to be very graceful. Because so few anchor points are used, much detail is lost, and the path wavers from the original dotted line of the Pencil tool by a significant amount. Even though it appears that all the anchor points are smooth points, they're actually curved corner points with two independent control handles.

Drawing open paths and closed paths

You can draw both open and closed paths with the Pencil and Pen tools. Paths in Illustrator may cross themselves. When these paths cross, the fills may look a little unusual. Strokes look normal; they just overlap where paths cross.

To create an open path, draw a path with the Pencil or Pen tool, but ensure that the beginning and end of the path are two separate points at different locations. Open paths with fills may look a little bizarre because Illustrator automatically fills in between the endpoints on the path, even if the imaginary line between the endpoints crosses the path. Figure 4.12 shows both open and closed paths drawn with the Pencil tool.

To create a closed path, end your path at the same place that you started the path. While drawing, press Alt (Option). When the Pencil cursor is directly over the location where the line begins, a little circle appears to the lower right of the Pencil. This change means that the path is a closed path if you release the mouse button when that particular cursor is showing.

FIGURE 4.12

The paths in this drawing were created with the Pencil tool.

Connecting Pencil paths

You can quickly connect the Pencil paths you draw in Illustrator. While drawing with the Pencil tool, press Alt (Option), and when you release the mouse button, a line automatically connects the beginning anchor point to the ending anchor point, resulting in a closed path. You can try to draw back to the beginning line, but they probably won't connect. You can also draw the paths close to one another: Select the two endpoints and then press Ctrl+J (⌘+J) to join the paths.

Adding to an existing open path

To continue drawing on an existing path (which could have been drawn with the Pencil tool or the Pen tool), the existing path must first be an open path with two distinct endpoints. Pass the Pencil tool over one end of the path and then watch for the cursor to change — the little x beside the Pencil disappears. This action means that if you click and drag, you can extend the path with the Pencil tool. If Caps Lock is engaged, the cursor changes from an X (crosshairs) to a +.

You can add on only to endpoints on an existing path. Anchor points that are within paths can't be connected to new (or existing, for that matter) segments. If you attempt to draw from an anchor point that isn't an endpoint, you create an endpoint for the path you're drawing that's overlapping but not connected to the anchor point you clicked.

Working with the Smooth tool

This extremely cool editing tool makes changing any path a breeze. The Smooth tool works on any path regardless of what tool created it. You can apply the Smooth tool in one of two ways:

- **Using the Tools panel:** Select the path you want to edit, click the Smooth tool found in the Pencil tool's popup tools, and then drag your mouse over a selected path to smooth out the line.

- **While using other tools:** You can also access the Smooth tool while using the Pencil tool by pressing Alt (Option). The tool changes to the Smooth tool while you keep Alt (Option) pressed.

Figure 4.13 shows a path before and after using the Smooth tool. The top path has more anchor points than the smoothed bottom path.

Double-clicking the Smooth tool opens a dialog box where, just as with the Pencil tool, you can set Fidelity and Smoothness values.

FIGURE 4.13

The top illustration is pretty bumpy. The same illustration below has the Smooth tool applied to it. Notice the smoothness, especially in the eye area.

Erasing with the Path Eraser tool

You find the Path Eraser tool with the Pencil tool in the Tools panel. Like the Smooth tool, the Path Eraser tool works on any path, no matter how you created it. The Path Eraser tool does what its name suggests: It erases a path at the point where you've dragged the Path Eraser tool over the path. You can use the Path Eraser tool to cut a path by first selecting the path and then dragging across a section with the Path Eraser tool. Illustrator removes the section you drag over. You can use the Path Eraser tool to cut a line, just as you would use the Scissors tool. If you just click one time on the path, Illustrator cuts the path exactly in that spot. Unlike Photoshop's clunky eraser-looking tool, this is much more refined and easier to use.

 **For more on the Scissors tool, see Chapter 6.**

Drawing with the Pen tool

The Pen tool is the most powerful tool in Illustrator's arsenal because you're dealing more directly with Bézier curves than with any other tool. Drawing objects with any other tool is one thing, but using the Pen tool to create paths out of nothing is dumbfounding.

During the first several months of using Illustrator, you may find yourself avoiding the Pen tool like the plague. Then, you slowly work up to where you can draw straight lines comfortably and, finally, curved segments. Even after you draw curved segments for a while, you still may not understand how the tool works, and you may miss out on many of its capabilities because of that lack of knowledge. While practicing with the Pen tool, you begin to understand the four types of anchor points — smooth points, straight corner points, curved corner points, and combination corner points — and you discover that understanding how anchor points work is the key to using the Pen tool. The first click of the Pen tool produces one anchor point. The second click (usually in a different location) creates a second anchor point that's joined to the first anchor point by a line segment. Clicking without dragging produces a straight corner point.

Although the Pen tool is a little frustrating and confusing to use at first, it's the most important tool to learn. It saves you so much time and effort because you can draw the most accurately and smoothly with fewer edits. After you master this tool, you will use it for most of your drawing and tracing needs.

Unfortunately, the Pen tool doesn't do all the work; you do have to perform some of the labor involved in creating curves and straight lines. Drawing with the Pen tool isn't just placing anchor points.

Here are some issues to consider when you're drawing with the Pen tool:

- **The first obstacle is determining where the heck those anchor points are going to go.** Two drawings with the same number of anchor points can look totally different, depending on anchor point placement. You have to think ahead to determine what the path will look like before you draw it. You should always locate points where you want a change in the path. That change can be a different curve or a corner. Look for these three changes:

- A corner of any type

- The point where a curve changes from clockwise to counterclockwise or vice versa

- The point where a curve changes *intensity*: from tight to loose or loose to tight (by far, the hardest change to judge)

- **The second obstacle is deciding what type of anchor point you want to use.** Remember that you have four different anchor points to choose from when drawing with the Pen tool — smooth, straight corner, curved corner, and combination corner. If the path is smoothly curving, you use a smooth point. If it has a corner, use one of the corner points.

- **The third obstacle arises when you decide that the anchor point should be anything but a straight corner point because all the other anchor points have control handles.** The obstacle is figuring out how to drag the control handles, how far to drag them, and in which direction to drag them.

Drawing straight lines with the Pen tool

The easiest way to start learning to use the Pen tool is by drawing straight lines. The lightning bolt in Figure 4.14 uses only straight lines. The great thing about straight lines drawn with the Pen tool is that you don't have to worry about or fuss over control handles.

The simplest straight line is a line drawn with only two anchor points. To draw straight lines, follow these steps:

1. **Click the Pen tool.** This tool is located on the third row of the first column in the Tools panel and looks like an old-fashioned ink pen tip.

2. **Click and release where you want the first endpoint to appear.** This becomes the beginning of your line.

3. **Click and release where you want the second endpoint (the end of the line) to appear.** A line appears between the two points. Too easy, isn't it?

 Hold Shift to keep the line constrained to a 45° angle (0, 45, 90, etc.).

4. **To draw another separate line, first click the Pen tool in the Tools panel or hold Ctrl (⌘) and then click on the Artboard.** Either action tells Illustrator that you're finished drawing the first line.

5. **Clicking and releasing again in one spot and then another draws a second line with two endpoints.** Be careful not to drag when clicking the Pen tool to form straight lines. If you drag the mouse, you create a smooth point and the path curves.

FIGURE 4.14

Straight lines drawn with the Pen tool are all you need to create something like this lightning bolt.

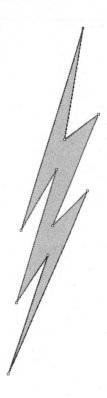

Paths drawn with the Pen tool, like the Pencil tool, may cross themselves. The only strange result you may see involves the fills for objects whose paths cross. In open paths created with the Pen tool, fills may look unusual because of the imaginary line between the two endpoints and any paths that the imaginary line crosses.

Closing paths with the Pen tool

If you want to create a closed path (one with no endpoints), after you finish whatever you're drawing, hover over the first anchor point in that segment. As the Pen tool crosses over the beginning anchor point, the cursor changes to a pen with a circle in the lower-right corner. Click the mouse on this anchor point to close the path. After you create a closed path, you don't need to click the Pen tool again. Instead, the next click of the Pen tool in the document automatically begins a new path.

 You must have at least three anchor points to create a closed path with straight lines.

Drawing curves with the Pen tool

Initially, you may find the whole process of drawing curves with the Pen tool rather disorienting. You actually have to think differently to grasp what the Pen tool is doing. To draw a curve, you need to drag with the Pen tool rather than click and release when you draw straight lines. This section gives two sets of instructions for creating two basic curve shapes: the bump and the S shape.

The most basic curve is the bump (a curved segment between just two points). Follow these steps to create the bump that's shown in Figure 4.15:

1. **Click with the Pen tool and then drag up about ½ inch.** You see an anchor point and a control handle line extending from it as you drag.

2. **Release the mouse button.** When you do so, you see the anchor point and a line extending to where you dragged, with a control handle at its end.

3. **Position the cursor about 1 inch to the right of the place you first clicked.**

4. **Click with the mouse and then drag down about ½ inch.** As you drag, you see a curve forming that resembles a bump.

5. **Release the mouse.** The curve fills with the current fill color. You also see the control handle you just dragged.

Before you try to draw another curve, remember that the Pen tool is still in a mode that continues the current path; it doesn't start a new one. To start a new path, choose Select ⇨ Deselect or press Shift+Ctrl+A (⌘+Shift+A). Alternatively, you can hold Ctrl (⌘) and then click an empty area on the Artboard. The next time you use the Pen tool, you can draw a separate path.

FIGURE 4.15

You can create a basic bump curve like this in five simple steps.

To create an S shape, one more set of steps is needed. With these steps, you can create the S shape, as shown in Figure 4.16:

1. **Click and drag with the Pen tool about ½ inch to the left.** An anchor point and a control handle line appear as you drag.

2. **Release the mouse button.** You should see the anchor point and the control handle that you just drew, with a control handle line between them.

3. **Position the cursor about 1 inch below where you first clicked.**

4. **Click and drag to the right about ½ inch.**

5. **Release the mouse button.**

6. **Position the cursor about 1 inch below the last point you clicked.**

7. **Click and drag to the left about ½ inch.** Now you have an S shape.

CROSS-REF For more on changing strokes and fills, see Chapter 6.

All the anchor points created in these two exercises are smooth points. You drag the control handles in the direction of the next curve that you want to draw. The lengths of the control handle lines on either side of the anchor point are equal. However, you don't have to make the lengths of the control handle lines on either side of the smooth point the same. Instead, you can make a smooth point have both long and short control handle lines coming out of it. The length of the control handle line affects the curve, as shown on the S curve in Figure 4.17.

FIGURE 4.16

It's also very easy to create a basic S curve like this one.

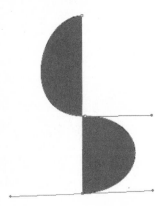

FIGURE 4.17

The length and direction of the control handle lines control the shape of the curve.

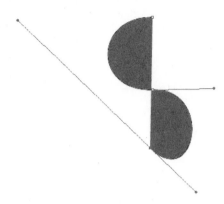

Follow these steps to create a smooth point with two control handle lines of different lengths:

1. **Create a smooth point along a path.** See the last set of steps to learn how to do so.

2. **Select the newly created smooth point with the Direct Selection tool.** For more on using the selection tools, see Chapter 6.

3. **Click and drag the control handle again.**

4. **Adjust the angle for both control handle lines and the length for the new control handle line that you're dragging.** Note that as you drag out this control handle line, the other control handle line wobbles to the angle that you're dragging. This happens because on any smooth point, the control handle lines must be at the same angle, and as you drag out the new control handle line, you're simultaneously changing the angle for both control handle lines.

Closing curved paths with the Pen tool

The majority of the paths you draw with the Pen tool will be closed paths, not the open ones you've drawn so far. Like open curved paths, any closed curved path must have at least two anchor points, just as paths with straight corner points need three distinct points to create a closed path.

When the Pen tool is placed over the starting point of the path you've drawn, a little circle appears to the right of the pen shape. This indicates that the path becomes a closed path if you click this anchor point.

Of course, to ensure that the initial anchor point remains a smooth point, you need to click and drag on the initial anchor point. Simply clicking produces a combination corner point, which has only one control handle associated with it.

Working with curved corner points

Curved corner points are points where two different, usually distinct, curved segments meet at an anchor point. Because the two curves meet this way, a smooth point doesn't provide the means for their joining correctly. Instead, a smooth point would make the two different curves smoothly blend into each other.

The main difference between a curved corner point and a smooth point is that a smooth point has two linked control handles on their ends; a curved corner point has two *independent* control handles. As the name indicates, control handles and their associated control handle lines move independently of each other, enabling two different, distinct types of curves to come from the same anchor point.

To create a curved corner point, create a smooth point in a path, press Alt (Option), and then drag the control handle of the point you just created. As you do this, you're creating the control handles independently. The next segment will curve as controlled by the newly split control handle, not by the original combined one.

 When creating curved corner points, you can press Alt (Option) to create independent points all the time, not just when starting a new segment.

Combination corner points

A combination corner point is a point where a curved segment and a straight segment meet each other. At this corner point, there's one control handle coming from the anchor point from the side where the curved segment is located, and on the other side, there's no control handle, indicating a straight segment.

To create a combination corner point with the Pen tool, draw a few curved segments and then go back to the last anchor point. You should see two linked control handles displayed at this point. Simply click once on the anchor point, and one of the two control handles disappears. The next segment then starts out straight.

 You can change existing smooth and curved corner points into combination corner points simply by dragging one of the control handles into the anchor points.

Using basic Pen tool drawing techniques

Now that you've gained some experience with the Pen tool, you'll benefit by living by the Pen Rules. The Pen Rules are laws to live by — or at least to draw by.

Follow these rules:

- **Remember not to drag where you want to place the next point; instead, go just one-third of that distance.** You must determine where you want to locate the next anchor point before you can determine the length of the control handle line you're dragging. Dragging by one-third is always a good approximation to make. You may run into trouble when the control handle line is more than half or less than one-quarter of the next segment. If your control handle line is too long or too short, chances are good that the line will curve erratically.

- **Don't get the outside of the curve and the outside of the shape you're drawing confused — they may well be two different things. Remember that control handle lines are always tangent to the curved segment they're guiding.** Tangent? Well, here's a simpler way of putting this rule: It's a line that touches the curve but doesn't cross or intersect the curve. If your control handle lies inside the curve you're drawing, it becomes too short and overpowered by the next anchor point. Control handles pull the curve toward themselves; this makes them naturally curve out toward the control handle lines. If you fight this natural pull, your illustrations can look loopy and silly.

- **Drag the control handle in the direction that you want the curve to travel at that anchor point.** The control handle pulls the curve toward itself by its very nature. If you drag backward toward the preceding segment, you create little curved spikes that stick out from the anchor points. This commandment applies only to Smooth points. If the anchor point is a curved corner point, you must make the initial drag in the direction the curve is traveling and the next drag (Alt [Option]+drag) in the direction that you want the curve to travel. If the anchor point is a combination curve point and the next segment is straight, make the dragging motion in the direction that the curve is traveling. Next, click and release the anchor point. If the combination curve point's next segment is curved, click and release the first click, and the second click should be dragged in the direction of the next curve.

- **Use as few anchor points as possible.** If your illustration calls for smooth, flowing curves, use very few anchor points. If, on the other hand, you want your illustration rough and gritty, use more anchor points. The fewer anchor points you use, the smoother the final result. When only a few anchor points are on a path, changing its shape is easier and faster. More anchor points mean a bigger file and also longer printing times. If you're not sure whether you need more anchor points, don't add them. You can always add them later with the Add Anchor Point tool.

CROSS-REF For more on the Add Anchor Point tool, see Chapter 6.

- **Place anchor points at the beginning of each different curve.** You should use anchor points as *transitional* points, where the curve either changes direction or increases or decreases in size dramatically. If it looks as though the curve changes from one type of curve to another, the location to place an anchor point is in the middle of that transitional section.

- **Don't overcompensate for a previously misdrawn curve.** If you really messed up on the last anchor point you've drawn, don't panic and try to undo the mistake by dragging in the wrong direction or by dragging the control handle out to some ridiculous length. Doing either of these two things may temporarily fix the preceding curve but usually wrecks the next curve, causing you to have to overcompensate yet again.

Using the various line tools

In addition to the Pencil and Pen tools, Illustrator includes several unique tools that you can use to create specialized types of lines. From straight lines with the Line Segment tool to spiral lines using the Spiral tool, these line tools fall into the convenience category. Housed with the Line Segment tool, these tools include the Arc, Spiral, Rectangular Grid, and Polar Grid tools.

Using the Line Segment tool

Now that you've learned how to create straight lines the hard way with the Pen tool, here's an easy way — use the Line Segment tool. After you learn to use the Line Segment tool, you'll think that using the Pencil or Pen tool to draw straight lines is just plain ridiculous. Any amount of caffeine in your system results in a jittery line with either tool. But using this tool is a breeze. Simply click and drag the line where you want it to go, as indicated in Figure 4.18. Holding Shift while drawing a line constrains the line to 45° increments. If you press Alt (Option) while drawing a line, your starting point begins in the middle of the line.

Double-clicking the Line Segment tool or clicking one time on the Artboard displays the Line Segment Tool Options dialog box, as shown in Figure 4.19. In this dialog box, you can set the length and angle and whether to fill the line with the defaulted fill color. You can use the Pen tool to draw straight lines, but when you have a tool specifically made for lines, use it.

TIP The Pen tool versus the Line Segment tool: The Pen tool can also draw straight lines and constrained lines, so why use the Line Segment tool at all? Well, one small slip of the Pen tool and you have a curved line. In addition, you can get the precise length and angle using the Line Segment tool because you actually see the line rubberbanding from the original point.

FIGURE 4.18

A line segment being drawn with the Line Segment tool

FIGURE 4.19

The Line Segment Tool Options dialog box lets you draw exactly the line you want without dragging the mouse.

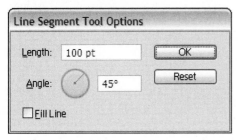

Working with the Arc tool

Arcs are now easily drawn using the Arc tool. The old-fashioned way used to be to draw an oval and remove the sections you didn't need via the Direct Selection tool or the Scissors tool. Figure 4.20 shows an arc drawn with the Arc tool.

The Arc tool is housed with the Line Segment tool. You can have an arc that sweeps inward or outward, depending on your settings. Double-clicking the Arc tool accesses the Arc Segment Tool Options dialog box, as shown in Figure 4.21.

FIGURE 4.20

An arc being drawn with the Arc tool

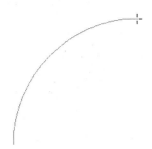

FIGURE 4.21

The Arc Segment Tool Options dialog box includes several options for the properties of an arc.

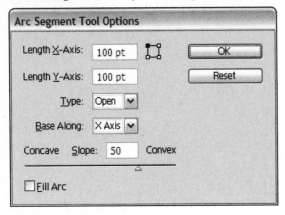

These are the Arc Segment Tool Options:

- **Length X-Axis:** Type the value for the length of the slope along the x-axis.
- **Length Y-Axis:** Type the value for the length of the slope along the y-axis.
- **Type:** Choose whether you want the arc to have an open or closed path.
- **Base Along:** This is where you choose the direction of the slope, either along the x-axis or the y-axis.
- **Slope:** Dragging the slider to the left results in a concave slope. Dragging the slider to the right results in a convex slope.
- **Fill Arc:** Clicking this check box fills the inside of the arc with the default color.

TIP When dragging out an arc, pressing F or X toggles the arc between convex and concave. Press the spacebar while you draw to move the whole arc. These keyboard shortcuts are true with all shapes that you draw in Illustrator.

Creating spirals with the Spiral tool

The Spiral tool (located with the Line Segment tool) makes spirals — all sorts of spirals. What can you use a spiral for? Well, you can use the Spiral tool to create a simulated record. Of course, the path is exceedingly long and refuses to print on most imagesetters. Other than that, you can use them to simulate nature patterns, such as snails, shells, a whirlpool, or a cinnamon roll. Figure 4.22 shows several spirals manufactured with the Spiral tool.

 Spirals beg to be stroked, not filled. Putting just a fill on a spiral makes it look lumpy and not quite round.

If you click in your document with the Spiral tool, the Spiral dialog box, as shown in Figure 4.23, opens, and you can type specific values for a spiral. This is handy for those times your client or boss wants that 82.5% decay spiral. Decay measures how tight the spiral is, while Segments controls the length of the spiral.

FIGURE 4.22

These spirals were created with the Spiral tool.

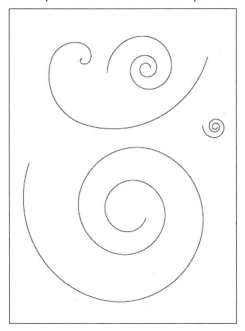

Making grid lines using the Rectangular Grid tool

You can easily create a grid using the Grid tool, which is housed with the Line Segment tool. For example, you could use a grid to create a perspective drawing. Use the Skew tool to give an angled view. You can create a unique Rubik's cube. You can also create grid paper or use the Grid tool to create a data chart. Figure 4.24 shows a drawn grid.

FIGURE 4.23

The Spiral dialog box allows you to modify how your spirals will look.

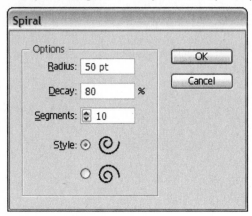

FIGURE 4.24

This grid was created using the Grid tool.

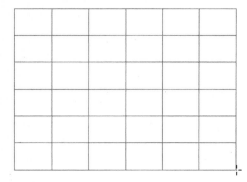

Pressing these keys while creating rectangular grids makes life easier:

- **Up or down arrow:** Increases or decreases the number of horizontal lines
- **Left or right arrow:** Increases or decreases the number of vertical lines
- **Shift:** Creates a perfect square grid
- **Alt (Option):** Creates a grid from a central point

Double-clicking the Grid tool accesses the Rectangular Grid Tool Options dialog box, as shown in Figure 4.25. Under the Grid Options, you can choose to skew the grid. That is, you can make the lines closer to the top or bottom and left or right. You can change the following options:

- **Default Size:** Type the width and height in points.
- **Horizontal Dividers:** Type how many dividers and how much they will skew.
- **Vertical Dividers:** Type the number of dividers and how much they will skew.
- **Use Outside Rectangle As Frame:** This option causes a rectangle to frame the grid.
- **Fill Grid:** Clicking this check box fills the grid with the default fill color.

FIGURE 4.25

The Rectangular Grid Tool Options dialog box lets you specify dividers.

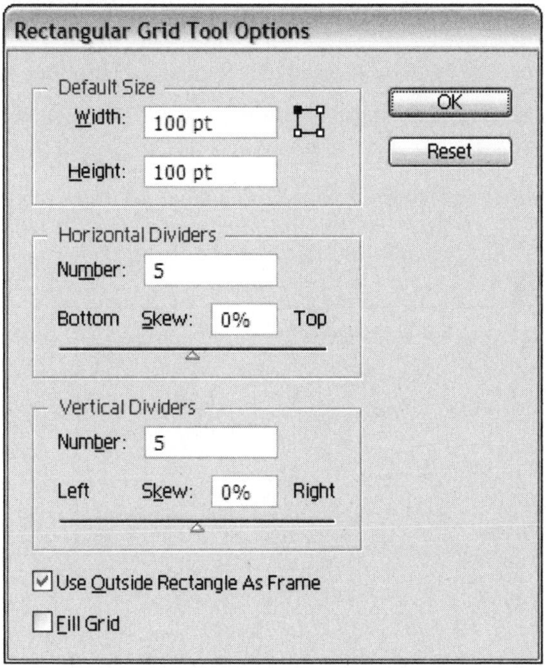

Understanding the Polar Grid tool

The Polar Grid tool is found with the Line Segment tool. A polar grid is also referred to as a radar grid. You would recognize it as similar to a dartboard or a bull's-eye, as shown in Figure 4.26.

The Polar Grid Tool Options dialog box, as shown in Figure 4.27, lets you set the same options as those found in the Rectangular Grid dialog box, except that the dividers are concentric and radial instead of horizontal and vertical:

- **Default Size:** Type the width and height in points.
- **Concentric Dividers:** Type how many dividers and how much they will skew (distributed) away from the center.
- **Radial Dividers:** Type the number of dividers and how much they will skew from top to bottom.
- **Create Compound Path From Ellipses:** Choosing this option causes ellipses to create a compound path, which is treated as a single path by Illustrator and results in a bull's-eye effect for the grid.
- **Fill Grid:** Clicking this check box fills the polar grid with the default fill color.

Pressing these keys while creating polar grids makes life easier:

- **Up or down arrow:** Increases or decreases the number of concentric circles
- **Left or right arrow:** Increases or decreases the number of radial lines
- **Shift:** Creates a perfectly round polar grid
- **Alt (Option):** Creates a polar grid from a central point

FIGURE 4.26

A polar grid looks like a dartboard or a bull's-eye.

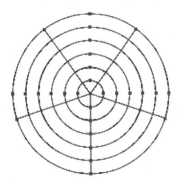

FIGURE 4.27

Use the Polar Grid Tool Options dialog box to adjust the settings for your polar grid object.

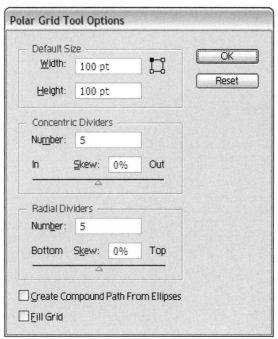

Using the Paintbrush tool

The Paintbrush tool draws a stroked path — that is, a path that's also a brushstroke. This makes life so much easier when it comes to editing. The Paintbrush tool is similar to paintbrush-type tools in painting programs. The Paintbrush has a certain width, and you can paint with this Paintbrush at this width anywhere in your document. The big difference between the paintbrushes in paint programs and Illustrator's Paintbrush tool is that when you finish drawing with Illustrator's Paintbrush tool, you create a stroked path.

To use the Paintbrush tool, click the tool, choose the brush from the Brush panel, and then start drawing. A free-form path appears wherever you drag. That's all there is to it — mostly. Figure 4.28 shows a drawing that was created with the Paintbrush tool set to a variable width with a pressure-sensitive stylus.

Drawing with the Paintbrush tool is a bit more complicated than I just explained. The most important consideration is the width of the paintbrush stroke. The paintbrush stroke can be as narrow as 0 points and as wide as 1296 points (that's 18 inches to you and me).

Although 0 is the smallest width, a paintbrush stroke drawn with a width of 0 points actually has a width bigger than 0 points. To change the paintbrush stroke width (the default is 9 points), open the Stroke panel (not the Tools panel) and then type a number in the Weight text field. Remember that you're actually changing the default brush.

FIGURE 4.28

This drawing of a horse was created with the Paintbrush tool by using a pressure-sensitive tablet and a stylus.

A mouse is not an intuitive drawing tool, and not being able to draw in the first place makes it even more difficult to draw with the Paintbrush tool. So, if artists have trouble with the mouse, what's the point of having the Paintbrush tool at all? Well, instead of a mouse, you can use several types of alternative drawing devices. The best of these is a pressure-sensitive tablet (for more information about pressure-sensitive drawing tablets, visit the Wacom Web site at www.wacom.com). Trackballs with locking buttons are also good for drawing with the Paintbrush tool; this allows more control over the direction and speed of the Paintbrush.

> **TIP** When you're drawing with any of the tools in Illustrator, dragging off the edge of the window causes the window to scroll, which creates a frightening effect for the uninitiated. If you don't want the window to remain where it scrolled to, don't let go of the mouse button; instead, drag in the opposite direction until the window returns to the original position.

To help you draw more precisely, you have the option of changing the cursor shape from the cute little brush into crosshairs. Press Caps Lock (to engage it), and the cursor changes into crosshairs with a dot in the center. Press Caps Lock again (to release it), and the cursor returns to the brush shape. The dot at the center of the crosshairs is the center of any paintbrush stroke drawn with the Paintbrush tool. Normally, when the cursor is in the shape of a paintbrush, the tip is the center of the paintbrush stroke. Some people find it easier to draw when the Paintbrush cursor is replaced with the precise crosshairs.

Using brushes

If you want to create a totally new brush, choose New Brush from the Brushes panel's popup menu to display the New Brush dialog box, as shown in Figure 4.29. You can then choose the type of new brush you want to create. You can choose from Calligraphic, Scatter, Art, and Pattern brushes. The Brushes panel includes samples of each of these brush types. Calligraphic brushes make strokes similar to a calligraphic pen. Scatter brushes scatter an object along the brushed path. The Art brush takes an object and stretches it along the brush path length. The Pattern brush uses repeated tiles along the brush path.

FIGURE 4.29

The New Brush dialog box lets you create one of four different brush types.

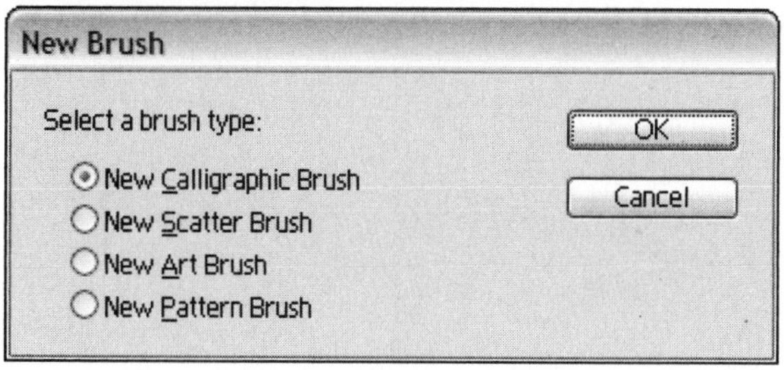

Using the Calligraphic brush

A Calligraphic brush was made to simulate an actual calligraphic pen tip. You set the angle and size and then draw to your heart's content. You can also create a perfectly round brush in the Calligraphic Brush Options dialog box by not typing an angle and by keeping the roundness at 100%.

The Calligraphic Brush Options, as shown in Figure 4.30, are as follows:

- **Name:** You can type a name here for your new brush or rename an existing brush (maximum of 30 characters).

- **Angle:** You can set the angle of the Calligraphic brush. The angle you should choose depends on what's going to be drawn. To mimic hand-drawn lettering in a calligraphic style, the angle should be set to 45° (or if you're left-handed, it should be set to –45°).

- **Roundness:** This does what you think it does. It sets the roundness of the brush. The higher you make the value, the rounder the brush.

- **Diameter:** The diameter value sets the maximum diameter of the brush.

- **Variation:** If you choose the Random option from the Angle or Roundness dropdown lists, you can then type a value for Variation. The Variation for the Angle value is in a degree that you want to vary from the original setting for each brushstroke. The Variation for the Roundness is set in percentages. A slider sets the Variation for the Diameter or you can type a number. The Diameter Variation goes from your original value up to the Variation value. This is a great way to simulate a hand-drawn look if you don't have a pressure-sensitive tablet.

FIGURE 4.30

The Calligraphic Brush Options dialog box allows you to customize a brush.

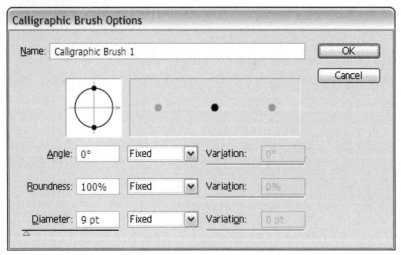

Creating a Calligraphic brush

You can use a Calligraphic brush in many ways. You can choose an existing brush and get started. If you load additional brush libraries, you'll find quite a variety of brushes to choose from. You can also create your own brush from an existing one or from scratch. To create a new brush, use an existing style that you like but that you want to alter. To create a brush like this, choose the brush that you want to duplicate and then choose Duplicate Brush from the Brush panel's popup menu. To edit that duplicated brush, double-click the duplicate brush or choose Brush Options from the popup menu. In the Brush Options dialog box, change the brush to your specifications.

Variable widths and pressure-sensitive tablets

If you have a pressure-sensitive tablet — some call them Wacom (pronounced walk 'em) tablets because a large majority are made by Wacom — you can choose the Pressure option beside the Diameter text field in the Brush Options dialog box (accessed by double-clicking a brush in the Brushes panel). If you don't have a pressure-sensitive tablet, the Pressure option is grayed out.

NOTE A pressure-sensitive tablet is a flat, rectangular device over which you pass a special stylus. The more pressure exerted by the stylus on the tablet, the wider a paintbrush stroke becomes, provided that you choose the Pressure option in the Calligraphic dialog box. When using the Pressure option, try to set the Variation different from the original specified diameter to see the difference when you press harder or softer.

Creating with the Scatter brush

The Scatter brush copies and scatters a predefined object along a path. Illustrator has a number of brush libraries containing artwork that you can use for a Scatter brush or you can choose a piece of artwork that you created to use as a Scatter brush. Choose Window ⇨ Brush Libraries to view the available brush libraries. Figure 4.31 shows an example of a path drawn with one of the available Scatter brushes.

These are your choices in the Scatter Brush Options dialog box, as seen in Figure 4.32:

- **Name:** You can type a name for your brush (up to 30 characters).
- **Size:** In the size area, you have several options. If you want really big images and small images that vary in size, then drag the sliders in opposite directions (there are two there, even though you can't see them when you first create the brush).
- **Spacing:** This option adjusts the space between each object.
- **Scatter:** This option adjusts how the objects follow the original path on each side of the path. If you set a high value, the objects are farther away from the original path.
- **Rotation:** This option adjusts how much the object rotates from its original position.

- **Rotation relative to:** This option gives you two choices from a popup menu. The Page option rotates objects according to the page setup. The Path option rotates objects tangent to the path.

- **Colorization:** You have four Colorization choices: None, Tints, Tints and Shades, and Hue Shift. Colorization and tips about colorization can be found later in this chapter.

 **TIP**   The Scatter Brush Options dialog box shows the brush preview only when you're creating a new brush.

FIGURE 4.31

The Scatter brush allows you to draw some very interesting paths.

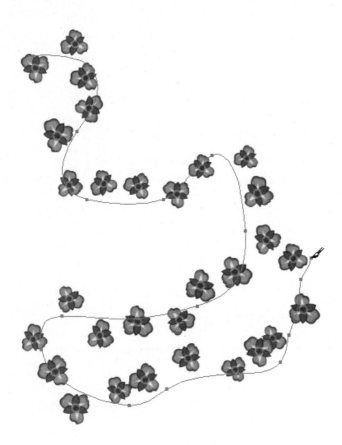

FIGURE 4.32

The Scatter Brush Options dialog box

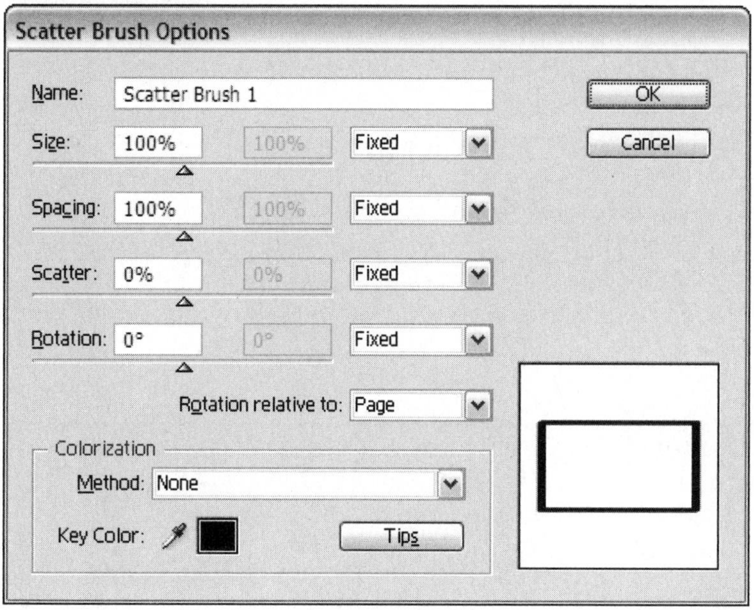

Scatter Brush Options

Name:	Scatter Brush 1

Size: 100% 100% Fixed

Spacing: 100% 100% Fixed

Scatter: 0% 0% Fixed

Rotation: 0° 0° Fixed

Rotation relative to: Page

Colorization

Method: None

Key Color:

OK

Cancel

Tips

Working with the Art brush

The Art brush, like the Scatter brush, uses an object along a path. The difference is that the Art brush stretches the object to the length of the path rather than repeating and scattering the object. Illustrator centers the object evenly over the path and then stretches it. Figure 4.33 shows several Art brush examples.

These are your choices in the Art Brush Options dialog box, as shown in Figure 4.34:

- **Name:** You can type a name your new Art brush or rename an existing Art brush (up to 30 characters).
- **Width:** This value scales the art when it's stretched. You can choose Proportional to keep the object in proportion.
- **Direction:** This option lets you choose from four directions. The directions are relative to how you drag the Paintbrush.
- **Flip:** This option lets you flip your object along or across the path.
- **Colorization:** You have four Colorization choices in the Method popup menu: None, Tints, Tints and Shades, and Hue Shift. The key color is the color that the colorization uses as a base. Colorization and colorization tips can be found later in this chapter.

FIGURE 4.33

The Art brush creates artistic-looking paths.

FIGURE 4.34

The Art Brush Options dialog box allows you to create your own Art brush.

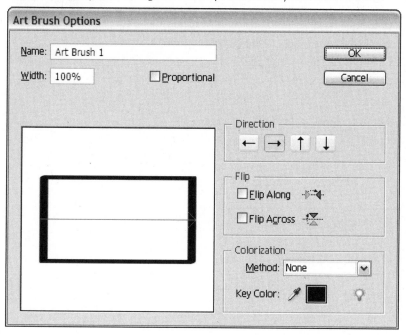

Creating tiles using the Pattern brush

The Pattern brush repeats a tiled object along a path. The Pattern brush can have tiles to display the sides, inner corner, outer corner, beginning, and end. If you think of a Pattern brush as you would a regular pattern tile but keep in mind the corners, you'll have no problem creating your own interesting Pattern brushes. Figure 4.35 shows an example of one of the Pattern brushes.

These are your choices in the Pattern Brush Options dialog box, as shown in Figure 4.36:

- **Name:** Type a new name or change an existing name (up to 30 characters).
- **Scale:** This option allows you to increase or decrease the size of the pattern relative to its original size.
- **Spacing:** This is the space between each tile of the pattern.
- **Tile buttons:** This is where you choose which of the five tiles you want to create.

- **Flip:** This option lets you flip the pattern along or across the path.

- **Fit:** In this option, you can choose Stretch to fit, Add space to fit, or Approximate path. Stretch lengthens or shortens a tile to fit your object. Add space adds a blank space between the tiles to fit the path proportionately. Approximate path makes the tile fit as close to the original path without altering the tiles.

- **Colorization:** You have four Colorization choices in the Method popup menu: None, Tints, Tints and Shades, and Hue Shift. The key color is the color that the colorization uses as a base. Colorization and colorization tips can be found later in this chapter.

The list in the Pattern Brush Options dialog box allows you to choose from four existing patterns instead of the selected artwork: None, Original, Polka Dot Pattern, and Waves Pattern. Any pattern in your document is listed here.

FIGURE 4.35

The Pattern brush draws a stroke by using a repeating pattern.

FIGURE 4.36

The Pattern Brush Options dialog box allows you to create some very interesting brushes.

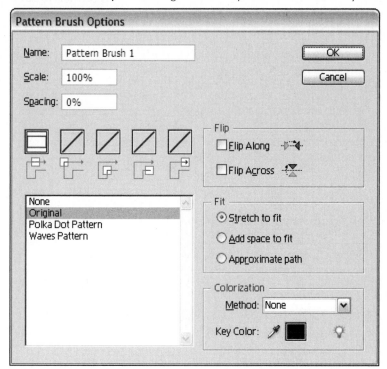

Making a custom brush

You can customize a brush in several ways. If you like a brush but not all aspects of it, you can duplicate that brush (by choosing Duplicate Brush from the Brushes panel menu) and edit its options to make it as you like. To edit a brush, double-click the brush, choose Brush Options from the popup menu, or click the Brush Options button at the bottom of the Brushes panel. You can also create a brush by choosing New Brush from the popup menu or clicking the New Brush button at the bottom of the Brushes panel. This displays a dialog box asking you to choose the type of brush you want to create.

NOTE You can create a Calligraphic brush by filling in the text fields of the Calligraphic Brush dialog box. To create any of the other brushes, you must have your art drawn first and then choose New Brush.

To create your own brush design, first create the object that you want to use. Next, select all the parts of the object that you want as a brush and then choose New Brush from the Brushes panel's popup menu. Then, choose the type of brush you want to create. The Brush Options dialog box opens, and you see your new design there. Now all you have to do is set the rest of the options, and you're ready to use your new brush.

Understanding colorization tips

The Tips button in the Art, Scatter, and Pattern Brush dialog boxes displays a dialog box explaining the different colorization options. Figure 4.37 shows the Colorization Tips dialog box, which has four areas of colorization: None, Tints, Tints and Shades, and Hue Shift.

To see how the Colorization options work, first create four copies of a brush. For the first copy, use the default of None. For the next three copies, change the stroke color (you won't see anything happen yet). Double-click the second copy and then choose Tint. Apply the stroke when asked to do so in the dialog box. The color should change at this point. Double-click the third copy and then choose Tints and Shades. Double-click the last copy and then choose Hue Shift. All the copies should look different.

FIGURE 4.37

The Colorization Tips dialog box provides visual examples of the various colorization options.

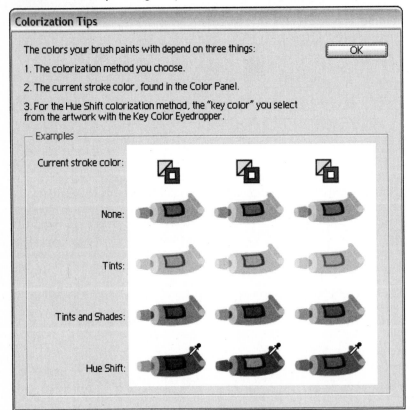

Checking out the Brush libraries

The Brush Library that displays when you choose the Brush panel is the default library. You have additional libraries from which to choose. Adobe has really come up with some cool brushes for your creative pleasures. The other libraries are found under the Window menu, as shown in Figure 4.38.

To use a brush from another Brush library, choose the brush you want from the scrolling list. Figure 4.39 shows just one of the many libraries that are included with Illustrator.

FIGURE 4.38

The Brush Library submenu under the Window menu contains many different libraries.

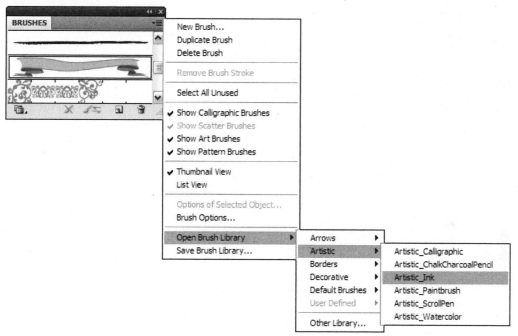

FIGURE 4.39

The Brush libraries include a variety of interesting brushes you can use.

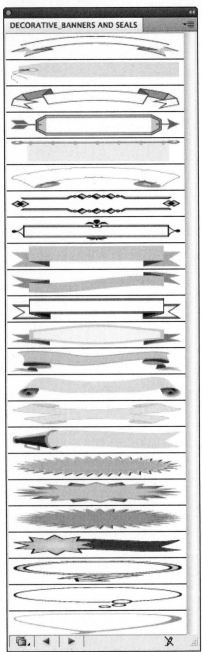

Summary

Illustrator's drawing tools provide you with many powerful methods of quickly creating artwork. In this chapter, you learned the following important points about using these tools:

- Illustrator includes four anchor point types: straight corner points, combination corner points, smooth points, and curved corner points.

- Edit curves with the control handles.

- Curves are based on the Bézier principle.

- Use the Pencil tool to create paths quickly.

- Use the Smooth and Path Eraser tools to edit your paths.

- Although the Pen tool is the most difficult to learn, it yields the smoothest results.

- The Paintbrush tool creates a free-formed stroked path.

- A pressure-sensitive tablet can mimic hand-drawn art.

- The Line Segment tool can create straight lines. Other tools with the Line Segment tool let you create arcs, grids, polar grids, and spirals.

- The Scatter brush repeats objects along a path rotated and sized differently.

- The Art brush stretches an object to the length of the path.

- The Pattern brush repeats a pattern on a path.

- You can create a new brush in the Brushes panel.

Chapter 5

Creating Objects, Graphs, and Symbols

In this chapter, you learn how to create objects, such as rectangles, ellipses, polygons, and stars. In addition, you find out how to create and enhance graphs, add touches of light with the Flare tool, and create really cool repeating effects with the Symbolism tools.

This is actually a very important chapter because it introduces the objects, graphs, and symbols that you will often use in later chapters. Be sure to take the time to understand the concepts that are presented in this chapter so that you have an easier time later.

Making Basic Shapes

Drawing the most basic shapes — rectangles, ellipses, polygons, and stars — is precisely what a computer is for. Try drawing a perfect ellipse by hand. Troublesome, isn't it? How about a square that doesn't have ink bubbles or splotches at the corners? A nine-pointed star? Drawing these objects and then coloring them in Illustrator is so easy and so basic that after a few weeks of using Illustrator, you never have to draw a shape by hand again without wincing — and maybe even shuddering.

Illustrator exemplifies the true power of object-oriented drawing programming. No matter what you draw, you can adjust and move each piece of the drawing independently until it's just right. Don't like the sun so high in your background? Pull it down and tuck it in just a bit behind those mountains. Is the tree too small for the house in your illustration? Scale it up a bit. This feature is great not only for artists but also for your pesky client (or boss) who demands that everything be moved except that darned tree.

IN THIS CHAPTER

Creating rectangles, ellipses, polygons, and stars

Using the Flare tool

Understanding fills and strokes

Designing graphs, charts, flowcharts, and diagrams

Using the Symbol Sprayer tools

Editing and altering symbols

And after you create the shape, you can move, rotate, scale, and manipulate it in any way you want. Figure 5.1 shows an illustration drawn one way and then modified in a matter of seconds by moving existing elements and adding a few anchor points.

FIGURE 5.1

A basic square (top) becomes a more interesting shape (bottom) with a few simple modifications.

Remember these general concepts when you draw basic shapes:

- **Creating common shapes:** You can draw common objects (or shapes) in Illustrator, including squares and rectangles, rectangles with rounded corners, circles and ellipses, polygons, and stars. Tools for creating these objects are found as popup tools in the Tools panel under the Rectangle tool. You basically use all these tools in the same manner. So, after you learn how to use the Rectangle tool later in this chapter, you'll know how to use the other tools.

CROSS-REF For more on paths, see Chapter 4. For more on selecting objects, see Chapter 6.

- **Lines and points that appear when you select an object:** After you draw a shape, an outlined closed path appears with blue points indicating the anchor points. The edge of the path has thin blue lines surrounding it. These blue lines indicate that the object is currently selected.

TIP Note that the closed path appears in black unless you've changed the default fill and line colors. For more on changing the fill or line color, see the section on this topic later in this chapter. Also, the anchor points appear as blue points only if you're in Preview mode, the default viewing mode. To learn more about the view modes in Illustrator, see Chapter 2.

- **Changing an object's shape:** The initial click you make with any of the shape tools is called the origin point. While you drag a shape, the origin point never moves, but the rest of the shape is fluid, changing shape as you drag in different directions and to different distances with your mouse. Dragging horizontally with almost no vertical movement results in a long, flat shape. Dragging vertically with very little horizontal movement creates a shape that's tall and thin. Dragging at a 45° angle (diagonally) results in a regular (in the geometric sense) shape.

- **Typing exact dimensions in a shape's dialog box:** If you click with a tool on the Artboard without dragging it, the shape's dialog box appears. The center of the shape is now where you clicked (normally, the corner of the shape is where you click). Unlike manually drawing (dragging) centered shapes, the dimensions you type are the actual dimensions of the shape. The dimension is not doubled as it is when you drag a centered shape.

- **Changing units of measure:** When you first run Illustrator, all measurements are set to points. Therefore, the values inside the various shape dialog boxes appear in so many points (12 points in a pica). To change the units of measure to something else (such as millimeters or inches) and to see how different units of measure compare, see Chapter 8.

- **Moving shapes while you draw them:** While drawing a shape, you may realize that you want to move it. In Illustrator, you can move any shape by holding the spacebar while depressing your mouse button and then dragging your shape to a new location. When you let up on the spacebar, you can continue to draw your object.

- **Deleting shapes:** Deleting the shape you've drawn is even easier than creating it — simply delete it by pressing Backspace or Delete.

NOTE Traditional bitmap paint applications don't have the capability to move sections of a drawing (with the exception of the use of layers in software such as Photoshop and Painter). After you move a section of an image in a bitmap program, a hole appears in the place where the section used to be. And if the new location already has an object, you delete this section of the object, replacing it with the new image.

Drawing shapes from their centers

When you draw a shape, Illustrator starts from the corner, and you have to move your mouse to form your shape. However, if you often place shapes on top of or under other objects, you may need to have an even amount of space between your shape and the object it surrounds. Instead of drawing a shape from a corner, you can draw one from its center. Drawing from the corner forces you to eyeball the space around the object, while drawing from the center of the other object ensures that space surrounding the object is the same.

To draw a shape from its center, hold Alt (Option) and then click and drag. The origin point is now the center of the shape. The farther you drag in one direction, the farther the edges of the shape go out in the opposite direction. Drawing from the center of a shape lets you draw something twice as big as the same shape drawn from a corner. As long as you press Alt (Option), the shape continues drawing from its center. If you release Alt (Option) before you release the mouse button, the origin of the shape changes back to a corner. You can press and release Alt (Option) at any time while drawing, toggling back and forth between drawing from a corner and drawing from the center. You can switch back and forth when drawing rectangles and ellipses only.

Drawing symmetric shapes

You can force Illustrator to create symmetric shapes by holding Shift as you draw a shape. For example, when you press Shift while drawing a rectangle, the rectangle constrains to a square. Likewise, you can draw a perfect circle by holding Shift as you draw an ellipse. You can do this for all the shape tools as well as the Line and Pencil tools.

You can also use the Rectangle (or Ellipse) dialog box to draw a perfect square (or circle) by typing equal values for the width and height. Simply click without dragging to get the dialog box to appear.

> **TIP** To draw shapes from their centers and to make them symmetric at the same time, draw the shape while holding both Alt (Option) and Shift. Ensure that both keys are still pressed when you release the mouse button.

Drawing shapes at an angle

Usually, when you draw a shape with a tool, the shape orients itself with the document and the document window. For example, the bottom of a rectangle aligns parallel to the bottom of the document window.

But what if you want to draw shapes that are all angled at 45° on the page? Well, one possibility is to rotate them after you draw them by using the Transform Each command or the Rotate tool. Better yet, you can set up your document so that every new shape automatically appears at an angle.

CROSS-REF For more on the Transform Each command and Rotate tool, see Chapter 11.

The angle of a shape depends on the Constrain Angle value. Usually, the Constrain Angle is 0°, where all shapes appear to align evenly with the borders of the document. To change the Constrain Angle, choose Edit (Illustrator) ⇨ Preferences ⇨ General and then type a new value in the Constrain Angle text field in the Preferences dialog box.

When you finish drawing these angled shapes, ensure that you change the Constrain Angle setting back to 0° or you create all new shapes at the altered Constrain Angle.

TIP Constrain Angle affects shapes and other objects created in Illustrator, including type. In addition, dragging objects while pressing Shift constrains them to the current Constrain Angle or to a 45° or 90° variation of it. The Constrain Angle is much easier to see if you turn on Grids by choosing View ⇨ Show Grid or pressing Ctrl+" (⌘+"). When the grid option is turned on, it's always aligned with the Constrain Angle.

Drawing rectangles using the Rectangle tool

The most basic shape you can draw is a rectangle. Although the following steps explain how to draw a simple rectangle, you essentially use these same steps for all the other shape tools in Illustrator.

1. **Click the Rectangle tool.** You can do this by clicking it in the Tools panel or by pressing the M on the keyboard. You find the Rectangle tool in the second column of the Tools panel on the fourth row from the top.

2. **Click your mouse on the Artboard and then hold the mouse button.** This sets the origin point of the rectangle. If you press Alt (Option) while you hold the mouse button, you create the rectangle from the center instead of the corner.

3. **Drag your mouse diagonally to the size you desire.** You can draw rectangles from any corner by clicking and dragging in the direction opposite from where you want that corner to be. For example, to draw a rectangle from the lower-right corner, click and drag up and to the left.

4. **Release the mouse button.** Illustrator creates a rectangle, as shown in Figure 5.2. The farther the distance from the initial click to the point where you release the mouse button, the larger the rectangle. As long as you have the Rectangle tool selected, dragging with it in the document window produces a new rectangle.

Click and drag to the opposite corner to draw a quick rectangle.

> **NOTE** Press the tilde (~) key while drawing with the Rectangle tool (as well as all the other shape tools) for a mind-bending, super-insta-duplication effect. Just be prepared to press Ctrl+Z (⌘-Z) afterward to undo the mess.

Defining properties with the Rectangle dialog box

If you want to create a rectangle with exact dimensions, all you have to do is open the Rectangle dialog box and type the dimensions. The steps that follow also apply to the other basic shape tools in Illustrator. To draw a rectangle of an exact size, follow these steps:

1. **Click and release the Rectangle tool where you want to place the upper-left corner.** The Rectangle dialog box, as shown in Figure 5.3, opens.

2. **Type the width and height.** When the Rectangle dialog box opens, values are usually already inside the text fields. These numbers correspond to the size of the rectangle you last drew. To create another rectangle of the same size, just click OK (or press Enter or Return). To make the rectangle a different size, replace the values with your own measurements. If a text field is highlighted, typing replaces the text in the text field and deletes what had been highlighted.

FIGURE 5.3

Use the Rectangle dialog box to specify the exact dimensions of a rectangle.

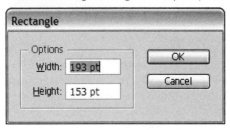

> **TIP** To highlight the next text field in a dialog box, press Tab. You can also highlight the preceding text field in a dialog box by pressing Shift+Tab. If you want to highlight any text field instantly, double-click the value or click the label next to that value.

3. **Click OK.** Illustrator draws the rectangle using precisely the size that you specified. To get out of the Rectangle dialog box without drawing a rectangle, click Cancel or just press Esc (⌘+period). Anything you type in that dialog box is then forgotten. The next time the dialog box opens, it still displays the size of the previously drawn rectangle.

Rectangles whose sizes are specified in the Rectangle dialog box are always drawn from the upper-left corner. The largest rectangle you can draw is about 19 feet by 19 feet. It's a wonder you can get anything done at all with these limitations!

Drawing rounded rectangles and squares

Sometimes, straight corners just aren't good enough. That's when it's time to create a rectangle with rounded corners. Why? Maybe you want your rectangles to look less computery. A tiny bit of corner rounding (2 or 3 points) may be just what you need.

Before getting into how to actually draw rounded rectangles, it helps to understand how Illustrator sets the roundness of your corners. It performs this feat in one of three ways:

- **Using the most recently drawn rounded-corner rectangle:** Illustrator sets the corner radius value using the dimensions of the most recently drawn rounded-corner rectangle and then places this value in the General Preferences dialog box. In other words, after you draw a rectangle using the Rounded Rectangle tool, Illustrator saves those dimensions for the next time that you draw a rounded rectangle.

- **Using the General Preferences dialog box:** What if you don't want to use the radius of the last rounded rectangle? You use the value in the General Preferences dialog box, of course. To do so, choose Edit (Illustrator)➪ Preferences➪ General or press Ctrl+K (⌘+K) and then set the corner radius you desire. All rounded rectangles are now drawn with this new corner radius until you change this value.

- **Using the Rounded Rectangle dialog box:** Changing the value in the Corner Radius text field in the Rounded Rectangle dialog box not only changes the current rounded rectangle's corner radius value but also changes the radius in the General Preferences dialog box. Illustrator uses this corner radius for all subsequently drawn rounded rectangles until you change the radius value again.

Now that you understand how Illustrator works when you draw rounded rectangles, the next step is to learn how to draw one. You can create a rounded rectangle in one of two ways: You can accept the current radius and draw or you can change the current radius and draw.

To draw a rounded rectangle with the current radius, use the Rounded Rectangle tool:

1. **Click the Rounded Rectangle tool.** You do this by clicking and holding the Rectangle tool in the Tools panel until a popup menu opens. Next, drag your mouse to the right to choose the Rounded Rectangle tool.

2. **Click and drag with the Rounded Rectangle tool as if you're drawing a standard rectangle.** The only difference is that this rectangle has rounded corners. The point at which you clicked is where the corner would be — if there were a corner. Of course, with rounded corners, there's no real corner, so the computer uses an imaginary point called the origin point as its on-screen corner reference.

Alternatively, you can specify a corner radius value in the Rounded Rectangle dialog box by following these steps:

1. **Click the Rounded Rectangle tool as before.**

2. **Click the Artboard with the Rounded Rectangle tool.** The Rounded Rectangle dialog box, as shown in Figure 5.4, opens.

FIGURE 5.4

The Rounded Rectangle dialog box includes a third text field for defining the corner radius.

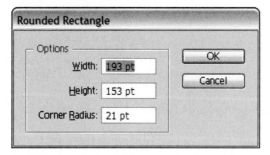

132

3. **Specify a value in the Corner Radius text field.** The third text field is for the size of the corner radius. This option makes the corners of the rectangle curved, although leaving the setting at a value of 0 keeps the corners straight. The corner radius in Illustrator is the length from that imaginary corner (the origin point) to where the curve begins, as shown in Figure 5.5. The larger the value you type in the Corner Radius text field of the Rectangle dialog box, the farther the rectangle starts from the imaginary corner and the bigger the curve. For example, if you set the corner radius at 1 inch, the edge of the rectangle starts curving 1 inch from where a real corner would normally appear.

FIGURE 5.5
_____

The corner radius defines the roundness of the corner.

Origin point   Corner radius

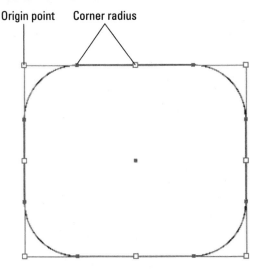

4. **Click OK.** Illustrator applies your changes.

5. **Click and drag with this tool as if you're drawing a standard rectangle.** Your rounded rectangle appears.

TIP If the corner radius is more than half the magnitude of either the length or width of the rectangle, the rectangle may appear to have perfectly round ends on at least two sides. If the corner radius is more than half the magnitude of both the length or width of the rectangle, then the rectangle becomes an ellipse!

TIP Need to draw a rounded rectangle from the center or create a rounded square? Use the Rounded Rectangle tool and then follow the instructions presented earlier in this chapter.

How the Corner Radius Really Works

For all you geometry buffs, the whole corner radius business works this way: The width of the Bounding Box of any circle is called the *diameter* of that circle; half the diameter is the *radius* of the circle, as indicated in the following figure.

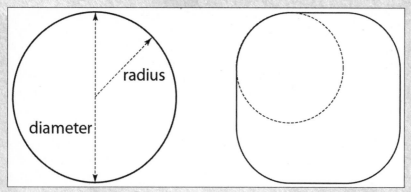

The diameter and radius of a circle

If you create a circle with a radius of 1 inch, the circle actually has a diameter of 2 inches. Put this 2-inch circle into the corner of the rectangle, as in the preceding figure, and the curve of the circle matches the curve of the rounded rectangle that has a corner radius of 1 inch.

To realistically determine the way a rounded corner will look, use the method that measures the distance from the imaginary corner to the place where the curve starts.

Using the Round Corners command to round straight corners

If you have an existing rectangle with straight corners and you want to make the corners round, neither of the methods presented earlier in this chapter is going to help you. Instead, you must choose Effect ➪ Stylize ➪ Round Corners and then type the value of the corner radius you want for the existing rectangle in the Round Corners dialog box. Using this command allows you to change straight-corner rectangles to rounded-corner rectangles. However, this effect is not recommended for changing rounded-corner rectangles to straight-corner rectangles because it usually results in an unsightly distortion.

Furthermore, this command can't change corners that you've rounded with either the Rounded Rectangle tool or through previous use of the Round Corners dialog box.

Rounding corners backward

What if you want your corners to round inward instead of out? Initially, it would seem that you're out of luck because Illustrator doesn't provide any way for you to type a negative value for a corner radius. However, you can manipulate the corners manually. The following steps explain how to create a reverse rounded-corner rectangle:

1. **Draw a rounded rectangle with the dimensions that you desire.** For more on drawing rounded rectangles, see the section on this topic earlier in this chapter.

2. **Select the leftmost point on the top of the rounded rectangle by dragging the Direct Selection tool (the hollow arrow) over it.** One control handle appears, sticking out to the left.

3. **Click and drag the control handle down below the anchor point while pressing Shift and then release the mouse button.** Holding Shift ensures that the control handle line is perfectly vertical.

4. **Select the topmost point on the left edge by dragging the Direct Selection tool over it.** A control handle appears, sticking straight up out of this anchor point.

5. **Click and drag the control handle to the right while pressing Shift and then release the mouse button.**

6. **Repeat these steps for each of the corners.** After you get the hang of it, the points start flying into position almost by themselves. Figure 5.6 shows an example of a rectangle with backward-rounded corners on the left side.

FIGURE 5.6

The final product of creating backward-rounded corners on a rectangle

Drawing ellipses

Drawing an ellipse is harder than drawing a rectangle because the point of origin is outside the ellipse. With a rectangle, the point of origin corresponds to a corner of the rectangle, which also happens to be an anchor point. The ellipse is completely within the rectangle. Figure 5.7 shows that the top edge of the ellipse is at the midpoint of the dragged rectangle.

 **Press Ctrl (⌘) while dragging to draw the ellipse from the edge of the ellipse itself, instead of the imaginary corner.**

Follow these steps (similar to those for drawing a rectangle) to create an ellipse:

1. **Click the Rectangle tool and then choose the Ellipse tool.** The Ellipse tool is housed with the Rectangle tool.

2. **Click and drag diagonally.** The outline of an ellipse forms.

3. **Release the mouse button.** The ellipse appears on-screen. Ellipses, like rectangles, have four anchor points, but the anchor points on an ellipse are at the top, bottom, left, and right.

 **Draw a circle by pressing Shift while drawing your ellipse.**

FIGURE 5.7

The curves of an ellipse extend to the boundaries of the dragged area.

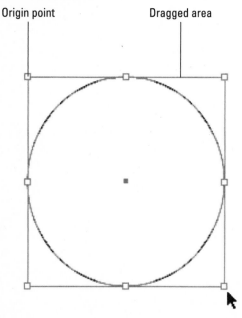

Creating polygons

Although creating more and more ellipses, rectangles, and rounded rectangles is loads of fun, sooner or later, you're going to get bored. I dare say that you can create more interesting shapes automatically by using some of the additional shape tools that come with Illustrator. Most of these tools are located in the Rectangle tool slot in the Tools panel, as shown in Figure 5.8.

FIGURE 5.8

The Rectangle tool slot, which appears here as a tearaway, and the tools housed with it allow you to draw many shapes.

To create a polygon, you first want to specify the number of sides for your polygon and then you can draw it following these steps:

1. **Click the Polygon tool.** This tool is located below the Ellipse tool in the Rectangle tool slot.

2. **Click the Artboard with the Polygon tool.** You want to do this before you draw the polygon. Clicking the Artboard displays the Polygon dialog box, as shown in Figure 5.9.

3. **Specify values for the polygon.** The Polygon dialog box has the following options, both of which you must specify:

   ▪ **Radius:** This is the distance from the center of the polygon to one of the vertices of the polygon. For even-sided shapes (4, 6, 8, 10, and so on, sides), the radius is half the width of the object, from one corner to the opposite corner. For odd-sided shapes, the radius is the distance from the center of the polygon to any of the vertices. Its diameter is twice that value.

   ▪ **Sides:** This is the number of sides that you want for the polygon.

4. **Click OK.**

FIGURE 5.9

Use the Polygon dialog box to create regular polygons.

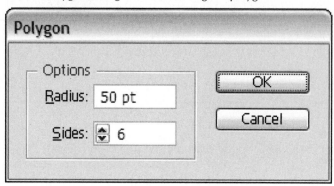

While drawing a polygon, you can change the number of sides on the fly without reopening the Polygon dialog box. To increase or decrease the number of sides, press the up or down arrow as you drag. Figure 5.10 shows different polygons drawn with the Polygon tool.

All polygons you create with the Polygon tool are regular polygons, meaning that they have sides of equal length. For this reason, every four-sided object that you create is a square and every six-sided object is a perfect hexagon. You may find the square capabilities of the Polygon tool useful; it can save you a step when you want to draw a square at an angle. You can't do this with the Rectangle tool unless you change the Constrain Angle in the General Preferences prior to drawing the square or use the Rotate tool on the square after you draw it.

CROSS-REF For more on the Rotate tool, see Chapter 11.

If you press Shift while dragging your mouse, the polygon you create is upright. It aligns to the current Constrain Angle (usually 0°). Therefore, if you create a triangle and you press Shift, the triangle has one side that's perfectly horizontal (the bottom) unless you have a different Constrain Angle, in which case one edge of the triangle aligns to that angle.

NOTE Press the spacebar to move your polygon around when dragging with the Polygon tool. You can do this at any time during the creation of a Polygon. When you release the spacebar, the tool functions as before.

FIGURE 5.10

The number of sides on polygons drawn with the Polygon tool can easily be adjusted as you drag by using the up and down arrows.

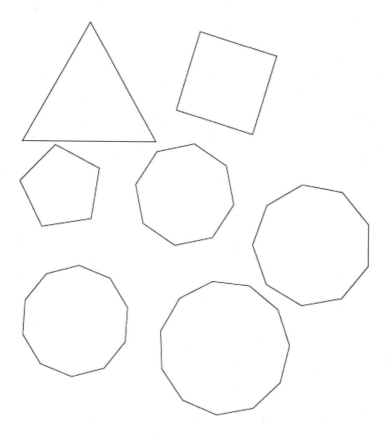

Seeing stars

To create stars, click the Star tool, which is in the Rectangle tool slot, and then drag in the document. As you drag, a star is created. Several stars are shown in Figure 5.11.

Stars have several of the same controls as polygons when you're drawing them: Pressing Shift aligns the star to the Constrain Angle, the spacebar moves the star around, and the tilde (~) key makes lots more stars. The up and down arrows work a bit differently; instead of adding and removing edges, they add and remove entire points. So, in a way, they're actually adding two edges. Stars must have an even number of sides or they're not really stars; they're the pointy lumps you doodled during your poly-sci classes as a sophomore.

The Star tool adds two additional keys for other functions: Pressing Alt (Option) positions the inner points relative to the outer points to produce a star with a corresponding side lying along the same line. Illustrator refers to them as fixed stars. And in case it's keeping you up at night, Alt (Option) has no effect on stars with three or four points.

Perhaps the most versatile function associated with the Star tool (and the Rectangle, Ellipse, Polygon, Spiral, and Ellipse tools) is what happens when using the tilde (~) key. When you press the tilde key and draw, several shapes appear rapidly. As Figure 5.12 shows, this technique can create all sorts of interesting designs.

FIGURE 5.11

Use the Star tool when you want to draw stars.

Stars can come in all shapes, not just the fixed and standard shapes. You create these shapes by pressing Ctrl (⌘) when you drag the mouse. When you hold Ctrl (⌘), only the outer points are extended; the interior points remain fixed. Using this feature allows you to build stars with long, thin points.

You can also specifically design a star by clicking with the Star tool to display the Star dialog box, as shown in Figure 5.13, where you can type the number of points and both the first and second radius of the points.

FIGURE 5.12

Press the tilde (~) key as you drag with most drawing tools to create some interesting designs.

FIGURE 5.13

The Star dialog box lets you specify both inner and outer radius values as well as the number of points.

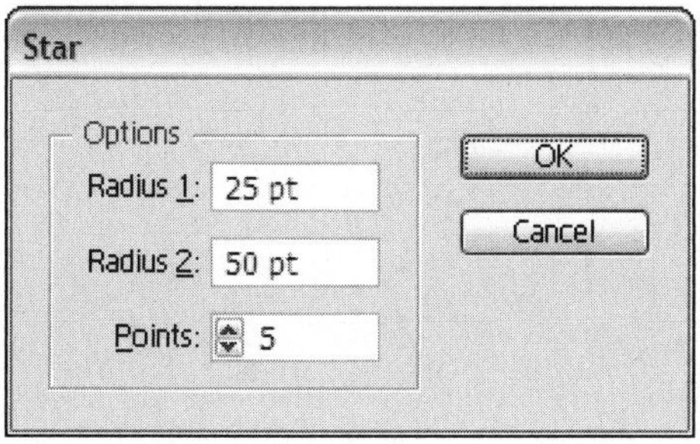

Turning Regular Stars into Something Spectacular

Of course, all the stars you create with the Star tool consist of regular-looking stars. However, using the steps that follow, you can turn an ordinary star into something spectacular. For example, you can use these stars to jazz up text for a more eye-catching look for an advertisement. Another good idea for using spectacular stars is for seals or official-looking approvals. For a more dramatic-looking starburst, follow these steps:

1. **Create a star with about 30 points.** Make it look something like the one in the first figure.

Start with a simple star.

2. **Choose Effect ⇨ Distort & Transform ⇨ Roughen to display the Roughen dialog box, as shown in the following figure.**

Add an effect.

3. **In the Roughen dialog box, change the Size to 5% and the Detail to 0.** Keeping the Detail at 0 won't let Roughen add any anchor points. Applying the Roughen effect makes some star points longer than others randomly, using 5% as the amount of change for any one point.

4. **Click the Corner radio button in the Points section (so you don't have curves on your starburst) and then click OK.** You can also click the Preview check box; each time you click and deselect it, a new preview results, regenerating the randomness each time. Clicking OK uses the Roughen preview you see on-screen, as shown in the next figure.

Apply your changes.

5. **Add any extras, such as a drop shadow, text, etc.** My end result is shown in the final figure.

And there you have it! A work of art!

Working with the Flare Tool

The Flare tool is more than a welcome complement to Illustrator's amazing tools. Housed with the Rectangle tool, the Flare tool is used to create a flare. Seems simple, but what exactly is a flare? A *flare* is a highlight or reflection from a light source. Figure 5.14 shows an Illustrator flare used in a movie poster.

Understanding Flare options

With most tools, you have options. To access the Flare tool options, double-click the Flare tool to display the Flare Tool Options dialog box, as shown in Figure 5.15.

In the Flare Tool Options dialog box, you can choose from many options, including these:

- **Center:** Sets the diameter, opacity, and brightness of the center of a flare.
- **Halo:** Sets the percentage of a halo's fade outward and its fuzziness. A low fuzziness results in a clean, crisp halo.
- **Rays:** Sets the number of rays, the longest ray length, and the fuzziness of rays. If you don't want rays, type **0** for the number of rays.
- **Rings:** Sets the distance of the path between a halo's center and the center of the farthest ring, the number of rings, the size of the largest ring, and the ring direction.

After you create a flare, you can always edit it by selecting the flare first and then clicking and dragging with the Flare tool to change the direction or length. If you expand the object, the flare changes to a blended object (one with smooth transitions between the colors). That way, you can change the number of blend steps or colors if necessary.

The Flare tool is perfect for making a nighttime sky of stars. You can use any backdrop with your graphic illustration. For variation, drag small, medium, and large flares for depth to the stars. Dragging a small amount outward creates a small flare; a little larger drag creates a medium flare; a big drag outward creates a large flare.

Using a flare to add highlight

The best use of flares is to add a highlight to an object. For example, you can drag out a flare on the corner of an object to simulate light reflecting off it. You simply click and drag to place the center of a flare, click to set the size of the center and the halo, and then rotate the ray angle.

FIGURE 5.14

The Flare tool creates flared light from a bright source, as shown in this movie poster.

FIGURE 5.15

The Flare Tool Options dialog box allows you to choose the settings for drawing flares.

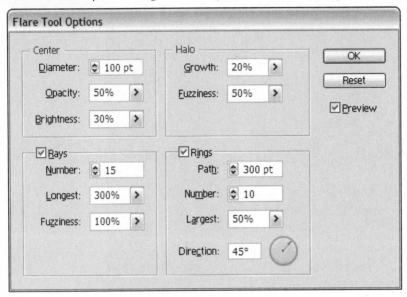

You can use keyboard commands while drawing to modify a flare:

- **Shift:** Constrains the rays of a flare to 45° increments.

- **Up arrow:** Adds rings. Each time you press the up arrow as you're drawing a flare, you add rings. Keep pressing for lots of rings.

- **Down arrow:** Deletes rings. Each time you press the down arrow as you're drawing a flare, it takes away rings.

- **Ctrl (⌘):** Press this key while dragging to hold the center of a flare constant.

Editing a flare

After you draw a flare, it's not set in stone. Maybe you don't like how far the flare is going out or maybe you want to see additional rings. You can always go back and edit the flare to remove rings, change the distance, etc. You have two ways to edit a flare:

- **Using the Flare tool:** Select the flare that you want to edit. Using the Flare tool, drag the endpoint to a new length or in a new direction. An example of this is shown in Figure 5.16.

- **Using the Flare Tool Options dialog box:** Select the flare that you want to edit. Double-click the Flare tool to open the Flare Tool Options dialog box. Change the values in the dialog box to edit the flare. Refer to Figure 5.15 to see the Flare Tool Options dialog box.

FIGURE 5.16

Editing a flare with the Flare tool produces a very different appearance.

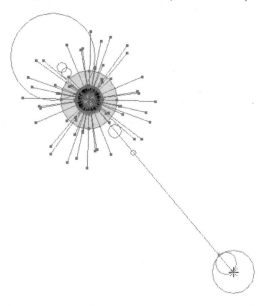

Filling and Stroking Shapes

One of the most powerful features of Illustrator is its ability to color objects. In Illustrator, you can color both the fill and the stroke of the paths that you create. The *fill* is the internal portion of a shape, while the *stroke* is the edge of a shape.

Using fills

The fill of an object is the color inside the shape. If a path is closed (a condition where there are no endpoints and the object's path is connected from end to end), the fill exists only on the inside of the path. If the path is open or has two endpoints, the fill exists between an imaginary line drawn from endpoint to endpoint and the path itself. Fills in open paths can provide some very interesting results when the path crosses itself or the imaginary line crosses the path. Figure 5.17 shows examples of fills in open and closed paths. Fills don't appear in Outline mode, only in Preview mode.

CROSS-REF For more on fills, see Chapter 10. For more on Preview and Outline modes, see Chapter 2.

Besides black and white, the fill color options include the following:

- **Process Colors:** A process color is made up of four inks: cyan, magenta, yellow, and black, also known as CMYK. Most commercial printers use these four colors to create your illustrations.

- **Spot Colors:** Spot color is created using inks that have been premixed. A spot color uses its own printing plate rather than the standard CMYK plates.

- **Patterns:** A pattern consists of created artwork that's repeated or laid out like tiles to fill a space.

- **Gradients:** A gradient blends two or more colors together for a smooth transition between colors.

- **Gradient Meshes:** A gradient mesh changes the object by adding blended lines to accommodate the changes in colors.

- **None:** This is where the fill is transparent. This option lets you see behind a path to what is underneath it when the stroke of an object is the visible part.

FIGURE 5.17

An open path (left) and a closed path (right) result in very different fills.

Using strokes

A stroke is defined as the outline or the path of an object. Any object you draw can have a stroke applied to it, including shapes, lines, paths, and even text. The stroke of an object is made up of three parts: color, weight, and attributes. Strokes appear where there are paths or around the edges of type. Like fills, any one path or object can have only one type of stroke on it; the color, weight, and style of the stroke are consistent throughout the length of the path or the entire text object. Individual characters in a text object can have different strokes only if you select them with the Type tool after you apply the stroke attributes.

CROSS-REF For more on how to apply strokes to text, see Chapter 9.

Setting stroke color

Besides black and white, the stroke color options are the same as those for fills, except that you can't apply gradients and gradient meshes to a stroke. To apply a stroke color, simply choose the stroke color at the bottom of the Tools panel or press X and then choose the color to use from the Color panel or from the Swatches panel.

Changing stroke weight

The weight of a stroke is how thick it is. On a path, Illustrator centers the stroke on that path, with half the thickness of the stroke on one side of the path and half the thickness on the other side of the path. So a 1-point stroke has $\frac{1}{2}$ point on each side of the path.

You set stroke weight in the Stroke panel's Weight menu or by typing a value in the Weight text field. Figure 5.18 shows the Stroke panel. You can also use the up and down arrows on the left of the Weight text box to incrementally change the stroke weight.

TIP Use mathematical operations in the Stroke panel! You can mathematically change the current stroke weight by adding, subtracting, multiplying, or dividing by any value. Just place the appropriate symbol (+ for add, - for subtract, * for multiply, and / for divide) after the current value and then the number by which you want to perform the operation. Use this when you're asked to increase the stroke weight by, say, 2 times the current value.

Strokes have upper and lower limits. You can never create strokes wider than 1000 points. A stroke with a weight of 0.001 can exist in Illustrator, although the recommendation is that you not choose such a value. Instead, set the stroke to 0. Because a stroke of 0.001 changes to match the output device (it appears 1 pixel thick or as a 1-point stroke on-screen), the potential changes in thickness can drastically change the way an image looks. Be very careful if you choose to venture into this area of Illustrator.

FIGURE 5.18

Choose from a preset stroke weight in the popup menu or type your own value in the Weight text box.

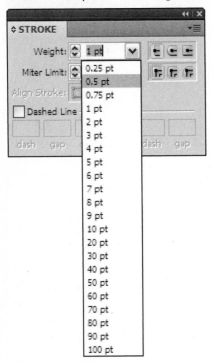

Modifying stroke attributes

The attributes of a stroke consist of several parts, including the cap style, join style, miter limit, and dash pattern. Figure 5.19 shows the Stroke panel where you choose these attributes.

The stroke attributes include the following options:

- **Cap style:** The way the ends of a stroke look. This style can be butt cap, rounded cap, or projected cap. Caps apply only to endpoints on open paths. You can choose a cap style for a closed path (with no endpoints), but nothing happens; if the path is cut into an open path, that cap style goes into effect.

  - **Butt Cap:** Chops the stroke off perpendicularly at the end of the path
  - **Round Cap:** Results in smooth, rounded ends that resemble a half-circle. These caps protrude from the endpoint one-half the stroke weight.

- **Projecting Cap:** Projects from the endpoint one-half the stroke weight and appear perpendicular to the direction of the path at its endpoint

- **Join style:** The join style is the manner in which the corner points on paths appear when you stroke them. You can apply one of three join styles to paths:

  - **Miter Join:** Causes the outer edges of the stroke to meet at a point. This join type is the only one affected by the miter limit.

  - **Round Join:** Rounds off the outside edge of corners

  - **Bevel Join:** Is cropped off before the angle can reach a corner

FIGURE 5.19

Use the options in the Stroke panel to set the stroke attributes.

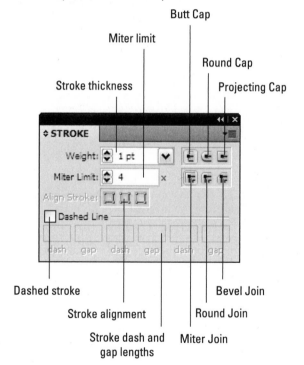

Joins affect only corner points, including straight corner points, curved corner points, and combination corner points. In all cases, join types affect only outside corners. Inside corners always appear mitered.

- **Miter Limit:** The Miter Limit option controls how far a corner can extend past the edge of the path. This is important for tight corners of paths with large weights because the place where the outside edges meet in a corner can be really far away from the original edges of the paths. The number in the Miter Limit controls how many times the width of the stroke the miter can extend beyond the point. The default is 4, which is good for the majority of applications.

- **Align Stroke:** Use this option to control how the stroke aligns with the path. It can be centered over the path, inside the path, or outside the path.

- **Dashed Line:** Usually, the dash pattern for a stroke is solid, but you can create various dash patterns for different effects. The bottom of the Stroke panel controls if and how dashed strokes should appear. Clicking the Dashed Line check box allows you to type different values for up to three dash and gap lengths.

Combining strokes with fills

Many times, paths in Illustrator require both fills and strokes. When you give both a fill and a stroke to a single path, the stroke knocks out the fill at the edges of the path by one-half the weight of the stroke. Figure 5.20 demonstrates this by using a dashed stroke to make the point a little more obvious.

FIGURE 5.20

A stroke knocks out a fill by one-half the weight of the stroke, as shown on the right circle.

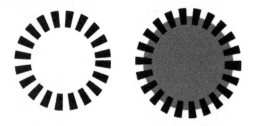

TIP If knocking out the fill of a path hides part of the pattern that you want to be seen, you can correct this problem by copying the path and pasting it in front, removing the frontmost path's stroke. Be warned, though, that the filled path, on top of the stroked path, knocks out the inner half of the stroke.

Applying fills and strokes

The Tools panel contains fill and stroke icons, which are located in the Paint Style section of the Tools panel and shown in Figure 5.21.

By default, the fill is set to White and the stroke is set to 1-point Black.

But you can reset to the default fill and stroke by clicking the Default Fill and Stroke icon in the lower-left corner of the Paint Style section.

You can also quickly swap between the colors in the Fill and Stroke icons by clicking the Swap Fill and Stroke icon located in the upper right of the Paint Style section.

When you first start Illustrator, the Fill icon is in front of the Stroke icon. This means that any changes made in the Color or Swatches panels affect the fill. When the Fill icon is in front of the Stroke icon, the fill is said to be in focus. You can change the focus to the stroke by clicking the Stroke icon. When the focus is on the stroke, changes made in the Color or Swatches panels affect the stroke, not the fill.

 **You can quickly reset the fill and stroke colors to their defaults by pressing D. You can quickly change the focus from the Stroke icon to the Fill icon by pressing Shift+X.**

The Fill and Stroke icons change in appearance to match the current fill and stroke. For example, if you have a purple fill and an orange stroke, the Fill icon is purple and the Stroke icon is orange, and you obviously slept through the color-coordination lectures in your design classes. The Fill icon displays a gradient or pattern if that's the current fill.

You use the three icons at the bottom of the Paint Style section to determine the type of fill or stroke:

- **Color:** You use this icon when you want to have a solid color or pattern for the fill or stroke. Press the comma (,) key to quickly activate the Color icon.

- **Gradient:** Use this icon when the fill contains a gradient. You can't color a stroke with gradients; clicking this icon when the Stroke icon is in focus changes the fill to gradient and also changes the focus to fill. Press the period (.) key to quickly activate the Gradient icon.

- **None:** This creates an empty fill or no stroke. Fills of None are entirely transparent. Strokes of None aren't colored and have no stroke weight. Press the forward slash (/) key to quickly activate the None icon.

FIGURE 5.21

The Paint Style section of the Tools panel

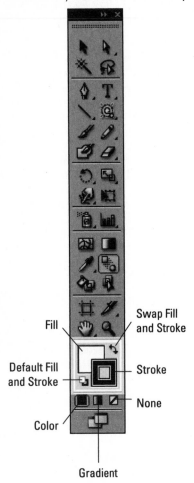

Swap Fill and Stroke

Fill

Default Fill and Stroke

Stroke

Color

None

Gradient

Oddly enough, you don't need to use the Color and Gradient icons to determine the type of fill when switching between color and gradient; you can simply click the appropriate swatch in the Swatches panel to change the fill type. No swatch for None is available; to change the fill or stroke to None, you must either click the None icon or press the forward slash (/) key. You can quickly combine pressing X and / to change the focus and apply None to the stroke or fill.

Creating and Embellishing Graphs and Charts

Graphs are most useful when they show numerical information that normally takes several paragraphs to explain or that you can't easily express in words. You can easily overlook a significant difference between two numbers until you use a graph to represent them. The Graphs feature is one of the most underused features in Illustrator. Most people use programs such as Microsoft Excel to design their graphs. You just wouldn't think Illustrator could do graphs with accuracy, but it can — and with more than just the boring graph visuals.

An exciting aspect about graphs in Illustrator is their fluidity. Not only can you create graphs easily, but you can also change them easily. In addition, if the data that you used to create a graph changes, you can type the new data and have it instantaneously appear in the graph.

All the graph tools work in a manner similar to that of the shape creation tools. For example, when you choose the Graph tool, you can click and drag to set the size of the graph or you can display the tool's dialog box (in this case, the Graph Size dialog box) by clicking the Artboard without dragging to type the size information.

The Graph Data box, as shown in Figure 5.22, looks like a simple spreadsheet with rows and columns. Using this box, you can type data to graph. After you type the data, click Apply (which looks like a check mark), and Illustrator updates your graph.

CAUTION Ensure that the graph is never ungrouped (a graph always has all its elements grouped together, meaning that you can select them with the Selection tool as a whole rather than individual pieces), at least not until you finish making all graph data and graph style changes. If you ungroup the graph, you can't use any of the graph options to change the ex-graph because Illustrator views it as just a set of paths and text.

CROSS-REF For more on grouping and ungrouping, see Chapter 8.

Importing Microsoft Excel graph data

You can import graph data in tab-delimited text files, such as those exported by Microsoft Excel. Tab-delimited files are text and numbers that are separated by tabs and newlines. To import data from another file, click Import, the leftmost icon at the top of the Graph Data box, and then choose the text file containing the information you want to graph.

CAUTION The text file that you import can't contain any punctuation except for decimal points. If you've formatted the text file with thousands separators (with commas), the numbers will not import correctly.

FIGURE 5.22

The Graph Data box resembles a simple spreadsheet.

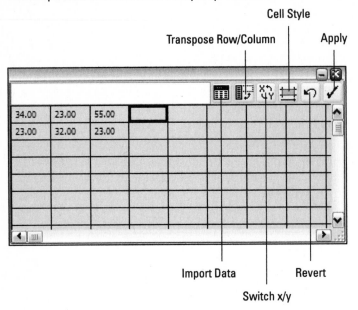

Because Illustrator is not really a graphing or spreadsheet program, many of the usual controls for arranging data in such programs aren't available, including inserting rows and columns and creating formulas.

The Cut, Copy, and Paste functions work within the Graph Data box, so you can move and duplicate information on a very basic level.

One very useful feature in the Graph Data box is the Transpose row/column button. This function switches the x- and y-axes of the data, thus swapping the row and column layout of everything that you've typed.

Making and editing graphs

Use the following steps to create a basic graph. The type of graph in this example is a grouped column graph, which you commonly use to compare quantities over time or between different categories:

1. **Click the Graph tool.** The tool is located midway down in the Tools panel and looks like a bar graph.

2. **Click and drag to form a rectangular area.** You do this as you would when using the Rectangle tool. The size of the rectangle that you create becomes the size of the graph.

3. **Release the mouse button.** As soon as you do so, an untitled floating window appears, containing a simple worksheet. This floating window is the Graph Data box (refer to Figure 5.22).

4. **Type your data into the Graph Data box.** Information that you type in the worksheet becomes formatted in graph form. The top row in the worksheet area should contain the labels for comparison within the same set. The items in the top row appear as legends outside the graph area. In the leftmost column, you can type labels that appear at the bottom of the grouped column graph as categories. In the remaining cells, type the pertinent information, as shown in Figure 5.23.

5. **Close the window.** This signals Illustrator to use the data that you typed in the graph. The graph appears, and it should look something like the one in Figure 5.24.

6. **Change your Graph styles.** After you create the graph, you can change the Graph styles to see which graph shows the information the best.

TIP To have the labels on the legends to read numbers only, you must place quotation marks (" ") around the numbers. If you don't use quotation marks, Illustrator considers the numbers as data, not labels.

You can change the numbers and the text in the Graph Data box at any time by selecting the graph and then choosing Object ⇨ Graph ⇨ Data. Illustrator re-creates the graph to reflect the changes you make. If you move some of the graph objects around, they may revert to their original locations when Illustrator re-creates the graph.

FIGURE 5.23

The graph data is now ready to be graphed.

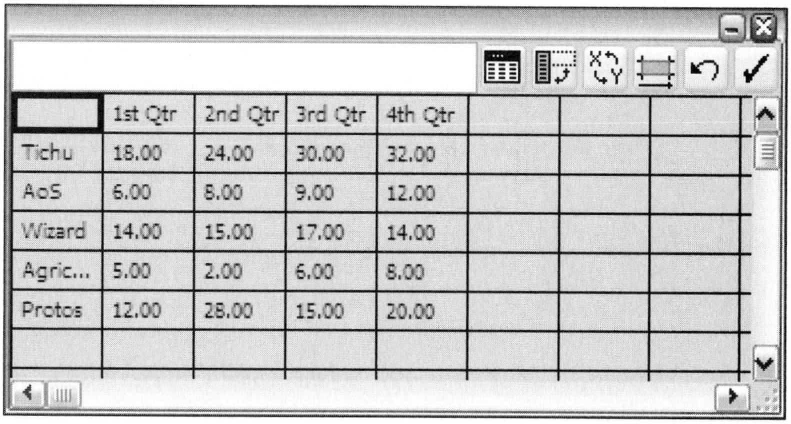

	1st Qtr	2nd Qtr	3rd Qtr	4th Qtr				
Tichu	18.00	24.00	30.00	32.00				
AoS	6.00	8.00	9.00	12.00				
Wizard	14.00	15.00	17.00	14.00				
Agric...	5.00	2.00	6.00	8.00				
Protos	12.00	28.00	15.00	20.00				

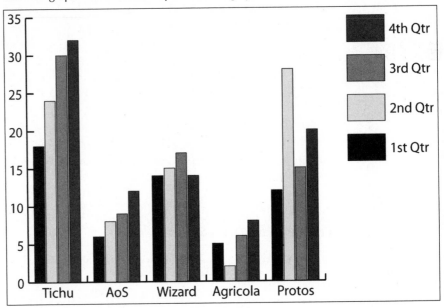

FIGURE 5.24

The final graph shown in a Grouped Column graph

Customizing graphs

When a graph is selected, you can choose Object ⇨ Graph ⇨ Type to open the Graph Type dialog box, as shown in Figure 5.25. Using this dialog box, you can quickly change between the different graph types while keeping the same data. Choosing a different graph type and then clicking OK changes the tool to represent the type of graph you select. You can choose from nine graph types; the column graph is the default.

The Graph Type dialog box includes several options for controlling the look of the graph, including the following:

- **Type:** Separate icon buttons are available for each of the graph types: Column, Stacked Column, Bar, Stacked Bar, Line, Area, Scatter, Pie, and Radar.

- **Value Axis:** The choices — On Left Side, On Right Side, On Both Sides — display the vertical values on the left side (the default), the right side, or both sides.

- **Style:** You can choose from these options to add a drop shadow or add a legend across the top of the graph. You can also opt to place the first row in front or the first column in front (for when the columns or rows stack closely together).

- **Options:** These settings are specific to the graph you select. The default graph (grouped column graph) has options to set the column and cluster width in percentage. Each type of graph has its own customization options.

 To make visually striking graphs, use a combination of graph types. Simply use the Group Selection tool to select all the objects that are one legend type, choose Object ⇨ Graph ⇨ Type, and then type the new graph type for that legend.

FIGURE 5.25

The Graph Type dialog box lets you choose the type of graph to use.

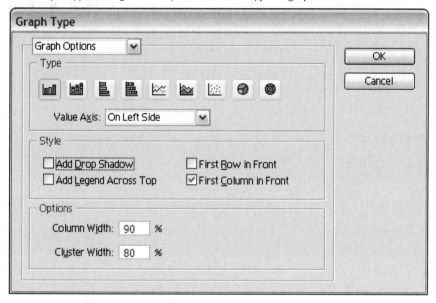

In the Graph Options popup menu in the Graph Type dialog box, you can find other options, such as Value Axis and Category Axis. These are the Value Axis and Category Axis options:

- **Tick Values:** This Value Axis option sets the minimum, maximum, and divisions and includes a check box to override calculated values.

- **Tick Marks:** This Value Axis option sets the length and how many ticks are drawn per division.

- **Add Labels:** This Value Axis option sets a prefix and/or a suffix for labels.

- **Tick Marks:** This Category Axis option sets the length and how many are drawn per division and includes a check box to draw tick marks between labels.

Choosing a graph type

You can choose from nine types of graphs in Illustrator. Each type gives a specific kind of information to the reader. Certain graphs are better for comparisons, others for growth, etc. The following sections describe the graphs, explain how to create them, and tell how you can use them.

Grouped-column graphs

You primarily use grouped-column graphs to show how something changes over time. Often, they're referred to as bar graphs because the columns that make up the graphs resemble bars.

The real strength of a grouped-column graph is that it provides for the direct comparison of different types of statistics in the same graph.

Column width and cluster width are two customizable options for grouped-column graphs and stacked-column graphs. Column width refers to the width of individual columns, with 100% being wide enough to abut other columns in the cluster. Cluster width refers to how much of the available cluster space is taken up by the columns in the cluster. At 80% (the default), 20% of the available space is empty, leaving room between clusters.

You can widen columns and clusters to 1000% of their size and condense them to 1% of the width of the original column or cluster.

Stacked-column graphs

Stacked-column graphs are good graphs for presenting the total of a category and the contributing portions of each category, as shown in Figure 5.26.

This graph shows the same amount of information as the grouped-column graph, but the information is organized differently. The stacked-column graph is designed to display the total of all the legends, and the grouped-column graph is designed to aid comparison of all individual legends in each category.

Line graphs

Line graphs (also known as line charts) show trends over time. They're especially useful for determining progress and identifying radical changes, as shown in Figure 5.27.

The Line graph of the Graph Type dialog box (Object ➪ Graph ➪ Type) has several unique options:

- **Mark Data Points:** This forces data points to appear as squares. If this box is not clicked, the data points are visible only as direction changes in lines between the data points.

- **Connect Data Points:** If you click this check box, Illustrator draws lines between each pair of data points.

- **Draw Filled Lines (and the corresponding text box for line width):** This creates a line filled with the data point legend color and outlined with black.

- **Edge-to-Edge Lines:** This stretches the lines out to the left and right edges of the graph. Although the result is technically incorrect, you can achieve better visual impact by using this feature, and depending on the type of graph you make, visual impact might be more important than getting it right.

FIGURE 5.26

This shows the data displayed in a stacked-column graph.

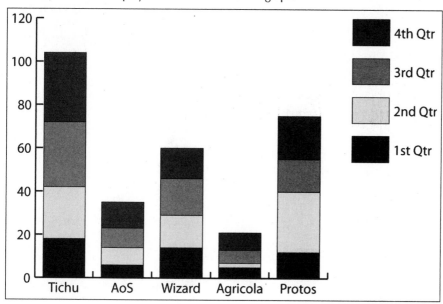

FIGURE 5.27

The graph type has been changed to a line graph.

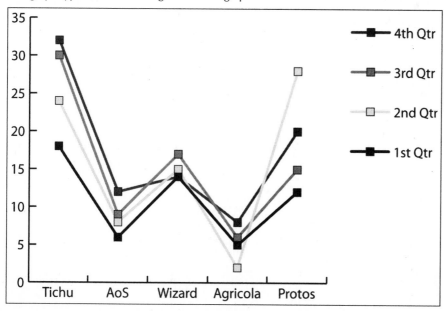

Area graphs

On first glance, area graphs may appear to be just like filled line graphs. Like line graphs, area graphs show data points that are connected, but area graphs, such as the one shown in Figure 5.28, stack data on top of each other to show the total area of the legend subject in the graph. In the Area Graphs dialog box, you can add style to the graph by choosing from these options: Add Drop Shadow, Add Legend Across Top, First Row in Front, and First Column in Front.

FIGURE 5.28

The data shown here is in an area graph.

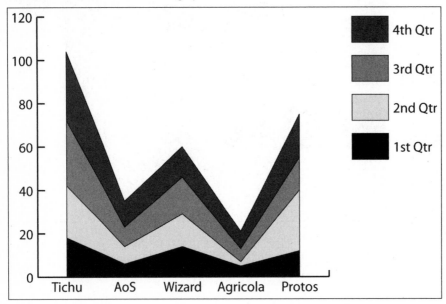

Pie graphs

Pie graphs are great for comparing percentages of the portions of a whole, as shown in Figure 5.29. The higher the percentage for a certain activity, the larger its wedge. Some of the options for pie graphs are Add Drop Shadow, Add Legend Across Top, First Row in Front, First Column in Front, Legend, Sort, and Position.

When you create pie graphs, you can remove the individual wedges from the central pie with the Group Selection tool to achieve an exploding pie effect.

FIGURE 5.29

These pie graphs display proportionally sized pies and pie wedges.

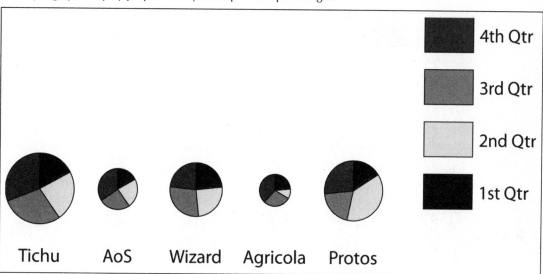

The Legends in Wedges option is the only option in the Graph Type dialog box that's specifically for pie graphs. If you choose this option, the name of each wedge centers within that wedge. Illustrator doesn't do a very good job of placing the legend names, many times overlapping neighboring names. In addition, the letters in the legend names are black, which can make reading some of the names difficult or impossible. Of course, you can always just add legends manually to any graph after the fact using Illustrator's Type tool, but then if the values change (and thus the graph), the graph has the wrong values displayed until you manually change them.

Scatter graphs and radar graphs

Scatter graphs, which are primarily used for scientific charting purposes, are quite different from all the other types of graphs. Each data point is given a location according to its x-y coordinates instead of by category and label. The points are connected, as are the points in line graphs, but the line created by the data point locations can cross itself and doesn't go in any specific direction. Scatter graphs have the same customization options as line graphs.

A radar (or web) graph compares values set at a certain point. This type of graph is viewed as a circle graph. Categories are spread around the circle, and the data with higher values extend farther from the center.

Creating Flowcharts, Diagrams, and Site Maps

Illustrator can create a chart for a company's organization. Using the Rectangle tool and some effects, you can make a clean organization chart.

To create an organization chart, whether it's for a business or simply a family tree, follow these steps:

1. **Click the Rectangle tool to draw a rectangle.** See the section on drawing rectangles for more on using this tool.

2. **Type a name inside the rectangle.** For more on typing text in graphics, see Chapter 9.

3. **Make copies of your rectangle.** Press Alt (Option) while dragging with the Selection tool to make copies of the first rectangle. Create as many rectangles as you need and then edit the names with the Text tool.

Figure 5.30 shows an organization chart created using Illustrator.

FIGURE 5.30

You can use Illustrator to create an organization chart that clearly defines your position.

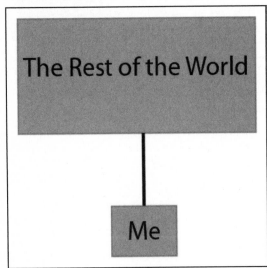

You can use the same principle for the organizational chart to create a sitemap for a Web site. The main difference is that you organize the sitemap from left to right rather than top to bottom as in an organizational chart. The point is to show the smoothest way that information flows.

Using Symbols

With the addition of the Symbol tools in Illustrator 10, small children can now, with ease, make a sensible drawing using the Symbol Sprayer tool. Adults and professionals alike can create amazing designs with very little effort. Illustrator has included a bunch of symbols to use with the Symbol Sprayer tool. If you want to, create your own and then add it to the Symbols panel.

Spraying with the Symbol Sprayer tool

To start using the Symbol Sprayer tool, follow these steps:

1. **Choose a symbol from the Symbols panel.** Figure 5.31 shows the Symbols panel, which you access by choosing Window ➪ Symbols or pressing Shift+Ctrl+F11 (Shift+⌘+F11).

2. **Click the Symbol Sprayer tool.** This tool is located midway down the left column of the Tools panel next to the Graph tool. It has an icon that looks like a spray can.

3. **Start spraying away.** The longer you hold the mouse button down, the more symbols are sprayed in that area. Figure 5.32 shows a bunch of butterflies sprayed on a page.

FIGURE 5.31

The Symbols panel contains various symbols that you can use in your drawings.

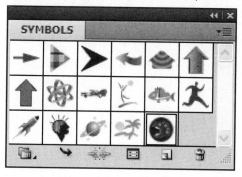

To change the size of the sprayer or related options, double-click the Symbol Sprayer tool to access the Symbolism Tools Options dialog box, as shown in Figure 5.33.

FIGURE 5.32

The butterfly symbol was sprayed on the Artboard by using the Symbol Sprayer tool.

FIGURE 5.33

Use the Symbolism Tools Options dialog box to modify the way the Symbol Sprayer tool functions.

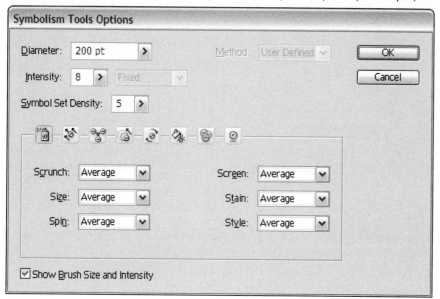

When you have a group of symbols, you can then alter them to look different. Editing the Symbol tools is done in the Symbolism Tools Options dialog box. Depending on the tool chosen from the icons along the top row, certain options might not be available. These options are:

- **Diameter:** This sets the diameter of the sprayer in points.

- **Method:** This sets the method to User Defined, Average, or Random. The User Defined method lets you manually scrunch, size, spin, screen, stain, and style the symbols. The Average method scrunches, sizes, spins, screens, stains, and styles the symbols by averaging the spaces between symbols. The Random method randomly scrunches, sizes, spins, screens, stains, and styles the symbols.

- **Intensity:** This determines how many instances Illustrator sets when you use the mouse. *Instances* is the term for the number of symbols Illustrator sprays when you either click the mouse just once or hold the mouse button down for a period of time.

- **Pressure Pen:** Use this dropdown list (popup menu) if you're using a pressure-sensitive tablet to choose the way that the Symbol Sprayer tool responds to different pen motions. This only appears if a pressure-sensitive pen is connected to your computer.

- **Symbol Set Density:** This sets the density of the symbol set for the tools. Density determines how close together the symbols are.

- **Scrunch, Size, Spin, Screen, Stain, and Style:** The Symbol Sprayer tool icon (on the far left) must be selected in order to access these options. Choose either User Defined or Average. The User Defined method lets you manually scrunch, size, spin, screen, stain, and style the symbols. The Average method scrunches, sizes, spins, screens, stains, and styles the symbols by averaging the spaces between symbols. The Random method randomly scrunches, sizes, spins, screens, stains, and styles the symbols.

- **Show Brush Size and Intensity:** Click this check box to see the actual size and intensity of the brush when using the Symbolism tools.

Making a new symbol

If you don't like the default images available in the Symbols panel, you can create your own. It's as simple as making your own symbol and then adding it to the panel. You can either create a new symbol or use an existing symbol as a base.

To modify an existing symbol and then add it to the panel, follow these steps:

1. **Click an existing symbol in the Symbols panel.** You can access the Symbols panel by choosing Window ⇨ Symbols or pressing Shift+Ctrl+F11 (Shift+⌘+F11).

2. **From the popup menu, choose Place Symbol Instance.** You find this option by clicking the triangle on the upper-right side of the Symbols panel. Alternatively, you can simply click and drag the symbol from the panel to the page, as shown in Figure 5.34.

FIGURE 5.34

Place a symbol instance by dragging the symbol from the panel to the Artboard.

3. **With the symbol selected, choose Object ⇨ Expand.** This displays the Expand dialog box so that you can choose the parts of the symbol you want to expand.

4. **Click OK to close the Expand dialog box.** This turns the object back into editable strokes and fills.

5. **Alter the object to your liking.** You may need to use the Object ➪ Ungroup command if you want to alter the existing design.

6. **Turn it back into a symbol by choosing New Symbol from the Symbols panel's popup menu, as shown in Figure 5.35.** Alternatively, you can drag the new symbol artwork over the Symbols panel, which also creates a new symbol.

You can also create your own new symbol. Simply draw the object you want as a new symbol and then drag it onto the Symbols panel (or choose New Symbol from the Symbols panel's popup menu). After you create a new symbol, you can use it the same way you use any of the built-in symbols.

FIGURE 5.35

Create a new symbol from an existing one and then either drag it to the Symbols panel or choose New Symbol from the popup menu.

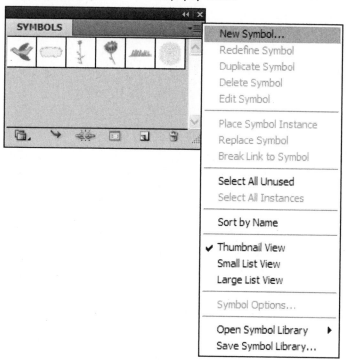

Using the Symbol tool

Illustrator gives you lots of ways to edit your symbols after you spray them on your Artboard. These Symbol tools change the spacing between the objects, their size, color, transparency, style, and direction. Located eight tools down on the left side of the Tools panel, you access these tools by simply clicking and dragging to the tool you want.

To apply the effects of these tools, click the tool and then click the Artboard. Generally speaking, the longer you hold the mouse button, the more Illustrator applies the effect. For example, the longer you wait to release the mouse after clicking with the Symbol Scruncher tool, the more your image contracts. If you hold Alt (Option) while clicking one of these tools, it reverses the effect of the tool. For example, pressing Alt (Option) while clicking the Symbol Scruncher tool pulls symbols apart. These tools are available:

- **Symbol Shifter tool:** Use the Symbol Shifter tool to totally move the symbols in the direction you drag. To change the stacking order with the Symbol Shifter tool, press Shift and then click the symbol to bring it forward. To send a symbol backward, hold Alt (Option) while pressing Shift and then click the symbol.

- **Symbol Scruncher tool:** This tool changes the location of your symbols by pulling them together and changing the density distribution of the sprayed symbols.

- **Symbol Sizer tool:** This tool increases the size of the symbols.

- **Symbol Spinner tool:** You use this tool to move symbols to a new location. Simply click the Symbol Spinner tool and then drag the symbols in the direction you want them to go.

- **Symbol Stainer tool:** The Symbol Stainer tool could possibly be the coolest Symbol tool of all. Use this tool to change the color of the symbols based on the Fill swatch in the Tools panel. Keep changing the color to make the symbols look totally different. The longer you hold the mouse pointer over the symbol, the more color is infused.

- **Symbol Screener tool:** This tool changes the transparency of the symbols. The longer you apply this tool, the more the transparency.

- **Symbol Styler tool:** Use this tool to apply a certain Style to a symbol. Choose the style from the Styles panel and then apply it to the symbol.

Summary

In this chapter, you learned how to use some of the more advanced and interesting drawing tools that Illustrator offers. These topics were covered:

- Even the most basic shapes, such as the rectangle and ellipse, can create some pretty cool artwork.

- The Flare tool can quickly add a highlight or create art on its own.

- Illustrator has a variety of graph styles from which to choose.

- You can always edit a graph's data as long as you don't ungroup the graph.

- The Symbol Sprayer tool creates a bunch of objects quickly and efficiently.

- Use the other Symbolism tools to alter the objects for variety.

- Change any of the Symbol tool options to create just what you want.

- You can alter the position, size, color, and transparency of the symbols at any time.

Chapter 6

Learning How to Select and Edit

In Chapter 4, you learned how to create paths. In Chapter 5, you learned how to create various objects. Now you need to know how to change them. This chapter explains how to select what you want to change and how to change it.

After you create, trace, or even legitimately borrow someone else's artwork, there's always that period where you look at the artwork and realize that it's not quite right. That's where this chapter comes in. No, I won't do your finishing for you, but I will show you how to take advantage of Illustrator's many tools to obtain the best end result, from slight control handle manipulations to massive scalings and rotations to dramatic effects created with the Pathfinder panel.

The focus of this chapter is modifying individual paths and the points on those paths by cutting them, combining them, and adjusting them.

Selecting a Path for Editing

The key to editing a path is learning how to select that path. Maybe you don't want the whole path, just a section, or maybe only a point. This section explains the selection tools and how to use them.

Understanding the selection methods

If there's one group of tools in Illustrator that you absolutely must have, it's the set of five selection tools (one of them is a popup tool). As in most applications, to alter something (move, scale, etc.), you must first select it. When you draw a new path or paste an object into Illustrator, the program automatically selects the object you're working on. However, as soon as you draw

173

another path, Illustrator deselects the preceding object and automatically selects the new path. The selection tools let you select paths and perform additional manipulations on them. Illustrator's five selection tools are the Selection tool, the Direct Selection tool, the Group Selection tool, the Magic Wand tool, and the Lasso tool, as shown in Figure 6.1.

FIGURE 6.1

The five selection tools are shown here. Clicking and holding the Direct Selection tool provides access to the Group Selection tool.

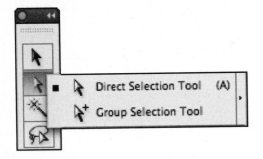

The following list details what these tools do. You can either click them in the Tools panel to select them (they're all housed together with the Selection tool) or you can press a keyboard shortcut to active them.

- **Selection tool:** This tool, which has a black arrowhead pointing diagonally up, allows you to select an object, a path, or a bunch of paths at one time. You can press V to activate it.

- **Direct Selection tool:** You use this tool, which has a white arrowhead diagonally pointing up, to select parts of an object or path. It's designed to select items on which you want to perform detailed work. You can press A to activate it.

- **Group Selection tool:** As its name suggests, this tool, which has a white arrowhead with a plus sign, allows you to select hierarchical groups of objects. Each click allows you to select a wider range of objects around the core object. You can quickly access the Group Selection tool when you have the Direct Selection tool selected by pressing and holding Alt (Option).

- **Magic Wand tool:** You use this tool, which looks like a magician's wand, to select groups of objects whose fills or strokes are similar in color. Because this tool detects drastic changes in color, you shouldn't use it for objects with subtle color differences. You can press Y to activate it.

- **Lasso tool:** This tool, which looks like — you guessed it — a lasso, lets you draw around the objects that you want to choose. You generally use this tool for unevenly shaped objects. Because this tool detects large differences in contrast, you use this tool if your object contrasts sharply with surrounding objects. You can press Q to activate it.

The specific function of each tool is discussed in greater detail later in this chapter. Before this discussion, however, you need to know that there are different categories of selecting, depending on what you want to select. These categories are Intrapath, Path, Group, IntraGroup, and Selecting All.

Using Intrapath selecting

Intrapath selecting means that you select at least one point or segment within a path — usually with the Direct Selection tool — to adjust individual points, segments, and series of points, as shown in Figure 6.2. Selected points appear as solid squares, and unselected points are hollow squares; in Figure 6.2, no points are selected (which is why they're all hollow squares). Intrapath selecting also allows you to use most of the functions in the Object menu, such as hiding, locking, or grouping. But these options lock, hide, or group the entire path. Using the Direct Selection tool, click the portion of the path you want to select, Shift+click portions to add them to or subtract them from the current selection, or drag a marquee around the area of the path that contains the portions you want to select.

FIGURE 6.2
_____

This shows an example of Intrapath selection on paths using the Direct Selection tool.

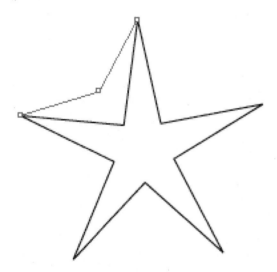

NOTE   Although you may select just a portion of a path, many features affect the entire path, not just the selected points. For example, most of the attributes available in the Object menu (including Pathfinder, Masking, and Compound Paths) affect the entire path even when only a point or segment is selected.

Using Path selecting

Path selecting means that all points and segments on a path are selected. When you click a path using the Group Selection tool or the Selection tool, Illustrator automatically selects the entire path. Drawing a marquee (a dotted rectangle indicating a selection) entirely around a path with the Direct Selection tool also selects the entire path. All the capabilities from Intrapath selecting are available, such as the entire Object menu and the Arrange submenu (located at the top of the Object menu). After you select a path, the entire path is affected by moving, transforming, cutting, copying, pasting, and deleting. An example of Path selecting is shown in Figure 6.3.

FIGURE 6.3

Path selection selects the whole path.

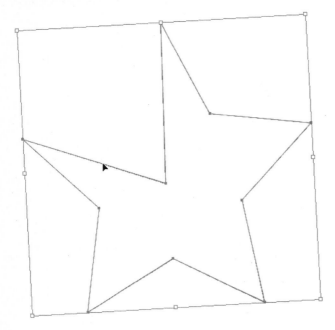

Using Group and IntraGroup selecting

You can select and affect a series of grouped paths as if it were a single object by using Group selecting. All paths in the group are affected in the same way as paths that you select with Path selecting. The Selection tool selects entire grouped paths at once. If you use the Group Selection tool instead, you need a series of clicks to select a group of paths. Figure 6.4 shows what you can accomplish with Group selecting.

You can also select and affect groups of paths within other groups by using IntraGroup selecting. All paths in the group are affected in the same way as paths that you select with Path selection.

Use the Group Selection tool to select a group of paths at once. Each successive click on the same path selects another set of grouped paths that the initial path is within.

CROSS-REF For more on groups, see Chapter 8.

FIGURE 6.4

Group selection affects the entire group.

Using Select All

To select everything in your document that hasn't been hidden or locked, choose Select ⇨ Select All or press Ctrl+A (⌘+A). This selects all the points and segments on every path that hasn't been locked in the document. You can also select everything in the document by drawing a marquee around all the paths with any selection tool.

Normally, after you select something new, everything that you've previously selected becomes deselected. To continue to select additional points, paths, or segments, you must hold Shift while clicking.

Shift normally works as a toggle when used with a selection tool, selecting anything that's not selected and deselecting anything that's currently selected. Each selection tool works with Shift a little differently, as described in the following sections.

> **TIP** To deselect everything that's selected, click a part of the document that's empty (where you can see the Pasteboard or Artboard) without using Shift. You can also deselect everything by choosing Select ⇨ Deselect All or by pressing Shift+Ctrl+A (Shift+⌘+A). Another choice under the Select menu is Reselect. This option allows you to reselect the last thing selected.

You can use the selection tools for manually moving selected points, segments, and paths. For example, you use automatic or computer-assisted manipulations when you type specific values in the Transform panel. The next few sections cover the selection tools and their functions.

Deciding which selection tool to use

After the brief overview of the selection tools, you need to decide which one works best in which cases. For specific path editing, use the Selection, Direct Selection, or Group Selection tools. For selecting areas or colored sections, use the Magic Wand or Lasso tools. The next sections describe the functions of the tools.

Using the Selection tool

The Selection tool selects entire paths or complete groups at one time. You can't select just one point or a few points on a path with the Selection tool. Instead, the entire path on which that point lies is selected (all the anchor points turn black). Drawing a marquee around parts of paths or entire paths also selects entire paths.

Each object in Illustrator has a Bounding Box that you can access when using the Selection tool. This Bounding Box, as shown in Figure 6.5, allows you to move or scale the selected objects by simply dragging the control handles. When you select an object, a Bounding Box appears around the whole object or around all the objects in a selected group. This Bounding Box has handles on the four corners as well as handles at the midpoint of each side of the box. These handles allow you to scale the object any way you want. By holding Shift and then dragging one of the corner handles, you can quickly scale the selected object proportionately. You can also rotate the object using the Bounding Box. Look for the curved arrow to indicate rotation (move the cursor just outside one of the box's corners to display the curved arrow).

> **TIP** You can enable or disable the Bounding Box by choosing View ⇨ Show Bounding Box/Hide Bounding Box or by pressing Shift+Ctrl+B (Shift+⌘+B). While the Bounding Box seems convenient initially, the more you use Illustrator, the more you find it getting in the way and want to hide it. Most seasoned Illustrator users never use the Bounding Box but instead press S to quickly access the Scale tool and R to quickly access the Rotate tool.

FIGURE 6.5

The Bounding Box provides quick access to scaling and rotating.

Using the Direct Selection tool

To select individual points, line segments, or a series of specific points within a path, you need to use the Direct Selection tool. This tool is the only tool that allows you to select something less than an entire path. You can also draw a marquee over a portion of a path to select only those points and segments within the area of the marquee. If the marquee surrounds an entire path, the entire path is selected. You can also select individual points or a series of points on different paths by drawing a marquee around just those points.

You use Shift with the Direct Selection tool to select additional points or segments or to deselect previously selected points. If you press Shift, the Selection tool works as a toggle between selecting and deselecting points or segments. You can use Shift in this way to add to or subtract from the current selection.

After you select a point or a series of points, you can manipulate those selected points by moving, transforming (via the transformation tools), and applying certain effects to them. You can select and modify individual segments and series of segments in the same way that you transform points.

Using the Group Selection tool

You can find the Group Selection tool in a popup menu under the Direct Selection tool. It first selects a path, then the group that the path is in, then the group that the other group with the path is in, etc.

For the Group Selection tool to work properly, select the first path or paths by either clicking them or drawing a marquee around them. To select the group that a particular path is in, however, requires you to click one of the initially selected paths. To select the next group also requires you to click; if you drag at any point, only the paths you drag over are selected. For example, suppose that you have a line of bicycles that belong to a group and each individual bicycle is also a group and each wheel on each bicycle is a group and each spoke is a separate path. Using the Group Selection tool, you can click once on a spoke to select it, and if you click it again, you select the wheel group; a third click selects the whole bicycle; and the fourth click selects the entire line of bicycles.

 When the Group Selection tool is active, you can switch to the Direct Selection tool by pressing A. You can toggle between the selection tools by pressing Alt (Option).

CAUTION Still confused about how Shift selects and deselects paths? Shift is an odd duck when used with the Group Selection tool. What happens when you click an unselected path with this tool while holding Shift? The path is selected. But what happens when you click a selected path? The process deselects just one path. What makes more sense is if you click again with Shift, and it then deselects the entire group. Nope. This isn't what happens. Shift works as a toggle on the one path you're clicking — selecting it, deselecting it, etc.

Dragging a marquee around paths with the Group Selection tool works only for the first series of clicks; dragging another marquee, even over the already-selected paths, just reselects those paths.

TIP You can use the keyboard to jump around each of the selection tools. No matter what tool you select in the Tools panel, pressing Ctrl (⌘) toggles to and allows the Selection tool while you hold Ctrl (⌘). You can switch between the Selection tool and the Direct Selection tool by pressing V for the Selection tool and A for the Direct Selection tool. When you have the Direct Selection tool active, press Alt (Option) to access the Group Selection tool!

If you have selected several paths at once, clicking a selected path selects only the group that the selected path is in. If other selected paths are in different groups, those groups aren't selected until you click those paths with the Group Selection tool. However, clicking multiple times on any of the paths in the selected group continues to select up in the group that the selected path is part of.

The Group Selection tool is most useful when dealing with graphs and blends, but it can be used in a number of other situations to greatly enhance your control of what is and isn't selected. People who are always ungrouping and regrouping paths can greatly benefit from using the Group Selection tool. In fact, proper use of this tool frees you from ever having to ungroup and regroup objects for workflow reasons.

The Group Selection tool also selects compound paths. One click selects an individual path within the compound path, and the second click selects the entire compound path.

Using the Magic Wand tool

The Magic Wand tool lets you make a selection based on the same stroke weight, fill color, stroke color, opacity, and blending mode. Choose the Magic Wand tool from the Tools panel (it looks like a magic wand) or press Y. To select with the Magic Wand tool, click the object that you want to select. All the objects with the same attributes are selected.

You can set the options on the Magic Wand tool for selecting objects. Access the Magic Wand panel by double-clicking the Magic Wand tool or choose Window ➪ Magic Wand. The Magic Wand panel is shown in Figure 6.6.

FIGURE 6.6

The Magic Wand panel allows you to fine-tune the operation of the Magic Wand tool.

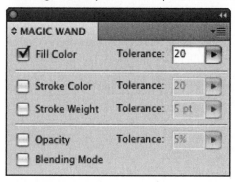

You can set the following options in the Magic Wand panel:

- **Fill Color:** Click this check box to make your Magic Wand selection based on the object's fill color.

- **Stroke Color:** Click this check box to make a Magic Wand selection based on the object's stroke color.

- **Stroke Weight:** Click this check box to base your Magic Wand selection on the object's stroke weight.

- **Opacity:** Click this check box to base your Magic Wand selection on the object's opacity.

- **Blending Mode:** Click this check box to make a Magic Wand selection based on the object's blending mode.

- **Tolerance:** Set the tolerance for the Fill Color, Stroke Color, Stroke Weight, and Opacity. You can set the tolerance in pixels between 0 and 255 (for RGB objects) or between 0 and 100 (for CMYK objects). Setting the tolerance low results in a very close selection in the original selected object. A higher tolerance selects more objects.

Using the Lasso tool

The Lasso tool lets you make a freeform selection by dragging the mouse. Access the Lasso tool by choosing it from the Tools panel (it looks like a rope) or by pressing Q. The Lasso tool selects paths and anchor points by dragging around the path or line segment.

 With both the Magic Wand and Lasso tools, you can add to a selection by holding Shift while clicking with either tool. Subtract from a selection by holding Alt (Option).

Selecting, moving, and deleting entire paths

Usually, the best way to select a path that's not currently selected is by clicking it with the Selection tool, which highlights all the points on the path and allows you to move, transform, or delete that entire path.

To select more than one path, you can use a number of methods. The most basic method is to hold Shift and then click the successive paths with the Selection tool, selecting one more path with each Shift+click. Shift+clicking a selected path with the Selection tool deselects that particular path. Drawing a marquee with the Selection tool selects all paths that at least partially fall into the area drawn by the marquee. When drawing a marquee, be sure to start the cursor in an area where there's nothing. Finding an empty spot may be difficult to do in Preview mode because fills from various paths may cover any white space available. Drawing a marquee with the Selection tool while pressing Shift selects unselected paths and deselects currently selected paths.

CROSS-REF For more on Preview and Outline modes, see Chapter 2.

To select just a portion of a path, you must use the Direct Selection tool. To select an anchor point or a line segment, simply click it. To select several individual points or paths, click the points or paths that you want to select while holding Shift. You can also select a series of points and paths by dragging a marquee across the desired paths.

Individually selected points become solid squares. If these points are smooth, curved, or combination corner points, control handles appear from the selected anchor point.

The first time you click a straight line segment, all the anchor points on the path appear as hollow squares, telling you that something on that path is selected. Selected points turn black, and curved line segments have one or more control handles and control handle lines sticking out from the ending anchor points. Straight line segments don't do anything when selected. The inventive side of you may think that you can get around this problem by dragging the selected segments to a new location or by copying and pasting them and then undoing. However, this solution doesn't work because of Illustrator's habit of selecting all points on paths when undoing operations on those paths.

If paths are part of either a compound path or a group, all other paths in that compound path or group are also selected.

To move a path, click the path and then drag (in one motion) with the Selection tool. To move several paths, select the paths, click an already-selected path with the Selection tool or the Direct Selection tool, and then drag.

TIP   If you've been selecting multiple paths by using Shift, be sure to release Shift before clicking and dragging on the selection. If Shift is still pressed, the clicked path becomes deselected and no paths move. If this does happen, just Shift+click the path that was deselected and then drag.

To delete an entire path, select it with the Selection tool and press Backspace (Delete). To delete multiple paths, select them and press Backspace (Delete). Remember that line segments exist only when one point is on either side of the segment. Even if the line segment is not selected, if one of its anchor points is deleted, the line segment is also deleted. A path is made up of points, and those points are connected via segments. If the points are gone, the paths disappear along with them. But if you delete all the segments, all the points can still remain.

You can duplicate portions of paths by pressing Alt (Option) while releasing the mouse button. Duplicating segments also duplicates the anchor points on either side of that segment.

Using different selection options

Illustrator has several special select functions (they're found under the Select menu). You use the Select functions for selecting paths with common or specific attributes. The Select functions make mundane, repetitive tasks easy to accomplish by doing all the dirty work for you.

To access the Select functions, choose them from the Select menu, as shown in Figure 6.7.

You can find the following options under the Select menu:

- **All:** Choosing this selects everything in the document except locked objects.

CROSS-REF   For more on locking objects, see Chapter 8.

- **Deselect:** Choosing this function deselects everything in the document.
- **Reselect:** This function reselects the last selection.

 You can redo the last selection type by choosing Reselect from the Select menu or by pressing Ctrl+6 (⌘+6).

FIGURE 6.7

The Select functions found in the Select menu allow you to select objects.

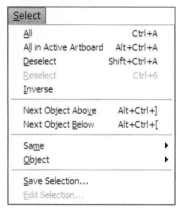

- **Inverse:** The Inverse function is perfect for selecting all paths that aren't selected. You can use this selection function to instantly select paths that are hidden, guides, and other unlocked objects that are hard to select.
- **Next Object Above:** Choosing this selects the next object above the selected object in stacking order (stacking order is the same as layer order). See Chapter 8 for more on stacking order and layering.
- **Next Object Below:** This function selects the next object below the selected object in stacking order.
- **Same:** Here, you can choose to select the same appearance, appearance attribute (the one currently selected in the Appearance panel), blending mode, fill and stroke, fill color, opacity, stroke color, stroke weight, graphic style, symbol instance, or threaded block series. Figure 6.8 shows these options. For more on threaded blocks, see Chapter 9.
- **Object:** In this area, you can choose to select all objects on the same layer, the object's direction handles, brushstrokes, clipping masks, stray points, text objects, Flash dynamic text, or Flash input text (text tagged to be editable within Flash player). Figure 6.9 shows these options.
- **Save Selection:** Use this to save a particular selection.
- **Edit Selection:** Use this to edit a saved selection.

FIGURE 6.8

The Same options found under the Select menu

FIGURE 6.9

The Object options found under the Select menu

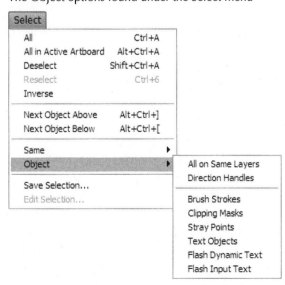

Select Inverse

Select Inverse (Select ⇨ Inverse) quickly selects all unlocked and unhidden objects that aren't currently selected while deselecting those objects that are currently selected. For example, if one object is selected and the document contains 15 other unlocked objects, the 15 objects become selected, but the one object that was selected originally becomes deselected.

CAUTION **Select Inverse doesn't cause locked or hidden objects to be selected and doesn't select guides unless guides aren't locked. Objects on layers that are locked or hidden aren't selected either.**

Select Inverse is useful because selecting a few objects is usually quicker than selecting most objects. After you select the few objects, Select Inverse does all the work of selecting everything else.

When no objects are selected, Select Inverse selects all the objects, just as choosing Select ⇨ Select All or pressing Ctrl+A (⌘+A) does. When all objects are selected, Select Inverse deselects all the objects, just as choosing Select ⇨ Deselect or pressing Shift+Ctrl+A (Shift+⌘+A) does.

Select Same Blending Mode

Same Blending Mode (Select ⇨ Same ⇨ Blending Mode) selects objects that have the same Blending mode attributes of the currently selected object. The objects are selected regardless of their other attributes as long as the Blending modes are the same.

Select Same Fill & Stroke

Same Fill & Stroke (Select ⇨ Same ⇨ Fill & Stroke) selects objects that have almost exactly the same paint style as the paint style of the selected object. The following information must be the same:

- Fill color (as defined in the next section)
- Stroke color
- Stroke weight

Some items in the object's paint style that don't matter (that is, they don't prevent Same Fill & Stroke from selecting an object) are any of the stroke attributes and the overprinting options.

TIP **If you select more than one object, don't select objects with different paint styles. The best thing to do with Same Fill & Stroke, as with Same Fill Color, is to select only one object.**

If you have a spot color selected, the Select functions select all other occurrences of that spot color, regardless of the tint. This can be troublesome when you want to select only a certain tint value of that spot color, not all the tint values.

Select Same Fill Color

Same Fill Color (Select ➪ Same ➪ Fill Color) selects objects that have the same fill color as the currently selected object. This function selects objects regardless of their stroke color, stroke weight, or stroke pattern. If you select objects with different fills, the Same Fill Color function won't work.

Same Fill Color considers different tints of spot colors to be the same color. This function works in two ways. First, if you select one object with any tint value of a spot color, Same Fill Color selects all other objects with the same spot color, regardless of the tint. Second, you can select more than one object, no matter what tint each object contains, provided that the selected objects have the same spot color.

CROSS-REF For more on spot colors, see Chapter 7.

CAUTION To be selected with Same Fill Color, process color fills (CMYK) must have the same values as the original. Even single colors, such as yellow, must be the same percentage. The Same Fill Color function considers 100% Yellow and 50% Yellow to be two separate colors. However, spot color fills are selected regardless of the tint percentage.

Same Fill Color also selects objects that are filled with the same gradient, regardless of the angle or the starting or ending point of the gradient. This function does not, however, select objects that have the same pattern fill.

Select Same Opacity

Same Opacity (Select ➪ Same ➪ Opacity) selects all the objects with the same Opacity value as the currently selected object, regardless of the other attributes of the objects.

Select Same Stroke Color

Same Stroke Color (Select ➪ Same ➪ Stroke Color) selects objects that have the same stroke color, regardless of the stroke weight or style and regardless of the type of fill.

The color limitations that are defined in the Same Fill Color section also apply to Same Stroke Color function.

Although you can choose a pattern for a stroke that makes the stroke look gray, the Same Stroke Color function doesn't select other objects that have the same stroke pattern.

Select Same Stroke Weight

Same Stroke Weight (Select ➪ Same ➪ Stroke Weight) selects objects that have the same stroke weight, regardless of the stroke color, the style, or the fill color.

Even if the stroke is a pattern, Illustrator selects other paths that have the same stroke weight as the patterned stroke when you apply this function.

Don't select more than one stroke weight if you select more than one object. If you've selected different stroke weights, Illustrator doesn't select any paths when you choose Select ⇨ Same ⇨ Stroke Weight. The best thing to do with the Same Stroke Weight function, as with Same Fill Color and Same Fill & Stroke, is to select only one object.

Select Same Style

Same Style (Select ⇨ Same ⇨ Style) selects objects that have the same Style attributes. Choosing Select ⇨ Same ⇨ Style selects all the objects with the same Style attributes as the currently selected object.

Select Same Symbol Instance

Same Symbol Instance (Select ⇨ Same ⇨ Symbol Instance) selects objects that have the same Symbol Instances. Choosing Select ⇨ Same ⇨ Symbol Instance selects all the objects with the same Symbol Instance as the currently selected object.

Select Same Link Block Series

Same Link Block Series (Select ⇨ Same ⇨ Link Block Series) selects all the threaded text link blocks with the initial selection. If you select only one block of text, choosing Select ⇨ Same ⇨ Link Block Series selects all the text that's linked with the currently selected text block.

Select Object All on Same Layers

Choosing Select ⇨ Object ⇨ All on Same Layers selects all objects on the currently selected objects' layers.

Select Object Direction Handles

Choosing Select ⇨ Object ⇨ Direction Handles selects all the direction handles on the currently selected object. This makes for easier editing of the object using its direction handles.

Select Object Brush Strokes

Choosing Select ⇨ Object ⇨ Brush Strokes selects all brushstrokes with the same attributes as the currently selected brushstroke.

Select Object Clipping Masks

Choosing Select ⇨ Object ⇨ Clipping Masks selects all unlocked or visible clipping masks in your document, but the objects they mask aren't selected. (A *clipping mask* is an object that hides other artwork that's outside the mask; see Chapter 12 for more information.) The only masks in the document that aren't selected are the masks that are locked or hidden and the masks that are on layers that are locked or hidden.

Select Object Stray Points

Choosing Select ➪ Object ➪ Stray Points selects all isolated anchor points in the document. Individual anchor points don't print or preview. You can see them in Preview mode only when they're selected. After you cut portions of line segments, stray points often appear. These individual points often interfere with connecting other segments. You can't use this selection function enough.

CROSS-REF For more on viewing modes, see Chapter 2.

You can mistakenly create stray points in various ways:

- Clicking once with the Pen tool creates a single anchor point.
- Deleting a line segment on a path that has two points by selecting the line segment with the Direct Selection tool and pressing Backspace (Delete) leaves behind the two anchor points.
- Using the Scissors tool to cut a path, and while deleting one side or another of the path, not selecting the points turns these points into stray points.

Bringing an Illustrator 4 or older document that has still-grouped rectangles or ellipses into the current version automatically deletes the center point and turns on the Show Center Point option in the Attributes panel (choose Window ➪ Attributes to display the Attributes panel).

CAUTION Center points of objects aren't stray points, and you can't select them without selecting the object to which they belong. Center points of objects are visible when you choose the Show Center Point option in the Attributes panel. Selecting the center point of an object selects the entire object, and deleting the center point deletes the entire object.

Select Object Text Objects

Choosing Select ➪ Objects ➪ Text Objects selects all unlocked and unhidden text objects in your document.

Select Flash Dynamic Text

Choosing Select ➪ Objects ➪ Flash Dynamic Text selects all unlocked and unhidden text objects that have been tagged as Flash Dynamic Text (allowing them to be edited programmatically within Flash Player) in your document.

Select Flash Input Text

Choosing Select ➪ Objects ➪ Flash Input Text selects all unlocked and unhidden text objects that have been tagged as Flash Input Text (allowing them to be edited manually within Flash Player) in your document.

Keeping and labeling a selection

After you've gone through any long process of selecting, you might want to save the selection, especially if you use a certain selection repeatedly. After you save a selection, you can make it reusable. To save a selection, create your selection first and then choose Select ⇨ Save Selection to display the Save Selection dialog box, as shown in Figure 6.10. By choosing Select ⇨ Edit Selection, you can change the name of the selection. You access a saved selection by choosing Select ⇨ name of selection, and you can edit saved selections under Select ⇨ Edit Selection.

The Save Selection dialog box allows you to name and save a selection.

Custom paint style selections

Unfortunately, you can't do multiple-type selections with any of the special selection functions. You can't, for example, select at one time all the objects that have the same stroke color and fill color but have different stroke weights.

The Lock Unselected command, which you activate by pressing Alt+Shift+Ctrl+2 (Option+Shift+⌘+2), is the key to specifying multiple selection criteria (this command doesn't appear on any of Illustrator's menus). The following steps describe how to perform multiple-type selections:

1. **Select a representative object that has the stroke and fill colors that you want.**

2. **Choose Select ⇨ Same ⇨ Fill Color.** Illustrator selects all objects having the same fill color as the original object, regardless of the objects' stroke color.

3. **Press Alt+Shift+Ctrl+2 (Option+Shift+⌘+2).** This locks any objects that aren't selected. This is a key step. The only objects that you can modify or select now are the ones that have the same fill color.

4. **Choose Select ⇨ Deselect or press Shift+Ctrl+A (Shift+⌘+A) and then select the original object.** The original object now has both the fill color and the stroke color that you want to select.

5. **Choose Select ⇨ Same ⇨ Stroke Color.** Only objects that have the same stroke and fill colors are selected, regardless of stroke weight.

6. Choose Object ⇨ Unlock All or press Alt+Ctrl+2 (Option+⌘+2) after you finish to make the other objects selectable.

Editing Paths in Illustrator

The path-editing tools are the Scissors tool; the Knife tool; and the Add Anchor Point, Delete Anchor Point, and Convert Anchor Point popup tools in the Pen tool slot. Clicking and holding the Pen tool displays the Pen, Add Anchor Point, Delete Anchor Point, and Convert Anchor Point tools. (Although the Slice tool might seem similar to the path-editing tools mentioned in this section, it actually serves a very different purpose, as discussed in Chapter 19.)

Dragging out to a path-editing tool replaces the default Pen tool with the newly selected popup tool. If you press Caps Lock at the same time that you choose a path-editing tool, the tool cursor resembles crosshairs. The crosshairs cursor allows precision positioning of cursors.

This list describes the purpose of each path-editing tool:

- **Add Anchor Point tool:** You use this tool to add anchor points to an existing path. If you add an anchor point to a straight segment (one that has no control handles on either end), the anchor point becomes a straight corner point. If the segment is curved — meaning that you have at least one control handle for that segment — the new anchor point becomes a smooth point.

- **Delete Anchor Point tool:** This deletes the anchor point you clicked. Illustrator creates a new segment between the anchor points that were on either side of the anchor point you clicked. If the anchor point on which you clicked is an endpoint, no new segment is drawn; instead, the next or previous anchor point on the path becomes the new endpoint.

- **Scissors tool:** You use this tool to split paths. Clicking with the Scissors tool on a closed path makes that path an open path, with the endpoints directly overlapping each other where the click occurred. Using the Scissors tool on an open path splits that open path into two separate open paths, each with an endpoint that overlaps the other open path's endpoint.

- **Knife tool:** This tool slices through path areas. It's the only path-editing tool that doesn't require you to have paths selected; it works on all unlocked paths that fall under the blade. Use this to cut an object into two closed-path objects.

- **Convert Direction Point tool:** This tool has two functions. The first is to simply change an anchor point from its current type to a straight corner point by clicking and releasing it. You can also change the current type to Smooth by clicking and dragging on the anchor point. The second function is to move control handles individually by changing smooth points to curved corner points and by changing combination corner points and curved corner points to smooth points. (Straight corner points don't have any control handles, so using this method can't change them.)

You can add and remove anchor points in two ways. I mentioned one method in Chapter 4, where I demonstrated how to add anchor points with the drawing tools and then remove them by simply selecting them and pressing Backspace (Delete).

The techniques covered in this chapter are unlike the methods discussed previously. Instead of adding new points that create an extension to an existing path, you learn how to add points in the middle of existing paths. Instead of deleting points and the line segments connected to them, you learn how to remove points between two anchor points and watch as a new line segment connects those two anchor points.

Editing with anchor points

To add an anchor point to an existing path, select the Add Anchor Point tool and then click a line segment of a path. You can't place an anchor point directly on top of another anchor point, but you can get pretty close. Figure 6.11 shows a path before and after several anchor points are added to it.

FIGURE 6.11

Adding anchor points to a path doesn't alter the shape of the path but allows the path to be modified more easily than if the points weren't added.

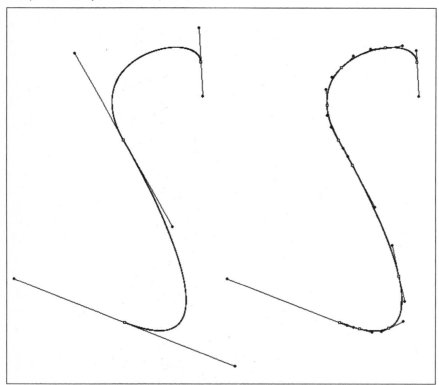

TIP I like to select the paths to which I'm adding anchor points before I start actually adding the points. This technique ensures that I don't accidentally get the annoying message "Can't Add Anchor Point. Please use the Add Anchor Point tool on a segment of a path." It seems that if there's just one point in the middle of a path, that's where I end up clicking to add the point. After I add one point, the path becomes selected automatically.

TIP If that annoying message really bugs you, click the Don't show again check box and instead you hear a quiet noise alerting you that you can't add the anchor point.

Anchor points added to paths via the Add Anchor Point tool are either smooth points or straight corner points, depending on the segment where the new anchor point is added. If the segment has two straight corner points on either side of it, then the new anchor point is a straight corner point. If one of the anchor points is any type of anchor point other than a straight corner point, the new anchor point is a smooth point.

The Add Anchor Points function

The Object ⇨ Path ⇨ Add Anchor Points command adds new anchor points between every pair of existing anchor points it can find. New anchor points are always added halfway between existing anchor points.

NOTE Add Anchor Points is related to the Add Anchor Point tool. This function adds anchor points the same way as the tool does — only more efficiently. Points that are added to a smooth segment are automatically smooth points; points added to a straight segment are automatically corner points.

For example, if you have one line segment with an anchor point on each end, Add Anchor Points adds one anchor point to the segment exactly in the middle of the two anchor points. If you draw a rectangle and apply the Add Anchor Points function, Illustrator adds four new anchor points: one at the top, one at the bottom, one on the left side, and one on the right side.

Figure 6.12 shows an object that has the Add Anchor Points function applied three times.

TIP Want to know how many points Illustrator adds to your path when you apply the Add Anchor Points function? Each time you reapply the function, the number of anchor points doubles on a closed path and is one less than doubled on an open path.

Adding anchor points is useful before using the Pucker & Bloat and Tweak effects and before using any other effect that bases its results on the number and position of anchor points.

CROSS-REF For more on effects, see Chapter 15.

FIGURE 6.12

Using the Add Anchor Points command doubles the number of anchor points, distributing new points midway between existing points. The original object (left) has four anchor points. Applying Add Anchor Points to it once (middle) results in eight anchor points. Applying Add Anchor Points a second time results in 16 anchor points (right).

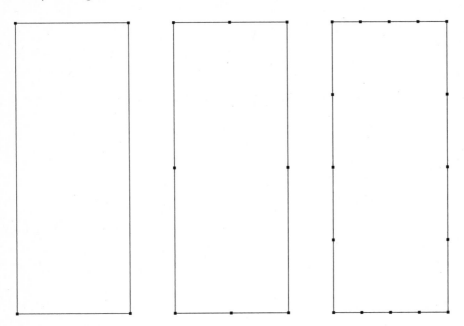

TIP If you need to add a large number of anchor points quickly, use the Roughen effect (found under Effect ⇨ Distort ⇨ Roughen) with a size of 0% and the detail set to how many anchor points you want per inch. When you use Roughen, the anchor points are equally distributed, regardless of where the original anchor points were in the selected path (as opposed to Add Anchor Points, which places new points between existing ones, resulting in clumping in detailed areas).

Removing anchor points

Removing anchor points is a little trickier than adding them. Depending on where you remove the anchor point, you may adversely change the flow of the line between the two anchor points on either side of it, as shown in Figure 6.13. If the point removed had any control handles, the removal usually results in a more drastic change than if the anchor point was a straight corner point. This situation occurs if control handles on the anchor point being removed are at least half the aspect of the curve. A straight corner point affects only the location of the line, not the shape of its curve.

FIGURE 6.13

Removing an anchor point can drastically alter the shape of the original path.

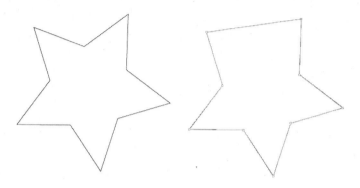

To remove an anchor point, click an existing anchor point with the Delete Anchor Point tool. Like the Add Anchor Point tool, you can remove points without first selecting the path, but, of course, if the path is not selected, you can't see it or the points that you want to remove. If you miss and don't click an anchor point, a message appears informing you that to remove an anchor point, you must click one.

After you remove anchor points, you can't usually just add them back with the Add Anchor Point tool. Considering that the flow of the path changes when you remove a point, adding a point — even the correct type of point — doesn't give the same result as just undoing the point deletion.

If only two points are on an open path, the anchor point you click is deleted and so is the segment connecting it to the sole remaining anchor point. If there are only two points on a closed path, both line segments from the anchor point you click are deleted along with that point, leaving only one anchor point remaining.

Simplifying paths by removing anchor points

Some artwork can be unnecessarily complicated with many more anchor points than are actually needed. These additional anchor points most often occur with artwork that has been traced by Illustrator's Live Trace tool or using clip art.

A solution for eliminating unneeded anchor points is to select the object and then choose Object ➪ Path ➪ Simplify, as discussed next. This removes anchor points evenly.

Removing anchor points using Simplify

Choosing Object ➪ Path ➪ Simplify displays the Simplify dialog box that you use to remove excess anchor points. The Simplify dialog box, as shown in Figure 6.14, has four areas to adjust:

- **Curve Precision:** Adjust the Curve Precision by dragging the slider. Be sure to click the Preview box first to see how the original curve changes based on the slider position. The closer the slider is to the right, the closer the path is to the original curve.

- **Angle Threshold:** This option adjusts the smoothness of the corners. The farther the slider is to the right, the wider the angles that are kept as corners.

- **Straight Lines:** Click this check box to create straight lines between anchor points, even if they were curved in the original.

- **Show Original:** Click this check box to see the original path behind the path you're simplifying.

Figure 6.15 shows the results of applying Simplify to an illustration with too many anchor points.

FIGURE 6.14

The Simplify dialog box helps you remove excess anchor points.

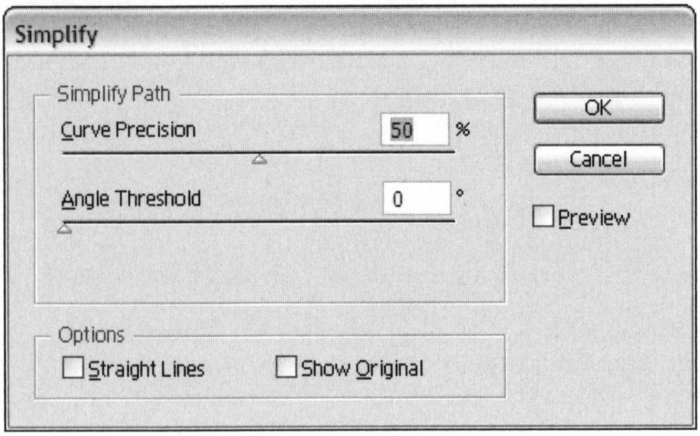

Splitting paths

To change a single path into two separate paths that together make up a path equal in length to the original, you must use the Scissors tool. You can also split paths by selecting and deleting anchor points or line segments, although this method shortens the overall length of the two paths.

To split a path with the Scissors tool, click anywhere on a path. Initially, it doesn't seem like much happens. If you clicked in the middle of a line segment, a new anchor point appears. (Actually, two appear, but the second is directly on top of the first, so you see only one.) If you click directly on top of an existing anchor point, nothing at all seems to happen, but Illustrator actually creates another anchor point on top of the one that you clicked.

FIGURE 6.15

The original artwork (left) has twice as many points as the artwork after using Simplify (right).

After clicking with the Scissors tool, you've separated the path into two separate sections, but it appears that there's still only one path because both sections are selected. To see the individual paths, deselect them by pressing Shift+Ctrl+A (Shift+⌘+A) and then select one side with the Selection tool. After you split a path, you may move one half independently of the other half, as shown in Figure 6.16.

The anchor points created with the Scissors tool either become smooth points or straight corner points, depending on the type of anchor point that's next along the path. If the line segment to the next anchor point has a control handle coming out of that anchor point that affects the line segment, the new endpoint becomes a smooth point. If there's no control handle for the line segment, the endpoint becomes a straight corner point.

 You can't use the Scissors tool on a line's endpoint — only on segments and anchor points that aren't endpoints.

Sectioning and repeating paths

Illustrator provides several capabilities that allow for multiple types of dividing and duplicating of paths, including paths that aren't selected. This section discusses those different features as well as the tool that makes this possible: the Knife tool.

FIGURE 6.16

The original path (left); the path after splitting and moving the two pieces apart (right)

The Knife tool

The Knife tool is located in the same area as the Scissors tool. The Knife tool divides paths into smaller sections as it slices through them because it goes through two sides of the closed path. Those sections are initially selected, but they're not grouped. Figure 6.17 shows a path before and after it crosses paths with the Knife.

> **TIP** Pressing Alt (Option) when using the Knife tool cuts in a straight line rather than a curved one. Pressing Shift constrains the straight line to a 45° angle when you also press Alt (Option).

> **CAUTION** Remember that the Knife tool works on all paths that are under the existing path, selected or not.

FIGURE 6.17

The original path (left) and the resulting paths (right) after being dragged apart

The Slice tool

Another tool that looks like it cuts is the Slice tool. It does cut a path into sections. If you're creating artwork for the Web, this is one of the tools to use. The Slice tool slices the artwork into sections that are independent, each with its own specific information.

CROSS-REF For more on slicing for the Web and the Slice tool, see Chapter 19.

Reshaping paths

You can reshape paths using the Reshape tool, which is housed with the Scale tool in the Tools panel. Using the Reshape tool gets results but maybe not exact editing. A great use for the Reshape tool is to edit multiple paths at the same time.

To use the Reshape tool on any path, just click where you want to bend the path and then drag. To use the Reshape tool on several paths at once, first select the paths with the Direct Selection tool or the Lasso tool and then use the Reshape tool to drag+select the point(s) you want to move. You must select at least one point that's not a straight corner point on each path. Then, drag on a reshape-selected point; Illustrator also moves all the curved corner points. Figure 6.18 shows what you can do with the Reshape tool.

FIGURE 6.18

A path being reshaped using the Reshape tool

Cleaning up a path

Clean Up removes three unwanted elements from Illustrator documents: stray points, unpainted objects, and empty text paths. Clean Up works on the entire document, regardless of what is selected. You apply this command by choosing Object ➪ Path ➪ Clean Up. The Clean Up dialog box is shown in Figure 6.19.

 Clean Up doesn't work on locked or hidden paths, paths turned into guides, or paths on locked or hidden layers.

These are the Delete options in the Clean Up dialog box:

- **Stray Points:** Selects and deletes any little points flying around. These points can cause all sorts of trouble, as a point can have paint attributes but can't print. This option actually deletes the points.

 Select All Stray Points under the Select menu selects the points, but you have to press Backspace or Delete to delete them.

- **Unpainted Objects:** Eliminates any paths that are filled and stroked with None and that aren't masks (masks always have fills and strokes of None)
- **Empty Text Paths:** Finds any text paths with no characters and then deletes them

FIGURE 6.19

Use the Clean Up dialog box to specify what elements you want to clean up.

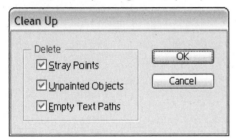

 Empty Text Paths isn't the same as the old Revert Text Paths from previous Illustrator versions, which changed empty text paths back into standard paths.

 For more on text paths, see Chapter 9.

If you aren't sure whether your document contains these three items, run Clean Up. If none of these items are found, a message box, as shown in Figure 6.20, appears and tells you so.

FIGURE 6.20

This message tells you that there was nothing to clean up in your document.

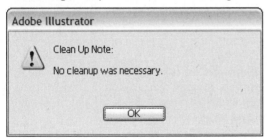

Offsetting a path

Offset Path, which you access by choosing Object ➪ Path ➪ Offset Path, draws a new path around the outside or inside of an existing path. The distance from the existing path is the distance that you specify in the Offset Path dialog box, which is shown in Figure 6.21. In a sense, you're creating a stroke, outlining it, and uniting it with the original — all in one action. You can specify the distance the path is to be offset by typing a value in the Offset box.

FIGURE 6.21

Use the Offset Path dialog box to specify how to create the new offset path.

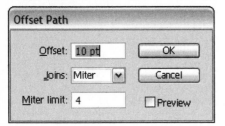

A positive number in the Offset Path dialog box creates the new path outside the existing path, and a negative number creates the new path inside the existing path. When the path is closed, figuring out where Illustrator will create the new path is easy. When working with an open path — such as a vertical line — the outside is the left side of the path and the inside is the right side of the path.

The Joins option allows you to select from different types of joins (which I discuss later in this chapter) at the corners of the new path. The choices are Miter, Round, and Bevel, and the result is the same effect that you get if you choose those options as the stroke style for a stroke.

The Miter limit affects the miter size only when you select the Miter option from the Joins drop-down list (popup menu). However, the option is available when you select Round and Bevel joins. Just ignore the Miter limit when you're using Round or Bevel joins. (You can't use a value that's less than 1.)

Often, when you're offsetting a path, the new, resulting path overlaps itself. This creates small, undesirable bumps in a path. If the bumps are within a closed-path area, select the new path and then choose Unite from the Pathfinder panel. If the bumps are outside the closed-path area, choose Divide from the Pathfinder panel and then select and delete each of the bumps.

TIP   If you're thinking of using the Scale tool rather than Offset Path, you should know that the Scale tool does something totally different from Offset Path. Offset Path offsets lines around the original path equally. The Scale tool enlarges or reduces the path but doesn't add lines. Unless you're using a perfect square or circle, stick to Offset Path. That way, you get an even placement of the new path accurately around or inside the selected path.

Outlining a path

Outline Path creates a path around an existing path's stroke. The width of the new path is directly related to the width of the stroke.

I use Outline Path for two reasons. The first and most obvious reason is to fill a stroke with a gradient. The second reason is that when you transform an outlined stroke, the effect is often different from the effect that results from transforming a stroked path. Scaling an outlined stroke changes the width of the stroke in the direction of the scale. The same is true when using the Free Distort effect (Effect ⇨ Distort & Transform ⇨ Free Distort), which also changes the width of the stroke in the direction of the scale. This sometimes results in a nonuniform-appearing stroke, which can't be achieved with a standard stroke. Figure 6.22 shows the difference between transforming/distorting a stroked path and an outlined stroke. Both copies were scaled vertically to more clearly demonstrate the different behaviors. With the stroked path, the transformation results in the stroke expanding far beyond the fill, while with the outlined stroke, the two remain in sync.

Consider these options for outlining a path:

- The End and Join attributes of the stroke's style determine how the ends and joins of the resulting stroke look.
- Outline Path creates problems for tight corners. It causes overlaps that are similar to those generated by Offset Path.

CAUTION Using a Dash pattern on the stroke and using Outline Path changes the stroke back to a solid line and then outlines it.

Looking under the Effect menu, you find a Path effect with the following options: Offset Path, Outline Object, and Outline Stroke. These are the same as what is found by choosing Object ⇨ Path. However, under Effect, you can always go back and edit the options. Choosing the Path functions from under the Object menu has a more permanent result.

CROSS-REF For more on the Effect menu, see Chapter 15.

Aligning and distributing points

Aligning and equally distributing points is very similar to aligning and distributing objects, except that you use the Direct Selection tool to select the points you want to align or distribute. After the points are selected, clicking the appropriate icon in the Control panel aligns or distributes the points, as shown in Figure 6.23. You can also align points by using the Average commands.

CROSS-REF For more on the Align and Distribute buttons, see Chapter 8.

CAUTION If you want to align all the points on a path horizontally or vertically, use the Average function (Object ⇨ Path ⇨ Average).

FIGURE 6.22

Both of these paths have been stretched vertically using the Scale tool. The original stroked path is on the left. The path on the right was outlined via Outline Path prior to being scaled.

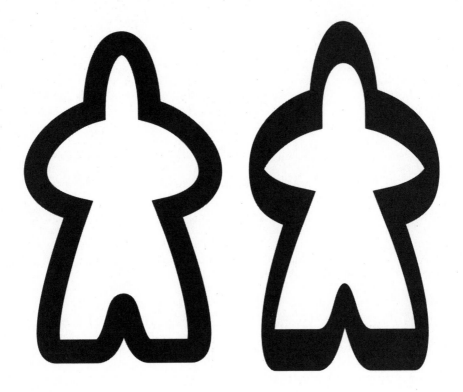

To average points vertically, choose the Vertical option in the Average dialog box, as shown in Figure 6.24. To average points both vertically and horizontally, choose Both. The Both option places all selected points on top of each other.

FIGURE 6.23

The path on top is the original one. The path below is what happens when all the points in the path are horizontally aligned (control handles create the bumpiness of the path).

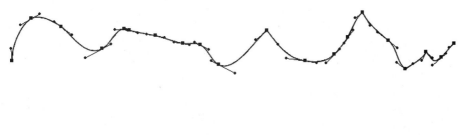

FIGURE 6.24

The Average dialog box lets you select Horizontal, Vertical, or Both.

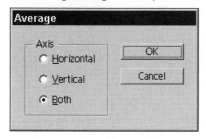

When averaging points using the Average dialog box, Illustrator uses the mean method to determine the center. No, Illustrator isn't nasty to the points that it averages; rather, Illustrator adds together the coordinates of the points and then divides by the number of points. This provides the mean location of the center of the points.

Joining

Joining is a tricky area to define. Illustrator's Join feature does two entirely different things. It joins two endpoints at different locations with a line segment, and it also combines two anchor points into one when they're placed on top of each other.

To join two endpoints with a line segment, select just two endpoints in different locations (not on top of each other) with the Direct Selection tool and then choose Object ➪ Path ➪ Join or press Ctrl+J (⌘+J). Illustrator forms a line segment between the two points, resulting in a closed path, as shown in Figure 6.25.

FIGURE 6.25

Join two endpoints with a line segment using the Object ➪ Path ➪ Join command.

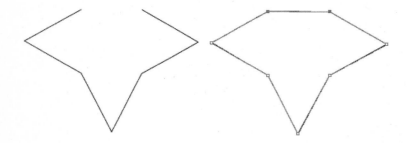

To combine two endpoints into a single anchor point, select the two points that are directly over one another and then choose Object ➪ Path ➪ Join or press Ctrl+J (⌘+J). Not only can you join two separate paths, but you can also join together the endpoints on the same open path (overlapping endpoints) to create a closed path in the same way that two endpoints from different paths are joined.

To ensure that endpoints are overlapping, drag one endpoint to the other with a selection tool. When the two points are close enough, the arrowhead cursor (normally black) becomes hollow (or white). Release the mouse button when the arrowhead is hollow, and Illustrator places the two points on top of each other.

Another way to ensure that the endpoints are overlapping is to select them and then choose Object ➪ Path ➪ Average or press Alt+Ctrl+J (Option+⌘+J). Next, select the Both option in the Average dialog box.

CAUTION When creating an anchor point out of two overlapping endpoints, ensure that the two points are precisely overlapping. If they're even the smallest distance apart, a line segment is drawn between the two points instead of transforming the two endpoints into a single anchor point.

Joining has these limitations:

- Joins can't take place when one path is part of a different group than the other path. If the two paths are in the same base group (that is, not in any other groups before being grouped to the other path, even grouped by themselves), the endpoints can be joined.

- If one path is grouped to another object and the other object has not been previously grouped to the path, the endpoints won't join.

- The endpoints on text paths can't be joined.

- The endpoints of guides can't be joined.

If all the points in an open path are selected (as if the path is selected with the Selection tool), then choosing Object ⇨ Path ⇨ Join or pressing Ctrl+J (⌘+J) automatically joins the endpoints. If the two endpoints are located on top of each other, the Join dialog box opens asking whether the new anchor point should be a smooth point or a corner point.

Joining is also useful for determining the location of endpoints when the endpoints are overlapping. Select the entire path, choose Object ⇨ Path ⇨ Join or press Ctrl+J (⌘+J), and then click the Smooth radio button. These steps usually alter one of the two segments on either side of the new anchor point. Undo the join, and you know the location of the overlapping endpoints.

 **If you're having trouble joining two open paths, ensure that they're not grouped. You can't join grouped paths.**

Converting Anchor Points

The Convert Anchor Point tool converts anchor points only by adjusting control handles. The Convert Anchor Point tool works differently with each type of anchor point.

 **For detailed definitions of the four types of anchor points and how they're drawn with the Pen tool, see Chapter 4.**

You can use the Convert Anchor Point tool either on extended control handles or on anchor points. When there are two control handles on an anchor point, clicking either control handle with the Convert Anchor Point tool does two things:

- It breaks the linked control handles so that when the angle of one is changed, the other is also not changed. As a result, the two handles can be dragged to different angles.

- It makes them independent so that the control handle's length from the anchor point and the angle can be altered individually.

Converting Smooth Points

Smooth points can be changed into the other three types of anchor points by using the Direct Selection and the Convert Anchor Point tools:

- To convert smooth points into straight corner points, click once with the Convert Anchor Point tool on the anchor point.

- To convert smooth points into combination corner points, use the Direct Selection tool or the Convert Anchor Point tool to drag one control handle into the anchor point.

- To convert smooth points into curved corner points, use the Convert Anchor Point tool to drag one of the control handles. After being dragged with the Convert Anchor Point tool, the two control handles become independent of each other (the movement of one won't affect the other).

The following steps show you how you can use the Direct Selection and Convert Anchor Point tools to change shapes — in this case, from a circle to a rhombus or diamond shape:

1. **Draw a circle with the Ellipse tool.** Remember to keep Shift pressed so you end up with a perfect circle.

2. **Click the Convert Anchor Point tool.**

3. **Click each of the anchor points and then release.** This converts the smooth anchor points to corner anchor points. The rhombus (diamond shape) should look like the illustration in Figure 6.26.

FIGURE 6.26

Convert the circle (left) to a diamond (right) by clicking each anchor point with the Convert Anchor Point tool.

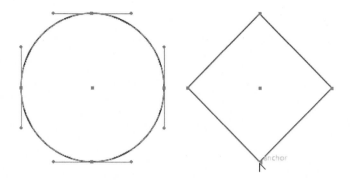

Converting straight corner points

You can change straight corner points into one of the other three types of anchor points by using the Convert Anchor Point and Direct Selection tools:

- To convert straight corner points into smooth points, use the Convert Anchor Point tool to click and drag on the anchor point. As you drag, linked control handles appear on both sides of the anchor point.

- To convert straight corner points into combination corner points, use the Convert Anchor Point tool to click and drag on the anchor point. As you drag, linked control handles appear on both sides of the anchor point. Select one of the control handles with the Convert Anchor Point tool or the Direct Selection tool and drag it toward the anchor point until it disappears.

- To convert straight corner points into curved corner points, use the Convert Anchor Point tool to click and drag on the anchor point. As you drag, linked control handles appear on both sides of the anchor point. Then, use the Convert Anchor Point tool to drag one of the control handles. After being dragged with the Convert Anchor Point tool, the two control handles become independent of each other.

Converting combination corner points

You can change combination corner points into one of the other three types of anchor points by using the Convert Direction Point and Direct Selection tools:

- To convert combination corner points into smooth points, use the Convert Anchor Point tool to click and drag on the anchor point. As you drag, linked control handles appear on both sides of the anchor point.

- To convert combination corner points into straight corner points, use the Convert Anchor Point tool to click once on the anchor point. The control handle disappears.

- To convert combination corner points into curved corner points, use the Convert Anchor Point tool to click and drag the anchor point. As you drag, linked control handles appear on both sides of the anchor point. Then, use the Convert Anchor Point tool to drag one of the control handles. After being dragged with the Convert Anchor Point tool, the two control handles become independent of each other.

The following steps are another example of how you can change shapes using the Direct Selection and Convert Anchor Point tools — this time, changing a circle into a heart:

1. **Draw a circle with the Ellipse tool.** Remember to keep Shift pressed so that you end up with a perfect circle.

2. **Click the lowest point on the circle with the Direct Selection tool.**

3. **Click the right control handle of that anchor point and then drag it up using your eye to judge the heart shape.**

4. With the Convert Anchor Point tool, click the left control handle of that point and then drag it up.

5. Click the anchor point at the top of the circle and then drag it down a little using the Direct Selection tool.

6. With the Direct Selection tool, click the left control handle of the topmost point and then drag it up.

7. Click the right control handle with the Convert Anchor Point tool and then drag it up.

8. Adjust the anchor points and control handles until the circle looks like a heart, as shown in Figure 6.27.

FIGURE 6.27

Convert a circle into a heart using the Direct Selection and Convert Anchor Point tools.

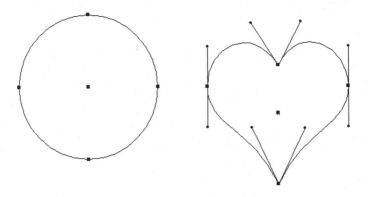

Converting curved corner points

You can change curved corner points into one of the other three types of anchor points by using both the Convert Anchor Point tool and the Direct Selection tool:

■ To convert curved corner points into smooth points, use the Convert Anchor Point tool to click and drag on the anchor point. You can then use the Direct Selection tool to adjust the angle of both control handles at once.

■ To convert curved corner points into straight corner points, use the Convert Anchor Point tool to click once on the anchor point. The control handles disappear.

■ To convert curved corner points into combination corner points, use the Direct Selection tool to drag one control handle into the anchor point.

Using Illustrator's Pathfinder Functions

The most powerful path functions in Illustrator are in the Pathfinder panel. They do tasks that would take hours to do using Illustrator's traditional tools and methods. The only drawback to the Pathfinder panel is that there are so many options that it's pretty hard to figure out which one to use for which job. Figure 6.28 shows the Pathfinder panel.

The Pathfinder options take over most of the mundane tasks of path editing that could otherwise take hours. Everything that the Pathfinder options do can be done manually with other Illustrator tools, but the Pathfinder options do them much more quickly. Common activities, such as joining two paths together correctly and breaking a path into two pieces, are done in a snap.

The Pathfinder options change the way that two or more paths interact. The cute little symbols on the Pathfinder options are supposed to clue you in to what each option can do, but the pictures are small, and most don't accurately depict exactly how each option works.

If you have the Show Tool Tips box selected — it's selected by default, but if it's deselected, choose Edit ➪ Preferences ➪ General (Illustrator ➪ Preferences ➪ General on the Mac) and then click the Show Tool Tips check box — the name of each of the Pathfinder options appears when you hold your cursor over its option symbol. However, these names can be a little confusing. The names were undoubtedly chosen to signify what each of the Pathfinder options can do, but most of them can't be defined easily with just one word.

FIGURE 6.28

The Pathfinder panel allows you to quickly edit paths.

Add to shape area

Subtract from shape area

Intersect shape areas

Exclude overlapping shape areas

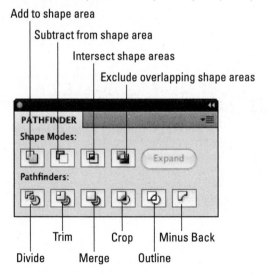

Divide Trim Merge Crop Outline Minus Back

Setting the Pathfinder options

To access the Pathfinder options, choose Pathfinder Options from the popup menu of the Pathfinder panel (accessed via the triangle in the upper right of the panel). This displays the Pathfinder Options dialog box, as shown in Figure 6.29, which allows you to customize the way that the Pathfinders work.

FIGURE 6.29

The Pathfinder Options dialog box allows you to configure the Pathfinders.

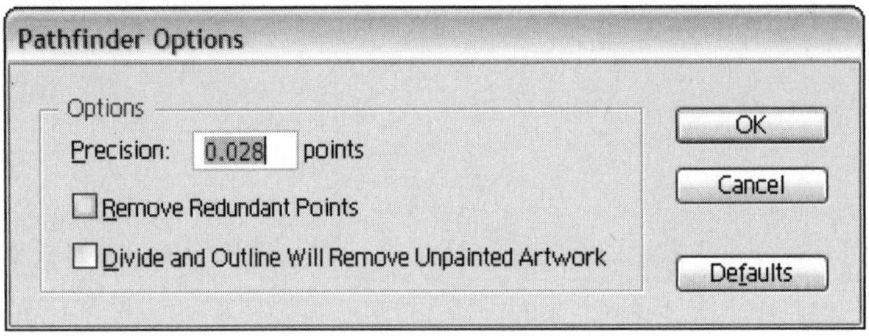

These are options in the Pathfinder Options dialog box:

- **Precision:** The value in the Precision text field tells Illustrator how precisely Pathfinders should operate. The more precisely they operate, the better and more accurate the results are but the longer the processing time is. This speed differential is most apparent when you apply Pathfinders — especially Trap (found in the Pathfinder panel's popup menu) — to very complex objects. The default value is 0.028 points, which seems to be accurate enough for most work.

- **Remove Redundant Points:** This option eliminates overlapping points that are side by side on the same path. I can't think of why you would want overlapping points, so keeping this option selected is a good idea.

- **Divide and Outline Will Remove Unpainted Artwork:** If you choose this option, Illustrator automatically deletes unpainted artwork. This relieves you from having to remove all those paths that Divide always seems to produce that are filled and stroked with None.

Usually, the defaults in the Pathfinder Options dialog box are the best options for most situations, except for Remove Redundant Points, which is off by default. If you change the options, be aware that the Pathfinder Options dialog box resets to the defaults when you quit Illustrator.

Adding to a shape

The Add to shape area mode unites the selected objects if they're overlapping. A new path outlines all the previously selected objects. There are no paths where the original paths intersected. The new object takes the paint style attributes of the topmost object. If any objects are within other objects, those objects are assimilated. If there are holes in the object, the holes become reversed out of a compound path.

You'll find that Add to shape area is one Pathfinder option that you'll use often. Play with combining various paths for a while so you know what to expect, and you develop a sense of when using Add to shape area is a better option than doing the same tasks manually.

Add to shape area combines two or more paths into one path, as described in these steps:

1. **Select the objects to which you want apply the Add to shape area mode.** In the example in Figure 6.30, the artwork is a rectangle with two ellipses resembling a can shape. Pathfinders work only with paths. You have to convert types into outlined paths, and you can't use Encapsulated PostScript (EPS) images.

2. **Choose Add to shape area from the Pathfinder panel.** Any overlapping artwork is united into one path. The color of the united path is always the color of the path that was the topmost selected path before you used Add to shape area.

When you use Add to shape area, paths that don't overlap but are outside of other paths become part of a group. Illustrator draws paths between endpoints of open paths before it unites those paths with other paths. Compound paths remain compound paths.

FIGURE 6.30

Two of the three objects on the left (the rectangle and one ellipse) were selected and then Add to shape area was clicked on the Pathfinder panel to create the cylinder on the right.

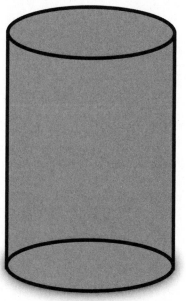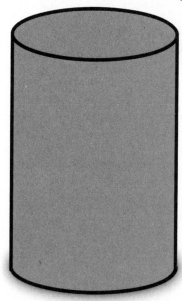

Subtracting from a shape

The Subtract from shape area mode does the opposite of Add to shape area. The topmost objects are subtracted from the bottom object. Figure 6.31 shows an object before (left) and after (right) using Subtract from shape area. The object retains the style (fill and stroke attributes) of the bottommost object.

FIGURE 6.31

The objects on the left before using Subtract from shape area and on the right after using Subtract from shape area

Intersecting and excluding shapes

The Intersect shape areas and Exclude overlapping shape areas modes are opposites. Using Intersect results in the opposite of what you get from using Exclude and vice versa.

The Intersect shape areas mode creates only the intersection of the selected paths. Any part of a selected path that doesn't intersect is deleted. If two paths are intersecting and selected, only the area that's common to both paths remains. If three or more paths are selected, all must intersect in a common area for the function to produce results. If the paths selected don't intersect at all, they all get deleted. If one selected path is contained within all the other selected paths, the result is that contained path. The resulting path has the paint style attributes of the topmost path.

After you select two or more paths and then click the Intersect button on the Pathfinder panel, only the overlapping portions of the paths remain. If you select three paths, the only area that remains is the area where all three selected paths overlap each other.

The Exclude overlapping shape areas mode is pretty much the opposite of Intersect. Choosing Exclude deletes the intersecting areas, grouping together the outside pieces. If you're having trouble making a compound path, use Exclude; any path within another path reverses, creating a compound path automatically.

If you use Exclude, only the areas that don't overlap remain. The color of the intersected or excluded path is always the color of the path that was the topmost selected path before you used Intersect or Exclude.

 **If you press and hold Alt (Option) when clicking any of the Pathfinder shape modes, the objects automatically expand.**

Using the Expand button

The Expand button in the Pathfinder panel is used to ungroup the original objects to which you applied a Pathfinder function. To use this button, first select a set of paths that had a Pathfinder function applied to them and then click the Expand button. The resulting paths form a new group.

Dividing paths

The Divide button in the Pathfinder panel checks to see where the selected paths overlap and then creates new paths at all intersections where the paths crossed, creating new paths if necessary. Fills and strokes are kept. In the process, the Divide command also groups the pieces of the fill together. Divide also keeps the original colors in the new paths; the illustration appears to look the same even if it previously had strokes. To keep the strokes, copy the paths before using Divide and then choose Edit ⇨ Paste In Back, which places a copy of the paths directly behind the original paths.

Simply put, Divide divides overlaying paths into individual closed paths, as described in the following steps and shown in Figure 6.32:

1. **Create the artwork that you want to divide into sections.**

2. **Create a path or paths where you want to divide the object.**

3. **Select all paths, both artwork and dividing paths, and then choose the Divide option in the Pathfinder panel.** The resulting paths are grouped, so either ungroup them or use the Direct Selection tool to move them apart.

FIGURE 6.32

Breaking a heart by using the Pathfinder Divide option

Trimming paths

The Trim button removes sections of paths that are overlapped by other paths. Frontmost paths are the only ones that remain. This Pathfinder is very useful for cleaning up complex overlapping illustrations, although it can take a bit of time to complete. Figure 6.33 shows overlapping outlined type before (top) and after (bottom) applying Trim. You can best see the overlapping objects removed in Outline mode.

CROSS-REF For more on Preview and Outline modes, see Chapter 2.

FIGURE 6.33

The original artwork (left) and after trimming (right). In order to show this clearly, I removed the fill on the left object. However, the Trim option only works with filled objects.

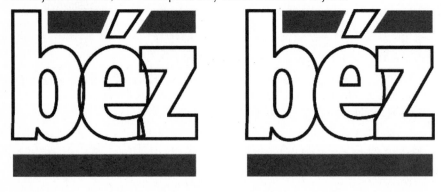

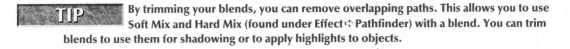

TIP By trimming your blends, you can remove overlapping paths. This allows you to use Soft Mix and Hard Mix (found under Effect ⇨ Pathfinder) with a blend. You can trim blends to use them for shadowing or to apply highlights to objects.

Merging paths

The Merge button combines overlapping paths that have an identical fill applied to them. Even if the fill is different by as little as 1%, Merge creates two separate paths. This Pathfinder is much more efficient than Add to shape area for making areas of the same color into one object.

The following steps describe how to use Merge:

1. **Create the artwork for which you want to use Merge.**

2. **Select the artwork you want to merge.**

3. **Choose the Merge option in the Pathfinder panel.** Illustrator removes all overlapped paths, leaving only the paths that have nothing in front of them. All adjacent areas that contain identical colors are united.

Cropping paths

The Crop button works in much the same way as masks work, except that anything outside the cropped area is deleted, not just masked. Figure 6.34 shows the original objects on the left and the cropped (and grouped) object on the right. The topmost object acts as the mask on the object(s) underneath.

Follow these steps to use the Crop command:

1. **Bring the object that you want to use as a cropper (in this case, the black outline of the meeple) to the front.**

2. **Select all the paths you want to crop as well as the cropper itself.**

3. **Choose the Crop option in the Pathfinder panel.** Illustrator deletes everything outside the cropper. The objects that were cropped are grouped together in the shape of the crop.

Unlike masks, there's no outside shape after a crop is made. The cropper used to crop the image is deleted when Crop is chosen. If there was a stroke on the cropping path, it disappears, as shown in Figure 6.34.

FIGURE 6.34

The artwork (left) before and after (right) cropping

CROSS-REF For more on masks, see Chapter 12.

Outlining paths

The Outline **button** creates small sections of paths wherever paths cross and color the strokes by using the fill of the path they were part of and giving the strokes a weight of 1 point. Outline is useful for spot color trapping because it automatically creates the sections needed that have to be chosen for overprinting, although the colors are often incorrect. (*Trapping* is a process whereby colors are printed slightly beyond the edge of an object so that there won't be white gaps between adjacent colored areas when the document is printed on a commercial printing press.)

Outline creates smaller path pieces than Divide does; but instead of making each section a closed path, each path maintains its individuality, becoming separate from adjoining paths. The result of outlining is several small stroke pieces. Instead of maintaining the fill color of each piece, each piece is filled with None and stroked with a fill color.

Using Minus Back

Each of the Pathfinders works on the principle that one path, either the frontmost or backmost path selected, has all the other overlapping paths subtracted from it.

The Minus Back button subtracts all the selected paths behind the frontmost selected path from the frontmost selected path. With two objects, it's also quite simple. The object in the back is deleted, and the area where the object in back was placed is also deleted. Understanding Minus Back gets a little more confusing when you have more objects, but it does the same thing, all at once, to all the selected paths. If the area to be subtracted is totally within the path it will subtract from, then a compound path results.

When you apply Minus Back, the color of the remaining path is the color of the frontmost path before you applied it.

Trapping

The Trap function in the Pathfinder panel is found under the popup menu. Trap takes some of the drudgery away from trapping. Traps solve alignment problems when color separations are produced. The most common problem that occurs from misalignment is the appearance of white space between different colors.

The only limitation for Trap is that it doesn't work well on extremely complex illustrations because of time and memory constraints. The other concern with Trap is that it leaves your illustrations pseudo-uneditable because it creates extra paths around your original trap and makes it really difficult to edit. It doesn't affect the existing paths, but if you do much editing, you have to delete the trap paths and retrap.

CROSS-REF For more on trapping, see Chapter 18.

TIP Prior to trapping, I create a layer called Traps. Immediately after trapping, I move all the trap objects to the Traps layer. This keeps the traps together in case I need to redo, adjust, or delete them.

Trap automatically creates a trap between abutting shapes of different colors. You set the amount (width) of trap in a dialog box that opens after choosing Trap.

To create a trap using the Trap option in the Pathfinder panel, follow these steps:

1. **Create and select the artwork that you want to trap.** If the artwork is overly complex, you may want to select only a small portion of the artwork before you continue.

2. **Choose the Trap option in the Pathfinder panel.**

3. **In the Trap dialog box, type the width of the trap in the Thickness text field (the default is 0.25 points).** Type the amount that you want the height of the trap to differ from the width, which allows for different paper-stretching errors. For example, typing the maximum, 400%, widens the horizontal thickness of the stroke to four times the amount set in the Thickness text field and leaves the vertical thickness the same.

4. **Type a Tint reduction value that specifies how much the lighter of the two colors should be tinted on that area.**

5. Click the Traps with Process Color check box to convert spot colors to process equivalents only in the resulting trap path that's generated from Trap.

6. Click the Reverse Traps check box to convert any traps along the object that are filled with 100% Black — but no other colors — to be less black and more of the lighter abutting color.

7. Click OK.

All traps generated by Trap result in filled paths, not strokes, and are automatically set to overprint in the Attributes panel.

Summary

Selecting the precise objects that you want to edit in an Illustrator document can be a little confusing until you learn the proper techniques. In this chapter, you learned how to select and edit. Specifically, this chapter covered the following topics:

■ The first step in path editing is choosing the right tool.

■ You can save selections and edit the names.

■ Using Add Anchor Points doesn't change the shape.

■ Using Delete Anchor Points changes the shape.

■ Use the Roughen effect to add anchor points evenly.

■ Use Clean Up to remove any hidden, unwanted, or stray anchor points.

■ Reshape paths with the Reshape tool.

■ Change the object's anchor points with the Convert Anchor Point tool.

■ Use the Pathfinder panel's shape modes to add, subtract, intersect, and exclude shape areas.

■ Use the Pathfinder panel's Pathfinder options to divide, trim, merge, crop, outline, or Minus Back.

■ Under the Pathfinder panel's popup menu is a trap function.

Chapter 7

Understanding Color, Gradients, and Mesh

This chapter covers color, gradients, and mesh. Gradients allow you to apply several different colors in a specific pattern across the surface of your image. You learn how to use and edit the preset gradients as well as how to create your own gradients.

Mesh changes your art into a grid of meshed lines, creating a 3-D color look. You use the Mesh tool to add realistic shadows to your object through a delicate balance of color shifts.

You find color options in the Swatches panel, the Color Guide panel, the Color panel, or the color picker. You can also apply color to fills and strokes.

Working with the Swatches Panel

You can access the Swatches panel by choosing Window ➪ Swatches. When you initially install Illustrator, the Swatches panel is housed with the Color panel, and you can switch between the panels by clicking their respective tabs.

By default, the Swatches panel contains and displays several commonly used colors, patterns, and gradients. You change what displays by clicking the buttons along the bottom of the panel. The following list describes the buttons from left to right:

- **Swatch Libraries menu:** This button displays all the swatch libraries that are installed for quick access. Choosing one brings up another swatch panel with that set of colors in it.

- **Show Swatch Kinds menu:** This button provides access to All swatches, Color swatches, Gradient swatches, Pattern swatches, or Color groups.

- **Swatch Options:** This button provides quick access to the Swatch Options dialog box for the currently selected button.

- **New Color Group:** Clicking this button creates a new color group.

- **New Swatch:** Clicking this button, which looks like a little piece of paper with a bent corner, creates a new swatch. You can also create a new swatch by dragging any single object into the Swatches panel.

- **Delete Swatch:** When you select a swatch and click the trash icon, Illustrator deletes it.

You can also view the swatches in either small or large thumbnail squares or view all the swatches in a list, with names if they have them. You can change the view mode by selecting the appropriate option from the Swatches popup menu. Figure 7.1 shows the default view of the Swatches panel.

FIGURE 7.1

The Swatches panel allows you to select and apply various swatch patterns.

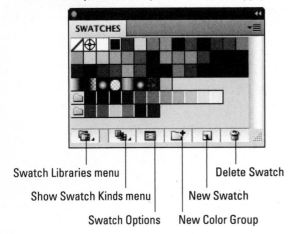

Swatch Libraries menu

Show Swatch Kinds menu

Swatch Options

Delete Swatch

New Swatch

New Color Group

Using the color swatches

You can create a new swatch based on the current paint style, which appears in the Paint Style section of the Tools panel, by clicking the New Swatch button along the bottom of the Swatches panel. If you press Alt (Option) when creating a new swatch, the New Swatch dialog box, as shown in Figure 7.2, opens. This dialog box allows you to initially name the swatch and set its color mode to either process color (CMYK) or spot color. *Process colors* are printed using a combination of the four standard printing inks — cyan, magenta, yellow, and black. *Spot colors* are printed using a special premixed ink that's exactly the color you want to print.

Under the Color Mode in the New Swatch dialog box, you can set Grayscale, RGB, HSB, CMYK, Lab, or Web Safe RGB. Most default process color swatches are set up with RGB. You can also create a new swatch by choosing New Swatch from the Swatches panel's popup menu, which you access by clicking the triangle on the upper-right corner of the panel.

FIGURE 7.2

The New Swatch dialog box lets you name the new swatch.

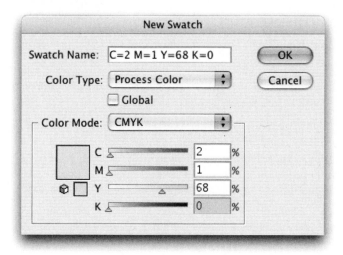

Double-clicking a swatch displays the Swatch Options for that swatch. The Swatch Options dialog box is exactly like the New Swatch dialog box, except that it includes a Preview check box. The Swatch Options dialog box has the following options:

- **Swatch Name:** Lets you change the name of the swatch, which you can view only in List view mode

- **Color Type:** Allows you to set the color type of the swatch to either process or spot

- **Global:** Specifies that the changes should be applied throughout the document

- **Color Mode:** Lets you change the mode to Grayscale, RGB, HSB, CMYK, Lab, or Web Safe RGB

CROSS-REF For more on Web-safe colors, see Chapter 19.

In addition, you can select one or more swatches to edit, duplicate, or remove from the Swatches panel. Click a swatch to select it; a frame appears on the selected swatch.

You can select more than one swatch by pressing Ctrl (⌘) and clicking additional swatches. If you press Shift and click additional swatches, a contiguous (connected) set of swatches is selected from where you initially clicked to where you Shift+clicked. You can deselect individual swatches by pressing Ctrl (⌘) and then clicking selected swatches. You deselect all the swatches by clicking an empty area of the Swatches panel. By selecting multiple swatches, you can duplicate and delete several swatches at once.

If you want to sort the swatches manually, you can do so by selecting any number of swatches and then dragging them to a new location within the Swatches panel.

Using the Swatches popup menu

The Swatches popup menu, shown in Figure 7.3, also has other functions, some of which were already mentioned:

- **New Swatch:** This option works the same as the New Swatch button at the bottom of the Swatches panel. A new swatch is created from whatever you select.

- **New Color Group:** This option creates a new color group at the bottom of the swatches panel (color groups are indicated by a folder on the left side of them).

- **Duplicate Swatch:** This option duplicates the selected swatches. You can also drag a selected swatch to the New Swatch button (the little piece of paper) to duplicate the swatch. If you press Alt (Option) while duplicating a swatch, the New Swatch dialog box opens.

- **Merge Swatches:** This option merges two or more selected swatches by using the first selected swatch's name and color. You must have two or more swatches selected to enable this option. It produces a new swatch that's a mixture of the selected swatches.

- **Delete Swatch:** To delete a swatch, select this option. You can also select the swatch and then click the trash icon. A warning dialog box appears asking whether you want to delete the swatch selection. Click Yes to delete the swatch.

- **Ungroup Color Group:** This option ungroups the selected color group.

- **Select All Unused:** This option selects the swatches in the Swatches panel that you aren't using in the current document. You can then delete those swatches if desired.

- **Add Used Colors:** This option adds a swatch for each color in your document. You don't need to select artwork in order for this to work; selecting this option simply adds a number of swatches equal to the different colors in your document.

TIP Use Add Used Colors in conjunction with New Color Group to quickly create a set of colors that are used in your document. For this to work, you need to select the swatches that were just created prior to choosing the New Color Group option.

- **Sort by Name:** This option organizes the swatches (regardless of which viewing mode the swatch panel is in) alphabetically.

- **Sort by Kind:** This option sorts the swatches to appear, starting with color, then gradients, and then patterns.

- **Show Find Field:** This option opens a Find field so you can type a specific swatch name to search for in the Swatches panel.

■ **The View options:** You can also view the swatches in small, medium, or large thumbnail squares or view all the swatches in a small or large list, with names if they have them. These different modes are shown in Figure 7.4.

■ **Swatch Options:** Selecting this option displays the Swatch Options for the selected swatch. This dialog box was discussed earlier in this chapter.

■ **Spot Colors:** This option displays the Spot Color Options dialog box so that you can choose whether to use Lab values or CMYK values to describe any spot colors.

■ **Open Swatch Library:** This option displays a submenu so that you can choose to open a different swatch library.

■ **Save Swatch Library as ASE:** Selecting this option presents the Save Panel as the Swatch Library dialog box, which allows you to save your custom swatches for future use.

■ **Save Swatch Library as AI:** Selecting this option also displays the Save Panel as the Swatch Library dialog box, except with the file type set to Swatch Exchange Files. Use this option if you're working with a group of people who all need to be using the same color swatches.

FIGURE 7.3

The Swatches popup menu provides additional options.

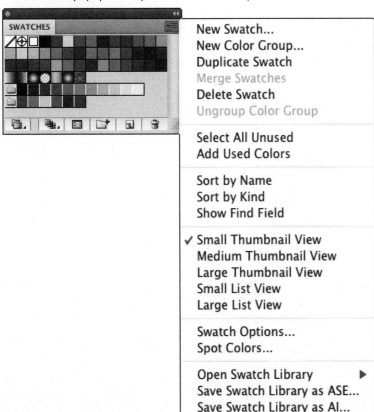

FIGURE 7.4

The five ways you can view the Swatches panel: small, medium, or large thumbnails (top row) or small or large lists

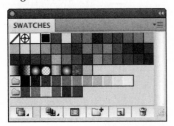
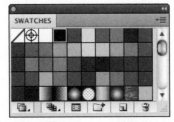
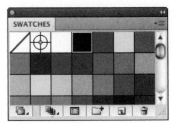
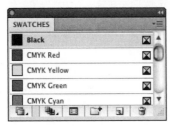

Using other swatch libraries

In addition to the standard Swatch Library panel, many other default Swatch Library panels are accessible from the Swatch Libraries submenu in the Window menu or from the Open Swatch Library submenu in the Swatches panel's popup menu, as shown in Figure 7.5. You can also create a new Swatch Library panel from any Illustrator document.

To view one of the other default Swatches panels, choose it from the Swatch Libraries submenu. You can't edit these swatch libraries; you can only add swatches from these libraries to your main Swatches panel. To add a swatch (or several selected swatches) to your main Swatches panel, follow these steps:

1. **Select the swatches you want to add.**
2. **Choose Add To Swatches from the library's popup menu.** You click the triangle on the upper-right corner of the panel to access this popup menu.
3. **Click and drag the swatches to the main Swatches panel or double-click the swatch.** Illustrator saves the main Swatches panel with your document. You can customize a panel for a specific document or edit the Adobe Illustrator Startup document's Swatches panel to use a certain set of colors in each new document you create.

Otherwise, these swatch libraries work the same way as your main Swatches panel; you can choose colors for fill and stroke, sort the swatches by Kind or Name, and view the swatches by List, Small Thumbnail View, or Large Thumbnail View. Figure 7.6 shows three swatch libraries.

FIGURE 7.5

The Open Swatch Library submenu allows you to choose different swatch libraries.

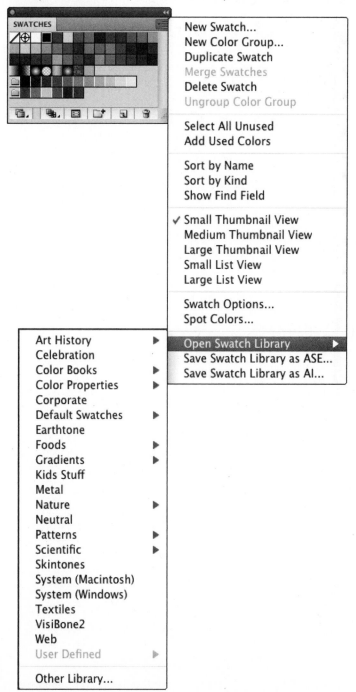

227

FIGURE 7.6

Three swatch libraries: Fruits and Vegetables, Pastels, and Water

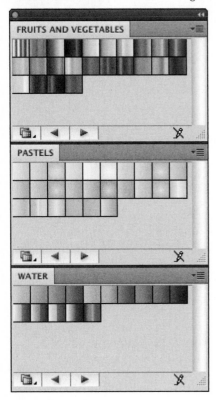

Using color space options in the Color panel

The Color panel provides basic color selection via the Color Ramp along the bottom of the panel and more precise control via sliders and percentage entries in Grayscale, RGB, HSB, CMYK, and Web Safe RGB. Most users of Illustrator use either RGB or CMYK color spaces. Heavy Web designers also use HSB and Web Safe RGB. If you're sure that you want to work only in black and white, choose Grayscale. Use the Color panel to add color to any object's stroke or fill. You can create any color to be used in an illustration by defining it in the Color panel, as shown in Figure 7.7. Access the Color panel by choosing Window ⇨ Color.

The Color panel has a popup menu (and arrowheads next to the panel's name) that allows you to toggle the display of the options and to choose from the available color spaces. The options are really the color-mixing sliders; I've never found a reason to hide them. In fact, the sliders take up such a small amount of space that after they're in view, you'll probably never hide them either.

FIGURE 7.7

The Color panel allows you to define colors precisely.

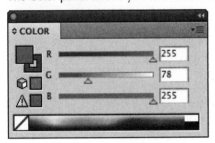

The color space options let you switch among the following:

- **Grayscale:** This option shows white to black with all shades of gray in between (see Figure 7.8).

FIGURE 7.8

The Color panel displaying the Grayscale color space

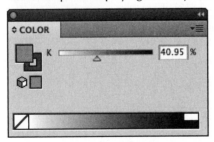

- **RGB:** The red, green, and blue color space is used by computer monitors, and it's perfect for multimedia and Web-page graphics. Refer to Figure 7.7 to see the RGB color space panel. You can type RGB values as percentages or as values from 0 to 255. Double-click to the right of the text fields to change the RGB measurement system from percentages to the numeric 0 to 255 system and back.

- **HSB:** Hue, Saturation, and Brightness comprise this RGB-derived color space, which is best for adjusting RGB colors in brightness and saturation. Figure 7.9 shows the HSB color space panel.

- **CMYK:** Cyan, magenta, yellow, and black are considered typical printing process colors, although Illustrator calls any colors process that aren't spot. Figure 7.10 shows the CMYK color space panel.

- **Web Safe RGB:** These colors are the 216 colors recognized by all graphic Web browsers on any platform (they use hexadecimal numbering). Web-safe colors are covered in more detail in Chapter 19. Figure 7.11 shows the Web Safe RGB color space panel.

FIGURE 7.9

The Color panel displaying the HSB color space

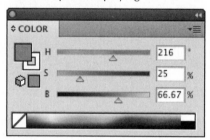

FIGURE 7.10

The Color panel displaying the CMYK color space

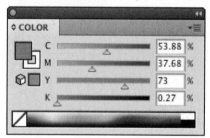

FIGURE 7.11

The Color panel displaying the Web Safe RGB color space

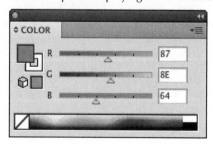

As you drag a specific color's slider, the other sliders also change in color. This gives you sort of a preview for what would happen if you were to drag along the sliders. The icon to the left of the sliders shows the current color and whether you're adjusting the fill (solid box) or stroke (box with a hole). Instead of dragging, you can also just simply click a different location along the slider to change its value.

> **TIP** **Press Shift to adjust RGB and CMYK sliders proportionately. This is a great way to tint process colors. Shift+drag the slider with the largest value (CMYK) or the smallest value (RGB) for the most control. When you release the mouse button, Illustrator makes the new color a tint of the original.**

You can also change the slider values by typing values for each of the individual color channels (for example, Cyan is a color channel in CMYK). Press Tab to highlight the next text field or press Shift+Tab to highlight the previous text field.

> **TIP** **Most of text fields in Illustrator's panels are mathematically adept. You can add, subtract, multiply, and divide in them. This is useful when typing color percentages in the text fields of the Color panel. To add 5% to the current value, type +5 after the current value. To subtract 5%, type -5 after the current value. To divide the current value by 2, type /2 after the current value. To multiply the current value by 2, type *2 after the current value.**

Using the Color Ramp

The Color Ramp is the bar along the bottom of the Color panel. It looks like a rainbow of colors. The Color Ramp allows you to quickly pick a color from the current color space. Resting your cursor above the Color Ramp area changes the cursor into an eyedropper.

When you change to a different color space, the Color Ramp along the bottom of the panel also changes to show the rainbow of colors in that particular color space.

> **TIP** **Shift+click the Color Ramp to cycle through the color spaces; this is much faster than choosing a color space from the popup menu.**

Click any portion of the Color Ramp to select that color. Illustrator provides large rectangles of black and white to make choosing black or white easier. The Grayscale and Spot Color Ramps have large areas for both 0% and 100% to make selecting those percentages easier. You can also drag over the Color Ramp, watching the large square in the top of the Color panel (if Options are showing) to see the color you're dragging over. If Options aren't shown, look at the active Fill/Stroke icons in the Tools panel to see the color you're currently positioned over. (This works only when the mouse button is pressed as you pass across the Color Ramp.)

> **TIP** **You can press X while dragging around the Color Ramp to switch between the fill and stroke focus. This way, you can quickly select colors for both fill and stroke with one mouse click. If the fill is in focus, click and drag through the Color Ramp to the appropriate color. Then, with the mouse button still pressed, press X; you'll now be picking a color for the stroke. Want to change the fill again? Just press X while holding down the mouse button.**

Press Alt (Option) and then click anywhere on a Color Ramp to affect the opposite attribute. For example, if stroke is in focus on the Tools panel, pressing Alt (Option) and clicking on a Color Ramp changes the fill color, not the stroke. Be aware, however, that Alt (Option)+clicking on a swatch in the Swatches panel doesn't affect the opposite attribute; this works only on a Color Ramp (and the color box in the Color panel).

Working with gamut

If you choose certain colors, a little icon appears in the center left of the Color panel, as shown in Figure 7.12. This icon indicates that the current color is out of gamut with the color space. Therefore, the particular color you chose isn't within the range of colors that can be displayed or printed for the selected color space. This issue is generally important only if you plan to print the document using CMYK process colors.

If you plan to use the image on-screen, such as in Web or multimedia publishing, whether the color is in gamut doesn't really matter.

FIGURE 7.12

The In Gamut indicator appears when the current color can't be accurately displayed or printed.

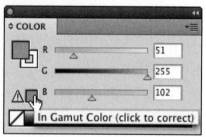

The best way to reset the current color is to click the In Gamut icon. The RGB or HSB values change so that the resulting color is well within CMYK color space. Another way to change the current color to CMYK color space is to choose CMYK from the Color panel's popup menu.

If you want to change the color space of several objects — or perhaps your entire document — to CMYK, select the objects that you want to change and then choose Effect ➪ Colors ➪ Convert to CMYK. To change the whole document to a different color space, choose File ➪ Document Color Mode ➪ CMYK Color or RGB Color.

Spot colors

Spot colors are colors in Illustrator that aren't separated into process colors (cyan, magenta, yellow, and black) when printed. Instead, they're printed on a different separation. A commercial printer uses special ink (commonly Pantone) for this spot color. Spot colors are indicated in the Swatches panel in

Small Thumbnail and Large Thumbnail views by a white triangle containing a black dot in the lower right of the spot color swatch. The List view mode shows a square with a circle inside of it (a spot) on the right edge of the swatch listing. In List view mode, both the color space (grayscale, RGB, or CMYK) and Process/Spot status are indicated to the right of the color chip and name.

You can use as many spot colors in an illustration as you want, although it isn't usually practical or desirable to have more than four in one document. (Because CMYK printing can duplicate most colors, process colors are often a better choice than four spot colors.) Illustrator's default Swatch libraries, accessible by choosing Window ⇨ Swatch Libraries, mostly contain spot colors that you can choose among or you can create your own. Follow these steps to create your own spot color:

1. **Create a new swatch with the appearance you want.** Use the color sliders to do this.

2. **Double-click the newly created swatch.** This opens the Swatch Options dialog box.

3. **Change the Swatch type from Process to Spot.** Now, when you use that swatch as a fill or stroke, Illustrator considers it a spot color when it comes time to print.

TIP You can convert any spot color to a standard CMYK color (the color, not the swatch) by selecting the spot color and then changing the color space in the Color panel to CMYK. You can even change the color space to grayscale, RGB, or HSB in this way. This works only on the selected paths; the swatch is not affected.

Applying colors with the Color panel

Now you know how the panels work, but how do you change the color of paths to what's in the panels? The easiest thing to do is to select the path you want to change the fill or stroke (or both) of, change the focus (if necessary) of the Fill/Stroke icons, and select a color from either the Color or Swatches panel. Press X to change the color for the other (fill or stroke).

The key here is selecting. If you have selected paths, any changes you make affect those selected paths.

When you create a new path, Illustrator uses the fill and stroke that are currently displayed in the Paint Style section of the Tools panel.

To apply colors to text, you can either select an entire text area with a Selection tool or select individual characters with a Type tool.

TIP Selecting Type with a Selection tool can cause type paths, type areas, and type itself to be filled and stroked. You can use the Group Selection tool to deselect the associated paths. Or better yet, just use the Type tool to drag across the characters you want to select.

Transferring color from one object to another

The Eyedropper and Paint Bucket tools are lifesavers for those who constantly use self-stick notes to jot down the percentages of CMYK (cyan, magenta, yellow, and black) in one path so that those same amounts can be applied to another path. A good reason to use the Paint Bucket and Eyedropper tools is to ensure that your colors are consistent throughout an illustration. So, for example, if you used a custom color somewhere that you want to use again somewhere else, you don't try to duplicate it with a CMYK mix that may not be an exact match. With a couple of clicks or keystrokes, you can easily transfer the color properties of one object to another. The tools work with paths, objects, type, and placed images.

The Eyedropper and Paint Bucket tools work similarly to the other tools in Illustrator in that their properties stay the same until you change them — in this case, by clicking a new path or object with a different color. The Eyedropper tool sucks up color from where you click. Use this to see the breakdown of a color in the area you clicked. The Paint Bucket tool fills in an area with the active color in the Color Swatch. Just click the Paint Bucket tool on the shape you want to fill with color. To give you more control over what the tools can pick up and apply, Illustrator gives you an exhaustive list of properties to select in the Eyedropper Options dialog box. Double-clicking the Eyedropper tool displays this dialog box, as shown in Figure 7.13, where you can select or deselect options depending on what attributes you want to apply. So, for example, you can have the Eyedropper tool pick up the color and stroke weight of a path without transferring the path's transparency properties.

CROSS-REF For more on paths, objects, and type, see Chapters 4, 5, and 9, respectively. Most of the properties listed in the Eyedropper Options dialog box are also discussed in these chapters. For more on placed images, see Chapter 3.

At the bottom of the Eyedropper Options dialog box is the Raster Sample Size menu. From this menu, you can choose whether you suck up a Point Sample (samples the color from the point where you click), 3×3 Average (averages the color in an area of 3 pixels by 3 pixels), or 5×5 Average (averages the color in an area of 5 pixels by 5 pixels).

The Eyedropper tool

The Eyedropper tool samples paint style information from a path and stores it in the Fill and Stroke boxes on the Tools panel without selecting that path. The information stays there until you change the information in the color panel, select another path with different paint style information, or click any other path or placed image with a different paint style.

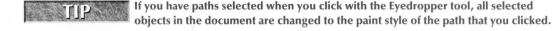 **TIP** If you have paths selected when you click with the Eyedropper tool, all selected objects in the document are changed to the paint style of the path that you clicked.

The Live Paint Bucket tool

You use the Live Paint Bucket tool to apply the current paint style to both paths and Live Trace images. You can also apply any attribute that's active in the Appearance panel. Using the Live Paint Bucket tool is a quick and painless way to apply a set style or group of attributes you like to other objects.

CROSS-REF For more on the Live Paint Bucket tool, see Chapter 14. For more on Live Trace, see Chapter 13.

FIGURE 7.13

The Eyedropper Options dialog box allows you to fine-tune the operation of the Eyedropper tool.

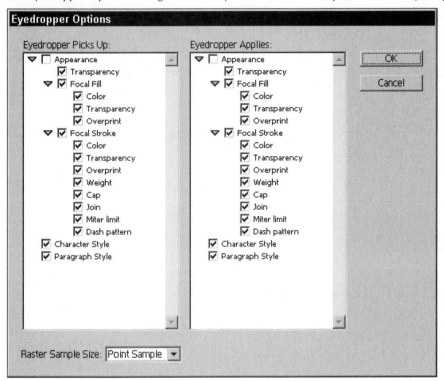

Using Transparency

Transparency has changed the face of Illustrator. Being able to apply transparent live effects to any object in Illustrator is just plain amazing. It opens up many doors and lets in a kaleidoscope of colors to see through. Transparency is like looking through stained glass, a piece of plastic, anything you can see through. You can adjust the blending modes for a variety of effects. Blending modes are the interaction of the colors of an object with the objects underneath that object. Imagine that you're playing with Plexiglas blocks in three dimensions. You can see what is behind or in front of those blocks. You can even go as far as thinking that you're Superman looking through objects with X-ray vision. You can create stained-glass effects, mix color effects, and so much more. You can apply transparency to objects, groups of objects, or a whole layer.

In Illustrator, you apply transparency in the Transparency panel (shown in Figure 7.14). If the Transparency panel isn't showing when you start up Illustrator, choose Window➪ Transparency. To see the options available in the Transparency panel, click the upper-right triangle and then choose Show Options. In the preview pane on the left side of the panel, you can see a thumbnail view of the current Opacity setting applied to the selected object.

FIGURE 7.14

The Transparency panel allows you to create transparent objects.

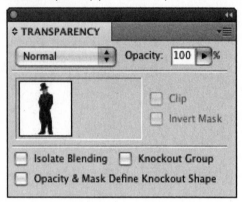

These options, which are discussed in more detail later in this chapter, are available in the Transparency panel:

- **Mode:** Use this option to choose the method used in the blend.
- **Opacity:** Adjust this slider to determine how much you can see through that object.
- **Clip:** This option gives the masks a black background.
- **Invert Mask:** This option reverses luminosity and opacity values of the masked objects.
- **Isolate Blending:** Select this option to affect only the group or layer opacity.
- **Knockout Group:** Selecting this option means that the opacity doesn't affect the group or layer, just the object.
- **Opacity & Mask Define Knockout Shape:** Selecting this option means you can use a mask to delineate where Illustrator applies the transparency settings.

Defining transparency between objects, groups, and layers

You can apply transparency to an object, group of objects, sublayer, or the entire layer. You can also apply transparency to symbols, patterns, type, 3-D objects, graphic styles, strokes, and brush-strokes. To define an object's transparency, select the object first and then drag the Opacity slider in the Transparency panel to the desired opacity. Figure 7.15 shows an example of changing the top object's opacity.

FIGURE 7.15

The R on top of the image was changed to 60% so you can see the picture through it.

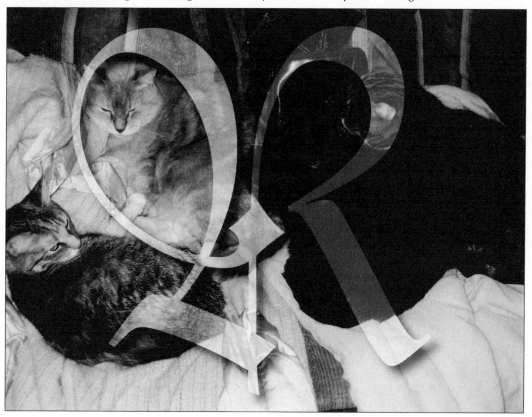

Working with opacity

You adjust the transparency in the Transparency panel by clicking and dragging the Opacity slider. You access the slider by clicking the arrow on the side of the Opacity box. As mentioned previously, opacity is how see-through the object is. Applying no opacity makes an object totally transparent. Applying any amount of opacity makes the object partially transparent. An opacity value of 100% makes the object totally opaque, which mean you can't see through it at all. If you check the Appearance panel, it shows you the amount of opacity applied to that particular object.

To apply opacity to a group of objects or to a whole layer, start with the Layers panel and follow these steps:

1. **In the Layers panel, click the layer you want to adjust.**

2. **In the Transparency panel, adjust the Opacity slider or type the Opacity value.**

Using blending modes

Within the Transparency panel, you find 16 blending modes similar to Photoshop's blending modes. Each mode creates a different effect when applied to the same object. Blending modes can totally change the look of the opacity applied to an object. Using blending modes lets you choose a variety of ways the colors of the objects blend when on top of another object. You create blending modes by combining a base color (the bottom object), the blend color (of the object on top), and the resulting color from the overlapping.

Illustrator supplies a variety of blending modes in the Transparency panel. Figure 7.16 shows the list of blending modes found in the Transparency panel's popup menu:

- **Normal:** Use this for no interaction with the base color, only the blend color result.
- **Darken:** This mode uses the darker color (base or blend) as the resulting color.
- **Multiply:** This mode multiplies the base color by the blend color, creating a darker color.
- **Color Burn:** Use this to darken the base color.
- **Lighten:** This mode uses the lighter color (base or blend) as the resulting color.
- **Screen:** This multiplies the opposite color of the blend and base colors, creating a lighter color.
- **Color Dodge:** Use this to lighten and brighten the base color.
- **Overlay:** This mode either multiplies or screens, depending on the base color. The base color is mixed with the blend color, resulting in the lightness or darkness of the original color. With patterns or graphic styles, the highlights and shadows of the base color are kept and the blend color is mixed in to create lightness or darkness of the beginning color.
- **Soft Light:** This mode is like shining a softened light on the object. Blends less than 50% gray get lightened, and blends greater than 50% get darkened. If the blend is 50%, it's left alone.
- **Hard Light:** This mode is similar to soft light but with a harsh light shining on the object. If the blend color is lighter than 50% gray, the object becomes lightened. If the blend color is darker than 50% gray, the object becomes darkened.
- **Difference:** This mode chooses the brighter color (either base or blend) and subtracts it from the other color.
- **Exclusion:** This mode is similar to the Difference mode but with a lower contrast.
- **Hue:** This creates a result having the base color's saturation and the blend color's hue.
- **Saturation:** This creates a result having the base color's hue and the blend color's saturation.
- **Color:** This creates a result having the base color's luminance and the blend color's hue and saturation.
- **Luminosity:** This mode is the opposite of the Color mode. The result is the base color's hue and saturation and the blend color's luminance.

FIGURE 7.16

In the Transparency panel's popup menu, you see all the blending modes.

Normal
Darken
Multiply
Color Burn
Lighten
Screen
Color Dodge
Overlay
Soft Light
Hard Light
Difference
Exclusion
Hue
Saturation
Color
Luminosity

Isolating blending

Isolating blending is a necessary evil when too many objects are involved in an illustration that has transparency. When patterns are involved, you may lose the clarity of your artwork unless you limit how far the blending goes with the Opacity settings. In the Transparency panel, there's a check box for Isolate Blending. Use this to pick and choose how far you want the opacity to affect the underlying objects.

Follow these steps to apply a blending mode to an object:

1. **Click the dropdown list (popup menu) in the Transparency panel and then select a choice to apply that blending mode to the selected object.**

2. **Group together the objects that you want in the blend.** For more on grouping objects, see Chapter 7.

3. **In the Layers panel, click the radio button to the right of the layer that contains the selected group of objects to target the group of objects you want to isolate.**

4. **Click the Isolate Blending check box in the Transparency panel.**

Knocking out a group

Along with Isolate Blending is the Knockout Group check box in the Transparency panel. Knockout Group does the opposite of Isolate Blending. That is, you use the Knockout Group option to block the view of objects under the group.

Using opacity, clipping, and invert masks

A clipping mask crops the objects behind the mask to the edges of the mask. An opacity mask is similar to a clipping mask. Instead of clipping away other objects, it clips the objects to the defined area (mask) to show transparency. The opacity mask in Illustrator is like the layer mask concept in Photoshop. Use the opacity mask to clip objects to the top shape and apply the opacity mask's luminosity to the underlying objects. Where the top mask is white, you can see the artwork underneath, and where the mask is black, it's opaque. Figure 7.17 shows a group of rectangles on a grid background. The rectangles were added, and an opacity mask consisting of a gradient was applied to the objects, as shown in Figure 7.18. Select Make Opacity Mask from the Transparency panel's popup menu to apply an opacity mask.

FIGURE 7.17

The artwork before (left) and after (right) an opacity mask was applied to the set of rectangles

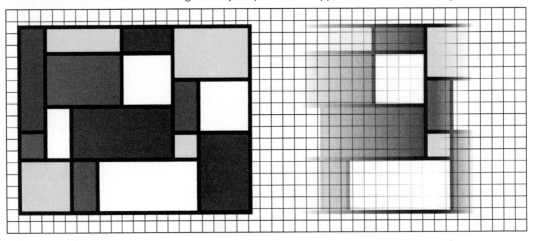

After applying an opacity mask, the original shape disappears. If you don't believe me, check Outline mode. To get the shape back, simply release the opacity mask. You can release the opacity mask under the Transparency panel's popup menu. Choose Release opacity masks, and the objects return to their original state.

CROSS-REF For more on the viewing modes, see Chapter 2.

Other choices under the Transparency menu are to unlink or relink an opacity mask. An opacity mask is automatically linked to the object that it's masking. To unlink the opacity mask, click the link symbol between the opacity mask and the object or choose Unlink Opacity Mask in the Transparency panel's popup menu. When you unlink the object from the mask, you can move the object(s) around under the opacity mask, and the mask stays put. To relink the two back together, click the link between the two thumbnails or choose Link Opacity Mask from the Transparency panel's popup menu.

FIGURE 7.18

The Transparency panel shows the opacity mask used in Figure 7.17.

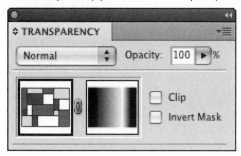

You can disable an opacity mask, and Illustrator removes the mask from its masking task but doesn't delete the objects you used to make the mask from the file. To get the mask back, choose Enable Opacity Mask from the Transparency panel's popup menu.

You can edit opacity masks if you click the thumbnail of the mask in the Transparency panel. Use Illustrator's editing tools to change the mask shape. Other options in the Transparency panel for the opacity mask are to make the opacity mask act as a clipping mask with the Clip option. Select this to have the mask clip the area around the selected mask (like the clipping mask function). You can also use the Invert Mask option. Selecting this option inverts the dark and light, which reverses the original opacity.

 **When using the Make Opacity Mask function, all the objects in the mask are automatically grouped together.**

Viewing the transparency grid

Now that you're getting into this whole transparency thing, you may find it hard to see which objects have transparency applied to them. To see these transparent objects, you can enable the transparency grid. This grid shows up as a gray-and-white checkered pattern positioned behind all other objects.

To view the transparency grid, choose View ⇨ Show Transparency Grid or press Ctrl+Shift+D (⌘+Shift+D). If you want to change the look of the transparency grid, choose File ⇨ Document Setup; the transparency section is in the center of the dialog box, as shown in Figure 7.19. You can also access the Document Setup by pressing Alt+Ctrl+P (⌘+Option+P).

Using these options, you can set the Grid Size and change the Grid Colors. A preview of the grid is also shown next to the color selection boxes. The Simulate Colored Paper option shows you what your objects look like when printed on colored paper. At the bottom of the Document Setup dialog box are options for setting the Transparency Flattener Settings.

Figure 7.20 shows an example of several objects as they appear above the transparency grid. Objects that are opaque completely block the view of the transparency grid, while those that are partially transparent allow the grid to show through.

FIGURE 7.19

In the Document Setup dialog box, you can change the transparency grid.

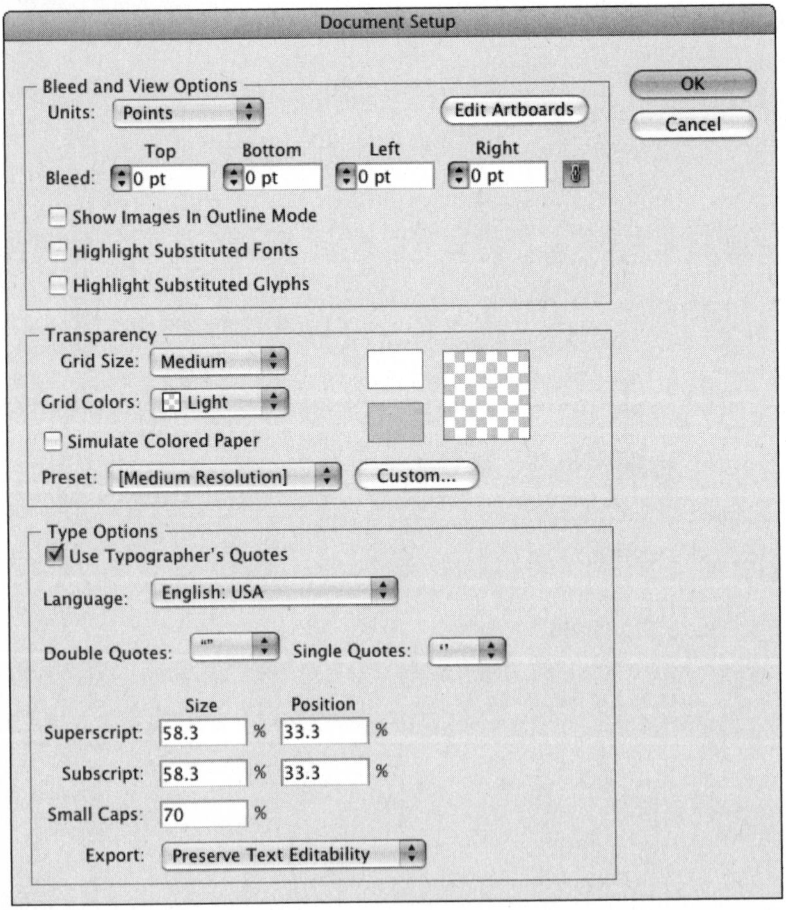

FIGURE 7.20

Opaque objects (the figure) block the transparency grid, while transparent ones (the R and its drop shadow) allow it to be seen.

Printing and flattening

Flattening is a process that removes transparency from objects and substitutes objects that have a similar appearance — only without any transparency. Flattening happens when transparency is not supported by other applications. Flattening actually creates more pieces of the objects. Flattening also changes your transparency. You lose transparency, and instead, a color is applied that reflects the opacity color. If you have two objects overlapping and you flatten the image, a third object is created where they overlap.

For more precise control over flattening, you can use the options that are available in the Flatten Transparency dialog box, as shown in Figure 7.21. To use this option, select the object(s) you want to flatten and then choose Object ⇨ Flatten Transparency. In the Flatten Transparency dialog box, choose your settings and then click OK. You also have the option to preview the settings by clicking the Preview check box.

FIGURE 7.21

The Flatten Transparency dialog box provides more precise control over flattening.

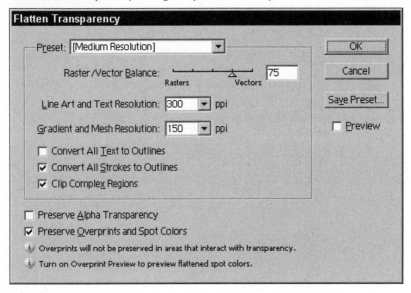

You can set these options in the Flatten Transparency dialog box:

- **Preset:** Choose from preset transparency flattening options of high, medium, or low resolution. Typically, you want to choose higher resolution for final printouts and lower resolution for draft output.

- **Raster/Vector Balance:** This option lets you choose the amount of rasterization. Set the balance high to retain as much vector information as possible. Set the balance lower so that more objects are rasterized into pixels.

- **Line Art and Text Resolution:** Set the resolution of the vector objects when they're rasterized.

- **Gradient and Mesh Resolution:** Set the resolution of the gradients and mesh objects when they're rasterized.

- **Convert All Text to Outlines:** This option changes all text to outlined paths.

- **Convert All Strokes to Outlines:** This option changes all the strokes to outlined paths.

- **Clip Complex Regions:** This option reduces the patching that happens to an object that's partially rasterized and partially vectored. This option can also result in very complex paths, making the image hard to print.

- **Preserve Alpha Transparency:** This option saves the opacity of flattened objects.

- **Preserve Overprints and Spot Colors:** This option saves the overprinting and spot color objects.

Transparency and type

Now that you have the basics, let's delve into using transparency on objects. You can create a plethora of different effects using transparency. The following sections cover just a few of the amazing things you can do with transparency.

Transparency is not limited to objects. It's also fantastic to use on type. Take some text and then give it a three-dimensional feel by choosing Effect ⇨ 3D ⇨ Extrude & Bevel (you must use the Selection tool to select the text before you can apply the effect). Then, with color, highlights, and a background added, you can use the Transparency panel to really make the text sing. Figure 7.22 shows an illustration done with text and transparency.

Separating transparent objects

Transparency is useful with many different types of objects. Use it in a brushstroke, creating fills, styles, multiple fills, and more. If you choose to flatten the transparency, Illustrator actually cuts it into sections. To flatten transparent objects, first select them and then choose Object ⇨ Flatten Transparency. The Flatten Transparency dialog box opens.

FIGURE 7.22

Text and transparency create some fantastic effects.

3-D, symbols, and transparency

Transparency is not limited to basic objects. You can use transparent effects on symbols, effects, patterns, brushstrokes, and 3-D objects. Figure 7.23 shows three-dimensional gears with different opacity settings. Anything you can do in Illustrator can have transparency applied. The Symbol tool has a Symbol Screener tool, which applies transparency in a brush-like fashion. You can also apply opacity to the whole group of sprayed symbols using the Transparency panel.

CROSS-REF For more on the Symbol Screener tool, see Chapter 5.

FIGURE 7.23

Three-dimensional gears with different transparency effects applied

Using type with brushstrokes and transparency can also result in some eye-catching effects. To create embossed type, follow these steps:

1. **Enter the type you want.** Don't worry about the typeface; just pick something plain.

2. **Choose the Selection tool in the Tools panel.** This ensures that you're working with the text as an object, not as individual characters.

3. **Give the type a White fill color and a different stroke color (something medium that's not too dark or light).** For more on stroke and fill colors, see Chapter 10.

4. **In the Appearance panel, choose Add New Stroke from the Appearance panel's popup menu.** A new stroke line item appears in the Appearance panel.

5. In the Appearance panel, click on the new stroke item, change the color of it to something lighter than the original stroke, and then drag it down below the original stroke.

6. Choose Effect ➪ Distort and Transform ➪ Transform and then move the stroke -1 point horizontally and +1 point vertically.

7. With the stroke you just modified selected, click the Duplicate Stroke button at the bottom of the Appearance panel and then drag the new stroke down below both of the other strokes.

8. Change the color of the new stroke to something a little darker than the original stroke.

9. Double-click the Transform item in the new stroke (in the Appearance panel) and then change the move values to +1 horizontal and -1 vertical.

This creates an embossed stroke effect. Add a background, and the text lets the background shine through. Figure 7.24 shows an example of this embossed effect.

FIGURE 7.24

This type was embossed using the previous steps.

Creating Gradients

The Gradient feature has no rivals. It's by far the most powerful gradient-creating mechanism available anywhere. Gradients in Adobe Illustrator can have 32 different colors from end to end in a linear gradient and from center to outside in a radial gradient. Gradients can consist of custom colors, process colors, or just plain black and white. Each gradient stop can have any level of opacity applied to it. The midpoint of two adjacent colors can be adjusted smoothly and easily toward either color. You can make the Gradient panel available at all times because it's a floating panel. You can access it or view it by choosing Window ➪ Gradient or by pressing Ctrl+F9 (⌘+F9).

 You can apply gradients only to the fills of paths, not to strokes or text objects. You can't use gradients in patterns either.

Using preset gradients

To choose a preset gradient, select a path and then ensure that the Fill box is active in the Tools panel. In the Swatches panel, click the gradient swatch icon at the bottom of the panel. The four default gradient presets appear alone in the swatches. When you click a gradient swatch, Illustrator applies the gradient to the selected path.

Using the Gradient panel

The Gradient panel, if nothing else, is really neat-looking, with all sorts of nifty little controls at your disposal for creating and modifying gradients; it's shown in Figure 7.25.

FIGURE 7.25

The Gradient panel allows you to create your own gradients.

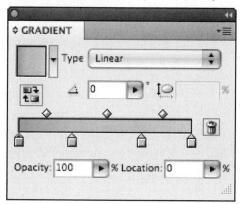

The Type list box (popup menu) at the top of the Gradient panel lets you select from Radial or Linear gradient types. Radial gradients move from that center location of an object radial outward in all directions. Linear gradients move in one direction across the object. If you choose a radial gradient, you can change the distortion of the gradient by editing the value in the Aspect Ratio field (it has a little oval next to it). The Angle field controls the angle of the gradient.

The bottom of the Gradient panel is where you control what colors are in the gradient and where the colors are in relation to one another.

The default gradient is black and white and moves from white on the left to black on the right. To add a new color to the bar, click below the bar where you want the new color to appear. This causes a color marker (which appears as a small square). The new color becomes a step between the left color slider and the right color slider. The Location percentage value defines how close you click to either end with 0% on the left and 100% on the right. In other words, the closer you click to the left end, the closer that color is to the left slider.

If you then click the square marker, it becomes selected. You can tell when a gradient marker is selected because the small triangle above it turns dark. When selected, you can change its color by selecting a new color in the Color panel. You can add up to 32 color stops between the two end colors. When a color stop is selected, typing a different percentage in the Location field on the right changes the color stop's position. When a color stop is selected, you can also change its opacity by typing a value in the Opacity field in the lower left of the panel.

> **TIP** Double-clicking on a gradient stop displays a temporary Color/Swatch panel that allows you to quickly change the color of the gradient stop.

The diamonds above the color bar show the midpoint between two color stops. By moving the midpoint left or right, you alter the halfway color between two color stops. When a diamond is selected, typing a different percentage in the location field below changes the diamond's position.

> **TIP** If you start with a black-and-white gradient and want to add color to the gradient, click and drag the color you want from the Color panel onto the marker to change the marker's color mode.

Working with the Gradient tool

You use the Gradient tool to give a more 3-D look to an object by changing the angle and the starting and ending points for a linear gradient as well as the location of the center and edges of a radial gradient. The tool is also used to offset the highlight on a radial gradient.

> **NEW FEATURE** Illustrator CS4 allows you to do many of the Gradient panel changes directly on your artwork by displaying a little gradient stop bar, as shown in Figure 7.26. This is extremely handy for tiny adjustments of the gradient stops, especially if you're zoomed in tightly. You can even access the temporary Color/Swatch panel by double-clicking on a gradient stop in this floating bar.

Gradients are created with the Gradient panel and applied from the Gradient tool or panel. Follow these steps:

1. **Double-clicking the Gradient tool displays the Gradient panel.** The Gradient tool in the Tools panel looks like a blended rectangle.

2. **Select a gradient type.** Choose Radial or Linear.

3. **Select at least one path that's filled with a gradient.**

4. **Drag with the Gradient tool on the object.** Dragging on linear gradients changes the angle and the length of the gradient as well as the start and end points. Dragging with the Gradient tool on radial gradients determines the start position and end position of the gradient. Clicking with the Gradient tool resets the highlight to a new location.

Figure 7.27 shows a gradient original and after changing the start position of the gradient.

The Gradient tool places a live gradient stop bar on your selected artwork.

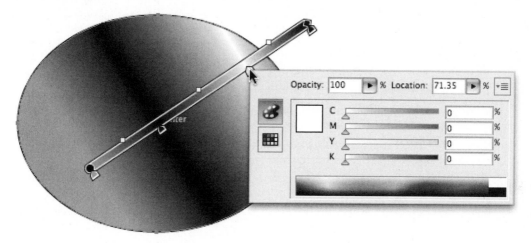

The circle on the left has a radial gradient applied to it. The circle on the right has the same gradient, but it's positioned differently within the object by using the Gradient tool.

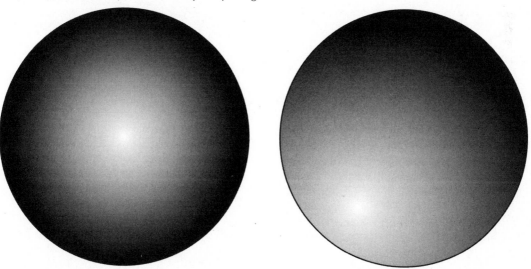

Using Gradients to Create Bubbles

Gradients are a great tool to use when creating objects with a three-dimensional look. You can create great molecular pieces for a chemistry drawing or bubbles for a fun illustration. Start out by drawing circles and then using the Gradient tool to change the angle of the gradient. Use the Gradient tool to click where you want the highlight to be and then drag where you want the darker area to be. You can create a set of random bubbles quite easily using gradients. To create bubbles, follow these steps:

1. **Draw a circle using the Ellipse tool while holding Shift.**

2. **Fill the circle with a radial gradient in a blue color.**

3. **Duplicate the fill in the Appearance panel, changing the new fill's gradient location and setting it to Overlay 60% in the Transparency panel.**

4. **With the object selected, change the transparency to 80% and then choose the Multiply blend mode.** The first figure shows a bubble as well as the Appearance panel, which shows the settings I used for creating a bubble.

5. **Drag the bubble to the Symbol panel to create a new bubble symbol.**

6. **Using the Symbol Sprayer tool, first select the bubble in the Symbol panel and then spray out a bunch of bubbles.** Use the Symbol Sizer tool to adjust their size, as shown in the last figure.

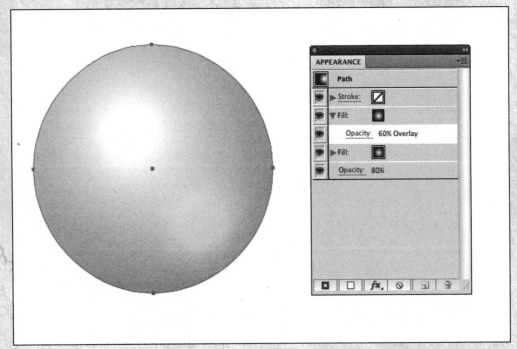

The Appearance panel with the bubble setup

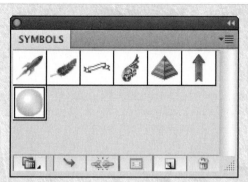

The Symbol panel with the new bubble in place

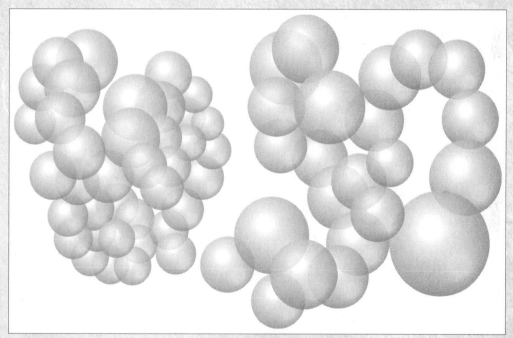

The resulting bubbles sprayed from the Symbol Sprayer tool after some adjustment from the Symbol Sizer tool

    7. Using the other Symbolism tools, change the location, tint, and transparency of the bubbles to give them a more realistic look.

For more on using symbols and the tools related to them, see Chapter 5.

Expanding gradient objects

In Illustrator, you can automatically change gradients into blends by selecting the gradient you want to change and then choosing Object ➪ Expand. You might want to expand a gradient into a blend to add special effects to the object with the paths rather than a gradient fill. Because you expand the object into paths, there are many more paths to change, twist, or mangle, creating lots of options for your object. Expanding the object changes the fill to a blend of paths. The Expand dialog box, as shown in Figure 7.28, allows you to choose to expand the object, fill, or stroke. You also choose whether to expand the gradient to a mesh or the number of steps in the blend.

CROSS-REF For more on blending, see Chapter 12.

FIGURE 7.28

The Expand dialog box can convert a gradient into a blend.

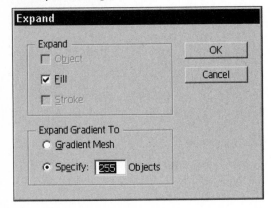

Printing gradients

Selecting the Compatible Gradient and Gradient Mesh Printing option in the Print dialog box prevents most gradient problems from occurring. Choose File ➪ Print and then choose Graphics from the list on the left side, as shown in Figure 7.29. When you print to PostScript Level 1 printers, clicking this check box speeds gradient printing dramatically. If your target printer is not a PostScript printer, then this check box is disabled. Compatible gradients bypass a high-level imaging system within Illustrator that older printers and printers without genuine Adobe PostScript may not be able to understand. Clicking this check box may cause documents to print slower on printers that would ordinarily be able to print those documents.

FIGURE 7.29

Select the Compatible Gradient and Gradient Mesh Printing option in the Graphics pane to resolve printing problems with certain printers.

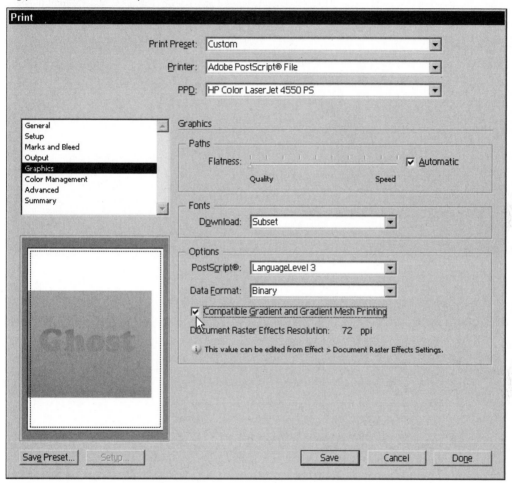

Adding Realism with Mesh

The Mesh tool changes a normal filled path into a multicolored object with the click of a button. You use the Mesh tool to add highlights, shading, and three-dimensional effects. Figure 7.30 shows an object created with the Mesh tool. You click and then create a new color at the clicked point. The new color blends smoothly into the object's original color. This section demonstrates how you enhance highlights and color and add multiple highlights.

FIGURE 7.30

The Mesh tool was used to create these realistic-looking clouds.

Enhancing with highlights and color

The Mesh tool, which is found in the Tools panel, looks like a rectangle with squiggly lines inside. The Mesh tool adds highlights or shading with the click of a mouse. Follow these steps to apply a mesh:

1. **Deselect the object to which you want to add a point.**

2. **Pick the color of the highlight point in the Color panel.** If it isn't visible, choose Window ⇨ Color.

3. **Select the Mesh tool from the Tools panel.**

4. **Click to set the point.**

5. **To change the highlight color, use the Direct Selection tool to select a point on the mesh and then change its color values in the Color panel.**

The Create Gradient Mesh dialog box, as shown in Figure 7.31, is accessed by choosing Object ⇨ Create Gradient Mesh, and it allows you to create your own gradient meshes to use with the Mesh tool. To display this dialog box, you must have something selected; otherwise, Illustrator grays out the option. In the Create Gradient Mesh dialog box, you can set how many mesh lines form a row and a column; whether the appearance is flat, to center, or to the edge; and the highlight intensity from 0% to 100%.

FIGURE 7.31

The Create Gradient Mesh dialog box allows you to customize the mesh settings.

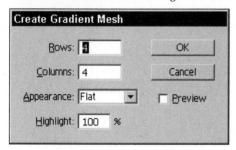

Adding multiple highlights

Clicking more than once on an object with the Mesh tool adds more blends to the object. Each click creates new horizontal and vertical axes. For this reason, the tool is called a mesh. The more clicks that are created, the more individual lines appear until the base object appears as a complex mesh of lines. Each intersection of lines is a point of color that can be changed. However, when you change a color, adjacent intersecting points aren't updated. The following steps give you an example of what happens when you add multiple highlights to an object:

1. **Create a dark-colored rectangle and then deselect it.**

2. **Change the color in the Color panel to a bright color.**

3. **With the Mesh tool, click in the middle of the rectangle.** A point of light appears, creating a sort of radial gradient.

4. **Deselect the rectangle, change the fill color to another bright color, and then click another point.** When you do this, two additional points that are somewhere between the dark background and the two bright highlights appear. Click again for yet another highlight. Figure 7.32 shows an example of this.

TIP If you never manually change the color of the two new points, they continue to update to match the color of the surrounding points. But if you change the color of one of those points, they're no longer smart and remain that color regardless of the colors of the points around them.

You can create very complex mesh objects with just a dozen or so clicks. These objects are editable, but you need to somehow keep track of which points were the originals so that all the other ones update automatically.

TIP   You can change the background color of the object you're editing after several highlights have been added by selecting all the points on the perimeter of the original object with the Direct Selection tool. Every click with the Mesh tool adds four points to the perimeter of the object.

The Mesh tool can be used to create realistic shading and some really impressive effects, such as the comic book cover shown in Figure 7.33.

FIGURE 7.32

A rectangle with a highlight in the middle and additional highlights at each corner

FIGURE 7.33

The Mesh tool was used to create this comic book cover.

Summary

In this chapter, you learned some very important points about adding a bit of splash to your Illustrator documents by using colors, gradients, and mesh. In particular, this chapter covered the following topics:

- You use the Swatches panel to store and apply commonly used colors.

- The Color panel allows you to choose colors from a Color Ramp and to mix colors using interactive sliders.

- You change the color space from grayscale to CMYK to RGB to HSB by selecting one from the Color panel's popup menu.

- You can color paths and type quickly by using the Eyedropper tool to sample colors from paths or placed images.

- You can also create your own gradients and then save them in the Swatches panel.

- Gradients can consist of gradient stops that have different opacities.

- You can quickly turn gradients into blends by selecting the gradient and then applying the Expand option.

- The Mesh tool can be used to add shading effects to flat colored areas.

Part II

Putting Illustrator to Work

Chapter 8

Using Illustrator to Organize Objects

As more and more objects are added to a document, the artwork can very quickly become unmanageable. To address this problem, Illustrator includes many features for organizing the various objects in the document. From locking or hiding objects that you don't want to accidentally move to grouping a set of objects so they can all move together, these features are keys to success in Illustrator.

Another key way to organize objects covered in this chapter is by using the Layers panel. The Layers panel offers precise control over different objects by placing them on different layers and controlling what effects are applied to them.

This chapter shows you how to use Illustrator's features to organize the objects in your documents.

Locking and Hiding Objects

All objects in Illustrator can be locked or hidden — including guides. The process of locking and hiding work is about the same, and the results are only marginally different. In a way, hiding is an invisible lock. Locking the artwork still leaves it visible and printable. When you hide an object, it's for all intents and purposes gone until you show it again. Locking is great to use when you still need to see the location of the object but don't want to accidentally move or transform it. Hiding works well when you need the object out of the way but not gone.

CROSS-REF You can quickly lock and hide layers using the Show/Hide and Lock/Unlock columns in the Layers panel.

Locking objects

Locking can be applied to more than just objects that you draw. Under the Object ⇨ Lock menu, you can choose to lock a selection, all artwork above, or other layers. To lock an object, select it and choose Object ⇨ Lock ⇨ Selection. You can also press Ctrl+2 (⌘+2). Illustrator not only locks the object, but it also deselects it. In fact, you can't select an object after you lock it. You can't move or change locked objects nor can you hide them. Because you can't select a locked object, you can't change it — in Illustrator, as in most applications, you can modify objects only when you select them.

A locked object remains locked when you save and close the document. As a result, locked objects remain locked the next time you open the document. Because locked objects are always visible, they always print. You can't tell from the printed item whether or not it's locked.

To change a locked object, choose Object ⇨ Unlock All. You can also press Ctrl+Alt+2 (⌘+Option+2). This command unlocks (and selects) all objects. There's no way to unlock just a few objects locked with the Lock command. That's one reason why you may want to use the Layers panel to lock specific objects instead of using the Object ⇨ Lock command: Objects locked using the Layers panel can be individually unlocked.

> **TIP** A tricky way to invisibly copyright your illustration is to create a small text box in a far corner of the Pasteboard with your copyright information in it, color the text white, and lock the text box. No one knows it's there, and it can't be easily selected. In fact, it'll even print if it's placed on top of a background in another program.

You should consider locking objects under the following circumstances:

- **When the document is full of complex artwork.** You can do a Select All and not have to wait forever for the Selection tool to finish selecting all parts of the complex art before locking the artwork.
- **When you don't want to accidentally move or change certain artwork.**
- **When you can't easily select paths that are under other paths.** In this case, you lock the ones on top.
- **When you have to fit an illustration into a certain area.** In this situation, you create a box of that size and lock it so you have an instant boundary with which to work.

Hiding objects

Sometimes, you don't want to see certain objects on your document page — perhaps because they obstruct your view of other objects or they take a long time to redraw. In these cases, it's a good idea to hide the objects in question. To do so, select them and then choose Object ⇨ Hide ⇨ Selection. Alternatively, you can press Ctrl+3 (⌘+3).

Hidden objects are invisible and unselectable; they still exist in the document, but they don't print. When a document is closed and reopened, hidden objects reappear.

To show (and select) all hidden objects, choose Object ⇨ Show All. Alternatively, you can press Ctrl+Alt+3 (⌘+Option+3). Think of it as unhide. There's no way to show just a few of the hidden objects when using the Show All command.

Setting object attributes

Choosing Window ⇨ Attributes (Ctrl+F11/⌘+F11) displays the Attributes panel, as shown in Figure 8.1. In this panel, you have these options:

- The Overprint Fill and Overprint Stroke options control how Illustrator handles overlapping areas of different colors when printing the document.

- The Show or Hide Object's Center Point buttons let you choose whether to view the center point of a closed path.

- The Reverse Path Direction buttons are used when working with compound paths. Use these to reverse a path's direction when a multiple compound path isn't working.

- The Use Non-Zero Winding Fill Rule and Use Even-Odd Fill Rule buttons control how Illustrator fills areas defined by compound paths.

- The Image Map list box allows you to specify the shape of an area in an image map.

- The URL field allows you to specify a URL for a selected object or objects.

FIGURE 8.1

The Attributes panel allows you to set object attributes.

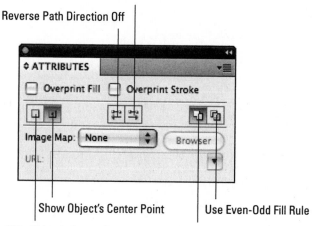

Reverse Path Direction On

Reverse Path Direction Off

Show Object's Center Point   Use Even-Odd Fill Rule

Hide Object's Center Point   Use Non-Zero Winding Fill Rule

Understanding Object Stacking Order

Stacking order is a crucial concept that you need to understand in the world of Adobe Illustrator. This concept is not the same as the layer concept; rather, it's the forward/backward relationship between objects within each layer.

After you create the first object, Illustrator places the next object you create in front (on top) of the first object. Likewise, Illustrator places the third created object in front of both the first and second objects. This cycle continues indefinitely, with objects being stacked one in front of another.

To make your life much more pleasant, Illustrator lets you move objects forward or backward through the stack of objects. In fact, Illustrator's method of moving objects forward and backward is so simple and basic that it's also quite limiting. You can also move objects via the Layers panel, which offers a wide range of moving and organizing options.

Controlling the stacking order for objects

You can change the stacking order of objects in Illustrator from front to back or you can move objects up or down through the stacking order. Figure 8.2 shows two versions of the same illustration after one object was moved up in the stacking order. Use these commands for moving objects in the stacking order:

FIGURE 8.2

The stacking order changes the look of the illustration; by moving the large circle up, it hides part of the three outer objects.

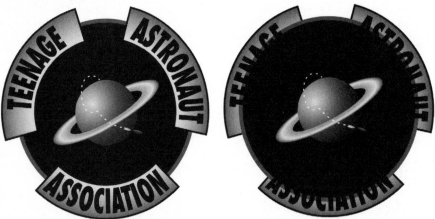

- **Bring to Front:** To move an object to the front, choose Object ➪ Arrange ➪ Bring to Front or press Ctrl+Shift+] (⌘+Shift+]). Illustrator moves the selected object forward so that it's in front of every other object (but only in that layer). Bring to Front isn't available when no objects are selected. Multiple selected paths and grouped paths still retain their front/back position relative to each other.

- **Bring Forward:** To move selected objects forward one object at a time, choose Object ➪ Arrange ➪ Bring Forward or press Ctrl+] (⌘+]).

- **Send Backward:** To move selected objects backward one object at a time, choose Object ➪ Arrange ➪ Send Backward or press Ctrl+[(⌘+[).

- **Send to Back:** To move an object to the back, choose Object ➪ Arrange ➪ Send to Back or press Ctrl+Shift+[(⌘+Shift+[). Illustrator sends the selected object to the back so that it's behind every other object. Send to Back is not available when there are no objects selected. Multiple selected paths and grouped paths still retain their front/back position relative to each other.

- **Send to Current Layer:** Choose Object ➪ Arrange ➪ Send to Current Layer to move the selected object to a different layer. You must first select the object and then select the destination layer in the Layers panel before choosing this command.

Understanding the stacking order for text

Individual characters in a string of text work in a similar manner to their object cousins when it comes to front/back placement. The first character typed is placed at the back of the text block, and the last character typed is placed at the front, as shown in Figure 8.3. To move individual characters forward or backward, you must first choose Type ➪ Create Outlines or press Ctrl+Shift+O (⌘+Shift+O) and then select the outline of the character that you want to arrange. The outlined text is now treated as an object. Use the same arranging commands from the Object ➪ Arrange submenu that you use for other types of objects to move the stacking order of the outlined type.

FIGURE 8.3

Text characters that overlap each other demonstrate a stacking order.

CROSS-REF   For more on creating and modifying text, see Chapter 9.

Using a stacking order for strokes and fills

Try as you might, you can't change the front/back relationship of strokes and fills. Strokes are always in front of fills for the same path. To get the fill to cover or overlap the stroke, you must copy the path, use the Paste in Front command by choosing Edit ⇨ Paste in Front or pressing Ctrl+F (⌘+F), and then remove the stroke from the path that you pasted.

CROSS-REF   For more on strokes and fills, see Chapter 10.

Pasting objects in front of and behind selected objects

Choosing Edit ⇨ Paste in Front or pressing Ctrl+F (⌘+F) pastes any objects you have on the Clipboard in front of any selected objects or at the top of the current layer if no objects are selected.

Choosing Edit ⇨ Paste in Back or pressing Ctrl+B (⌘+B) pastes any objects on the Clipboard behind any selected objects or at the bottom of the current layer if no objects are selected. When you paste an object in front or behind, you're also pasting the attributes of that object (such as the stroke and fill).

In addition, both Paste in Front and Paste in Back paste objects in the same location as the copied object, even from document to document. If the documents are different sizes, Illustrator pastes them in the same location relative to the center of each document. If the Clipboard is empty or if type selected with a Type tool is on the Clipboard, these options aren't available.

NOTE   Copied items in Illustrator retain their layer names and related layer information. When you copy an item that's on layer X-Flies and paste that item in another document that contains an X-Flies layer, the item appears on the X-Flies layer. If the document doesn't contain that layer, Illustrator creates a new layer with that name and then the item appears on that layer. This works only if you select the Paste Remembers Layers option item from the Layers panel's popup menu.

Creating and Deconstructing Groups

Grouping is the process of putting together a series of objects that need to remain spatially constant in relationship to each other. You generally group objects if you intend to move them, flatten them, or perform one effect on all of them at once. Your group may contain as little as one path to an unlimited number of objects. You generally ungroup a group of objects when you no longer need the grouping. For example, you may ungroup objects so that you can edit one of them. When you have objects that go together, such as the figure of a person you created, you may want to group all parts of that person to keep the figure neatly together. That way, when you want to move the person, all pieces move together as one unit. Often, you try to move a collection of objects, and you miss one or more pieces. When you group the pieces together, they all move together when one object is selected. Ungrouping is necessary when you want to separate the objects to make them a part of another group or you want them to stand individually. When applying transformations or special effects, you should ungroup them so that a specific object can have the effect applied.

Grouping objects

In any illustration, objects are much easier to manipulate if they're grouped. Grouping similar areas is helpful for moving entire areas forward or backward as well as for doing any type of horizontal or vertical movement or transformation upon a set of objects. Suppose that you drew a tree with a bunch of apples. You want to group the apples together so you can edit the apples all at one time, such as changing the color or the size.

To group objects together, follow these steps:

1. **Select the items you want to group with any of the selection tools.** For more on the selection tools, see Chapter 6.

2. **Choose Object ⇨ Group or press Ctrl+G (⌘+G).** This command makes the separate objects stay together when you select them.

Now, when you select any object in a group with the Selection tool, Illustrator selects all the objects in that group and makes all the points in a path solid (selected).

Not only can you group several objects together, but you can also group groups together to form a group of groups in which there's a hierarchical series of grouped groups. In addition, groups can be grouped to individual objects or to several other objects.

After a set of objects or groups is grouped together, grouping it again produces no effect. The computer doesn't beep at you, display a dialog box, or otherwise indicate that the objects or groups you're attempting to group together are already grouped. Of course, it never hurts to again choose Object ⇨ Group if you're not sure whether they're grouped. If they weren't grouped before, they now are, and if they were grouped before, nothing unusual or unexpected happens.

TIP If you group several objects that are on different layers, all the objects move to the topmost layer that contains one of the grouped objects and form a group there. This means that the perceived stacking order may change, which can change the appearance of your Illustration.

Ungrouping

If you want to apply a specific effect to one object in the group, you have to ungroup the object so the whole group isn't affected. Suppose, in the apple tree, that you want to make one apple really big and rotten-looking. First, ungroup the apples, regroup all but one of the other apples (to keep them organized), and then apply the effect to just one apple. To ungroup groups (separate them into individual paths and objects), follow these steps:

1. Select the group with either the Group Selection tool or the Selection tool.

2. Choose Object ➪ Ungroup or press Ctrl+Shift+G (⌘+Shift+G). Any selected groups become ungrouped.

Ungrouping, like grouping, works on one set of groups at a time. For example, if you have two groups that are grouped together, ungrouping that outer group results in the two original groups. If you again choose Ungroup, Illustrator also ungroups those two groups. Another way to understand grouping is to think of nesting. Each operation adds or subtracts only one level of nesting.

> **TIP** When you absolutely don't want anything in a group grouped with anything else — and you suspect that there may be several mini-groups within the group you have selected — simply press Ctrl+Shift+G (⌘+Shift+G) several times. You don't need to select the subgroups individually to ungroup them. To eliminate all the groups in your illustration, choose Select ➪ All or press Ctrl+A (⌘+A) and then proceed to ungroup by pressing Ctrl+Shift+G (⌘+Shift+G) several times. To remove certain objects from a group or compound path, select just those objects, cut them, and then Paste in Front (or Paste in Back).

Layering Your Artwork

Illustrator's layering feature provides an easy and powerful way to separate artwork into individual sections. A layer is a separate section of the document that's on its own level or is above, under, or in between other layers but never on the same level as another layer. You can view these sections separately, locked, hidden, or rearranged around each other. Figure 8.4 shows the Layers panel displaying various layers that I use for my comic strips. In this case, the layers have been named to make it easier to keep track of what is on each layer.

Having the various elements of your illustration on separate layers helps you organize them. Each area of the illustration has its own layer. You use these layers to create the stacking order as well as to keep the text on one layer for easier editing. Artists use layers to organize the different grouped objects, shadows, borders, and backgrounds. You can also turn layers off and on to give a client different options on a logo, Web site, or business theme. Using the Layers panel, you can create, control, and manipulate layers to suit your needs. Another use for layers is to trace placed images.

> **CROSS-REF** For more on Live Trace, see Chapter 13.

For my comic strip, I pretty much always keep the title and frames, ground, and sky layers locked so I don't accidentally move the elements on those layers when I marquee-select objects. Keeping distinct elements on separate layers, such as the lines for text and the characters, ensures the proper stacking order at all times, so there's no chance a line becomes hidden behind a character.

The biggest advantage for layers is that you can color-code them to further organize your work. By choosing Select ➪ All or pressing Ctrl+A (⌘+A), you can quickly see which objects are on which layers just by the color of the paths and points. The selection boxes for each layer match the color shown in the right column of the Layers panel (which is displayed when objects on that layer are selected). Using the same colors for all layers makes you miss out on half the power of layers. Use vivid, distinct colors for each layer.

Of course, having too many layers can pose problems. Layers take up RAM and computer power. Therefore, the more layers you have, the slower your system operates. For this reason, you should create layers only when they help you better organize an illustration. Even setting up one additional layer can dramatically ease selection and moving problems.

> **TIP** You can create as many layers as you want, up to the limitations of application memory. Suffice it to say, however, that the more layers you create after a certain point (several hundred), the slower Illustrator runs.

FIGURE 8.4

The Layers panel for my comic strip; keeping elements on separate layers allows for faster editing and fewer mistakes.

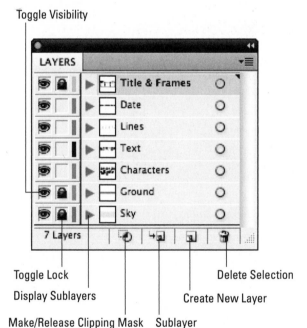

Toggle Visibility

Toggle Lock

Display Sublayers

Make/Release Clipping Mask   Sublayer

Delete Selection

Create New Layer

Getting started with layers

After you realize that you need to use layers, what do you do? The only way to manipulate, create, and delete layers is by using the Layers panel. If the Layers panel isn't showing, choose

Window⇨Layers or press F7. When you open the Layers panel for the first time in a new document, you see only Layer 1 listed.

To create a new layer, follow these steps:

1. **Click the Create New Layer button at the bottom of the panel.** The button looks like a piece of paper with the bottom-left corner folded over and is to the left of the trash icon in Figure 8.4. You can also click the triangle in the upper right of the panel to display a popup menu. Clicking the first item, New Layer, displays the Layer Options dialog box, as shown in Figure 8.5. You can also display this dialog box by double-clicking a layer's name.

2. **Change the name of your layer.** In the Layer Options dialog box, the name of the new layer is highlighted. To change this name, type a new name to replace the generic name.

FIGURE 8.5

The Layers Options dialog box lets you name the layer.

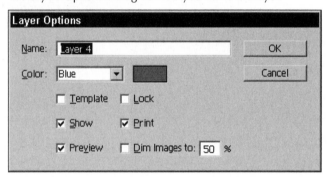

3. **Select any of the options that you want for this layer.** The options below the name in the Layer Options dialog box affect how you view the layer and make it function. The options are as follows:

   ▪ **Color:** The first option is the color of the paths and points when objects on that layer are selected. Choose one of the preset colors from the dropdown list (popup menu) or select the Other option to use a Custom Color. Each time you create a new layer, a different color (going in order from the list) is applied to that layer.

   ▪ **Template:** Use this option when you want to trace something but not have it print. If you click the Template check box, Illustrator automatically deselects the Print option and allows the Dim Images option.

   ▪ **Show:** This option makes the objects in the layer visible.

   ▪ **Preview:** This option lets you see a preview of objects on this layer.

■ **Lock:** This option prevents objects on this layer from being selected and prevents any objects from being put on this layer.

■ **Print:** This option allows you to print objects that are on this layer.

■ **Dim Images to:** This option dims any placed images on the layer. The default value is 50% lighter or you can type a value.

4. **Click OK.** The new layer appears above the existing layer in the Layers panel.

If you want the objects on the new layer to appear below the objects on the existing layer, click the name of the new layer and then drag it below the existing layer. Be careful not to drop the new layer on top of the existing layer — doing so makes the new layer into a sublayer of the existing layer.

To modify the existing layer, double-click it. The Layer Options dialog box opens again. Make the changes and select the options that you want for this layer and then click OK.

Using the Layers panel

The Layers panel is the control center where all layer-related activities take place. Most activities occur in the main section of the Layers panel, which is always visible when the Layers panel is on-screen. Other activities take place in the popup menu that appears when you click the triangle in the upper right of the panel.

Illustrator has wonderful options in the Layers panel. First is the capability to thin the display of layers in the panel for those illustrations with tons of layers. Second is the capability to drag to a hidden layer. Third is that Illustrator displays in italic those layers that you don't have set to print so that you can see quickly what will and what won't print.

Clicking the Close button in the Layers panel closes the Layers panel. You can also close the Layers panel by choosing Window ⇨ Layers or by pressing F7. To bring the Layers panel back to the screen, choose Window ⇨ Layers or press F7 again.

Using the Layers panel columns

Aside from the standard Minimize and Close (Zoom and Close) buttons at the top of the panel, the following is a list of the options in the Layers panel:

■ **Show/Hide column:** The far-left column controls how you view each layer. If this column has a solid eye icon, the layer is in Preview mode. The hollow eye icon means that the layer is in Outline mode. No eye indicates a hidden layer. Clicking a solid or hollow eye icon toggles it from showing to hidden. Clicking in the Show/Hide Column when no eye is present shows the layer. Pressing Ctrl (⌘) and clicking the eye toggles it from solid (Preview mode) to hollow (Outline mode) and then back again. Pressing Alt (Option) and clicking an eye shows or hides all other layers. Layers that are set as template layers display a little icon with an overlaid square, triangle, and ellipse to indicate a template layer.

- **Lock/Unlock column:** The second column is the Lock/Unlock column. The lock icon indicates whether a layer is locked. An empty column means that the layer isn't locked. A lock icon means that the layer is locked from use.

- **Layer Names:** The column in the center of the panel lists the names of all the layers in the document. When no documents are open, no layers are listed. If one layer is high-lighted and has a triangle in the upper-right corner, that layer is active. All new objects are created on the active layer. You can select a range of layers by Shift+clicking each layer. Pressing Ctrl (⌘) allows you to select or deselect additional layers. The layer at the top of the column is the layer that's on top of all the other layers. The layer at the bottom of the column is the layer that's at the bottom of all the other layers. To move a layer, click and drag it up or down. As you drag, a dark horizontal line indicates where the layer is placed when you release the mouse button.

 **Ctrl+Alt+click (⌘+Option+click) on a specific eye icon to turn all layers into Outline mode, except the selected layer.**

 **You can undo all layer changes after they happen by choosing Edit ➪ Undo or by pressing Ctrl+Z (⌘+Z) immediately afterward.**

- **Target icon:** When an object is selected, the target icon (to the right of the layer name) displays as a double ring. It appears as a single ring when the object is not selected. You can also click the icon to select the object.

- **Object status:** To the right of the target icon is the object status of the layer. If a square appears in that column, at least one object on that layer is selected.

Using the Layers panel buttons

The four buttons along the bottom of the Layers panel make layer manipulation very easy. This section explains what these buttons do:

- **Make/Release Clipping Mask:** This button, which looks like an overlapping rectangle and circle, lets you create a clipping mask in the layer. The topmost object in the layer acts as the masking shape. The difference between using Make/Release Clipping Mask from the Layers panel rather than choosing Object ➪ Clipping Mask ➪ Make is that the objects won't be grouped when using the Layers panel.

CROSS-REF For more on clipping masks, see Chapter 12.

- **Create New Sublayer:** You use this button, which looks like an arrow pointing to a piece of paper with the bottom-left corner turned down, to add sublayers. To do so, select the layer and then click the Create New Sublayer button or choose Create New Sublayer from the popup menu in the Layers panel. You can have as many sublayers inside a layer as you want. To see the sublayers, click the triangle to the left of the layer name. You can also change a layer into a sublayer by dragging it under the layer you want it to go to. Figure 8.6 shows the sublayers within a layer. A sublayer is indicated by brackets (< >) and is indented. Some sublayers have a triangle indicating that there are more sublayers within that sublayer. The sublayers also tell you what is in that layer, such as <Path>, <Compound Path>, etc.

- **Create New Layer:** Clicking this button, which looks like a piece of paper with the bottom-left corner turned down, creates a new layer instantly, without the New Layer dialog box appearing. If you press Alt (Option) and then click the New Layer button, Illustrator creates a new layer by way of the Layer Options dialog box. Dragging a layer to the New Layer button duplicates that layer and everything on it.

- **Delete Selection:** Clicking this button, which looks like a trash can, deletes the selected layers. If there's art on a layer that's about to be deleted, a dialog box appears to ensure that you really want to delete that layer; Figure 8.7 shows the warning you receive. Alt (Option)+clicking the trash icon deletes selected layers without a warning dialog box, whether or not art is on the selected layers. You can also drag layers to the trash icon; Illustrator deletes the layers without a warning dialog box.

FIGURE 8.6

The sublayers of a layered illustration show you the document layout.

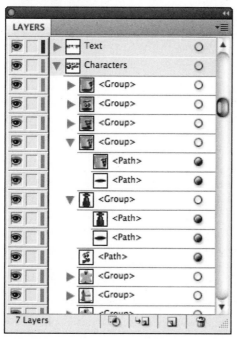

FIGURE 8.7

If you attempt to delete a selected layer that contains artwork, Illustrator warns you before actually deleting the layer.

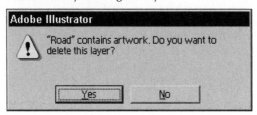

Moving and layers

You can move selected objects to another layer. A selected object appears on its layer with a square in the upper-right corner of that layer. Dragging that square to another layer moves the selected object to that layer. Figure 8.8 shows a selection marker being dragged to another layer. You can drag only to a layer that isn't hidden or locked. Only one object at a time can be moved to another layer.

FIGURE 8.8

The selected object is being moved to another layer.

This box shows the items being dragged.

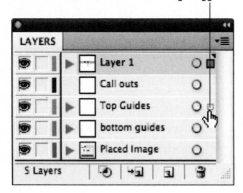

Using the Layers panel's popup menu

Clicking the triangle in the upper right of the Layers panel displays a popup menu that shows the different options that are available relative to the selected layers; Figure 8.9 shows this popup menu. These options are available:

■ **New Layer:** This option creates a new layer above the currently selected layer or, if no layer is selected, at the top of the list. When you select this option, the Layer Options dialog box opens. When you create a new layer, Illustrator automatically assigns the next color in the color list.

TIP If you press Alt (Option) before you click the popup menu triangle, the first menu item reads New Layer Above First Layer or New Layer Above whatever the name of the active layer is.

■ **New Sublayer:** This option creates a new sublayer below the selected layer.

■ **Duplicate Layer:** This option duplicates selected layers, along with any objects that are on those layers. You can also duplicate layers by dragging them to the New Layer icon at the bottom of the Layers panel.

■ **Delete Layer:** This option deletes the layer and any artwork on the layer. If the layer you want to delete contains artwork, a dialog box warns you that you're about to delete it. If one or more objects are selected, the popup menu says Delete Selection. If you select several layers, the entry reads Delete Layers, and all selected layers are deleted. You can undo layer deletions using the Edit ➪ Undo command.

■ **Options for Layer:** This option is called Options for whatever the name of the active layer is. The menu item reads Options for Selection if you select more than one layer. Clicking Options for Selection displays the Layer Options dialog box. If more than one layer is selected, the layer options affect all selected layers.

■ **Make/Release Clipping Mask:** This option creates a clipping mask in the layer. The topmost object in the layer acts as the masking shape.

■ **Locate Object:** Use this to find where an object is located in the Layers panel. Choose an object in the document and then select this option to see where it is in the Layers panel.

■ **Merge Selected:** This option combines selected layers into one. Merging layers does two important things: First, in just one step, it places art together that you want on the same layer. Second, it automatically eliminates all those empty layers.

■ **Flatten Artwork:** This option takes all your layers and combines them into one layer.

■ **Collect in New Layer:** This option moves the selected objects to a new layer.

■ **Release to Layers (Sequence):** Use this option to move the selected objects to new individual layers.

■ **Release to Layers (Build):** Use this option to move the selected objects to layers in a cumulative sequence. You mainly use this option to create animation sequences where the first layer contains the first object, the second layer contains the first and second objects, the third layer contains the first three objects, etc.

■ **Reverse Order:** Use this to reverse the stacking order of the selected layers. The layers must be adjoining in the Layers panel.

■ **Template:** You use this option to make your selection a template.

- **Hide Others:** This option hides all the layers except the selected ones.

- **Outline Others/Preview All Layers:** This option changes all unselected layers to Outline view or changes all unselected layers to Preview view.

- **Lock Others/Unlock All Layers:** This option locks all layers except the selected ones or unlocks all layers except the selected ones.

- **Paste Remembers Layers:** This option causes Illustrator to paste all objects on the layer from which you copied them, regardless of which layer is currently active. Deselecting this menu item causes objects on the Clipboard to be pasted on the current layer.

- **Panel Options:** Use this option to change the Row Size, Thumbnail views, and whether to Show Layers Only.

 Double-clicking a layer name displays the Layer Options dialog box.

FIGURE 8.9

The Layers panel's popup menu gives you more options for working with layers.

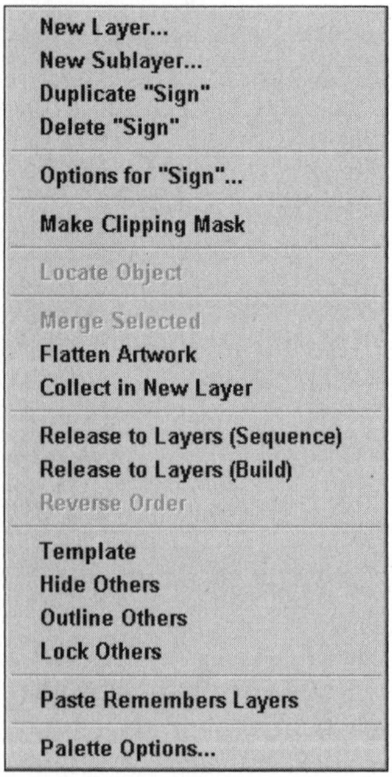

| New Layer... |
| New Sublayer... |
| Duplicate "Sign" |
| Delete "Sign" |
| Options for "Sign"... |
| Make Clipping Mask |
| Locate Object |
| Merge Selected |
| Flatten Artwork |
| Collect in New Layer |
| Release to Layers (Sequence) |
| Release to Layers (Build) |
| Reverse Order |
| Template |
| Hide Others |
| Outline Others |
| Lock Others |
| Paste Remembers Layers |
| Palette Options... |

Working with Templates in Illustrator

It's often much easier to create artwork in Illustrator by starting with something to trace, whether it's a logo, a floor plan, or your cousin Fred's disproportionate profile. Even the best artists use some form of template when they draw to keep proportions consistent, to get angles just right, and for other reasons that help them to achieve the best possible results.

This section discusses methods and techniques for manually tracing different types of artwork within Illustrator. First, you place an image — the image that you eventually want to trace — on a layer, which is your template layer. Next, you use the template layer to trace your image.

CROSS-REF For more on Live Trace, see Chapter 13.

Placing a template on a layer

You can create a template in Illustrator by placing any image into a template layer. That image can then be used for tracing or as a guide for creating or adjusting artwork.

Follow these steps to create a template layer:

1. **Double-click the layer that you want to modify.** The Layer Options dialog box opens.
2. **In the Layer Options dialog box, click the Template check box.** By default, the Dim Images check box is selected and all other options are grayed out.
3. **Type a value in the Dim Images text field.** The lower the percent value, the lighter the image appears in Illustrator.
4. **Click OK to apply the change.** Illustrator creates a template layer from the image you selected.

NOTE Paths that you place on template layers don't appear when they're selected. Instead, an icon appears in the Layers panel's view column to indicate that the current layer is a template layer. Template layers don't print.

TIP You can make any vector artwork into a template by rasterizing it and then placing that layer into a template layer.

Figure 8.10 shows an image before and after dimming.

Placed images work well as templates because their resolutions are independent of the Illustrator document. You can scale placed images up or down, changing their on-screen resolution as you change their size. For example, if you scale a 72 dpi (dots per inch) image down to one-fourth of its imported size (making the dpi of the placed image 4×72, or 288 dpi), you can zoom in on the image in Illustrator at 400%. At 400%, the placed image still has a 72 dpi resolution because one-fourth of 288 dpi is 72 dpi. The more you increase the placed image's dpi by scaling it down, the more you can zoom in to see the details of the image. Here's another plus: A placed image template is a full-color template that keeps all the shading and colors and allows you to see all the fine details easily. That way, you can trace all the tiny details that the color brings out.

FIGURE 8.10

The original image (left) and after dimming (right)

Using a template to trace an image

Now that you have your template (placed image) all set up, you're ready to trace it — or so you would think. You can go about tracing in lots of different ways, and I include the best of the best techniques in this section to help you muddle through this mess.

You can trace templates in two ways: manually and automatically. Manually tracing consists of using the Pencil and Pen tools to tediously trace the edges of a template — often a very time-consuming task. You manually trace an image when you have lots of time on your hands and when you want to retain every single detail of the traced image. As an alternative, you can use the Live Trace function, discussed in Chapter 13, to speed up the process.

Some designers prefer manually tracing templates. Using the Pen and Pencil tools allows illustrators to add detail, remove oddities, and change curves, angles, etc., to their satisfaction. Using a pressure-sensitive tablet makes for clean, accurate tracing. The Pencil tool is great to use when creating more bumpy lines, as in map drawing. The Pen tool is fantastic for creating smoother, more accurate lines.

CROSS-REF For more on using the Pen and Pencil tools, see Chapter 4.

NOTE If you use a pressure-sensitive drawing tablet, you may find that manually tracing a printed copy of an image that you place under the clear plastic overlay on the surface of the tablet is easier than attempting to trace the image on the screen. You may need to experiment to see which method best suits your working style.

Using Align and Distribute

The Align panel contains several buttons for aligning and distributing objects with a simple click of a button. Align treats paths, type objects, and groups as single objects, allowing for quite a bit of flexibility when aligning and distributing. Aligning objects moves them to line up along a specified area (horizontal left, horizontal middle, horizontal right, vertical top, vertical center, and vertical bottom). Select the objects first, then choose an alignment. Figure 8.11 shows a bunch of objects before and after being horizontally aligned. Distribute takes the selected objects and evenly moves them a specified amount from each other (vertical distribute top, vertical distribute center, vertical distribute bottom, horizontal distribute left, horizontal distribute center, and horizontal distribute right).

FIGURE 8.11

Objects before horizontal alignment (top) and after (bottom)

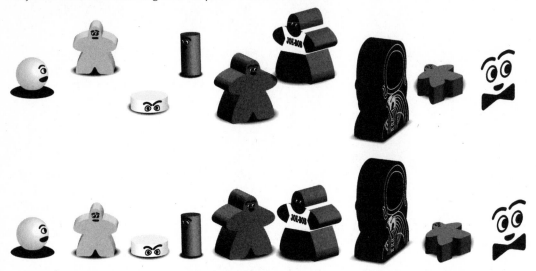

To use the Align panel, follow these steps:

1. **Select the objects you want to align and/or distribute.** For more on selecting objects, see Chapter 6.

2. **Click the appropriate button in the panel.** The panel has two areas: Align Objects and Distribute Objects:

   - **The Align area:** In order from left to right, the buttons in this area are Horizontal Align Left, Horizontal Align Center, Horizontal Align Right, Vertical Align Top, Vertical Align Center, and Vertical Align Bottom.

   - **The Distribute areas:** In order from left to right, the buttons in this area are Vertical Distribute Top, Vertical Distribute Center, Vertical Distribute Bottom, Horizontal Distribute Left, Horizontal Distribute Center, and Horizontal Distribute Right.

 Each click in the panel counts as a change in Illustrator, which means that if you click 20 times, you need to undo 20 times to return to where you started.

Measuring an Image

So, you're drawing the blueprints for that new civic center downtown, and your boss wants everything to scale. Wouldn't it be great if Illustrator helped you with your gargantuan task? But wait! It does! You can measure objects or distances between objects in Illustrator in several ways:

- Using the Measure tool
- Using the Transform panel
- Using the rulers along the side of the document window
- Placing objects whose dimensions are known against the edges
- Using Offset Path
- Eyeballing it (popular since the first artist painted his recollections of the preceding day's battle with the saber-toothed animals of his time)

Different methods of measuring are appropriate for different needs. For example, you want to use the Measure tool to check the accuracy between objects or the size of the objects. When using the Transform panel, you can type exact measurements of scaling, moving, rotating, shear, and reflecting. The rulers let you drag out guidelines for keeping your objects accurately sized and aligned. Offset Path duplicates the selected path, offsetting it from the original by the specified distance. Eyeballing is fine as long as accuracy isn't a condition of your illustration.

The default unit of measure for all the measurement methods listed above is points. Before I discuss the various ways to measure, I want to mention how to change units.

Changing the measurement units

The default of using points for measurement is great for type, but when was the last time your art director said, "I'd like you to design a 360-point × 288-point ad and make the logo at least 144 points high." And your grandmother isn't likely to say to you, "Gosh, you must be at least 5,600 points tall, maybe taller. You've grown at least 100 points since I last saw you. Does your mother let you wear that to school?!"

Points don't work for everything, so Adobe lets you change the measurement units to picas, inches, centimeters, millimeters, or pixels. The way to choose from these measurements is to temporarily indicate a different unit of measurement each time you type a value by appending a character or two to the end of your numerical value.

In the metric system, there are 100 centimeters in a meter and 10 millimeters in a centimeter. The other system, which is much more significant to Illustrator users, is the pica/point system. When the pica measurement system is selected in the Units & Display Performance section of the Preferences dialog box, measurements are displayed using the common (common to typesetters and designers, anyway) system of picas followed by points. So, a distance of 3 picas and 6 points is displayed as 3p6. Such a measurement is displayed as 42 points using the point system.

You can change to a different unit of measure in one of three ways:

- **Using the Preferences dialog box:** Choose Edit (Illustrator) ⇨ Preferences ⇨ Units & Display Performance and then select the measurement system you want by using the General list box. This permanently alters your measurement units. In other words, all dialog boxes in all new documents express their measurements in the specified units, not points (unless you choose points).

- **Using the Document Setup menu:** Choose File ⇨ Document Setup and then choose the appropriate unit of measure from the Units list box. This changes the units in that document only.

- **Using any dialog box:** Type the appropriate unit abbreviation, listed in Table 8.1, after the number in whatever dialog box you open, even if the text fields show points. Illustrator does conversions from points to inches and centimeters (and vice versa) on the fly, so after you type a point value, the program converts the points into inches as soon as you press Tab. This little feature can be an excellent way for you to become more comfortable with points and picas. To get picas, type **p0** after the number.

TABLE 8.1

Illustrator Unit Abbreviations

Unit of Measure	Abbreviation	Example
Inches	inch, in, or "	For 2 inches, type 2 inch, 2 in, or 2".
Millimeters	mm	For 2 millimeters, type 2 mm.
Centimeters	cm	For 2 centimeters, type 2 cm.
Points	pt	For 2 points, type 2 pt or 0p2.
Picas	p	For 2 picas, type 2p.
Picas and points	p	For 2 picas 6 points, type 2p6.
Pixels	px	For 2 pixels, type 2px.

A quick refresher on measurement units and their relations:

$$1" = 6p = 72 \text{ pt} = 25.4 \text{ mm} = 2.54 \text{ cm}$$

$$.16667" = 1p = 12 \text{ pt} = 4.2 \text{ mm} = .42 \text{ cm}$$

$$.01389" = 0p1 = 1 \text{ pt} = .35 \text{ mm} = .035 \text{ cm}$$

$$.03931" = p2.83 = 2.83 \text{ pt} = 1 \text{ mm} = .1 \text{ cm}$$

$$.39305" = 2p4.35 = 28.35 \text{ pt} = 10 \text{ mm} = 1 \text{ cm}$$

Pixels can't be directly related to the other measurement units because the size of each pixel varies according to screen resolution.

Using the Measure tool

The fastest way to obtain a precise, exact measurement in Illustrator is to use the Measure tool, as shown in Figure 8.12. Follow these steps to use the tool:

1. **Click and hold the Eyedropper tool.** The Measure tool is a popup tool found with the Eyedropper and Paint Bucket tools.

2. **Click the Measure tool.** The icon looks like a ruler.

3. **Click an object where you want to begin measuring with the Measure tool.** The Info panel of the Measure tool opens.

4. **Click where you want to end your measurement.** The Info panel shows the distance between the location first clicked and the next location clicked or the distance between where the tool was first clicked and where the mouse was released after dragging.

Double-clicking the Measure tool displays the Guides & Grid section of the Preferences dialog box, where you can set the distance between grid lines if you use the grid to help in making more accurate drawings. For more on the Guides & Grid options, see the section on this topic later in this chapter.

You can use the measurements that you obtain with the Measure tool to move your object the distance you want. As soon as the Measure tool measures a distance, it routes that information to the Move dialog box, as shown in Figure 8.13. The next time you open the Move dialog box, it holds the values sent by the Measure tool. You open the Move dialog box by choosing Object ⇨ Transform ⇨ Move or by double-clicking the Selection tool. If you hold Shift, you can constrain the movement of the measuring line to 45° or 90°.

FIGURE 8.12

The Measure tool allows you to make very precise measurements.

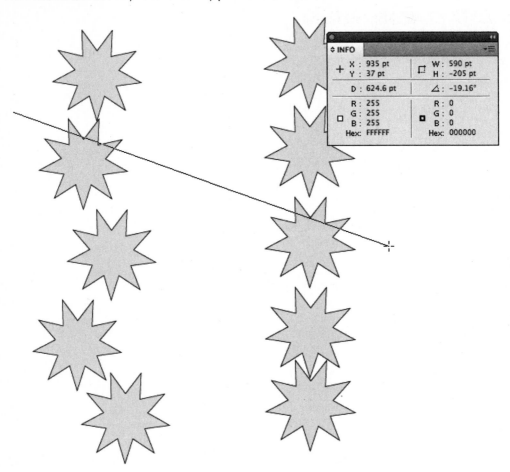

Sizing objects with the Transform panel

A great way to resize objects is by using the Transform panel. When you have an object selected, you can type a new height and width in the Transform panel, and the object immediately changes to match the new measurements. The Transform panel also lets you know the placement of the object via the X and Y values. The Transform panel, which you open by choosing Window➪Transform, shows the height, width, and location of any selected path or paths, as shown in Figure 8.14.

FIGURE 8.13

The Move dialog box allows you to move objects with great precision.

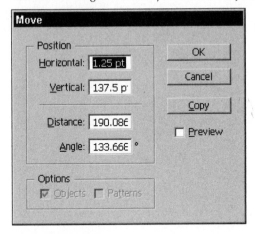

FIGURE 8.14

Use the Transform panel to set objects to specific sizes.

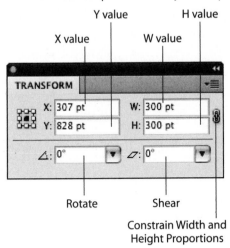

The options for the Transform panel are:

- **X and Y:** These two options show the location of the object on the page, measured from the lower-left corner.

- **W:** This option shows the width of the selected object (or the total width of the selected objects when more than one is selected).

- **H:** This option shows the height or total height of the selected object or objects.

- **Rotate:** Located on the bottom left of the panel, you use this option to rotate an object by typing a value in degrees.

- **Shear:** Located on the bottom right, you can type a value to slant the object along a horizontal or vertical axis.

To change the object's size, select the object first and then type a new value for the height and width in the Transform panel. If you want the object to move, type new X and Y values in the Transform panel.

Using rulers

You can toggle rulers on and off by choosing View ⇨ Show/Hide Rulers or by pressing Ctrl+R (⌘+R). Normally, the rulers measure up and across from the Artboard's lower-left corner; however, you can alter this orientation by dragging the ruler origin (where the zeros are) from its position in the upper-left corner, between where the two rulers meet. Because rulers take up valuable on-screen real estate, it's usually a good idea to leave them turned off unless you're constantly measuring things or you want to display your illustration at a higher magnification. Rulers are easy to show and hide — just press Ctrl+R (⌘+R) when you want to see them and press Ctrl+R (⌘+R) again to hide them. To reset the rulers to their original location, double-click in the origin box of the rulers.

TIP If you change the ruler origin to the middle of the document page, move it back to a corner when you're finished. When you zoom in, rulers may be the only indicator of your location within the document.

One of the rulers' neatest features is the display of dotted lines on the rulers that correspond to the cursor's position. And yet, at times, measuring with rulers works no better than eyeballing; although the process requires precision, you're limited by the rulers' hash marks in pinpointing the cursor's exact position. The rulers are best suited for measuring when the document is at a very high zoom level.

Measuring with objects

Using objects to compare distances can be more effective than using either the Measure tool or the rulers, especially when you need to place objects precisely — for example, when you want several objects to be the same distance from one another.

If you place a circle adjacent to an object (so that the objects' edges touch), you know that the second object is placed correctly when it's aligned to the circle's other side. (A circle is the object most commonly used because the diameter is constant.)

You can use other objects for measuring, including:

- ■ **Squares:** When you need to measure horizontal and vertical distances
- ■ **Rectangles:** When the horizontal and vertical distances are different
- ■ **Lines:** When the distance applies to only one direction

To gain better precision, turn the measuring object into a guide by choosing View ➪ Guides ➪ Make Guides. Guides are discussed later in this chapter.

Using Offset Path (for equidistant measuring)

Suppose that you want to place several objects the same distance from a central object. You may find that using any of the previously mentioned measuring techniques is time-consuming and even inaccurate, especially when you deal with complex images. However, Illustrator's Offset Path dialog box allows you to automatically align objects equidistantly from a central object.

To use Offset Path to measure objects that are equally spaced apart, follow these steps:

1. **Select the central object.** For more on selecting objects, see Chapter 6.

2. **Choose Object ➪ Path ➪ Offset Path.** The Offset Path dialog box, as shown in Figure 8.15, opens.

3. **Type the desired distance in the Offset text field.** You can type a distance in points, millimeters, inches, or pixels.

CROSS-REF For more on the Offset Path dialog box and its settings, see Chapter 6.

FIGURE 8.15

The Offset Path dialog box creates an offset path you can use for the precise placement of objects.

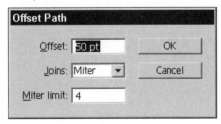

4. **Click OK.** Illustrator creates the new Offset Path.

5. **Change the new path into a guide.**

6. **Align your objects to this guide.**

Working with Grids

Nothing I've found is more useful on a day-to-day basis than the Grid feature. Grids act as a framework for your artwork, providing an easy method for aligning and positioning images. Figure 8.16 shows an Illustrator document that has grids turned on. One advantage of using grids is the Snap to Grid feature. With this feature, you can move objects near a gridline, and Illustrator automatically snaps the object directly on the grid line.

Grids start from the origin of your Artboard (usually the lower-left corner). If you want to change the position of the grid, you can do so by dragging the origin point (at the Origin Marker where the rulers meet) to the new starting position for the grid. You reset the grid position (and the ruler origin) by double-clicking the Origin Marker.

Instead of gridlines, you may want to use guides for layout purposes. For example, you may need a few lines in different locations to set a page for a flyer advertisement. Use guides by dragging them out from the rulers to the exact locations where you want to place art and enter type. Gridlines are great for using lines that are set a specific distance apart. Use gridlines to create a perspective drawing or to place objects a specific distance apart.

This list shows the commands for displaying gridlines and the various Snap to Grid features, which are available only when gridlines are displayed:

- **Display grid lines:** Choose View ⇨ Show Grid or press Ctrl+" (⌘+").
- **Turn off grids:** Choose View ⇨ Hide Grid or press Ctrl+" (⌘+").
- **Snap to Grid:** Choose View ⇨ Snap to Grid or press Ctrl+Shift+" (⌘+Shift+"). This feature snaps the object to the nearest grid.
- **Snap to Point:** Choose View ⇨ Snap to Point or press Ctrl+Alt+" (⌘+Option+"). This feature snaps the dragged object to another object's point. More importantly, you can see this happen. As you drag, the cursor turns from black to white when you're directly over another point.

> **TIP**   If you want to display grids in each new document, open your Illustrator startup file and then turn on grids in that document. Then, save the startup file. All new documents display grids when you first create them.

Creating grid color, style, and spacing

You can customize the way grids look by changing the Grid preferences. Choose Edit (Illustrator) ⇨ Preferences ⇨ Guides & Grid to display the Guides & Grid section of the Preferences dialog box, as seen in Figure 8.17. Here, you can change the grid color, style, and spacing.

FIGURE 8.16

A document with Illustrator's Grid function turned on

FIGURE 8.17

The Guides & Grid section of the Preferences dialog box allows you to set up the appearance options.

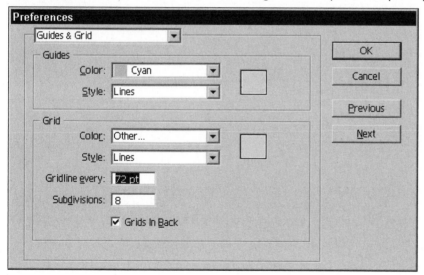

These options are available in the Grid section of the Preferences dialog box:

- **Color:** In this area, you can pick a new color from the list of colors. If you choose Other, you can use the color picker to the right of the Color area to pick a new color for your grids.

- **Style:** You can also choose between lines and dots as the grid style. I prefer to use lines for my grid because dots can turn an already busy-looking page into one with all sorts of, well, dots all over the place.

- **Gridline every:** Type the distance you want between gridlines. To change the space between the major (darker) gridlines, type a value in the Gridline every text field.

- **Subdivisions:** To create subdivisions (minor) between the dark values, type a number for how many sections should be created between the main lines. If you type **1** as the value, no subdivisions are created. Because you're defining the number of divisions, not the number of lines, typing 2 creates one line between the two main lines. The standard 1-inch gridline with eight subdivisions creates $\frac{1}{8}$-inch squares.

- **Grids In Back:** You can deselect the Grids in Back check box to make your gridlines appear in front of your artwork. The box is selected by default so that the gridlines aren't running on top of your artwork.

Spinning grids

Your grid doesn't have to consist of just vertical and horizontal lines. You can rotate the grid to any angle you want by changing the Constrain Angle in the General section of the Preferences dialog box. This is perfect for working with angled artwork; even if only a portion of the artwork is at an angle, the Constrain Angle can be set temporarily to the angle of the artwork.

Using Guides

Guides are dotted or solid lines that help you align artwork. Guides don't print, and they're saved with documents. In Illustrator and most desktop-publishing software, guides are straight lines extending from one edge of a document to the other. But in Illustrator, you can also turn any path into a guide.

For the most part, guides behave exactly like their path counterparts. As long as you have them unlocked, you may select them, hide them, group them, and even paint them (although paint attributes aren't be visible on-screen or on a printout until the guides are converted back into paths).

Creating guides

You can create guides in two ways: by pulling them out from the rulers and by transforming paths into guides.

To pull a guide from a ruler, first make the vertical and horizontal rulers visible by choosing View ➪ Show Rulers or by pressing Ctrl+R (⌘+R). To create guides that span the entire Pasteboard, click the vertical or horizontal ruler and then drag out.

To transform an existing path into a guide, select the path and then choose View ➪ Guides ➪ Make Guides or press Ctrl+5 (⌘+5).

> **TIP** And now a word about the Magic Rotating Guide (possibly the coolest tip you'll ever learn): When you drag a guide out from the vertical ruler and press and hold Alt (Option), the vertical guide becomes a horizontal guide. And vice versa.

Locking, unlocking, and moving guides

When you create a guide, you may want to ensure that it doesn't get moved when you're selecting and moving your objects. Locking your guide is a great way to ensure that the guide doesn't get picked up and moved. Moving a guide is necessary if you create a specific guide like the outline of a business card and you want to move it to create a different business card. Moving an unlocked guide is simple — click and drag it. If guides are locked, unlock them by choosing View ➪ Guides ➪ Lock Guides or by pressing Ctrl+Alt+; (⌘+Option+;).

If you aren't sure whether the guides in your document are locked or unlocked, click and hold the View ➪ Guides menu. If you see a check mark next to Lock Guides, Illustrator locks the guides and also locks all new guides. To unlock all the document's guides, choose View ➪ Guides ➪ Lock Guides; to lock guides again, choose View ➪ Guides ➪ Lock Guides (yes, it's a toggle).

Releasing guides

Now that you're getting the hang of using the guides, you may want to delete them or release them to move. You can also release a guide if you've decided to make it into an object that you can stroke and fill. To release a guide or change it into a path, select the guide and choose View ➪ Guides ➪ Release Guides. Alternatively, you can press Ctrl+Alt+5 (⌘+Option+5).

To release multiple guides first, ensure that the guides are unlocked; in other words, ensure that no check mark appears next to Lock Guides in the View ➪ Guides menu. Select the guides and then choose View ➪ Guides ➪ Release Guides or press Ctrl+Alt+5 (⌘+Option+5).

> **NOTE** You select multiple guides in the same way you select multiple paths: Drag a marquee around the guides or press Shift and then click each guide. For more on selecting paths, see Chapter 6.

> **TIP** Selecting all guides — even those that are currently paths — by dragging a marquee or Shift+clicking can be a chore. Here's another way: First, ensure that the guides aren't locked. Next, choose Select ➪ All or press Ctrl+A (⌘+A). Choose View ➪ Guides ➪ Release Guides or press Ctrl+Alt+5 (⌘+Option+5). This releases all guides and, more importantly, selects all paths that were formerly guides (all other paths and objects are deselected). Finally, choose View ➪ Guides ➪ Make Guides or press Ctrl+5 (⌘+5), and all selected paths become guides again and are selected.

Deleting guides

Suppose that you've just finished a fantastic drawing that you created with the help of many guides. Now that the image is complete, you want to delete those guides. Sure, you can unlock them and select them by holding Shift. Or if you were really thinking, you could put those guides on a layer and simply Select All and then Delete. Well, Illustrator has just made your life even easier. By choosing the Clear Guides option under the View menu's Guides submenu, all guides are miraculously deleted.

Changing guide preferences

In the Guides & Grid section of the Preferences dialog box (refer to Figure 8.17), you can change the style and the color of the guides. To open the Guides & Grid section of the Preferences dialog box, choose Edit (Illustrator) ➪ Preferences ➪ Guides & Grid.

In the Guides section of this dialog box, you have the following options:

- **Color:** Choose a color from the list box or select Other to choose a color from the color picker. With guides, I like to use a darker, more vibrant color than a watered-down cyan. No matter which color you choose, keep it different from the Grid color, and ensure it contrasts with the colors you're using in your document.

- **Style:** You can set the guide style to dots or lines; which you choose is a matter of preference. However, you may want to pick the opposite of what you've chosen for grids to further differentiate the two.

Understanding Smart Guides

Smart Guides pop up to help you create a shape with precision, align objects with accuracy, and move and transform objects with ease. Figure 8.18 shows an example of a Smart Guide. To activate Smart Guides, choose View ➪ Smart Guides or press Ctrl+U (⌘+U).

NEW FEATURE   Smart Guides in Illustrator CS4 are really, really smart.

Check boxes allow you to turn these options on and off in the Smart Guides section of the Preferences dialog box, as shown in Figure 8.19. These are some of the Smart Guides display options:

- **Alignment Guides:** These let you view guidelines (thin lines that pop up when moving or copying objects) when using Smart Guides.

- **Anchor/Path Labels:** These hints pop up when you drag over your object. They tell you what each area is. For example, if you drag over a line, the hint pops up with the word "path." If you drag over an anchor point, the hint reads "anchor point."

- **Object Highlighting:** When you select this option, the object to which you point is highlighted.

- **Measurement Labels:** When you select this option, measurement labels are shown.

- **Transform Tools:** When you're rotating, scaling, or shearing an object with this option selected, Smart Guides appear to help you out.

- **Construction Guides:** As you create objects, these guides appear at the angles specified. You can choose presets in this dropdown list (popup menu). The preset angles are 0, 45, 90, and 135. The angles are shown in the box at the right. When you add a custom angle, it appears with the preset lines.

- **Custom Angles:** You can create a Custom Angle of your own in the boxes below the dropdown list (popup menu). To do so, simply type the angle in one of the empty boxes.

- **Snapping Tolerance:** Snapping Tolerance lets you choose how close an object must be to another object before the first object automatically snaps to the second object. You set the Snapping Tolerance in points; the lower the number, the closer you have to move the objects to each other. If the number is pretty high, an object snaps to another object if it's merely passing by.

FIGURE 8.18

With Smart Guides on, I rested the cursor on the object on the left. Smart Guides highlighted the path used to create the object and indicated that it's a path.

FIGURE 8.19

The Smart Guides section of the Preferences dialog box

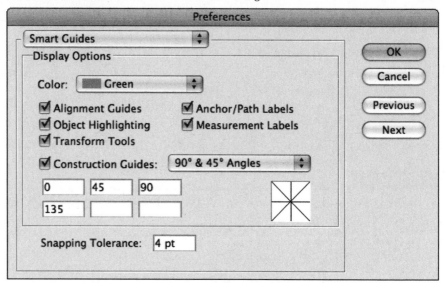

Measuring for Printing

Thinking ahead to the time when your job will print is always a good thing. Two of the most important areas of printing are the placement and sizing of your artwork within the Illustrator document. This section deals with production-oriented issues you may face while using Illustrator to create printable pieces.

Tiling

Often, you create something that's quite small, and you need to have several similar (but slightly different) copies of the artwork on the page at once. Setting up your artwork for optimal spacing and printing is referred to as tiling.

Illustrator can do tiling automatically if you have identical artwork to be tiled and provides a different set of tools you need to tile your artwork when each item will be a little different. A sample of tiled artwork is shown in Figure 8.20.

CROSS-REF For more on tiling, see Chapter 15.

To tile your artwork, follow these steps:

1. **Select the finished artwork.** For more on selecting artwork, see Chapter 6.

2. **Open the Move dialog box.** You can do this by double-clicking the Selection tool or by choosing Object ⇨ Transform ⇨ Move.

3. **Type the width of the art in the Horizontal field plus the distance you want for spacing.** You may need to experiment to find the correct value to use here.

4. **Type 0 (zero) in the Vertical field.**

5. **Click Copy.**

6. **Choose Object ⇨ Transform ⇨ Transform Again.** You can also press Ctrl+D (⌘+D). This creates another duplicate of the artwork. Do this until you have the right number of pieces across the page.

7. **Select the entire row of artwork.**

8. **Open the Move dialog box again.**

9. **Type 0 (zero) in the Horizontal field.**

10. **Type the height of the art in the Vertical field plus the distance you want for spacing.**

11. **Click Copy.**

12. **Choose Object ⇨ Transform ⇨ Transform Again.** Alternatively, you can press Ctrl+D (⌘+D). Again, this creates another duplicate of the row of artwork. Do this until you have the right number of pieces down the page, as shown in Figure 8.20.

13. **Using the appropriate tools, edit the individual copies of the artwork.**

Creating crop marks

Crop marks are little lines that are designed to help you cut (or crop) along the edges of your illustration after the document has been printed. Crops (that's the slang term; if you're even half cool, you won't say crop marks) don't intrude on the edges of the artwork but instead are offset a bit from the corners of where the edges are.

FIGURE 8.20

Artwork that has been tiled and repeated on a page. Then, each instance has been modified by using a different 3-D rotation.

You add crop marks using the Marks and Bleed pane of the Print dialog box, as shown in Figure 8.21.

Instead of using standard crop marks, you can choose to use Japanese Crop Marks, which look different yet are seemingly no more functional than regular crop marks. You make this selection in the Printer Mark Type dropdown list (popup menu) of the Print dialog box.

CROSS-REF For more on printing, see Chapter 18.

FIGURE 8.21

Use the Print dialog box to add crop marks.

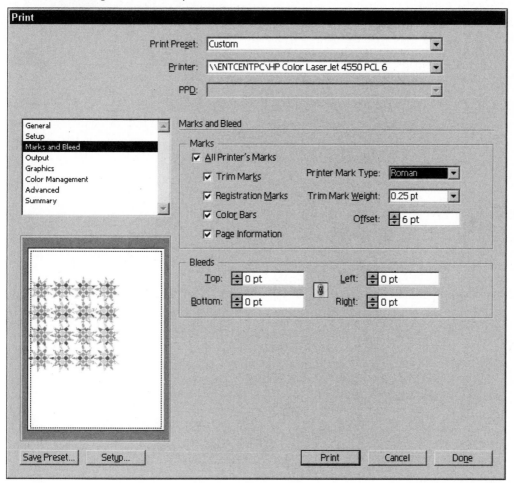

Summary

Illustrator documents can quickly become very complex. You need to learn how to organize the objects in your documents in order to work efficiently. In this chapter, you learned valuable organization techniques, including:

- Locking and hiding objects can help in creating illustrations.
- Grouping objects keeps artwork organized.
- You can use layers to effectively separate different sections of your artwork.
- Template layers are used in Illustrator to make your drawing easier and more precise, and it distinguishes them from template documents.
- Manual tracing allows you to produce unique effects.
- The Measure tool provides a quick way to measure distances in Illustrator documents.
- Measurements generated by the Measure tool appear in the Move dialog box the next time you open it.
- Guides can be created from any object.
- You can quickly create document guides by dragging out from the rulers.
- Use the Copy button within the Move dialog box to tile and repeat artwork.
- Use the Smart Guides feature to make aligning objects much easier.

Chapter 9

Working with Type

Fonts are a big deal to Illustrator users. For the seasoned graphic artist, the thousands of typefaces that are available provide a typesetting heaven on Earth. For a newcomer to Illustrator and typesetting, fonts can be overwhelming. Illustrator ships with about 300 Adobe PostScript Type 1 fonts; other fonts are available for purchase at costs that range from about $2 per face to hundreds of dollars for a family. (A font face is a single variation, while a font family typically includes quite a few variations.)

This chapter covers creating type with various type tools, all the different formatting available, and cool things to do with type on a path and outlined type.

Understanding Fonts

Fonts come in various formats, with each format having advantages and disadvantages over other formats. Fonts fall into the following categories: bitmap fonts, PostScript fonts (Type 1), TrueType fonts, OpenType fonts, and Multiple Master fonts.

Understanding bitmap fonts

Bitmap fonts are the original fonts used for computers. They consist of a series of dots inside a grid pattern and worked well both on-screen and on the dot-matrix printers that were prevalent at the time of their introduction.

Each character in a bitmap font has a certain number of dots that define its shape. Some bitmap fonts include different point sizes, with the smaller point sizes having fewer dots than the larger point sizes. The larger the point size of the bitmap fonts, the more detail is available and the better the letter looks.

Because bitmap fonts were originally designed for a computer screen, the dots in a bitmap font are set at 72 dpi (dots per inch). When you print a bitmap font on a laser printer, which has a resolution of at least 300 dpi, the letters tend to look blocky, even when their sizes are supported by the typeface.

Understanding PostScript fonts

Although PostScript fonts have in the past been the most popular font format in professional publishing circles, they're also the most confusing and frustrating fonts to use because they have two parts: the screen fonts (which are really bitmap fonts) and the printer fonts.

You need the printer fonts, as their name implies, for printing. Printer fonts consist of outlined shapes that get filled with as many dots as the printer can stuff into that particular shape. Because these printer fonts are mathematical outlines and not a certain number of dots, they make characters look good at any point size. In fact, PostScript printer fonts are device-independent, meaning that the quality of the type depends on the dpi of the printer (which is device-dependent). The higher the dpi, the smoother the curves and diagonal lines look. If printer fonts are missing, the printer either uses the corresponding bitmap font or substitutes another font whose printer font is available.

Adobe, just by coincidence, created the PostScript page description language based on outlines instead of dots, developed PostScript fonts, and also created typefaces in PostScript format called Type 1 format and Type 3 format. Since the rise of desktop publishing, the font standard has been PostScript.

Understanding TrueType fonts

The greatest advantage of TrueType fonts is that they have only one component — not separate screen fonts and printer fonts. Actually, many TrueType fonts do include screen fonts because hand-tuned screen fonts at small sizes tend to look better than filled outlines at screen resolution.

The quality of TrueType fonts is comparable to, if not better than, that of PostScript typefaces. Apple includes TrueType fonts with every new computer it sells. Microsoft includes a boatload of fonts with Windows, Office, and all the other applications it sells and licenses.

Understanding OpenType fonts

OpenType fonts take TrueType fonts a step further by including PostScript information. They also include a variety of features, such as *ligatures* (typographic replacement characters for certain letter pairs) and alternate *glyphs* that PostScript and TrueType don't offer. A glyph is the form of a character, such as a capital letter with a swash, making it a bit more exciting than the regular capital letter. Glyphs are covered in more detail later in this chapter. Ligatures are replacement characters for paired letters, such as ff, fi, and ffl. Illustrator offers an OpenType panel for you to specify alternate characters, such as ligatures. You open the OpenType panel by choosing Window ⇨ Type ⇨ OpenType. The OpenType option lets you enhance the look of your OpenType fonts.

Adding type with Multiple Master fonts

Multiple Master fonts, again from Adobe, provide a somewhat complex way to vary fonts. Normally, a typeface may come in several weights, such as bold, regular, light, and black. But what if you want a weight that's between bold and black? Usually, you're out of luck.

The theory behind Multiple Master fonts was that a font has two extremes — black and light, for example. Multiple Master technology creates any number of in-betweens that range from one extreme to the other. Multiple Masters don't stop with weights though. They also work to step between regular and oblique, wide and condensed, and serif (fonts that include the little detailed hooks on the end of most strokes) and sans serif (fonts without those hooks).

Although it seemed like a good idea when Adobe introduced the idea of Multiple Master fonts back in 1991, little interest was generated among users, and Adobe no longer develops this technology.

Understanding Basic Type Menu Commands

The Type menu, as shown in Figure 9.1, contains all of Illustrator's type controls (with the exception of the type tools).

FIGURE 9.1

The Type menu allows you to choose from various type-related commands.

You can change most of the Type options in the Character panel, as shown in Figure 9.2, by choosing Window ➪ Type ➪ Character or by pressing Ctrl+T (⌘+T). You can also change many text-related options using the Paragraph panel by choosing Window ➪ Type ➪ Paragraph or by pressing Alt+Ctrl+T (Option+⌘+T).

FIGURE 9.2

The Character panel provides access to many Type options.

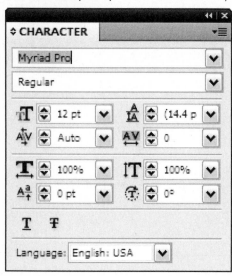

Type is set in Illustrator in blocks of continuous, linked text. In most cases, text blocks in Illustrator are *threaded* — meaning that the text automatically reflows to fit the linked text boxes if they're resized.

NOTE   When the term *paragraph* is mentioned, it's usually referring to the characters that are between Returns. If there are no Returns in a story, then that story is said to have one paragraph. Returns end paragraphs and begin new ones. There's always exactly one more paragraph in a story than there are Returns.

The following sections describe each of the Type menu options. The next four sections discuss the first four of these commands. The rest of the options are covered throughout this chapter.

Using the Font submenu

The Font submenu of the Type menu displays the typefaces in their actual form. The Font submenu displays all the fonts that are accessible from your user account (not necessarily all the fonts currently installed on your computer). A check mark appears next to the font that's currently selected; an indicator as to whether it's a TrueType, Type 1, or OpenType font also appears. If no check mark appears next to any of the fonts, more than one font is currently selected. Figure 9.3 shows the Font submenu.

FIGURE 9.3

Use the Font submenu to choose a typeface.

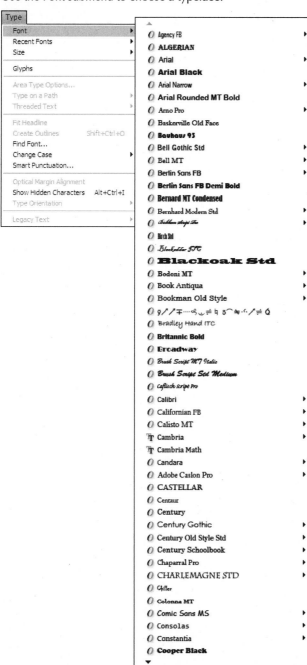

Understanding the Recent Fonts submenu

The Recent Fonts submenu of the Type menu displays the most recent fonts you've used in that document. The default setting for Recent Fonts is 5. You can change that number in the Type section of the Preferences dialog box. Access the Type preferences by choosing Edit ➪ Preferences ➪ Type (Illustrator ➪ Preferences ➪ Type). In this dialog box, you can set the number of recent fonts using the Number of Recent Fonts dropdown list (popup menu). The minimum for Recent Fonts is 1, and the maximum is 15.

Choosing a font size

Choose Type ➪ Size to display a submenu with Other and various point sizes listed. Choosing Other displays the Character panel with the font size text field highlighted so that you can type a specific font size. You can type any point size from 0.1 to 1296 in this text field.

A check mark appears in the Size submenu next to the point size that's currently selected. If the point size currently selected doesn't correspond to a point size in the Size submenu, a check mark appears next to the Other menu item. Point size for type is measured from the top of the ascenders (such as the top of a capital letter T) to the bottom of the descenders (such as the bottom of a low-ercase g). If no check mark appears next to any of the sizes, more than one size is currently selected (even if the different sizes are all Other sizes).

You can also increase and decrease the point size of type by using the keyboard shortcuts. Pressing Ctrl+Shift+> (⌘+Shift+>) increases the point size by the amount specified in the Size/Leading text field of the Type section of the Preferences dialog box. Pressing Ctrl+Shift+< (⌘+Shift+<) decreases the point size.

Yet another way to change point size is to use the Scale tool. Using the Scale tool to change point size lets you change to any size; that size is displayed in the Character panel as soon as you're finished scaling. Again, remember that the limit in scaling type is 1296 points; you can't exceed that limit even with the Scale tool unless the type has been converted to outlined paths, at which time you can scale to any size.

Using alternate glyphs

A glyph is the form of a character of text. Some fonts have multiple forms for a letter, and the Glyphs panel is where you can choose those other options. Glyphs are also the ornamental forms, swashes, ligatures, and fractions that are part of OpenType fonts. Choosing Glyphs from the Type menu displays the Glyphs panel, as shown in Figure 9.4. If no type is selected, the panel displays Entire Font in the Show list (popup menu). The other choice in the Show list (popup menu) is for Alternates for Current Selection. Use this panel to view some of the special character fonts, such as Symbol or Zapf Dingbats.

FIGURE 9.4

The Glyphs panel allows you to choose alternate glyphs for use in your documents.

Using the Type Tools

You use the type tools to create and later edit type. The default tool is the standard Type tool, which creates both individual type and area type. Individual type is created when you click with the Type tool, creating a point for the type to begin. Area type is created by dragging a box that the type then fills. The popup tools on the tearaway Type panel, as shown in Figure 9.5, are the Type tool, the Area Type tool, the Type on a Path tool, the Vertical Type tool, the Vertical Area Type tool, and the Vertical Type on a Path tool. Each of the type tools displays a different cursor.

FIGURE 9.5

The type tools provide many different ways to create interesting text.

Type tool   Type on a Path tool   Vertical Area Type tool

Area Type tool   Vertical Type tool   Vertical Type on a Path tool

You can select type in Illustrator with the Selection tool, in which case all the type in the text block is modified. You select type with a type tool by dragging across either characters or lines — every character from the initial click until the release of the mouse button is selected. Double-clicking with a type tool highlights the entire word you clicked, including the space (but not the punctuation) after it. Triple-clicking (clicking three times in the same place) highlights an entire paragraph.

You can add new type to an existing story by clicking with a type tool where you want the new type to begin and then typing. If type is highlighted when you begin typing, the highlighted type is replaced with the new type.

The original reason for the inclusion of a vertical type capability in Illustrator was for Japanese type (commonly referred to as Kanji) compatibility. Vertical type can also have a number of specialized uses. The following sections that discuss the different kinds of type blocks (Point, Rectangle, Area, and Path) address both normal (horizontal) type and vertical type capabilities.

Using the Type tool

With the Type tool, you can do everything you need to do with type. Clicking in any empty part of your document creates *individual type*, an anchor point to which the type aligns. Type created as individual type doesn't wrap automatically; instead, you must manually press Enter (Return) and start typing the next line. Individual type is usually used for creating smaller portions of type, such as labels and headlines.

Clicking and dragging with the Type tool creates *area type* — type that's bordered by a box.

As the Type tool passes over a closed path, it changes automatically into the Area Type tool. Clicking a closed path results in type that fills the shape of the area you clicked. Holding Alt (Option) as you pass over a closed path changes the tool into the Type on a Path tool.

If the Type tool crosses over an open path, it becomes the Type on a Path tool. Clicking an open path places type on the path, with the baseline of the type aligning along the curves and angles of the path. Holding Alt (Option) when the Type tool is over an open path changes it into the Area Type tool.

This intelligent switching of type tools by Illustrator keeps you from having to choose different type tools when you want a different kind of type.

You can toggle between the Type tool and the Vertical Type tool by pressing Shift. In fact, pressing Shift with the Area Type and Type on a Path tools automatically toggles those tools to their Vertical Type counterparts. This holds true even if you press Shift along with Alt (Option) (when toggling between Area Type and Type on a Path tools).

Using the Area Type tool

You use the Area Type tool for filling closed or open paths with type. You can even fill compound paths in Illustrator. Figure 9.6 shows an example of how the Area Type tool fills a path.

Using the Type on a Path tool

You use the Type on a Path tool for running type along any path in Illustrator. This is a great tool for placing type on the edges of a circle or wiggly lines. Figure 9.7 shows an example of type on a path.

FIGURE 9.6

The Area Type tool creates text that fills a path.

Area type fills
path areas with type,
 much like this text is doing
   right now. You use the Area Type tool for filling closed or
    open paths with type. You can even fill compound paths in Illustrator.
     Figure 9.6 shows an example of how the Area Type tool fills a path. Area
      type fills path areas with type, much like this text is doing right now. You
       use the Area Type tool for filling closed or open paths with type. You
        can even fill compound paths in Illustrator. Figure 9.6 shows an
         example of how the Area Type tool fills a path. Area type fills path
          areas with type, much like this text is doing right now. You use the
           Area Type tool for filling closed or open paths with type. You
            can even fill compound paths in Illustrator. Figure 9.6 shows
             an example of how the Area Type tool fills a path. Area
              type fills path areas with type, much like this text is
               doing right now. You use the Area Type tool for
                filling closed or open paths with type. You
                 can even fill compound paths in Illus-
                  trator. Figure 9.6 shows an
                   example of

FIGURE 9.7

The Type on a Path tool can create text that follows a path.

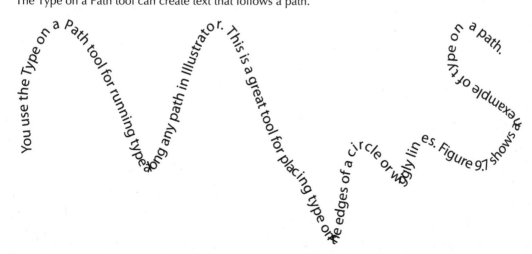

Using the Vertical Type tool

Vertical type will probably remind you of the signs on the front of an old-time movie theater where the letters of the theater's name were stacked vertically rather than horizontally. The effect can be rather stunning when used properly. For the most part, the Vertical Type tool works like the regular Type tool, but instead of placing characters side by side, characters are placed from top to bottom, as shown in Figure 9.8. Note that this is not the same as simply rotating the text 90°. Vertical text really isn't that common, as it was added to Illustrator primarily to allow Kanji (such as Chinese and Japanese characters) writing, which is usually done vertically instead of horizontally.

FIGURE 9.8

Vertical type can create an interesting effect.

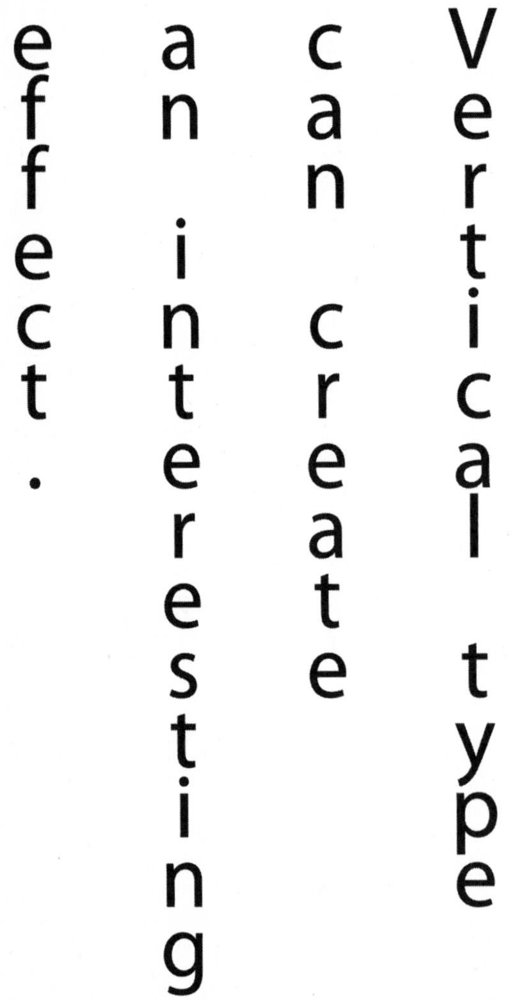

Creating Individual Type

To create type with a single point defining its location, use the Type tool to click a single location within the document window where there are no paths. A blinking insertion point appears, signifying that type will appear where that point is located. When you type on the keyboard, text appears in the document at that insertion point.

> **CAUTION** When creating individual type, remember that only a hard return forces a new line of text to be created. If no returns are used, text eventually runs right off the document. When importing text used as individual type, be sure that the text contains hard returns; otherwise, the text will run into oblivion. Hard returns can be added after importing (via the File ⇨ Place command), but doing so may be difficult.

Placing Area Type in a Rectangle

You can create type in a rectangle in two ways. The easiest way is by clicking and dragging the Type tool diagonally, which creates a rectangle as you drag. The blinking insertion point appears in the top row of text, with its horizontal location dependent on the text alignment choice. Choosing flush-right alignment forces the insertion point to appear in the upper-right corner; centered alignment puts the insertion point in the center of the top row; and flush-left alignment, or one of the justification methods, makes the insertion point appear in the upper-left corner. Choose any alignment option in the Paragraph panel or by pressing the appropriate keyboard command (refer to the Appendix for a list of type alignment keyboard commands). Access this panel by choosing Window ⇨ Type ⇨ Paragraph or by pressing Alt+Ctrl+T (Option+⌘+T).

If you press Shift while drawing the rectangle, the rectangle is constrained to a perfect square. There's no need to drag from the upper left to the lower right — you can drag from any corner to its opposite, whichever way is most convenient.

To create type in a rectangle of specific proportions, click once in the document window with the Rectangle tool. The Rectangle Size dialog box opens, and you can type the information needed. Choose the Type tool and then click the edge of the rectangle. The type fills the rectangle as you type.

> **CROSS-REF** For more on the using the Rectangle tool, see Chapter 5.

> **NOTE** If you use a rectangle as a type rectangle, it's always a type rectangle, even if you remove the text.

If you need to create a type container that's a precise size but don't want to draw a rectangle first, open the Info panel by choosing Window ⇨ Info or by pressing F8. As you drag the Type cursor, watch the information in the Info panel, which displays the dimensions of the type area. When the W text field is the width you want and the H text field is the height you want, release the mouse button.

Working with Type Areas

For type to exist in Illustrator, you must first define a type area. You can never have type outside these areas because type is treated very differently from any other object in Illustrator.

You can create different kinds of type areas:

- **Individual type:** Type that exists around a single point clicked with the standard Type tool
- **Area type:** Type that flows within a specific open or closed path
- **Type on a path:** Type whose baseline is attached to a specific open or closed path
- **Vertical type:** Type that flows vertically rather than horizontally. As with normal horizontal type, vertical type can be individual type, area type, or type on a path.

Figure 9.9 shows examples of the variations of type you can create in Illustrator. In the figure, all the paths are selected to provide a clearer picture of how the type areas compare.

FIGURE 9.9

This figure shows the different kinds of type areas that you can create using the type tools.

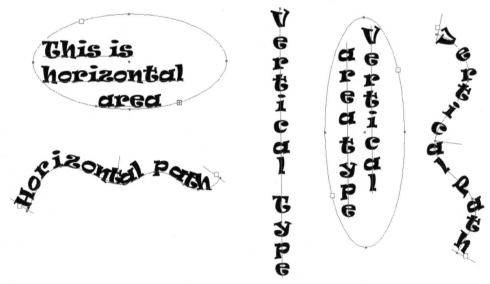

Creating Area Type

To create type within an area, first create a path that confines the area of your type. You can make the path closed or open and any size. Remember that the area of the path should be close to the size needed for the amount of text (at the point size that it needs to fit). After you create the path, choose the Area Type tool, position the type cursor over the edge of the path, and then click.

The type in Figure 9.10 flows into the outline of a polygon that has been distorted.

FIGURE 9.10

Area type created so the text flows inside the outlines of a modified polygon

To   create
type within an area, first
create a path that confines the area
of your type. You can make the path closed or
open, and any size. Remember that the area of the
path should be close to the size needed for the
amount of text (at the point size that it needs to fit). After
you create the path, choose the Area Type tool and position
the type cursor over the edge of the path and click. To create
type within an area, first create a path that confines the area
of your type. You can make the path closed or open, and any
size. Remember that the area of the path should be close to
the size needed for the amount of text (at the point size that
it needs to fit). After you create the path, choose the Area
Type tool and position the type cursor over the edge of the
path and click. To create type within an area, first create
a path that confines the area of your type. You can
make the path closed or open, and any size.
Remember that the area of the path
should be close to the size
needed for the
a m o

Using area type functions

When working with area type, you can choose several options. First, you need to have some area type selected. Then, double-click the Area Type tool or choose Type ➪ Area Type Options to access the Area Type Options dialog box, as shown in Figure 9.11.

You can set these options:

- **Width/Height:** Defines the area of the type
- **Rows/Columns:** Sets the number, size, and gutter of the horizontal rows and vertical columns
- **Offset:** Determines how far the text is offset from the edge of the path area
- **Text Flow:** Sets whether the text flows left to right and top to bottom or top to bottom and left to right

Click the Preview check box to see the settings you set before clicking OK or pressing Enter (Return) or clicking Cancel.

FIGURE 9.11

The Area Type Options dialog box allows you to set several parameters for area type.

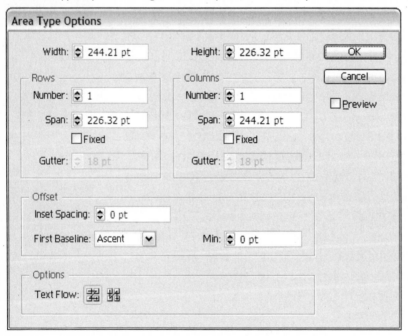

Choosing good shapes for area type

What exactly constitutes a good shape to use for area type? As a rule, gently curved shapes are better than harsh, jagged ones. Type tends to flow better into the larger lumps created by smoothly curving paths.

Try to avoid creating paths with wild or tight curves. Other designs that can cause problems are hourglass shapes or any closed path that has an area where the sides are almost touching. Type flows into a smoothly curved area, but it has trouble flowing into a sharp, spiky shape.

Try to make the top and bottom boundaries of the path have less bumpiness than the sides. This reduces the number of times that type jumps from one area to another.

TIP For the best results with area type, make the type small relative to the path and justify it by pressing Ctrl+Shift+J (⌘+Shift+J). This ensures that the type flows up against the edges of the path.

Outlining areas of area type

Placing a stroke on the path surrounding area type can be a great visual effect, but doing so and getting good results can be a bit tricky. If the stroke is thicker than 1 or 2 points, and you don't want the type to run into the edges of the stroke, there are a few things you can do. The best way to set the offset value is to use the Area Type Options dialog box to type the value you want the text to offset away from the path. To do so, follow these steps:

1. **Create a path for your Area type with any drawing tool — for example, the Rectangle tool is a good tool to use.** For more on the drawing tools, see Chapters 4 and 5.

2. **Click the shape with the Area Type tool.**

3. **Type your text.**

4. **With the text selected, double-click the Area Type tool or choose Type ⇨ Area Type Options.** This opens the Area Type Options dialog box. For more on the options in this box, see the section on this topic earlier in this chapter.

5. **Type the value by which you want to offset the type away from the edge of the path.** You type this in the Inset Spacing area under the Offset section of the dialog box.

6. **Click Preview to see the result.**

7. **If you like what you see, click OK.**

Selecting carefully with area type

Probably the most overlooked rule when it comes to manipulating area type and the paths that create the type boundaries is the simple fact that Illustrator treats the path and the type equally, unless you choose the path with the Direct Selection (or Group Selection) tool. Area type is selected when you see an underline under all the characters in the area.

When using the transformation tools, be sure that if you don't want to change any of the characteristics of the type that you select just the path. Use the Group Selection tool to click once on the deselected path, and Illustrator selects only the path, not the type. If you transform the area text when you have both selected, the transformation applies to the text as well as the path.

 If you have both the type and the path selected, the transformations affect both the type and the path.

 For more on the selection tools, see Chapter 6.

Changing the area, not the type

Sometimes, you need to adjust the path that makes up the area of the area type — for example, when you scale a path up or down so that the text flows better. The trick here is to ensure that you select the entire path without selecting any of the characters. To do this, deselect the type and then select the path with the Group Selection tool (the hollow [white] arrow with the + sign).

Now any changes you make affect only the path, allowing you to scale it, rotate it, or change its paint style attributes without directly affecting the text within it. Figure 9.12 shows a transformed path, which allows the text inside to flow differently.

You can also use the Direct Selection tool to move individual points and control handles, and you can also use path editing tools to add, modify, and delete anchor points.

Type Color and the Color of Type

Color of type and type color are two different things. You can paint type in Illustrator and make it any one of millions of different shades, which determines the color we normally think of.

The color of type, on the other hand, is the way the type appears in the document and is more indicative of the light or dark attributes of the text. The actual red-green-blue (RGB) colors of the type do work into this appearance, but the weight of the type and the tracking and kerning (discussed later in this chapter) often have a much more profound effect on the color of type.

To easily see the color of type, unfocus your eyes as you look at your document or turn the page upside down. Obviously, this works better on a printed area than on-screen (boy, those monitors get heavy when you hold them upside down). But you can still get the gist of the way the document appears when you view it on your monitor. Dark and light areas become much more apparent when you can't read the actual words on the path. This method of unfocusing your eyes to look at a page also works well when trying to see the look of a page and how it was designed. Often, unfocusing or turning the page upside down emphasizes the fact that you don't have enough white space or that all the copy seems to blend together.

Heavy type weights, such as bold, heavy, and black, make type appear darker on a page. Type kerned and tracked very tightly also seems to give the type a darker feel.

The x-height of type (the height to which the lowercase letters, such as an x, rise) is another factor that determines the color of type. Certain italic versions of typefaces can make the text seem lighter, although a few typefaces make text look darker because of the additional area that the thin strokes of the italic type cover.

With RGB colors, you can make type stand out by making it appear darker or you can make it blend into the page when you make it lighter. When you add smartly placed images near the type, your page can come alive with color.

FIGURE 9.12

You can edit the original area type shape (left) to change only the text flow, not the type (right). (Poem by John Keats)

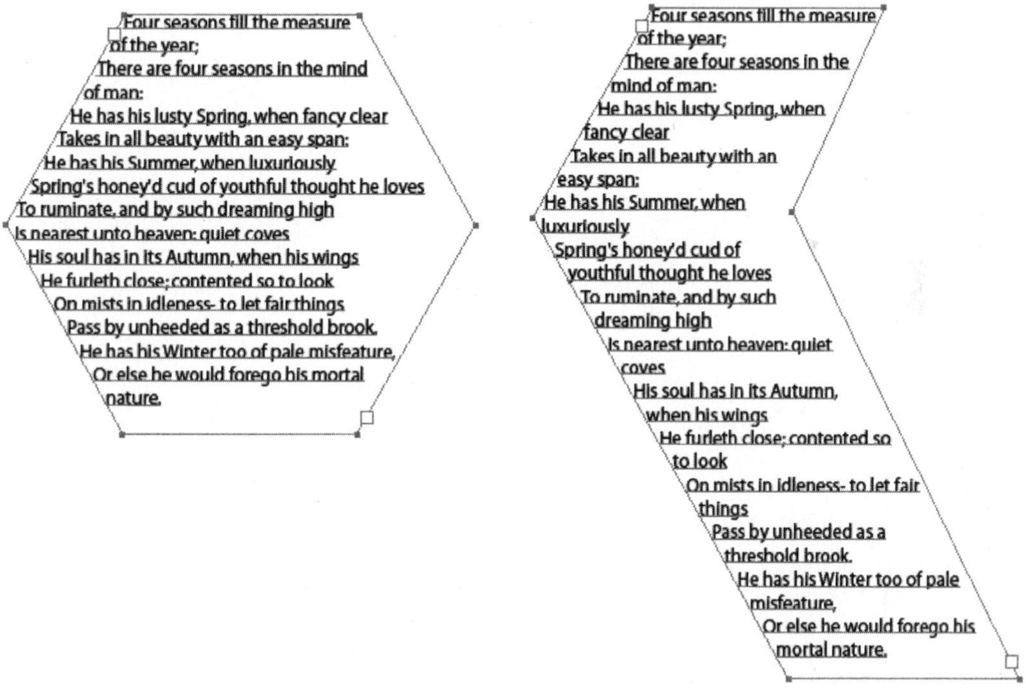

Flowing area type into shapes

You can do all sorts of nifty things with type that you flow into areas — from unusual column designs to fascinating shapes. Using nonrectangular columns can liven up a publication quite easily. Some magazines use curved columns that are easy to read and lend a futuristic, hip look to the publication. Angled and curved columns are simple to make in Illustrator by creating the shape of the column and flowing area type from one shape to the next.

Traditionally, forcing type into an irregular (nonrectangular) area was quite a task. The typesetter had to set several individual lines of type, each specified by the art director or client to be a certain length so that when all the text was put together, the text formed the shape. This is probably the main reason the world has not seen much of this, except in the portfolios of overly zealous art students.

For example, you can give a report on toxic waste more impact by shaping the text into the form of a hypodermic needle. Or you can make a seasonal ad in the shape of a Christmas tree. Look at some of the Absolut Vodka ads to see what has been done to flow text onto that all-too-familiar bottle.

Wrapping type around paths

You can have type wrap around any path. To do this, select the path (or paths) you want to have the type wrap around and then choose Object ➪ Text Wrap ➪ Make. In the dialog box that appears, type the distance of how far you want the text to be from the path in the Offset field and then click OK.

In order for type to wrap around paths, the type must be under (below) the path and on the same layer as the path.

Placing Type on a Path

The unique thing about type on a path is that when the path is not visible, the type becomes the path, as shown in Figure 9.13. This can produce some really fascinating results, especially when combined with various fonts of different weights, styles, colors, and special characters. You can even give the path a fill or stroke by selecting it with the Direct Selection tool and then applying a fill or stroke.

Although using the Type on a Path tool can create some great effects, it has one glitch. You usually run into trouble when the path you're using has either corner anchor points or very sharp curves. Letters often crash (run into one another) when this occurs. Besides the most obvious way to avoid this problem, which is to not use paths with corner anchor points and sharp curves, you can sometimes *kern* (add or subtract space between specific pairs of characters) the areas where the letters crash until they aren't touching anymore.

When kerning type on a path, be sure to kern from the flush side first. For example, if the type is flush left, start your kerning from the left side and then work to the right. If you start on the wrong end, the letters you kern apart move along the path until they aren't in an area that needs kerning, but other letters appear there instead.

FIGURE 9.13

Type set on a path actually becomes the path.

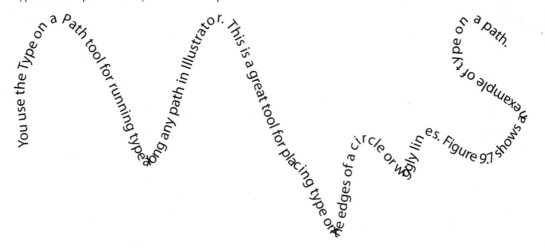

Another method of fixing crashed letters is to tweak the path with the Direct Selection tool. Carefully adjusting both anchor points and control handles can often easily fix crashes and letters that have huge amounts of space between them.

To create type on a path:

1. **First, create a path in your document.** You should create a path that doesn't cross over itself.

2. **Click the path with the Type on a Path tool.** This creates an insertion point along the path. This works whether the path is a closed path or an open path.

3. **Start typing your text.** Type aligns to the insertion point; if the type is set to flush left, the left edge of the type aligns to the location where the Type on a Path tool was first clicked.

TIP Instead of typing your text in Illustrator, you can copy and paste it from another application using the Edit ➪ Paste command.

Adding effects to type on a path

Under the Type menu, you can wrap type on a path by changing some of the settings. After you create type on a path, choose from the following effects: Rainbow, Skew, 3D Ribbon, Stair Step, or Gravity. To adjust the settings, choose Type ➪ Type on a Path ➪ Type on a Path Options to display the Type on a Path Options dialog box, as shown in Figure 9.14, or double-click the Type on a Path tool.

FIGURE 9.14

The Type on a Path Options dialog box allows you to add some special effects to type.

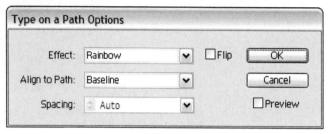

In this dialog box, you can choose the following:

- **Effect:** Choose from Rainbow, Skew, 3D Ribbon, Stair Step, and Gravity, as shown in Figure 9.15. The Rainbow effect places each letter's baseline along a path curved like a rainbow. Skew keeps all the letters' vertical edges strictly vertical. 3D Ribbon keeps all the letters' horizontal edges strictly horizontal. Stair Step does exactly what you expect: It raises (or lowers, depending on the settings) each letter as if the text were climbing (or descending) stairs. Gravity puts the center of each letter on the baseline of the path with increasing rotation.

- **Align to Path:** This option alters the path's alignment, with the choices being Ascender, Descender, Center, or Baseline, as shown in Figure 9.16. Choosing Ascender aligns the type higher on the path in line with the top of the highest part of the letter (an h, for example). The Descender option aligns the type lower on the path in line with the hanging part of the letter (a g, for example). Choosing Center aligns the type equally on the path, with half being above the line and half being below the path. The Baseline option aligns the base of the type (not the descender) to the path.

- **Spacing:** This allows you to space the path up or down from its original position.

- **Flip:** This option flips the type to the opposite side.

- **Preview:** This allows you to preview your changes before you click OK to commit to them.

FIGURE 9.15

The Type on a Path Effect options

FIGURE 9.16

The Align to Path options

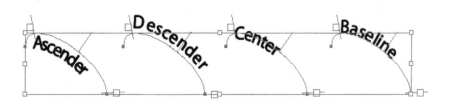

Using vertical type

Vertical type is a fascinating capability in Illustrator. If you use Kanji (including Japanese or Chinese) characters, you'll find it invaluable. But even if you don't, you may find some interesting uses for setting type vertically rather than horizontally.

You can make your type appear vertical instead of horizontal in two ways. You can create type using any of the three Vertical Type tools or you can convert horizontal type into vertical type with Type ⇨ Type Orientation ⇨ Vertical. Figure 9.17 shows area type both horizontally and vertically. Note that vertical type takes up a great deal more space than horizontal type and flows top to bottom and right to left.

Most of Illustrator's standard character and paragraph panel changes work with vertical type but not always in ways you expect. For example, type is set on a centerline, not a baseline. The centerline runs vertically through the center of each character. Table 9.1 lists the differences in the way each major function works.

TABLE 9.1

Vertical Type Functions

Function	Difference
Font	Same as standard
Size	Same as standard
Leading	Changes the amount of space between the vertical lines of type, measured from centerline to centerline
Kerning/Tracking	Kerning changes the amount of space between each pair of characters. Tracking changes the amount of space between characters. Because very few Roman characters have both ascenders and descenders, tracking and kerning substantially can really help eliminate the excess white space between characters that makes vertical type so hard to read.
Vertical Scale	Changes the width of the characters
Horizontal Scale	Changes the height of the characters
Baseline Shift	Moves the type left (negative values) and right (positive values) along the centerline
Flush Left	Words are flush top
Center	Words are vertically centered
Flush Right	Words are flush bottom
Justify Full Lines	Words on full (vertical) lines are justified from top to bottom
Justify All Lines	This vertically justifies all the lines.
Left Indent	Top is indented. Positive numbers move the text down, and negative numbers move the text up.
Right Indent	Bottom is indented, with numbers working like Left Indent
First Line Indent	The rightmost line is indented. Again, positive numbers move the text down, and negative numbers move the text up.
Space Before Paragraph	Paragraphs go from right to left, so this control increases the space to the right of the selected paragraph(s).
Auto Hyphenate	Hyphenates words the same way as horizontal type, but the hyphens appear at the bottom of each line.
Hang Punctuation	Punctuation hangs above and below the text area
Tab Ruler	Appears to the right of text areas in vertical form
Create Outlines	Same as standard

FIGURE 9.17

Vertical type (left) and the same type reoriented to horizontal (right)

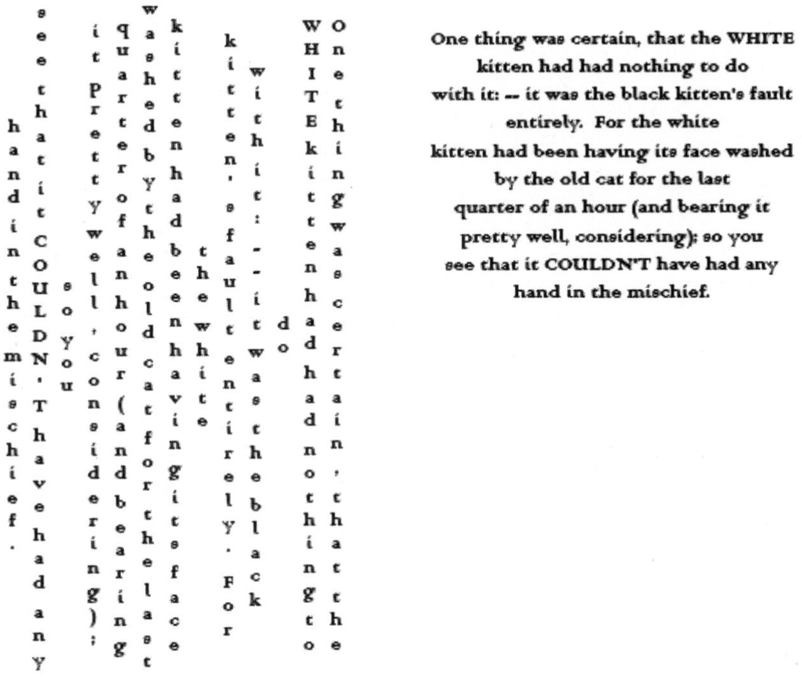

One thing was certain, that the WHITE
kitten had had nothing to do
with it: -- it was the black kitten's fault
entirely. For the white
kitten had been having its face washed
by the old cat for the last
quarter of an hour (and bearing it
pretty well, considering); so you
see that it COULDN'T have had any
hand in the mischief.

Selecting Type

Before you can make changes to text, you must first select it. You can select text in two ways: You can select type areas with a selection tool, which selects every character in the type area, or you can select characters individually or in groups with any of the type tools.

To select the entire type area or multiple type areas, click the type or the baseline of a line of type within the type area you want to select. Any changes made in the Type menu, Font menu, Character panel, or Paragraph panel affect every character in the selected type areas.

To select individual characters within a type area, you must use a type tool. As you near text that has been typed in the document, the dotted lines surrounding the cursor disappear. The hot spot of the type cursor is the place where the short horizontal bar crosses the vertical bar.

To select an individual character, drag across the character you want to select. As you select a character, its color reverses, so black text appears white. To select more than one character, drag left or right across multiple characters; all characters from the location you originally clicked to the current location of the cursor are highlighted. If you drag up with the cursor over straight text, you select all the characters to the left and all the characters to the right of the cursor's current location. Dragging down does the reverse. The more lines you drag up or down, the more lines you select.

To select one word at a time (and the space that follows it), double-click the word you want to select. The word and the space after it reverse. The reason that Illustrator selects the space following the word has to do with the number of times you copy, cut, and paste words from within sentences. For example, to remove the word Lazy in the phrase "The lazy boy," you double-click the word "lazy" and press Backspace (Delete). The phrase then becomes "The boy," which only has one space where the word Lazy used to be. To select several words, double-click and drag the Type cursor across the words you want to select. Illustrator selects each word you touch with the cursor, from the location you initially double-click to the current location. Dragging to the previous or next line selects additional lines, with at least a word on the first line double-clicked and one word on the dragged-to line.

For the nimble-fingered clickers, you can also click three times to select a paragraph. Triple-clicking anywhere inside the paragraph selects the entire paragraph, including the hard Return at the end of the paragraph (if there is one). Triple-clicking and dragging selects successive paragraphs if you move the cursor up or down while pressing the mouse button during the third click.

To select all the text within a type area with a type tool, click once in the type area and then choose Select ➪ Select All or press Ctrl+A (⌘+A). You can select text only in contiguous blocks. You have no way to select two words in two different locations of the same type area without selecting all the text between them.

You can also select type through the use of Shift. Click one spot (I'll call it the beginning) and then Shift+click another spot. The characters between the beginning and the Shift+click are selected. Successive Shift+clicks select characters from the beginning to the current location of the most recent Shift+click.

Editing Type

Illustrator has limited text-editing features. By clicking once within a type area, a blinking insertion point appears. If you begin typing, characters appear where the blinking insertion point is. Pressing Delete removes the character to the right of the insertion point.

The arrow keys on your keyboard move the blinking insertion point around in the direction of the arrow. The right arrow moves the insertion point one character to the right, and the left arrow moves the insertion point one character to the left. The up arrow moves the insertion point to the previous line; the down arrow moves the insertion point to the next line.

Pressing Ctrl (⌘) speeds up the movement of the insertion point. Ctrl+→ (⌘+→) or Ctrl+← (⌘+←) moves the insertion point to the next or preceding word, and Ctrl+↓ (⌘+↓) or Ctrl+↑ (⌘+↑) moves the insertion point to the next or preceding paragraph.

TIP **Pressing Shift while moving the insertion point around with the arrows selects all the characters that the insertion point passes over. This also works for the Ctrl+arrow (⌘+arrow) movements.**

When you select characters with a type tool, typing anything deletes the selected characters and replaces them with what you're currently typing. Pressing Backspace (Delete) when characters are selected deletes all the selected characters. If you paste type by pressing Ctrl+V (⌘+V) when you have characters selected, the selected characters are replaced with the pasted characters.

Using the Type Panels

Illustrator offers a variety of type panels. The Character, Paragraph, and OpenType panels are tabbed together. The Tabs panel is on its own. There's also a Glyphs panel. You can create character and paragraph styles and keep them in the Character Styles or Paragraph Styles panel. You can change typeface, style, alignment, kerning, and so much more with the panels.

Working with the Character panel

The easiest way to change the attributes of characters is by using the Character panel, as shown in Figure 9.18. Many of the changes in the Character panel are also available as options in the Type menu. As a rule, if you've more than one change to make, it's better to do it in the Character panel than the menu, even if just so that everything you need is in one place.

Character attribute changes affect only the letters that are selected, with the exception of leading (explained later), which should probably really be in the Paragraph panel.

TIP **You can change several character attributes by increments. The increments are set in the General and Type sections of the Preferences dialog box. You can change increments for point size, leading, baseline shift, and tracking/kerning values. Where appropriate, the key commands for each attribute change are listed in the following sections.**

You can use Tab to move across the different text fields in the Character panel. In addition to Tab tabbing forward through the text fields, pressing Shift+Tab tabs backward through the text fields.

FIGURE 9.18

The Character panel allows you to set a number of character properties in one place.

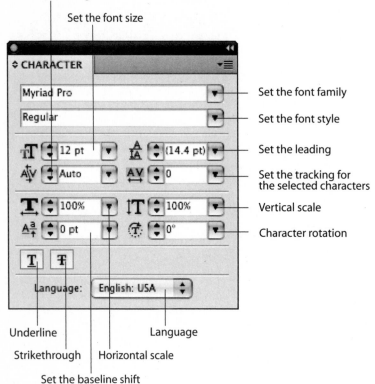

Set the kerning between two characters

Set the font size

Set the font family

Set the font style

Set the leading

Set the tracking for the selected characters

Vertical scale

Character rotation

Underline

Strikethrough

Set the baseline shift

Horizontal scale

Language

NOTE   Choosing Edit ⟳ Undo or pressing Ctrl+Z (⌘+Z) doesn't undo items typed in the Character panel while you're still in the text field. To undo something, you must first move along (by tabbing) to the next text field, undo the change, and then Shift+Tab back. Canceling (Esc) doesn't cancel what you've typed but instead bounces you back to editing the text (if you choose a type tool).

TIP   All the text fields in the Character panel have both a list with common values in them for quick access and up and down arrows to the left of each text field. These arrows increase (up) and decrease (down) the values of each of the currently selected text fields. Pressing Shift while clicking the little arrow buttons makes the change with each press even greater.

You can use the keyboard to press these buttons. When the text field is highlighted, press the up arrow on your keyboard to press the up arrow button; press the down arrow on your keyboard to press the down arrow button. Press Shift at the same time to jump the value by a greater amount.

Changing fonts and styles

The top field on the Character panel is called Set the font family. When you click the Set the font family field triangle, the list of fonts and how they look displays (that is, the fonts are displayed using actual characters from the font family). This also happens when you choose Font from the Type menu.

You can change the font style by clicking the Set the font style field triangle. The options that appear are based on the current font that's selected — typically, styles such as bold and italic appear here.

Measuring type

At 72 points, the letter I is about 50 points tall. In inches, that's just under ¾ inch. To get better results for specially sized capital letters, a good rule is that every 100 points is about a 1-inch capital letter (because the height of a font includes the descenders). This works for most typefaces and only for the first several inches, but it's a good start to getting capital letters that are sized pretty accurately.

Curves in capital letters are yet another wrench thrown into the equation. In many typefaces, the bottom and top of the letter O go beneath the baseline and above the ascender height of most squared letters. Serifs on certain typefaces may also cross these lines.

You measure type from the top of the ascenders (such as the top of a capital T) to the bottom of the descenders (such as the bottom of a lowercase p). So, when people tell you they want a capital I that's 1-inch high, you can't just say, "Oh, there are 72 points in an inch, so I'll create a 72-point I for them."

Changing type size

The text field on the left below the Set the font style text field is the Set the font size text field. You type the desired point size (from 0.1 point to 1296 points in increments of .001 point), and any selected characters increase or decrease to that particular point size. Next to the Set the font size text field, you find a menu triangle, which lists the standard point sizes available. The point size for type is always measured from the top of the ascenders to the bottom of the descenders. You can increase or decrease the point size with the keyboard by typing Ctrl+Shift+> (⌘+Shift+>) to increase and Ctrl+Shift+< (⌘+Shift+<) to decrease the point size by the increment specified in the Preferences dialog box. Figure 9.19 shows the results of changing the font size of various individual characters using the keyboard commands.

FIGURE 9.19

Original type on top; adjusted point size using the key commands on bottom

illustrator

illustrator

> **TIP** The keyboard commands for increasing and decreasing typographic attributes, such as point size, leading, baseline shift, and tracking, are more than just other ways to change those attributes. Instead, they're invaluable for making changes when the selected type has more than one different value of that attribute within it. For example, if some of the characters have a point size of 10 and some have a point size of 20, using the keyboard command (with an increment set to 2 points) changes the type to 12 and 22 points. This is tedious to do separately, especially if there are multiple sizes or just a few sizes scattered widely about. See Appendix A for a thorough list of keyboard commands for type functions.

Adjusting the leading

Next to the Set the font size text field, you find the Set the leading text field. Leading is the spacing between lines. In this text field, you type the desired leading value between 0.1 point and 1296 points, in increments of .001 point. To the right of the Set the leading text field is a popup menu triangle, from which you can choose common leading values. In Illustrator, leading is measured from the baseline of the current line up to the baseline of the preceding line, as shown in Figure 9.20. The distance between these two baselines is the amount of leading. The type in this figure is set to 24 points, with various leading amounts between different lines.

If you change the Character panel's leading text field from the number that displays there by default, the Auto entry in the Set the leading list becomes deselected. The Auto option, when clicked, makes the leading exactly 120% of the point size. This is just great when the type is 10 points because the leading is 12 points, a common point size-to-leading relationship. But as point size goes up, leading should become proportionately less, until, at around 72 points, it's less than the point size. Instead, when Auto Leading is clicked (or you can type it into the field), 72-point type has an 86.5-point leading. That's lots of unsightly white space.

You can also set Leading increments in the Type section of the Preferences dialog box.

FIGURE 9.20

This shows how leading affects the appearance and readability of text.

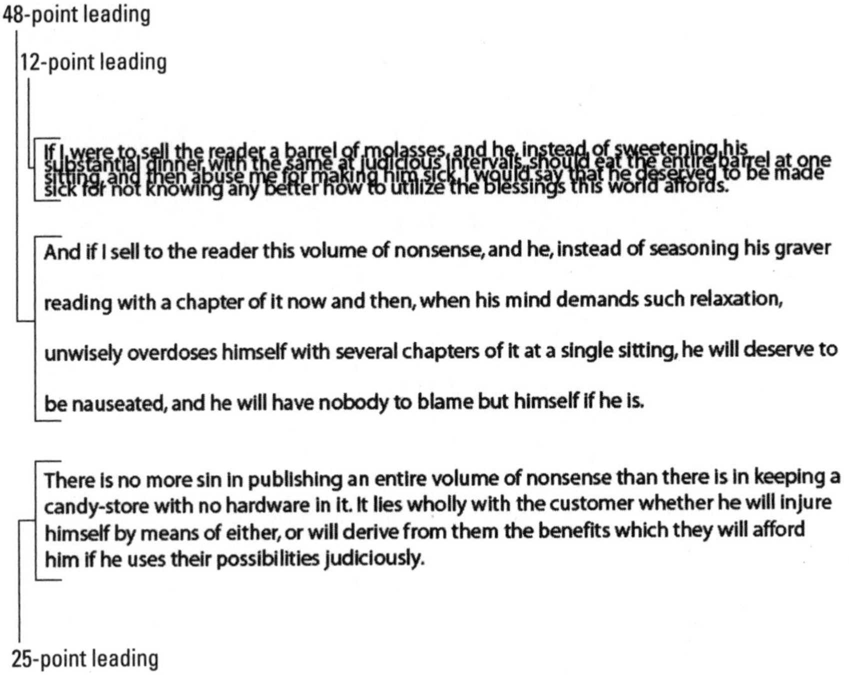

48-point leading

12-point leading

If I were to sell the reader a barrel of molasses, and he, instead of sweetening his
substantial dinner with the same at judicious intervals, should eat the entire barrel at one
sitting, and then abuse me for making him sick, I would say that he deserved to be made
sick for not knowing any better how to utilize the blessings this world affords.

And if I sell to the reader this volume of nonsense, and he, instead of seasoning his graver

reading with a chapter of it now and then, when his mind demands such relaxation,

unwisely overdoses himself with several chapters of it at a single sitting, he will deserve to

be nauseated, and he will have nobody to blame but himself if he is.

There is no more sin in publishing an entire volume of nonsense than there is in keeping a
candy-store with no hardware in it. It lies wholly with the customer whether he will injure
himself by means of either, or will derive from them the benefits which they will afford
him if he uses their possibilities judiciously.

25-point leading

Kerning and tracking

Kerning is the amount of space between any specific pair of letters. You can change kerning values only when there's a blinking insertion point between two characters.

Tracking is the amount of space between all the letters currently selected. If you select the type area with a selection tool, it refers to all the space among all the characters in the entire type area. If you select characters with a type tool, tracking affects only the space among the specific letters selected.

Although they're related and appear to do basically the same thing, tracking and kerning actually work quite independently of each other. They only look like they're affecting each other; altering one never actually changes the amount of the other. The Set the kerning between two characters text field appears directly below the Set the font size text field, while the Set the tracking for the selected characters text field appears below the Set the leading text field. Figure 9.21 shows examples of both leading and kerning.

The Set the kerning text field often reads Auto instead of a value when you select several letters. If Auto appears in that text field, the kerning built into the font is used automatically. Choosing a different value overrides the Auto setting and uses the value you type. If you select several letters, you can choose only 0, but you can type any number if a blinking insertion point appears between the letters. Auto kerning works by reading the kerning values of the typeface that were embedded by the type designer when the typeface was originally created. The typeface designer normally defines the space between letters; different typefaces look like they have different amounts of space between letters. There are usually a couple hundred preset kerning pairs for common Adobe type-faces, although the expert sets have quite a few more. When Auto kerning is in effect, you can see those preset kerning values by clicking between kerned letter pairs (capital T with most vowels is a good one to check) and then reading the value in the Set the kerning text field. If you use Auto kerning, Illustrator displays the value in parentheses when the cursor is positioned between any two characters. Different typefaces have different kerning pairs, and kerning pairs change from typeface to typeface as well as from weight to weight and style to style.

FIGURE 9.21

The top line is the original, the second line has tracking set close, the third has tracking set apart, the fourth shows an example of kerning set close, and the last shows kerning set farther apart.

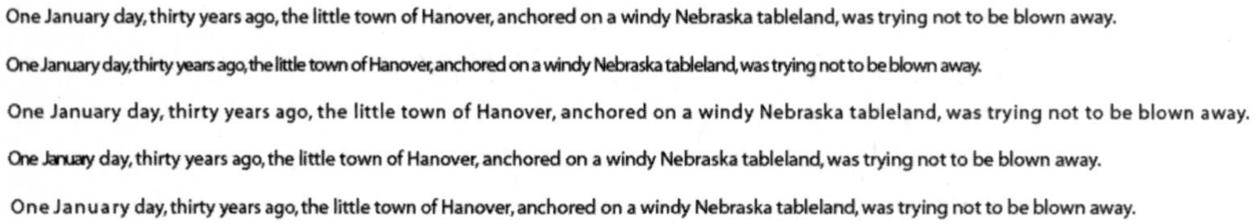

One January day, thirty years ago, the little town of Hanover, anchored on a windy Nebraska tableland, was trying not to be blown away.

One January day, thirty years ago, the little town of Hanover, anchored on a windy Nebraska tableland, was trying not to be blown away.

One January day, thirty years ago, the little town of Hanover, anchored on a windy Nebraska tableland, was trying not to be blown away.

One January day, thirty years ago, the little town of Hanover, anchored on a windy Nebraska tableland, was trying not to be blown away.

One January day, thirty years ago, the little town of Hanover, anchored on a windy Nebraska tableland, was trying not to be blown away.

For example, a kerning pair of the letters AV in Times New Roman Bold, when Auto kerning is on, is set to (−129). If you type a value of −250, that value overrides the Auto kerning, turning it off and using your new value of −250 (tracking and kerning are both measured in .001 em, a unit of measure that's relative to the current type size). Figure 9.22 shows the difference between a kerning value of −129 and −250.

 An em space is the width of a capital M in a particular font at a particular point size.

To use the keyboard to decrease or increase the kerning or tracking by the increments specified in the Preferences dialog box, click between two letters with the Type tool and press Alt+← (Option+←) or Alt+→ (Option+→). To increase or decrease the tracking or kerning by a factor of five times the amount in the Preferences dialog box, press Alt+Ctrl+→ (Option+⌘+→) or Alt+Ctrl+← (Option+⌘+←).

The values entered for tracking and kerning must be between −1000 and 10,000. A value of −1000 results in stacked letters that overlap each other. A value of 10,000 makes enough space between letters for 10 em spaces. That's lots of space.

FIGURE 9.22

The top letters are using Auto kerning (–129). The bottom letters are using –250 kerning.

NOTE Different software works with kerning and tracking differently. In programs that do offer numerical tracking, it's usually represented in some form of a fraction of an em space, but the denominator varies from software to software. Fortunately, all Adobe software is consistent here.

Using vertical scale and horizontal scale

Also in the Options section of the Character panel are the Horizontal Scale and the Vertical Scale text fields. These options are just below the kerning and tracking text fields. Horizontal scale controls the width of the type, causing it to become expanded or condensed horizontally. Vertical scale controls the height of the type. You can type values from 1% to 10,000% in these text fields. Like most other text fields in the Character panel, the values entered are absolute values, so whatever the horizontal scale is, changing it back to 100% returns the type to its original proportions.

Using baseline shift

The lower portion of the Character panel contains the Set the baseline shift text field, which, unlike leading, moves individual characters up and down relative to their baseline (from leading). Positive numbers move the selected characters up, and negative numbers move the characters down by the amount specified. The maximum amount of baseline shift is 1296 points in either direction. Baseline shift is especially useful for type on a path. You can change baseline shift via the keyboard by selecting a letter with the Type tool and pressing Alt+Shift+↑ (Option+Shift+↑) to increase. Pressing Alt+Shift+↓ (Option+Shift+↓) decreases the baseline shift by the increment specified in the Preferences dialog box.

Using character rotation

Along with the scale and baseline options, the Character panel also contains the Character Rotation text field. This somewhat odd option tilts individual characters by rotating them relative to the baseline without changing the direction of the baseline. Figure 9.23 shows an example of how this works. In this case, the baseline is a line segment that slants downward at a 45° angle. The characters on the left use normal character rotation, while those on the right are rotated 45° counterclockwise, producing a very interesting visual effect of letters falling down a hill.

FIGURE 9.23

The characters on the right are rotated along the baseline to produce a greater visual impact.

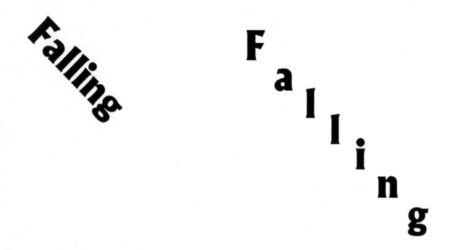

Using text underlining and strikethrough

To underline or strikethrough text, you simply click the Underline or Strikethrough button at the bottom left of the Character panel.

Understanding the language barrier

If you're reading a translation of the Illustrator Bible in a language other than English, I'd like to welcome you by saying hello in your native language: "Hello." Okay, I'm probably not fooling you here; through the magic of translators who speak several languages much more fluently than I speak westernized American English, my current language of choice, this book is translated into other languages without one iota of input from me.

If your language of choice is not English, you'll be interested in the Language option along the bottom of the Character panel. You can change to your language of choice so that functions such as the spelling dictionary and hyphenation dictionary work for words that you'll be typing.

More multinational options

The other options along the bottom of the Character panel are specifically designed for Kanji (such as Japanese or Chinese) character operations. To even see these options, you first have to choose Edit ➪ Preferences ➪ Type (Illustrator ➪ Preferences ➪ Type) and then click the Show Asian Options box. This reconfigures the Character panel to show the Asian options for kerning and tracking.

Working with the Paragraph panel

Some of the changes you make to text affect entire paragraphs at once. Paragraph attributes include options such as alignment, indentation, hyphenation, spacing, and line breaking.

Adding paragraph options

You can change paragraph attributes if you first select a type area using a selection tool, in which case the changes affect every paragraph within the entire type area. If you use the Type tool to select one or more characters, changes you make to paragraph attributes affect the entire paragraphs containing the selected characters.

To display the Paragraph panel, as shown in Figure 9.24, choose Window ➪ Type ➪ Paragraph or press Alt+Ctrl+T (Option+⌘+T).

The bottom part of the Paragraph panel contains information that isn't changed often, so it almost doesn't need to be displayed. If you want to display it, choose Show Options from the Paragraph panel's popup menu.

FIGURE 9.24

The Paragraph panel

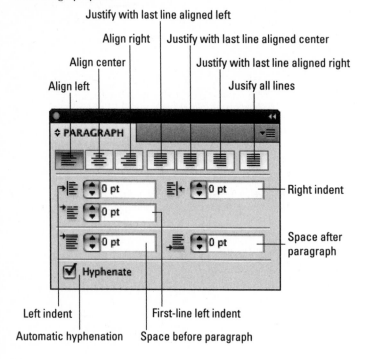

Aligning type

You can align paragraphs in different ways. Each way is represented by an icon in the Paragraph panel that shows a graphical representation of what multiple lines of type look like when that particular alignment is applied. Each alignment type has a specific function:

■ **Align left:** Moves all your text so that it lines up with the left side of your page. The most common and the default setting, experienced typesetters often refer to this option as ragged right due to the uneven right side of the text. You can also apply this type of alignment by pressing Ctrl+Shift+L (⌘+Shift+L).

■ **Align center:** All lines of type in the paragraph are centered relative to each other, to the point clicked, or to the location of the I-bar in type on a path. You can also apply this type of alignment by pressing Ctrl+Shift+C (⌘+Shift+C).

■ **Align right:** Use this option to create a smooth, even right side and an uneven left side (no, ragged left isn't really a correct term). You can also apply this type of alignment by pressing Ctrl+Shift+R (⌘+Shift+R).

■ **Justify with last line aligned left:** You apply this to make both the left and right sides appear smooth and even, except for the last line, which is aligned left.

- **Justify with last line aligned center:** Use this option to make both the left and right sides appear smooth and even, except for the last line, which is aligned in the center.

- **Justify with last line aligned right:** With this option, both the left and right sides appear smooth and even, except for the last line, which is aligned right.

- **Justify all lines:** Sometimes called Force Justify, this option is the same as Justify, except that the last line of every paragraph is justified along with the other lines of the paragraph. This can create some really awful looking paragraphs, and it's done mainly for artistic emphasis, not as a proper way to justify type. The Justify all lines option is particularly useful for stretching a single line of type across a certain width. You can also apply this type of alignment by pressing Ctrl+Shift+F (⌘+Shift+F).

NOTE Justification works only on area type. Illustrator doesn't allow you to choose Justify or Justify all lines for type on a path or individual type.

Indenting paragraphs

Paragraphs can be indented within the Paragraph panel by choosing different amounts of indentation for the left edge, the right edge, and first line of each paragraph. The maximum indentation for all three text fields is 1296 points and the minimum is –1296 points.

Using indents is a great way to offset type, such as quotes, that needs to have smaller margins than the rest of the type surrounding the offset type. Changing the indentation values is also useful for creating hanging indents, such as numbered or bulleted text.

To create hanging indents easily, make the Left indent as large as the width of a bullet or a number and a space and then make the First-line value the negative value of that. If the Left indent is 2 picas, the first line is –2 picas. This creates great hanging indents every time.

Spacing before or after paragraphs

Illustrator lets you place additional space between paragraphs by typing a number in the Space before paragraph text field or the Space after paragraph text field. You add this measurement to the leading to determine the distance from baseline to baseline before the selected paragraphs. You can also type a negative number to decrease space between paragraphs, if necessary. You can make the values for Space before paragraph between –1296 and 1296 points.

Spacing through justification

Illustrator allows you to control the spacing of letters, words, auto leading, and glyphs in text by changing the values you find in the Justification dialog box. You access this dialog box by choosing the Justification option in the Paragraph panel's popup menu, as shown in Figure 9.25. You can control these options in the Justification dialog box:

- **Word Spacing:** Word spacing is the space between the words that you create by pressing the spacebar. Set the Minimum, Desired, and Maximum values. The word space can range from 0% to 1000%; 100% is the default, where no additional space is added. The minimum is the least amount of word spacing in percentage that you want to accept.

Type the exact percentage for the Desired setting. The maximum is the most amount of spacing you accept.

- **Letter Spacing:** Letter spacing is the space between letters of words. The Letter spacing can be set from –100% to 500%. A value of 0% means that no space is added. Set the Minimum, Desired, and Maximum values.

- **Glyph Scaling:** A glyph refers to any font character. Glyph scaling lets you change the width of the character as a percentage of the original. Set the Minimum, Desired, and Maximum scaling percentages. The range of glyph scaling is from 50% to 200%; 100% is the default, where no scaling occurs.

- **Auto Leading:** Set the auto leading as a percentage, which ranges from 0% to 500%, with 120% being the default.

- **Single Word Justification:** When there's a single word for the last line justification, choose one of these options from the popup menu: Full Justify, Align Left, Align Center, and Align Right.

FIGURE 9.25

The Justification dialog box allows you to control how Illustrator applies paragraph justification.

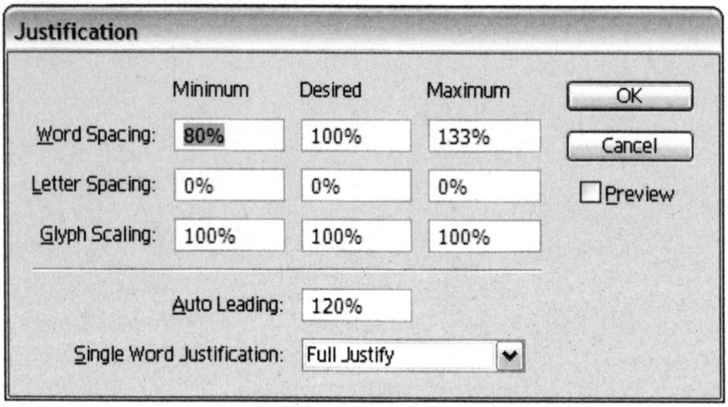

Justification				
	Minimum	Desired	Maximum	OK
Word Spacing:	80%	100%	133%	Cancel
Letter Spacing:	0%	0%	0%	☐ Preview
Glyph Scaling:	100%	100%	100%	
Auto Leading:		120%		
Single Word Justification:	Full Justify			

Spacing affects the space between letters and words regardless of the alignment, although Justified text has even more spacing control than Flush Left, Flush Right, or Centered text.

When you choose Flush Left, Flush Right, or Centered alignment, the only text fields in the dialog box that you can change are the Desired text fields for Letter Spacing and Word Spacing.

The Minimum and Maximum boxes in the Word Spacing, Letter Spacing, and Glyph Scaling areas are mainly used to control where the extra space goes and where it's removed from when stretching out and compressing the lines of text.

Hyphenating text

Hyphenation? In a drawing program? Unbelievably, but yes, and it's a neat addition to Illustrator's text-handling capabilities. Hyphenation works in the background, silently hyphenating when necessary.

To use Illustrator's hyphenation, you must click the Automatic hyphenation check box in the lower left of the Paragraph panel.

Hyphenation in Illustrator works from a set of hyphenation rules that you define in the Hyphenation dialog box, as shown in Figure 9.26. View the Hyphenation dialog box by choosing Hyphenation from the Paragraph panel's popup menu. Here, you can specify how many letters must fall before the hyphen can appear and how many letters must fall after the hyphen. You can also limit the number of consecutive hyphens that appear at the end of a line of text to avoid the ladder look of multiple hyphens, where they all line up in a vertical column above each other.

FIGURE 9.26

The Hyphenation dialog box allows you to fine-tune the way Illustrator hyphenates text.

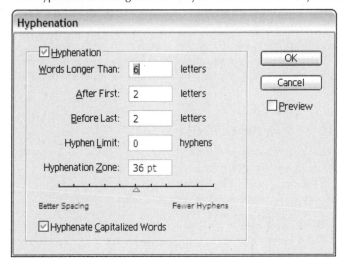

Using Every-line and Single-line Composer

In Illustrator, you can choose from two composition methods: Adobe Every-line Composer or Adobe Single-line Composer. These composer options are found in the Paragraph panel's popup menu. What this means is that in a paragraph, the composer checks and chooses the best breaks, hyphenation, and justification for the specific paragraph.

Every-line Composer checks all the lines in the paragraph and makes its evaluation based on the paragraph as a whole. Single-line Composer looks at each line of type rather than the whole paragraph to determine the best breaks, hyphenation, and justification.

Controlling punctuation

Roman Hanging Punctuation handles the alignment of punctuation marks for a specified paragraph. With the Roman Hanging Punctuation option turned on, apostrophes, quotes, commas, periods, and hyphens are 100% outside the margin or type area. Characters — such as asterisks, tildes, ellipses, en dashes, em dashes, colons, and semicolons — are 50% out of the margin.

If you click the Roman Hanging Punctuation option in the Paragraph panel's popup menu, punctuation at the left edge of a flush left, justified, or justified last line paragraph appears outside the margin or type area. Punctuation on the right edge of a flush right, justified, or justified last line paragraph also appears outside the margin or type area. Strangely enough, Illustrator is one of the few programs that support this very hip feature, which allows tiny pieces of punctuation to exist outside solid blocks of type.

Another choice for punctuation is Optical Margin Alignment. Optical Margin Alignment handles the punctuation marks alignment for all paragraphs inside a type area. With this option turned on, all punctuation hangs outside the margin or type area so the type is aligned. You can find this feature under the Type menu.

> **NOTE** Additional options in the Paragraph panel's popup menu are Burasagari, Kinsoku Shori Type, Bunri-Kinshi, and Kurikaeshi Moji Shori. To see these options, you first must turn on Asian Options in the Type preferences. To do this, choose Edit ⇨ Preferences ⇨ Type (Illustrator ⇨ Preferences ⇨ Type) and then click the Show Asian Options check box. Use these options for aligning double-byte punctuation marks, which aren't affected by choosing Roman Hanging Punctuation.

Working with the OpenType panel

Choose Window ⇨ Type ⇨ OpenType or press Alt+Ctrl+Shift+T (Option+⌘+Shift+T) to access the OpenType panel. Use this panel to apply specific options to alternate characters with OpenType fonts. Figure 9.27 shows the OpenType panel. The OpenType panel provides options that OpenType fonts may have, such as automatic fractions, small caps, and other goodies.

> **NOTE** Different OpenType fonts vary greatly in the features they offer. If you attempt to choose one of the options in the OpenType panel that isn't offered in the font you have selected, Illustrator changes the mouse pointer to a slashed circle to indicate that you can't select that option.

Working with the Tabs panel

You use the Tabs panel to set tabs the same way you would in your word-processing or page-layout program. To display the Tabs panel, as shown in Figure 9.28, choose Window ⇨ Type ⇨ Tabs or press Ctrl+Shift+T (⌘+Shift+T). The Tabs panel appears above the type you have selected and automatically assumes the width of the type area.

FIGURE 9.27

The OpenType panel

Contextual ligatures

Swash

Titling alternates

Fractions

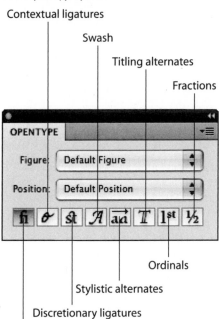

Ordinals

Stylistic alternates

Discretionary ligatures

Standard ligatures

FIGURE 9.28

The Tabs panel allows you to set tabs in your text blocks.

Center-justified tab

Decimal-justified tab

Tab leader

Position Panel Above Text

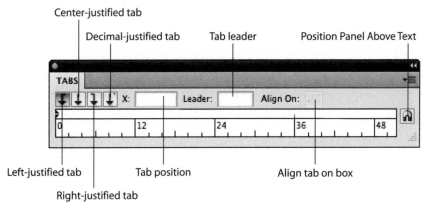

Left-justified tab

Tab position

Align tab on box

Right-justified tab

To change the width of the Tabs panel, click and drag on the resize triangle in the lower-right corner of the panel. The Tabs panel can be made wider but not taller. To reset the Tabs panel to the exact size of the type area, drag the resize box back.

 **The Position Panel Above Text button moves the Tabs panel to make it flush left with the type and moves it up or down so that it's right above the selected text area.**

Illustrator automatically sets tabs at every half-inch. These are called Auto tab stops. After you set a tab, all the Auto tab stops to the left of the tab you have set disappear. The Auto tab stops work like left-justified tabs.

If you click the Snap to Unit check box in the Tabs panel's popup menu, tab stops correspond to the ruler tick marks.

The measurement system shown on the ruler is the same system that the rest of the documents use. You can change the measurement system in the Units & Display Performance section of the Preferences dialog box. You can access this by choosing Edit ➪ Preferences ➪ Units & Display Performance (Illustrator ➪ Preferences ➪ Units & Display Performance).

To set a tab, choose a tab from the four Tab style buttons on the upper left of the Tabs panel and then click the ruler below to set exactly where you want the new tab. After the tab has been set, you can move it by dragging it along the ruler or remove it by dragging it off the top or bottom edge of the ruler.

You can set four types of tabs:

- **Left-justified:** This option makes type align to the right side of the tab, with the leftmost character aligning with the tab stop.

- **Center-justified:** This option makes type align to the center of the tab, with half the characters aligning on either side of the tab stop.

- **Right-justified:** This option makes type align to the left side of the tab, with the rightmost character aligning with the tab stop.

- **Decimal-justified:** This option makes type align to the left side of the tab, with a decimal or the rightmost character aligning with the tab stop.

To change a tab from one style to another, choose a tab stop and then click the Tab style button you want to use for the tab stop. To deselect all tabs, click in the area to the right of the Tab position box. (If you don't click far enough away from the Tab position box, you end up changing the units.) It's a good idea to deselect tabs after setting them so that when you define a new Tab style for the next tab stop, it doesn't change the tab stop that you just set.

Using Advanced Type Functions

Illustrator has built in some more advanced type functions that go beyond the basic user. In these functions, you find Threading Text, Wrapping Text, Fitting Headlines, Find Font, Check Spelling, and Change Case. You find each of these functions under the Edit and Type menus.

Threading text

The Threading Text option links text from one area to another, continuing a story from one area to another, as shown in Figure 9.29. Linked blocks act like groups, enabling you to use the Selection tool and then click just one area to select all areas. (You can still select individual blocks with the Direct Selection tool.) Whenever you have more text than can fit into a text area, a tiny red plus sign in a box appears, alerting you that there's more text in the box than you can see.

FIGURE 9.29

Text blocks are threaded together in the order of the arrows.

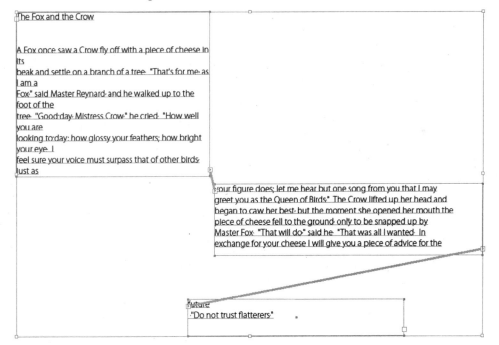

To use threaded text, select a text area or rectangle and any other shapes, even text rectangles and areas, and then choose Type ➪ Threaded Text ➪ Create. The text areas then act as if they're grouped. Text flows from the backmost shape to the frontmost in any group of linked blocks, so be careful to order your boxes correctly when setting up linked text. In fact, if you send a box to the back, Illustrator starts the thread from that location, then goes to the next box forward, and then the next, etc. You can't choose Type ➪ Threaded Text ➪ Create unless at least one text area and one other path or text area are selected. You can do this before you start typing/placing your text or afterward.

Unthreading text

You can unthread text in various ways. To release the object from the text thread, choose Type ➪ Threaded Text ➪ Release Selection. This removes the text from the objects. To remove the thread but leave the type in the objects, choose Type ➪ Threaded Text ➪ Remove Threading. You can also break the threads by double-clicking on an out port (the text doesn't get split or deleted but instead is still waiting to be threaded to somewhere it can be displayed). The out port is the little box with the outward-pointing arrow at the edge of the object that the type is flowing from.

When you double-click the out port again, the text flows forward into the next object.

Fitting a headline

The Type menu's Fit Headline option is designed to automatically increase the width of type in order to fit type perfectly from the left side of a type area to the right side of that same type area, as shown in Figure 9.30. In this case, the Fit Headline option was used on the headline over the right-side text, while the left side uses normal text. Another option is to use Justify all lines in the Paragraph panel, but it doesn't do as good of a job as Fit Headline.

Finding and replacing text

Under the Edit menu are more choices for text editing. Illustrator lets you find certain text and then replace it with other text by choosing Edit ➪ Find and Replace to open the Find And Replace dialog box, as shown in Figure 9.31. Use this to replace specific letters, words, or characters. In the Find And Replace dialog box, you have the following options:

- **Match Case:** Selects the characters only if they have the same uppercase and lowercase attributes as the characters you type in the Find text field
- **Find Whole Word:** Tells Illustrator that the characters you type in the Find text field are an entire word and not part of a word
- **Search Backwards:** Tells Illustrator to look before the current insertion point for the next instance of the characters, instead of using the default, which is to look after the current insertion point
- **Check Hidden Layers:** Instructs Illustrator to look in the text in hidden layers
- **Check Locked Layers:** Instructs Illustrator to look in the text in locked layers

FIGURE 9.30

The Fit Headline option makes headlines fit across the entire text block, as shown on the right.

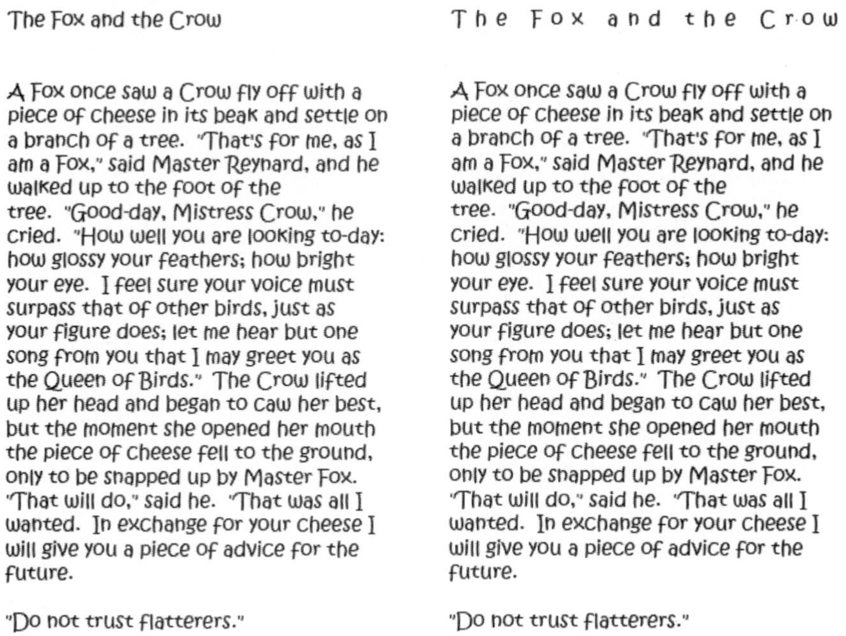

The Fox and the Crow

A Fox once saw a Crow fly off with a piece of cheese in its beak and settle on a branch of a tree. "That's for me, as I am a Fox," said Master Reynard, and he walked up to the foot of the tree. "Good-day, Mistress Crow," he cried. "How well you are looking to-day: how glossy your feathers; how bright your eye. I feel sure your voice must surpass that of other birds, just as your figure does; let me hear but one song from you that I may greet you as the Queen of Birds." The Crow lifted up her head and began to caw her best, but the moment she opened her mouth the piece of cheese fell to the ground, only to be snapped up by Master Fox. "That will do," said he. "That was all I wanted. In exchange for your cheese I will give you a piece of advice for the future.

"Do not trust flatterers."

The Fox and the Crow

A Fox once saw a Crow fly off with a piece of cheese in its beak and settle on a branch of a tree. "That's for me, as I am a Fox," said Master Reynard, and he walked up to the foot of the tree. "Good-day, Mistress Crow," he cried. "How well you are looking to-day: how glossy your feathers; how bright your eye. I feel sure your voice must surpass that of other birds, just as your figure does; let me hear but one song from you that I may greet you as the Queen of Birds." The Crow lifted up her head and began to caw her best, but the moment she opened her mouth the piece of cheese fell to the ground, only to be snapped up by Master Fox. "That will do," said he. "That was all I wanted. In exchange for your cheese I will give you a piece of advice for the future.

"Do not trust flatterers."

FIGURE 9.31

Use the Find And Replace dialog box to edit your text.

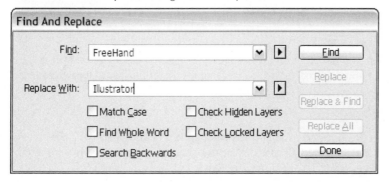

The following steps describe how to use these options to find and replace text:

1. **Choose Edit ⇨ Find and Replace.** The Find And Replace dialog box opens.

2. **Type the word(s), phrase(s), or character(s) that you want to find in the Find text field.**

3. **In the Replace With text field, type the word(s) or character(s) that you want to use to replace the text.**

4. **Click the appropriate check boxes described in the previous section.**

5. **Click Find to find the first occurrence of the word(s) or character(s).**

6. **Click Replace to replace the selected text.** Click Replace & Find to first replace the text and then locate the next occurrence. If you want to change all occurrences, click Replace All.

NOTE You don't need to select areas of type with the selection or type tools in order to search for text — all that's necessary is that the document that you want to search is the open and active document.

Finding fonts

The Find Font option looks for certain fonts in a document and replaces them with fonts you specify. This can be especially handy if you've pasted in text from other applications and you want to make certain that your Illustrator document has a uniform appearance throughout.

To locate the fonts in your document, choose Type ⇨ Find Font to display the Find Font dialog box, as shown in Figure 9.32.

To change all occurrences of a certain font to another font, choose the font you want to change in the top list, titled Fonts in Document. Choose a font in the box in the lower section of the dialog box and then click Change All. To change one particular instance, click Change. To find the next occurrence of that font, click Find Next. The Skip button skips over the currently selected text and finds the next occurrence of that font. Keep in mind that choosing System from the Replace With Font From list can take a while for Illustrator to build and display the font list, especially if you have a ton of fonts on your system.

Clicking Save List allows you to save your font list as a text file. You can deselect any of the options at the bottom of the Find Font dialog box to avoid searching within those types of type areas.

Checking spelling

Spell-check checks all text in a document to see whether it's spelled (and capitalized) correctly. To use this feature, choose Edit ⇨ Check Spelling to display the Check Spelling dialog box, as shown in Figure 9.33. You can also use Ctrl (⌘)+I to check spelling.

NOTE Check Spelling uses a standard user dictionary as well as all foreign language and hyphenation dictionaries that are available.

FIGURE 9.32

The Find Font dialog box helps you change the fonts that are in your document.

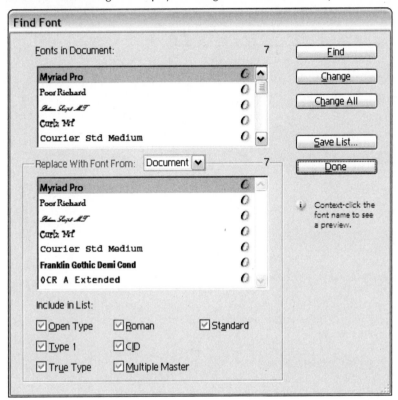

If you have any misspelled words or words that aren't in the available dictionaries, those words are listed at the top of the Check Spelling dialog box in the Misspelled Words list. Choosing a word from this list displays similar words below in the Suggestions list.

Some of the options you can change are to find repeated words or lowercased words at the start of a sentence. Other options are to ignore uppercase words, Roman numerals, and words with numbers.

You use the Add button when you want to add the selected misspelled word to your custom dictionary.

As you're checking your spelling in the Check Spelling dialog box, clicking Change replaces the misspelled word with the highlighted word in the Suggested Corrections list. Clicking Change All replaces all misspelled occurrences of that word throughout the entire document with the correctly spelled word.

FIGURE 9.33

Use the Check Spelling dialog box to make certain your documents don't contain embarrassing spelling errors.

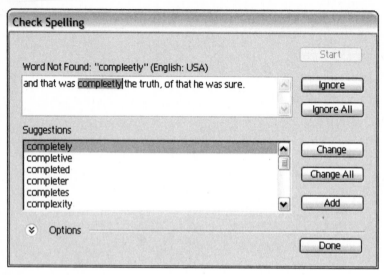

Clicking Ignore ignores that occurrence of the misspelled word. Clicking Ignore All skips all occurrences of that word in the document.

Clicking Done closes the Check Spelling dialog box.

Changing case

The Change Case option converts selected text to one of a variety of case options. To use this feature, select type with a type tool and then choose Type ⇨ Change Case. The four submenu choices are UPPERCASE, lowercase, Title Case, and Sentence case.

The four Change Case options affect only letters, not numbers, symbols, or punctuation. The options are as follows:

- **UPPERCASE:** Converts all selected letters into uppercase, regardless of whether any letters were uppercase or lowercase

- **lowercase:** Converts all selected letters into lowercase, regardless of whether any letters were uppercase or lowercase. It also doesn't matter if the letters were originally uppercase because they were typed with Caps Lock engaged or if the uppercase letters were uppercase because of a style format.

- **Title Case:** Capitalizes the first letter of each word (except articles and prepositions that aren't the first word or last word or don't follow punctuation)

■ **Sentence case:** Uses periods, exclamation points, and question marks as the end of the sentence to capitalize the first letter of each sentence

 **Be sure to check your text for proper capitalization after using any of these options. You're almost certain to find errors in things, such as proper names and acronyms.**

Using Smart Punctuation

The Smart Punctuation option looks for certain characters in a document and replaces them with characters you specify. To use this feature, select type with either a selection tool or a type tool. Then, choose Type ⇨ Smart Punctuation. The Smart Punctuation dialog box, as shown in Figure 9.34, opens.

FIGURE 9.34

Use the Smart Punctuation dialog box to replace ordinary punctuation with typographer's punctuation.

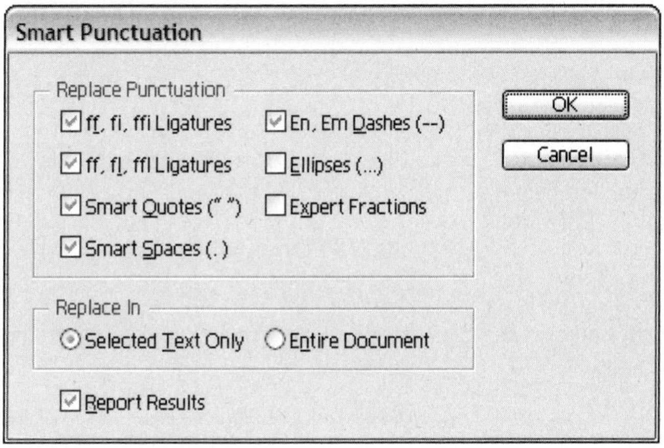

Smart Punctuation

Replace Punctuation
- ☑ ff, fi, ffi Ligatures
- ☑ ff, fl, ffl Ligatures
- ☑ Smart Quotes (" ")
- ☑ Smart Spaces (.)
- ☑ En, Em Dashes (--)
- ☐ Ellipses (...)
- ☐ Expert Fractions

[OK]
[Cancel]

Replace In
- ◉ Selected Text Only ○ Entire Document

☑ Report Results

The Smart Punctuation option works after the fact, making changes to text already in the Illustrator document. There are no settings, for example, to convert quotes to curved quotes as you're typing them (once they're curved quotes, they stay that way). The types of punctuation to be changed are determined by a set of check boxes in the Smart Punctuation dialog box. Clicking this check box causes Illustrator to look for these certain instances and, if it finds them, corrects them with the proper punctuation.

The first two options are used for replacing ff, fi (or fl), and ffi (or ffl) with ligatures. Ligatures are characters that represent several characters with one character that's designed to let those characters appear better-looking when placed next to each other. Most fonts have fi and fl ligatures, which look like fi and fl, respectively.

The remaining Smart Punctuation options work as follows:

- Smart Quotes replaces straight (or dumb) quotes (" " and ' ') with curly (smart) quotes (" " and ' '), also known as typesetter's quotes or printer's quotes.

- Smart Spaces replaces multiple spaces after a period with one space. (In typesetting, there should only be one space following a period.)

- En, Em Dashes replaces hyphens (-) with en dashes (–) and double hyphens (--) with em dashes (—).

- Ellipses replaces three periods (...) with an ellipsis (…).

- Expert Fractions replaces fractions with expert fractions if you have the expert fractions for the font family you're using. Adobe sells Expert Collection fonts that contain these fractions. If you don't have expert fractions, your fractions remain unchanged.

Other options are to replace in Selected Text Only or in Entire Document. Clicking the Report Results check box displays a dialog box once changes have occurred, telling you how many of the punctuation changes were made.

Adding rows and columns

Area Type Options divides rectangular paths (text rectangles) into even sections. You can add rows, columns, or both to a text area using these options.

To add Rows and Columns, select a path and then choose Type ⇨ Area Type Options to display the Area Type Options dialog box, as shown in Figure 9.35.

You can select any text path, open or closed, and divide it into rows and columns. The Area Type Options dialog box has the following options:

- You can set the Width of the columns and the Height of the rows in the text fields or by using the up and down arrows.

 NOTE All measurements in the Area Type Options dialog box are displayed in the current measurement system.

- In the Rows section, the Number text field sets the number of rows for the original path.
- The Span text field is the height of each of the rows.
- Click the Fixed check box to prevent the row height from changing if the text block is resized.
- The Gutter text field specifies the space between rows.
- In the Columns section, the Number text field sets the number of columns for the original path.

- The Span text field determines the width of the columns.
- Click the Fixed check box to prevent the column width from changing if the text block is resized.
- The Gutter text field specifies the space between columns.

FIGURE 9.35

The Area Type Options dialog box allows you to create additional columns and rows in your text blocks.

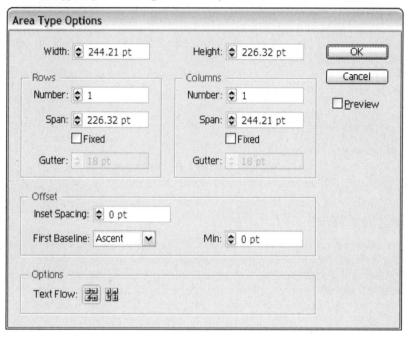

Remember that using the Area Type Options feature actually divides the selected rectangle into several pieces.

- The Offset options are for Inset Spacing (from the edge of the object area) and First Baseline. Use the settings in this section to move text slightly away from the baseline for improved readability.

- The Text Flow options determine the direction of text as it flows from one section to the next. You may choose between text that starts along the top row and flows from left to right and then goes to the next lowest row, flowing from left to right, etc. The second option is to have text start in the left column, flowing from top to bottom, and then to the next column to the right, flowing from top to bottom.

- Clicking the Preview check box displays changes as you make them in the Area Type Options dialog box.

Showing hidden characters

When you type, you typically add certain special characters — such as spaces, returns, and tabs. Typically, you don't see these characters. You can choose to view the hidden characters by choosing Show Hidden Characters from the Type menu. This option can be especially useful when you're working with imported text because it allows you to find any extra hidden characters that can interfere with proper text formatting.

Changing type orientation

You can easily change the orientation of your type by choosing Type Orientation from the Type menu. You then choose either Horizontal or Vertical from the Type Orientation submenu. That way, if you wanted vertical type and did it as horizontal, you can easily change it without retyping it.

Updating legacy text

Legacy text is any text created in version 10 and earlier. Because Illustrator now uses a new Adobe Text Engine, the older text must be converted to take advantage of this new type engine. The changes are character positioning with tracking, leading, and kerning, shifts in the words (resulting in different hyphenation), and changes in word flow from threaded text. When you open an older file, a dialog box appears asking if you want to update all legacy text. If you decline to do the update when opening the file, you can use the Legacy Text submenu entries to update all or selected legacy text while editing the file.

Exporting and placing

You can export text from your Illustrator documents for use in other applications. To export text, select the text you want to export and then choose File ➪ Export to display the Export dialog box, as shown in Figure 9.36. In the Export dialog box, choose Text Format from the Save as type drop-down list (popup menu) and then type a file name for the exported file. Click the Export button to save the file.

Word-processing software, page-layout software, or any other software that can read text files can open and use text that you save in Illustrator.

To place text in Illustrator, choose File ➪ Place and then choose a text file for placement. Illustrator allows you to drag a type area rectangle to place the text or you can just click to place the text as point type.

FIGURE 9.36

The Adobe Export dialog box is similar to the standard file dialog box that may appear.

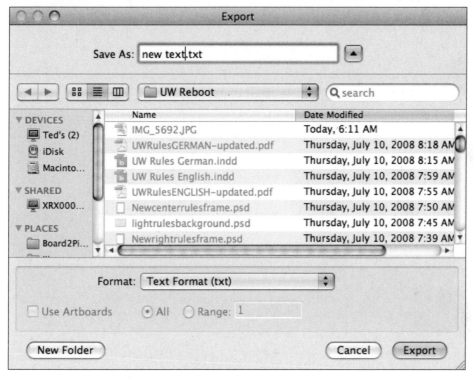

Creating Outlines

After you create, edit, and spell-check your text, you may want to create outlines from the characters so that you can modify the characters to produce some interesting visual effects. To do so, choose Type ➪ Create Outlines or press Ctrl+Shift+O (⌘+Shift+O), and the selected type converts into editable paths, like those shown in Figure 9.37. To convert type to outlines, you need to select the type with a selection tool, not a type tool. Each letter is its own compound path, and you can edit each path with the Direct Selection tool as you would edit any other path.

CROSS-REF For more on the Direct Selection tool, see Chapter 6.

OpenType and TrueType combine the screen and printer fonts into one file — if you can choose any of these font types in Illustrator, you can create outlines from them. Illustrator locates the font file and uses that information to create the outlines.

After you convert type to outlines, you can apply gradients to its fill, and you can apply patterns to its fill, which you can preview on-screen. You can also apply patterns to nonoutline type by clicking a pattern in the Swatch panel for the file or stroke of the character.

FIGURE 9.37

Type converted into outlines can result in some cool effects.

CAUTION Although you can undo Create Outlines, be forewarned that you can't convert back to type in case you make a spelling error or want to change the font or any other type attribute.

You can convert all forms of type, including individual type, type on a path, area type, and type containers to outlines.

TIP Creating outlines out of type is also very useful when you want to send the file to be outputted and the person doing the output doesn't have the font you're using. Simply use the Create Outlines option before you send the file, and it prints just fine. (This is not advised for 4-point type or smaller, as described later in this chapter.)

The process of creating editable type outlines has many uses, including distorting mild-mannered characters into grotesque letters. More practical uses for editable type outlines include making type-based logos unique, arcing type (where one side is flat and the other is curved), special effects and masking, and avoiding font-compatibility problems.

Initially, when type is converted into outlines, individual characters are turned into compound paths. This ensures that holes in letters, such as in a lowercase a, b, or d, are transparent and not just white-filled paths placed on top of the original objects.

CROSS-REF For more on warp effects, see Chapter 11. For more on compound paths, see Chapter 12.

Distorting characters for special effects

After letters have been turned into outlines, there's nothing to stop you from distorting them into shapes that resemble letters only in the most simplistic sense of the word.

The results of letter distortion usually aren't all that eye-pleasing, but they can be fun. Few things in life are as pleasing as taking a boring letter Q and twisting it into the letter that time forgot. Or fiddling around with your boss's name until the letters look as evil as your boss does. Or adding pointed ears and whiskers to a random array of letters and numbers and printing out several sheets of them with the words "Mutant kittens for sale."

When modifying existing letters, use the Direct Selection tool. Select the points or segments you want to move and then drag them around to your heart's content. This can be great practice for adjusting paths, and you might accidentally stumble onto some really cool designs.

Type outlines provide you with the flexibility to manipulate letters to turn an ordinary, boring, letters-only logo into a distinct symbol embodying the company's image. Outlines are flexible enough that there really are no limits to what can be done with something as simple as a word of type.

Masking and other effects

Standard type or type that has been converted into outlines can be used as a mask or filled with a placed image or any objects, as shown in Figure 9.38.

FIGURE 9.38

This shows masking an image.

For outlined words to work as a single mask, you must first change them into a compound path. Usually, individual letters of converted type are changed into individual compound paths, whether the letter has a hole in it or not. For masks to work properly, you must select the entire word or words you want to use as a mask and then choose Object ➪ Compound Path ➪ Make or press Ctrl+8 (⌘+8). This changes all the selected letters into one compound path.

After the words are a compound path, place them in front of the objects to be masked, select both the words and the masked objects, and then choose Object ➪ Clipping Mask ➪ Make or press Ctrl+7 (⌘+7).

TIP   In some third-party (non-Adobe) and shareware typefaces, making a compound path out of a series of letters can produce results where the holes aren't transparent. This issue is usually one of path direction, which can be corrected by selecting the inner shape (the hole) and changing the direction with the path direction buttons on the Attributes panel (accessed by choosing Window ➪ Attributes).

CROSS-REF   For more on masks, see Chapters 7 and 12.

Avoiding font conflicts by creating outlines

If you ever give your files to a service bureau or to clients, you've probably already run into some font-compatibility problems. A font-compatibility problem usually means that the place you gave your file to doesn't have a typeface that you used in your Illustrator document or that it has a different version of the same typeface with different metrics.

This is a problem to which there's no great solution, and the trouble seems to be worsening as more font manufacturers spring up. And then there are shareware typefaces, some of which resemble Adobe originals to an uncanny degree of accuracy. All this leads to a great deal of confusion and frustration for the average Illustrator user.

But there's a way around this problem — at least most of the time. Convert your typefaces into outlines before you send them to other people with other systems — they don't need your typefaces for the letters to print correctly. In fact, converted letters aren't really considered type anymore, just outlines.

TIP   Save your file before converting the text to outlines and then save it as a different file name after converting the text to outlines. This allows you to do text editing later on the original file, if necessary.

Understanding hinting

Most Type 1 fonts have *hinting* built into them. Hinting is a method for adjusting type at small point sizes, especially at low resolutions. Although hinting is built into the fonts, when those fonts are converted into paths via the Create Outlines command, the hinting functionality is gone. This is part of the reason that type converted to outlines can look heavier than it does otherwise.

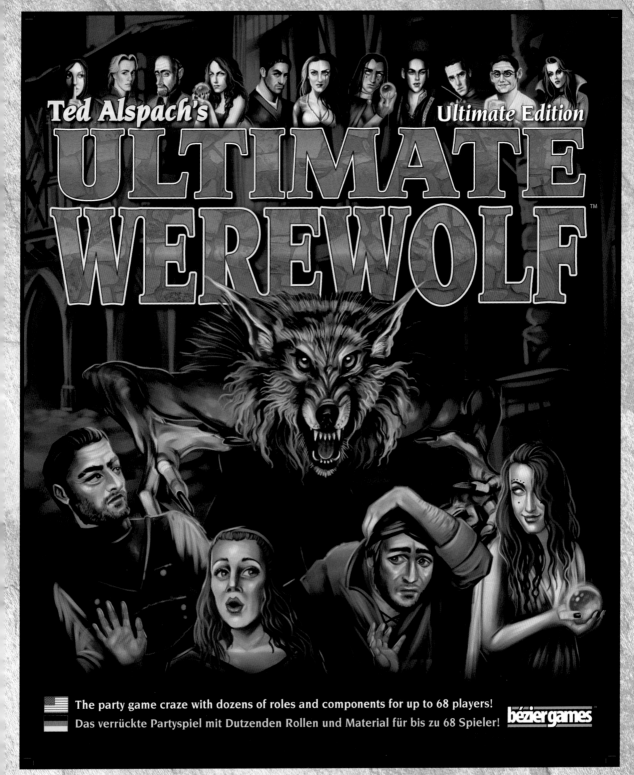

This is a design for a booth poster that shows off the artwork for the *Ultimate Werewolf* game. Illustrator was used as an assembly tool for the various pieces of art, the logo, and the text.

SORCERER

-3

Each card in the *Ultimate Werewolf* set was saved from Illustrator as a PDF with marks set as shown here. Even though the corners are die-cut curved, that isn't indicated on the file; it simply shows trim marks.

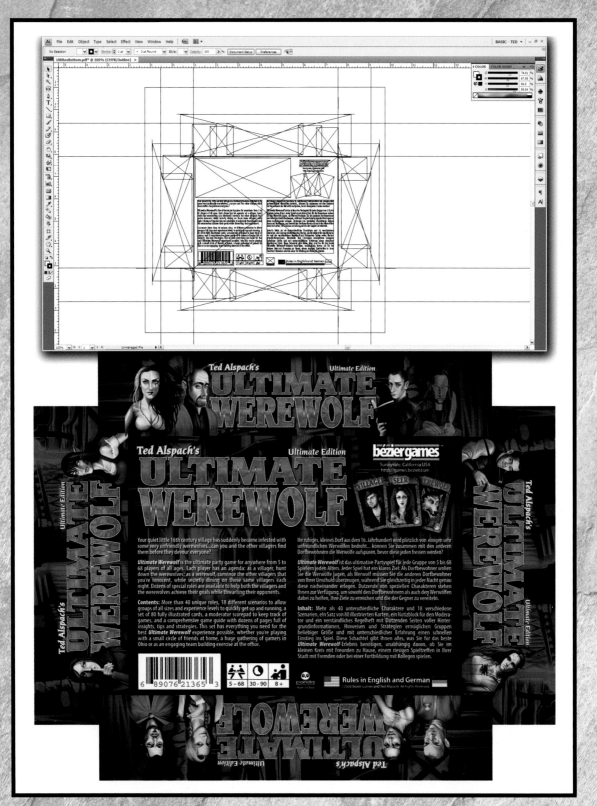

This shows the bottom of the box in Outline mode (top) and in full color (bottom). While the *Ultimate Werewolf* logo was created in Illustrator, it was placed into this Illustrator document as a linked image, which is why you see boxes for the logo.

Ted Alspach's

Ultimate Edition

ULTIMATE WEREWOLF

Clipping Mask

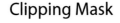

The *Ultimate Werewolf* logo consists of two distinct parts: The top part is the stone texture, which is masked by the letters in the logo. The bottom part is the colorization of the letters. By setting the top part to an opacity of 50% and the transparency blend mode to Lighten, the result is textured text.

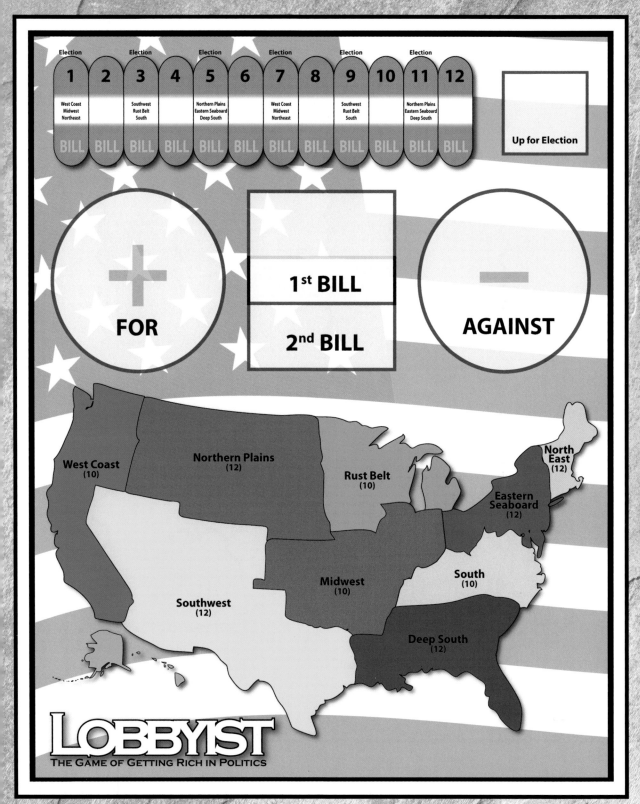

Everything here was created in Illustrator. Liberal use of transparency was applied to allow the otherwise disparate illustrations to work together.

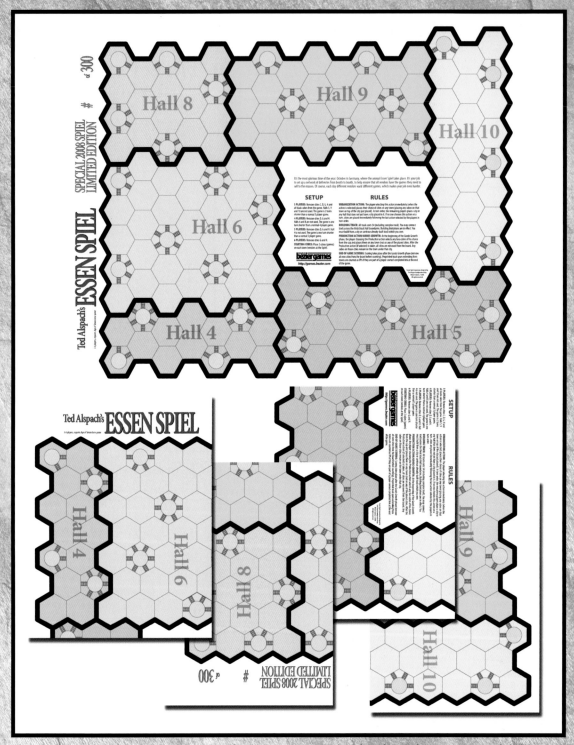

The challenge for creating this map was that it was going to be sliced into four pieces, and the text, if at all possible, couldn't be cut, as that would make it difficult to read. Guides were used within Illustrator to determine where the cut lines would be so that the file could be created in such a way to guarantee that the pieces would line up properly without slicing through text.

bézier games

TED ALSPACH'S
Vermont
New Hampshire
Central New England*

Vermont, New Hampshire and Central New England provide 3-8 players a unique Age of Steam experience in the heart of 1840's America. The Vermont and New Hampshire expansions feature unique twists on basic gameplay such as alternating seasons in Vermont where prices and income increase every other turn, and anti-competitive restrictions in New Hampshire which prevent players from building duplicate track and using other players' track to deliver goods. Central New England takes place on an absolutely grand scale', with two full maps side-by-side allowing up to 8 players to play together as they compete to deliver goods across state lines.

Vermont, New Hampshire und Central New England bieten 3-8 Spielern eine einzigartige Age of Steam-Erfahrung, im Herzen von Amerika in den 1840ern. Die Erweiterungen Vermont und New Hampshire bieten besondere Variationen des gewohnten Spielablaufs, wie sich ändernde Jahreszeiten in Vermont, bei denen sich Kosten und Einnahmen jeden zweiten Zug erhöhen, sowie die Konkurrenz unterdrückenden Einschränkungen in New Hampshire, durch die die Spieler daran gehindert werden, doppelte Strecken zu bauen und die Strecken der anderen Spieler für den Warentransport zu nutzen. In Central New England spielt man in einem besonders großen Maßstab, mit zwei kompletten Spielplänen Seite an Seite, so dass bis zu 8 Spieler teilnehmen können, wenn sie darum wettstreiten, Waren über die Staatsgrenzen zu transportieren.

These expansions require an Age of Steam base game

*Central New England requires two copies of this expansion. Vermont, New Hampshire and Central New England expansions designed by Ted Alspach, 2008. http://games.bezier.com

6 89076 21325 7

The front cover to this game was assembled in Illustrator, and with the exception of the snowy background and train image (which were assembled together in Photoshop), the rest of the graphics were created in Illustrator. Of note is the top map section that blends into the snowy image below. This effect was achieved by masking the map portion with an opacity mask consisting of a gradient.

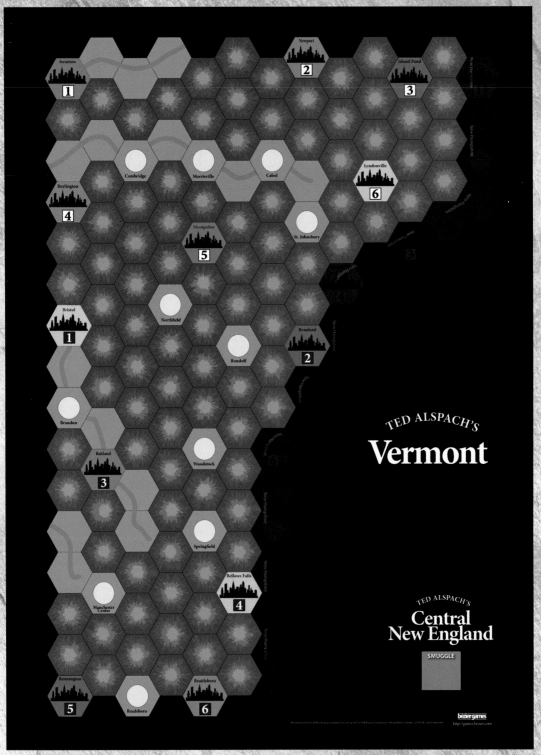

This is the complete *Vermont* board, created entirely in Illustrator. Each of the mountain hexes was created with an appearance that had three additional fills, each of which was scaled down and roughened considerably as well as given a slightly different fill. Illustrator treats each hex independently in order to achieve a totally random effect for each of the hexes this is applied to.

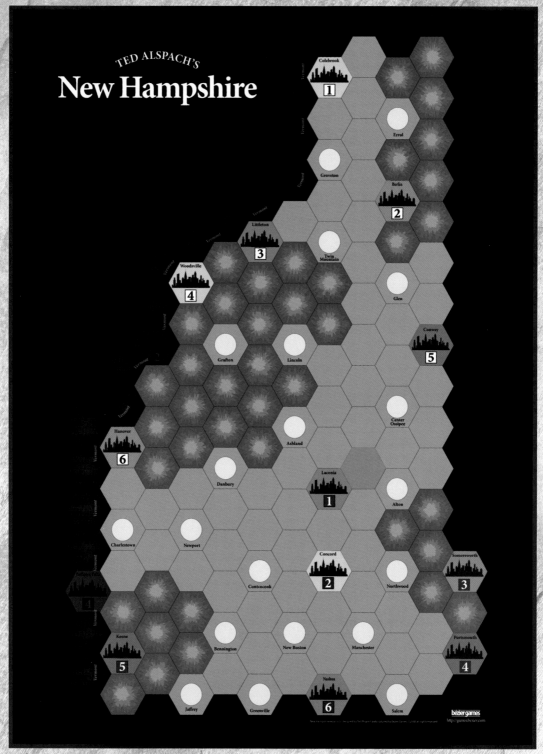

In order to make the two maps work together when lying side by side, a column of faded hexes was created on the edge of each map, simply copied from one map and pasted on the other, with the opacity set to 30%. The background black is a rich black consisting of 60% Cyan, 60% Magenta, 60% Yellow, and 100% Black, making the faded hexes look much more vivid.

While working on the international version of *Start Player,* I needed to set it so that the title text (in the orange box at the top of the card), the description text (in the box below), and the character statements were all printed in 100% Black set to overprint. Overprint is important because that way all languages could share the CMY plates, while only the Black one is different.

For the election strips of *Board 2 Pieces*, I changed the title to a stars-and-stripes theme with meeples as stars. I created the patterns for each and then filled the text objects with those patterns to achieve the end result.

A close-up of Venus was to appear on the Illustrator CS box, with all sorts of additional detail to Venus's eye and lips. But then the Flower took over for the CS versions.

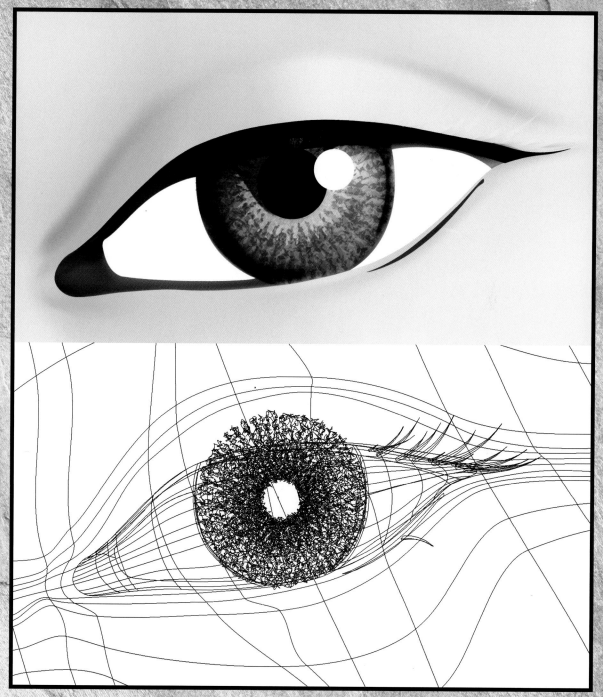

This is a super close-up of Venus's eye, with the color version above and the artwork version below.

Drop shadows and bright distinctive colors make this classic *Buffy the Vampire Slayer* quote from Season 3 pop.

This dramatically colored live trace of a cat was then modified to give it a loopy, free-flowing appearance.

This *Rapscallion* booth poster uses 100% Illustrator-generated imagery.

Creating outlines shouldn't cause that much of a problem when the type is to be output to an imagesetter because the high resolution of the imagesetter makes up for the loss of hinting. However, very small type — 4 points or less — could be adversely affected.

NOTE Converting typefaces to outlines removes the hinting system that Adobe has implemented. This hinting system makes small letters on low-resolution (less than 600 dpi) devices print more accurately, controlling the placement and visibility of serifs and other small, thin strokes in characters. Type at small point sizes looks quite different on laser printers, although it retains its shape and consistency when it's output to an imagesetter or an output scanner system.

Understanding Other Type Considerations

When you're using type in Illustrator, remember these things if you want to get good results:

- Ensure that the person you're sending the Illustrator file to has the same fonts you have. It isn't enough just to have the same name of a font; you need the exact font that was created by the same manufacturer.

- Try not to mix TrueType fonts with PostScript fonts. This usually ends up confusing everyone involved.

- If the person you're sending Illustrator files to doesn't have your typeface, select the type in that font and then choose Type ⇨ Create Outlines or press Ctrl+Shift+O (⌘+Shift+O).

- If you're saving your illustration as an EPS file to be placed into another program and you're not going to open the file, you can choose Include Document Fonts in the EPS Save dialog box. This forces any fonts used in the illustration to be saved with the illustration and allows the illustration to print as a placed image from within another program or to print from Illustrator as a placed EPS. The same goes for PDF files.

Summary

Text can be an important part of Illustrator documents. Understanding how Illustrator handles text-related issues is vital to getting the best results. In this chapter, you learned about the following important topics in this area:

- Individual type has one point as its anchor, and the type is aligned to that point.

- There are four ways to put type on a page: individual type, type containers, area type, and type on a path.

- Type containers exist within a rectangle drawn with the Type tool.

- Type can be selected all at once by clicking the path (or point) of the type with the Selection tool.

- Individual characters, words, and paragraphs can be selected by using any of the type tools.

- Area type is type that exists within the confines of any path.

- Type on a path is type that runs along the edge of a path.

- The Character panel, accessed by pressing Ctrl+T (⌘+T), contains all the character-specific information about selected type and can be used to change that information.

- Tracking and kerning remove or add space between groups or pairs of letters, respectively.

- The Paragraph panel contains all the paragraph-specific information about selected type and can be used to change that information.

- Most of the options used to control type can be found in the Type menu.

- Type can be set to wrap around selected paths by using the Text Wrapping feature.

- Type can be set to jump from text block to text block by threading text blocks together.

- The Tabs panel is used to set tabs for text areas.

- If you have both the screen font and the printer font of a Type 1 typeface, or if you have an OpenType or TrueType font installed, you can convert the font into outlines via the Create Outlines command.

- After type has been changed to outlines, you can use those outlines as a mask or fill those outlines with gradients or patterns.

Chapter 10

Using Creative Strokes and Fills with Patterns

N o Illustrator book would be complete without discussing the how-tos of creating creative strokes, patterns, and textures with the Scribble effect. Sure, you can create these by simply drawing them, but Illustrator makes their creation a breeze. Illustrator allows you to create a pattern as well as save it for future use.

We all have the desire to add some texture to make flat images pop up. The Scribble effect lets you add some sketchy or computery effects to an otherwise boring illustration, giving the drawing a loose, free, quality look.

Using Creative Strokes

In Chapter 4, I discuss how to apply strokes to paths, and in Chapter 5, I discuss all the attributes of a stroke and how to apply them to objects. In this chapter, you learn how to use strokes to create something spectacular.

The ability to stroke a path in Illustrator is greatly underrated. Strokes can do more than just outline shapes and vary thickness and patterns. You can enhance illustrations with a combination of strokes, including easily creating a filmstrip or a railroad track with some stroke attribute changes.

The first part of this section explains some of the greatest mysteries and unlocks some of the deepest secrets that surround strokes. If that sounds at all boring, take a look at the figures in this chapter. I created most of them by using strokes, not filled paths.

You create most effects with strokes by overlaying several strokes on top of each other. By using the Appearance panel's popup menu to add a new stroke, you place an exact duplicate of the original path on top of itself.

Changing the weight and color of the top stroke gives the appearance of a path that's a designer, or custom, stroke. You can add strokes on top of or under the original stroke to make the pattern more complex or to add more colors or shapes.

Stroke essentials

Strokes act and work differently than fills. Remember these basic rules when using strokes:

- **Even distribution:** The most important thing to remember when using strokes is that you should evenly distribute stroke-weight width on both sides of a path. In other words, for a stroke with a 6-point weight, each side of the stroke's path should have 3 points of weight.

- **Using patterns in strokes:** You can place patterns in strokes, and you can see the pattern on the stroke.

- **No gradients allowed:** Due to PostScript limitations, you can't use gradients to color strokes. The workaround for this is to choose Effect ⇨ Path ⇨ Outline Stroke so you can edit later to fill with a gradient. Choosing Object ⇨ Path ⇨ Outline Stroke creates path outlines around the width of the stroke. When you convert a stroke to an outline, it's really an outlined path object, and you can fill it with patterns and gradients (both of which appear when previewing and printing).

- **Consistent stroke weight:** Stroke weight never varies on the same path.

- **No stroke weight:** A stroke with a color of None has no stroke weight.

- **Strokes and Pathfinder functions:** Strokes are, for the most part, ignored when combining, splitting, or modifying paths with the Pathfinder functions. Strokes are never considered when the Pathfinder functions search for the locations of the paths.

CROSS-REF For more on gradients, see Chapter 7. For more on stroke weights as they relate to paths and objects, see Chapters 4 and 5. For more on the Pathfinder functions, see Chapter 6.

Using the stroke charts

The stroke charts in Figures 10.1 through 10.3 show how some of the basic stroke-dash patterns look with various options chosen, at different weights, and in different combinations. The great advantage of these charts is that you can find a style similar to the one you want and then modify it to suit your situation. The charts should help you determine when to use certain types of stroke patterns because some patterns work better than others with curves and corners. All the paths in the charts were taken from an original shape that included a straight segment, a corner, and a curve.

The first chart, shown in Figure 10.1, consists of thirty-two 3-point stroke paths that have a variety of dash patterns and end and join attributes. The second chart, shown in Figure 10.2, shows eighteen 10-point stroke paths with similar attributes. These charts show stroke effects with only one path. The area in the middle of each path in the charts describes the path.

The third chart, shown in Figure 10.3, contains paths that have been copied on top of the original by using the Appearance panel. To copy the path this way, select the path and then choose Add New Stroke from the Appearance panel's popup menu. The paths are listed in the order that they were created. The first path is described at the bottom of the list. The first path is duplicated in the Appearance panel by choosing Add New Stroke from the popup menu and then given the paint style attributes of the item in the list. In the case of blended paths (the fourth one down in the first row of Figure 10.3), you need to copy the original line and then choose Edit ➪ Paste In Front or press Ctrl+F (⌘+F) rather than use the Appearance panel to duplicate the path (this keeps the paths in place). You can't blend multiple paths in the Appearance panel because Illustrator reads the paths as one path. So, in the case of blends, invoke the Paste in Front option before blending. You can just select all paths and then choose Object ➪ Blend ➪ Make.

> **TIP** To create some really great effects, such as a pearl necklace, you need to blend the paths. You can blend paths from one to another. Simply select the paths and then choose Object ➪ Blend ➪ Make. You can change the blend amount if necessary by choosing Object ➪ Blend ➪ Blend Options.

> **CROSS-REF** For more on blends, see Chapter 12.

When you create a stroke pattern, the original path is frequently selected in the Appearance panel and then copied on top of the original by using the Appearance panel's popup menu (select the path and then choose Add New Stroke) several times.

FIGURE 10.1

Thirty-two 3-point stroke paths

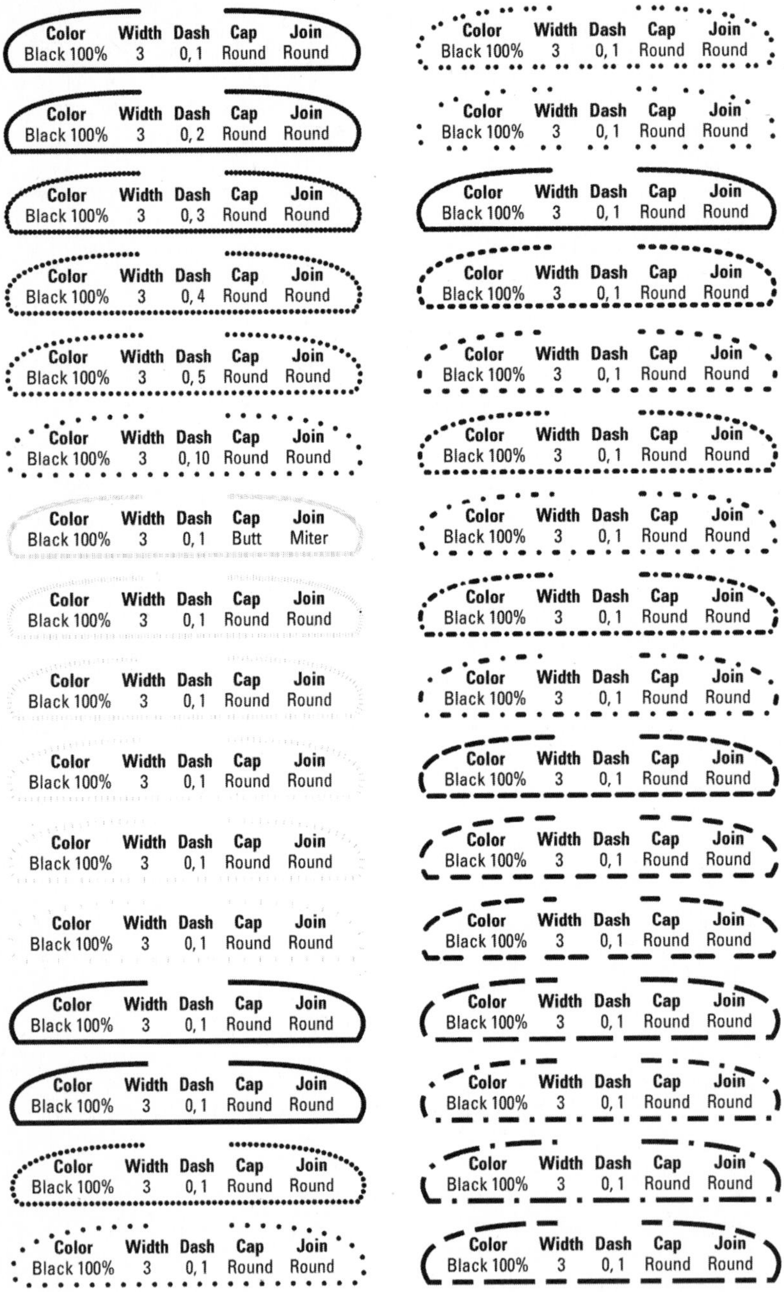

Color	Width	Dash	Cap	Join
Black 100%	3	0, 1	Round	Round

Color	Width	Dash	Cap	Join
Black 100%	3	0, 2	Round	Round

Color	Width	Dash	Cap	Join
Black 100%	3	0, 3	Round	Round

Color	Width	Dash	Cap	Join
Black 100%	3	0, 4	Round	Round

Color	Width	Dash	Cap	Join
Black 100%	3	0, 5	Round	Round

Color	Width	Dash	Cap	Join
Black 100%	3	0, 10	Round	Round

Color	Width	Dash	Cap	Join
Black 100%	3	0, 1	Butt	Miter

Color	Width	Dash	Cap	Join
Black 100%	3	0, 1	Round	Round

Color	Width	Dash	Cap	Join
Black 100%	3	0, 1	Round	Round

Color	Width	Dash	Cap	Join
Black 100%	3	0, 1	Round	Round

Color	Width	Dash	Cap	Join
Black 100%	3	0, 1	Round	Round

Color	Width	Dash	Cap	Join
Black 100%	3	0, 1	Round	Round

Color	Width	Dash	Cap	Join
Black 100%	3	0, 1	Round	Round

Color	Width	Dash	Cap	Join
Black 100%	3	0, 1	Round	Round

Color	Width	Dash	Cap	Join
Black 100%	3	0, 1	Round	Round

Color	Width	Dash	Cap	Join
Black 100%	3	0, 1	Round	Round

Color	Width	Dash	Cap	Join
Black 100%	3	0, 1	Round	Round

Color	Width	Dash	Cap	Join
Black 100%	3	0, 1	Round	Round

Color	Width	Dash	Cap	Join
Black 100%	3	0, 1	Round	Round

Color	Width	Dash	Cap	Join
Black 100%	3	0, 1	Round	Round

Color	Width	Dash	Cap	Join
Black 100%	3	0, 1	Round	Round

Color	Width	Dash	Cap	Join
Black 100%	3	0, 1	Round	Round

Color	Width	Dash	Cap	Join
Black 100%	3	0, 1	Round	Round

Color	Width	Dash	Cap	Join
Black 100%	3	0, 1	Round	Round

Color	Width	Dash	Cap	Join
Black 100%	3	0, 1	Round	Round

Color	Width	Dash	Cap	Join
Black 100%	3	0, 1	Round	Round

Color	Width	Dash	Cap	Join
Black 100%	3	0, 1	Round	Round

Color	Width	Dash	Cap	Join
Black 100%	3	0, 1	Round	Round

Color	Width	Dash	Cap	Join
Black 100%	3	0, 1	Round	Round

Color	Width	Dash	Cap	Join
Black 100%	3	0, 1	Round	Round

Color	Width	Dash	Cap	Join
Black 100%	3	0, 1	Round	Round

Color	Width	Dash	Cap	Join
Black 100%	3	0, 1	Round	Round

FIGURE 10.2

Eighteen 10-point stroke paths

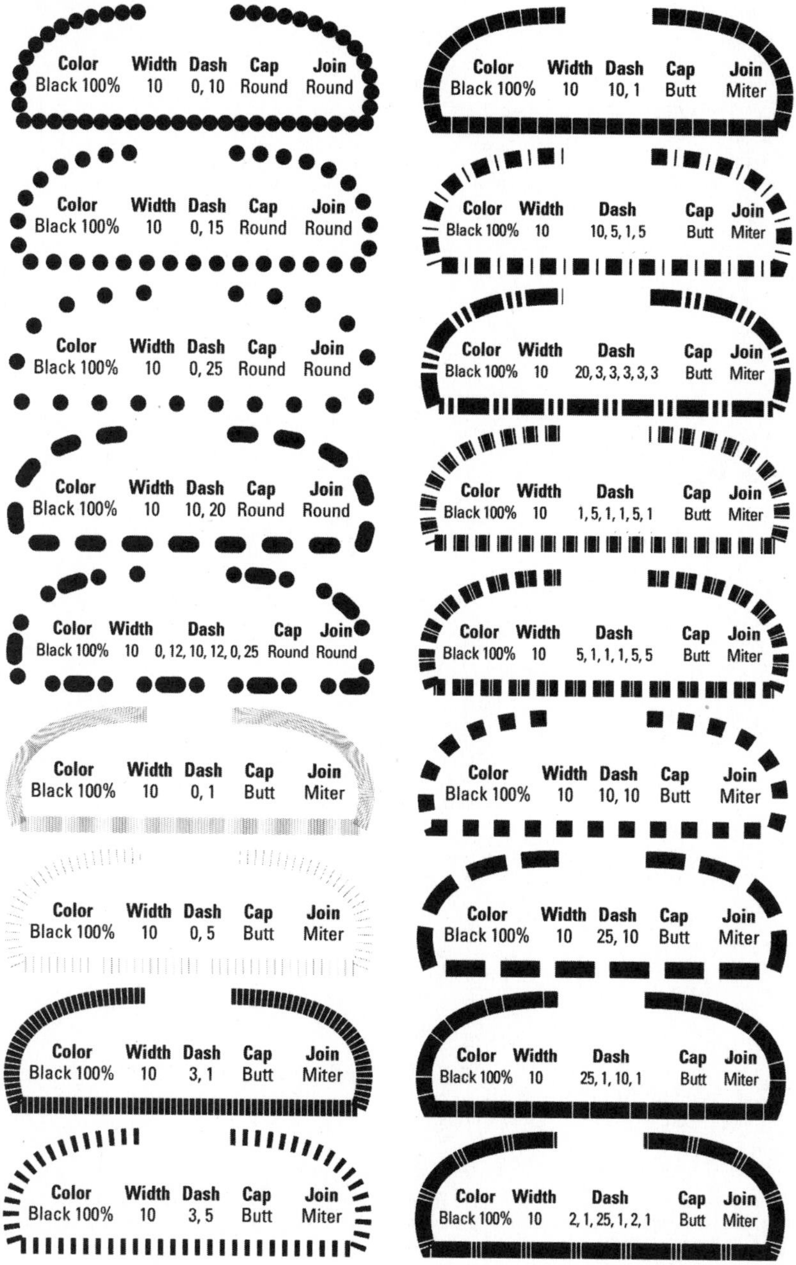

Color	Width	Dash	Cap	Join
Black 100%	10	0, 10	Round	Round

Color	Width	Dash	Cap	Join
Black 100%	10	0, 15	Round	Round

Color	Width	Dash	Cap	Join
Black 100%	10	0, 25	Round	Round

Color	Width	Dash	Cap	Join
Black 100%	10	10, 20	Round	Round

Color	Width	Dash	Cap	Join
Black 100%	10	0, 12, 10, 12, 0, 25	Round	Round

Color	Width	Dash	Cap	Join
Black 100%	10	0, 1	Butt	Miter

Color	Width	Dash	Cap	Join
Black 100%	10	0, 5	Butt	Miter

Color	Width	Dash	Cap	Join
Black 100%	10	3, 1	Butt	Miter

Color	Width	Dash	Cap	Join
Black 100%	10	3, 5	Butt	Miter

Color	Width	Dash	Cap	Join
Black 100%	10	10, 1	Butt	Miter

Color	Width	Dash	Cap	Join
Black 100%	10	10, 5, 1, 5	Butt	Miter

Color	Width	Dash	Cap	Join
Black 100%	10	20, 3, 3, 3, 3	Butt	Miter

Color	Width	Dash	Cap	Join
Black 100%	10	1, 5, 1, 1, 5, 1	Butt	Miter

Color	Width	Dash	Cap	Join
Black 100%	10	5, 1, 1, 1, 5, 5	Butt	Miter

Color	Width	Dash	Cap	Join
Black 100%	10	10, 10	Butt	Miter

Color	Width	Dash	Cap	Join
Black 100%	10	25, 10	Butt	Miter

Color	Width	Dash	Cap	Join
Black 100%	10	25, 1, 10, 1	Butt	Miter

Color	Width	Dash	Cap	Join
Black 100%	10	2, 1, 25, 1, 2, 1	Butt	Miter

FIGURE 10.3

Paths that have been copied on top of the original paths

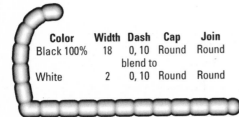

Color	Width	Dash	Cap	Join
White	8	0, 28	Round	Round
White	2	0, 14	Round	Round
Black 100%	4	0, 14	Round	Round
Black 100%	10	0, 28	Round	Round
Black 100%	2	Solid	Round	Round

Color	Width	Dash	Cap	Join
White	1	Solid	Butt	Round
White	18	1, 9, 0, 9	Butt	Round
Black 100%	8	1, 18	Round	Round
White	14	1, 18	Round	Round
Black 100%	18	1, 18	Round	Round

Color	Width	Dash	Cap	Join
White	9	0, 15	Round	Round
Black 100%	10	0, 15	Projected	Round
Black 100%	4	Solid	Round	Round

Color	Width	Dash	Cap	Join
Black 100%	18	0, 1 blend to	Butt	Miter
White	2	0, 1	Butt	Miter

Color	Width	Dash	Cap	Join
Black 100%	18	0, 10 blend to	Round	Round
White	2	0, 10	Round	Round

Color	Width	Dash	Cap	Join
Black 100%	18	Solid blend to	Round	Round
White	16	Solid blend to	Round	Round
Black 100%	14	Solid	Round	Round
White	14	Solid	Round	Round
Black 100%	11	Solid blend to	Round	Round
White	9	Solid blend to	Round	Round
Black 100%	7	Solid	Round	Round
White	7	Solid	Round	Round
Black 100%	2.5	Solid blend to	Round	Round
White	1	Solid	Round	Round

Color	Width	Dash	Cap	Join
Black 50%	12	20, 10	Butt	Round
Black 100%	14	Solid	Projected	Round
White	16	1, 2	Butt	Round
Black 100%	18	Solid	Projected	Round

Color	Width	Dash	Cap	Join
Black 100%	6	0, 10	Round	Round
White	8	0, 10	Round	Round
Black 100%	10	0, 10	Round	Round

Color	Width	Dash	Cap	Join
Black 100%	6	0, 10	Projected	Miter
White	8	0, 10	Projected	Miter
Black 100%	10	0, 10	Projected	Miter

Creating parallel strokes

Do you need to create a railroad track or a racetrack quickly? Creating the curvy parallel lines to make your illustration realistic is easier than you think. The following steps describe how to create a specialty stroke that looks like parallel strokes:

1. **Use the Pen tool to draw a short curved line similar to the line at the top in Figure 10.4.** The example uses a fill of None and a stroke-path weight that's 42-point Black (use the Stroke panel to set the size of the stroke).

2. **In the Appearance panel's popup menu, choose Add New Stroke.** You access the popup menu by clicking the triangle in the upper-right corner of the Appearance panel. The new stroke appears just above the existing stroke in the Appearance panel.

3. **Change the stroke weight of the new stroke to 30-point White.** Make certain that the new stroke is selected in the Appearance panel before making these changes. This overlays the new, narrower white stroke on top of the wider black stroke.

4. **Choose Add New Stroke from the Appearance panel's popup menu.**

5. **Change the stroke weight of the new stroke to 18-point Black.**

6. **Again, choose Add New Stroke from the Appearance panel's popup menu.**

7. **Change the stroke weight of the new stroke to 6-point White.** In the final product, shown in Figure 10.4, the 30-point stroke is 12 points more than the 18 points of the black stroke — or 6 points on each side. The 42-point stroke is 12 points more than the white 30-point stroke.

CAUTION The order in which the overlapping strokes appear in the Appearance panel is very important. The widest stroke must be at the bottom of the list, the next widest just above that, etc. If you don't have the strokes in the proper order, narrower strokes that are below wider strokes will not be visible (unless you change the opacity of the thicker strokes). If necessary, you can drag the strokes in the Appearance panel to rearrange them into the correct order.

This example is just the tip of the iceberg in creating custom strokes. Not only can you have paths that overlap, but you also can give the stroke on each path different dash patterns, joins, and caps. You can even add fills to certain paths to make the stroke different on both sides of the path. And if all that isn't enough, you can use Outline Path to outline strokes.

TIP When you create parallel strokes, determine how thick each of the visible strokes should be, multiply that number by the black and white visible strokes that you want for the base stroke, and work up from there. For example, if you want 10-point strokes and there are four white strokes and five black strokes, make the first stroke 90-point Black. Then, make the next strokes 70-point White, 50-point Black, 30-point White, and 10-point Black.

Knowing the secrets doesn't let you in on the really good stuff though. Read on to learn how to apply these techniques to achieve truly amazing effects with strokes.

FIGURE 10.4

The original 42-point stroke at the top and the final parallel stroke that results from overlaying new, smaller, contrasting strokes over existing ones

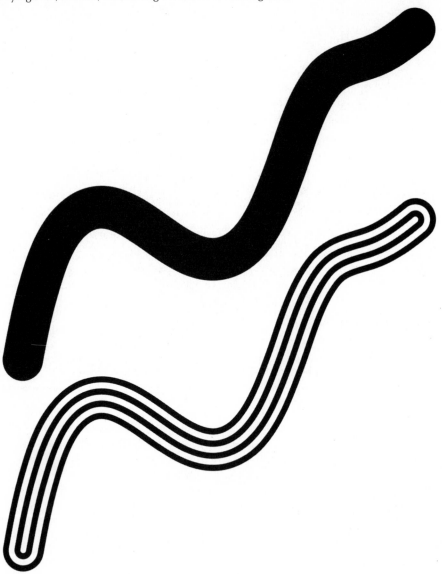

Creating a Filmstrip Stroke

The stroke examples shown earlier in this chapter can help you find a specific style, which you can then modify for your situation. As an example, the second stroke from the top in the right column in Figure 10.3 is a stroke that looks like filmstrip. The following steps describe how to create this filmstrip stroke, which is a basic stroke that produces a stunning effect.

1. **Draw a wavy path with the Pen tool.** For more on using the Pen tool, see Chapter 4.

2. **Change the stroke of the path to 18-point Black and the fill to None.**

3. **Choose Add New Stroke from the Appearance panel's popup menu.** Change the new stroke to 16-point White and then use a dash pattern of Dash 1, Gap 2.

4. **Choose Add New Stroke from the Appearance panel's popup menu again.** Change the new stroke to 14-point Black.

5. **Choose Add New Stroke from the Appearance panel's popup menu once more.** Change the new stroke to 50% Black, 12 points, with a dash pattern of Dash 20, Gap 10.

The figure that follows shows the final filmstrip, and the Appearance panel displays the list of strokes. You can use this procedure to create any of the strokes in Figure 10.3 or substitute the values that are listed in the chart to create custom strokes.

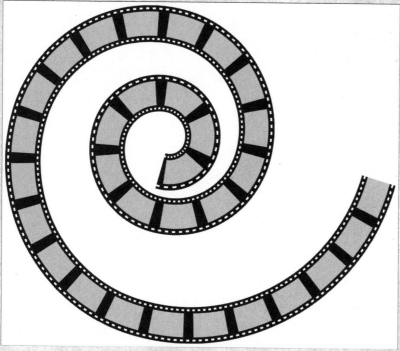

Creating cinematic celluloid

Creating map elements

Several effects that you can create with paths have a traveling theme, mainly because a path starts somewhere and finishes somewhere else. Railroad tracks, roads, highways, trails, and rivers all have a tendency to neatly conform to stroke effects with paths.

Creating a railroad track with a gradient

One of the trickiest traveling paths to create is a railroad track. The practical point of creating this railroad track is to illustrate how to change a stroke into a gradient. As mentioned at the beginning of this chapter, you can do this only if you convert your stroke into an outline. Then, you can fill it with the gradient of your choosing. To get the real railroad track look, some innovative thinking is necessary, as described in the following steps:

1. **Draw a line with the Pen tool to represent the railroad track.** Set the fill to None.

2. **Give the path a desired stroke weight.** This example uses a stroke weight of 60 points, as shown in Figure 10.5.

FIGURE 10.5

Begin by drawing a 60-point line with no fill.

3. **Copy the path by choosing Edit ⇨ Copy.** Alternatively, you can press Ctrl+C (⌘+C).

4. **Choose Edit ⇨ Paste in Front.** Alternatively, you can press Ctrl+F (⌘+F). You're still pasting the original copied path from the Clipboard. This creates a second path, which is the area between the two metal rails of the railroad.

5. **Give the inside path a desired stroke weight.** The example uses a stroke weight of 40 points, which is the inner section of the train track.

6. **Select both paths by dragging a marquee around them with the Selection tool and then choose Object ⇨ Path ⇨ Outline Stroke.** This changes the paths into outlined paths because strokes can't contain gradients.

7. **Fill the paths with a metallic gradient, as shown in Figure 10.6.** For more on applying gradients, see Chapter 7.

8. **Select both paths and then click the Exclude overlapping shape areas button in the Pathfinder panel.** This command subtracts the inner section of the track from the two outer sections. Now you have two metal rails, as shown in Figure 10.7.

9. **Choose Edit ⇨ Paste in Back.** This pastes the original copied path from the Clipboard directly behind the original path. Alternatively, you can press Ctrl+B (⌘+B).

10. **Give the new path a stroke weight that you want.** This example uses a stroke weight of 80 points. This part becomes the wooden railroad ties that support the rails.

11. **Choose Object ⇨ Path ⇨ Outline Stroke.** This changes the strokes into outlined paths. Fill this path with a gradient consisting of several wood-like browns, as shown in Figure 10.8. The ties are still one big solid chunk of wood (I split them later).

12. **Choose Edit ⇨ Paste in Front.** You can also press Ctrl+F (⌘+F). This pastes a path right on top of the wooden area.

13. **Give the stroke the same color as the background, give it a weight of 50, and give it a dash pattern of Dash 20, Gap 10.** The gaps are the see-through areas, showing the wood-filled path below them. Figure 10.9 shows the final result.

Outline Stroke is often used on this type of stroke design because strokes can't have gradient fills. The reason that the railroad ties were not given a dash pattern before Outline Path was applied is that Outline Path doesn't work with dash patterns.

FIGURE 10.6

Fill both paths with a metallic gradient.

FIGURE 10.7

Use the Pathfinder panel to create the rails.

FIGURE 10.8

Add the stroke for the ties.

FIGURE 10.9

The final railroad track looks pretty realistic.

Creating a highway

Figure 10.10 shows a stroke design that I discovered a few years back while I was playing with Illustrator. It has the makings of a cute parlor magic trick that you can use to impress your friends. Back when you had to work in Artwork mode — that is, before Illustrator 5.0 — creating designs with strokes was much more difficult. Artists couldn't see what they were drawing on-screen, so they had to envision it in their minds. Editing dashes and weights is almost a pleasure now that you can use the Stroke panel and undo multiple changes.

Follow these steps to create a four-lane highway by drawing just one path:

1. **Use the Pen tool to draw a slightly wavy path from the left side of the Artboard to the right.**

2. **Change the Path to a fill of None and then create a 400-point stroke in green.** This path is the grass next to the highway.

3. **Choose Add New Stroke from the Appearance panel's popup menu.** Change the paint style of the stroke to 25% Cyan, 25% Yellow, and 85% Black, with a weight of 240 points. This path creates the shoulders on the highway. Remember to double-click the

stroke color picker to display the Color Picker dialog box and to use the Stroke panel to set the stroke width.

4. **Choose Add New Stroke from the Appearance panel's popup menu.** Change the paint style to 5% Cyan and 10% Black, with a weight of 165 points. This path creates the white lines at the edges of the shoulders.

5. **Choose Add New Stroke from the Appearance panel's popup menu.** Change the paint style to 15% Cyan, 10% Yellow, and 50% Black, with a weight of 160 points. This path is the highway's road surface.

6. **To create the dashed white lines for the lanes, choose Add New Stroke from the Appearance panel's popup menu.** Change the paint style to 5% Cyan and 10% Black, with a weight of 85 points, a dash of 20, and a gap of 20.

7. **Choose Add New Stroke from the Appearance panel's popup menu.** Change the paint style to 15% Cyan, 10% Yellow, and 50% Black, with a weight of 80 points. Deselect the Dashed line check box. This path is the inner part of the highway's road surface.

8. **To create the two yellow lines, choose Add New Stroke from the Appearance panel's popup menu.** Change the paint style to 15% Cyan, 20% Magenta, and 100% Yellow, with a weight of 8 points.

9. **Choose Add New Stroke from the Appearance panel's popup menu.** Change the paint style to 15% Cyan, 10% Yellow, and 50% Black, with a weight of 3 points. This path is the piece of highway that divides the yellow lines.

FIGURE 10.10

The final highway design that results from this exercise

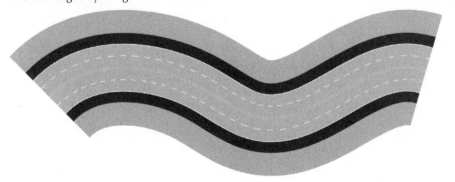

Creating Perfect Patterns

"The Perfect Pattern is one in which you cannot determine the borders of its tiles," according to the *Chinese Book of Patterns*. If that's true, you can use Illustrator to create perfect patterns.

The Pattern function in Illustrator is twofold. First, you can fill or stroke any path with a pattern. Second, you can edit existing patterns or create new ones from Illustrator objects. The real strength of Illustrator's pattern features is that you can create patterns as well as apply them on-screen in almost any way imaginable.

A *pattern* in Illustrator is a series of objects within a rectangle that's commonly referred to as a *pattern tile*. When you choose a pattern in the Swatches panel, Illustrator repeats the selected pattern as necessary to fill the object, as shown in Figure 10.11.

Illustrator places the pattern tiles together for you. After you apply a pattern to an object, you can use any of the transformation tools (discussed later in this chapter) to alter it.

FIGURE 10.11

The pattern repeats to fill the object.

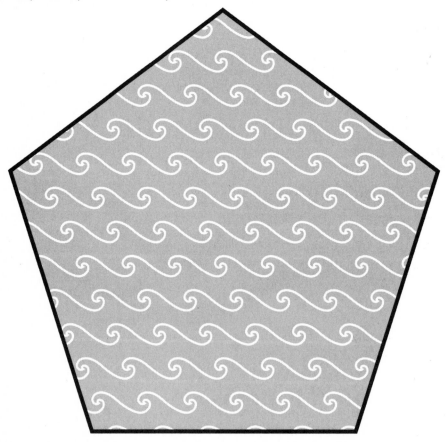

 Tile patterns can either have a background color or they can be transparent. Transparent patterns can overlay other objects, including objects filled with patterns.

CROSS-REF For more on creating objects with fills, see Chapter 5.

Using the default patterns

A few patterns are available at all times in Illustrator. You can open other libraries from the Swatch Libraries submenu of the Window menu. Under the Swatch Libraries submenu, you have a variety of libraries from which to choose. The last option is Other Library. Through Other Library, you can bring in saved libraries as well as the sample libraries that ship with Illustrator. Figure 10.12 shows one of the sample pattern libraries.

To fill a path with a pattern, select that path, ensure the Fill icon is active, and click the corresponding pattern swatch in the Swatches panel. Illustrator fills the path with the pattern you select.

Although there are a few different default fill patterns, each one can take on a whole new perspective if you use the various transformation functions — move, rotate, scale, reflect, and skew — on them. The default patterns are stored in the Adobe Illustrator Startup file.

FIGURE 10.12

The Decorative_Classic pattern library is one of several sample libraries you can use in your Illustrator documents.

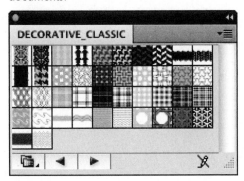

CROSS-REF For more on the move, rotate, scale, reflect, and skew functions, see Chapter 11.

Creating custom patterns

In addition to using the patterns provided with Illustrator, you can create custom patterns by following these steps:

1. **Create the artwork that you want to appear in the pattern tile.** This example uses a bunch of different stars created and arranged in a specific order.

2. **Select the artwork with the Selection tool.** For more on the Selection tool, see Chapter 6.

3. **Drag your artwork into the Swatches panel.** A swatch with your new pattern appears on the panel.

4. **Select the object first and then choose the new pattern you created in the Swatches panel.** This applies the new pattern to your object.

Figure 10.13 also shows the artwork applied as the fill of another shape. Patterns can contain paths, symbols, and text but can't contain masks, gradients, placed images, or other patterns.

FIGURE 10.13

The final basic pattern tile (left) is used here as a fill pattern for a shape (right).

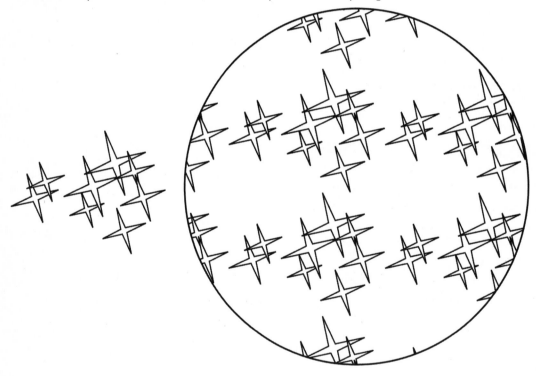

Understanding pattern backgrounds and boundaries

Any pattern tile you create can have the color background you specify simply by making a rectangle the size of the tile and placing it behind the objects in the pattern. When you create the pattern on top of the background rectangle, just select the entire background along with the pattern objects to create the pattern.

If you don't create a background rectangle, Illustrator uses the Bounding Box, as shown in Figure 10.14, of the selected objects to determine the size of the pattern tile. The Bounding Box is the smallest rectangle that completely encloses all selected objects and paths.

FIGURE 10.14

The Bounding Box is the smallest rectangle that completely encloses your selected objects and paths.

But what happens if you want the edge of the pattern tile to be somewhere inside the Bounding Box? Illustrator provides a way for you to create a Bounding Box to define pattern tiles that consist of objects that extend beyond the pattern edges. You create a Bounding Box by creating a rectangle with the Rectangle tool, fill it with None, and make it the backmost object in the pattern tile.

CROSS-REF For more on drawing rectangles and using fills, see Chapter 5.

Making seamless patterns

To make patterns seamless, you need to remember that objects that lie across the edge of the pattern border are cut into two sections, the outside section of which is invisible. You also need to ensure that lines that stretch from one edge of a pattern border to the other side connect to another line on the opposite edge of the boundary. The second problem is more difficult to deal with than the first one. To make a line match well from one side to the other, you usually have to move one or both of the ends up or down slightly.

For patterns to appear seamless, you can't make the edges of the pattern noticeable. Avoiding this sounds rather easy.

All you have to do is avoid placing any objects that touch the edges of a background rectangle. Well, that technique will do it, but when you use such a pattern, the lack of any objects along the borders of the tile can make the pattern look strange.

Creating symmetrical patterns

You can easily create symmetrical patterns in Illustrator. The key to creating them is to draw the Bounding Box after you create the rest of the objects, drawing outward from the center point of one of the objects.

When you create symmetrical patterns, the main difficulty is judging the space between the objects in the pattern. Objects can seem too close together or too far apart, especially in patterns that have different amounts of horizontal and vertical space between the objects. The solution is to use a square as the pattern tile boundary. This ensures that you have an equal amount of space from the center of one object to the center of the next object, both vertically and horizontally.

Creating line patterns and grids

Using lines and grids for patterns is ideal because they're so easy to create. The key in both types of patterns is the size of the bounding rectangle. You use a grid to draw accurate floor plans or even for drawing perspective scenes. Line patterns are great for creating fences or any repeating linear paths.

Creating line patterns

Follow these steps to create a line pattern:

1. **Decide what point size you want for the lines and how far apart you want them.**

2. **Draw a rectangle, making the height match the separation you want between the lines.** Ensure you draw the rectangle with a fill and stroke of None.

3. **Draw a horizontal line with a fill of None and a stroke of the point size you want from outside the left edge of the rectangle to outside the right edge of the rectangle.**

4. **Make a pattern from the two objects.** You make a pattern by adding the image to the Swatches panel.

5. **Apply the pattern to the object of your choice.** You can apply a pattern by selecting the object and then choosing the pattern from the Swatches panel. The triangle in Figure 10.15 shows the results.

You can also use this technique with vertical lines. Just make the bounding rectangle's width the distance from line to line.

Creating grid patterns

You can use a grid pattern to create graphing paper for a logo. Another good use of grid patterns is for grates or windows because you can use the transformation tools to add perspective. Creating grids is even easier than creating evenly spaced lines:

1. **Create a rectangle that's the size of the grid holes.** For example, for a 1/4-inch grid, you make the rectangle 1/4 inch × 1/4 inch. For more on creating rectangles, see Chapter 5.

2. **Apply a stroke to the object.** Make the stroke the weight that you want the gridlines to be.

CROSS-REF For more on stroke weights and applying strokes, see Chapter 5.

3. **Make that rectangle into a pattern.** You make a pattern by adding your object to the Swatches panel. That's it. You now have a pattern grid that's as precise as possible.

TIP If you want the space between gridlines to be an exact measurement, make the rectangle bigger by increasing the stroke weight. A 1/4-inch grid (18 points) with 1-point gridlines requires a rectangle that's 17 points × 17 points.

FIGURE 10.15

You can easily make a pattern from straight lines and then apply it to any object.

Using diagonal-line and grid patterns

Shading effects, such as hatched lines, are easily created with a diagonal-line and grid pattern. Figure 10.16 shows text shaded using a diagonal-line pattern rotated and scaled to show a shaded effect. You may find creating diagonal-line and grid patterns difficult if you try to make a rectangle; instead, draw a path at an angle and then use the rectangle with the path in it as a pattern. Joining diagonal lines at the edges of the pattern is nearly impossible.

Using this technique is also a great way to avoid making several patterns when you need line patterns that are set at different angles. Just make one horizontal line pattern and rotate the patterns within the paths.

Follow these steps for a better method of creating a shaded effect:

1. **Create a Bounding Box using the Rectangle tool.**

2. **Create lines (or grids) in horizontal or vertical alignment that extend beyond the Bounding Box.**

3. **Make the lines (or grids) into a pattern.** You can do this by dragging the lines (or grids) to the Swatches panel.

4. **Apply the pattern to an object.** You do this by selecting the object and then clicking the pattern in the Swatches panel.

5. **Double-click the Rotate tool.** The Rotate dialog box opens.

6. **In the Rotate dialog box, type the angle to change the lines, deselect the Objects check box, and click the Patterns check box.** The pattern rotates to the desired angle inside the path.

FIGURE 10.16

A line pattern applied to an object to create a shaded effect

Using transparency and patterns together

Transparent patterns are great to use over the top of color, or gradients, or even other patterns. Instead of creating a bunch of specific patterns that use other patterns, use the transparent pattern option to layer over the top of other patterns. A great use of this option is to use a gradient and then use a line pattern to add a hatched shading look. To make the background of a pattern transparent, don't use a background rectangle. Only the objects in the pattern will be opaque.

You can use the simple line pattern with a transparent background alone or over another pattern. Figure 10.17 shows the same text from Figure 10.16 but with the transparent pattern over a gradient.

FIGURE 10.17

A transparent pattern applied over a gradient

One way to achieve interesting effects is by making a copy of the object behind the original. Follow these steps:

1. **Select the object.**

2. **Choose Edit ➪ Copy.** Alternatively, you can press Ctrl+C (⌘+C). This creates a copy of the object.

3. **Choose Edit ➪ Paste in Back.** You can also press Ctrl+B (⌘+B). This pastes the object behind the original object.

4. **Change the fill in the copy of the object to a solid, a gradient, or another pattern.**

5. **Use the Opacity slider in the Transparency panel to change the appearance as desired.**

Transforming patterns

After you create patterns and place them within paths, you may find that they're too big or at the wrong angle for the path. Likewise, they may start in an awkward location. You can use the transformation tools and the Move command to resolve these problems.

To transform a pattern inside a path, follow these steps:

1. **Select the path.**

2. **Double-click the transformation tool that corresponds to the change that you want to make to the pattern.** The transformation tool's dialog box, as shown in Figure 10.18, opens.

3. **In this transformation (Rotate, Scale, etc.) dialog box, deselect the Objects check box.** This selects the Patterns check box. The Patterns and Objects check boxes are grayed out if the selected object doesn't contain a pattern.

Any changes that you make in a transformation dialog box when only the Patterns check box is clicked affect only the pattern, not the outside shape.

FIGURE 10.18

The Rotate dialog box (along with the other transformation dialog boxes) lets you transform patterns independently of objects.

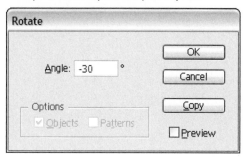

CROSS-REF For more on transforming objects, see Chapter 11.

To move a pattern within a path, choose Object ➪ Transform ➪ Move (or double-click the Selection tool). The Move dialog box also contains Patterns and Objects check boxes. If you deselect the Objects check box, which selects the Patterns check box, only the pattern is moved.

Summary

Using patterns and strokes creatively makes drawing objects a far easier task. In this chapter, you learned about the following topics:

- The most attractive aspect of strokes is that you can use them on top of each another.

- The stroke charts provided in this chapter show some of what you can do with strokes.

- Use Outline Path to create filled paths from strokes.

- Use fills to create half-stroked paths.

- Patterns are a type of fill that provides texture to any path.

- Illustrator supplies several default patterns. You can transform these patterns in the same ways that you can transform other Illustrator objects.

- You can use almost anything you create in Illustrator as a pattern, with the exception of masks, gradients, placed images, and other patterns.

- You construct diagonal-line patterns by creating a horizontal-line pattern and rotating it with the Rotate tool when the pattern is filling a path.

Chapter 11

Applying Transformations and Distortions

Illustrator has the capability to transform any object by scaling it, rotating it, reflecting it, shearing it, or reshaping it. In this chapter, you learn how to take advantage of this power by using transformation functions with menus, panels, and certain tools.

In addition to transformations, Illustrator really gets fun when you work with distortions. Distortions are accomplished with a number of different effects, warps, and the amazing Liquify tools.

Adding a Transformation with Tools

Although there are many places to find the transformation functions, the first stop is the transformation tools. The transformation tools in the Tools panel address fundamental functions, such as scaling, rotating, reflecting, shearing, and reshaping. Before you can use any of these tools, however, you must select one or more objects (including paths, points, and segments). The selected paths are the paths that are transformed.

Using the various transformation tools, you can transform selected objects in five ways:

- Click with a transformation tool to set an origin point and then drag from a different location. This is called a manual transformation.

- Click and drag in one motion to transform the object from its center point or last origin point.

- Press Alt (Option), click to set the origin, and then type exact information in the tool's dialog box. This method is more precise than manually transforming.

- Double-click a transformation tool to set the origin in the center of the selected object and then type information in the tool's dialog box.

- Use the Transform panel (discussed later in this chapter).

All the transformations have additional options in their dialog boxes. Clicking Copy makes a copy of the original and then transforms it to your settings. Clicking the Object check box applies the transformation only to the object (not the fill pattern inside). Clicking the Pattern check box applies the transformation to just the pattern (not the object). Clicking both check boxes applies any transformations to both the object and the pattern.

All the transformation tools work on an accumulating basis. For example, if you scale an object 150% and then scale it again by 150%, the object becomes 225% of its original size (150% × 150% = 225%). If the object is initially scaled to 150% of its original size and you want to return it to that original size, you must do the math and figure out what percentage you need to resize it — in this case, 66.7% (100% ÷ 150% = 66.7%) — or you could just use the Undo feature. Typing 100% in the Scale dialog box leaves the selected objects unchanged.

Illustrator automatically creates a visible origin point, as shown in Figure 11.1, when you use any of the transformation tools. Because the origin is in the center of the selection, if you just click and drag with a transformation tool, the origin point is visible as soon as you click a transformation tool. If you click without dragging to set the origin, it appears at that location until the origin is reset. Having the origin point visible as a blue crosshair makes the transformation tools much more useable and functional.

When manually transforming objects, you can make a copy of the selected object — and thus leave the original untransformed — by holding Alt (Option) before and after releasing the mouse button. In a transformation tool's dialog box, you can make a copy by clicking Copy.

If the Patterns check box is available (you must have a pattern in one of the selected paths; otherwise, this option is grayed out) in any of the transformation tool dialog boxes, you can click its check box to transform your pattern and the object. You can also transform the pattern only, leaving the object untransformed, by deselecting the Objects check box.

CROSS-REF   For more on patterns, see Chapter 10.

TIP   You can manually transform just patterns (and not the objects themselves) by pressing the grave (`) key while using any of the transformation tools, including the Selection tool.

Manually transforming objects is fairly simple if you remember that the first place you click (the point of origin) and the second place should be a fair distance apart. The farther your second click is from the point of origin, the more control you have when dragging to transform.

FIGURE 11.1

The origin point that appears when using any of the transformation tools

All the transformation tools perform certain operations that rely on the Constrain Angle as a point of reference. Normally, this is set to 0°, which makes your Illustrator world act normally. You can change the setting by choosing Edit (Illustrator)⇨Preferences⇨General or by pressing Ctrl+K (⌘+K) and then typing a new value.

You can access each of the transformation tool dialog boxes by choosing Object⇨Transform, as shown in Figure 11.2.

FIGURE 11.2

The Transform submenu under the Object menu

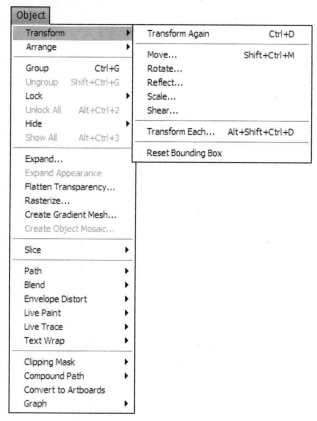

NOTE If the Bounding Box (the blue box that surrounds selected objects) is visible (View ⇨ Show Bounding Box), you can use the Selection tool to rotate, scale, or move the object.

Rotating with the Rotate tool

The Rotate tool is found in the Tools panel, and it rotates selected objects within a document. Double-clicking the Rotate tool or choosing Object ⇨ Transform ⇨ Rotate opens the Rotate dialog box, as shown in Figure 11.3, where you type the precise angle of the selected item's rotation in the Angle box. The object rotates around its origin, which by default is located at the center of the object's Bounding Box. A positive number between 0 and 180 rotates the object counterclockwise that many degrees. A negative number between 0 and −180 rotates the selected object clockwise. The Rotate tool works on a standard 360° circle of rotation.

Click once to set the origin point, which is the object's center of rotation, and then click fairly far from the origin and drag in a circle. The selected object spins along with the cursor. To constrain the angle to 45° increments as you drag, press and hold Shift. This angle is dependent on the Constrain Angle box and is in 45° increments plus the angle in this box. Figure 11.4 shows an illustration before and after rotation.

FIGURE 11.3

The Rotate dialog box allows you to precisely rotate objects.

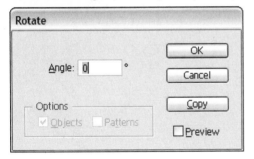

FIGURE 11.4

The object before (left) and after (right) rotation

Reflecting with the Reflect tool

The Reflect tool makes a mirror image of the selected objects, reflected across an axis of reflection. You can find the Reflect tool as a popup tool under the Rotate tool. Double-clicking the Reflect tool or choosing Object ➪ Transform ➪ Reflect reflects selected objects across an axis of reflection that runs through the horizontal center or the vertical center of the selected objects. In the Reflect dialog box, as shown in Figure 11.5, you can type the axis of reflection. If you want to reflect the object through either the horizontal or vertical axis, click the appropriate radio button.

NOTE Pressing Alt (Option) and then clicking in the document window with the Reflect tool selected also opens the Reflect dialog box; however, the axis of reflection is now not in the center of the selected object but passes through the location in the document where you Alt (Option)+clicked.

FIGURE 11.5

Use the Reflect dialog box to create mirror images of objects.

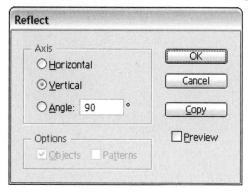

Manual reflecting is done by clicking once to set the origin point (the center of the axis of reflection) and then again somewhere along the axis of reflection. If you click and drag after setting your origin point, you can rotate the axis of reflection and see what your objects look like reflected across various axes. Pressing Shift constrains the axis of reflection to 90° angles relative to the Constrain Angle. Holding Alt (Option) during the release of the click leaves a copy of the original object. Figure 11.6 shows an illustration before and after being reflected.

Scaling with the Scale tool

The Scale tool resizes objects either uniformly or nonuniformly. You can also use the Scale tool to flip objects but without the precision of the Reflect tool. It's impossible to keep both the size and proportions of an object constant while flipping and scaling using the Scale tool.

FIGURE 11.6

An object before (left) and after (right) being reflected across the vertical axis

Double-clicking the Scale tool or choosing Object ➪ Transform ➪ Scale opens the Scale dialog box, as shown in Figure 11.7. All selected objects are scaled from their origins, which by default is located at the center of the object's Bounding Box. If the Uniform option is chosen, numbers typed in the Scale text field result in proportionately scaled objects, where the width and height of the object remain proportional to each other. Numbers less than 100% shrink the object; numbers greater than 100% enlarge it.

Nonuniform scaling resizes the horizontal and vertical dimensions of the selected objects separately, distorting the image. Nonuniform scaling is related to the Constrain Angle you set in the General Preferences dialog box; the angle set there is the horizontal scaling, and the vertical scaling is 90° from that angle.

> **TIP**   Pressing Alt (Option) and then clicking in the document window with the Scale tool selected also opens the Scale dialog box, but the objects are now scaled from the location in the document that was Alt (Option)+clicked.

You can achieve manual resizing by clicking your point of origin and then clicking away from that point and dragging to scale. If you cross the horizontal or vertical axis of the point of origin, the selected object flips over in that direction. Holding Shift constrains the objects to equal proportions if you drag the cursor at approximately 45° from the point of origin. Alternatively, holding Shift constrains the scaling to either horizontal or vertical scaling only if you drag the cursor at about a 90° angle from the point of origin relative to the Constrain Angle.

FIGURE 11.7

The Scale dialog box allows you to specify exactly how objects are scaled.

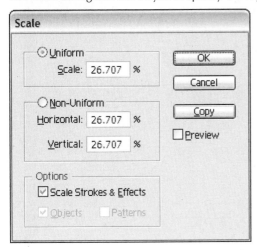

Shearing with the Shear tool

You find the Shear tool as a popup tool under the Scale tool. The Shear tool is somewhat tricky to use until you get the hang of it. Essentially, it pulls all points above the origin point to the side and pushes all points below the origin point in the opposite direction. The farther the points are from the origin, the farther to the side they're moved. The effect gives a slanted, perspective-like look to your object. Use the Shear tool to add a shadow to an object or text. Another great use of shear is to make an object or text look like it's in perspective.

Double-clicking the Shear tool opens the Shear dialog box, as shown in Figure 11.8, which allows more precise control. Double-clicking causes the origin to be in the center of the selected object. The Shear Angle box is simple enough; you type the angle amount the object should shear. Any amount over 75° or less than –75° typically renders the object into an indecipherable mess because at this angle or higher, the art has been flattened into a straight line. The Shear tool reverses the positive-numbers-are-counterclockwise rule.

To shear an object clockwise, type a positive number; to shear counterclockwise, type a negative number. The Axis Angle box is for shearing an object along a specified axis, as opposed to the standard 0/45/90 angle.

TIP Pressing Alt (Option) and then clicking in the document window with the Shear tool selected also opens the Shear dialog box, with the origin of the shear being the location of the Alt (Option)+click.

Manual shearing is something else again because while you click, hold, and drag with the Shear tool, you're doing two things at once. From the beginning of the second click until you release the mouse, you change the angle of shearing. Usually, it's best to start your second click fairly far away from the point of origin. Pressing and holding Shift constrains the axis of shearing to a 45° angle relative to the Constrain Angle. Figure 11.9 shows an illustration before and after being sheared.

FIGURE 11.8

The Shear dialog box allows you to apply a shear transformation to an object.

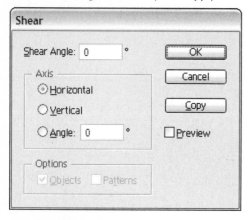

FIGURE 11.9

The sun god Ra before (left) and after (right) being sheared shows how the Shear tool affects objects.

Reshaping with the Reshape tool

You use the Reshape tool to select one or multiple anchor points in order to change an object's shape. You can also select parts of paths to change. Located as a popup tool under the Scale tool, you use the Reshape tool on any path by clicking where you want to bend the path and then dragging. To use the Reshape tool on several paths at once, use the Reshape tool to select the points you want to move first. You must select at least one point that isn't a straight corner point on each path. You then drag on a selected point; all the curved points also move. Figure 11.10 shows an example of what the Reshape tool does.

 **The Reshape tool works best on curved objects, such as spirals, ovals, etc.**

FIGURE 11.10

The spiral before (left) and after (right) using the Reshape tool

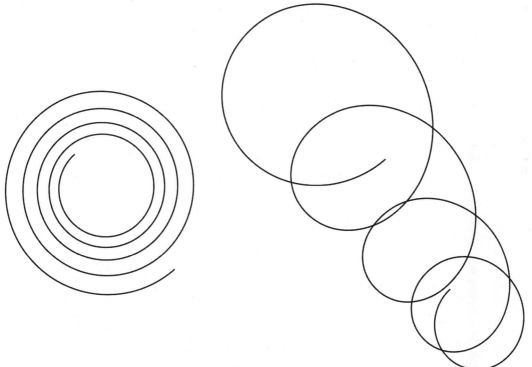

Moving objects

The most common way to move an object is to use a selection tool and then drag the selected points, segments, and paths from one location to another.

The precise way to move an object is to use the Move dialog box, as shown in Figure 11.11, or the Transform panel (discussed later in this chapter). Select the object you want to move and then choose Object ➪ Transform ➪ Move. The Move dialog box opens, and you can type the appropriate values in the horizontal or vertical text fields. If you want to move an object diagonally, type a number in the Distance text field and then type the angle of movement direction in the Angle text field.

You can move any selected object (except for text selected with a Type tool) via the Move dialog box, including individual anchor points and line segments.

By default, the Move dialog box contains the distance and angle that you last moved an object, whether manually with a selection tool or in the Move dialog box. If you use the Measure tool (found in the Tools panel) prior to using the Move dialog box, the numbers in the Move dialog box correspond to the numbers that appeared in the Info panel (choose Window ➪ Info to open it) when you used the Measure tool.

 **TIP** Double-clicking the Selection tool in the Tools panel also opens the Move dialog box.

FIGURE 11.11

The Move dialog box allows you to specify an exact distance and direction to move objects.

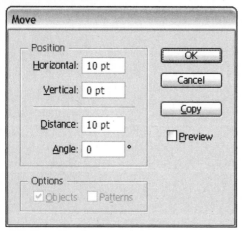

In the Move dialog box, positive numbers in the Horizontal text field move an object to its right, while negative numbers move an object to its left. Positive numbers in the Vertical text field move an object up, while negative numbers move an object down. Negative numbers in the Distance text field move an object in the opposite direction of the Angle text field. The Angle text field works a bit differently. Negative numbers in the Angle text field move the angle in the opposite direction from 0°, so typing –45° is the same as typing 315 and typing –180 is the same as typing 180.

The measurement system in the Move dialog box uses the units set in the General Preferences dialog box. To use units other than those of the current measurement system, use these indicators:

- **For inches:** 1", 1in, or 1 inch
- **For picas:** 1p, 1pica, or 1 pica
- **For points:** 1pt or 1 point
- **For picas/points:** 1p1, 1 pica, or 1 point
- **For millimeters:** 1mm or 1 millimeter
- **For centimeters:** 1cm or 1 centimeter

The Horizontal and Vertical text fields are linked to the Distance and Angle text fields; when you change one of the Horizontal or Vertical fields, Illustrator alters the Distance and Angle fields accordingly.

Clicking Copy duplicates selected objects in the direction and distance indicated, just as holding Alt (Option) when dragging duplicates the selected objects.

TIP The Move dialog box is a great place to type everything via the keyboard. Press Tab to move from text field to text field, press Enter (Return) instead of clicking OK, and press Esc (⌘+period) instead of clicking Cancel. Pressing Alt (Option)+Enter (Return) or pressing Alt (Option) while clicking OK is the same as clicking Copy. The same is true for all the transformation tool dialog boxes.

Using the Free Transform tool

Free Transform allows you to rotate, scale, reflect, and shear all with one tool. This way, you can create multiple transformations at one time. The Free Transform tool is located directly below the Scale tool in the Tools panel.

What is unique about this tool is that you can select more than one object to change the size, shape, and placement in one step. The Free Transform tool doesn't replace the Free Distort effect. Using this cool tool to create distorted effects is different from using the Free Distort effect.

CROSS-REF For more on the Free Distort effect, see Chapter 11.

At first glance, they may seem the same, but they aren't. The Free Transform tool actually adds perspective, while the Free Distort effect mimics the shape but keeps the spacing uniform. This sounds confusing, but the visual example in Figure 11.12 may help. The middle image shows the application of the Free Transform tool to the top and bottom of the fence. This gives a tree-line effect with perspective. The bottom image shows the application of the Free Distort effect to the top and bottom of the fence. Note the different results.

TIP To apply the Free Transform tool to the top and bottom of an image at the same time, hold Alt (Option). For more control, hold Ctrl (⌘) as you start to drag.

FIGURE 11.12

The middle fence was created using the Free Transform tool. The bottom fence was created using the Free Distort effect.

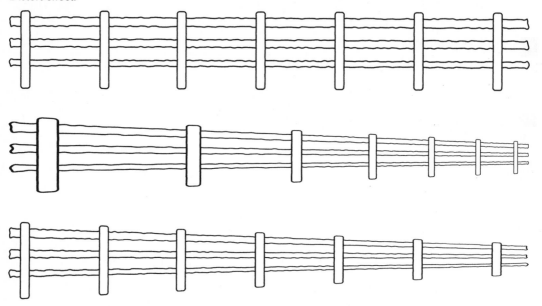

Working with the Transform Panel

Imagine a panel that combines four of Illustrator's five transformation capabilities into one place. Then, look at Figure 11.13, which shows Illustrator's Transform panel in all its glory.

The Transform panel provides a way to move, scale, rotate, and shear selected artwork. You don't have a Reflect option; you need to use the tool or the Transform submenu option to reflect artwork. Instead of manually setting an origin point or transforming from the center by default, the Transform panel gives you nine fixed origin points based on the Bounding Box of the selected objects. You can select these fixed origin points by using the square set of points in the right side of the panel. Choose an origin point before typing values in the panel, and the transformations originate from the corner, the center of a side, or the center of selected objects.

The text fields in the Transform panel are as follows:

- **X:** This is the horizontal location of the artwork, measured from the left edge of the document or horizontal ruler origin (if it's been moved from the left edge).

- **Y:** This is the vertical location of the artwork, measured from the bottom edge of the document or vertical ruler origin (if it's been moved from the bottom edge).

- **W:** This is the width of the artwork's Bounding Box.

- **H:** This is the height of the artwork's Bounding Box.

- **Rotate:** This field lets you apply a rotation to the selected artwork.

- **Shear:** This field lets you apply a shear to the selected artwork.

FIGURE 11.13

The Transform panel allows you to apply several transforms in one place.

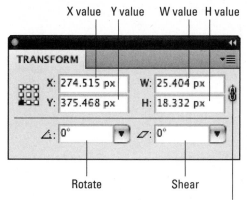

To use the panel, type the new value you want to use into any text field and then press Enter (Return). If you have another value to type, press Tab to go to the next text field or Shift+Tab to go back a text field. Pressing Alt (Option) when you press Enter (Return) or Tab creates a duplicate of the selected artwork with the transformations you specified.

For scaling, you can type either absolute measurements (the size in inches, picas, etc., that you want the artwork to be) or as a percentage by adding the percent (%) symbol after your value. You can also force Illustrator to scale uniformly, regardless of whether you're using absolute measurements or percentages, by clicking Constrain Width and Height Proportions on the right side of the panel.

Using Transform Each

Transform Each provides a way to do several transformations in one shot, but that's only the beginning. The unique thing about Transform Each is that each selected object is transformed independently, as opposed to having all the selected objects transformed together. Figure 11.14 shows the difference between normal rotating and scaling and the rotate and scale functions in Transform Each.

FIGURE 11.14

The original logo (top) and changes applied using the Transform Each dialog box (middle) as well as with changes using the Random check box (bottom)

To access the Transform Each dialog box, as shown in Figure 11.15, choose Object ⇨ Transform ⇨ Transform Each. In the dialog box, use the sliders/dial or type values for each transformation. If you click the Random check box on the right side of the dialog box, you can give each object selected a random value that falls between the default (100% for Scale; 0 for Move and Rotate) and the value set by the sliders/dial.

In addition to controls for setting the Scale, Move, and Rotate values, the Transform Each dialog box includes check boxes to reflect the selected objects about the x- or y-axis and an icon for selecting an origin point. But of all the offerings, the Random option of Transform Each is its most powerful asset. Clicking the Random check box can turn a grid into a distinct random texture, as shown in Figure 11.16.

FIGURE 11.15

The Transform Each dialog box allows you to apply transformations to several objects at the same time.

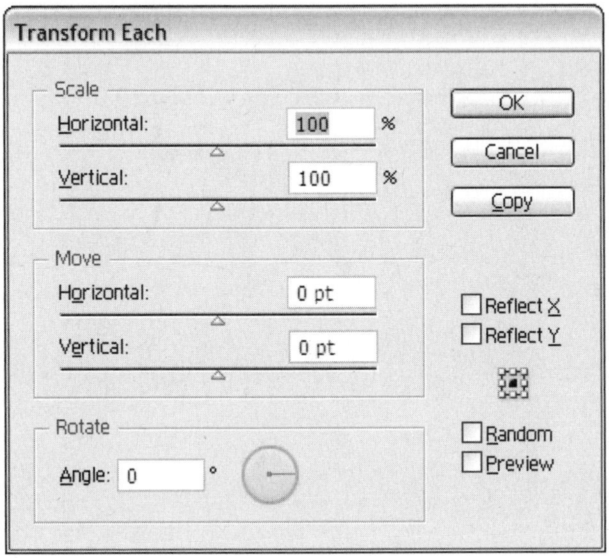

FIGURE 11.16

Transform Each's Random function applied to a pattern of columns of squares really mixes things up.

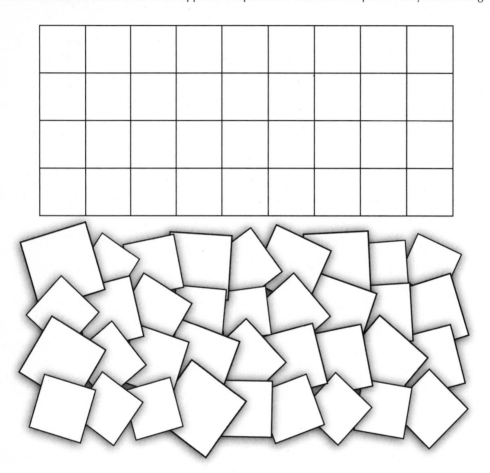

Using Transformations

The transformation tools open a world of possibilities within Illustrator. The following tips and ideas should give you a head start in exploring the amazing power of transformations.

Choosing Object ⇨ Transform ⇨ Transform Again or pressing Ctrl+D (⌘+D) reapplies the last transformation that you performed on the selected object. Transform Again also makes a transformed copy if you made a copy either manually or by clicking Copy in the prior transformation tool's dialog box.

TIP Transform Again remembers the last transformation no matter what else you do, and it can apply that same transformation to other objects or reapply it to the existing transformed objects.

Creating shadows

You can create all sorts of shadows by using the Scale, Reflect, and Shear tools. To create a shadow, follow these steps:

1. **Select the path where you want to apply the shadow.**

2. **Click the bottom of the path once with the Reflect tool.** This sets the origin of reflection at the base of the image.

3. **Drag the mouse down while pressing Shift.** The image flips over, creating a mirror image under the original.

4. **Press Alt (Option) while keeping Shift pressed before and during the release of the mouse button.** This makes a copy of the image.

5. **Using the Shear tool, click the base of the reflected copy to set the origin.**

6. **Click and drag left or right at the other side of the reflection.** This sets the angle of the reflection.

7. **Using the Scale tool, click once again on the base of the reflected copy to set the origin.**

8. **Click and drag up or down at the other side of the reflection.** This sets how far away from the original object the shadow falls.

9. **Color the shadow darker than its background.** The resulting shadow is shown in the illustration in Figure 11.17. You may have to experiment with these steps a bit to achieve the results you really want.

FIGURE 11.17

A shadow created with the transformation tools

Rotating into a path

Clever use of the Rotate tool can create a unique-looking flower, as demonstrated in these steps:

1. **Start by creating a few overlapping ellipses and then group them together.**

2. **Select the group of ellipses and then choose Effect ⇨ Roughen.** Play with the values until the edges of the petal you're creating look slightly uneven.

3. **Click the Rotate tool.**

4. **Click to set an origin near one of the ends of the ellipse.**

5. **Click the other side of the group and then drag.** As you drag, the outline of the shape of the objects that you're dragging appears.

6. **When the ellipses have been rotated until they're only partially overlapping the original group, press Alt (Option).** This copies the group.

7. **Release the mouse button and then release Alt (Option).** A copy of the group appears.

8. **Press Ctrl+D (⌘+D) (Transform Again) to rotate another group of ellipses the same distance away.** Repeat this step several times.

9. **Draw a circle in the middle of the petals and then fill it with a gradient.**

Figure 11.18 shows the final flower. The farther you click from the ellipses to set the origin, the smaller the curve of the path of objects. Clicking right next to the objects causes them to turn sharply.

Making tiles using the Reflect tool

You can make symmetrical tiles with the Reflect tool. You can use a set of four differently positioned yet identical objects to create artwork with a floor-tile look. To do this, follow these steps:

1. **Create the path (or paths) that you'll make into the symmetrical tile.**

2. **Group the artwork together by selecting the artwork first and then choosing Object ⇨ Group or pressing Ctrl (⌘)+G.**

3. **Click the Reflect tool and then click off to the right of it to set the origin.**

4. **Click and drag on the left edge of the object and then drag to the right while pressing Shift+Alt (Option).** Using Shift reflects the image at only 45° angles.

5. **When the object has been reflected to the right side, release the mouse button while still pressing Alt (Option) and then release Alt (Option).** You now have two versions of the object.

6. **Select the original and reflected objects and then reflect again across the bottom of the objects.** You now have four objects — each mirrored a little differently — that make up a tile. You can use this tile to create symmetrical patterns.

The resulting tile pattern is shown in Figure 11.19.

FIGURE 11.18

Using the Rotate tool and the Transform Again menu command, you can quickly create a unique flower.

FIGURE 11.19

You can create symmetrical tiles with the Reflect tool.

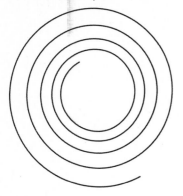
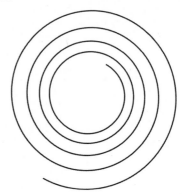
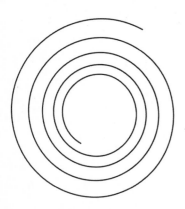
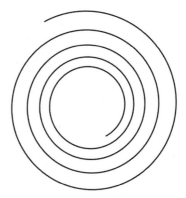

Using transformation tools on portions of paths

When using the transformation tools, you don't need to select an entire path. Instead, try experimenting with other effects by selecting single anchor points, line segments, and combinations of selected anchor points and segments. Another idea is to select portions of paths on different objects.

**TIP** When you're working with portions of paths, one of the most useful transformation tool procedures is to select a smooth point with the Direct Selection tool and then choose a transformation tool.

You can achieve precise control with the Rotate tool. Click the center of the anchor point and then drag around it. Both control handles move, but the distance from the control handles to the anchor point remains the same. This task is very difficult to perform with just the Direct Selection tool, which you can also use to accomplish the same task.

You can accomplish the exact lengthening of control handle lines by using the Scale tool. Click the anchor point to set the origin and then drag out from one of the control handles. Both control handles grow from the anchor point in equal proportions.

When working on a smooth point, you can use the Reflect tool to switch lengths and angles between the two control handles.

Here are some more portion-of-path transformation ideas:

- Select all the points in an open path except for the endpoints, and use all the different transformation tools on the selected areas.

- Select the bottommost or topmost anchor point in text converted to outlines, and scale, rotate, and shear for interesting effects.

- Select two anchor points on a rectangle, and scale and skew copies into a cube to create a 3-D appearance.

Transforming patterns

The option in all transformation tool dialog boxes and the Move dialog box to apply transformations to patterns can produce some very interesting results, as shown in Figure 11.20.

One of the most interesting effects results from using patterns that have transparent fills. Select an object that has a pattern fill and then double-click a transformation tool. Type a value, click the Patterns check box, deselect the Objects check box, and then click Copy. A new unchanged object overlaps the original object, but the pattern in the new object has changed. If desired, use the Transform Again command by pressing Ctrl+D (⌘+D) to create additional copies with patterns that have been transformed even more.

TIP You can transform patterns live by pressing the grave (`) key while dragging with any transformation tool (including the Selection tool for moving).

FIGURE 11.20

The pattern inside the arrow has been scaled and sheared.

Using Liquify Tools on Objects

Illustrator has another group of tools called the Liquify tools, which includes the Warp, Twirl, Pucker, Bloat, Scallop, Crystallize, and Wrinkle tools. These tools are housed with the Warp tool (a finger smushing a line) in the Tools panel. The Liquify tools give you freeform morphing abilities unlike any other drawing tools.

All these tools work with a brush interface. You can alter the brush options and the individual tool options by double-clicking the active tool. Figure 11.21 shows the Warp Tool Options dialog box. With all the Liquify tools, you can always adjust the Global Brush Dimensions and even set it to use a pressure pen. For all the tools, just click and drag them on any selected artwork to achieve the effect.

The Global Brush Dimensions section includes settings for the Width, Height, and Angle of the brush. The Intensity setting controls how hard you need to move against the path before a change appears. Using the Warp Options section, you can control the Detail and Simplify settings for each of the Liquify tools.

 Change the brush size while applying the tools by holding Alt (Option) before clicking with the tool. This allows you to drag the circle (brush) size out or in before you use the tool.

FIGURE 11.21

The Warp Tool Options dialog box gives you great latitude in warping objects.

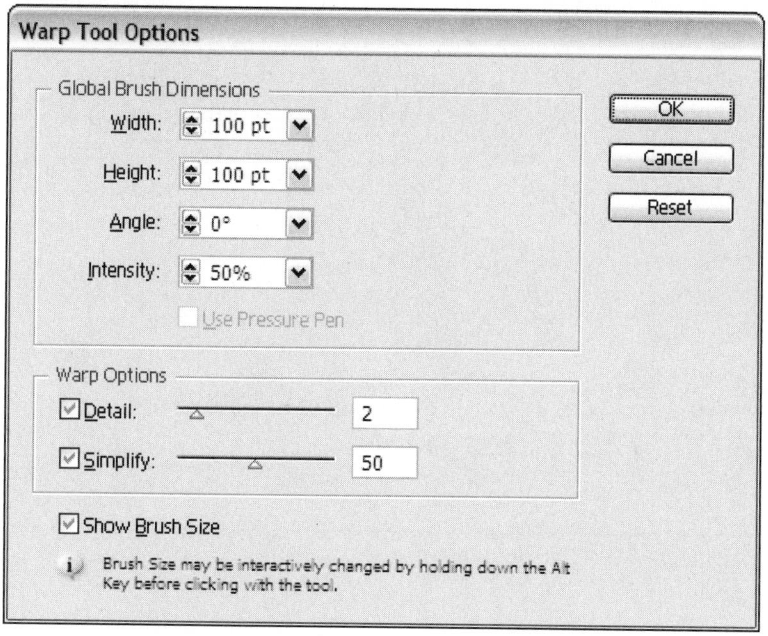

Warp Tool Options

Global Brush Dimensions
- Width: 100 pt
- Height: 100 pt
- Angle: 0°
- Intensity: 50%
- Use Pressure Pen

OK

Cancel

Reset

Warp Options
- ☑ Detail: △ 2
- ☑ Simplify: △ 50

☑ Show Brush Size

ⓘ Brush Size may be interactively changed by holding down the Alt Key before clicking with the tool.

Warping objects

The Warp tool treats objects like modeling clay. You stretch, drag, or pull areas of an object. Figure 11.22 shows the original object on the left and the warped one on the right. You can push out the shape by dragging outward. Put dents in the object by dragging from the outside in.

Twirling objects

The Twirl tool applies a spiraled effect to the object. Use this to swirl and ripple distortions on your artwork. Figure 11.23 shows the original object on the left and the swirled object on the right.

FIGURE 11.22

The object before (left) and after (right) using the Warp tool

FIGURE 11.23

The object before (left) and after (right) using the Twirl tool

Puckering

The Pucker tool is similar to the Pucker & Bloat effect (covered later in this chapter). Using this tool in a brush fashion applies a pinched or pulled-in look with spikes, as shown in Figure 11.24.

The object before (left) and after (right) using the Pucker tool

Bloating

The Bloat tool, like the Pucker tool, is similar to its effect counterpart. Use this to bulge out or puff out in a brushed, controlled fashion. Figure 11.25 shows the original object on the left and the bloated object on the right.

Scalloping

The Scallop tool is used to add arc shapes to your object. This tool randomly brushes arc shapes along the area you brush over. Figure 11.26 shows the original object on the left and the scalloped object on the right.

FIGURE 11.25

The object before (left) and after (right) using the Bloat tool

FIGURE 11.26

The object before (left) and after (right) using the Scallop tool

Crystallizing

The Crystallize tool applies arcs and spikes by using a brush on the object. Click and drag outward to push the path out. Click and drag inward to push the path inward. The object doesn't have to be selected; simply drag the brush over the top of the object you want to crystallize. Figure 11.27 shows an example of what this tool can do.

FIGURE 11.27

The object before (left) and after (right) using the Crystallize tool

Wrinkling

The Wrinkle tool applies a roughened edge to your artwork, similar to the Roughen effect but applied in a brush fashion. Figure 11.28 shows an application of the Wrinkling tool.

CROSS-REF For more on the Roughen effect, see Chapters 5 and 6.

FIGURE 11.28

The object before (left) and after (right) using the Wrinkle tool

Distorting with Effects

Effects provide changes in appearance to selected objects. You can go back and edit or remove just the effect without losing any of your other applied options.

CROSS-REF For more on effects, see Chapter 15.

All effects are fully editable via the Appearance panel. In the following examples, the commands used are those found by choosing Effect ➪ Distort & Transform.

Using free distortions

The first of the distortion effects is the Free Distort. This was discussed briefly with the Free Transform tool earlier in this chapter. The big difference between the Free Transform tool and the Free Distort command is that Free Distort keeps the spacing relevant and doesn't use the perspective as the Free Transform tool does.

The Free Distort command allows you to alter the shape of the selected object by dragging four corner points. Some may think of this as enveloping, but it's a much simpler effect. Figure 11.29 shows text that has the Free Distort command applied to it.

FIGURE 11.29

FIGURE 11.29

The Free Distort effect applied to type

Using Pucker & Bloat

Although the Pucker & Bloat command undoubtedly has the coolest sounding name that Illustrator has to offer, this command is also one of the least practical. But Illustrator is a fun program, right? And these commands make it lots of fun.

Puckering makes objects appear to have pointy tips sticking out everywhere, and bloating creates lumps outside of objects. Puckering and bloating are inverses of each other; a negative pucker is a bloat, and a negative bloat is a pucker. If you're bewildered by these functions, stop reading right here. The following information spoils everything.

Choosing Pucker & Bloat opens the Pucker & Bloat dialog box, as shown in Figure 11.30, where you can specify a percentage by which you want the selected paths to be puckered or bloated by either typing the amount or dragging the slider.

FIGURE 11.30

The Pucker & Bloat dialog box

Pucker & Bloat			
Pucker	0 %	Bloat	OK
			Cancel
			☐ Preview

Bloating causes the segments between anchor points to expand outward. The higher the percentage, the more bloated the selection is. You can bloat from –200 to +200. Using Bloat makes rounded, bubble-like extrusions appear on the surface of your object; using Pucker makes tall spikes appear on its path. When you drag toward Pucker, you can type how much you want to pucker the drawing. Pucker amounts can range from –200 to +200. The number of spikes is based on the number of anchor points in your drawing. Figure 11.31 shows the original text (top), the text being puckered (middle), and the text being bloated (bottom).

NOTE   **Text is great to play with using these distortion commands because it's still fully editable. You don't have to create outlines first.**

The Pucker & Bloat command moves anchor points in one direction and creates two independent direction points on either side of each anchor point. The direction points are moved in the opposite direction of the anchor points, and the direction of movement is always toward or away from the center of the object.

FIGURE 11.31

The original text (above) with Pucker applied (middle) and Bloat applied (below)

The distance moved is the only thing that you control when you use the Pucker & Bloat command. Typing a percentage moves the points that percentage amount.

NOTE Nothing about the Pucker & Bloat command is random. Everything about it is 100% controllable and, to some extent, predictable.

Roughening objects

Roughen adds anchor points and then moves them randomly by a percentage that you define. This gives objects a rough-appearing outline.

Because the Roughen commands work randomly, you obtain different results when you apply the same settings of the same command to two separate, identical objects. In fact, the results will probably never be duplicated. The Roughen command is a good reason for having the Undo command so you can apply the command, undo, and reapply using a different value until you achieve the desired effect. Figure 11.32 shows an example of using the Roughen command.

TIP Using the keyboard, you can continually reapply any command that works randomly and get different results. Select the object and then apply the command by choosing the menu item and typing the values. If you don't like the result, press Ctrl+Z (⌘+Z) to undo it. Press Ctrl+Shift+E (⌘+Shift+E) to reapply the last effect using a different random value.

One important limitation of the Roughen command is that it works on entire paths, even if only part of the path is selected. The best way to get around this limitation is to use the Scissors tool to cut the path into separate sections.

CROSS-REF For more on the Scissors tool, see Chapter 6.

The Roughen command does two things at once. First, it adds anchor points until the selection has the number of points per inch that you defined. Second, it randomly moves all the points around, changing them into straight corner points or smooth points, whichever you specified.

Choosing Roughen opens the Roughen dialog box, as shown in Figure 11.33, where you can type information to roughen the illustration — literally.

FIGURE 11.32

The original text (top) with Roughen applied to it (bottom)

BOARD2PIECES
BY TED ALSPACH

BOARD2PIECES
BY TED ALSPACH

FIGURE 11.33

The Roughen dialog box

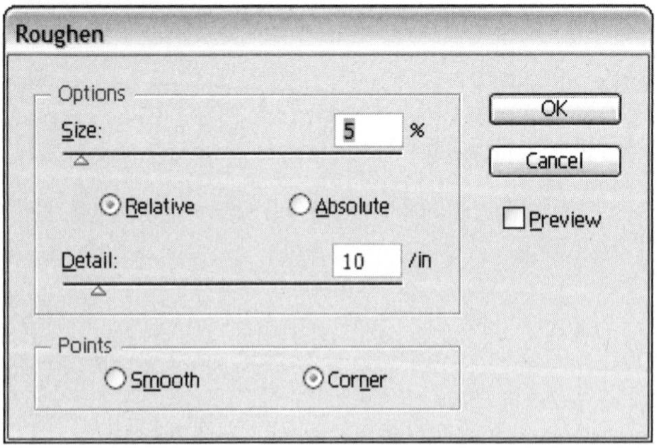

Three options are available:

- **Size:** How far points may move when roughened relative to the width or height (whichever is greater) of the selected path. Choose higher values to increase the apparent roughness.

- **Detail:** How many points are created per inch. Choose higher values to create more points.

- **Smooth or Corner Points:** If you click the Smooth radio button, all the anchor points added are smooth points. If you click the Corner radio button, all the points added are straight corner points. Use Smooth to create soft edges and Corner to create sharp edges.

Roughen never takes away points when roughening a path.

> **TIP** You can use the Roughen command as a very hip version of the Add Anchor Points command. If the Size text field is set at 0%, the added points are added along the existing path all at once. Instead of going to Add Anchor Points again and again, just try typing a value of 25 in the Detail text field of the Roughen dialog box. You have instant, multiple Add Anchor Points. This technique is great for Tweak (explained later in this chapter) or anything else where you need a bunch of anchor points quickly.

Transforming objects

You find the Transform command under the Distort & Transform submenu of the Effect menu. The transform effect is similar to the Transform panel, except that you can go back and edit as well as see the preview before applying.

Choosing Effect ➪ Distort & Transform ➪ Transform opens the Transform Effect dialog box, as shown in Figure 11.34. One really cool feature of this dialog box is the copies text field. Here, you can type a multiple number of copies, as shown in this duplication of a paper doll in Figure 11.35.

> **TIP** If the Transform effect doesn't come out quite the way you want, double-click the name of the effect in the Appearance panel to reopen the Transform Effect dialog box. Make any further changes you want and then click OK to modify the effect.

The Transform Effect dialog box

Transform Effect

Scale
Horizontal: 100 %
Vertical: 100 %

Move
Horizontal: 0 pt
Vertical: 0 pt

Rotate
Angle: 0 °

OK
Cancel

0 copies

Reflect X
Reflect Y

Random
Preview

Paper dolls created with the Transform effect

Tweaking transforms

Choosing Tweak opens the Tweak dialog box, as shown in Figure 11.36. In this dialog box, you define the amount of tweaking, including the horizontal and vertical percentages and which points are moved (anchor points, in control points, or out control points). Clicking the Relative radio button applies the effect to the Bounding Box edges of the object. Clicking the Absolute radio button moves the points based on the absolute measurements that you type.

FIGURE 11.36

The Tweak dialog box

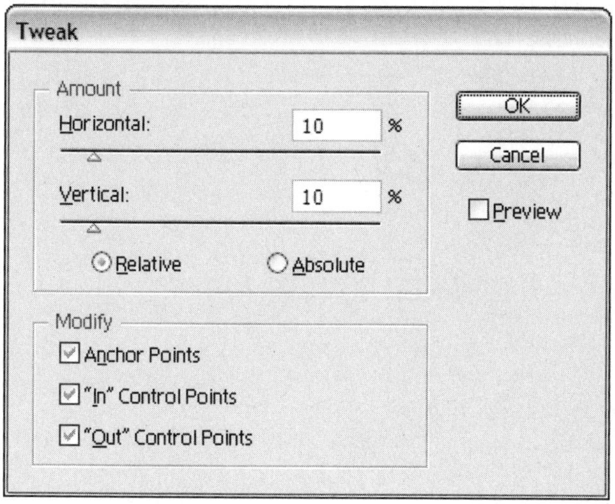

Tweak

Amount
Horizontal: 10 %

Vertical: 10 %

○ Relative   ○ Absolute

OK
Cancel
☐ Preview

Modify
☑ Anchor Points
☑ "In" Control Points
☑ "Out" Control Points

 **No anchor points are added with the Tweak dialog box.**

If you type **0** in either text field, no movement occurs in that direction. Illustrator bases the percentage on the width or height of the shape — whichever is longer. If you click the Anchor Points check box, all anchor points on the selected path move in a random distance corresponding to the amounts set in the Horizontal and Vertical text fields. If you click either the "In" Control Points or the "Out" Control Points check box, those points also move the specified distance. In control points are the points on one side of the anchor point that lead into the path. Out control points are the points on the other side of the anchor point that lead out of the path.

TIP **Consider using the Tweak option when you're not sure of the size of the selected artwork or when you can only determine that you want points moved a certain portion of the whole but can't determine an absolute measurement.**

Figure 11.37 shows an object that has the Tweak effect applied with the Relative option chosen (above) and the same values with the Absolute option chosen (below).

FIGURE 11.37

The top object was tweaked using the Relative option; the bottom object was tweaked using the Absolute option.

The percentages you type pertain to the Bounding Box dimensions and move points up to those limits. If the Bounding Box is 5 inches wide and 2 inches tall and you type a value of 10% for width and height, the points move randomly up to 0.5 inches horizontally and 0.2 inches vertically in either direction.

Using the Twist command

The Twist command is found by choosing Effect ⇨ Distort &Transform ⇨ Twist. This cool command rotates or twirls the selected object, with more action being in the center of the object. In the Twist dialog box, as shown in Figure 11.38, you set the Angle of the twist.

FIGURE 11.38

The Twist dialog box

You can twist paths and text (without converting to outlines) to create some really great effects. One of my favorite looks is to take a starburst of lines and twist them into a flower or spirographic shapes using the Twist and Tweak effects, as shown in Figure 11.39. The top-left image has no Twist applied, but a 10° Twist is added to each consecutive image. A positive number twists the object clockwise; a negative number twists the object counterclockwise.

FIGURE 11.39

A range from a 10° to a 110° Twist was added to the original object (top left).

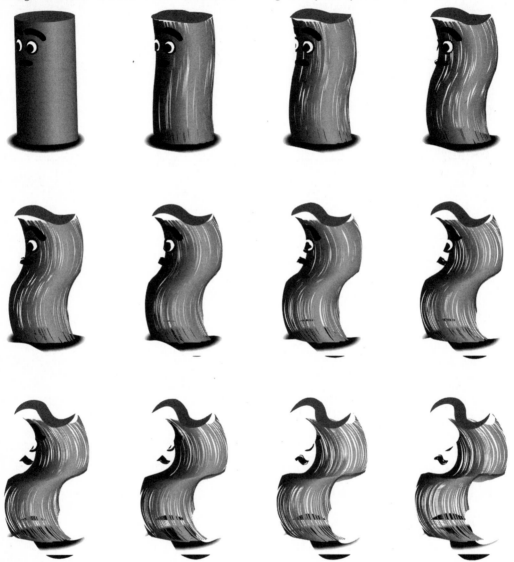

Working with the Zig Zag effect

The Zig Zag effect (Effect ⇨ Distort & Transform ⇨ Zig Zag) changes normally straight paths into zigzagged versions of those paths. When you first choose Zig Zag, the Zig Zag dialog box, as shown in Figure 11.40, opens.

The Zig Zag dialog box allows you to specify various parameters of the Zig Zag effect, including the Size, which is how large each zigzag is, and the Ridges per segment, which is the number of zigzags. In addition, you can specify whether you want the zigzags to be curved (click the Smooth radio button) or pointed (click the Corner radio button). Like most of the other Illustrator effects, Zig Zag has a handy Preview check box. The Relative and Absolute options work just like the similarly named options in the Tweak Effect. Figure 11.41 shows an example of zigzagged artwork.

FIGURE 11.40

The Zig Zag dialog box

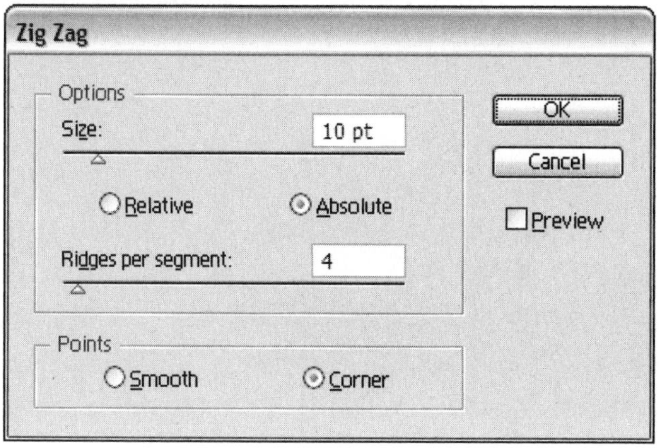

FIGURE 11.41

Art with a zigzag applied to it

Using Warp Effects

Warp effects are also known as envelopes. Warp effects bend objects into a selected shape. Unlike Free Distort, you have many points to work with and a variety of preset options. You can choose from a variety of predefined warp effects: Arc, Arc Lower, Arc Upper, Arch, Bulge, Shell Lower, Shell Upper, Flag, Wave, Fish, Rise, Fisheye, Inflate, Squeeze, and Twist.

You can find all these warp effects by choosing them from the Effect ➪ Warp submenu. Each of these predefined styles for Warp can also be altered into your own design in the Warp Options dialog box, as shown in Figure 11.42.

In all the preset options, you have Warp Options to edit to your heart's desire. You can set these options:

- **Style:** Pick from 15 predefined warps.
- **Horizontal or Vertical:** This affects either the horizontal areas or the vertical areas of the shape.
- **Bend:** Change how much of an effect is applied in percentage.
- **Distortion Horizontal:** This option allows you to increase or decrease the horizontal distortion in percentage.
- **Distortion Vertical:** This option allows you to increase or decrease the vertical distortion in percentage.

FIGURE 11.42

The Warp Options dialog box

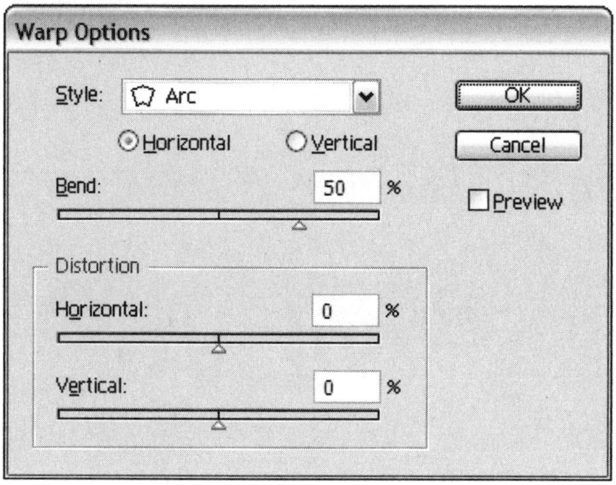

Understanding Warp types

This section provides more information on the 15 Warp Style presets:

- **Arc:** Bends a shape's top and bottom into an arc
- **Arc Lower:** Bends just the lower half of the shape into an arc
- **Arc Upper:** Bends just the upper half of the shape into an arc
- **Arch:** Bends the upper, middle, and lower areas into an arch
- **Bulge:** Pushes out the top and bottom of the shape

- **Shell Lower:** Squeezes in the middle and bulges out the lower area of the shape
- **Shell Upper:** Squeezes in the middle and bulges out the upper area of the shape
- **Flag:** Pushes the shape on the top and bottom into an upper and lower curve
- **Wave:** Pushes the shape on the top, middle, and bottom into an upper and lower curve
- **Fish:** Squeezes the shape into a fish shape
- **Rise:** Pushes the shape upward from lower left to upper right
- **Fisheye:** Bulges out just the center of the shape
- **Inflate:** Bulges out the whole shape instead of just the center
- **Squeeze:** Pushes in the left and right sides of the shape
- **Twist:** Twists the object around the center

Figure 11.43 shows all 15 presets applied to text.

FIGURE 11.43

Each warp style is shown in its own name.

Summary

Distortions and transformations are some of the most fun effects that are built into Illustrator. In this chapter, you learned the following:

- You can transform an object multiple ways. You can use the transformation tools, the Transform menu, the Transform panel, or the transform effects.
- Add awesome effects by using the Liquify tools in a brush-like fashion.
- The Distort effects work by moving points around selected paths.
- The Pucker and Bloat features create spiked and bubbled effects, respectively.
- Roughen can be used to intelligently add anchor points.
- Use either the Twist effect alone or with the Twirl tool to twist artwork.
- Twirling adds anchor points as needed when twirling.
- Tweak is used to randomly move existing points and control handles.
- The Zig Zag effect creates wavy or spiky paths.
- Warps push an object into a specific shape.

Chapter 12

Using Path Blends, Compound Paths, and Masks

Three of the more difficult areas of Illustrator to master are path blends, compound paths, and masks. Of course, these are also three of the more powerful functions in Illustrator. A blend is a bunch of paths created from two original paths. Compound paths consist of two or more separate paths that Illustrator treats as a single path. You use a mask to hide portions of an image or mask them out. This chapter shows you how to get to know these three functions so that you can use them in your documents.

Understanding the Difference between Blends and Gradients

In Illustrator, a *blend* is a series of paths that Illustrator creates based on two other paths. A series of paths transforms from the first path into the second path, changing fill and stroke attributes as it moves. A *gradient* is a smooth blend of colors between two or more colors. The big difference is that the gradient appears as a box rather than a series of paths, as in a blend. With a gradient, you use a panel to signify where the colors start and stop.

At first glance, blends and gradients seem to do the same things but in different ways — so why have both? The Blend tool, moreover, seems to be much harder to use than the Gradient Vector tool. On the surface, it seems that you can do more with gradients than with blends. Blends take a long time to redraw; gradients take a fraction of the time.

After all, if gradients are so much easier to use and produce so much better results, is it really necessary to have a Blend tool or a Blend function? Students, clients, and the occasional passerby have asked me this question quite often, and they seem to have a good point at first. Upon further study, however, it becomes apparent that blends are quite different from gradients, both in form and function.

You use gradients only as fills for paths. You can make gradients either linear or radial, meaning that color can change from side to side, top to bottom, or from an interior point to the outside. Every gradient can have as many distinct colors in it as you can create. Gradients are simply an easier way to create blends that change only in color, not in shape or size.

CROSS-REF For more on gradients, see Chapter 7.

Blends, on the other hand, are a series of transformed paths between two end paths. The paths between the end paths mutate from one end path into the other. All the attributes of the end paths change throughout the transformed paths, including shape, size, and all paint style attributes. The major benefit is that you can blend multiple colors at one time.

Blends can be incredibly flexible when it comes to creating photorealistic changes in color if you plan ahead. Changes to blends aren't really changes at all; instead, they're deletions of the transformed objects and changes in the attributes of the end paths. If you know what you want, blending colors can take on an incredibly realistic look by changing the shapes of the blend's end paths just slightly.

But even more useful than creating realistic changes in color is blending's capability to transform shapes from one shape to another (this is typically called *morphing*), as shown in Figure 12.1. With a bit of practice (and the information in this chapter), you can transform any illustration into another illustration. There's a limit to the complexity of the illustrations that you can transform, but the limit is due more to the time it takes to create the blends than to limitations inherent in Illustrator.

Because blends work on both stroke and fill attributes of objects, you can create some really exciting effects that aren't possible by using any other technique, electronic or traditional.

FIGURE 12.1

Blending to transform (or morph) a shape

Creating Path Blends

Originally, Adobe marketed the Blend tool as a tool whose primary purpose was to transform shapes, not blend colors. Instead, designers used the tool for blending colors to create what were known as vignettes or what traditional artists called gradients.

The Blend tool creates in-between steps in the area between two paths, where the paint style and shape of one path transform themselves into the paint style and shape of the second path.

Version 8 of Illustrator dramatically enhanced the Blending function. The big change is that blends became live, or editable. This huge change allows users to change the color, shape, and location of the blend shapes. The blend instantly reblends to the new changes. Another great change is the capability to blend along a path.

Although any blend takes into account both color and shape, I treat color and shape separately in this chapter because people using the Blend tool are often trying to obtain either a color effect or a shape effect rather than both at once.

You use the Blend tool to create blends, which are a group of paths (commonly referred to as blend steps) that change in shape and color as each intermediate path comes closer to the opposite end path. Follow these steps to create a blend:

1. **Using a shape tool, create a small (1-inch) vertical shape.** This example uses a rectangle. For more on creating shapes, see Chapter 5.

2. **With the Selection tool, click on the rectangle, press Alt (Option), and then drag a few inches to the right.** This copies the path a few inches to the side. Press Shift as you drag horizontally to constrain the movement of the path.

3. **On the left shape, change the fill and stroke to desired values.** This example uses a fill of Black and a stroke of None. For more on changing the fills and strokes for shapes, see Chapters 4 and 5.

4. **For the right rectangle, change the fill and stroke to desired values.** This example uses a fill of White and a stroke of None.

5. **Select the Blend tool by pressing W, click the top-left point of the left path, and then click the top-left point of the right path.** This step tells Illustrator to blend between these two paths, and it uses the top-left points as reference. The Blend tool cursor changes from x to + in the lower-right corner. Illustrator creates a spine between the two end paths, which are now transparent. Figure 12.2 shows the resulting blend.

6. **Press Ctrl+Shift+A (⌘+Shift+A).** This deselects all previously selected paths. The default Blend Option creates smooth color between the two shapes. The blend consists of 256 paths, including the two end paths. In the example, each path is a slightly different tint of black.

FIGURE 12.2

This blend moves from black to white.

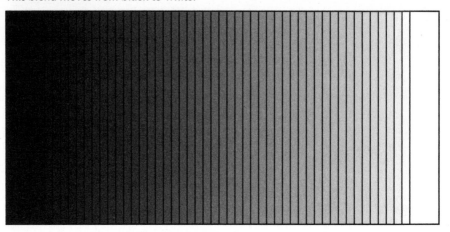

Defining Linear Blends

You create color blends by making two end paths, usually identical in shape and size, giving each path different paint style attributes, and generating a series of steps between them with the Blend tool. The more end paths you create, the more colors you can create.

NOTE The examples in this chapter are easier to understand when you work in Preview mode. For more on Preview mode, see Chapter 2.

Follow these steps to create a basic linear blend:

1. **Draw a curved path with the Pen tool, filling and stroking it as desired.** The example has a fill of None and a stroke of 2-point Black.

2. **Alt+copy (Option+copy) the path to the right, filling and stroking the copied path as desired.** The example gives the new path a stroke of 2-point Yellow.

3. **With the Blend tool, click the path on the left and then the path on the right.** Alternately, you can select both objects and then choose Object ⇨ Blend ⇨ Make.

4. **Deselect all by pressing Ctrl+Shift+A (⌘+Shift+A) to see the result, as shown in Figure 12.3.**

NOTE The blend shown in Figure 12.3 demonstrates one of the hazards of creating blends — something often referred to as *banding*. See the sidebar on banding later in this chapter to learn what to do to reduce or eliminate banding.

You have a variety of ways to blend objects. Keep in mind these suggestions when blending objects:

- You can edit blends by using the Selection, Rotate, or Scale tools.
- You can perform blending with any number of objects, colors, opacities, and gradients.
- You can't apply blending with mesh objects.
- You can't edit the path (or *spine*, as it's called) that the blend creates.
- The fill of the topmost object is used when blending patterns.
- When intermixing process and spot colors, the blend is colored with process colors.
- When blending with transparent objects, the topmost object's transparency is used.
- You can blend symbols.
- You can change the number of steps that Illustrator uses in the Blend Options dialog box.
- Blends create a knockout with transparency groups. (If you don't want this, change it in the Transparency panel by deselecting the Knockout Group option.)

FIGURE 12.3

The final result is a linear blend.

Working with Blend Options

Adobe has enhanced the Blending functions of Illustrator by making the Blend tool easier to use and faster and by adding a Blend submenu under the Object menu. The Blend options are Make, Release, Blend Options, Expand, Replace Spine, Reverse Spine, and Reverse Front to Back. With Illustrator's Blend capability, you may not need to release a blend to change it. You can use the Direct Selection tool to select the end paths and edit the paths or change their color, and the blend instantly updates. Live Blending is the capability to change the shape or color of a blend and update it automatically.

Using the Blend option

The Blend Options dialog box lets you change the Spacing and Orientation aspects. Select the blend that you want to adjust, and either double-click the Blend tool or choose Object ⇨ Blend ⇨ Blend Options to open the dialog box to change the settings.

Figure 12.4 shows the Blend Options dialog box. The three Spacing choices are Smooth Color, Specified Steps, and Specified Distance. The Orientation options are Align to Page and Align to Path.

FIGURE 12.4

The Blend Options dialog box allows you to set up blends the way you want.

These are the Blend options:

- **Smooth Color:** This option automatically determines the best number of steps needed to make this blend look very smooth.

- **Specified Steps:** This option lets you choose the number of intermediate steps you want in the blend.

- **Specified Distance:** This option allows you to type the distance between steps.

- **Align to Page:** This option runs the blend vertically or horizontally, depending on your page orientation.

- **Align to Path:** This option runs the blend perpendicular to the path.

Blending multiple objects

Illustrator has the capability to blend multiple objects in one step. Long gone are the days of blending, hiding, blending, hiding, etc. Select all the objects that you want to blend and then choose Object ➪ Blend ➪ Make or use the Blend tool to click all the objects that you want to blend. Figure 12.5 shows a blend that uses four different-shaped rectangles. To create this effect, I first drew four rectangles, each with a different fill. You need to use different fills in the objects to see a blend effect like this one.

FIGURE 12.5

Blends can use multiple objects.

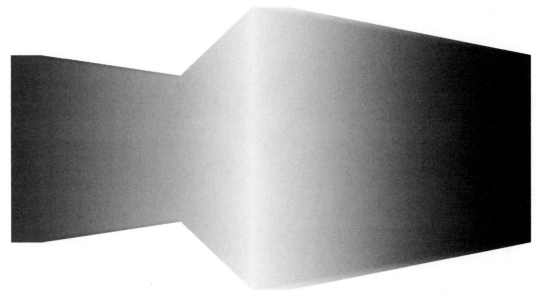

Editing a blended object

Blend functionality lets you change the colors of a blend without having to redo the whole blend. With the Direct Selection tool, select the path whose color you want to change in the blended shape. Choose a new fill and/or stroke color. The blend updates instantly with the new color.

Another great aspect of Live Blend is the capability to edit the blend at any time and have it automatically update on the fly. As mentioned before, Illustrator creates a path, or spine, when you create a blend. With the Direct Selection tool, you can select an anchor point on the spine and move it. This changes the location of that point, and the blend updates accordingly.

Now you can edit lines by adding, deleting, or moving any part of your blend, and it updates automatically. You can delete and add points or change the shape of a path with the Direct Selection tool. Figure 12.6 shows a figure before and after editing the blend. In this case, the meeple that begins the blend was modified in the lower blend by dragging the point at the top of his head up.

FIGURE 12.6

The original figure (top) and the edited blend (bottom) show how a simple modification can create a vastly different object.

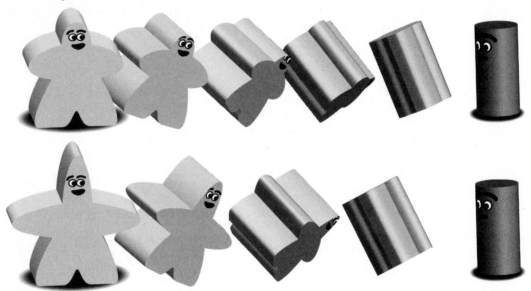

Releasing a blend

If you want to redo a blend, you have to release it first by choosing Object ➪ Blend ➪ Release. This command eliminates the intermediate objects and leaves you with just the original ones.

Expanding blends

If you want to retain the intermediate objects, choose Object ➪ Blend ➪ Expand. Choosing Object ➪ Blend ➪ Expand expands the blend into a series of individual shapes. You can then move or edit these shapes independently of the other shapes.

Replacing the spine

The Replace Spine option allows you to make a blend follow a selected path. Follow these steps to apply this effect:

1. **Create the blend as described earlier in this chapter.** For example, create a blend that blends a mostly vertical ellipse into a mostly horizontal ellipse.

2. **Draw a path in the shape that you want the spine of the blend to follow.** In this case, draw a large diameter circle to use as the path for the blend.

3. **Select the blend with the spine that you want to change and the path that you want to become the new spine.**

4. **Choose Object ➪ Blend ➪ Replace Spine.** The blend updates automatically, in this case adding a new step, with the objects distributed evenly from their centers. Figure 12.7 shows before and after a blend has been applied to a path. In this case, the path used in the lower instance is a circle.

FIGURE 12.7

This demonstrates how the original blend (top) is changed after applying Replace Spine (bottom).

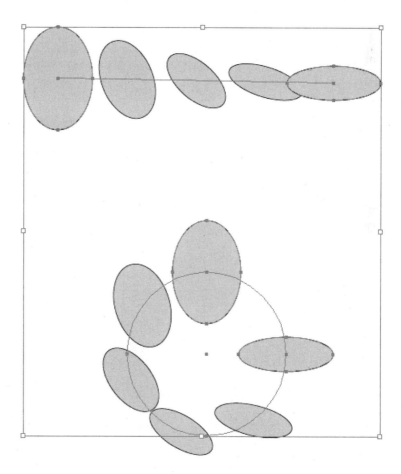

Reversing the spine

This menu option reverses the sequence of the objects that you're blending. If you have a rectangle on the right blended to a circle on the left, choosing Object ⇨ Blend ⇨ Reverse Spine places the circle on the right and the rectangle on the left. Reversing the spine flips the position of the shapes on the spine, as shown in Figure 12.8.

Reversing front to back

The Reverse Front to Back option reverses the order in which your paths were drawn when you created your blend. If you drew a small circle first and a large circle second, choosing Object ⇨ Blend ⇨ Reverse Front to Back places the small circle underneath and the large circle on top, as shown in Figure 12.9.

FIGURE 12.8

Reversing the spine changes the original (top) by swapping the position of the shapes (bottom).

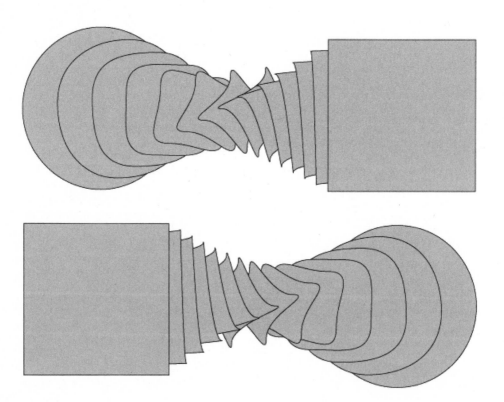

FIGURE 12.9

Reversing the spine front to back changes the stacking order of the original (top), creating the effect shown (bottom).

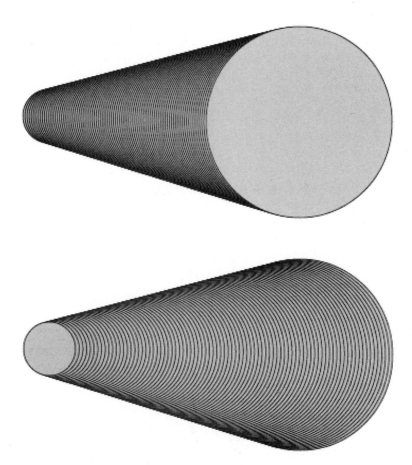

Using nonlinear blends

End paths on a blend with two endpoints (linear segments) used to make blends don't have to be just horizontal or vertical. And when you create multiple color blends, you don't have to align the intermediate end paths the same way as you align the end paths. Careful setup of intermediate blends can create many interesting effects, such as circular and wavy appearances, all created with straight paths.

> **NOTE** End paths that cross usually produce undesirable effects; if carefully constructed, however, the resulting blends can be quite intriguing. Blending crossed end paths creates the appearance of a three-dimensional blend, where one of the end paths blends up into the other.

To create nonlinear blends, set up the end paths and either rotate them or change their orientation by using the Direct Selection tool on one of the endpoints. Then, blend from one end path to the intermediate end paths and then to the other end path. Figure 12.10 shows an example of a non-linear blend.

Another good example of a nonlinear blend is to create a color wheel by aligning straight lines in a hexagon shape with differing colors and then blending between them, as shown in Figure 12.11.

FIGURE 12.10

On the left are the lines before blending and on the right are the lines blended with the Blend tool (Smooth Color option).

 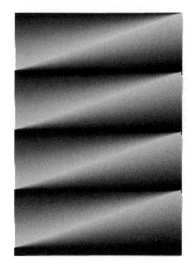

FIGURE 12.11

This is a linear blend applied in a perimeter fashion.

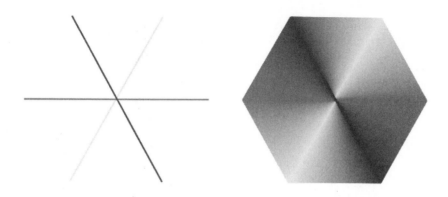

Finding end paths for linear blends

You can also use rectangles with fills and no strokes to achieve a linear blend effect. Figure 12.12 shows both lines and rectangles used for end paths.

Although you can use a rectangle as an end path, you should use a single line with two endpoints instead. In fact, lines are better than rectangles for three reasons. First, lines use half as much information as rectangles because lines have two anchor points, while rectangles have four anchor points. Second, it's much easier to change the width of a line (stroke weight) after you create the blend (just select the lines and then type a new weight in the Stroke panel) than it is to change the width of rectangles (you would have to use Transform Each's Scale option). Third, creating a linear blend with lines (strokes) creates a thick mess of paths, but creating a linear blend with rectangles creates a thicker mess, so much so that it's difficult to select specific rectangles.

> **TIP** You can blend an open path with a closed path and vice versa. You can blend open or closed paths to any path by choosing Object ➪ Blend ➪ Make or using the Blend tool. However, the end result is usually not very desirable.

Calculating the number of steps

Whenever you create a blend, Illustrator provides a default value in the Specified Steps text field of the Blend Options dialog box that assumes that you want to print your illustration to an imagesetter or another high-resolution device capable of printing all 256 levels of gray that PostScript allows.

FIGURE 12.12

Lines and rectangles are both used for end paths in blends here.

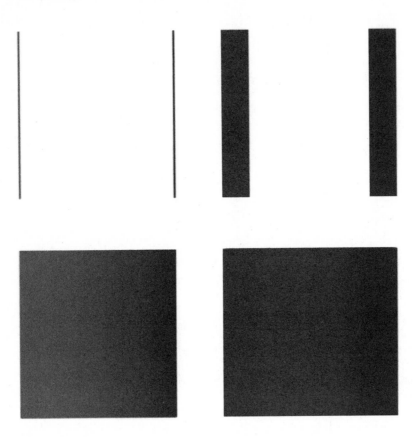

The formula that Illustrator uses is quite simple. It takes the largest change that any one color goes through from end path to end path and multiplies that percentage by 256. The formula looks like this:

```
256 × largest color change % = the number of steps you want to create
```

For example, using a linear blend example where the difference in tint values is 100% (100% – 0% = 100%), when you multiply 100% by 256, you get 256. Because the total number of grays must be 256 or fewer, Illustrator creates only 254. When you add this to the two ends, you have 256 tints.

But, of course, not everything you create outputs on an imagesetter. Your laser printer, for example, can't print 256 grays unless you set the line screen extremely low. To determine how many grays your laser printer can produce, you must know both the dpi (dots per inch) and the line screen (refer to the printer documentation). In some software packages, you can specify the line screen, but unless the printer is a high-end model, it's usually difficult to specify or change the dpi. Use the following formula to find out how many grays your printer can produce:

```
(dpi/line screen) × (dpi/line screen) = number of grays
```

For a 300-dpi printer with a typical line screen of 53, the formula looks like this:

```
(300/53) × (300/53) = 5.66 × 5.66 = 32
```

A 400-dpi printer at a line screen of 65 has the following formula:

```
(400/65) × (400/65) = 6.15 × 6.15 = 38
```

A 600-dpi printer at 75 lines per inch uses this formula:

```
(600/75) × (600/75) = 8 × 8 = 64
```

Sometimes, you may want to reduce the number of blend steps in a blend from the default because either your printer can't display that many grays or the distance from one end path to another is extremely small (see the sidebar on stroke blends later in this chapter).

When reducing the number of blends, start by dividing the default by two and then continue dividing by two until you have a number of steps with which you're comfortable. If you aren't sure how many steps you need, do a quick test of just that blend with different numbers of steps specified and print it out. If you're going to an imagesetter, don't divide by two more than twice; otherwise, banding can occur.

Creating radial blends

To create a radial blend (one that goes from a larger shape to a smaller shape), follow these steps:

1. **Make a shape about 2 inches in diameter.** See Chapter 4 for more on creating shapes. Fill the shape. The example uses a fill of 100% Black.

2. **Make a smaller shape inside the larger shape and then fill it as desired.** The example fills the smaller shape with White.

3. **Select both shapes using the Direct Selection tool and then choose Object ➪ Blend ➪ Make.** You can also use the Blend tool by clicking on the two selected shapes.

4. **To change the number of steps, choose Object ➪ Blend ➪ Blend Options.** When blending black to white, Illustrator automatically uses 255 steps. When blending other colors, Illustrator automatically chooses the best amount. Feel free to experiment with changing the number of steps.

You can create radial blends with almost any object. Figure 12.13 shows a radial blend using a star.

CAUTION   As with most other blends, when blending from two identically shaped end paths, always click the anchor point in the same position on each object. Figure 12.13 shows the difference between clicking the anchor points in the same position (left) and clicking those that aren't in the same position (right).

FIGURE 12.13

Here are two examples of radial blends that differ because different anchor points were selected.

One of the great things about creating radial blends manually (not using the gradient feature) is that by changing the location and the size of the inner object, you can make the gradient look vastly different. The larger you make the inner object, the smaller the blended area becomes.

The Gradient tool allows you to change the highlight point on a radial gradient without changing the source, or angle, of the highlight.

CROSS-REF   For more on gradients and meshes, see Chapter 7.

Avoiding Banding

This is the graphic artist's worst nightmare.

Smooth blends and gradations turn into large chunks of tints and suddenly become darker or lighter instead of staying neat and smooth. *Banding*, as this nightmare is called, is an area of a blend where the difference from one tint to the next tint changes abruptly and displays a defining line showing the difference between the two tints. Individual tints appear as solid areas called bands.

Avoiding banding is easier when you know what causes it. Usually, one of two factors in Illustrator is the cause: too few blend steps or too little variation in the colors of the end paths. Preventing banding due to any of these causes depends on the line screen setting and the capability of your printer to print it.

These causes pretty much make sense. Take the linear blend example earlier in this chapter. If you have only three intermediate steps between end paths, you have only five colors in the blend, thus creating five bands. If you place each of the end paths on one side of a 17-inch span, each created blend step takes up the 5 points of width of the stroke, making each shade of gray 5 points wide. If you make the color on the left 10% Black instead of 100% Black, Illustrator creates only 26 color steps between the two end paths. So, to avoid banding, use the recommended number of steps over a short area with a great variation of color.

If you find it hard to fix the banding problem and your blend consists of process colors, try adding a small amount of an unused color (black, for example) to cover up the banding breaks. A 5% to 30% change over distances may provide just enough dots to hide those bands. Keeping this in mind, you've more of a chance for banding if you use the same tints for different process colors. Alter the tint values for one of the colors at one of the end paths just a little, and this alteration staggers the bands enough to remove them from sight.

For more on calculating the needed steps, see the section on this topic earlier in this chapter.

Making a Color Blend

Using colors in a blend is really no different from using black and white, except for the spectacular results. The only difficulty in using colors in blends is whether the colors look good together.

Using multiple colors with linear blends

To create linear blends that have multiple colors, you must create intermediate end paths, one for each additional color within the blend. Follow these steps:

1. **Create two end paths at the edges of where you want the entire blend to begin and end.** Don't worry about colors at this time.

2. **Select the two paths and then choose Object ⇨ Blend ⇨ Make.** Alternatively, you can press Ctrl+Alt+B (⌘+Option+B) or click the objects with the Blend tool.

3. **Choose Object ➪ Blend ➪ Blend Options.** This opens the Blend Options dialog box.

4. **Choose the values you want for the blend.** Change the Spacing option to Specified Steps. Choose your orientation and then type a number for the steps. (I typed 3 to create three evenly spaced paths between the two end paths.)

5. **Expand the newly created strokes by choosing Object ➪ Blend ➪ Expand.** Color each of the strokes of the paths differently and then give them a desired weight. The example uses a weight of 2 points.

6. **Select all the paths using the Selection tool and then choose Object ➪ Blend ➪ Make.** Alternatively, you can press Ctrl+Alt+B (⌘+Option+B). The result should look like the blend of colors in Figure 12.14.

FIGURE 12.14

This is a multiple color linear blend with the paths and spine selected.

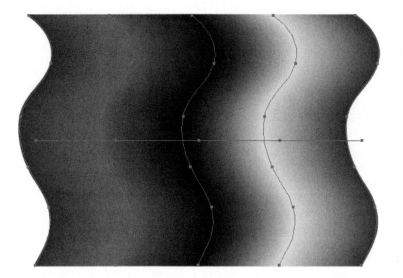

Using guidelines for creating color linear blends

Although the preceding procedure should have gone smoothly with no problems, follow these guidelines when creating blends to obtain good results each time you print:

■ **For linear blends, use either rectangles with only four anchor points or a basic 2-point path.** If you use a shape with any more anchor points or if you use a curved shape with any paths that aren't perfectly straight, you get extra information that isn't needed to create the blend and printing takes much longer than usual.

- **When creating linear blends, use one rectangle per end path and color the fills of the paths, not the strokes.** Coloring the strokes may appear to work, but it usually results in a moiré (wavy) pattern when you print. Ensure that you set the stroke to None, regardless of what you have for the fill.

- **Don't change the number that appears in the Specified Steps text field in the Blend Options dialog box if you want smooth color.** Making the number higher creates additional paths that you can't print; making the number lower can result in banding when you print (see the sidebar on banding earlier in this chapter).

Creating Shape Blends

The difference between color blends and shape blends is in their emphasis. Color blends emphasize a color change; shape blends emphasize blending between different shapes.

You have a number of details to remember when creating the end paths that form a shape blend. You must make both paths either open or closed. If open, you can only click endpoints to blend between the two paths. If the shapes also change color, be sure to follow the guidelines in the section related to color blends earlier in this chapter.

For the best results, both paths should have the same number of anchor points selected before blending, and you should have the selected points in a relatively similar location. Illustrator pairs up points on end paths and the segments between them so that when it creates the blend steps, the lines are in about the same position.

Complex-shape blending

Whenever a shape is complex (that is, it isn't a perfectly symmetrical shape), you may have to perform a number of functions to create realistic and eye-pleasing effects. Figure 12.15 shows a complex-shape blend.

FIGURE 12.15

It can be a little difficult to get the results you want with complex-shape blends.

One function that you can perform to improve the blend involves adding or removing anchor points from the end paths. Even if you select the same number of points and those points are in similar areas on each path, Illustrator may not give you an acceptable result. The Add Anchor Point and Delete Anchor Point tools become quite useful here. By adding points in strategic locations, you can often fool Illustrator into creating an accurate blend; otherwise, the blend steps can resemble a total disaster.

TIP As a general rule, you disturb the composition of the graphic less if you add anchor points rather than remove them. On most paths, removing anchor points changes the shape of the path dramatically.

Another method of getting the paths to blend more accurately involves shortening them by splitting a long, complex path into one or two smaller sections that aren't nearly as complex. You must blend each path, which you can do in one step by choosing Object ➪ Blends ➪ Make.

Creating realism with shape blends

To create a realistic effect with shape blends, the paths you use to create the blends need to resemble objects you see in life, which are generally curved rather than straight. Take a look around you and try to find a solid-colored object. Doesn't the color appear to change from one part of the object to another? Shadows and reflections are everywhere. Colors change gradually from light to dark — not in straight lines but in smooth, rounded curves.

You can use blends to simulate reflections and shadows. You usually create reflections with shape blends and create shadows with stroke blends.

This section shows you how to simulate reflections with shape blends. This procedure is a little tricky for any artist because the environment determines a reflection. The artwork you create may be viewed in any number of environments, so the reflections have to compensate for these differences. Fortunately, unless you create a mirror angled directly at the viewer (impossible, even if you know who the viewer is in advance), you can get the person seeing the artwork to perceive reflection without really being aware of it.

The chrome-like type in the word DON'T in Figure 12.16 was created by masking shape blends designed to look like a reflective surface.

1. **Type the word or words you want to use for masking the reflective surface.** The typeface and the word itself have an impact on how an observer perceives the finished artwork. The example uses the word DON'T and the typeface Stencil. The example also required a great deal of tracking to make all the letters touch so that the word looks like one piece of material. In addition, the example uses baseline shift to move the apostrophe up several points.

2. **Select the text using the Selection tool.**

3. **Choose Type ➪ Create Outlines or press Ctrl+Shift+O (⌘+Shift+O).** At this point, most of the serifs on the letters overlap.

4. **Select all the letters and then choose Add to Shape Area from the Pathfinder panel.** This command eliminates any unsightly seams between the letters. If desired, create a rectangle and then place it behind the letters. This makes the letters of the word stand out.

5. **Using the Pencil tool, draw a horizontal line from left to right across the rectangle.** Alt+drag (Option+drag) several of this pencil-drawn path from the original down to the bottom of the rectangle to create copies. The example required the creation of five more paths.

6. **With the Direct Selection tool, randomly move around individual anchor points and direction points on each path, but try to avoid overlapping paths.**

7. **Color the stroke of each path differently, going from dark to light to dark.** In my example, I went from dark to light to dark to light and back to dark again.

8. **Blend the stroked paths together.**

9. **Open the Transparency panel and then choose Make Opacity Mask from the popup menu to mask the blend with the type outlines.** The mask you're creating is an opacity rather than a clipping mask. Your results should look similar to Figure 12.16.

FIGURE 12.16

This shows a reflective surface type blend created by blending and masking.

In the preceding steps, you press Alt (Option) to copy the path not only because it makes things easier but also to ensure that the end paths in the blends have the same points in the same locations. This technique is much more effective than adding or deleting points from a path.

TIP   With slight transformations, you can use the same reflection blend for other objects in the same illustration and no one is the wiser. A method that I often use is to reflect the original, scale it to 200%, and then use only a portion of the blend in the next mask.

Figure 12.17 shows how to use shape blends to create the glowing surface of a lit object — in this case, a light bulb. The key to successfully achieving this effect is to draw the shape first and then use a copy of the exact same path for the highlights. The relative locations of anchor points stay the same, and the number of anchor points never changes.

FIGURE 12.17

A light bulb created with blends almost seems to glow.

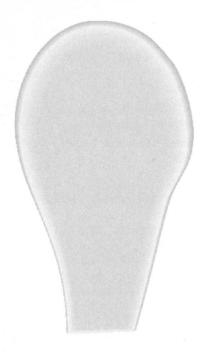

1. **Draw the shape you want to light.** Take your time to get it exactly the way you want it because this path is the basis for everything else in this example. The example of the light bulb uses a fill of 30% Magenta and 80% Yellow and a stroke of None.

2. **Copy the object and then scale it down just a little bit, setting the origin on the base of the bulb.** Make two more copies of the object, each a little smaller than the previous copy.

3. **Change the color of each copy slightly.** In the example, the light bulb's paths from inside to outside are as follows: Color the first (inside) path as 5% Magenta and 10% Yellow; the next path as 10% Magenta and 30% Yellow; and the last path as 15% Magenta and 40% Yellow. The outermost path should still be 30% Magenta and 80% Yellow.

4. **The paths should be in the correct top-to-bottom order, but if they aren't, fix them.** To see if they're in the correct order, go to Preview mode. If the smaller paths aren't visible, then send the outer paths to the back by choosing Object ➪ Arrange ➪ Send to Back.

CROSS-REF For more on Preview mode, see Chapter 2.

5. **Blend the paths together by selecting similar anchor point locations in each step.**
    Figure 12.17 shows the result. You can, of course, make additional modifications for an
    even more realistic appearance should you desire.

Blending symbols

The Blend tool can also blend symbols. Use the Symbol Sprayer tool to spray symbols or drag
some symbols from the panel. Select the symbols and then blend them together. You can blend
similar or different symbols. Figure 12.18 shows a basic blend from a large flower symbol to a
small flower symbol, and the spine was edited to an arch shape.

CROSS-REF For more on the Symbol Sprayer tool, see Chapter 5.

FIGURE 12.18

Here is a flower symbol sized large and small and blended.

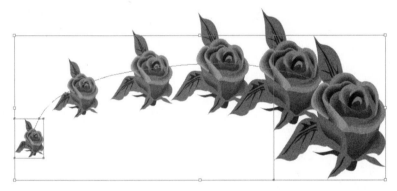

In blending different symbols, the blend may be a bit distorted. Even expanding the symbol won't
change the blend outcome. Figure 12.19 shows several sets of blends between different symbols.

FIGURE 12.19

A blend between different symbols can produce some very interesting results.

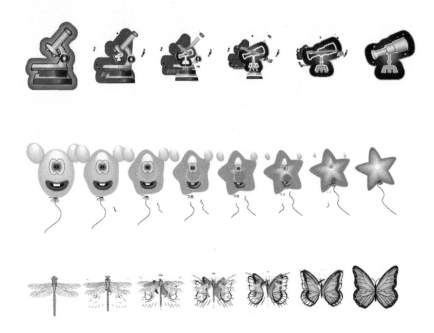

Blending envelopes

Not only can you blend symbols, but you also can take a blend and stuff it in an envelope-like shape with warp effects. Simply select the blend and then choose Effect ➪ Warp ➪ Arc and then either click OK or choose another preset or create your own warp. Figure 12.20 shows two blends with two different warp effects applied.

CROSS-REF   For more on warp effects, see Chapter 11.

Blending 3-D objects

Another great use of blending is to blend 3-D objects. You create a 3-D object, either create another one or duplicate and alter the original, and then press Ctrl+Alt+B (⌘+Option+B) to blend the two together. To change anything, select one of the objects in the blend and then use the Appearance panel to make your edits. Figure 12.21 shows a 3-D star blended with another 3-D star on a curved spine.

FIGURE 12.20

You can create unusual effects by warping a blend's envelope.

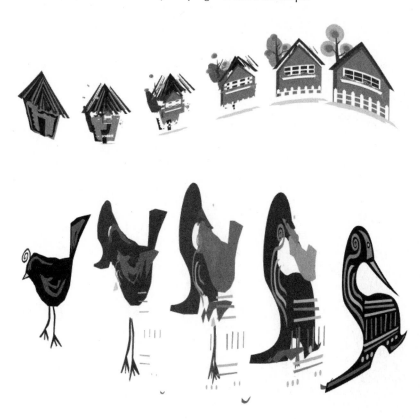

CROSS-REF For more on the Appearance panel, see Chapter 15. For more on using 3-D, see Chapter 16.

TIP A really cool thing to do with the 3-D stars is to select all objects and the blend and then open the Layers panel. Choose Release to Layers (Sequence) from the panel menu. After you do this, choose File ⇨ Export and then choose Flash (swf) from the Save as type box (Format popup menu). Choose AI Layers to SWF Frames as the export type to create a file that you can open in your browser that becomes animated. It creates three files: an HTML file, a JPEG file, and an SWF file. When you open the HTML file in your browser, it plays the SWF file using the JPEG file.

FIGURE 12.21

These 3-D stars are blended together and are still fully editable.

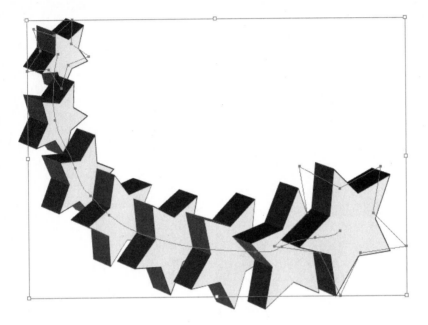

Airbrushing and the Magic of Stroke Blends

Blending can create effects that are usually reserved for bitmap graphics functions, such as the Glow, Drop Shadow, and Feather effects in Illustrator or the Layer Effects in Adobe Photoshop, but without the limitation of pixels. Blending identical, overlapping paths together and varying their stroke weights and colors create most of the effects described in this section. This technique can provide some of the best effects that Illustrator has to offer.

An important key to getting shape blends to look really good is to blend from the color of the shape to the first blend or to make that first blend the background color. This flows the blend smoothly into the background, so you can't exactly tell where the blend starts and stops.

Usually, the bottommost stroke has a heavier weight than the topmost stroke, and as the color changes from bottom stroke to top stroke, the colors appear to blend in from the outside.

It's always faster to simply use the effect instead of created stroke-based blends, and by using an effect, you gain the ability to edit your artwork and have the effect quickly regenerate. But strokes allow you to scale your images to any size without dramatically increasing file size, especially if you're taking the AI image into InDesign or Photoshop.

Airbrushing shadows

To create a realistic shadow effect, the edges of an object must be a little fuzzy. The amount of fuzziness on the edges of the path is relative to the distance of the object from its shadow and the strength of the light source. These two areas also affect how dark the shadow is.

To make really cool shadows, you can use the drop shadow effect to create soft- or hard-edged shadows, which are usually good for quickly creating text shadows.

A second way to create smooth shadows is to use stroke blends. Stroke blends can allow the shadows to fade smoothly into the background with a Gaussian blur-like effect. Follow these steps to create this effect:

1. **Copy the object/path and then paste it behind the original object by choosing Edit ⇨ Paste In Back.** At this point, you may want to hide the object from which you're creating the shadow so that it doesn't get in your way, especially if this object is right above where you want to place the shadow.

2. **Fill the shadowed path with the color you want the shadow to be and then make the stroke the same color, with a 0.5-point stroke weight.** In this case, if your text is black, you might want to use gray.

3. **Copy the shadow and then choose Edit ⇨ Paste in Back or press Ctrl+B (⌘+B).** Then, change the stroke color to whatever the background color is (usually white, unless something else is under the shadow). Make the stroke weight twice the distance to which you want the shadow to fade out. In my example, I made the stroke 12 points.

4. **Now blend these two paths.** Blending is easy using the Object ⇨ Blend ⇨ Make command or by pressing Ctrl+Alt+B (⌘+Option+B). The shadow slowly fades in from the background color to the shadow color. Show the hidden objects (you may have to bring them to the front), and your shadow effect is created, as shown in Figure 12.22.

FIGURE 12.22

Blends can produce an effect similar to airbrushed shadows.

Creating glows

Glows are very similar to soft-edged shadows, but instead of a dark area fading into the background, a lighter area fades into the background. You can create a glow by using the Glow effect or maintain much more control over the glow by using stroke blending.

Follow these steps to create a stroke-blended glow behind an object:

1. **Draw an object around which you want to create a glow.** In this example, the Ellipse tool is used to draw a circle with a red fill.

2. **Change the stroke to 6% Magenta, 60% Yellow, and 100% Black, and make the stroke about 40 points wide.** You can make the stroke wider if you want the glow to spread over a larger area.

3. **Select the object and then choose Edit ⇨ Copy or press Ctrl+C (⌘+C) to copy it.**

4. **Choose Edit ⇨ Paste in Front or press Ctrl+F (⌘+F) to paste a copy in front of the existing object.**

5. **Give the copied object a stroke of 6% Magenta and 62% Yellow and a weight of 1 point.**

6. **Select both objects by choosing Select ⇨ All or by pressing Ctrl+A (⌘+A).**

7. **Blend the two edge paths together to create the glow behind the object.**

8. **Draw a Black rectangle around the outside edge of the object and then send it to the back by choosing Object ⇨ Arrange ⇨ Send to Back.** Figure 12.23 shows the result.

> **NOTE**   When creating glows, make the initial glow area (around the edge of the object) lighter than the object's edges if there are bright highlights in the object. Make the initial glow darker than the edges if the edges of the object are the brightest part of the object.

Softening edges

You can soften edges of objects in a manner very similar to that of creating shadows. The reason you soften edges is to remove the hard, computer-like edges from objects in your illustration. You can soften edges to an extreme measure so that the object appears out of focus or you can soften just a tiny bit for an almost imperceptible change.

When determining how much of a distance you want to soften, look at the whole illustration, not just that one piece. Usually, the softening area is no more than 1 or 2 points (unless you're blurring the object).

FIGURE 12.23

A glow added behind this object makes it look like a sun shining in the blackness of space.

To soften edges on an object, follow these general steps:

1. **Draw the object you want to soften.**

2. **Choose Edit ⇨ Copy or press Ctrl+C (⌘+C) to copy the object.**

3. **Change the stroke to the color of the background and the weight to twice the width you want for the softening edge.** An amount of 3 or 4 points produces a good result in most cases.

4. **Choose Edit ⇨ Paste in Front or press Ctrl+F (⌘+F).**

5. **Click the object to ensure the front object is selected.**

6. **Make the stroke on the object 0.25 points, and use the same color as the fill.**

7. **Choose Object ⇨ Blend ⇨ Make to blend the two objects.**

8. **Choose Edit ⇨ Paste in Front or press Ctrl+F (⌘+F) to place a copy of the original object on top of the blended object.**

9. **Click outside the objects to deselect them.** Figure 12.24 shows an example of how a softened edge looks when zoomed in to 800%.

FIGURE 12.24

Zooming in shows how the softened edge effect appears.

To blur an object, just make the bottom layer stroke extremely wide (12 to 20 points or more, depending on the size of the illustration) and then blend as described in the preceding instructions.

Designing neon effects

To create neon effects with stroke blends, you need to create two distinct parts. Part one is the neon tubing, which by itself is neat, but it doesn't really have a neon effect. The second part is the tubing's reflection off the background, which usually appears as a glowing area. These two separate blends give the illusion of lit neon.

 Neon effects work much better when the background is very dark, although some interesting effects can be achieved with light backgrounds.

Basically, creating a neon effect simply requires that you make two copies of the blended object. The copy in front requires a blend where the top object has a smaller stroke weight and a brighter color to emulate the glow of a neon tube. The copy in the rear uses a wider stroke that blends to the darker color of the background. Figure 12.25 shows an example of the neon effect.

 Try crossing paths with neon, or for an even more realistic look, create unlit portions of neon by using darker shading with no reflective glow.

FIGURE 12.25

A neon candle is a good example of how you can use two blends to create an interesting effect.

Another interesting effect that you can create that's similar to the neon effect is a backlighting effect. You can accomplish backlighting effects by creating a glow for an object and then placing that same object on top of the glow. By making the topmost object filled with black or another dark color, a backlit effect is produced.

Using Compound Paths

Compound paths are one of the least understood areas of Illustrator, but after you understand a few simple guidelines and rules, manipulating and using them correctly is easy.

Compound paths are paths made of two or more open or closed paths. Where the paths cross with fills is a transparent hole. You can specify which paths create the holes by changing the direction of the paths by selecting them with the Direct Selection tool and then choosing the reverse path direction option in the Attributes panel. The general rule is that paths traveling in the opposite direction of any adjoining paths form holes.

Creating compound paths

You can create compound paths of all sorts by using the following steps. Ensure that none of the paths are currently compound paths or grouped paths before creating a new compound path and then follow these steps:

1. **Create all the paths that you need for the compound path, including the outside path and the holes.**

2. **Select all the paths and then choose Object ⇨ Compound Path ⇨ Make or press Ctrl+8 (⌘+8).** Illustrator now treats the paths as one path. When you click one of the paths with the Selection tool, the other paths in the compound path are also selected. Fill the object with any fill.

3. **Place the compound path over any other object.** I used a placed EPS image for this example. The inner paths act as holes that allow you to see the object underneath. Figure 12.26 shows a before and after example of creating a compound path.

You can select individual paths by clicking them once with the Group Selection tool. As always, you can select points and segments within each path by using the Direct Selection tool. Clicking only once with the Group Selection tool on paths that you want to select is important. Clicking those paths more than once with the Group Selection tool selects all the other paths in the compound path. To click (for moving or copying purposes) the selected individual paths after the Group Selection tool has clicked them once, click them with the Direct Selection tool.

> **NOTE** Paths belonging to different groups can't be made into a compound path unless all paths in all the groups are selected.

Here are some things you need to understand about compound paths:

■ When you create a compound path, it takes on the paint style attributes of the bottom-most path of all the paths that were selected and have become part of that compound path.

■ You can create a compound path that's only one path, although there are few reasons to do so.

■ If the singular compound path is selected as part of a larger compound path (with either the Direct Selection tool or the Group Selection tool), the path directions may be altered.

■ If you aren't sure whether an individual path is a compound path, choose the Release option from the Object ⇨ Compound Path submenu. If the Release option is available, then it's a compound path; if not, then it isn't a compound path.

Compound paths don't work in a hierarchical process as groups do. If a path is part of a compound path, it's part of that compound path only. If a compound path becomes part of another compound path, the paths in the original compound path are compounded only with the new compound path.

FIGURE 12.26

The left side shows the paths before being combined; the right side shows how the inner paths become holes in a compound path, showing through to the placed image behind them.

Blending between Multiple-Path Compound Paths

Here's how to blend between multiple-path compound paths:

1. **Click the Blend tool and then click from one compound shape to another compound shape.**

2. **While the initial blend between the two objects is still selected, double-click the Blend tool in the Tools panel to open the Blend Options dialog box.**

3. **Click the Spacing dropdown list (popup menu), choose Specified Step, and then type a number. Remember that the larger the number you type, the smoother the blend is.**

4. **Click the Preview check box to see the results before you close the dialog box.**

For really cool results, ensure that the two objects are different colors. For the smoothest blends, ensure that you don't have a stroke color applied to your shapes.

Releasing compound paths

When you want to release a compound path, select the path and then choose Object ➪ Compound Path ➪ Release or press Shift+Ctrl+Alt+8 (Shift+⌘+Option+8). The path changes into regular paths.

If any of the paths appear as holes, they're instead filled with the fill of the rest of the compound path. The results may be a little confusing because these holes then seem to blend right in to the outer shape of the compound paths.

If the compound path that you're releasing contains other compound paths, they're also released because Illustrator doesn't recognize compound paths that are within other compound paths.

Understanding holes

Holes for donuts, Life Savers, and rings are quite simple to create. Just select two circles, one smaller than and totally within a larger circle, and then choose Compound Path ➪ Make or press Ctrl+8 (⌘+8). The inside circle is then a hole.

A compound path considers every path within it to lie along the borders of the compound path. Path edges within an object appear to you to be on the inside of an object, but they appear to Illustrator to be just another edge of the path.

With this concept in mind, you can create a compound path that has several holes, such as a slice of Swiss cheese or a snowflake. Just create the outermost paths and the paths that you want to make holes, select all the paths, and then choose Object ➪ Compound Path ➪ Make.

 You aren't limited to one set of holes. You can create a compound path with a hole that has an object inside it with a hole. In that hole can be an object with a hole, etc.

Overlapping holes

Holes, if they really are paths that are supposed to be empty areas of an object, shouldn't overlap. If anything, you can combine multiple holes that are overlapping into one larger hole, possibly by using Unite in the Pathfinder panel (accessed via Window ➪ Pathfinder).

If holes within a compound path do overlap, the result is a solid area with the same fill color as the rest of the object. If multiple holes overlap, the results can be quite unusual, as shown in Figure 12.27. (A section later in this chapter discusses reversing path directions.)

NOTE In most cases, you get the desired results with holes only if the outermost path contains all the holes. As a rule, Illustrator uses the topmost objects to poke holes out of the bottommost objects. If you want holes to overlap, ensure that the holes are above the outside border.

FIGURE 12.27

This figure shows overlapping holes before being made into compound paths (left) and after (right).

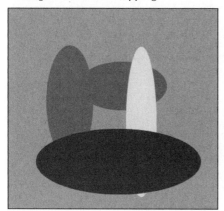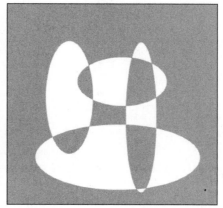

Creating compound paths from separate sets of paths

Compound paths are very flexible. You can choose two sets of paths, each with an outline and a hole, and make them into one compound path. This technique is especially useful for making masks, but you also can use it to alleviate the repetition of creating several compound paths and selecting one of them at a time.

For example, if you have two shapes, a square and a circle, and want a round hole in each of them, you draw two smaller circles and put them into place. After you position the two shapes in the correct locations, you select them and the round paths inside each of them and then you choose Object ➪ Compound Path ➪ Make or press Ctrl+8 (⌘+8). Each of the objects now has a hole, and they act as if they're grouped, as indicated in Figure 12.28. If you don't see a hole in each of the two objects, try again, but make certain that the small circles are above the other objects in the front-to-back order.

To move separate objects that are part of the same compound path, select each object with the Group Selection tool, which selects an entire path at a time, and then move them. Remember that after they're selected, you should use the Direct Selection tool to move the selected portions of a compound path.

Compound paths can include separate shapes with holes.

Working with type and compound paths

You've been using compound paths as long as you've been using computer PostScript typefaces. All PostScript typefaces are made of characters that are compound paths. Letters that have holes, such as uppercase B, D, and P and lowercase a, b, and d, benefit from being compound paths. When you place them in front of other objects, you can see through the empty areas to objects behind them that are visible in those holes.

Each character in a PostScript typeface is a compound path. When you convert characters to editable outlines in Illustrator, each character is still a compound path. If you release the compound paths, the characters with empty areas appear to fill with the same color as the rest of the character, as shown in Figure 12.29, because the holes are no longer knocked out of the letters.

> **NOTE** Many times, type is used as a mask, but all the letters used in the mask need to be one compound path. Simply select all the letters and then choose Object ⇨ Compound Path ⇨ Make or press Ctrl+8 (⌘+8). This action creates a compound path in which all the letters form the compound path. Usually, all the holes stay the same as they were as separate compound paths (unless there's overlap between the objects).

Any letters that overlap in a word that you make into a compound path can change path directions and thus affect the emptiness of some paths. If letters have to overlap, use the Pathfinder Unite feature on them first, select all the letters, and then choose Object ⇨ Compound Path ⇨ Make or press Ctrl+8 (⌘+8).

FIGURE 12.29

Type as it normally appears after you convert it to outlines (top) and after you release compound paths (bottom)

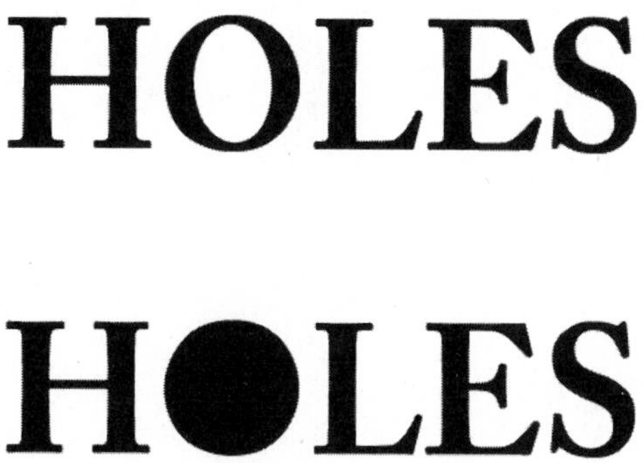

HOLES

H●LES

Finding Path Directions

Each path in Illustrator has a direction. For paths that you draw with the Pen or Pencil tool, the direction of the path is the direction in which you draw the path. When Illustrator creates an ellipse or a rectangle, the direction of the path is clockwise.

If you're curious about which way a path travels, click any spot of the path with the Scissors tool and then choose Effect ⇨ Stylize ⇨ Add Arrowheads. In the Add Arrowheads dialog box, ensure that only the End button area is selected and then click OK. An arrowhead appears, going in the direction of the path. Figure 12.30 shows several paths that include an arrowhead to indicate the direction for each path.

FIGURE 12.30

The arrows represent the directions of the paths.

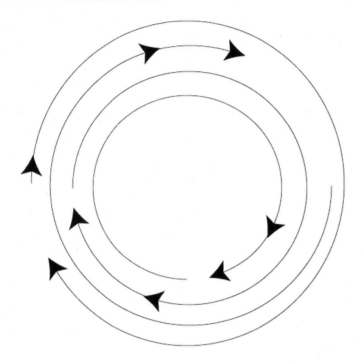

Paths have directions for one purpose (one purpose that you need to know about anyway) and that's to determine what the solid areas of a compound path and the empty areas become. The individual paths in a compound path that create holes from solid paths go in opposite directions.

If two smaller circles are inside a larger circle, they still punch holes in the larger circle because both of them are traveling in the same direction. But what happens when the two inside circles overlap? The area where they overlap is inside the empty area, but both holes go in the same direction. The intersection of the two holes is solid because of the winding path rule (see the next section for an explanation of winding).

Figuring out which way to go

Understanding the Winding Numbers Rule is helpful when you're dealing with compound paths. The Winding Numbers Rule counts surrounded areas, starting with 0 (outside the outermost edge) and working inward. Any area with an odd number is filled, and any area with an even number (such as 0, the outside of the path) is empty, or a hole.

You can apply this rule to most compound paths — although taking the time to diagram the paths you've drawn and place little numbers in them to figure out what is going to be filled and what isn't is usually more time-consuming than doing it wrong, undoing it, and doing it right.

Reversing path directions

To change the direction of a path, select just the path using the Group Selection tool and then choose Window➪Attributes. In the Attributes panel, as shown in Figure 12.31, click the other (not darkened) direction button.

When you convert a path into a compound path, its direction may change. One element that's consistent when dealing with path directions is that holes must travel in the opposite direction from the outside path. As a result, if the Reverse Path Direction button is on for the holes, it's not on for the outside path. That's the normal scenario when you create compound paths with holes. You can, if you desire, click Reverse Path Direction On for the outside path and Reverse Path Direction Off for the inside path. The resulting image has the same holes as produced by the reversing of the path. Figure 12.32 shows a compound path and its path directions before and after some of the paths were reversed.

FIGURE 12.31

The Attributes panel allows you to control the path directions and fill rules.

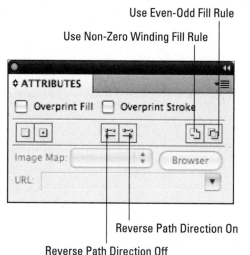

Use Even-Odd Fill Rule

Use Non-Zero Winding Fill Rule

Reverse Path Direction On

Reverse Path Direction Off

CAUTION   Never attempt to change path direction when all paths of a compound path are selected. Clicking once on either button makes all the paths in the compound path go in the same direction at this point, which means that no holes appear.

FIGURE 12.32

Reversing the direction of the paths in the illustration on the left fills those holes, as shown in the illustration on the right.

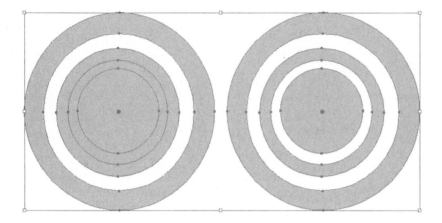

Faking a compound path

At times, using a compound path just doesn't work. You may need to cheat a little. Except in the most extreme circumstances, you can fake compound paths, but you need to make quite an effort.

If the background is part of a gradient, select the hole and the object that's painted with the gradient, apply the gradient, and then use the Gradient tool to make the gradient spread across both objects in exactly the same way. This trick can fool even the experts.

TIP   One way to fake a compound path is by selecting the background, making a copy of it, making the hole a mask of the background area, and then grouping the mask to the copy of the background.

Using Clipping Masks

In Illustrator, you use clipping masks to mask out parts of underlying objects that you don't want to see. The path that you draw in Illustrator defines the shape of the mask. Anything outside the mask is hidden from view in Preview mode and doesn't print.

CROSS-REF   For more on Preview mode, see Chapter 2. For more on masks, see Chapter 7.

Clipping masks are objects that mask out everything but the paths made up by the mask, as shown in Figure 12.33. Clipping masks can be open, closed, or compound paths. The masking object is the object whose paths make up the mask, and this object must be in front of all the objects that are being masked.

FIGURE 12.33

FIGURE 12.33

This shows an object, its mask, and the resulting masked object.

You can make clipping masks from any path, including compound paths and text. You can use masks to view portions of multiple objects, individual objects, and placed images.

Creating masks

To create a mask, the masking object (the path that's in the shape of the mask) has to be in front of the objects that you want it to mask. You select the masking object and the objects that you want to mask. Then, you choose Object ⇨ Clipping Mask ⇨ Make or press Ctrl+7 (⌘+7). In Preview mode, any areas of the objects that are outside the mask vanish, but the parts of the objects that are inside the mask remain. Figure 12.34 shows an illustration with masks and without them.

 **Masks are much easier to use and understand in Preview mode than in Outline mode. For more on these modes, see Chapter 2.**

If you want to mask an object that isn't currently being masked, select the new object and all the objects in the mask, including the masking object. Then, choose Object ⇨ Clipping Mask ⇨ Make or press Ctrl+7 (⌘+7). The mask applies to the new object as well as to the objects that were previously masked. The new object, like all others being masked, must be behind the masking object.

Like compound paths, masking doesn't work in hierarchical levels. Each time you add an object to a mask, the old mask that didn't have that object is released, and a new mask is made that contains all the original mask objects as well as the new object. Releasing a mask affects every object in the mask, as discussed later in this chapter.

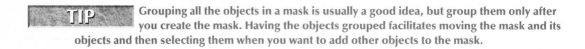

TIP Grouping all the objects in a mask is usually a good idea, but group them only after you create the mask. Having the objects grouped facilitates moving the mask and its objects and then selecting them when you want to add other objects to the mask.

FIGURE 12.34

The image on the left uses masks to hide portions of objects. The image on the right is the result of releasing those masks.

Masking raster images

There are two ways to mask raster images. You accomplish the first method in Photoshop by creating a clipping path and then saving it as an EPS image. For the second method, you use a clipping mask in Illustrator.

Each method has its strengths and weaknesses. The best solution is a combination of both methods. The main advantage to creating a clipping path in Photoshop is that you can adjust the path while viewing the image clearly at 16:1. (Viewing an image at 1600% in Illustrator displays chunky, unrecognizable blocks of color.) In this manner, you can precisely position the path over the correct pixels so that the right pixels are selected for masking. A disadvantage to using a clipping path is that compound paths in Photoshop adhere to one of two different fill rules, which control the way holes appear for differing path directions. Illustrator is much more flexible in this respect because you're able to change the path direction of each individual path with the Reverse Path Direction option in the Attributes panel.

Using a mask with other masks

You can mask objects that are masking other objects. Just ensure that you select all the objects in each mask and that, as with other objects, they're behind the path that you want to use for a masking object.

NOTE You can apply a stroke or fill to a masking object. A fill and stroke of None replace any paint style attributes that you applied to the object prior to transforming it into a mask. But if you select the object after it's a mask, you can apply a stroke or fill to that mask. If you release the mask, the path that was the masking object continues to have a fill and stroke of None.

Releasing masks

To release a mask, first select the masking object (you can also select other objects). Then, choose Object ⇨ Clipping Mask ⇨ Release or press Ctrl+Alt+7 (⌘+Option+7), and the masking object is no longer a mask.

If you aren't sure which object is the masking object or if you're having trouble selecting the masking object, choose Select ⇨ Select All or press Ctrl+A (⌘+A) and then choose Object ⇨ Clipping Mask ⇨ Release or press Ctrl+Alt+7 (⌘+Option+7). Of course, this action releases all other masks that are in the document — unless they were separate masks that were being masked by other masks.

To release all the masks in the document, even those masks that are being masked by other masks, choose Select All (Edit ⇨ Select All) or press Ctrl+A (⌘+A) and repeatedly choose Release Mask. Usually, repeating Release Masks three times gets everything, unless you went mask-happy in that particular document. You can also choose Select ⇨ Clipping Masks to check if any masks remain. If the Release menu option is enabled, then a mask still remains.

Masking and printing

As a rule, PostScript printers don't care too much for masks. They care even less for masks that mask other masks. And they really don't like masks that are compound paths.

Unfortunately, because of the way that Illustrator works, every part of every object in a mask is sent to the printer, even if you only use a tiny piece of an object. In addition, controlling where the masking object slices objects requires a great deal of computing power and memory. You can have a problem, for example, when you have more stuff to mask than the printer can handle.

More important than any other issue involved with masks and printing is the length and complexity of the masking path.

The more objects in a mask, the more complex it is. More anchor points and direction points coming off those anchor points add more complexity to the document. In other words, your printer enjoys a mask only if the masking object is a rectangle and you're not masking other objects.

Masking and compound paths

Creating masks from compound paths is especially useful when you're working with text and want several separate letters to mask a placed EPS image or a series of pictures that you created in Illustrator.

The reason that you need to transform separate objects into compound paths is that a masking object can be only one path. The topmost object of the selected objects becomes the masking object, and the others become objects within the mask. Creating a compound path from several paths makes the masking feature treat all the objects as one path and makes a masking object out of the entire compound path.

You can use compound paths for masking when you're working with objects that need to have holes as well as when you're working with text and other separate objects. Figure 12.35 was created by making one compound path from all the parts of the window frame and using that compound path as a mask.

FIGURE 12.35

Creating a compound path from all the parts of the window frame made this window frame a clipping mask for the background.

Summary

Path blends, compound paths, and masks allow you to create some really fancy effects in your Illustrator documents. In this chapter, you learned the following important information about these topics:

- Using blends rather than gradients can produce some pretty cool and realistic results.
- With Blend options, you can change the blend to steps, distance, or smooth color.
- You can blend from 3-D objects to symbols and use different objects.
- Compound paths are one or more paths that Illustrator treats as a single path.
- Compound paths give you the ability to put holes in your paths.
- Changing the direction of a path via the Attributes panel can change the holes in the compound path.
- Each character of type converted to outlines consists of a compound path.
- Masks are paths that overlay other Illustrator objects, showing the objects only through the masking path.
- When using text outlines as a mask, ensure that all the paths making up the text outlines are joined into a single compound path.

Chapter 13

Using Live Trace

I n this chapter, I introduce Live Trace, which takes the art of using bit-map images as the basis for Illustrator documents to a new and exciting level. You can use this tool to create vector-based graphics from raster images, but that description hardly even hints at the possibilities that Live Trace opens up for you.

Understanding Live Trace

As you're aware by now, Illustrator is primarily a vector-based graphics application. Quite simply put, Illustrator is able to handle vector images with far more adeptness than it can raster (or bitmap) images. To most people, however, the format of an image is far less important than how that image appears. Sometimes, only a bitmap will do the job. For example, digital photos are always bitmap images — never vector images. If you need to use a digital photo in your Illustrator document, you have to import it as a bitmap image.

Even though you have to import digital photos as bitmap images, you may not have to leave them in that format inside of Illustrator. There are many instances where a vector-based representation of the photo is just what you need. Consider the example shown in Figure 13.1. The image on the left is a digital photo, and on the right is the result of using the Live Trace tool to convert the image into a drawing that looks like a hand-drawn sketch. If you create an image to use for a logo for a Web site that advertises a pet-sitting business, the hand-drawn sketch appearance may well serve your needs better than the digital photo.

IN THIS CHAPTER

Understanding Live Trace

Learning Live Trace modes

Setting Live Trace options

Tracing with Live Trace

FIGURE 13.1

The left image is the raw imported bitmap, and the right image was traced using the Live Trace tool to produce a hand-drawn sketch appearance.

So, just what does Live Trace do? Live Trace uses color or contrast information in an imported bitmap to create path and anchor points so that the bitmap image can be converted into a vector-based image. The tool uses the parameters that you set in the Tracing Options dialog box to determine how closely the vector image matches the bitmap image. Using various presets and options that are available in the dialog box, you can create a result that looks virtually identical to the bitmap or you can go to the other extreme of having a result that contains only a few strokes that look like a very basic sketch with almost no detail. The important point to remember is that the Live Trace tool is extremely versatile, so you need to spend a little time trying out various options in order to achieve the final results you want.

Learning Live Trace Modes

Live Trace has three tracing modes. These modes create very different end results, so a good place to start in understanding how Live Trace functions is to examine each tracing mode.

You choose a tracing mode by using the choices in the Vector dropdown list (popup menu) in the Tracing Options dialog box, as shown in Figure 13.2. Choose Object ⇨ Live Trace ⇨ Tracing Options to open the Tracing Options dialog box.

FIGURE 13.2

Choose a tracing mode from the Vector list in the Tracing Options dialog box.

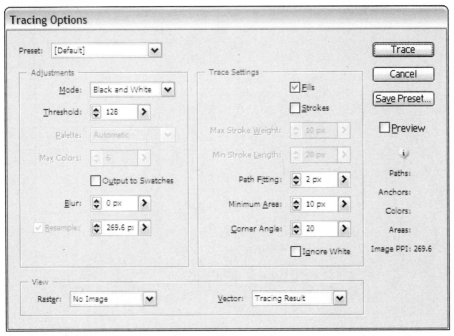

Getting to know Outline mode

In Outline mode, the Live Trace tool creates strokes that outline any shapes in the bitmap image that seem to be a single fill area. Figure 13.3 shows an example of using Outline mode to trace a bitmap image.

CROSS-REF For more on Outline mode, see Chapter 2.

TIP Outline mode is also called Fill mode because it outlines the fills in the image.

As Figure 13.3 shows, Outline mode creates an image lacking any fills. You can, of course, add a fill to any area, but this mode is probably most appropriate for images where you want to produce a pen-and-ink style of drawing.

FIGURE 13.3

This shows how the Live Trace tool traces an image in Outline mode.

Using Tracing Result mode

In Tracing Result mode, the Live Trace tool creates stroked paths of variable widths, as shown in Figure 13.4. In this example, I chose the Color 6 preset to make it easier to see the differences between the tracing modes. The end result is an image that has fills without outlining strokes.

 Tracing Result mode is sometimes called Stroke mode because it fills the strokes that are traced in the image.

The image in Figure 13.4 shows just one possible result you might see when using Tracing Result mode.

FIGURE 13.4

This shows how the Live Trace tool traces an image in Tracing Result mode, with the left side being the original image and the right side showing how the image looks when traced.

Combining Outline and Tracing Result modes

If you choose the Outlines with Tracing option in the Vector dropdown list (popup menu), Illustrator combines Outline and Tracing Result modes, as shown in Figure 13.5.

> **TIP** When a traced image is selected, you can use the Preview different views of the vector result button on the Control panel to see each of the different tracing modes. Likewise, you can use the Preview different views of the raster image button to see different views of the bitmap image.

Although you can achieve many effects just by changing the tracing mode, that's only the beginning. In the following sections, you learn how to use the other options in the Tracing Options dialog box to create the exact effect you want.

FIGURE 13.5

This shows how the Live Trace tool traces an image combining Outline and Tracing Result modes.

Setting Live Trace Options

If you were to simply choose Object ➪ Live Trace ➪ Make or click the Live Trace button on the Control panel without exploring the Live Trace options, you probably wouldn't gain much respect for the Live Trace tool. This tool is likely the most customizable tool contained in Illustrator. In fact, I can't even show you more than a very small sampling of the possibilities because it has so many options.

Understanding the Live Trace presets

Probably the best place to begin experimenting with the Live Trace options is by choosing one of the settings in the Preset dropdown list (popup menu) in the Tracing Options dialog box. After you choose a preset that produces results close to your desired end result, you can play around with the remaining options in the dialog box to fine-tune the output.

 Always ensure that you click the Preview check box in the Tracing Options dialog box. That way, you can immediately see the results of any selections you make.

Figure 13.6 shows an example of the Default preset option. In this case, the output is a black-and-white image with no shading.

FIGURE 13.6

Using the Default tracing preset produces a black-and-white image like this.

The next preset is the Color 6 preset, as shown in Figure 13.7. In this preset, the vector image has six colors.

FIGURE 13.7

Using the Color 6 tracing preset produces a color image that uses six colors.

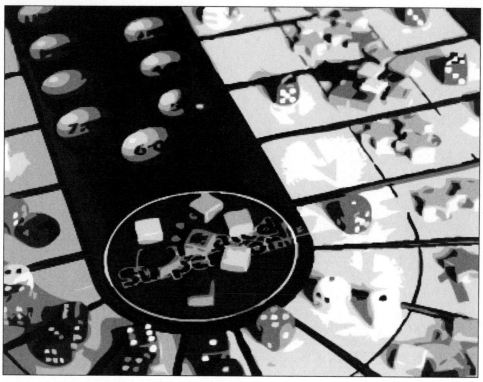

Figure 13.8 shows an example of the Color 16 preset. Although the appearance is similar to the Color 6 preset, Color 16 uses 16 shades for a more realistic appearance.

Using the Color 16 tracing preset produces a color image that uses 16 colors and has more subtle shading.

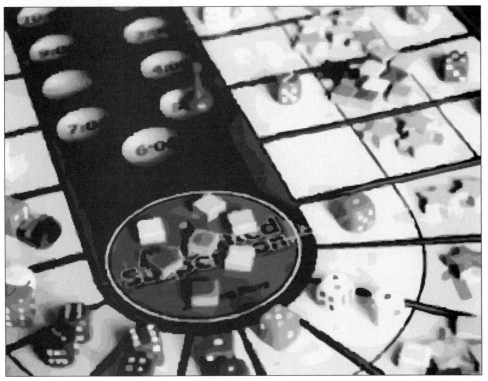

Figure 13.9 shows an example of the Photo Low Fidelity preset. It can be a bit difficult to see the differences between Color 16 and Photo Low Fidelity, but Photo Low Fidelity tends to have fewer paths and anchor points than does Color 16.

FIGURE 13.9

Using the Photo Low Fidelity tracing preset produces a color image that uses 16 colors but has a slightly different appearance than the Color 16 preset.

The Photo High Fidelity preset shown in Figure 13.10 produces a very realistic-looking image. In this preset, 64 colors are used, and the result looks very much like the original raster image.

FIGURE 13.10

Using the Photo High Fidelity tracing preset produces a color image that uses 64 colors for an almost photographic appearance.

The Grayscale preset shown in Figure 13.11 produces a result similar to the Color 6 preset but with all the colors replaced by shades of gray.

FIGURE 13.11

Using the Grayscale tracing preset produces a grayscale image that uses six shades of gray.

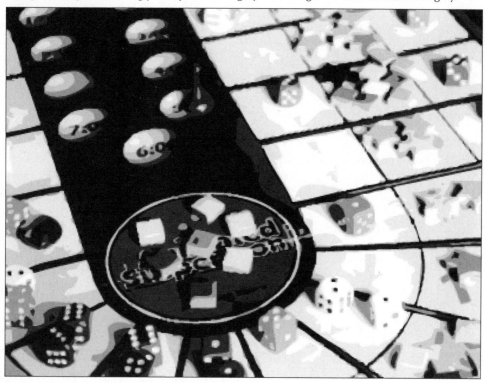

Believe it or not, the example shown in Figure 13.12 is the same image used in the previous examples. The only difference is the selection of the Hand Drawn Sketch preset. Obviously, this preset works better with other raster images, but comparing the results for the same image throughout is interesting.

FIGURE 13.12

Using the Hand Drawn Sketch tracing preset produces a very different result with the sample image.

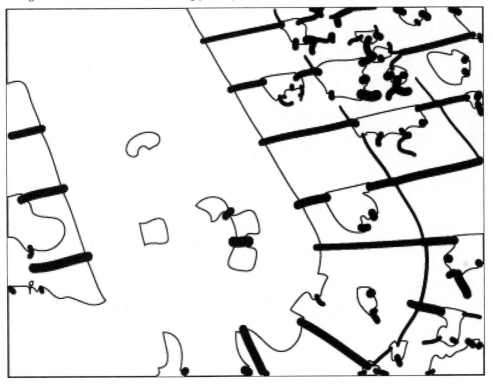

Figure 13.13 shows how the Detailed Illustration preset renders the image. In this case, the result is similar to the Default preset but with slightly more detail.

FIGURE 13.13

Using the Detailed Illustration tracing preset produces a black-and-white image.

Figure 13.14 shows an example of the Comic Art preset. Again, this preset is probably best suited to images other than this example, such as ones with a lot of contrasting colors. This shows less detail than the Default setting.

Using the Comic Art tracing preset produces a black-and-white image that can be very difficult to discern.

Figure 13.15 shows the image traced by using the Technical Drawing preset.

Using the Technical Drawing preset produces a black-and-white line drawing.

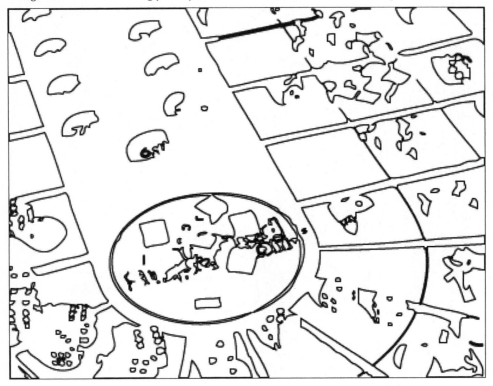

The Black and White Logo preset shown in Figure 13.16 is somewhat similar to the Default and the Detailed Illustration presets, but for this image, the results seem a bit more pleasing, with just a hint of more detail and smoother curves.

FIGURE 13.16

Using the Black and White Logo preset produces a black-and-white image that's fairly striking.

Figure 13.17 shows the Inked Drawing preset. Although the results are similar to the Black and White Logo preset results, this preset has a very different overall effect.

FIGURE 13.17

Using the Inked Drawing preset also produces a black-and-white image that has some interesting differences from similar presets.

The final preset, Type, is shown in Figure 13.18. Again, the preset options produce a black-and-white image, but the end result shows more detail than some of the other images.

Choosing custom Live Trace options

After you choose a preset that gets you at least close to your desired result, you likely want to experiment with the other options in the Tracing Options dialog box. In doing so, you have the opportunity to fine-tune the appearance of the vector output.

FIGURE 13.18

Using the Type preset also produces a black-and-white image but with more detail than some of the other black-and-white presets.

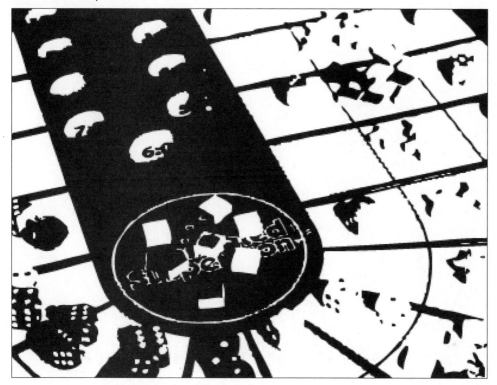

These are the available options:

- **Mode:** This option allows you to choose Color, Grayscale, or Black and White for the format of the vector image.

- **Threshold:** This option allows you to choose the threshold between black and white (only for black and white images).

- **Palette:** This option allows you to choose a custom library for color selection for color and grayscale images. The only choice here is Automatic, unless you've loaded a custom swatch library by choosing Window ⇨ Swatch Library ⇨ [library name].

- **Max Colors:** Use this option to specify the number of colors to use (between 2 and 256) for color and grayscale images.

- **Output to Swatches:** Choose this option to output the colors used to the Swatches panel.

- **Blur:** Use this to specify the size of the Blur effect to apply during raster image processing to remove small jagged edges. The higher the value, the more detail around edges is lost, resulting in smoother lines.

- **Resample:** This option allows you to specify the sampling resolution to use on the raster image. You may want to choose a lower resolution to reduce the size of the document.

- **Tracing Fills/Strokes:** These options allow you to choose the desired Trace mode.

- **Max Stroke Weight:** Use this to specify the maximum weight of a stroke that's converted into a stroked path.

- **Min Stroke Length:** Use this to specify the minimum length of a stroke that's converted into a stroked path.

- **Path Fitting:** Use this to control how closely paths should be traced.

- **Minimum Area:** This option allows you to specify the area (in pixels squared) that's rejected during trace. Use this setting to reduce the complexity of the resulting vector image.

- **Corner Angle:** Use this to specify the sharpness of a turn in the raster image that's turned into a corner in the vector image.

It's probably best to experiment with small changes in a single option at a time to narrow in on your desired results. As long as the Preview check box is selected, Illustrator redraws the vector image after each change you make. If you find that it takes too long to generate the previews, you can work with Preview off, but doing so makes it more difficult to fine-tune the results.

Tracing Raster Images with Live Trace

Aside from choosing the set of options that best suits your particular needs, actually using the Live Trace tool is quite simple. Follow these steps to trace a raster image using the Live Trace tool:

1. Choose File ➪ Place to display the Place dialog box, as shown in Figure 13.19.

2. Choose the bitmap image that you want to trace.

3. Click Place to close the dialog box and return to your document.

4. **Ensure that the newly placed image is selected.** If the image is not selected, click it with the Selection tool.

5. Choose Object ➪ Live Trace ➪ Tracing Options to display the Tracing Options dialog box.

6. Choose a preset from the Preset dropdown list (popup menu).

7. Click the Preview check box to preview the tracing.

8. Choose any options in the Tracing Options dialog box that you want.

9. Click Trace to close the Tracing Options dialog box and return to your document.

FIGURE 13.19

Open the Place dialog box to choose a bitmap image to place into your document
(Windows at top and Mac at bottom).

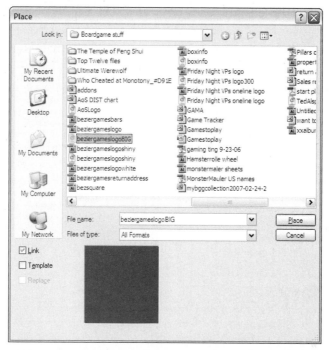

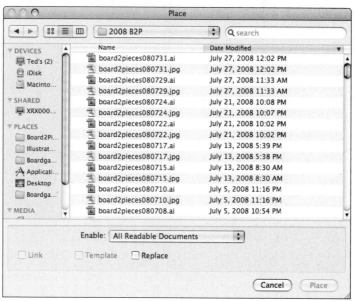

You can also click the Tracing Presets and Options dropdown list (popup menu) on the Control panel and then choose a preset or the Tracing Options command from the dropdown list (popup menu). Then, click the Live Trace button on the Control panel to trace the image.

TIP   **Instead of using the up/down arrows to change the settings for one of the Live Trace options, click the existing value and then type the new value. This is especially important when the Preview option is selected or when you're typing values using the Control panel because Illustrator redraws the tracing whenever there's a value change.**

After an image is traced, you can modify the image in several ways. As explained in Chapter 14, you can use the Live Paint tool to change the colors in the image. Even if you trace the image in black and white, you can still colorize it. Another way to modify the traced image is to choose Object ➪ Expand (or click the Expand button on the Control panel). If you expand the traced image, it becomes an ordinary Illustrator object and is no longer live. This means that you can't make any additional changes with the Live Trace tool, but you can use the other drawing tools to modify the image.

You can quickly trace a raster image and then expand it into editable paths by using the Object ➪ Live Trace ➪ Make & Expand command. This saves you a step, but unlike the name, it isn't really live anymore — it's just paths after you do this command.

Summary

In this chapter, you learned how to use the Live Trace tool, which can quickly create vector graphics from raster-based images. Here are some important things you learned:

- Live Trace has three modes for tracing raster images.
- Live Trace has a number of presets that you can use to quickly trace raster images.
- The Tracing Options dialog box offers an almost unlimited range of tracing options.
- You can convert traced images into ordinary Illustrator objects by expanding them.

Chapter 14

Using Live Paint

Illustrator does its best to prove it's indeed much smarter than you with the Live Paint feature. Instead of requiring you to create the specific shape you want to fill with color, Live Paint does this intelligently, secretly creating those shapes so you don't have to. It sounds really easy, right?

Understanding Live Paint

Bitmap-image editing and creation programs have long had a fun yet often frustrating tool that's typically called Paint Bucket. With just a click of the Paint Bucket tool, you can fill an enclosed area with a solid color. The Paint Bucket tool icon is always some variation on paint spilling out of a paint can, which seems like a very good icon for something that can be so hard to control. A single missing pixel around the perimeter of the area that you want to fill provides an escape route so that the fill spills out into areas you don't intend to paint. It's almost like trying to paint a room when a nosy cat is prowling around just waiting for a chance to cause some mischief.

When vector-based graphics applications, such as Illustrator, took on the paint bucket metaphor, things were considerably different than they had been in the bitmap world. For one thing, in a vector-based application, objects are typically treated as a unit. If you want to change the fill color of an object, you typically don't have to worry about the dreaded missing pixel paint spill because each object is independent.

So, at this point, you're probably wondering how the Live Paint Bucket tool improves on the Paint Bucket tool in previous versions of Illustrator. This tool is better in a couple of subtle but very helpful ways. First, with the Live

Paint Bucket tool, it's much easier to modify specific areas of an object, such as an image you traced with the Live Trace tool. That's because the Live Paint Bucket tool automatically detects the various independent regions as you move the tool over an object. As it detects each region, the Live Paint Bucket tool highlights the detected region, as shown in Figure 14.1. In this image, I used the Live Trace tool to trace an old greeting card that I scanned. The highlighted areas are surrounded with a bright contrast to show the detected regions.

The Live Paint Bucket tool allows you to easily fill individual regions within an object rather than the object as a whole. Also, because the paint remains live, any changes you make to the regions are also reflected in the paint fill.

FIGURE 14.1

This image shows how Live Paint highlights a region (in this case, her right lapel) as it's detected.

NOTE Clicking a Live Trace object with the Live Paint Bucket tool converts the object into a Live Paint object. This precludes making additional changes to the object using Live Trace, so it's important to complete all your Live Trace adjustments before you use the Live Paint Bucket tool.

In addition to the Live Paint Bucket tool, Illustrator offers the Live Paint Selection tool. This tool allows you to select Live Paint regions without making any changes to those regions. In effect, the Live Paint Selection tool could be called the selection-only portion of the Live Paint Bucket tool. Using the Live Paint Selection tool, you can select more than one Live Paint region at a time, as shown in Figure 14.2 (the selected regions are filled with a dotted pattern to show that they're selected). The highlighted area indicates the current region that's added to the selection.

FIGURE 14.2

The Live Paint Selection tool allows you to select regions without immediately modifying them.

 Clicking a Live Paint object with the Live Paint Selection tool makes it easier to preview the areas that the Live Paint Bucket tool will modify without actually making those changes.

Setting the Live Paint Options

You should probably become familiar with the options that are available for controlling how the Live Paint Bucket tool works before you use the tool. It has only a few options, but they can have quite an effect on how well the tool meets your expectations.

The first set of Live Paint Bucket tool options are contained in the Live Paint Bucket Options dialog box, as shown in Figure 14.3. Double-click the Live Paint Bucket tool in the Tools panel to display the dialog box.

FIGURE 14.3

The Live Paint Bucket Options dialog box allows you to choose basic settings for the Live Paint Bucket tool.

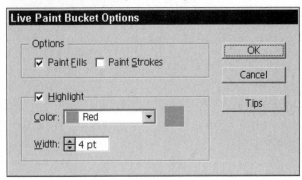

These settings are available in the Live Paint Bucket Options dialog box:

- **Paint Fills:** When selected, this option allows the Live Paint Bucket tool to add the current fill color or pattern to the fill of a region you click.

- **Paint Strokes:** When selected, this option allows the Live Paint Bucket tool to add the current stroke color to the stroke of a region you click.

- **Highlight:** When selected, this option outlines the region that's automatically detected as you move the mouse pointer over a Live Paint object.

- **Color:** This setting allows you to choose the color of the outline.

- **Width:** Use this setting to set the width of the outline that the Live Paint Bucket tool draws around the region.

By default, the Paint Fills option is selected and the Paint Strokes option is deselected. Selecting both options and using a contrasting color for the stroke color can produce some interesting effects.

In addition to the options shown in the Live Paint Bucket Options dialog box, you can also control how the Live Paint Bucket tool responds to gaps. Set the gap options in the Gap Options dialog box, as shown in Figure 14.4. Choose Object ⇨ Live Paint ⇨ Gap Options to display this dialog box.

These settings are available in the Gap Options dialog box:

- **Gap Detection:** Click this check box to turn on gap detection. This option is off by default.

- **Paint stops at:** Choose Small Gaps, Medium Gaps, or Large Gaps from the dropdown list (popup menu). Illustrator finds fewer gaps when you choose a larger setting.

- **Custom:** Click this check box if you want to specify the size of the gap rather than using one of the preset options. If you select this option, use the text box to specify the size of gap you want to detect.

- **Gap Preview Color:** Choose a contrasting color to make the detected gaps stand out from your artwork.

- **Close gaps with paths:** Click this button to remove the gaps by inserting paths in place of the gaps.

Depending on the result that you're attempting to produce, using gap detection improves the smoothness of the Live Paint Bucket tool's results. With fewer gaps to contend with, the Live Paint Bucket tool generally finds simpler paths than it would in a drawing with many gaps.

FIGURE 14.4

The Gap Options dialog box allows you to choose settings for how the Live Paint Bucket tool deals with gaps in objects.

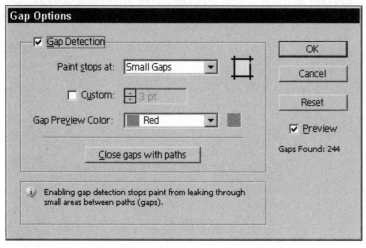

499

Using Live Paint

You can use the Live Paint Bucket tool to fill objects that you've drawn or you can use it to fill images that you created using the Live Trace tool. Either way, you begin by creating a Live Paint group so that Illustrator knows which objects you want to modify.

To create a Live Paint group, use the Selection tool to select the object (or objects) that you want to include in the group. Then, click the selected object with the Live Paint Bucket tool. After an object is part of a Live Paint group, Illustrator displays outlines around the detected regions as you move the Live Paint Bucket tool over the group. If the Paint Strokes check box is selected in the Live Paint Bucket Options dialog box, the Live Paint Bucket tool's icon changes when the tool is over a stroke. Clicking the Live Paint Bucket tool over a stroke fills the stroke with the current stroke color. Figure 14.5 shows an entire illustration that's been converted to a Live Paint group and then selected.

You can also click a region in a Live Paint group by using the Live Paint Selection tool to pick up the color from that region. You may, for example, decide that you want to pick up a color from one area to use to fill several other areas to reduce the clutter in a vector image traced by the Live Trace tool.

FIGURE 14.5

This shows the result of converting an entire image to a Live Paint object.

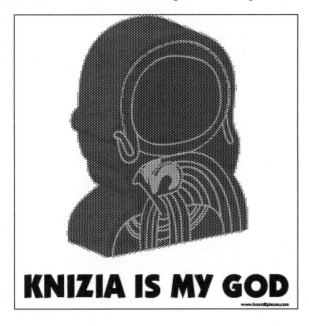

Summary

The Live Paint Bucket tool provides you with a flexible vector-based paint tool that's considerably more powerful than the paint bucket tools you find in bitmap-image editors. In this chapter, you learned the following:

- The Live Paint Bucket tool is the replacement for the Paint Bucket tool found in earlier versions of Illustrator.

- Live Paint groups remain live so that any changes you make to the paths are reflected in the fill you added using the Live Paint Bucket tool.

- Live Trace objects must be converted to Live Paint groups before you can use the Live Paint Bucket tool on them. This prevents you from making further modifications with the Live Trace tool.

- You can use the gap detection options to control how the Live Paint Bucket tool deals with gaps in the paths.

- You can choose to have the Live Paint Bucket tool paint fills, strokes, or both.

Part III

Mastering Illustrator

Chapter 15

Working with Graphic Styles and Effects

Probably some of the most amazing illustrations you see in Illustrator come from using graphic styles and effects. Graphic styles can increase your productivity with any type of repeating symbol or set of attributes that you use daily. Set as a style, you can use it over and over again.

Those of you looking to create special effects, look no further. In this chapter, you discover when to use effects.

Along with effects, you also see a variety of artwork that combines effects with graphic styles.

Understanding How Graphic Styles Work

Graphic styles have brought Illustrator to the front of the pack in illustration software. Graphic styles give you the ability to save all of an object's attributes in a panel. You can use the Graphic Styles panel to quickly add the attributes, such as transparency, effects, strokes, and fills, to another object. Creating a style is pretty darn easy. Simply create the look you want on an object. Then, with your object selected, choose New Graphic Style from the Graphic Styles panel's popup menu. That's it! Now you can use that style anytime you want. It seems like a breeze, but before diving headfirst into the Graphic Styles panel, first check out the Appearance panel.

The Appearance panel houses all the information about a selected object. The information includes the stroke information, fill information, any effects from the Effect menu, and transparency information. In this Appearance panel, you can continually edit, rearrange, and delete this style information.

 **You can't apply graphic styles to type unless you change the type to outlines. For more on changing type to outlines, see Chapter 9.**

Using the Appearance panel

The Appearance panel shows all strokes, fills, transparency, multiple fills, and any effects or transformations applied to that selected object. You open the Appearance panel by choosing Window ⇨ Appearance. Figure 15.1 shows the Appearance panel.

FIGURE 15.1

With an object selected, the Appearance panel displays that object's information.

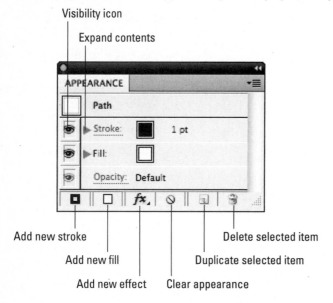

The panel area shows the sequential order of the attributes that make up the object. Each time you add to the object, it becomes listed above the previous entry. With this stacking order, you can drag other information, such as stroke weight, above or below the other entries, creating a different look to the object.

The Appearance panel's popup menu, as shown in Figure 15.2, has a few options from which to choose. To access this menu, simply click the triangle on the upper right of the panel. Under this menu, you can find the following: Add New Fill, Add New Stroke, Duplicate Item, Remove Item,

Clear Appearance, Reduce to Basic Appearance, New Art Has Basic Appearance, Hide Thumbnail, Redefine Graphic Style, and Show All Hidden Attributes. Each of these items is discussed in detail later in this chapter.

The Appearance panel's popup menu gives you additional options.

```
Add New Fill
Add New Stroke
Duplicate Item
Remove Item

Clear Appearance
Reduce to Basic Appearance

✓ New Art Has Basic Appearance

Hide Thumbnail

Redefine Graphic Style

Show All Hidden Attributes
```

Editing and adding strokes and fills

Editing an item is as easy as clicking. Click the item you want to edit and then make your changes, and the object immediately updates to your edits. When you click an effect in the Appearance panel, Illustrator displays the dialog box for that particular effect.

You can click a stroke or a fill in the Appearance panel and then make edits in the miniature Stroke or Fill panel that opens, as shown in Figure 15.3. To edit a stroke or a fill, click one time in the Appearance panel to select the stroke or fill and then change the color of the stroke or fill and the stroke weight.

To edit the stroke weight and color by using the Appearance panel, follow these steps:

1. **Select the object with the Selection tool.** For more on the Selection tool, see Chapter 6.
2. **In the Appearance panel, change the stroke weight by clicking and holding it and then choosing a new stroke width and other stroke attributes in the miniature Stroke panel.**
3. **In the Appearance panel, choose a new color by clicking and holding on the drop-down arrow to display the Color/Swatch miniature panel, as shown in Figure 15.4.** The color is automatically updated for the object.

FIGURE 15.3

When you click a stroke or a fill in the Appearance panel, Illustrator displays a miniature panel for it.

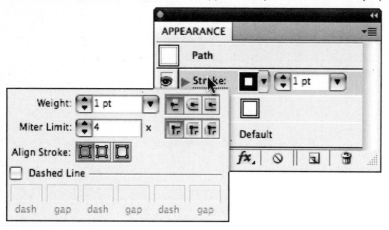

FIGURE 15.4

Clicking and holding the dropdown arrow on the stroke allows you to quickly change its color.

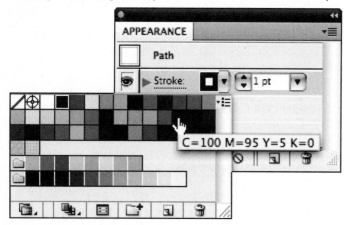

Duplicating and removing items

Under the Appearance panel's popup menu is a menu item you can use to remove an item — such as the stroke or the fill — in the object's list. Click the item to select it and then choose Remove Item from the popup menu (or click the Delete Selected Item button at the bottom of the panel). The item is removed from the list and the object. Use this to edit a preset style to customize it.

You can also duplicate an object in the Appearance panel. Select the item you want to duplicate in the list in the Appearance panel and then choose Duplicate Item from the popup menu or click the Duplicate icon at the bottom of the panel. This comes in handy when you want to use some of the item's attributes but not all. Duplicate the item and then edit it as you want.

Clearing an appearance

Clearing an appearance removes the effects and changes the stroke and fill to None. If there are multiple fills or strokes, all are reduced to one stroke and one fill. You find the Clear Appearance option in the popup menu.

Reducing to basic appearance

Choosing Reduce to Basic Appearance from the Appearance panel's popup menu removes all but one stroke and one fill and all the effects. The remaining stroke and fill are assigned the default attributes (typically the bottommost stroke and fill color and the stroke weight of the bottommost stroke). If you didn't use a stroke, Illustrator reduces the object to the original fill color only. Similarly, if you didn't use a fill, Illustrator reduces the object to the original stroke color and weight. Figure 15.5 shows the object before and after applying Reduce to Basic Appearance. The end result looks a bit bland compared to the original.

FIGURE 15.5

The object on the left has all its graphic styles and attributes. The object on the right has been reduced to a basic appearance.

> **NOTE** Reducing an object to the basic appearance is not the same as clearing the appearance. Clearing the appearance removes all the attributes, while reducing to basic appearance only simplifies the object to a single stroke and fill.

Showing and hiding Appearance panel attributes

Clicking the eyeball to the left of any Appearance panel attribute, such as fill, stroke, opacity, and any applied effect, allows you to temporarily hide that attribute. Click it again to show the hidden attribute.

Setting New Art preferences

If you select the New Art Has Basic Appearance option (from the Appearance panel's popup menu), all art created afterward has a basic appearance of a white fill and a black stroke. If you don't select this option, as shown in Figure 15.6, all art created after using a style has the appearance of the last used style.

FIGURE 15.6

If the New Art Has Basic Appearance option isn't selected, all new art has the same attributes as the last style used.

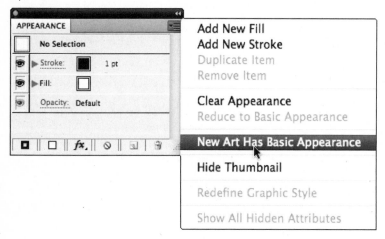

Viewing thumbnails

In the Appearance panel, you have the option to view a small thumbnail of the selected object's style. The thumbnail appears in the upper left of the Appearance panel. If you don't want to see this little thumbnail, choose Hide Thumbnail from the Appearance panel's popup menu. To see the thumbnail again, choose Show Thumbnail from the menu. I can't think of a good reason to hide the thumbnail, but the option is available if you want to use it.

Redefining graphic styles

The Redefine Graphic Style option is available only when you apply one of the preset styles from the Graphic Styles panel. When you use the Redefine Graphic Style option, your new changes overwrite the original, and any objects that use that style immediately update to your new changes.

In order to redefine a graphic style, you must first select the style you want to redefine in the Graphic Styles panel. Then, select an object that has the characteristics that you want to apply to the style. Finally, choose Redefine Graphic Style from the Appearance panel's popup menu.

CAUTION   Redefining a style completely replaces that style with the new style. The existing name is retained, but all other attributes are replaced. Unless you're absolutely sure that you want to replace all the style's attributes, it's probably safer to simply create a new graphic style by using the Graphic Styles panel.

Working with the Graphic Styles panel

Now that you understand the Appearance panel, it's time to dive headfirst into the Graphic Styles panel. This magnificent little panel contains lots of creativity and amazing preset effects. The Graphic Styles panel, as shown in Figure 15.7, has but a few buttons: Break Link to Graphic Style, New Graphic Style, and Delete Graphic Style. You find the guts of the panel in the popup menu, which you access by clicking the triangle on the upper right of the panel. The following sections explain all the options found in the Graphic Styles panel's popup menu.

FIGURE 15.7

The Graphic Styles panel allows you to create and use graphic styles.

New Graphic Style

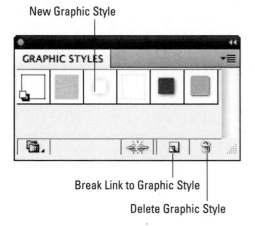

Break Link to Graphic Style

Delete Graphic Style

Creating a new graphic style

Click the New Graphic Style button to make your selected object's attributes into a new style in the Graphic Styles panel. You can also create a new style by choosing New Graphic Style from the popup menu in the Graphic Styles panel. To create a new style, follow these steps:

1. **Create an object.** For more on creating objects, see Chapter 5.

2. **Add color to the fill and/or stroke, a stroke weight, and a dash pattern if desired.**

3. **Add effects from the Effect menu.** You can include transformations, twists, distortions, or anything you want.

4. **After the object looks just right, select the whole object.**

5. **Choose New Graphic Style from the popup menu in the Graphic Styles panel.** This displays the Graphic Style Options dialog box, as shown in Figure 15.8, so that you can name the new style. Clicking the New Graphic Style button bypasses the Graphic Style Options dialog box (unless you Alt (Option)+click the button) and simply gives the new style a default name of Graphic Style *x*, where *x* is a number starting with 1.

FIGURE 15.8

The Graphic Style Options dialog box allows you to name the new style.

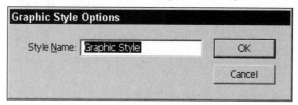

6. **Type a name for the New Graphic Style and then click OK.** This adds the new style to the Graphic Styles panel. The new graphic style now appears in the Graphic Styles panel.

7. **You can apply that new graphic style to any object you create.**

TIP Another way to create a new graphic style is to drag the object thumbnail from the Appearance panel into the Graphic Styles panel. This automatically creates a new graphic style. If you want to name it, you can either double-click it in the Graphic Styles panel or select it and then choose Graphic Style Options from the popup menu.

Duplicating and merging graphic styles

Using the Graphic Styles panel's popup menu, you can duplicate a style. Select a style in the panel and then choose Duplicate Graphic Style from the popup menu in the panel. This creates a duplicate swatch at the end of the list of graphic style swatches. Use this to alter and create your own custom style. You use Duplicate Graphic Style to duplicate a default swatch so that you don't over-write the original swatch.

You can also take two different styles and combine them as one. Use the Merge Graphic Styles command found in the Graphic Styles panel's popup menu. To combine two or more graphic styles, follow these steps:

1. **Press and hold Shift.**

2. **Click the graphic styles that you want to combine in the Graphic Styles panel.** To select noncontiguous graphic styles, press Ctrl (⌘) instead of Shift.

3. **Choose Merge Graphic Styles from the popup menu in the Graphic Styles panel.** The new combined graphic style is added to the end of the swatches in the Graphic Styles panel.

Deleting a graphic style

To delete a graphic style, select the graphic style in the Graphic Styles panel and then choose Delete Graphic Style from the popup menu. Alternatively, you can click the Delete button (the trash icon) at the bottom of the panel. A warning message appears asking "Delete the Style Selection?" Click Yes to delete the style or No to cancel the action.

Breaking the link to a graphic style

You use the Break Link to Graphic Style option to break the graphic style from the object. The object still retains the appearance of the graphic style, but changes to the graphic style's definition no longer alter the object's appearance. A good use of this option is to find a graphic style that you like but want to change. Fill an object with that graphic style, click the Break Link to Graphic Style button, and then alter the object as you want. When you have an object as you like it, you can turn its attributes into a new style. Another good use for this option is when you want several objects to have the same basic style, but you want to make some subtle changes to some of them. If you break the link to the style for the objects that you don't want to change, you can quickly modify the remaining objects simply by modifying the style.

Understanding the other Graphic Styles panel options

Choosing Select All Unused selects all graphic styles that aren't used in the document. You can then choose to delete the unused graphic styles from the Graphic Styles panel.

Sort by Name sorts the graphic style swatches alphabetically. You probably won't find this very useful unless you choose one of the list views.

In the Graphic Styles panel, you can choose how you view the graphic style swatches. Choosing Thumbnail shows you a swatch of the graphic style. Choosing Small List View displays a small swatch next to the name of the graphic style. The Large List View displays a larger swatch next to the name of the graphic style.

The Override Character Color option overrides the object's original color with the graphic style. If you want to retain the original color qualities, deselect the Override Character Color option in the Graphic Styles panel's menu.

The Graphic Style Options lets you name or rename a graphic style swatch. You may not want to rename the standard swatches because doing so makes it harder to remember if you have a particular swatch open when you're looking at the names in a library.

Opening and saving Graphic Style Libraries

After you create a bunch of cool styles, you should save them as a library for future use. To save a Graphic Style Library, follow these steps:

1. **Choose Save Graphic Styles as Library from the Graphic Styles panel's popup menu.** The Save Graphics Styles as Library dialog box, as shown in Figure 15.9, opens. (Your dialog box may look a little different if you choose to display the standard dialog box instead of the Adobe dialog box.)

2. **Type a name for the library in the File name text box.**

3. **Click Save to save the file.**

FIGURE 15.9

Use the Save Graphics Styles as Library dialog box to save your graphic styles in your own library.

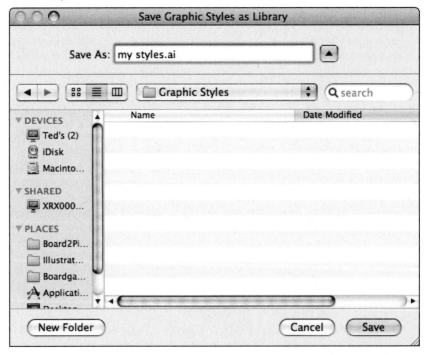

To open a saved library, follow these steps:

1. **Choose Other Library from the Open Graphic Style Library under the Graphic Styles panel's popup menu.** The Open dialog box opens.

2. **Choose the saved file.**

3. **Click Open to open the library file.**

Using Effects

Effects are an intense set of commands. They apply their magic to any of the appearance attributes. Effects are fully editable at any time, and any effect you apply shows up in the Appearance panel, where you can also edit any of the applied effects.

To quickly apply the last used effect to another object, choose Effect ➪ Apply Last Effect or press Ctrl+Shift+E (⌘+Shift+E). If you like the effect but want to change some of the parameters, choose Effect ➪ Last Effect or press Ctrl+Shift+Alt+E (⌘+Shift+Option+E).

Effects aren't limited to vector-based objects. You can also apply effects to raster images.

Understanding 3-D effects

One of the biggest features in Illustrator is three-dimensional abilities. Because this is such a cool and intense feature, it's being covered in its own chapter.

 **For more on creating 3-D effects, see Chapter 16.**

Using Convert to Shape effects

The Convert to Shape effects take any selected object and fit it into a rectangle, a rounded rectangle, or an ellipse. The Convert to Shape effect puts a frame around your selected object. The frame is in one of the shapes that you choose (rectangle, rounded rectangle, or ellipse). Convert to Shape creates a new shape based on the original object's dimensions. Setting a negative value in the relative area decreases the size of the frame, and a positive number increases the size of the frame relative to the original size. To set the new size of the shape, type the height and width values.

Figure 15.10 shows the Shape Options dialog box that opens when you choose any of the Convert to Shape effects. In this dialog box, you can choose the type of shape that you want to create from the Shape dropdown list (popup menu). You can also choose to create a shape that's set to a specific size by clicking the Absolute radio button or a shape that's resized by clicking the Relative radio button. The Corner Radius text field is used to specify the amount of corner-rounding for rounded rectangles.

Figure 15.11 shows an example of applying the Effect ⇨ Convert to Shape ⇨ Ellipse command to a star-shaped object. In this example, the Relative option was used, and 18 extra points were added to both the height and width.

FIGURE 15.10

Use the Shape Options dialog box to specify how the Convert to Shape effects function.

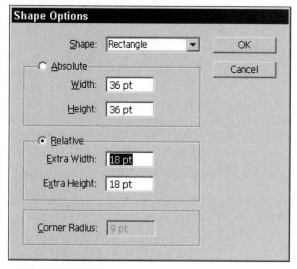

FIGURE 15.11

The original shape (left) and the shape that results from applying the Convert to Shape effect (right)

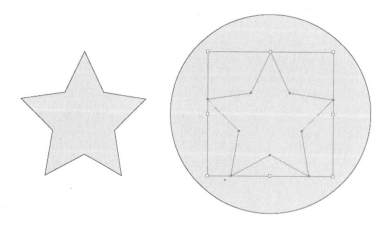

Distorting and transforming effects

The Distort & Transform effects include Free Distort, Pucker & Bloat, Roughen, Transform, Tweak, Twist, and Zig Zag. You may wonder why Transform effects appear in the Effect menu when you can do transformations in the Object menu. The big reason for applying a transformation under the Effect menu is that you can go back and edit that particular transformation at any time.

CROSS-REF For more on distortions and transformations, see Chapter 11.

Creating Path effects

The Path effects that you can apply are Offset Path, Outline Object, and Outline Stroke. As with the Transform options, the Path options are the same as under the Object menu. The Path effects under the Effect menu are exactly the same as under the Object menu, except that the effects are live and editable at any time. This means that you can go back at any time and change any of the Path effects that you've applied.

CROSS-REF For more on Path effects, see Chapter 6.

Understanding the Rasterize effect

The Rasterize effect has the same effect as the Object ➪ Rasterize menu command, but when applied as an effect, you can easily remove it at a later time by using the Appearance panel.

The Photoshop effects are on the bottom half of the Effect menu. These effects can be applied only to a rasterized image. To use these effects, first choose Effect ➪ Rasterize to display the Rasterize dialog box, as shown in Figure 15.12.

In the Rasterize dialog box, you can set the resolution (from low to high or set your own). Choose from white or transparent background and the type of anti-aliasing. Other options are clipping mask or adding space around the object.

Stylizing effects

Under the Stylize effects are options that you can use to embellish paths and add effects to objects. The Stylize options are Add Arrowheads, Drop Shadow, Feather, Inner Glow, Outer Glow, Round Corners, and Scribble.

FIGURE 15.12

The Rasterize dialog box allows you to convert objects to raster objects by using an effect that can be edited later.

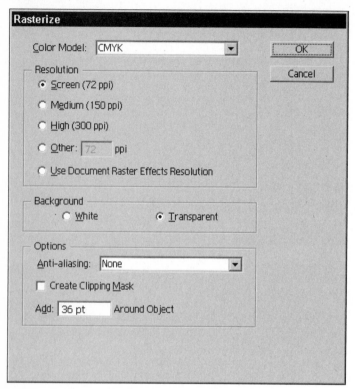

Using the Add Arrowheads effect

The Add Arrowheads effect is a boon to technical artists, sign makers, and anyone in need of a quick arrow. The number one complaint about the Add Arrowheads effect is that Illustrator offers too many arrowheads from which to choose. Some complaint!

Choose Effect ⇨ Stylize ⇨ Add Arrowheads to add an arrowhead (or two) to any selected open path. If more than one path is selected, arrowheads are added to each open path. To use Add Arrowheads, select an open path and then choose Effect ⇨ Stylize ⇨ Add Arrowheads to display the Add Arrowheads dialog box, as shown in Figure 15.13. In this box, you can pick which of the 27 different arrowheads you want to stick on the end of your path. Scale refers to the size of the arrowhead relative to the stroke weight of the path; you can type any number between 1% and

1000% in this box. Choosing Start places the arrowhead at the beginning of the path (where you first clicked to draw it); choosing End places the arrowhead at the end of the path (where you last clicked to draw it); and choosing Start and End places the same arrowhead on both the beginning and end of the path. Reapplying this effect to the same paths continues to put arrowheads on top of arrowheads.

FIGURE 15.13

Use the Add Arrowheads dialog box to add markers to one or both ends of a path.

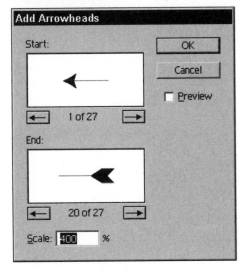

Figure 15.14 shows customized arrowheads created in Illustrator.

 **Add Arrowheads doesn't work on closed paths.**

Arrowheads are grouped to the paths that were selected when they were created; it's sometimes necessary to rotate the arrowhead by either ungrouping it or choosing it with the Direct Selection tool.

The size of the arrowheads is based on the width of the stroke, but you can alter each arrowhead's dimensions in the Scale text field in the Add Arrowheads dialog box.

FIGURE 15.14

You can create many different types of customized arrowheads.

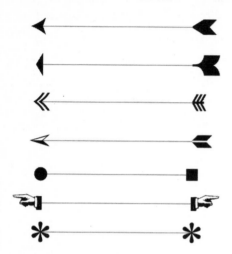

Using the Drop Shadow effect

The Drop Shadow effect makes creating drop shadows for most paths a relatively simple task.

Selecting Drop Shadow affects both stroke and fill. In the Drop Shadow dialog box, as shown in Figure 15.15, you can specify the offset of the drop shadow by typing values for how far across the drop shadow should move (X) and how far up or down it should move (Y). Positive numbers move the shadow to the right and down; negative numbers move the shadow to the left and up.

You have these options in the Drop Shadow dialog box (among others):

- **Mode:** Use this to choose the blending mode to apply.
- **Opacity:** This lets you set how much you can see through the shadow.
- **X and Y Offset:** The general rule in drop-shadowing is that the more the drop shadow is offset, the more elevated the original object looks. To make an object look as if it's floating far above the page, type high offset values.
- **Blur:** This lets you type how far the blur goes outward in pixels.
- **Color:** You choose this to set the shadow color to something other than black.
- **Darkness:** The percentage entered here is how much black is added to the fill and stroke colors. Darkness doesn't affect any of the other custom or process colors.
- **Create Separate Shadows:** Choose this to make the shadow separate from the object (ungrouped).

To create a drop shadow, do the following:

1. **Create and select the artwork to which you want to give a drop shadow.**

2. **Choose Effect ➪ Stylize ➪ Drop Shadow to display the Drop Shadow dialog box.**

3. **Type the amount that you want the drop shadow to be offset.**

4. **Type the Opacity value.** This determines how see-through Illustrator makes the shadow.

5. **You can also set the mode for the shadow.** I chose Multiply. For more on various modes, see Chapter 7.

6. **Type a value for Darkness.** The value that you type in the Darkness field determines how much black Illustrator adds to the shadow to make it appear darker. Alternatively, you can choose a color for the shadow.

7. **Click OK.** If the shadow isn't what you want, click the underlined Drop Shadow link on the Appearance panel and then change the settings.

FIGURE 15.15

The Drop Shadow dialog box allows you to quickly produce drop shadow effects.

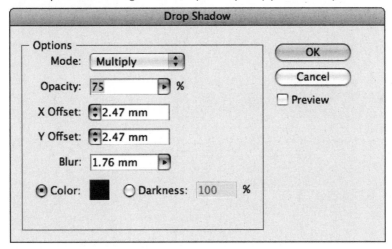

Understanding the Feather effect

The Feather effect adds a fade out to the selected object. Feather fades the object to transparent over a specified distance in points. To add a Feather effect to an object, follow these steps:

1. **Select the object to which you want to apply the Feather effect.**

2. **Choose Effect ➪ Stylize ➪ Feather to open the Feather dialog box, as shown in Figure 15.16.**

FIGURE 15.16

Use the Feather dialog box to set the distance over which objects fade out.

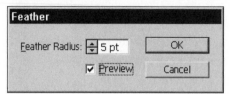

3. Type the Feather Radius in points that you want in the Feather dialog box.

4. Click OK to see the Feather effect, as shown in Figure 15.17.

FIGURE 15.17

This shows the original text (top) and the faded-out text (bottom) created using the Feather effect.

Using the Inner Glow and Outer Glow effects

The Inner Glow and Outer Glow effects create a softened glow on the inside or outside edge of an object. Choose Effect ⇨ Stylize ⇨ Inner Glow or Effect ⇨ Stylize ⇨ Outer Glow. In the Inner Glow dialog box, as shown in Figure 15.18, choose the blending mode for the glow as well as the Opacity, Blur distance, and whether the glow starts from the center or the edge. The outer glow dialog box works the same way, but the glow appears on the outside of the object.

FIGURE 15.18

The Inner Glow dialog box allows you to create glowing effects in objects.

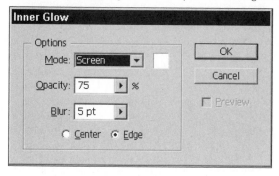

Using the Round Corners effect

Choose Effect ➪ Stylize ➪ Round Corners to use the Round Corners effect to create round corners just like (snap your fingers) that. This effect works on any path that has corner points, but the best results seem to be on polygons and stars or on type with very sharp corners.

In the Round Corners dialog box, as shown in Figure 15.19, you specify what the radius of the Round Corners should be. The larger the number you type for the radius, the bigger the curve is.

NOTE Don't apply the Round Corners effect to a rounded rectangle to make the corners more rounded. Instead of making the corners rounder, the flat sides of the rounded rectangle will curve slightly.

FIGURE 15.19

The Round Corners dialog box allows you to create smooth rounded corners where previously there were sharp ones.

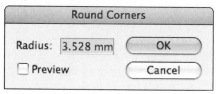

Understanding Scribble

The Scribble effect adds a sketchy quality to an illustration. You can choose from a variety of presets or create your own. The scribble effect can create a mass-produced, mechanical look or a loose, flowing, childlike scrawl. The breakdown of what Scribble does is that it converts an object's stroke and fill to lines divided by transparency. The Scribble Options dialog box lets you alter the line style, density, looseness of the lines, and stroke width.

You find the Scribble effect under the Stylize submenu of the Effect menu. Figure 15.20 shows a portrait with two different Scribble effects applied. Within the Scribble Options dialog box are options that you can choose to change or customize your scribbled art or to choose from preset Scribble effects.

FIGURE 15.20

Two different Scribble effects result in two very different portraits.

Using the Scribble presets

In the Scribble Options dialog box, you find a variety of preset options. Figure 15.21 shows the Scribble Options dialog box, which offers these presets:

- **Custom:** Remembers the last settings you typed

- **Default:** Applies 30° angled lines, with varying thickness to the fill and stroke

- **Childlike:** Applies 10° loopy angled lines that look very loose and as if a child had sketched them

- **Dense:** Applies very tight 45° angled lines, with little space between lines

- **Loose:** Applies very loose loopy –20° angled lines, with lots of spacing between lines

- **Moiré:** Applies tight –45° lines so close they actually create a moiré (wavy) pattern with the fill

- **Sharp:** Applies –30° angled lines tightly, with little space between lines (similar to Dense)

- **Sketch:** Applies −30° angled lines, with a thicker stroke for the lines but with little space between lines

- **Snarl:** Applies 60° angled lines tightly together, with loopy lines and a thin stroke weight

- **Swash:** Applies a figure eight loop to the object, with a thinner stroke weight and a symmetrical look to the lines

- **Tight:** Applies a 30° angled line, with tight lines and a thin stroke weight for an even, line-filled area

- **Zig-Zag:** Applies a −20° angled line, with a thin stroke weight for an even symmetrical look to the lines in the filled area

FIGURE 15.21

The Scribble Options dialog box provides enough options to create hundreds of very different scribble effects.

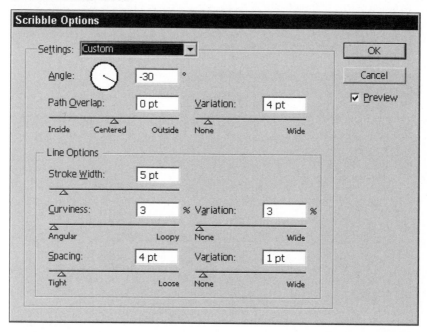

Working with the Scribble options

In the Scribble Options dialog box, you can find a variety of additional options to set — from Angle and Path Overlap to a Variation setting for Path Overlap. Line options are Stroke Width, Curviness, and Spacing, the latter two of which can have a Variation applied. You can choose from a preset value or click the Preview check box and type your own values to see immediate results.

You can set the following options for the Scribble effect:

- **Path Overlap:** This sets the amount the scribble lines stay inside or go beyond the object's edge.

- **Variation:** This sets how the scribble line lengths differ (loopy or angled) and how close together they're set.

- **Stroke Width:** This sets the width of the scribble lines.

- **Curviness:** This sets how far the different scribble lines curve from each other.

- **Variation:** This sets a range for how much the curviness may vary from line to line.

- **Spacing:** This sets the spacing amount between scribble lines.

- **Variation:** This establishes the range in which spacing magnitudes fall.

- **Preview:** Click this check box to see the effect before applying it.

Using SVG Filters effects

You find SVG Filters under the Effect menu. These filters are XML-based and resolution-independent, a perfect fit for vector art.

CROSS-REF For more on XML and SVG, see Chapter 19.

To access the SVG Filters, choose Effect ⇨ SVG Filters. You've many different SVG filters from which to choose:

- **Alpha:** Creates transparent fluctuations

- **Bevel Shadow:** Creates a beveled shadow that's softened

- **Cool Breeze:** Creates fluctuations on the top edge of the object (as shown in Figure 15.22)

- **Dilate:** Takes the fill outward to the edge of the object

- **Erode:** Takes away the fill from the edge of the object

- **Gaussian Blur:** Adds a soft shadow by blurring the object's edge

- **Pixel Play:** Uses light effects on the object

- **Shadow:** Creates a harsh shadow on the object

- **Static:** Uses a static fill in place of the original fill color

- **Turbulence:** Creates transparent fluctuations to the object

- **Woodgrain:** Creates a woodgrain effect to the object

FIGURE 15.22

The Cool Breeze SVG filter applied to text

Warp effects

The Warp effects are also part of the Effect menu. Chapter 11 extensively covers these effects.

Creating Photoshop effects

You can apply tons of Photoshop filter effects to any rasterized image. Turn your vector art into raster art, and apply effects from artistic to texturizing. The main effects are Artistic, Blur, Brush Strokes, Distort, Pixelate, Sharpen, Sketch, Stylize, Texture, and Video.

These filters are the same as the ones you find in Photoshop, but you don't have to go back and forth between the applications to access them. Use them to create more exciting rasterized artwork.

 Be sure that you change the document colors space to RGB (File ➪ Document Color Mode ➪ RGB Color); otherwise, the Photoshop filter effects are grayed out.

Summary

Graphic styles, filters, and effects provide some very powerful tools for manipulating objects in your Illustrator documents. In this chapter, you learned about these tools and the following related topics:

- Graphic Styles are where you can access saved Appearance settings.
- Choose from a wide range of graphic styles from the Graphic Style Libraries.
- Use the Appearance panel to edit an object's attributes.
- Effects let you go back and edit at any time.
- Scribble effects can add a softer, sketchy look to your illustration.
- Reapply the last effect quickly by pressing Ctrl+Shift+E (Ô+Shift+E).
- Access the last effect's dialog box by pressing Ctrl+Shift+Alt+E (Ô+Shift+Option+E).

Chapter 16

Creating 3-D in Illustrator

Creating depth and adding perspective has been the desire of many illustrators. This chapter shows how you can create three-dimensional images in Illustrator. Adding 3-D to your package design, logo, or any illustration is a breeze. Take any path, type, or object and then model it into a 3-D form, adding lighting and rotating it in three dimensions. Use 3-D to take your artwork to the next level. Imagine a logo in three dimensions rotating 360° on a Web site. The possibilities are endless.

Using 3-D in Illustrator

One of the really cool features in Illustrator is the ability to create 3-D inside the application. You use the Extrude command to pop a two-dimensional item into a three-dimensional world. You can revolve a path into a three-dimensional object with highlights and even map artwork onto an image in 3-D. Not only can you revolve and extrude, but you can also rotate the object. Because your 3-D object is an effect, you can edit it at any time.

Take any flat shape and then add depth with 3-D, and you still retain all the editing abilities of the flat shape. Illustrator takes any changes you make later and incorporates them in the 3-D form. Using the Preview option, you can see what the object will look like. The extrude, revolve, rotate, and map artwork functions all appear in one neat dialog box.

In the past, Adobe offered Adobe Dimensions, which was a three-dimensional creation program. With Dimensions, you could extrude and revolve two-dimensional paths to create three-dimensional art. You could also add depth and lighting effects to make the object appear realistic. Most of Dimensions' capabilities are now inside Illustrator. The main difference in Illustrator is that you can't position multiple objects in 3-D space. You can only position one object at a time. And Illustrator creates the 3-D effect live rather than having to render, as Dimensions did.

Many 3-D packages are on the market, ranging from high-end software, such as Caligari trueSpace, 3ds max, and Maya, to low-end programs. They all handle transforming high-end 3-D into video, creating special effects, and making movies. And video artists use them in upscale game designs and animation. The low-end 3-D programs include Swift 3D, Poser, and Strata. Poser allows you to create 3-D models (people and animals) right down to the facial hair and realistic skin. Strata can create a model, render the 3-D, and animate the 3-D objects. Illustrator's 3-D abilities don't quite go that far, but it has come a long way for an illustrating program. Adobe took the three-dimensional qualities of Adobe Dimensions, created a cleaner, user-friendlier interface, and put it inside Illustrator.

Understanding the Three-Dimensional World

The concept of three dimensions should be more intuitive and easy to understand because we are three-dimensional creatures who live in a three-dimensional world. But because most of our media are two-dimensional (reading, watching TV, working on a computer), adjusting to a three-dimensional digital world can be confusing and frustrating.

Changing from two dimensions to three dimensions

Television is a two-dimensional medium. The picture tube has height and width. Computer screens are two-dimensional. The pages of books are two-dimensional. Maps are two-dimensional, even though the world is round. Most people think in two dimensions.

Most of the two-dimensional objects that we deal with may very well be replaced with three-dimensional objects. Three-dimensional life will become a complete reality as soon as technology makes it so. Holograms have been around for a while, and technology is making them more accurate and lifelike. Video games and virtual-reality glasses already simulate three dimensions through the use of holograms and computer-generated imagery.

Three-dimensional positioning

When you're trying to understand the concept of three dimensions on a computer screen, the most difficult aspect to grasp is depth. Left, right, up, and down are all simple concepts, but what about things that are closer or farther away? Maybe sometime in the future, we'll have to look up and down when we're driving.

NOTE You're already thinking in three dimensions if you're familiar with Illustrator's Send to Back and Bring to Front commands. If you feel comfortable with stacking order and layers, then you're one step closer to working with three-dimensional positioning.

CROSS-REF For more on Send to Back and Bring to Front, see Chapter 8.

You use three indicators to position objects in the 3D Extrude & Bevel Options dialog box, which you access by choosing Effect ⇨ 3D ⇨ 3D Extrude & Bevel:

- **X is the object's horizontal location.** A value greater than 0 means that the object is positioned to the right of center (0). A value less than 0 (any negative number) represents an object to the left of center.

- **Y defines the object's vertical position.** A value that's greater than 0 means that the object is above center. A value that's less than 0 means that the object is below center.

- **Z represents the object's depth.** This variable indicates how far forward or backward the object is from the center. A value less than 0 means that the object is behind 0, or farther away. A value greater than 0 means the object is in front of 0, or closer to you.

Figure 16.1 shows the X, Y, and Z values as you would see them initially in the 3D Extrude & Bevel Options dialog box. In the dialog box, relative X (horizontal), Y (vertical), and Z (depth) positions of selected objects can be rotated around those axes. In a direct, straight-from-the-front view, you can't determine an object's Z position. From the default position, which is a view of the object from above and to the right of the front, you can determine all three positions visually.

FIGURE 16.1

The rotational values in the 3D Extrude & Bevel Options dialog box allow you to view an object in three dimensions.

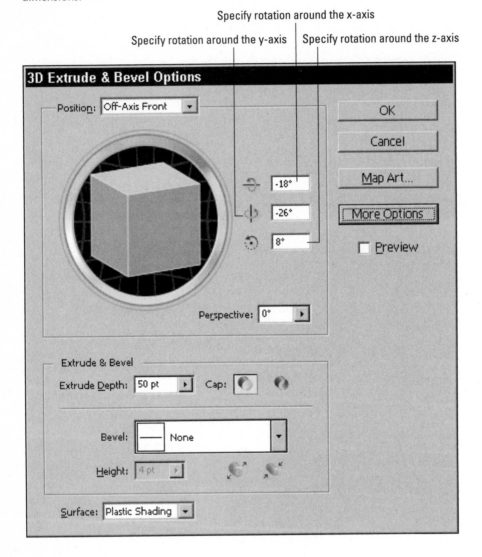

Extruding and Revolving 2-D Objects

Illustrator's Extrude command adds sides, a top, and a back to an object. When extruding an object, you can fill the object or leave a hole in the middle (extruding the path but not the fill). Another option is to bevel the edges, which creates an amazing look for 3-D text.

The Revolve command turns a path around a center axis, creating a 3-D effect in a circular fashion. This is a great way to create a bottle, a chess piece, or any other revolved shape. Not only can you apply light and shading to the revolved object, but you can map artwork directly onto the face of the object.

Extruding flat art

Extruding is the process of giving two-dimensional art depth that's equal on every part of the artwork. Figure 16.2 shows flat art and the same art extruded. When extruding art, you can retain the default depth (50 pt) or set the Extrude Depth slider to anywhere from 0 to 2000 points.

FIGURE 16.2

The original flat art (left) and the extruded art (right)

To create a basic extrusion on an object, follow these steps:

1. **Create an object to extrude.**
2. **Select the object with the Selection tool.** For more on selecting objects, see Chapter 6.
3. **Choose Effect ⇨ 3D ⇨ Extrude & Bevel to display the 3D Extrude & Bevel Options dialog box.**
4. **Click the Preview box.** This lets you see the default settings on your selected object.
5. **Click OK.** Illustrator applies the 3-D extrusion to your object by using the default settings (unless you made any changes in the dialog box).

You can choose these options in the 3D Extrude & Bevel Options dialog box:

- **Position:** This lets you choose from a variety of positions for your selected object. Choose a view from the Front, Back, Left, Right, Top, Bottom, Off-Axis Back, Off-Axis Left, Off-Axis Right, Off-Axis Top, Off-Axis Bottom, Isometric Left, Isometric Right, Isometric Top, and Isometric Bottom. The default position is Off-Axis Front. You can also click and drag the box around to create a custom rotation.

- **Extrude Depth:** This option lets you control how far in points the object's path is extruded. Drag the slider (which appears when you click next to the word Extrude) with the Preview button selected to see a live preview of the depth.

- **Cap:** Choose whether to have the cap turned on for a more solid look or off for a hollow look.

- **Rotate:** Use this option to rotate your object around the x-, y-, and z-axes.

- **Views:** This option lets you change the view around the x-, y-, and z-axes.

That was just a basic extrusion. There's so much more you can do. To begin with, you can cap or uncap an object (see Figure 16.3). Uncapping removes the front and back panes, making the object hollow. Capping puts front and back panes on the object, making the object solid.

Figure 16.3 shows a meeple with extrusion, lighting, and altered views applied in 3-D.

Extruding a stroke

One visually appealing effect that you can achieve is to take a dashed-stroked line and use Extrude to make it 3-D. This technique creates a bamboo look or individual bars.

NOTE 3-D objects are inherently extremely visual subjects, and most of the changes you make to them are quickly visible in a preview. Rather than giving you exact settings to reproduce the objects shown in the illustrations, I suggest you experiment to achieve results that please you. Your final results probably won't look just like the illustrations, but you'll have fun and learn more about how the settings interact.

Follow these steps to extrude a dashed line:

1. **Create an object with a dashed line stroke and no fill.** I used outlined text with a dashed stroke but no fill.

2. **Choose Effect ➪ 3D ➪ Extrude & Bevel.** The Extrude & Bevel Options dialog box opens.

3. **Click the Preview check box.** This lets you preview the image as you modify it.

4. **Set the Extrude depth in points.** Alternatively, you can click and drag the slider, change the views by picking an option from Position, or drag the box to a different view.

5. **Click OK to see the extruded dashed lines.** Figure 16.4 shows the resulting effect.

FIGURE 16.3

A meeple with caps that was extruded (top left), lighted (top middle), and rotated (top right). The bottom row shows the same variations without caps.

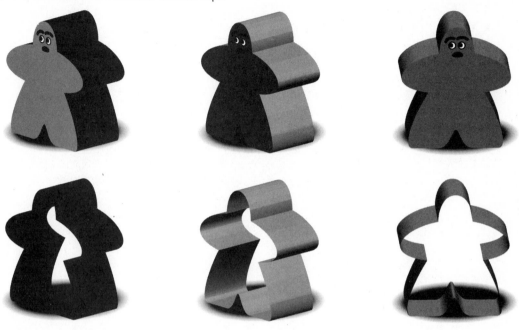

FIGURE 16.4

The extruded dashed stroke has a bamboo-type appearance.

TIP Try using any of the graphic styles (Window ➪ Graphic Styles) on your object before using the 3D Extrude & Bevel Options dialog box. You can come up with some pretty cool results. For more on graphic styles, see Chapter 15.

Understanding bevels

The use of bevels can make or break your artwork. Bevels give an edge to your 3-D object. You can use Illustrator's preset bevels or, if you feel ambitious, you can create your own bevel.

Follow these steps to add a bevel to an object:

1. **Create an object to which you want to add 3-D.**

2. **Choose Effect ➪ 3D ➪ Extrude & Bevel.** The Extrude & Bevel Options dialog box opens. (You can also apply an extrusion and change the position.)

3. **Choose a bevel from the Bevel dropdown list (popup menu).**

4. **Choose the height of the bevel and whether it bevels in or out.** The height option is how large or small you want the bevel to be. You set this option by clicking and dragging the Height slider to a bevel in points. The other option is whether you want to add the bevel to the outside of the object or subtract it from the inside of the object. To make this determination, you click either the Bevel In button or the Bevel Out button.

5. **Click the Preview check box to see the bevel.** Leave the Preview check box deselected until you're done with your settings; otherwise, it may take awhile to preview your object.

6. **Click OK to see the final results.** Figure 16.5 shows the resulting bevel along the edge of the extruded path.

Although the preset bevels are good to use, you can also create your own custom bevel.

Follow these steps to add your own bevel to the Bevel list:

1. **Make a copy of the** `Bevels.ai` **file to use as a backup in case you munge the file accidentally.**

2. **Open the** `Bevels.ai` **file found in the Adobe Illustrator Plug-ins folder.**

3. **Create the path you want to be your bevel in the** `Bevels.ai` **document.**

4. **Turn that path into a symbol.** Do this by choosing Window ➪ Symbols. Either drag the path to the Symbols panel or select the path and then click the New Symbol button in the Symbols panel. Or with the path selected, choose New Symbol from the Symbols panel's popup menu.

CROSS-REF For more on symbols, see Chapter 5.

5. **Rename the symbol.** To rename the symbol, double-click the symbol in the Symbols panel. Type a name in the Symbol Options dialog box and then click OK.

6. **Choose File ➪ Save.** This saves the new path symbol in the `Bevels.ai` file.

7. **Quit Illustrator and then restart Illustrator.** When you look at the Bevel list in the 3D Extrude & Bevel Options dialog box, your new bevel is listed there. You can now apply the custom bevel as you would any other bevel.

FIGURE 16.5

Adding a bevel to artwork results in a very realistic-looking 3-D effect.

Revolving objects

Revolving, also called *lathing*, is the process of spinning a 2-D object around an axis a specified number of degrees in order to create a 3-D object. You can create new objects by revolving different objects around different axes. You can create a lamp, a chess piece, a wedge of cheese, and more.

Follow these steps to revolve a path:

1. **Draw a path with any of the drawing tools (Pen, Pencil, or Line Segment).** Figure 16.6 shows a simple path. For more on the different drawing tools, see Chapter 4.

2. **Select the path and then choose Effect ➪ 3D ➪ Revolve to display the 3D Revolve Options dialog box, as shown in Figure 16.7.**

3. **Click the Preview check box to see the revolved object displayed using the default settings.**

4. **Click OK to finish the revolving.** Figure 16.8 shows the result of revolving the path you created. In this case, the object is tilted a little to better show off the effect.

FIGURE 16.6

Draw the path to be revolved.

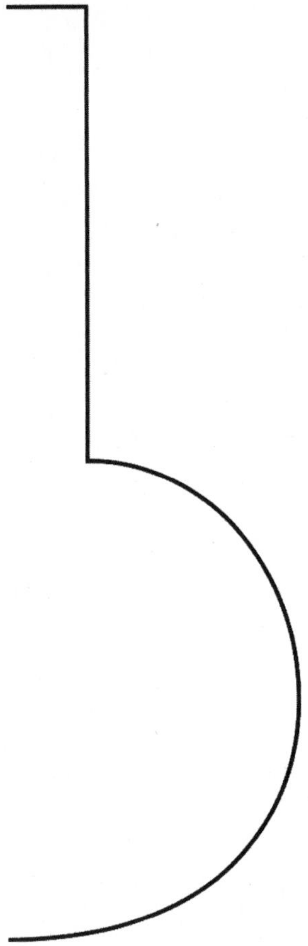

Use the 3D Revolve Options dialog box to create 3-D objects by revolving a path.

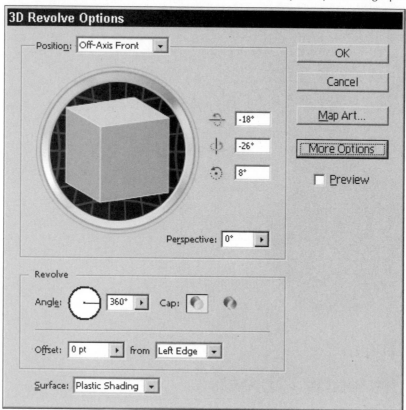

The default option is to revolve the path 360°. You can change that to any number between 1 and 360. A number less than 360 creates an open section like a wedge taken out of a round of cheese.

FIGURE 16.8

The revolved path looks like a 3-D object (the lighting area in the lower portion happens automatically as part of the effect).

Rotating Objects

You can use the Rotate function found under an Effect submenu to rotate 2-D and 3-D objects. This rotation happens in 3-D space. This is a great way to apply a sheared effect or perspective to an object that's 2-D.

3-D rotation is done in its own dialog box. Choose Effect ⇨ 3D ⇨ Rotate to open the 3D Rotate Options dialog box, as shown in Figure 16.9. In this dialog box, you can type values in the text fields or you can click and drag the box to the rotation you want. Ensure that you click the Preview check box so you can see the rotation happen live.

> **NOTE**　In most cases, you want to edit the existing effect by double-clicking it in the Appearance panel (Window ⇨ Appearance) rather than using the Effect ⇨ 3D ⇨ Rotate menu option to rotate the existing object. Adding the Rotate effect to existing 3-D objects can produce some very confusing results.

FIGURE 16.9

The 3D Rotate Options dialog box allows you to rotate an existing object.

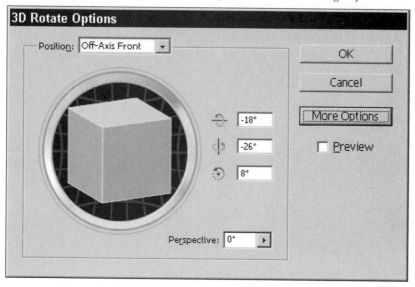

Changing the Appearance of Three-Dimensional Objects

Objects created in the 3D Extrude & Bevel Options dialog box are not only colored but also lit. Additional specifications come with lighting: shading and reflectivity. You control the light by its surface characteristics. If you don't see any lighting options, click More Options on the right side of the 3D Extrude & Bevel Options dialog box. This opens the shading and light areas, as shown in Figure 16.10.

The Surface characteristics

The Surface properties control the look of the outside surface of the 3-D object. You can create 3-D objects that are just outlined, have no shading, have soft shading, or have intense, glossy shading. Your options are Wireframe, No Shading, Diffused Shading, and Plastic Shading. Figure 16.11 shows one object with each of the following surface characteristics applied to it:

- **Wireframe** traces the curves of the object's geometric shape and fills the shape with transparent fill (there are no lighting options with this surface characteristic).
- **No Shading** fills the object with the same color as the original 2-D object (there are no lighting options with this surface characteristic).
- **Diffuse Shading** adds a soft diffused light source on the object's surface.
- **Plastic Shading** adds a bright shiny light as if the object were made of plastic.

FIGURE 16.10

The shading and light areas of the 3D Extrude & Bevel Options dialog box allow you to exercise control over the lighting effects.

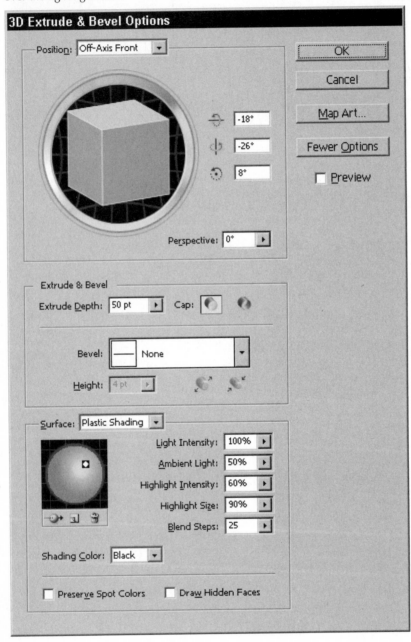

FIGURE 16.11

An object with all four surfaces applied (from left to right): Wireframe, No Shading, Diffuse Shading, and Plastic Shading

Understanding lighting

Lighting can be a little confusing in a 3-D program. Because lights in 3-D are positioned an infinite distance from objects, shading for different objects is the same, no matter what the position of the objects. For example, if the lights are in the upper left, objects on the far left have the same lighting as objects on the far right. If the lights were positioned closer, the shading would appear differently.

A good way to think of the lights that you create is that they resemble sunlight to us earthbound creatures. Light from the sun shines on an object in New York City almost exactly the same way it shines on an object in Boston. Because the sun is so far away, the difference in the position of the sun relative to the two cities is minute. If the sun were an infinite distance away and Earth were flat, the two cities would have exactly the same sunlight.

Because there are no shadows in Illustrator's 3D Extrude & Bevel Options dialog box, objects that are between the light source and another object let light pass through them so that the light can reach the hidden object.

Lighting options

In the lighting sphere in the 3D Extrude & Bevel Options dialog box, you can set a variety of lighting choices on your object. These buttons appear below the lighting preview sphere from left to right: Move selected light to back of object, New Light, and Delete Light.

You have these lighting options for Diffuse Shading or Plastic Shading:

- **Light Intensity** controls how intense the light is. The values are from 0 to 100.
- **Ambient Light** changes the brightness of all the surfaces of an object. The values are from 0 to 100.
- **Blend Steps** adjusts how smooth the shading flows across an object. A lower number creates a more matte look. A higher number creates a glossy, shiny look.

If you're just using Plastic Shading, you can use these additional options:

- **Highlight Intensity** controls the reflecting light. A low number creates a matte look. A high number creates a glossy look.
- **Highlight Size** controls the size of the highlight on the object from 0 (none) to 100 (all).

Along with the lighting is the Shading Color. The default is Black, but you can choose Custom, click the swatch that appears, and access the color picker, where you can choose any color you want.

CROSS-REF   For more on color, see Chapter 7.

The lighting sphere shows the light on a surface. You can move the light around by dragging it to a new location. By clicking the New Light icon (the one in the middle), you can add additional lights to the surface. The active light has a box around it. Each light can have different settings applied to it.

NOTE   The default setting is that all 3-D objects must have one light. You can add as many as you want in addition to the default.

The trash icon (on the right) lets you delete lights. Select a light and then click the trash icon to delete the light. The first button is Move selected light to back of object. It sends that light behind the object for backlighting. Figure 16.12 shows an object with different lighting features applied to it.

FIGURE 16.12

This figure shows an object with different lighting effects applied by using the lighting options in the 3D Extrude & Bevel Options dialog box.

Spot colors are automatically changed to process colors unless you click the Preserve Spot Colors check box. When you click the Draw Hidden Faces check box, you can view the back faces through transparent surfaces.

 If you hold Shift while adjusting lighting in the 3D Extrude & Bevel Options dialog box, you see the changes update as you move the lights in real time.

Using the Appearance panel with 3-D

The Appearance panel works wonders with 3-D objects. If you have complex artwork with a 3-D effect applied, you can reduce screen redraw time by clicking the eyeball (hiding the effect) in the Appearance panel. If you have an object with multiple strokes and fills and 3-D, try moving the 3-D entry to different areas of the Appearance panel. Move it above a fill or under a stroke, and see how different the object can look. Figure 16.13 shows an object with multiple attributes. I moved the 3-D section to different areas to create different looks.

FIGURE 16.13

An original object (left) and the object after different attributes were moved in the Appearance panel (right)

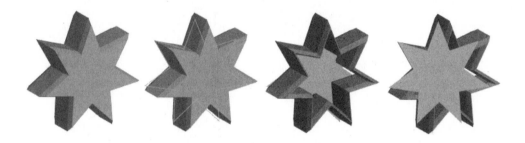

Mapping 2-D art to 3-D surfaces

One of the most powerful features of 3-D is the ability to wrap 2-D objects around 3-D surfaces. This feature alone makes upgrading or buying Illustrator worth the money. The mapping feature is a great way to add a label to a bottle or any type of package design. Now your clients can see how their product looks before printing and packaging.

The most important concept to understand when you're mapping artwork is that each 3-D object usually has several different surfaces, and each of those surfaces can have separate mapped artwork. The key to mapping 2-D to 3-D is to make a map out of the 2-D object that you want to use and then turn it into a symbol. Any of Illustrator's symbols can be mapped onto 3-D objects.

Follow these steps to create a 3-D map out of a 2-D object:

1. **Create the text (or another object) that you want to map onto 3-D art.**
2. **Drag the created text into the Symbols panel.** This makes the text a new symbol. See instructions earlier in this chapter for adding symbols to the Symbols panel. For more on symbols, see Chapter 5.

3. **Create the path that you want to turn into 3-D.** I chose a path to indicate a sign.

4. **Choose Effect ⇨ 3D ⇨ Extrude & Bevel to display the 3D Extrude & Bevel Options dialog box, as shown in Figure 16.14.**

This figure shows the 3D Extrude & Bevel Options dialog box along with the path for a sign.

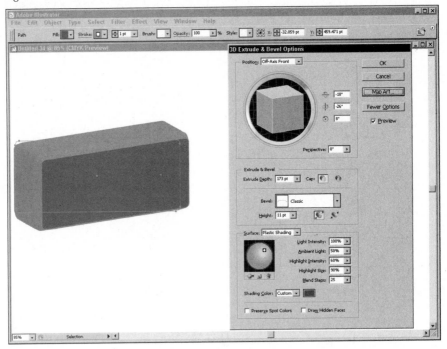

5. **Click Map Art to display the Map Art dialog box, as shown in Figure 16.15.** In this dialog box, you can see the number of surfaces on the object, starting with surface 1.

6. **Choose the surface that you want to map.**

NOTE   As you choose a surface, the original highlights in red wireframe the surface you're selecting to make it easier for you to see where the mapping will occur.

7. **When you have the surface that you want to map, choose a symbol from the Symbol menu.** The symbol you created is listed there, as shown in Figure 16.16.

FIGURE 16.15

The Map Art dialog box allows you to place art on the surface of a 3-D object.

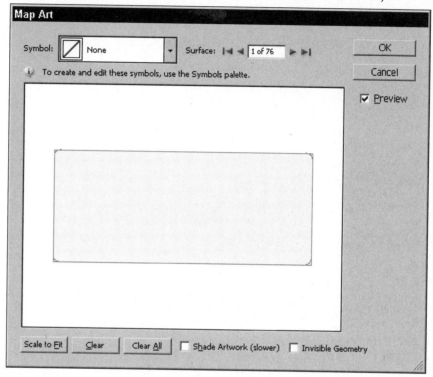

8. After you choose the art for all the surfaces, click OK to exit the Map Art dialog box.

9. Change the rotation or axis view if you want.

10. **Click OK.** The final results are shown in Figure 16.17.

When you choose a symbol in the Map Art dialog box to map, the symbol appears in the center of the screen with a Bounding Box around it. This box gives you the ability to stretch, rotate, or move the object to fit the area you want.

The Map Art dialog box also has a Preview check box, which allows you to see the object mapped onto the shape. A cool thing to do is to use a cube and then map artwork on all surfaces of the cube to make custom dice. You could use the dice in animation for a Web page.

CROSS-REF For more on creating art for the Web, see Chapter 19.

FIGURE 16.16

Your created symbol appears in the Symbol box.

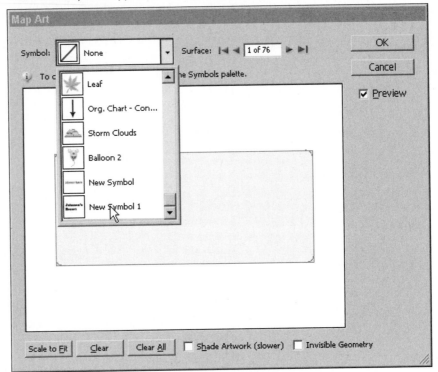

FIGURE 16.17

The final artwork is mapped onto the extruded object.

The Map Art dialog box has several other useful features:

- **Surface:** All the object's surfaces are listed here. Apply mapped art to one surface or as many as you want.
- **Scale to Fit:** Choose this option to scale the mapped artwork to fit the whole surface.
- **Clear:** Use this to remove mapped artwork from the selected surface.
- **Clear All:** Use this to remove all mapped artwork from all surfaces.
- **Shade Artwork (slower):** This option shows the mapped artwork along with the shade and lighting applied. A preview takes longer with this option selected.
- **Invisible Geometry:** Clicking this check box previews just the mapped art on the object, with the object showing in wireframe.

Using Other 3-D Techniques

Using Illustrator's 3-D effects isn't the only way to create depth in illustrations. You can do many things in Illustrator to create the illusion of depth. Drop shadows (Effect ➪ Stylize ➪ Drop Shadow) help define depth, but the most useful thing that you can do is to think about how a light source would hit an object and then reflect back to the viewer.

Using gradients to make bumps and dents

When you place gradients on themselves and one gradient has a different direction than another, 3-D effects appear. If you remember that highlights reflect off surfaces that bounce light to your eye, that principle should help you determine the direction of the gradients.

Of course, whether an object is coming at you or going away from you should be obvious, shouldn't it? Figure 16.18 shows ten buttons. See whether you can determine which buttons are innies and which buttons are outies. To assist you further, each button is on a standard background and has a button ring. The ring makes the direction of several of the buttons quite obvious.

Perspective drawing

Another newer aspect to Illustrator is the addition of perspective. The perspective option is found in the 3D Extrude & Bevel Options dialog box. This option gives your 3-D object a perspective look. The perspective option ranges from 0° to 160°. The perspective is a simulated distance from the object in the actual file, as shown in Figure 16.19.

FIGURE 16.18

Innie and outie buttons show another 3-D technique.

FIGURE 16.19

A 3-D object with perspective applied

Summary

Creating 3-D objects from 2-D ones really brings your Illustrator documents alive. In this chapter, you learned about Illustrator's 3-D effects, including the following:

- You can extrude or revolve 2-D objects to create 3-D objects.
- You can add multiple lights and change the color of the shading on a 3-D object.
- You can change the surface characteristics to be wireframe, no shading, diffuse shading, or plastic shading.
- You can map 2-D artwork onto 3-D objects.
- Layering gradients creates a 3-D look.

Chapter 17

Customizing and Automating Illustrator

Y ou know that you can use Illustrator to do all types of incredible art-work, but you should also see the practical, real-world side of Illustrator where deadlines must be met and there's little or no time for play. This chapter focuses on the real-world applications of Illustrator and how to get the most out of the software.

Who's Responsible for Illustrator?

Under the Help menu (Illustrator menu on a Mac), you find some useful information about the creators of Illustrator and its plug-ins.

About Illustrator displays a dialog box, as shown in Figure 17.1, with the user information and credits for the Illustrator team (click Credits to see the list). The Credits box lists everyone who ever helped with getting Illustrator updated and created and makes you aware of the large number of people who are involved in creating, maintaining, and updating the software.

IN THIS CHAPTER

Customizing Illustrator

Altering preferences

Creating actions

Customizing actions

FIGURE 17.1

The Adobe Illustrator dialog box tells you information about your copy of Illustrator.

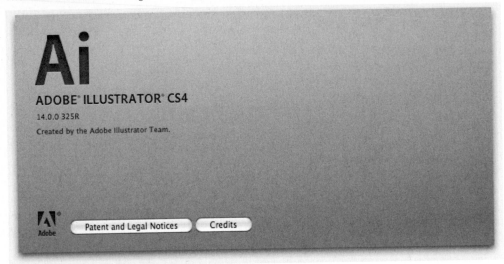

Customization Options

No two illustrators work the same. To accommodate the vast differences among styles, techniques, and habits, Illustrator provides many settings that each user can modify to personalize the software.

Illustrator provides four major ways to change preferences:

- You can control how Illustrator works by accessing the Preferences submenu, which you do by choosing Edit ⇨ Preferences (Illustrator ⇨ Preferences) or by pressing Ctrl+K (⌘+K). Within the Preferences dialog box, a number of different preference panes can be selected from the dropdown list (popup menu) at the top of the dialog box. You can go through each of the preference panes one by one by clicking Next and/or Previous or simply by choosing a preference pane from the Preferences submenu. The preference panes are General, Selection & Anchor Display, Type, Units & Display Performance, Guides & Grid, Smart Guides, Hyphenation, Plug-ins & Scratch Disks, User Interface, File Handling & Clipboard, and Appearance of Black.

- A second way to make changes is by changing preferences relative to each document. You usually make these changes in the Document Setup dialog box, but a few other options are available. You can find more information on document-specific preferences later in this chapter.

- The third way to customize preferences happens pretty much automatically. When you quit Illustrator, it remembers many of the current settings for the next time you run it. These settings include panel placements and values in Tools panel settings.

- The fourth way is to use the Window ⇨ Workspace commands to save your favorite workspace configuration or to reset the workspace to the default when you really mess things up.

Illustrator has a few settings that you can't customize. These features can really get under your skin because most of them seem like things that you should be able to customize. A section later in this chapter discusses what you can't customize.

Changing Preferences

The General section of the Preferences dialog box, accessed by choosing Edit ⇨ Preferences ⇨ General (Illustrator ⇨ Preferences ⇨ General) or pressing Ctrl+K (⌘+K), contains most of the personalized customizing options for Illustrator. The options in this box affect keyboard increments, measuring units, and the way that objects are drawn. These options are considered personalized options because they're specific to the way that each person uses the program. Few people have the same preference settings as others have (unless they never change the defaults). Figure 17.2 shows the General section of the Preferences dialog box.

FIGURE 17.2

The General section of the Preferences dialog box enables you to customize Illustrator.

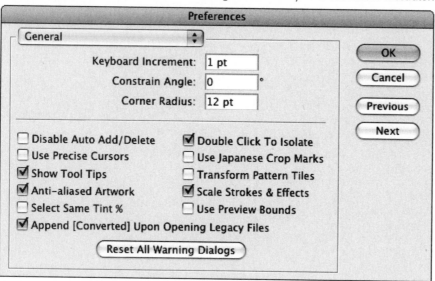

Altering the Keyboard Increment option

The cursor key increment that you specify in this setting controls how far an object moves when you select it and press the keyboard arrows.

The default for this setting is 1 point, which many people feel is small enough. I make my increment smaller when I'm working in 800% or 1600% views.

 While the arrow keys move selected objects the distance that's set in the Keyboard Increment option, press Alt (Option)+arrow key to make a copy of the object in that direction.

Using the Constrain Angle option

The Constrain Angle setting controls the angle at which all objects are aligned. By default, rectangles are always drawn flat, aligning themselves to the bottom, top, and sides of the document window. When you press Shift, lines that you draw with the Pen tool and objects that you move align to the Constrain Angle, or 45°, 90°, 135°, or 180°, plus or minus the constraining angle.

The Constrain Angle also affects how the four transformation tools transform objects. The Scale tool can be very hard to use when the Constrain Angle is not 0°, and the Shear tool becomes even more difficult to use than normal at different constrained angles. Pressing Shift when using the Rotate tool constrains the rotational angle to 45° increments added to the Constrain Angle.

CROSS-REF For more on the Rotate tool and the other transformation tools, see Chapter 11.

In Illustrator, 0° is a horizontal line and 90° is a vertical line. Figure 17.3 shows Illustrator angles.

If you set the Constrain Angle to 20°, objects are constrained to movements of 20°, 65°, 110°, 155°, and 200°. Constrain Angles of 90°, 180°, and –90° (270°) affect only type, patterns, gradients, and graphs; everything else works normally.

When copying objects using the Alt (Option) shortcut, you can press Shift in conjunction with a Constrain Angle to duplicate objects at a specific angle. To copy with the Alt (Option) shortcut, press Alt (Option) while dragging an object and then release the mouse button before releasing Alt (Option) to produce a duplicate of the object at the new location.

FIGURE 17.3

Angles in Illustrator are measured in a counterclockwise direction.

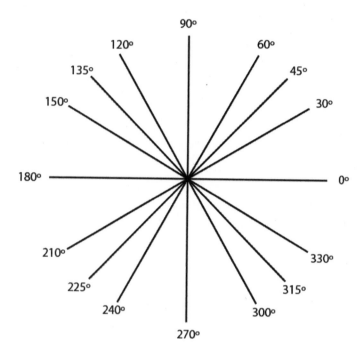

Changing the Corner Radius option

The Corner Radius option affects the size of the curved corners on a rounded rectangle.

CROSS-REF For more on the Corner Radius option and rounded rectangles, see Chapter 5.

The corner radius value changes each time you type a new value in the Rounded Rectangle dialog box. This dialog box opens when you click the Rounded Rectangle tool without dragging in a document. If, for example, you create one rounded rectangle with a corner radius of 24 points, all rounded rectangles that you create from that point forward have a radius of 24 points. You can change the corner radius in only two ways:

- Click the Rounded Rectangle tool without dragging in a document and then type a new value in the Rounded Rectangle dialog box.
- Type a new value in the Corner Radius text field in the Preferences dialog box.

The real advantage to changing the corner radius in the Preferences dialog box is that the corner radius affects manually created (dragged with the Rounded Rectangle tool) rounded rectangles immediately. Changing the corner radius in the Rectangle dialog box requires that you know the exact dimensions of the rectangle or that you draw a rectangle by typing information in the Rounded Rectangle dialog box (clicking with the Rounded Rectangle tool without dragging) and then specify the corner radius. You must then delete the original rectangle in order to manually draw a rounded rectangle with the correct corner radius.

CAUTION Because you can change the corner radius setting easily, be sure to check it before you manually draw a series of rounded rectangles. You can't easily or automatically change the corner radius on existing rounded rectangles.

If you use 0 points as the corner radius setting, the corners aren't rounded at all.

Adjusting the General options

The 11 check boxes in the General section of the Preferences dialog box are Illustrator's version of the *Battlestar Galactica* ragtag fleet of unwieldy spacefaring craft. Some are quite powerful, and others seem like they aren't capable of transferring millions of people across the galaxy, much less defending themselves against the evil menace of the Cylon Empire. Okay, that wasn't the best analogy. The fact is, you won't find another place in Illustrator where so many totally unrelated options share the same dialog box, and I had to come up with a snazzy introduction.

Use Precise Cursors

Precise cursors are cursors that appear as a variation of a crosshair instead of in the shape of a tool. Figure 17.4 shows cursors that are different when the Use Precise Cursors option is selected.

TIP Caps Lock toggles between standard cursors and precise cursors. When the Use Precise Cursors option is selected, Caps Lock makes the cursors standard. When the Use Precise Cursors option is deselected, Caps Lock activates the precise cursors.

I usually keep this option selected and rarely engage Caps Lock to change the cursors back to normal. In particular, I find the precise cursor for the Brush tool to be quite useful because the standard Brush cursor is a giant amorphous blob.

Show Tool Tips

This option displays little popup names for the tools if you rest your cursor above them for one second. It's a great idea to keep this option selected because not only do you see the name of the tool but also the key to press to access that tool.

TIP Illustrator lets you see the name of each swatch as you pass your cursor over it if you have Tool Tips active.

FIGURE 17.4

This shows the regular cursors on the left and the precise cursors on the right.

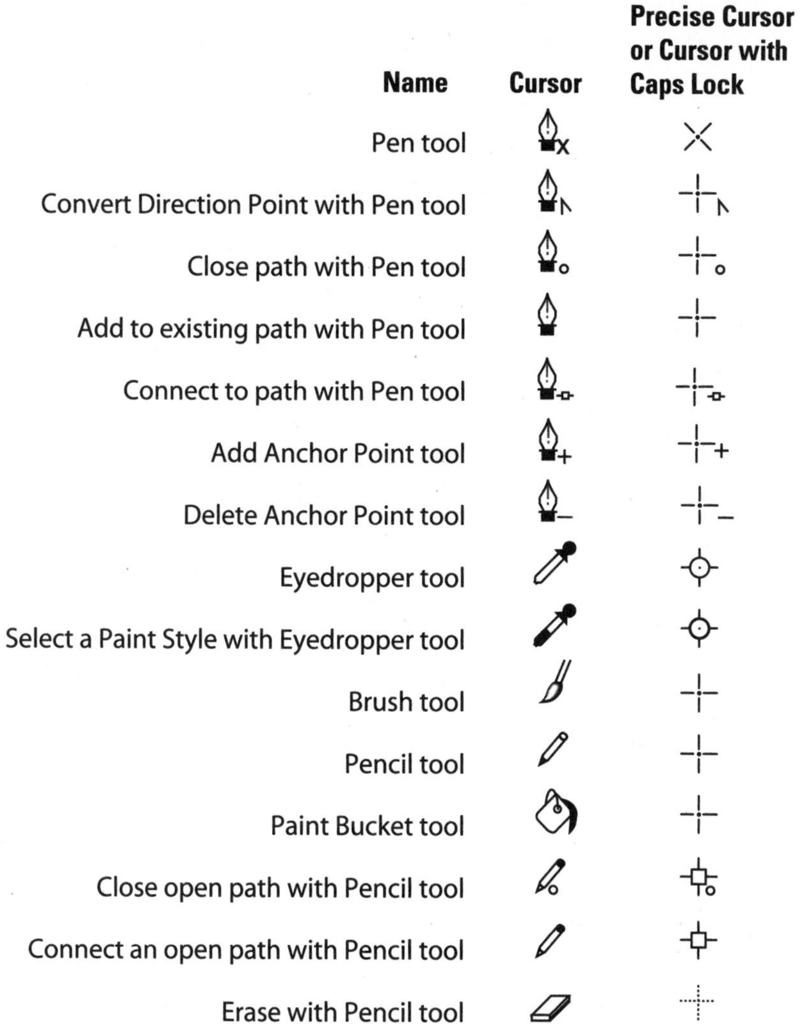

Name	Cursor	Precise Cursor or Cursor with Caps Lock
Pen tool		
Convert Direction Point with Pen tool		
Close path with Pen tool		
Add to existing path with Pen tool		
Connect to path with Pen tool		
Add Anchor Point tool		
Delete Anchor Point tool		
Eyedropper tool		
Select a Paint Style with Eyedropper tool		
Brush tool		
Pencil tool		
Paint Bucket tool		
Close open path with Pencil tool		
Connect an open path with Pencil tool		
Erase with Pencil tool		

Anti-aliased Artwork

The Anti-aliased Artwork option turns on anti-aliasing for on-screen representation of vector objects. Curved and diagonal edges appear smooth instead of jagged (or stairstepped). The resulting effect is for on-screen viewing only, and it won't affect output or rasterization of your artwork.

Select Same Tint %

This option specifies that the objects must have the same tint percentage when selecting objects with the same color. If this option isn't selected and you select a color, all tints of that color are selected.

Append [Converted] Upon Opening Legacy Files

When you open an older version of an Illustrator file (prior to Illustrator CS), a dialog box appears with the following message: "This file contains text that was created in a previous version of Illustrator. This legacy text must be updated before you edit it." Because the text engine was revamped in Illustrator CS, all old type needs to be updated. By default, this option is selected so that all files with legacy type or other functions, such as older files before gradients and transparency, are updated when opening the file.

Disable Auto Add/Delete

This option controls how the Pen tool behaves. With the option deselected (the default), clicking on an anchor point on an existing path deletes the point, and clicking on an existing path adds a new anchor point. If you click this check box, the Pen tool doesn't add or remove points from existing paths but instead always creates a new path/segment when selected.

Use Japanese Crop Marks

When selected, the Use Japanese Crop Marks option changes the standard crop marks, usually created with Effect ⇨ Crop Marks, to Japanese Crop Marks, as shown in Figure 17.5.

Transform Pattern Tiles

Select the Transform Pattern Tiles option if you want patterns in paths to be moved, scaled, rotated, sheared, or reflected when you use the transformation tools. When this option is selected, opening a transformation dialog box (Move, Scale, Rotate, Shear, or Reflect) automatically selects the Pattern check box. When the option is deselected, the Pattern check box is not selected in a transformation dialog box. This option controls whether selected patterns are transformed when the Transform panel is used.

I usually click the Transform Pattern Tiles check box, which sets all patterns to automatically transform and move with the objects that are being transformed and moved. This feature is especially useful when you want to create perspective in objects because the transformations of patterns can enhance the intended perspective.

FIGURE 17.5

Standard crop marks (top) and Japanese crop marks (bottom)

Scale Strokes & Effects

When the Scale Strokes & Effects feature is on, it automatically increases and reduces line weights and applied effects relative to an object when you uniformly scale that object manually. For example, if a path has a stroke weight of 1 point and you reduce the path uniformly by 50%, the stroke weight changes to 0.5 points.

 Scaling objects nonuniformly (without pressing Shift) doesn't change the stroke weight on an object, regardless of whether the Scale Strokes & Effects feature is on or off.

Use Preview Bounds

When you select the Use Preview Bounds option, it affects how the Info panel measures the dimension of the selected object. With the Use Preview Bounds option selected, Illustrator's Info panel includes the size of the stroke width and other elements, such as feathered shadows, in the dimensions.

Reset All Warning Dialogs

The Reset All Warning Dialogs option reverts all of Illustrator's lovely warnings. For example, a warning appears when you try to delete a point and don't click the point. You can turn this off by clicking the Don't show this again check box. When you choose to reset all warning boxes, it's turned on again.

Changing the Selection & Anchor Display options

As shown in Figure 17.6, this section controls how paths are selected as well as how anchor points and their handles are displayed.

Tolerance

This setting controls how far away from an object you can be in order to select it, measured in screen pixels.

Object Selection by Path Only

With Object Selection by Path Only selected, you must select the object's path with a Selection tool to select the object rather than click the fill. If you deselect this option, you can click the fill with the Selection tool to select it.

Snap to Point

This option makes it easier to select an anchor point (as opposed to selecting another part of a path or object). The pixel amount is measured in screen pixels.

Anchors/Handles

For each of these, click the appropriate check box to select how anchors and handles appear when selected.

Highlight anchors on mouse over

This option highlights anchors (in the color of the layer where the path resides) as the tip of your mouse passes over them.

Show handles when multiple anchors are selected

Clicking this check box shows all the control handles for all points selected when you're using the Direct Selection tool.

The Selection & Anchor Display section of the Preferences dialog box enables you to select the options for Selection & Anchor Display.

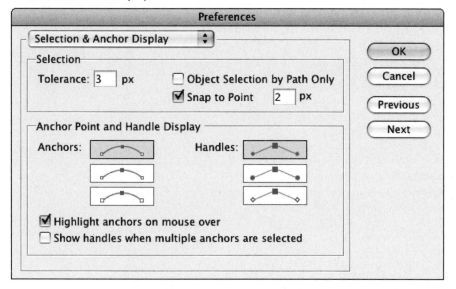

Changing Preferences for Type

The Type preferences enable you to customize your type options. You have nine type options to choose from. Figure 17.7 shows the Type section of the Preferences dialog box.

You can set these 10 type preference options:

- Size/Leading
- Baseline Shift
- Tracking

- Type Object Selection by Path Only
- Show Asian Options
- Show Font Names in English
- Number of Recent Fonts
- Font Preview
- Enable Missing Glyph Protection
- Use Inline Input for Non-Latin Text

When you select Font Preview, you have an additional option of Size.

FIGURE 17.7

The Type section of the Preferences dialog box enables you to select the options for type used in your documents.

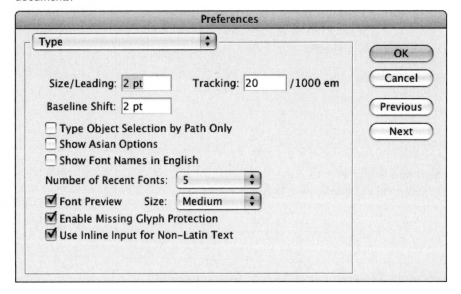

The Size/Leading option

You can use the keyboard to increase and decrease type size by pressing Ctrl+Shift+> (⌘+Shift+>) and Ctrl+Shift+< (⌘+Shift+<), respectively. You can increase and decrease leading by pressing Alt+↑ (Option+↑) and Alt+↓ (Option+↓), respectively. In the Size/Leading text box, you specify the increment by which the size and leading change.

You can increase or decrease the type size and leading only until you reach the upper and lower limits of each. The upper limit for type size and leading is 1296 points; the lower limit for each is 0.1 points.

 I keep my settings fairly high, at 10 points, because I have found that I require large point changes, usually quite a bit more than 10 points. If I need to do fine-tuning, I either type the exact size that I want or use the Scale tool.

The Baseline Shift option

The Baseline Shift feature moves selected type up and down on the baseline, independent of the leading. The increment specified in this box is how much the type is moved when you press the arrow keyboard commands. To move type up one increment, press Alt+Shift+↑ (Option+Shift+↑). To move type down one increment, press Alt+Shift+↓ (Option+Shift+↓).

I keep the Baseline shift increment at 1 point so that I can adjust path type better; specifically, I like to be able to adjust the baseline shift of type on a circle.

The Tracking option

Tracking changes the amount of space between selected characters, and the setting in this text field represents the amount of space (measured in thousandths of an em space) that the keyboard command adds or removes. To increase tracking, press Ctrl+→ (⌘+→); press Ctrl+← (⌘+←) to decrease it.

To increase the tracking by five times the increment in the Type & Auto Tracing section of the Preferences dialog box, press Shift+Alt+Ctrl+\ (Shift+Option+⌘+\). To decrease the tracking by five times the increment, press Shift+Alt+Ctrl+Backspace (Shift+Option+⌘+Backspace).

The value in the Tracking text field also affects incremental changes in kerning. *Kerning* is the addition or removal of space between one pair of letters only. Kerning is done instead of tracking when a blinking insertion point is between two letters, as opposed to at least one selected character for tracking.

The Type Object Selection by Path Only option

Selecting this option makes it possible to select text by clicking on the text path itself. The default is turned off, allowing you to click anywhere on the type with the Selection tool to select the type.

The Show Asian Options option

Select the Show Asian Options option to view and set the options for Asian fonts. The Asian fonts include Chinese, Japanese, and Korean.

The Show Font Names in English option

If you have a font from another language installed on your system (like Kanji, a Japanese character set), this option allows you to see these typefaces in the font/type menus as English words.

Setting the Number of Recent Fonts option

Use the Number of Recent Fonts setting to specify how many font names are displayed in the Type ⇨ Recent Fonts submenu. You can choose a value between 1 and 15 from the dropdown list (popup menu). This option is especially useful if you have a large number of fonts installed on your system and you reuse several of the same fonts often. Choose a value that represents the largest number of fonts that you typically use in a single document.

Choosing a Font Preview size

When the Font Preview check box is selected, Illustrator displays fonts in the Type ⇨ Font menu by using characters from the font. You can choose small, medium, or large characters for the font preview from the Size dropdown list (popup menu). A smaller size allows more fonts to appear in the list without scrolling, while larger sizes make the subtle differences between certain fonts easier to see.

Enable Missing Glyph Protection

This option removes characters that aren't present when a font is missing. It helps avoid those nasty boxes that can appear for missing characters.

Use Inline Input for Non-Latin text

For special characters, this allows typing those characters directly into a text box instead of being forced to use the Glyph panel.

Using Units & Display Performance

The Units & Display Performance preferences enable you to select the measurement system you want to use and set the performance of the Hand tool. Figure 17.8 shows the Units & Display Performance section of the Preferences dialog box.

FIGURE 17.8

The Units & Display Performance section of the Preferences dialog box allows you to choose the measurement units for Illustrator.

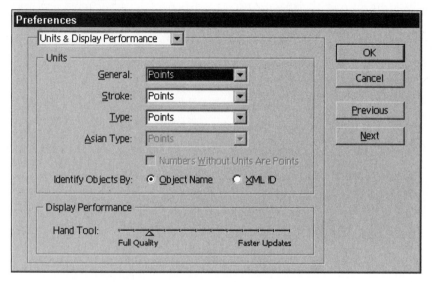

Changing Units settings

The General dropdown list (popup menu) in the Units section changes the measurement system for the current document and all future new documents. Illustrator contains five measurement units: inches, picas, points, millimeters, and centimeters. The areas for which the measurement can be specified are the following:

- **General:** Applies to the Measure tool and the rulers
- **Stroke:** Applies to the weight of the path's stroke
- **Type:** Sets the type measurement increments
- **Asian Type:** Sets the type measurement increments for Asian type

CAUTION Changing the General units in the Units & Display Performance Preferences dialog box changes the ruler units in the Document Setup dialog box. Access this dialog box by choosing File ⇨ Document Setup or pressing Ctrl+Alt+P (⌘+Option+P).

The other areas under Units that can be changed are the Numbers Without Units Are Points check box and Identify Objects By (Object Name or XML ID) radio buttons:

- **Numbers Without Units Are Points:** When you type a number with no measurement indicator (in for inches, pt for points, etc.), the default is points.

- **Identify Objects By:** In this area, click a radio button to identify objects by name or XML ID. If you save your document in SVG format for use with other Adobe products, select XML ID to ensure that object names conform to XML naming conventions.

Being aware of which measurement system you're working in is important. When you type a measurement in a dialog box, any numbers that aren't measurement system–specific are applied to the current unit of measurement. For example, if you want to move something 1 inch and you open the Move dialog box by choosing Object ➪ Transform ➪ Move or double-clicking the Selection tool, you need to add either the inch symbol (") or the abbreviation after you type 1 in the dialog box if the measurement system is not inches. If the measurement system is points or picas, typing 1 moves the object 1 point (or 1 pica), not 1 inch. If the measurement system is already in inches, typing just the number 1 is fine.

Usually a corresponding letter or letters indicates the measurement system: *in* for inch, *pt* for points, and *cm* for centimeters.

 The default measurement is points, so if you ever toss your preferences file or reinstall Illustrator, be aware that you may have to change the measurement system.

Changing Display Performance

The Hand tool's viewing performance is what you're adjusting under the Display Performance area. Click and drag the slider to the left so you see more quality when moving around your screen. Drag the slider to the right to get a quicker update with less quality viewing. A quicker update shows a rough preview as you're dragging rather than an exact preview of your illustration as you move around.

Changing Guides & Grid Preferences

The Guides & Grid section of the Preferences dialog box lets you control the color and style of your guides and grids as well as the spacing of your grid. Figure 17.9 shows the Guides & Grid section of the Preferences dialog box. For more on grids and guides and their options, see Chapter 8.

 You can place grids in back of or in front of your image by selecting or deselecting the Grids In Back option in the Guides & Grid section of the Preferences dialog box.

FIGURE 17.9

The Guides & Grid section of the Preferences dialog box enables you to fine-tune the guides and grid settings.

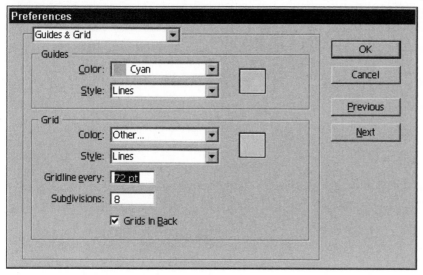

Adjusting Smart Guides

Smart Guides are helpers that show you the angle of the line and list the line as a path. You can select or deselect four Display Options as well as adjust the angles and snapping tolerance. The Smart Guides snap to other objects, aiding you in aligning, editing, and transforming. Figure 17.10 shows the Smart Guides section of the Preferences dialog box.

Changing Display Options

These hints and lines pop up when you drag your mouse over an object. They tell you what each area is. For example, if you drag your mouse over a line, the hint pops up with the word "path." If you drag your mouse over an anchor point, the hint says "anchor point." As you move your cursor around, lines appear to help you align new objects and existing ones. The options below control which hints and lines appear when Smart Guides are on:

- **Color:** This popup menu allows you to select the color of the hints.
- **Alignment Guides:** These are incredibly handy lines that appear when the object you're dragging is aligned to any edge or center of another object on your screen.
- **Object Highlighting:** This option highlights the object to which you're pointing.
- **Transform Tools:** When you're rotating, scaling, or shearing an object with this option selected, Smart Guides show up to help you out.

- **Anchor/Path Labels:** This displays the words "anchor" and "path" when the cursor is over one of these.

- **Measurement Labels:** These labels display how far from your last click, how big objects are that you're creating, etc.

- **Construction Guides:** This lets you view guidelines when using Smart Guides.

FIGURE 17.10

Use the Smart Guides section of the Preferences dialog box to set up the Smart Guides.

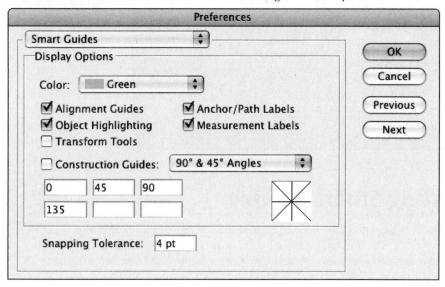

Altering angles (for construction guides)

The angles that you can choose in the Smart Guides section of the Preferences dialog box let you pick what angles display construction guides when you drag an object. You can choose from seven presets or create custom angles. The lines indicate the standard guide angles. When you add your own angled lines, a line appears representing the particular angle you typed.

Changing the Snapping Tolerance

The Snapping Tolerance setting allows you to choose how close one object must be to another object before the first object automatically snaps to the second object. Set the Snapping Tolerance in points; the lower the number, the closer you must move the objects to each other. The Snapping Tolerance default is 4 points. That means when you're within 4 points to another object, your selected object snaps to the second object. I tend to stick with the default.

Adjusting Slices Preferences

Slices are subdivisions of a Web-based graphic and used for Web pages. Options under Slice are the Show Slice Numbers check box and Line Color dropdown list (popup menu). If selected, the Show Slice Numbers option shows the numbers for each slice. The Line Color option lets you change the slice lines to a color of your choice. The default is to use a contrasting color.

 For more on slicing, see Chapter 19.

Changing Hyphenation

The Hyphenation section of the Preferences dialog box contains options for customizing the way Illustrator hyphenates words. At the top of the dialog box is a dropdown list (popup menu) that lists various languages. Select a default language. Typically, if you use Illustrator in English, you don't have to change anything. If you use a different language, you need to have that language installed on your computer. Then, you can choose the language you want to use as the default. At the bottom of the dialog box is an area where you can add to the list of hyphenation exceptions. These exceptions are words that you don't want Illustrator to hyphenate under any circumstances. Figure 17.11 shows the Hyphenation section of the Preferences dialog box.

FIGURE 17.11

The Hyphenation section of the Preferences dialog box enables you to control how special words are hyphenated.

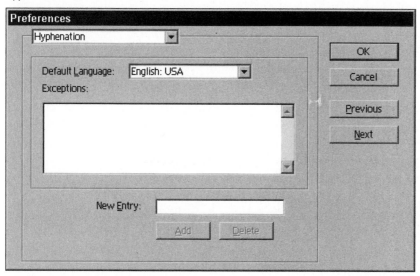

Adjusting the Plug-Ins & Scratch Disks

The next item in the dropdown list (popup menu) in the Preferences dialog box is a two-trick pony, the Plug-ins & Scratch Disks section, as shown in Figure 17.12. The first section in this dialog box enables you to specify a folder for plug-ins. The default is the plug-ins folder in the Adobe Illustrator folder.

FIGURE 17.12

Use the Plug-ins & Scratch Disks section of the Preferences dialog box to specify file locations.

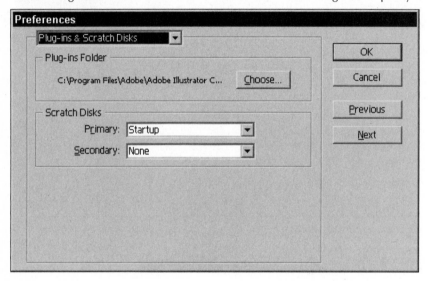

The second section in the Plug-in & Scratch Disks section of the Preferences dialog box lets you define what drives to use as scratch disks (places where Illustrator stores information when it runs out of RAM). Typically, you should assign the fastest, largest drive to be your primary scratch disk. The settings you choose don't take effect until you restart Illustrator.

Customizing the User Interface

The User Interface preferences let you change how bright the UI (mostly panels) is. In addition, you can set Icon panels to automatically collapse after you access a control in them and whether to use the tabbed document interface (deselecting this option removes the tabs from the top of the document work area, making the documents only accessible via the Window menu). You set these preferences in the User Interface section of the Preferences dialog box, as shown in Figure 17.13.

FIGURE 17.13

The User Interface section of the Preferences dialog box enables you to specify how bright the UI appears.

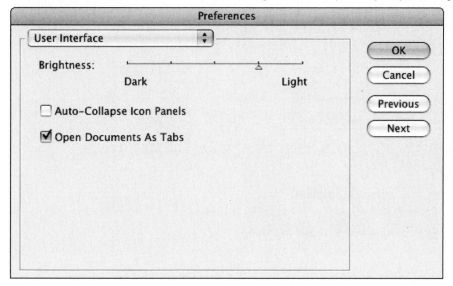

Customizing the File Handling & Clipboard

The File Handling & Clipboard preferences let you change how files are saved with extensions and links and how to handle the Clipboard files. You set these preferences in the File Handling & Clipboard section of the Preferences dialog box, as shown in Figure 17.14.

The File Handling preferences are used when saving and updating files. Click the Use Low Resolution Proxy for Linked EPS check box to display a low-resolution image for a linked EPS to save file space. You can also set how links are updated; choose from Automatically, Manually, or Ask When Modified in the Update Links dropdown list (popup menu).

The Clipboard is another area that can be altered in preferences. When you copy and paste, the Clipboard holds that information. Objects copied to the Clipboard are PDF files by default. You can change that to AICB (Adobe Illustrator Clip Board), and you won't have any transparency support. Under the AICB option, you can select Preserve Paths or Preserve Appearance and Overprints. All the AICB options enable you to do more with editing but also take up more file space.

FIGURE 17.14

The File Handling & Clipboard section of the Preferences dialog box enables you to specify file sharing and the Clipboard options.

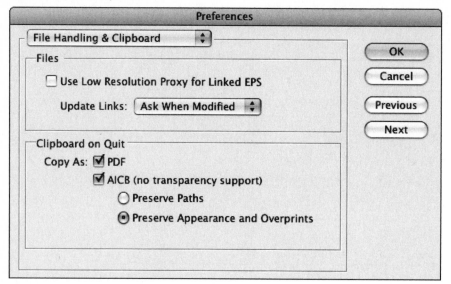

Setting the Appearance of Black Options

In the Appearance of Black section of the Preferences dialog box, you have two options for controlling how Illustrator displays and prints black. In each case, you can choose to accurately depict black or make black into a deeper, richer-appearing color. Figure 17.15 shows the Appearance of Black section of the Preferences dialog box.

FIGURE 17.15

The Appearance of Black section of the Preferences dialog box enables you to control how Illustrator treats black sections of your documents.

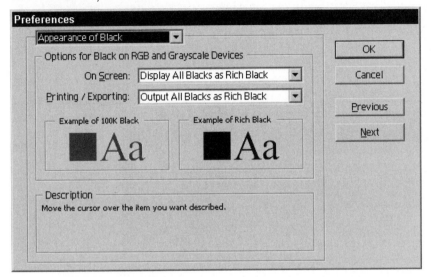

Altering Placement and Tools Panel Value Preferences

Most Illustrator users take many preferences for granted. But if Illustrator didn't remember certain preferences, most Illustrator users would be quite annoyed.

Panels (including the Tools panel) remain where they were when you last used Illustrator. Illustrator remembers their size and whether they were open. Values in the Tools panel are still whatever you set them to the last time you used a specific tool. For example, the options in the Paintbrush/Eyedropper dialog box remain the same between Illustrator sessions.

Adding Keyboard Customization

Longtime users of Illustrator have noticed keyboard shortcut changes. Although they may be frustrating, there's a method to Adobe's madness. It wants to make working between programs seamless, and that means making keyboard shortcuts the same throughout its programs. If you liked a certain keyboard command, you can always customize the keyboard to what you like.

Choose Edit ➯ Keyboard Shortcuts to access the Keyboard Shortcuts dialog box, as shown in Figure 17.16, where you can change and save your own settings. After you start to edit the Keyboard Shortcuts, Defaults changes to Custom. Next time you start Illustrator, your custom settings are available under the Illustrator Defaults dropdown list (popup menu).

 **You can't use Ctrl (⌘), Alt (Option), or function keys with other keys for shortcuts.**

FIGURE 17.16

The Keyboard Shortcuts dialog box allows you to set up your own set of shortcuts.

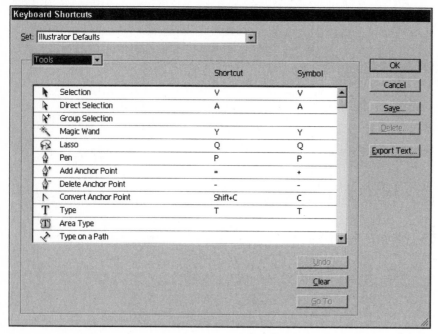

Knowing What You Can't Customize

Several things can't be customized in Illustrator, and they can be annoying:

- Type information always defaults to 12-point Myriad Pro, Auto Leading, 100% Horizontal Scale, 0 Tracking, Flush Left, Hyphenation Off.
- Every new document begins with only one layer. It's called Layer 1 and is light blue.

- When you create new objects, they always have a 0% Black fill and a 1-point stroke.
- The Selection tool is always the active tool when you first launch Illustrator.

Using Actions

Adobe has brought the same technology from Photoshop into Illustrator to ease repetitive tasks. The tasks of applying color, object transformations, and text functions are easily automated using the Actions panel. Illustrator comes with some prerecorded actions, and you can create your own.

In the Actions panel, the box on the far-left side toggles an item off or on. The next box toggles the dialog box off or on. The buttons at the bottom enable you to record your own actions.

Using a Default Action

Accessing Default Actions requires little effort. To activate a Default Action, click the action to highlight it and then click the Play Current Selection button.

Creating a new action

If the numerous default actions aren't enough, you can create your own actions. To start recording a new action, you need to create a new action. Click the Create New Action button at the bottom of the Actions panel or choose New Action from the Actions panel's popup menu to open the New Action dialog box so that you can name the action. After typing a name (I prefer to give it a descriptive name so I know what action it does), click Record and then start doing your action. After you finish, you can move the order or delete parts of your action.

 **Not everything can be recorded. If an action can't be recorded, Illustrator displays a warning dialog box.**

Creating a new set

When you create a new action, it's put into a folder with a set of actions. You can have multiple actions in a folder or just one. A new action needs to be a part of a set (or in a folder). It can be an existing set or a new set. Think of actions as packages. To create a new set, click the Create New Set button at the bottom of the panel or select New Set from the Actions panel's popup menu.

FIGURE 17.17

The Actions panel helps you automate Illustrator.

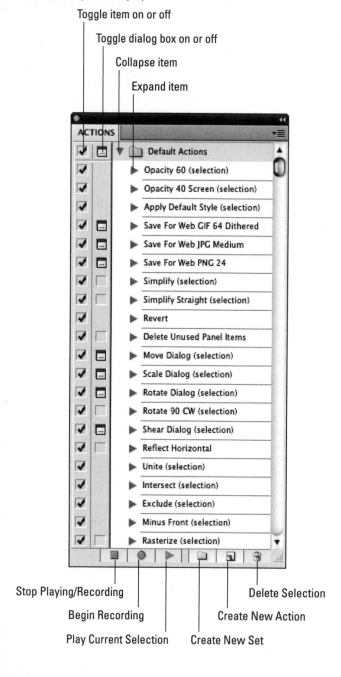

Toggle item on or off

Toggle dialog box on or off

Collapse item

Expand item

Stop Playing/Recording

Begin Recording

Play Current Selection

Create New Set

Create New Action

Delete Selection

What is recordable?

In Illustrator, not everything is recordable. As with anything, there are limits. The following actions are recordable in the Actions panel:

- **File:** New, Open, Close, Save, Save as, Save for Microsoft Office, Save a Copy, Revert, Place, and Export
- **Edit:** Cut, Copy, Paste, Paste in Front, Paste in Back, Clear, Select All, and Deselect All
- **Object:** Transform Again, Move, Scale, Rotate, Shear, Reflect, Transform Each, Arrange, Group, Ungroup, Lock, Unlock All, Hide Selection, Show All, Expand, Rasterize, Blends, Mask, Compound Path, and Cropmarks
- **Type:** Block, Wrap, Fit Headline, Create Outlines, Find/Change, Find Font, Change Case, Rows & Columns, Type Orientation, and Glyph Options
- **Effects:** Colors, Create, Distort, and Stylize
- **View:** Guides-related only
- **Panels:** Color, Gradient, Stroke, Character, MM Design, Paragraph, Tab Ruler, Transform, Pathfinder, Align, Swatch, Brush, Layer, and Attribute
- **Tools panel:** Ellipse, Rectangle, Polygon, Star, Spiral, Move (Selection tool), Rotate, Scale, Shear, and Reflect
- **Special:** Bounding Box Transform, Insert Select Path, Insert Stop, and Select Objects

Duplicating and deleting an action

You can duplicate an action when you want to modify an existing action but don't want to record the whole darn thing again. To duplicate an action, first select an action in the Actions panel and then choose Duplicate from the Actions panel's popup menu. This makes a copy of the action.

To change the name of the action, double-click the action to open the Action Options dialog box, as shown in Figure 17.18. You can change the name of an action this way but not the name of the action set. You can also see which set the selected action is a part of. Assign a function key here, especially if it's an action that you use repeatedly. You can also change the color of the action button listed in the Actions panel.

Deleting an action is pretty easy. Select the action that you want to delete and then drag it to the trash icon at the bottom of the panel or use the Actions panel's popup menu.

FIGURE 17.18

The Action Options dialog box enables you to rename or assign a shortcut key to an action.

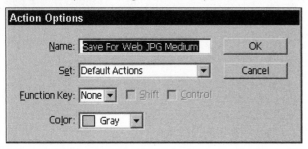

Starting and stopping recording

To start recording, do one of the following:

- Create a new action set and action.
- Select an existing action and then click the Begin Recording button at the bottom of the panel.
- Activate an action and then select Start Recording in the Actions panel's popup menu.

To stop recording, do one of the following:

- Click the Stop Playing/Recording button.
- Select Stop Recording in the Actions panel's popup menu.

Inserting a menu item

If you have either duplicated an action or want to add to an action, you may want to insert an item into the action. To insert a menu item, activate an action, start recording, and then select Insert Menu Item from the Actions panel's popup menu. This allows you to record most menu items, such as File, Edit, Object, Type, Effect, and guide-related Views. You don't have to use this to record a menu item.

Inserting a stop

Record Stop enables you to stop the playback of an action at a point where you may want to make the action stop so you can add something to a certain area each time you replay it. During your recording, select Insert Stop in the Actions panel's popup menu. You can have some fun with this one. You're creating your own dialog box when you insert a stop, as shown in Figure 17.19.

Put a message in this dialog box just for fun. Always allow the user to continue if he or she wants. That way, you continue with the rest of the action after the stop. This is great for using Actions to partially do the creation but pauses so you can type specifics in a dialog box.

FIGURE 17.19

The Record Stop command lets you create your own dialog boxes.

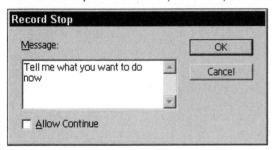

Action Options

The Action Options are where you name or rename the action, move it to a set, assign a function key, or assign a color to the action. The function key option is a cool feature that lets you assign a function key to an action so you can just press F5, for example, and your action starts.

Playback Options

The Playback Options dialog box, which you access by choosing Playback Options from the Actions panel's popup menu, lets you customize your actions even further. This dialog box is shown in Figure 17.20.

FIGURE 17.20

Use the playback options to control how fast your recorded action plays.

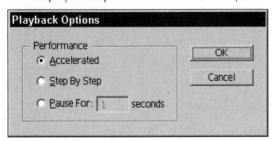

You can accelerate, step through, or pause your Actions as follows:

- **Accelerated:** Plays the action all at once — and quickly. This is great for monotonous, repetitive actions, such as renaming figures or adding a tagline.

- **Step By Step:** Plays the action one step at a time. This lets you decide whether you want to perform a step or add in-between steps.

- **Pause For:** Stops at each step for the specified time. This is a good choice if you want to closely examine how something was recorded and want to stop the recording at a certain spot.

Inserting a selected path

You can't record the Pen tool or the Pencil tool, but you can record a path. Follow these steps:

1. **Draw a path.**
2. **While the path is selected, start recording.**
3. **Choose Insert Select Path from the Actions panel's popup menu.**
4. **Stop recording.**

You've just created an action to place a path.

Selecting an object

If you want to select an object to use later in your recording, you need to apply text to it and then select an object or path first. Follow these steps:

1. **Select the object or path.**
2. **Select Show Note from the Attributes panel's popup menu.**
3. **Type the text you want to apply to the object in the bottom field and then click the Begin Recording button on the Actions panel to record the new setting.**
4. **When you need to select the object or path, choose Select Object from the popup menu to display the Set Selection dialog box, as shown in Figure 17.21, type the name you gave it in the Attributes panel, and then click OK.** The object or path is now selected.

Clearing, resetting, loading, replacing, and saving actions

Whew! Even after creating a bunch of cool actions, you want more options. You can clear, reset, load, replace, and save actions. Now you can create, delete, load sets, and save to your heart's content by choosing the appropriate item in the Actions panel. The following describes what each option does:

- **Clear Actions:** Deletes all the action sets in the Actions panel

- **Reset Actions:** Resets the panel to the Default Actions

- **Load Actions** or **Replace Actions:** Lets you navigate to a folder where the action sets are and lets you select one. You can find a ton of prerecorded actions and action sets on the application CD.

- **Save Actions:** Lets you save actions after you record them. You must save your new action just like a file if you want to use it the next time you launch Illustrator. Select Save Action from the popup menu and then navigate to where you want to save your action set (maybe the Action Sets folder within the application folder).

FIGURE 17.21

You can use the Set Selection dialog box to select objects by name.

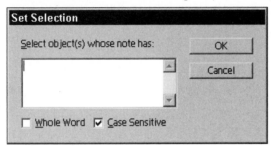

Summary

You can customize and automate Illustrator to make the program work the way you want. In this chapter, you learned about the following topics:

- The different preference areas can be changed in Illustrator.

- You can customize many preferences, including keyboard shortcuts, in the various panes in the Preferences dialog box.

- The Constrain Angle option controls the angle at which objects are drawn and moved when Shift is pressed.

- The General Units option controls the measurement units for Illustrator.

- Use the Actions panel to streamline repetitive tasks in Illustrator.

Part IV

Getting Art Out of Illustrator

Chapter 18

Understanding PostScript and Printing

Until the mid-1980s, computer graphics were, well, crusty. Blocky. Jagged. Rough. If you looked at graphics that were done on computers in 1981 and printed to a black-and-white printer, you'd laugh so hard you couldn't breathe, stopping the laughter only when you realized that you actually could not breathe. Of course, in 1981, the world was gaga over the capabilities of computers and computer graphics. Those same pictures were admired, and the average person was generally amazed. The average designer, on the other hand, shuddered and prayed that this whole computer thing wouldn't catch on.

Desktop publishing was pushed to a level of professionalism in 1985 by a cute little software package called PageMaker. With PageMaker, you could do typesetting and layout on the computer screen, seeing everything on-screen just as it would eventually be printed. Well, almost. Aldus was the company that created PageMaker. In 1994, Adobe swallowed Aldus.

Problems aside, PageMaker would not have been a success if the laser printer hadn't handily arrived on the scene. Even so, there were problems inherent with laser printers too.

At 300 dots per inch (dpi), there were 90,000 dots in every square inch. A typical 8½-inch × 11-inch page of type had 8.5 million dots to put down. Computers were finally powerful enough to handle this huge number of dots, but the time it took to print made computers pretty much useless for any real work.

Several systems were developed to improve the printing process, and the one standout was PostScript from Adobe Systems. Apple licensed PostScript from Adobe for use on its first LaserWriter, and a star was born. Installed on every laser printer from Apple were two things from Adobe: the PostScript page description language and the Adobe base fonts, which included Times, Helvetica, Courier, and Symbol.

PostScript became fundamental to Apple computers and laser printers and became the standard. To use PostScript, Apple had to pay licensing fees to Adobe for every laser printer it sold. Fonts were PostScript, and if there ever was a standard in graphics, the closest thing to it was PostScript (commonly called EPS, for Encapsulated PostScript).

Today, the majority of fonts for both Mac and Windows systems are OpenType fonts, and many of the typefaces used in professional work are OpenType. However, almost all graphics and desktop-publishing software can read PostScript in some form (especially since OpenType is a derivative of PostScript).

You can print Illustrator documents in two ways: as a composite, which is a single printout that contains all the colors and tints used, or as a series of color separations, with a printout for each color. Color separations are necessary for illustrations that are printed on a printing press.

Understanding the Benefits of PostScript

A typical graphic object in painting software is based on a certain number of pixels that are a certain color. If you make that graphic larger, the pixels become larger, giving a rough, jagged effect to the art. To prevent these jaggies, two things can be done: Ensure that enough dots per inch are in the image so that when the image is enlarged, the dots are too small to appear jagged. Or define graphics by mathematical equations instead of by dots.

PostScript is a mathematical solution to high-resolution imaging. Areas, or shapes, are defined and then these shapes are either *filled* or *stroked* with a percentage of color. The shapes are made up of paths, and the paths are defined by a number of points along the path (anchor points) and controls off those points (control handles, sometimes called curve handles or direction points) that control the shape of the curve. Those paths fill up with dots at print time, but the higher number of dots per inch (commonly referred to as *dpi*) give the illusion of a perfectly smooth edge.

Because the anchor points and control handles have real locations on a page, mathematical processes can be used to create the shapes based on these points. The mathematical equation for Bézier curves is quite detailed (at least for someone who, like me, fears math).

PostScript is not just math though. It's actually a programming language and, more specifically, a page description language. Like BASIC, Pascal, Forth, SmallTalk, and C, PostScript is made of lines of code that are used to describe artwork.

Fortunately, the average user never has to deal directly with PostScript code; instead, the average user uses a simplified interface, such as Illustrator. Software that has the capability to save files in

PostScript or to print to a PostScript printer writes this PostScript code for you. Printers that are equipped with PostScript then take that PostScript code and convert it to dots on a printed page.

Using PostScript

That most applications can handle EPS files and that most printers can print PostScript are of great benefit to users, but the strength of PostScript is not really in its widespread use.

If you create a 1-inch closed path in pixel-based drawing software and then enlarge that same path in any application, the path begins to lose detail. A 300-dpi path at twice its original size becomes 150 dpi. Those jagged edges become more apparent than ever.

If you create a 1-inch circle in Illustrator, you can enlarge it to any size possible without losing one iota of resolution. The Illustrator circle stays perfectly smooth, even enlarged to 200%, because the circle's resolution depends on the laser printer or imagesetter that prints it. Therefore, a perfect 1-inch circle has the potential to be a perfect 2-foot circle (providing you can find a printer or imagesetter that can print a 2-foot-diameter circle).

But scaling objects is only the beginning. You can distort, stretch, rotate, skew, and flip objects created in Illustrator to your heart's content, and the object still prints to the resolution of the output device.

Here's an example: A company wants its tiny logo on a 3-foot-wide poster. If you use raster methods, the edges become fuzzy and gross-looking — pretty much unacceptable to your client. Your other conventional option is to redraw the logo at a larger size or to trace the blown-up version — a time-consuming proposition either way.

Illustrator's solution is to scan the logo, trace it either in another software tracing program or with the Live Trace tool, and then allow you to touch it up and build your design around it. Afterward, output the illustration to a printer that can handle that size poster. There's no loss of quality; instead, the enlarged version from Illustrator often looks better than the scanned original.

Knowing What to Do Prior to Printing

Before you start the printing process, you may need to change or adjust a few items. For example, you may need to change the page size and orientation or set how certain colors should separate. This section deals with the issues you should be aware of before you press Ctrl+P (⌘+P) to send your file to the printer.

Changing the Artboard size

Clicking the Artboard tool in the Tools panel allows you to specify the size of the Artboard in your document. If the Artboard is smaller than the printable page, then anything entirely outside the edges of the Artboard is cropped off when you print the illustration through Illustrator. Any objects that are partially on the Artboard print. Figure 18.1 shows how you can use the Artboard tool to change the Artboard size.

When the Artboard tool is selected, you can change the Artboard size of your document (represented by the dashed line).

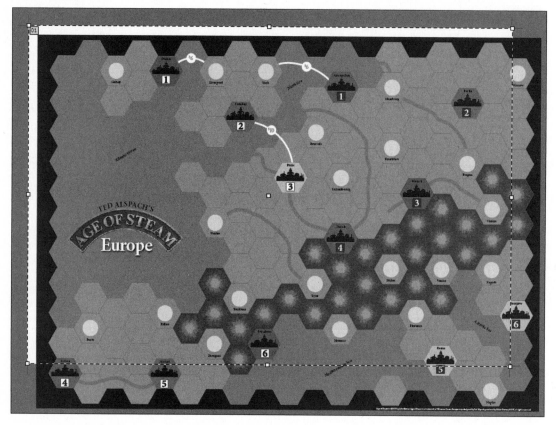

Printing composites

A composite printout looks very much like the image that appears on the screen. If you have a color printer, the image appears in color; otherwise, the colors are replaced by gray tints.

NOTE   Objects that are hidden or that exist on layers that are currently hidden don't print. Objects that exist on layers that have the printing check box deselected in the Layer Options dialog box also don't print.

When you're ready to print your document, choose File➪Print or press Ctrl+P (⌘+P). This action opens the Print dialog box, as shown in Figure 18.2, where you can choose which pages to print, how many of each to print, and several other options. If you click Cancel or press Esc, the dialog box disappears and no pages are printed. To print, click Print or press Enter (Return).

The Print dialog box has a number of areas. You display each area by choosing an item from the list that appears along the left side of the dialog box.

FIGURE 18.2

The Print dialog box provides many options for controlling how your Illustrator documents print.

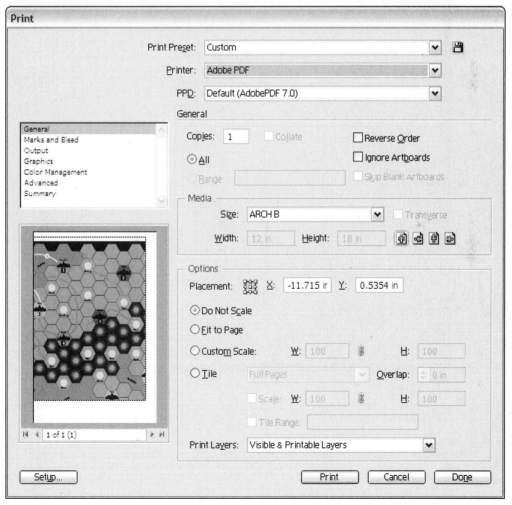

The General pane offers these options:

- **Copies:** The number that you type here determines how many copies of each page print.
- **Pages:** If you click the All radio button, all the pages that have art on them print. If you click the Range radio button and type numbers in the text field, only the pages that those numbers refer to print.
- **Media:** This handles the Size, Width, Height, and Orientation of the document.
- **Options:** This section determines how to print the layers and includes scaling options. In the Print Layers dropdown list (popup menu), choose from Visible & Printable Layers, Visible Layers, and All Layers. The Scaling options are Do Not Scale, Fit to Page, and Custom Scale (type a width and height in percentages).

The Setup (Page Setup on the Mac) button offers these options:

- **Crop Artwork to:** Choose from Artboard, Artwork Bounding Box, or Crop Area.
- **Placement:** Choose where you want the printing origin to start from relative to the edge of the paper.
- **Tiling:** This relates to paging. You can print Single Full Page, Tile Full Pages, or Tile Imageable Areas.

The Marks & Bleed pane offers these options:

- **Marks:** This lets you click or deselect the following options: All Printer's Marks, Trim Marks, Registration Marks, Color Bars, and Page Information. As for Printer's Mark Type, choose from Roman or Japanese. You can also set the Trim Mark Weight and offset from the art.
- **Bleeds:** This relates to how the art bleeds or extends off the page. This is used to ensure the art prints to the edge. Choose the top, bottom, left, and right. There's a Link button that's on by default, so if you change one, the rest change in synchrony.

The Output pane offers these options:

- **Mode:** This controls whether the print is a Composite (all colors together) or a Separation (each color plate printed on its own page). Depending on your printer configuration, you may have an In-Rip Separation option. This option is for raster-image processors that can perform the separation.
- **Emulsion:** This controls the positioning of the emulsion layer. Up (Right Reading) means that the layer is facing you, and you can read the text. Down (Right Reading) means that the layer is facing away from you, and the type is readable when facing away.
- **Image:** This controls whether the print is a Negative or a Positive.
- **Printer Resolution:** This lets you change the printer's resolution (lines per inch/dots per inch). You can go only as high in resolution as your printer allows. You can always go lower in resolution.

- **Convert All Spot Colors to Process & Overprint Black check boxes:** These check boxes control whether all spot colors print as process or black overprints.

- **Document Ink Options:** This controls how the ink is printed or converts a spot color to a process color.

The Graphics pane offers these options:

- **Paths:** The Flatness setting adjusts the lines. Curved lines are defined by lots of tiny straight lines. The more accurate to the curved path, the better the quality and the slower it is to print. The lower accuracy to the path, the faster it prints, but the quality may not be as high as you might want.

- **Fonts:** This controls how PostScript fonts are downloaded to the printer. Some fonts are stored in the printer, but others that aren't standard on your printer can either be held on the printer or your computer.

- **Options:** The other options under Graphics are setting the PostScript language and Data format for type. You can check the Compatible Gradient and Gradient Mesh printing by converting the gradient or gradient mesh to a JPEG format. This area is also where you're informed of your Document Raster Effects Resolution (choose Effect ⇨ Document Raster Effects Settings).

The Color Management pane offers these options:

- **Print Method:** The Print Method lists the Color Handling (whether the printer or Illustrator handles the colors), Printer Profile (the color management profile that you want to use), and Rendering Intent (the rendering intent to use when converting colors to a profile space).

The Advanced pane offers these options:

- **Print as Bitmap:** Click this check box to have your file print as a bitmapped image. This is useful to see a quick printout without the quality.

- **Overprint and Transparency Flattener Options:** In this area, you choose whether you want to Simulate, Preserve, or Discard Overprints. You also choose the resolution from three presets or specify a custom resolution.

The Summary area lists the summary of the whole file. All the printing options you've chosen are listed here, and any warnings are listed at the bottom.

 **Choosing Level I PostScript options reduces errors when printing to an older printer.**

 **When an illustration doesn't print, always choose Print Detailed Report. That way, you can read exactly what the error was.**

 **Always save your file before printing.**

Working with gray colors

When you print a full-color illustration on a black-and-white printer, Illustrator substitutes gray values for the process colors. In this way, the program creates the illusion that each color has a separate, distinct gray value. Of course, each color can't have its own unique gray value, so the colors have to overlap at some point.

Magenta is the darkest process color, ranging from 0% to 73% gray. Therefore, the darkest magenta prints is 73% gray. Cyan is the next darkest, ranging from 0% to 57% gray. Yellow is extremely light, ranging from 0% to only 11% gray. Figure 18.3 shows a comparison of the four process colors at various settings and their printed results. The four bars show different values, indicated above the bars, for each process color. Within each bar is the percent of black that prints when you print that color at that percentage to a black-and-white printer.

FIGURE 18.3

This shows how colors appear when printed on a black-and-white laser printer.

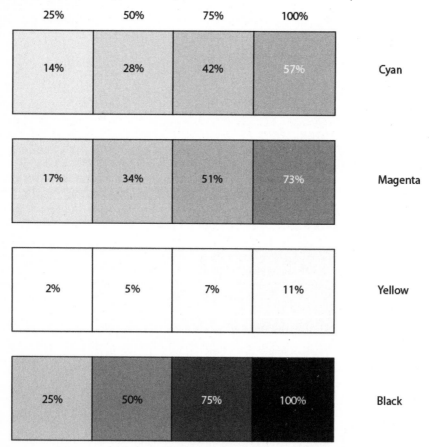

Different printers may produce different tints of gray. Lower-resolution printers, such as 300-dpi laser printers, don't create an accurate gray tint because they use dots that are too large to create accurate tint patterns.

Using the Separation Setup

After you choose File ➪ Print and then click the Output option on the left, the Print dialog box presents the Output pane, as shown in Figure 18.4. The left side shows how the illustration is aligned on the page and which elements print with the illustration. The right side contains all the options for how the illustration is to print on the page.

The picture on the left side initially shows the illustration on a portrait-oriented page, even if land-scape is selected in Illustrator.

Understanding the printer's marks and bleeds

The various marks shown on the page are the printer's marks defaults. The *trim marks* are used for cutting the image after it's printed. The *registration marks* are used when printing separations, and you can line up the registration marks to ensure that the print doesn't shift and all looks as you planned.

The *bleeds* define how much of the illustration can be outside of the Bounding Box and still print. The default for bleed is 18 points, regardless of the size of the Bounding Box. To change the bleed, type a distance in points in the Bleed text field in the Marks and Bleed area. As you type the num-bers, the bleed changes dynamically.

Bleeds are useful when you want an illustration to go right up to the edge of the page. You need to account for bleed when you create an illustration in Illustrator so that the illustration is the correct size with x amount of bleed.

Changing printer information

Illustrator uses a *PostScript Printer Description* (PPD) file to customize the output for your specific printer. To change the PPD, click the arrow at the right edge of the PPD dropdown list (popup menu) in the Output area of the Print dialog box. Choose the PPD file that's compatible with your printer.

NOTE PPDs were created with specific printers in mind. Unpredictable and undesirable results can occur when you use a PPD for a different printer than the one for which it's intended. If you don't have a PPD for your printer and must use a substitute, always test the substitute PPD before relying on it to perform correctly.

FIGURE 18.4

This shows the Output options, with a separation setup selected.

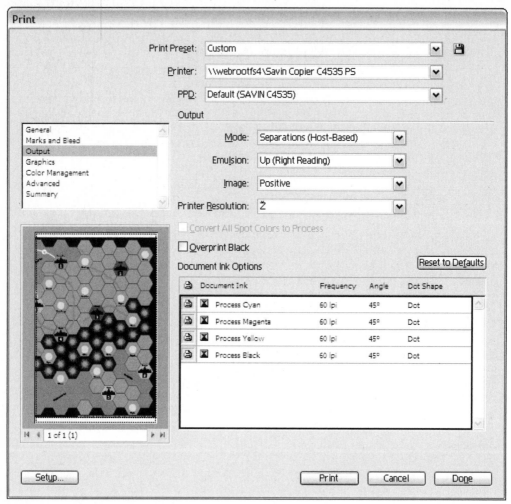

If your printer's PPD is not included with Illustrator, you may be able to get it directly from the printer manufacturer by visiting the manufacturer's Web site.

When you choose a different PPD file, the information in the main panel changes to reflect the new selection. Certain default settings in the lists are activated at this time. You can change the settings at any time, but most of them revert to the defaults if you choose a new PPD.

Changing the page size

In the General pane of the Print dialog box, the Media section has a dropdown list (popup menu) that shows the available page sizes for the printer whose PPD is selected. For laser printers, few page and envelope sizes are supported. For imagesetters, many sizes are supported, and an Other option allows you to specify the size of the page on which you want to print.

Imagesetters print on rolls of paper or film. Depending on the width of the roll, you may want to print the image sideways. For example, on a Linotronic 180 or 230 imagesetter, paper and film rolls are commonly 12 inches wide. For letter-size pages, you should click the Transverse check box to print the letter-size page with the short end along the length of the roll. For a tabloid page (11 inches × 17 inches), don't click the Transverse check box because you want the long edge (17 inches) of the page to be printed along the length of the roll. If you click Transverse for a tabloid-size document, 5 of the 17 inches are cropped off because the roll is not wide enough. As always, when trying something new with printing, run a test or two before sending a large job.

NOTE The page size that you choose in the Size dropdown list (popup menu) determines the size of the page on the left side of the main panel. The measurements next to the name of the page size aren't the page measurements; instead, they're the measurements of the imageable area for that page size. The imageable-area dimensions are always less than the dimensions of the page so that the margin marks can fit on the page with the illustration.

Changing the orientation

The Orientation setting controls how the illustration is placed on the page. You have four choices: portrait, landscape, portrait reversed, and landscape reversed.

Choosing Portrait causes the illustration to print with the sides of the illustration along the longest sides of the page. Choosing Landscape causes the illustration to print with the top and bottom of the illustration along the longest sides of the page.

Usually, the orientation reflects the general shape of the illustration. If the illustration is taller than it is wide, you usually choose Portrait orientation. If the illustration is wider than it is tall, you usually choose Landscape orientation.

NOTE It doesn't matter to Illustrator whether the illustration fits on the page in one or both of these orientations. If you can't see all four edges of the Bounding Box, chances are good that the illustration will be cropped. Orientation is quite different from Transverse. Orientation changes the orientation of the illustration on the page, but Transverse changes the way the page is put on the paper. It's a seemingly small difference but an important one to understand.

Figure 18.5 shows an illustration that's placed on a page in both portrait and landscape orientations, with and without the Transverse option selected.

FIGURE 18.5

An illustration placed on a page in portrait orientation (upper left), landscape orientation (lower left), portrait with Transverse selected (upper right), and landscape with Transverse selected (lower right)

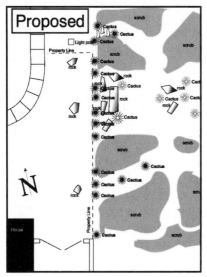

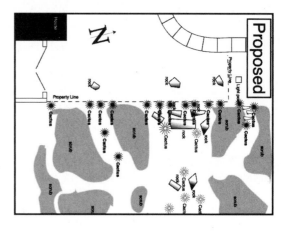

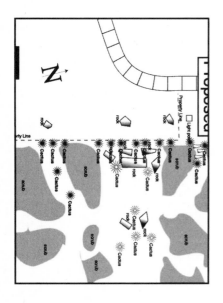

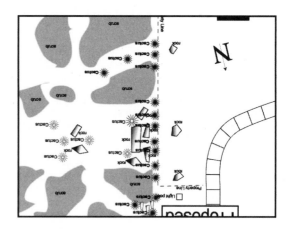

Understanding emulsion

Hang out around strippers (at a commercial printing company . . . get your mind out of the gutter!), and you hear them constantly talk about emulsion up and emulsion down. In printing, *emulsion* is a photosensitive coating that's applied, dried, exposed, and then washed off, leaving the areas to be printed open for ink to pass through. The nonprinting areas retain the emulsion to prevent the ink from passing through. If you have a piece of film from a printer lying around, look at it near a light. One side is shinier than the other side. That side is the side without emulsion. When you're burning plates for presses, the emulsion side (dull side) should always be toward the plate.

In the Output area of the Print dialog box, you use the Emulsion option to control which side the emulsion goes on. If you're printing negatives on film, choose Down (Right Reading) from the Emulsion dropdown list (popup menu). For printing on paper, just to see what the separations look like, choose Up (Right Reading). Always consult with your printer for the correct way to output film.

> **TIP** Although wrong reading isn't an option in the Separation Setup dialog box, you can reverse an illustration by choosing the opposite emulsion setting. In other words, Down (right reading) is also Up (wrong reading), and Up (right reading) is also Down (wrong reading).

Thinking of the emulsion as the toner in a laser printer may help you understand this concept better. If the toner is on the top of the paper, you can read it fine, as always (Up emulsion, right reading). If the toner is on the bottom of the paper and you can read the illustration only when you place the paper in front of a light, the emulsion is Down, right reading. Thinking along these lines helped me when I was new to the printing industry, and it should also help you.

Changing from positive to negative to positive

You use the Image dropdown list (popup menu) to switch between printing positive and negative images. Usually, you use a negative image for printing film negatives and a positive image for printing on paper. The default for this setting, regardless of the printer chosen or PPD selected, is Positive.

Working with different colors

At the lower right of the Output pane of the Print dialog box, the Document Ink Options list displays where you can choose different colors and then set them to print or not print and also set Custom Colors to process separately.

The list of colors contains only the colors that are used in that particular illustration. At the top of the list of separation colors are the four process colors if they or spot colors that contain those process colors are used in the illustration. Below the process colors is a list of all the spot colors in the document.

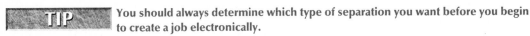

TIP   If the illustration has any guides in it, their colors are reflected in the Document Ink Options list. From looking at the preview of the illustration in the Output options in the Print dialog box, you can't easily determine that these blank separations will print. The best thing to do is clear all guides by choosing View ➪ Guides ➪ Clear Guides.

By default, all process colors are set to print, and all spot colors are set to convert to process colors. Clicking the Convert All Spot Colors to Process check box toggles between converting everything (selected) and retaining spot colors (deselected).

Each color in the list has its own frequency and angle. Don't change the angle or frequency for process colors because the separator has automatically created the best values for the process colors at the halftone screen you've specified. Instead, ensure that any spot colors that may print have different angles from each other so that no moiré (wavy) patterns develop from them.

As soon as you type new values or choose different options using the color list, the changes are applied.

Outputting a Color-Separated File

Color separations are necessary to print a color version of an illustration on most printing presses. Each separation creates a plate that's affixed to a round drum on a printing press. Ink that's the same color as that separation is applied to the plate, which is pressed against a sheet of paper. Because the ink adheres only to the printing areas of the plate, an image is produced on paper. Some printing presses have many different drums and can print a four-color job in one run. Other printing presses have only one or two drums, so the paper has to pass through the press four or two times, respectively, to print a four-color job.

The two types of color separations are process color separations and spot color separations. Each type has its own advantages and drawbacks, and you can use either type or a combination of both types for any print job. Process color separations typically use four colors (cyan, magenta, yellow, and black) to reproduce the entire range of colors. Spot color separations use a custom-mixed ink to precisely render a specific color.

TIP   You should always determine which type of separation you want before you begin to create a job electronically.

Using spot color separations

Jobs that are printed with spot colors are often referred to as two-color or three-color jobs when two or three colors are used. Although you can use any number of colors, most spot color jobs contain only a few colors.

Spot color printing is most useful when you're using two or three distinct colors in a job. For example, if I need only black and green to create a certain illustration, I would use only black and a green custom color for all the objects in the illustration.

There are three main reasons for using spot color separations rather than process color separations:

- It's cheaper. Spot color printing requires a smaller press with fewer drums. For process color separations, you usually need to use a press with four drums or run the job through a smaller press a number of times.

- Spot colors are cleaner, brighter, and smoother than the same colors that you create as process colors. To obtain a green process color, for example, you need to mix both cyan and yellow on paper. Using one spot color results in a perfectly solid area of color.

- You can't duplicate certain spot colors, especially fluorescent and metallic colors, with process colors.

Learning Printing from the Experts

If you've never visited a printing company, make a point to visit one and take a tour. Most printing companies have staff members who are more than willing to explain their equipment and various printing processes. In a 30-minute tour with a knowledgeable guide, you can learn enough to save yourself hours of work, money, and misunderstandings.

When you talk to printing reps, find out what type of media they want your work on. Printing companies commonly use imagesetters that can output the job for you, and some companies even perform this service at no charge or for a significant discount if you have the job printed there.

Imagesetters are similar to laser printers, except that they produce images with a very high dpi, from 1273 to 3600 and sometimes higher. Imagesetters can print directly to RC (resin-coated) paper or to film negatives (or positives). The paper or film runs through the imagesetter and then must run through a developing process for the images and text to appear.

Most printing company salespeople can tell you when to give them negs (film negatives) and paper and which service provider to use if they don't have an imagesetter in-house. Many can tell you which software their clients prefer and which software packages create problems, and they can give you tips that can help you get your project through the process without problems.

A service provider is a company that has on its premises an imagesetter and whose function is to provide the general community of desktop publishers with imagesetter output at a cost between $7 and $40 per page. Service providers often have color output capabilities and offer disk conversion and other services that are sometimes needed by desktop publishers.

continued

continued

Better yet, do what I did: Work at a printing company for a short period of time. The first job I had out of college, working in the prepress department of a four-color commercial printer, taught me more than I learned in four years of school. The experience instilled in me some of the most important basic skills for graphics design that I still use and need every day. Ever wonder why your printer gets so grumpy when you say your files won't be available until two days past the promised date? Working at a printing company can give you an understanding of job scheduling — an art of prophecy and voodoo that gives ulcers to printing company managers and supervisors.

The more you know about printing and your printer, the better your print job will turn out and the fewer hassles you have to deal with.

Illustrator creates spot colors whenever you specify a spot color in a swatch. If you use six spot colors and black, you could print seven spot color separations.

Spot colors do have their limitations and disadvantages. The primary limitation of using only spot colors is that the number of colors is restricted to the number of color separations that you want to produce. Remember that the cost of a print job is directly related to the number of different inks in the job.

The cutoff point for using spot colors is usually three colors. When you use four spot colors, you limit yourself to four distinct colors and use as many colors as a process color job that can have an almost infinite number of colors. However, spot color jobs of six colors aren't unusual. Sometimes, people use more than three spot colors to keep colors distinct and clear. Each of the six colors is bright, vibrant, and distinct from its neighbors, whereas different process colors seem to fade into each other.

NOTE Spot colors are often incorrectly referred to as Pantone colors. Pantone is a brand name for a color-matching system. You can choose Pantone colors as custom colors and use them in Illustrator, and you can print them as either spot colors or as process colors.

Printing process color separation

Process color separation, also known as four-color separation, creates almost any color by combining cyan, magenta, yellow, and black inks. By using various combinations of different tints of each of these colors, you can reproduce many of the colors (more than 16 million of them) that the human eye can see.

Process printing uses a subtractive process. You start with bright white paper and darken the paper with various inks. Cyan, magenta, and yellow are the subtractive primaries (unlike additive monitor colors of red, green, and blue), and black is added to create true black, a color that the primaries together don't do very well.

The use of process color separation is advisable in two situations:

- When the illustration includes color photographs
- When the illustration contains more than three different colors

Choosing numerous colors

Everyone always says that you can create as many colors as you could ever want when you're using process colors. Maybe.

In Illustrator, you can specify colors up to $^1/_{100}$% accuracy. As a result, 10,000 different shades are available for each of the four process colors. So, theoretically, $10,000^4$, or 10,000,000,000,000,000, different colors should be available, which is 10 quadrillion or 10 million billion. Any way you look at it, you have a heck of a lot of color possibilities.

Unfortunately, most imagesetters and laser printers can produce only 256 different shades for each color. This limitation of the equipment (not PostScript) drops the number of available colors to 256^4, or 4,294,967,296, which is about 4.3 billion colors — only 1 billionth of the colors that Illustrator can specify.

This limitation is fortunate for humans, however, because the estimate is that we can detect a maximum of 100 different levels of gray — probably less. As a result, we can view only 100^4, or 100,000,000, different colors.

You can, though, run into a problem when you preview illustrations. An RGB monitor (which is the color format used on computers) can theoretically display up to 16.7 million colors if each red, green, and blue pixel can be varied by 256 different intensities.

Another problem is that about 30% of the colors that you can view on an RGB monitor can't be reproduced by using cyan, magenta, yellow, and black inks on white paper. You can't create these unprintable colors in Illustrator, but you can create them in most other drawing and graphics software packages. These colors are for on-screen viewing pleasure only.

The secret to process color separation is that the four colors that make up all the different colors are themselves not visible. Each color is printed as a pattern of tiny dots, angled differently from the dots of the other three colors. The angles of each color are very important. If the angles are off even slightly, a noticeable wavy pattern commonly known as a moiré emerges.

The colors are printed in a specific order — usually cyan, magenta, yellow, and then black. Although the debate continues about the best order in which to print the four colors, black is always printed last.

To see the dots for each color, use a magnifying device to look closely at something that's pre-printed and in full color. Even easier, look at the Sunday comics, which have bigger dots than most other printed pieces. The different color dots in the Sunday comics are quite visible, and the only colors used are cyan, magenta, yellow, and black.

The size of the dots that produce each of these separations is also important. The smaller the dots, the smoother the colors appear. Large dots (such as those in the Sunday comics) can actually take away from the illusion of a certain unified color because the different color dots are visible.

Figure 18.6 shows how process colors are combined to create new colors. In the figure, the first four rows show very large dots. The top three rows are cyan, magenta, and yellow. The fourth row is all four process colors combined, and the bottom row shows how the illustration looks when you print it.

Process color printing is best for photographs because photographs originate from a continuous tone that's made on photographic paper from film instead of dots on a printing press.

In Illustrator, you can convert custom colors to process colors either before or during printing. To convert custom colors to process colors before printing, select any objects that have a specific custom color and tint and then click the Process Color icon that appears in the Color panel. The color is converted to its process color counterpart, and all selected objects are filled with the new process color combination.

After you click the Process Color icon, if the selected objects become filled with white and the triangles for each process color are at 0%, you've selected objects that contain different colors or tints. Undo the change immediately.

To ensure that you select only objects that have the same color, select one of the objects and then choose Select ➪ Same ➪ Stroke Color. Objects that have different strokes or objects with different tints of the same color aren't selected.

You can convert custom colors to process colors in the Output options in the Print dialog box and in many page-layout programs.

Combining spot and process color separations

You can couple spot colors with process colors in Illustrator simply by creating both process and named spot colors in a document.

Usually, you add spot colors to process colors for these reasons:

- You're using a company logo that has a specific color. By printing that color as a spot color, you make it stand out from the other coloring. In addition, color is more accurate when it comes from a specific ink rather than from a process color combination. Often, the logo is a Pantone color that doesn't reproduce true to form when you use process color separation.

- You need a color that you can't create by using process colors. Such colors are most often metallic or fluorescent, but they can be any number of Pantone colors or other colors that you can't match with process colors.

FIGURE 18.6

The top three rows display cyan, magenta, and yellow. The fourth row displays their combination. The fifth row displays the colors when they print.

- You need a varnish for certain areas of an illustration. A varnish is a glazed type of ink that results in a shiny area wherever you use the varnish. You commonly use varnishes on titles and logos and over photographs.

- You need a light color over a large area. The dots that make up process colors are most noticeable in light colors, but by using a spot color to cover the area with a solid sheet of ink that has no dots, you can make the area smoother and enhance it visually.

In some circumstances, you need to use a spot color as both a spot color and a process color. Normally, you can't do both, but the following steps describe one way to circumvent this problem:

1. If the color doesn't exist as a swatch, create a swatch for the color.

2. In the Swatch Options dialog box (double-click the swatch), choose Spot Color from the dropdown list (popup menu) and then click OK.

3. Duplicate the swatch by dragging it on top of the New Swatch icon (the little piece of paper).

4. In the Swatch Options dialog box for the duplicated swatch, choose Process Color from the dropdown list (popup menu) and then click OK.

 **You can tell which swatch is which by looking at the lower-right corner of the swatches; the spot color swatch has a white triangle with a spot in it, whereas the process swatch is solid.**

Using Other Applications to Print

Many other software programs, particularly page-layout software programs, incorporate color-separation capabilities. These programs usually allow you to import Illustrator files that have been saved as Illustrator EPS files.

When you produce color separations from other software, ensure that any custom colors in the Illustrator illustration are present and accessible in the document that the illustration is placed within. Usually, you can set the custom colors to process separately or to spot separately.

 **You can't change the colors of an imported Illustrator EPS document in a page-layout program, so be sure that the colors are correct for the illustration while it's in Illustrator.**

Understanding Trapping

Trapping is one of the most important but least understood issues in all of printing. Trapping is the process of overprinting different colored areas so there won't be any gaps between them.

Traps solve alignment problems when color separations are produced. The most common problem that occurs from misalignment is the appearance of white space between different colors.

NOTE Although Illustrator incorporates a trapping effect, it's not a trap-happy piece of software. For detailed illustrations, it usually isn't worth your time to set the trapping inside Illustrator; instead, you want to have your printer do the work for you.

NOTE The thought of trapping scares many graphic designers, not just because they don't know how to do it but also because they aren't sure what trapping is and what purpose it serves. Understanding the concept of trapping is the hard part; trapping objects is easy (although somewhat tedious in Illustrator).

Figure 18.7 shows a spot color illustration with four colors. The top row shows each of the individual colors. The first illustration in the second row shows how the illustration prints if all the separations are aligned perfectly. The second illustration in the second row shows what happens when the colors are misaligned. The third illustration in the second row shows how the illustration looks when trapped, with black indicating where two colors overprint each other.

This example shows extreme misalignment and excessive trapping; I designed it just as a black-and-white illustration for this book. Ordinarily, the overprinting colors may appear a tiny bit darker, but they don't show as black. I used black so that you can see what parts of the illustration overlap when trapping is used. The trapping in this case is more than sufficient to cover any of the white gaps in the second illustration.

Trapping is created by *spreading* or *choking* certain colors that touch each other in an illustration. To spread a color, enlarge an object's color so that it takes up more space around the edges of the background area. To choke a color, expand the color of the background (by scaling the paths/objects in the background or by stretching the edges with the Direct Selection tool) until it overlaps the edges of an object.

The major difference between a spread and a choke has to do with which object is considered the background and which object is the foreground. The foreground object is the object that traps. If the foreground object is spread, the color of the foreground object is spread until it overlaps the background by a certain amount. If the foreground object is choked, the color of the background around the foreground object is expanded until it overlaps the foreground object by a certain amount.

TIP To determine whether to use a choke or a spread on an object, compare the lightness and darkness of the foreground and background objects. The general rule is that lighter colors expand or contract into darker colors.

Figure 18.8 shows the original misaligned illustration and two ways of fixing it with trapping. The second star has been spread by 1 point, and the third star has been choked by 1 point.

FIGURE 18.7

This spot color illustration shows individual colors (top) and aligned, misaligned, and trapped composites.

Orange

Yellow

Blue

Red

Perfect alignment

Poor alignment

Poor alignment
trapped
(yellow spread)

FIGURE 18.8

The original illustration (left), fixing the star by spreading it 1 point (middle), and fixing the star by choking it 1 point (right)

Original

Blue (star shape)
1-pt spread

Blue (star shape)
1-pt choke

Understanding misaligned color separations

Three common reasons why color separations don't align properly are that the negatives aren't the same size, the plates on the press aren't aligned perfectly when printing, or the design gods have decided that a piece is too perfect and needs gaps between abutting colors. Trapping is required because it's a solution for covering gaps that occur when color separations don't properly align.

Negatives can be different sizes for a number of reasons. When the film was output to an imagesetter, the film may have been too near the beginning or the end of a roll or separations in the same job may have been printed from different rolls. The pull on the rollers, while fairly precise on all but top-of-the-line imagesetters — where it should be perfect — can pull more film through when there's less resistance (at the end of a roll of film) or less film when there's more resistance (at the beginning of a roll of film). The temperature of the film may be different if a new roll is put on in the middle of a job, causing the film to shrink (if it's cold) or expand (if it's warm).

The temperature of the processor may have risen or fallen a degree or two while the film was being processed. Again, cooler temperatures in the chemical bays and in the air dryer as the film exits the process have an impact on the size of the film.

Film negatives usually don't change drastically in size, but they can vary up to a few points on an 11-inch page. That distance is huge when a page has several abutting colors throughout. The change in a roll of film is almost always along the length of the roll, not along the width. The quality of the film is another factor that determines how much the film stretches or shrinks.

Most strippers are quite aware of how temperature affects the size of negatives. A common stripper trick is to walk outside with a freshly processed negative during the colder months to shrink a negative that may have enlarged slightly during processing.

Check with your service provider staff to see how long the processor is warmed before sending jobs through it. If the answer is less than an hour, the chemicals will not be at a consistent temperature, and negatives that are sent through too early will certainly change in size throughout the length of the job. Another question to ask is how often the chemicals are changed and the density checked from the imagesetter. Once a week is acceptable for a good-quality service provider, but the best ones change chemicals and check density once a day.

The plates on a press can be misaligned by either an inexperienced press operator or a faulty press. An experienced press operator knows the press and what to do to get color plates to align properly. A faulty press is one where plates move during printing or aren't positioned correctly. An experienced press operator can determine how to compensate for a faulty press.

No press is perfect, but some of the high-end presses are pretty darn close. Even on those presses, the likelihood that a job with colors that abut one another can print perfectly is not very great.

If a job doesn't have some sort of trapping in it, it probably won't print perfectly, no matter how good the negatives, press, and press operator are.

Knowing how much you need to trap

The amount of trap that you need in an illustration depends on many things, but the deciding factor is what your commercial printer tells you is the right amount.

The most important thing to consider is the quality of the press that the printer uses. Of course, only the printer knows which press your job will run on, so talking to the printer about trapping is imperative.

Other factors to consider include the colors of ink and types of stock used in the job. Certain inks soak into different stocks differently.

Traps range from $^4/_{1000}$ of an inch to $^6/_{1000}$ of an inch. Most traditional printers refer to traps in thousandths of inches, but Illustrator likes values in points for this sort of operation. Figure 18.9 is a chart with traps in increments of $^1/_{1000}$, from $^1/_{1000}$ of an inch to $^{10}/_{1000}$ of an inch, and gives their point measurements. The trapped area is represented by black to be more visible in this example.

FIGURE 18.9

Different trap amounts

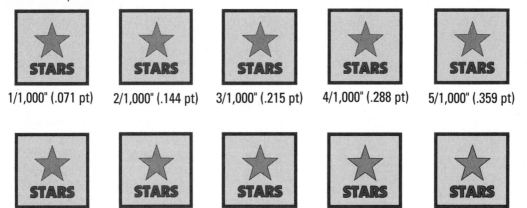

1/1,000" (.071 pt)   2/1,000" (.144 pt)   3/1,000" (.215 pt)   4/1,000" (.288 pt)   5/1,000" (.359 pt)

6/1,000" (.432 pt)   7/1,000" (.503 pt)   8/1,000" (.576 pt)   9/1,000" (.647 pt)   10/1,000" (.720 pt)

Remember that the greater the trap, the less chance that any white gaps will appear, but the trap may actually be visible. Visible traps of certain color pairs can look almost as bad as white space.

Trapping Illustrator files

In Illustrator, you accomplish manual trapping by selecting a path's stroke or fill and setting it to overprint another path's stroke or fill. Overprint can be turned on and off for each object by using the Attributes panel, which is accessed by choosing Window ➪ Attributes. The degree to which the two paths' fills or strokes overlap and overprint is the amount of trap that's used.

The most basic way to create a trap on an object is by giving it a stroke that's either the fill color of the object (to create a spread) or the fill color of the background (to create a choke).

> **TIP** Be sure to make the width of any stroke that you use for trapping twice as wide as the intended trap because only half the stroke (one side of the path) actually overprints a different color. In some circumstances, fixing a stroke that's initially not wide enough can be difficult.

Another way to create a trap is to use the Pathfinder panel. Follow these steps:

1. **Select all pieces of art that are overlapping or abutting.**

2. **Choose Trap from the Pathfinder panel.** The Trap button appears when you choose Options from the Pathfinder panel's popup menu.

3. **Type the width into the Height/Width text field.**

4. **Click OK to apply the trap.**

Using complex trapping techniques in Illustrator

The preceding trap explanations are extremely simplified examples of trapping methods in Illustrator. In reality, objects never seem to be a solid color, and if they are, they're never on a solid background. In addition, most illustrations contain multiple overlapping objects that have their own special trapping needs.

I consider trapping to be complex when I can't just go around selecting paths and applying the trap quickly. Complex trapping involves several techniques:

- **Create a separate layer for trapping objects.** By keeping trapping on its own layer, you make myriad options available that aren't available if the trapping is intermixed with the rest of the artwork. Place the new layer above the other layers. Lock all the layers but the trapping layer so that the original artwork is not modified. You can turn trapping on and off by hiding the entire layer or turning off the Print option in the Layers Options dialog box.

- **Use the round joins and ends options in the Stroke portion of the Stroke panel for all trapping strokes.** Round joins and ends are much less conspicuous than the harsh corners and 90° angles of other joins and ends, and they blend smoothly into other objects.

- **Trap gradations by stroking them with paths that are filled with overprinting gradients.** You can't fill strokes with gradients, but you can fill paths with gradients. You can make any stroke into a path by selecting it and then choosing Outline from the Pathfinder panel. After you transform the stroke into a path, fill it with the gradient and then click the Overprint Fill check box (in the Attributes panel) for that path.

> **NOTE** Whenever I start a heavy-duty trapping project, I always work on a copy of the original illustration. Wrecking the original artwork is just too easy when you add trapping.

When Trapping Yourself Isn't Worth It

Before you spend the long amounts of time that complex trapping entails and modify your illustration beyond recognition (at least in Outline mode), you may want to reconsider whether you should do the trapping yourself.

If you estimate that trapping your job requires several hours of work, the chances of doing it correctly dwindle significantly. If the illustration includes many crisscrossing blends and gradations or multiple placed images, you may not have the patience to get through the entire process with your sanity intact.

If you determine that you can't do the trapping yourself, you can have it done after the fact with Luminous TrapWise or Island Trapper or you can have a service provider with special output devices create trapping automatically. These services undoubtedly cost more than doing the trapping yourself, but it gets done right, which is the important thing.

Summary

Printing Illustrator documents can often be quite a bit more complex than simply choosing File ➪ Print. In this chapter, you learned about a number of issues that directly affect the quality of the final printed output, including these:

- Illustrator can be interpreted as a good front end for the PostScript page description language.
- Print separations from within Illustrator.
- Choose whether to print a composite or separations from the Print dialog box.
- Determine separation information in the Output section of the Print dialog box.
- Prevent potential white strips that can appear when a printer isn't perfectly aligned with trapping.
- Output options in the Print dialog box let you specify which colors print and at what angle and frequency they print.

Chapter 19

Creating Web Graphics

In concept, designing for the Web and designing for print are very similar, but in practice, they both offer special tests to the patience of an Illustrator user. In this chapter, I discuss challenges that the designer faces when attempting to present ideas graphically that appeal to the eye and get the right point across. Web design encompasses more than just converting your picas to pixels.

Designing for the Web versus Designing for Print

A Web designer faces specific issues that a print designer never even thinks about. Consider these:

- **A print designer chooses the specific color inks and paper with which to print, giving the designer complete control over how a reader sees it.** A Web designer has no way of knowing what kind of monitor a reader is using to view his or her Web site — a strong yellow color on one screen may look orange or green on another monitor. Monitors also display at different resolutions (older machines may be set to 1024×768, while newer ones may be 1600×1080 or higher), meaning Web designers must make their Web sites work for all of them.

■ **A Web designer is always at the mercy of the Web browser.** In our ever-changing world, you can't know what a reader will use to view your Web site. When the Web first became popular, Netscape Navigator was the browser of choice. Microsoft's Internet Explorer is by far the most prevalent browser out there now. Apple introduced a browser called Safari to run specifically on the Mac platform (and now also runs on Windows). Firefox is also rapidly becoming very popular, as is Opera. Because each browser displays type, uses styles, handles animation, shows frames, and even formats links differently, a Web site in Explorer can look very different from the same Web site in Firefox, Opera, or Safari.

■ **A Web designer must be conscious of how long it takes an average reader to download a page or graphic.** Although high-speed broadband connections are more popular, this is still an issue and limits Web designers from using large full-color images or graphics. You still need to consider how many colors to use, what file types to use, and even what fonts to use.

■ **The most alluring aspect of the Web is interactivity.** Web designers can take advantage of technologies that print designers can only dream of. Examples include having graphics change when a user moves his or her mouse (rollovers), making images come alive with animation. Other advantages are utilizing advanced programming techniques (called scripting) to deliver customized graphics tailored specifically to the reader or displaying a greeting based on the time of day.

> **TIP**   Sometimes, a Web designer actually does know what monitor or system his or her viewers are using. When creating Web sites for use on intranets, which are employee-accessible internal company or organization networks, a designer can take advantage of that knowledge and use it to his or her benefit. For example, if a designer knows that everyone has a Windows computer running Internet Explorer, he or she can design just for that browser and not worry or care what the site may look like in Netscape, Safari, Opera, or Firefox.

Illustrator and the Web — the Basics

Illustrator is a great tool for creating Web graphics because it possesses all the necessary production tools, supports all the standard file types, and offers superb integration with other Web applications, such as Adobe Photoshop, Adobe Dreamweaver, Adobe GoLive, and Adobe Flash. Even more important, because Illustrator is a vector-based application, you can easily repurpose graphics for both print and the Web, which means that you don't have to re-create your artwork for one or the other.

Although in theory you could create an entire HTML Web page using only Illustrator, no one would mistake Illustrator as the only tool you need for Web design. Illustrator's strength is creating graphics for a Web page or designing Web pages for assembly in an HTML editor, such as GoLive or Dreamweaver. Brave designers may also utilize text-based HTML editors, such as BBEdit. Illustrator is also perfect for creating vector-based graphics that you import into Flash for creating truly interactive content.

Illustrator is well-equipped to handle Web graphics, and before you actually run off and start creating them, I want to discuss some of the fundamental tools and functions that you need to understand. The first idea to remember is that all Web graphics are in RGB mode, so when you create a new document, ensure that you choose RGB. If you forget, you can always choose File ⇨ Document Color Mode ⇨ RGB to change to RGB color mode, as shown in Figure 19.1.

FIGURE 19.1

Be sure to specify RGB for the document's color mode for Web documents.

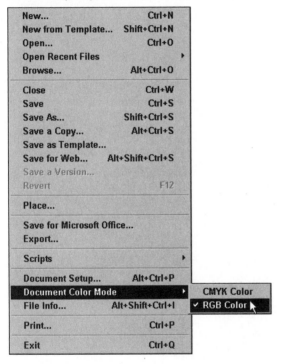

Understanding Pixel Preview mode

Sometimes, you just have to face the facts.

Web graphics are always displayed in pixels. Even vector-based Web formats, such as Flash and SVG, end up displaying on a computer screen, which means that they're viewed in pixel form. Although some monitors display at 96 ppi or 105 ppi (pixels per inch), most still display graphics at 72 ppi. In either case, the resolution is much less than the 3450 dpi (dots per inch) that you see from your high-end imagesetter or even the 600 dpi that you see on printouts from your laser printer.

At such a low resolution, curved lines and text appear jaggy and can make your graphics look like they came from the early 1980s (*Space Invaders* and *Asteroids* come to mind). To compensate for low resolution on monitors, software programs usually employ a technique called *anti-aliasing*. By applying a gentle blur to the edge of your text or graphics, you eliminate the jaggedness of your image, replacing it with a smooth transition and a clean look, as shown in Figure 19.2. Illustrator uses anti-aliasing to allow you to preview your graphics and text on-screen beautifully. Don't worry; your printed output remains unaffected and your text looks crisp and sharp when you print from your laser printer or imagesetter.

Because the delivery medium for Web graphics is a computer screen, a Web designer cares very much about anti-aliasing. For one reason, although soft edges on your graphic may make large text and graphics pretty on-screen, they can also make small text fuzzy and unreadable, as shown in Figure 19.3.

FIGURE 19.2

This demonstrates how art appears on a monitor with (left) and without (right) anti-aliasing.

Small anti-aliased text can be very hard to read.

Small size text can be hard to read

Illustrator has a special preview mode called Pixel Preview (choose View ➪ Pixel Preview) that displays the graphics on-screen as actual rasters — the exact way they would display in a Web browser. Using Pixel Preview mode lets you know exactly how anti-aliasing affects your graphics. Because anti-aliasing is based on your monitor's pixel grid (see the sidebar on comparing lines), moving your art around can affect its overall appearance. The first step in creating Web graphics from Illustrator is to turn on Pixel Preview. You can tell when you're in Pixel Preview mode by looking at the title bar of your document, as indicated in Figure 19.4.

The title bar indicates what view mode you're in (Windows is on top and Mac is on the bottom).

fg1903.ai @ 80% (RGB/Pixel Preview)

fg1903.ai @ 80% (RGB/Pixel Preview)

CROSS-REF For more on viewing modes, see Chapter 2.

TIP You can turn off anti-aliasing to see how it affects your display by going into the General Preferences dialog box (choose Edit (Illustrator) ➪ Preferences ➪ General) and deselecting the check box for Anti-aliased Artwork. All artwork also appears anti-aliased when you're in Pixel Preview mode. Disabling anti-aliasing doesn't make your graphics look pretty on-screen, but it does slightly enhance the performance of Illustrator.

Thin Black Lines versus Fat Gray Lines

Sometimes, the process of anti-aliasing produces results that are less appealing to the eye. Good examples of this are thin lines and small text. Anti-aliasing can make a thin black line look like a fat gray line or it can make small crisp text an unreadable mush of pixels. Fortunately, Illustrator provides you with the tools to avoid these issues.

First, you should understand why these things happen. A pixel can either be on or off — you can't have a pixel that's only half-colored. By default, Illustrator always draws objects that snap to an invisible pixel grid. (You can turn off this feature by deselecting View ⇨ Snap to Pixel when you're in Pixel Preview mode.) Illustrator also paints strokes on the center of a path. This means that if you choose a 1-pixel stroke, Illustrator centers it on the path, effectively placing half a pixel on either side of the stroke. However, because you can't fill only half a pixel with color, Illustrator uses anti-aliasing to turn that 1-pixel black line into a 2-pixel gray line. If you turn off the Snap to Pixel option and then move the line half a pixel in either direction (via the Move dialog box, accessed by double-clicking on the Selection tool), you see the 2-pixel gray line turn into a 1-pixel black line, as shown in this first figure.

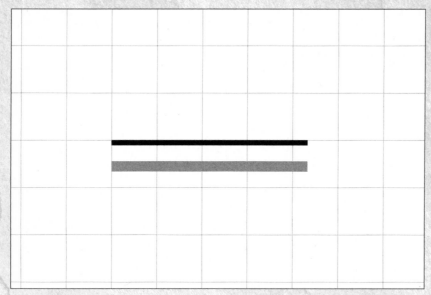

A 1-pixel black line snapped to the pixel grid appears as a 2-pixel gray line when anti-aliased.

Small text actually reads better without anti-aliasing at all. Here, you can use Illustrator's Effect menu to your advantage:

1. **Type some small text.**
2. **Choose Effect ⇨ Rasterize.** The Rasterize dialog box, as shown here, opens.

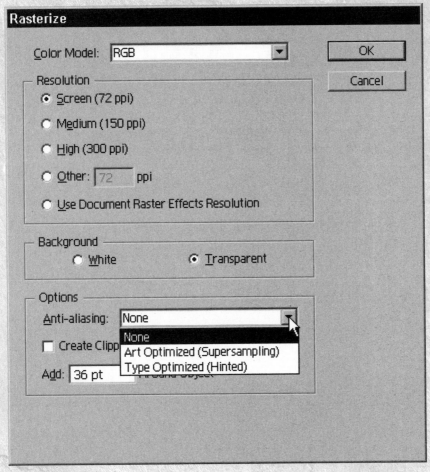

The Rasterize dialog box

continued

continued

3. **In the Anti-aliasing dropdown list (popup menu) in the Options section, choose None.**

4. **Click OK.** The next figure shows text with and without anti-aliasing.

Web design

Web design

Text with (top) and without (bottom) anti-aliasing applied

Because applying Rasterize in this way is a Live Effect, you can still make edits to your text with the Text tool as normal, yet the text can never be anti-aliased, as evidenced by the last figure. You can also use this technique for thin rules and lines.

Using Web-safe colors

This section looks at a topic that many Web developers consider ancient history. Although the idea of Web-safe colors was quite important in the dark ages of Web development 10 years or so ago, very few people still surf the Web using the antique computers whose extreme limitations caused the need for limiting to a select few the number of colors used. Sure, Illustrator still offers support for Web-safe colors, but you can probably ignore the whole issue safely and not lose any sleep over the possibility that someone visiting a Web site you designed can't see the exact color you intended.

As mentioned earlier, one of the problems that a Web designer faced in the past was choosing a color that looked consistent, no matter what computer you viewed the Web site on. First, I want to explore the way monitors displayed colors. The average monitor could display at least 256 different colors on-screen at any one time. So, what if one of the colors that you pick wasn't one of those 256 colors? In such cases, the monitor used a process called *dithering* to simulate that color on-screen.

Dithering is a process in which different colored pixels are placed in a pattern to match the desired color. This process is similar to four-color process printing, where dots of cyan, magenta, yellow, and black are used to simulate other colors. However, dithering can sometimes result in noticeable and ugly patterns, much like a moiré (wavy) pattern. Besides not displaying the exact color you want, dithering can make text or parts of your Web site unreadable (and you thought Web design was easy, right?).

To deal with this issue, developers came up with *Web-safe colors*, which are basically colors that you know display correctly without dithering on any computer. Is it magic? Believe it or not, it's actually math. Windows and Mac computers both had 256 standard system colors. But they didn't use the same 256 colors for their system palettes. When you actually matched the two standard system palettes, only 216 colors were identical; the other 40 were different. This means that you could safely specify 216 colors that were guaranteed to display without dithering on any computer.

Illustrator has long had a Web-safe color palette. You access this palette by going to the Swatches panel menu, choosing Open Swatch Library, and selecting Web. All colors listed in this palette are Web-safe colors. You can also pick Web-safe colors directly from the Color panel. To do so, choose Web Safe RGB from the Color panel's popup menu, as shown in Figure 19.5. When you drag the color sliders, Illustrator snaps to Web-safe colors. Clicking the color bar in the Color panel allows you to choose a color that's outside the Web-safe color gamut, and if you do so, Illustrator displays an out-of-gamut icon that looks like a 3-D cube, as shown in Figure 19.6. Clicking that cube snaps your color to the nearest Web-safe color.

Understanding hexadecimal colors

Hexa-*what?* No, I'm not trying to put a spell on you. In HTML-speak, colors are usually defined by hexadecimal code, which is based on a base-16 number system, where each digit is a number from 0 to F (15). Although you may not find it very intuitive to call a color FFFF00 (Red 255, Green 255, Blue 0) instead of yellow, hex values allow designers to use specific colors (after all, yellow comes in plenty of shades). When you have the Color panel set to Web Safe RGB mode, you can type hexadecimal values for a specific color. If you open the Web-safe color panel, Illustrator also displays hexadecimal codes if you mouse over the swatches, as shown in Figure 19.7. You can also type hex values directly into the Find text field to jump directly to a color.

FIGURE 19.5

Choosing the Web-safe RGB option in the Color panel's popup menu

FIGURE 19.6

The out-of-gamut warning informs you that your current color selection is not a Web-safe color.

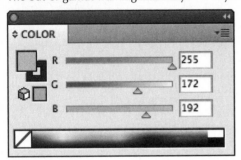

FIGURE 19.7

Hexadecimal values display in the Web-safe color panel when you point to a color swatch.

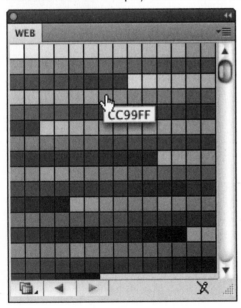

Optimizing and Saving Web Graphics

So, you've created your lovely graphic and now it's time to save it in a format that a Web browser can understand and display. Back in the old days, Web designers were forced to export graphics with all these different settings and then open those graphics in a Web browser to see how they looked. More often than not, they ended up repeating this process until the graphics looked just right.

The exporting process is difficult because there's an important balance between file size and file appearance. In general, the more colorful and complex a graphic is, the larger its file size. But the larger the file size, the longer it takes to download the image. Average Web surfers aren't very patient, and if it takes too long to load a page, they move on to another one. So, designers are forced to find that happy medium — an image that looks good enough but that also downloads fast enough.

 **Two kinds of compression are available to you to help make files smaller. One is called *lossless*, which compresses a file without losing any data. The other is *lossy*, which throws out data that's deemed not important (by the mercy of the compression gods). With lossy compression, you usually have control over how much information is tossed — the more data you choose to lose, the higher the compression rate and the smaller the file.**

Introducing the Save for Web & Devices dialog box

Back in the 1990s, Adobe released a product called ImageReady, which gave designers a way to preview how Web graphics look with different file types, compression settings, etc., and to obtain real-time feedback on file size. This product was so monumental that Adobe built the basic ImageReady functionality, called Save for Web & Devices, into Photoshop and Illustrator.

To use the Save for Web & Devices interface, choose File ➪ Save for Web & Devices and you're presented with a dialog box that takes up nearly the entire screen. There's good reason for this because Save for Web & Devices has many different settings and options, as shown in Figure 19.8. The next section discusses what all these options are about. Get comfy; this is where things get busy.

NOTE **As of CS3, all ImageReady functionality was moved into Photoshop.**

Previewing Web graphics

The most notable and most important part of the Save for Web & Devices dialog box is the Preview pane. You can choose to either view your art in Original mode, Optimized, 2 Up, or 4 Up (the latter of which I find the most useful), where you can view your image in up to four ways at once, allowing you to easily choose the best one. Here's how Save for Web & Devices works: You click one preview, choose settings, click another, choose different settings, etc., and then you compare the different versions. You can then pick the one you think is best (all without leaving the dialog box).

FIGURE 19.8

The Save for Web & Devices dialog box offers many options for optimizing your files for the Web.

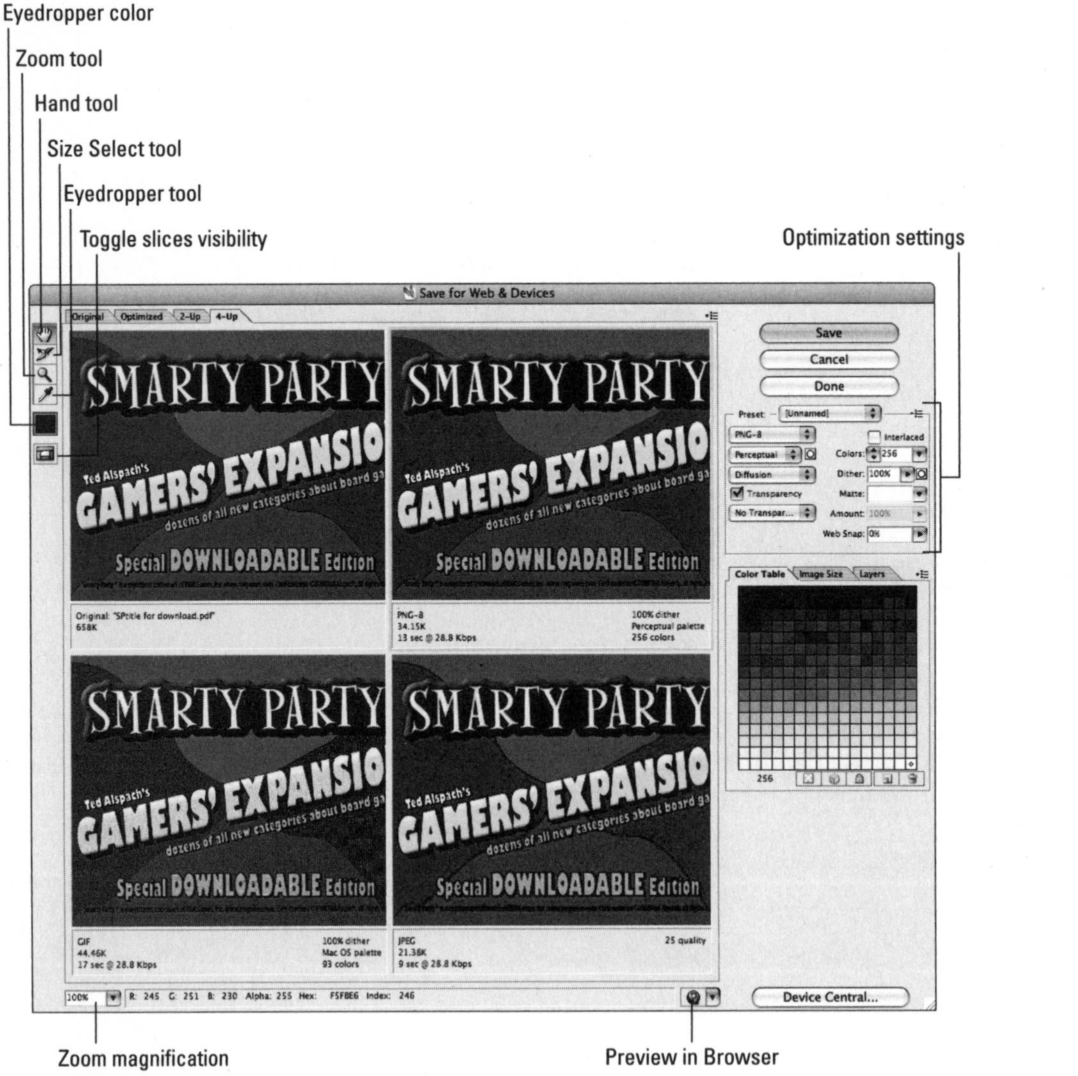

Eyedropper color

Zoom tool

Hand tool

Size Select tool

Eyedropper tool

Toggle slices visibility

Optimization settings

Zoom magnification

Preview in Browser

> **TIP** The Save for Web & Devices dialog box honors Illustrator's Crop Marks for clip
> sizes. So, if you want to easily export images for the Web in a particular size — even
> if you have other art on the page — you can draw a rectangle around the portion you want to
> export. You can then convert the rectangle to crops by choosing Object ⇨ Crop Area ⇨ Make and
> then choose File ⇨ Save for Web & Devices.

Along the left side of the dialog box are the four tools you use in Save for Web & Devices:

- **Hand tool:** Lets you move artwork around in the Preview pane
- **Slice Select tool:** Allows you to choose with which slice you want to work
- **Zoom tool:** Lets you increase or decrease the magnification of your image
- **Eyedropper tool:** Allows you to sample or choose colors from your image (some functions in the Color Table, located in the Preview pane, require you to choose a color)

You also find two additional buttons here:

- **Eyedropper color:** This indicates the color chosen with the Eyedropper tool or you can click it, which displays the color picker, allowing you to type in a specific color.
- **Slice Visibility:** Clicking this button either shows or hides the slices in your Preview pane (not the art that's in them, just the slice boundaries and numbers themselves).

Located on the upper-right side of the Preview pane is a popup menu, as shown in Figure 19.9, where you can choose a connection speed. Save for Web & Devices uses this setting to approximate how long it will take your graphic to load. Figure 19.10 shows that each Preview pane lists an optimization setting along with the estimated download time in the lower left of the pane.

FIGURE 19.9

Choosing a connection speed allows you to optimize the document for different types of connections.

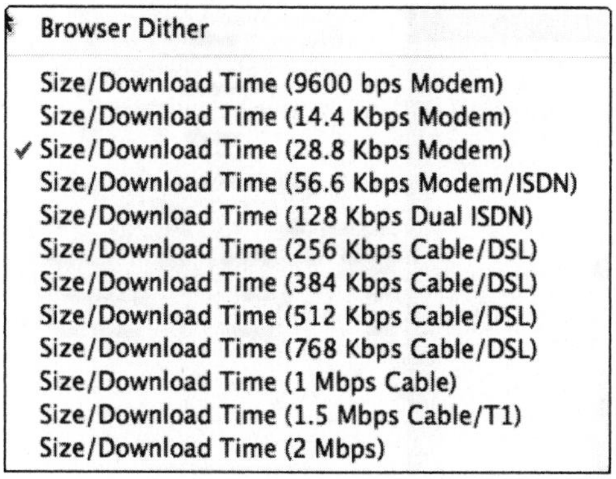

```
  Browser Dither

  Size/Download Time (9600 bps Modem)
  Size/Download Time (14.4 Kbps Modem)
✓ Size/Download Time (28.8 Kbps Modem)
  Size/Download Time (56.6 Kbps Modem/ISDN)
  Size/Download Time (128 Kbps Dual ISDN)
  Size/Download Time (256 Kbps Cable/DSL)
  Size/Download Time (384 Kbps Cable/DSL)
  Size/Download Time (512 Kbps Cable/DSL)
  Size/Download Time (768 Kbps Cable/DSL)
  Size/Download Time (1 Mbps Cable)
  Size/Download Time (1.5 Mbps Cable/T1)
  Size/Download Time (2 Mbps)
```

At the bottom of the panel, you have a zoom popup as well as feedback on colors and one of the handiest features — a button to preview your art in an actual Web browser of choice. Choosing this option launches a Web browser and not only displays the art but also all the information about the file, including the HTML source code to display it, as shown in Figure 19.11.

Along the right side of the Save for Web & Devices dialog box are all the settings you'd ever need (and some you'd probably never need) to customize your Web graphics to perfection. At the top are the Save, Cancel, and Done buttons (click Done if you just want to specify Web settings but don't want to export anything at that time). Pressing Alt (Option) turns the Cancel and Done buttons into Reset and Remember.

Directly below these buttons is where you set the file format options, such as choosing among GIF, JPEG, PNG-8, PNG-24, SWF, SVG, or WBMP and all the specific settings that go with them. Figure 19.12 shows the dropdown list (on a Windows computer) where you choose the file format. You also have a Color Table panel that lets you control specific colors in your image, an Image Size panel, and a Layers panel where you can specify the output of CSS (Cascading Style Sheets) layers (any top-level layer can be specified as a CSS layer here).

FIGURE 19.10

Each Preview pane lists a file-optimization setting and approximate download time in the lower-left corner of its box.

Approximate download times

Approximate download times

Cascading Style Sheets are part of what DHTML (or Dynamic HTML, which is now part of the HTML 4.01 specification) is all about. CSS layers give Web developers the ability to overlap images and slices and to interactively show and hide each layer. You learn more about CSS layers later in this chapter.

FIGURE 19.11

Along with a preview of your graphic, the browser displays all the file's settings.

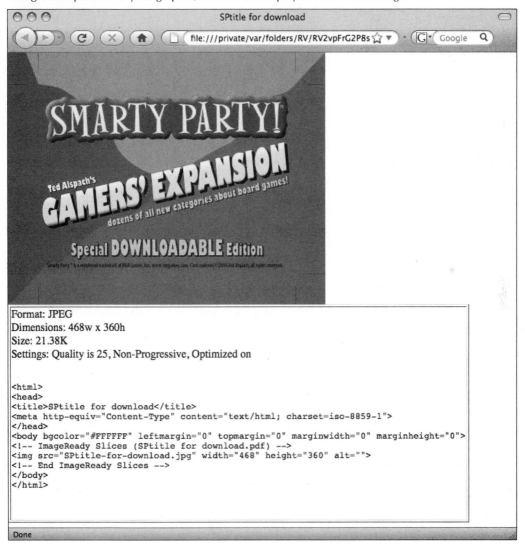

FIGURE 19.12

Choose a file format for the document from the dropdown list (popup menu).

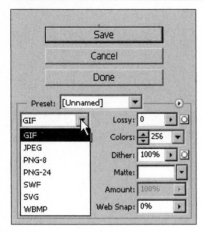

Learning the Web-graphic formats

As stated in the previous section, you have many options for formats in the Save for Web & Devices dialog box. Which one should you use? Each of these format types has advantages and disadvantages, and understanding the difference between them helps immensely as you design and build Web pages. This section thoroughly discusses each format and walks you through the various options associated with each one.

> **NOTE**   You should realize that no single setting is best suited for all Web graphics. Some settings are better suited for certain types of graphics. With experience, you'll come to understand and choose Web formats and settings with ease.

Understanding GIF

A GIF file can contain a maximum of 256 colors, and you can specify your image to have fewer colors to control file size. GIF uses a lossless compression algorithm and basically looks for large areas of pixels that are the same color to save file size. Lossless compression makes this format perfect for most flat color images, such as logos and text headlines.

GIF also has specific settings that can control how the GIF image displays in a Web browser. Because GIF supports a maximum of 256 colors, you have to choose a color-reduction algorithm, which is basically how Illustrator forces all the colors to fit within a specific table of colors. You can go a step further by also specifying exactly how many colors your GIF should contain, which can have a large impact on file size. If your image is just some black text, you can reduce your GIF to 4 or 16 colors with the same visual result — but reap major file size savings.

You can also choose different dither methods (to get colors that aren't in the Color Table to appear in your GIF). Here's where the different Preview panes can really help you choose the best setting for your graphic; GIF also supports transparency, so you can choose one color as a None color, allowing your image to have a transparent background (necessary for placing images on colored backgrounds). The Matte setting works in tandem with this. Anti-aliasing allows colors to blend into each other to create smoother transitions of color, but if you start off with art on a white background, you may see white pixels if you place that graphic on a nonwhite background. If you know the color on which you intend to display your graphic (that is, a background color), specifying that color as a matte ensures that the graphic blends perfectly into the background.

You can also interlace a GIF, which means that the image quickly appears in a browser at a low resolution and then improves in resolution and quality as it continues to load. This allows readers to start seeing graphics on-screen even while the page is still downloading. It's more of a psychological thing than anything else.

GIF files are becoming less and less common, as JPEG files have become the norm for most Web graphics.

Using the JPEG format

If GIF is perfect for flat color images, the JPEG format (pronounced jay-peg) is the perfect format for photos and continuous tone graphics. JPEG was originally created to allow photographers to easily transmit photos electronically. Utilizing a lossy compression algorithm, JPEG can achieve some astonishing file size savings by allowing you to compress a 10MB file to about 1MB in most cases.

Illustrator lets you set different levels of JPEG compression either by choosing options from a popup menu (Low, Medium, High, Very High, or Maximum) or by moving the Quality slider between 0 and 100. In the Save for Web & Devices dialog box, these settings refer to quality, not compression, so a setting of Maximum means maximum quality (and less compression), not maximum compression and lower quality. Because JPEG compression can result in files that have visible artifacts or look chunky (what you end up seeing are blocks of color rather than detail), you also have the option to apply a blur to minimize such artifacts. You can specify a blur setting of up to 2 pixels using the Blur slider (located under the Quality slider).

You can also set JPEG images to progressive, which means that they load incrementally in a browser (similar to GIF's interlacing). You can also specify a matte color for JPEG images (just as with GIFs).

Understanding the PNG format

When GIF became popular, an issue arose with regard to the patent holder who created the compression algorithm (Unisys). To get around possible legal issues, the PNG (Portable Network Graphics) format was born. Pronounced *ping*, the format offers lossless compression similar to GIF but can support up to 32-bit color images and 256-level alpha channels for transparency (far more than the 256-color limit and 1-color alpha of GIF). An *alpha channel* is another term for the part of a file that's transparent. Save for Web & Devices allows users to save PNG images in PNG-8 and PNG-24 format, which offers support for more colors.

Because PNG can support continuous-tone color, the format is great for both flat and photographic images. The additional settings you can apply to PNG images are similar to those that you can apply to GIF images.

Using the WBMP format

You use the Wireless Bitmap format specifically for graphics that you want to display on cell phones and PDA devices. The WBMP format is 1 bit, which means that pixels can be either black or white, so you're limited in choosing between different dithering methods (Diffusion, Pattern, and Noise) and a dithering amount.

 **Dithering** is a process in which different colored pixels are placed in a pattern to match the desired color.

The SWF and SVG options are covered later in this chapter.

Choosing output options

After you decide how to optimize your graphics, you can click Save. This opens the Save Optimized As dialog box, where you can choose to save your graphics in one of three formats. These options are available in the Save as type dropdown list (Format popup menu):

- **Images only:** Saves just the images themselves
- **HTML and Images:** Saves the images and an HTML page that contains them
- **HTML only:** Saves just the HTML code without the images

Not all Web designers work alone. In many cases, a Web designer works hand in hand with a Web developer or someone who either writes code or defines how it's written. Because there are so many ways of authoring HTML, many developers are very sensitive to how they write or how they build Web pages. Adobe is certainly aware of this because at the bottom of the Save Optimized As dialog is a dropdown list (popup menu) called Settings. If you choose Other from the list, as shown in Figure 19.13, you'll be rewarded with the Output Settings dialog box, which is a dream come true for even the pickiest developer.

Choosing Other from the Settings dropdown list (popup menu) gives you additional options.

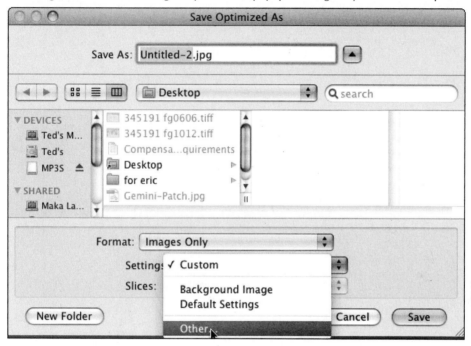

The Output Settings dialog box has four panes, each of which offers a wealth of options:

- **HTML:** Shown in Figure 19.14, this pane allows you to specify exactly how the HTML code is formatted, including options for better integration with other Adobe products. The Always Add Alt Attribute option includes Alt attributes in all img tags, even where you don't specify them, which is a Section 508 requirement (a federal regulation to provide accessibility for those with disabilities) as well as a requirement to pass an HTML 4 or XHTML validation check.

■ **Slices:** Shown in Figure 19.15, this pane gives you control over how tables are coded in HTML and whether CSS layers are generated. You can also choose exactly how each slice is named. Slicing is covered later in this chapter.

FIGURE 19.14

The HTML pane in the Output Settings dialog box

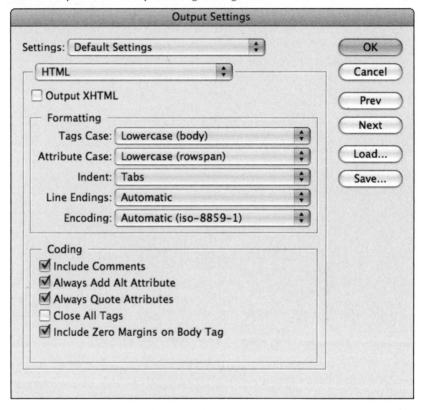

FIGURE 19.15

The Slices pane in the Output Settings dialog box

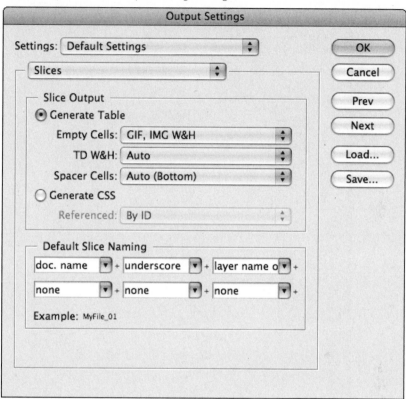

- **Background:** HTML allows you to specify a background color or a background image for the entire page (images *tile*, or repeat, to fill the entire page). In this pane, shown in Figure 19.16, you can specify what color or image you want for the background of your HTML page.

FIGURE 19.16

The Background pane in the Output Settings dialog box

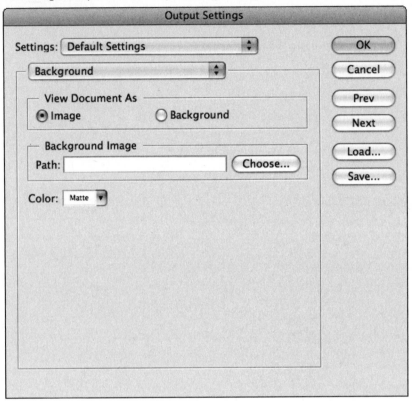

- **Saving Files:** Shown in Figure 19.17, this pane lets you specify exactly how to name your files as well as where you want to save them. The Include XMP option allows you to save metadata along with the files. XMP metadata comes from the File Info dialog box found under the File menu in Illustrator.

FIGURE 19.17

The Saving Files pane in the Output Settings dialog box

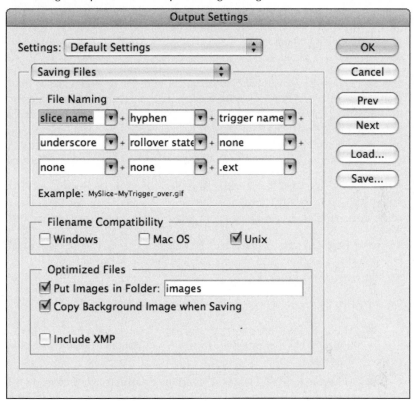

Creating Vector Graphics for the Web

Sure, the Web is a place where pixels abound, but that doesn't mean there's no room for vectors to play. In fact, vector-based Web graphics have become quite popular. They add the benefit of enlarging Web graphics without getting the jaggies and allow you to print better Web graphics from a browser. There are other benefits that I also talk about as I discuss the two most popular vector Web formats — Flash and SVG.

Using Flash graphics

Once upon a time, a company called FutureWave developed a program called FutureSplash Animator that created vectors that you could display in a Web browser. The program let you animate vector shapes and place some cool animation in a Web page. The downside was that very few people knew about it, and to play the animations in a Web browser, you had to install a special plug-in.

One day, a company called Macromedia bought FutureWave and renamed FutureSplash to Flash. It also provided a browser plug-in for Flash to go along with its already-popular Shockwave plug-in, calling it Shockwave Flash (SWF). Then, Adobe acquired Macromedia, and suddenly, the world now uses Adobe Flash. The Flash plug-in is now installed by default in every mainstream Web browser, and it has become the standard for creating interactive and engaging Web sites. Flash support is now even built into Apple's QuickTime video player, many cell phones, and PDAs.

Although Illustrator can't do anywhere near the kinds of things that Adobe Flash can do, it can export graphics in the SWF format. In fact, many designers who use Flash also use Illustrator to create their graphics and then import them into Flash to make them interactive.

To export graphics in the SWF format, choose File ➪ Export, choose Flash (SWF) from the Save as type dropdown list (Format popup menu), and then click Export to display the SWF Options dialog box, as shown in Figure 19.18.

For export options, you can choose from three settings:

- **AI File to SWF File:** This option creates a single static SWF file from whatever is in your Illustrator file. This is perfect for when you want to display a static SWF image in your Web page.

- **AI Layers to SWF Frames:** This option creates a single animated SWF file from the layers in your Illustrator file. Each Illustrator layer becomes its own frame, allowing you to export animations right out of Illustrator. When you choose this option, you can choose a frame rate as well as whether you want the animation to loop (see the next bulleted list for more on these options).

- **AI Layers to SWF Files:** This final option creates separate SWF files, each containing the contents of one layer in your Illustrator file. This is useful for designers who want to import individual art pieces into a Flash project.

FIGURE 19.18

The SWF Options dialog box allows you to save Illustrator documents in the SWF format.

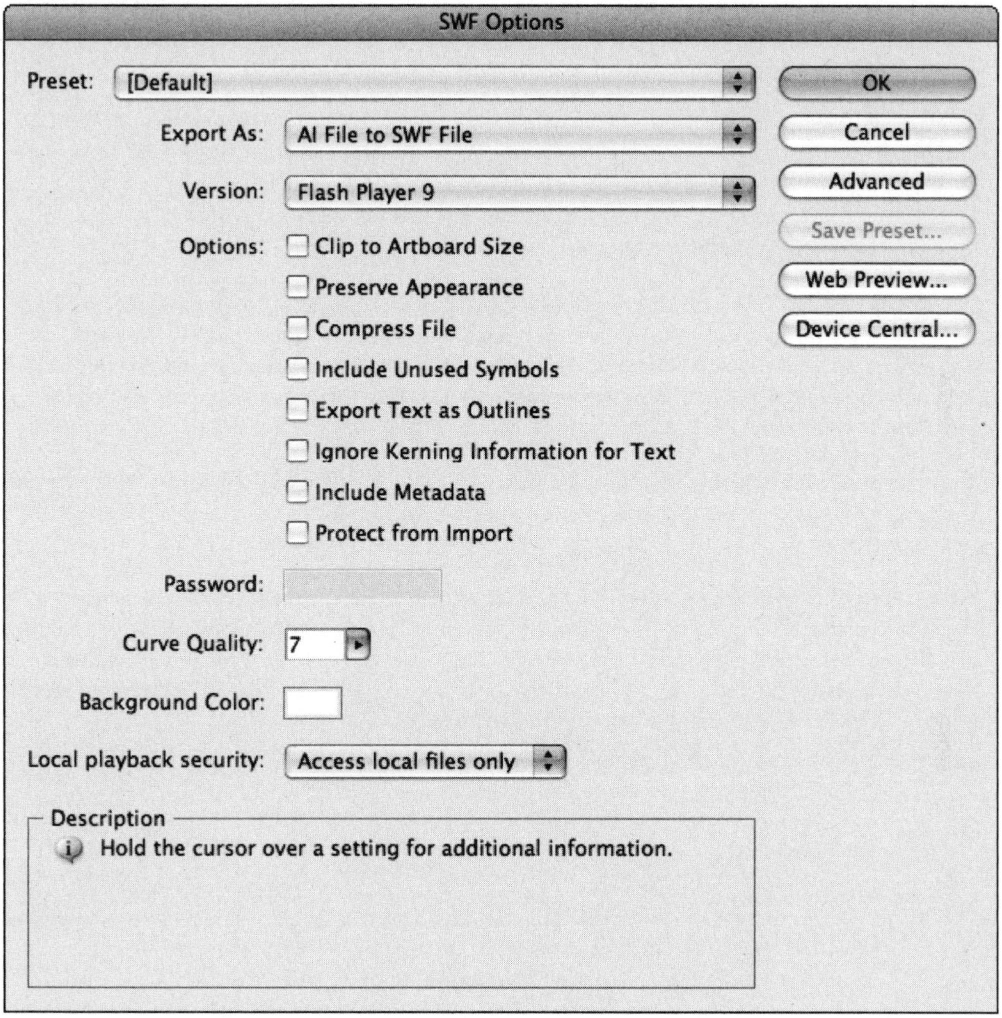

SWF Options

Preset: [Default]

Export As: AI File to SWF File

Version: Flash Player 9

Options: ☐ Clip to Artboard Size
☐ Preserve Appearance
☐ Compress File
☐ Include Unused Symbols
☐ Export Text as Outlines
☐ Ignore Kerning Information for Text
☐ Include Metadata
☐ Protect from Import

Password:

Curve Quality: 7

Background Color:

Local playback security: Access local files only

Description
ⓘ Hold the cursor over a setting for additional information.

OK
Cancel
Advanced
Save Preset...
Web Preview...
Device Central...

You can also save SWF files directly from the Save for Web & Devices dialog box — the benefit being that you can preview your art before you save.

TIP   Although the Save for Web & Devices dialog box can't preview SWF animations, you can use the Preview in Browser feature to see what your animation looks like before actually saving the file.

NOTE   Illustrator uses Apple's QuickTime plug-in to preview SWF files in Save for Web & Devices. If you can't see a preview of your image when you choose SWF in the Save for Web & Devices dialog box, ensure that you have QuickTime installed.

Creating SVG files

SVG stands for Scalable Vector Graphics and is an open standard format based on XML. To view SVG files in a Web browser, a plug-in is required, although future versions of Web browsers (Explorer, Opera, Safari, etc.) will most likely provide built-in SVG support because the format is becoming increasingly popular. One cool aspect of SVG is that you can edit it in any text editor and change values easily, thus changing the look of your graphic.

Illustrator is actually one of the most robust tools available for creating SVG graphics. Not only can Illustrator save files in the SVG format, but it can also open SVG files — even if they weren't created in Illustrator.

You can save SVG files directly out of Illustrator by choosing File ➪ Save and then choosing SVG from the Save as type dropdown list (Format popup menu), as shown in Figure 19.19. You can also choose to save SVG files via the Save for Web & Devices dialog box, as mentioned earlier in this chapter. Of course, the advantage to saving them from the Save for Web & Devices dialog box is that you can preview the results before you save them.

FIGURE 19.19

Choosing to save your file in the SVG format

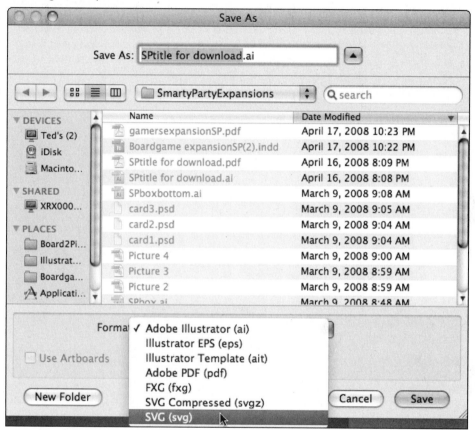

When you save an SVG file, you can choose to embed fonts (where the font license agreement allows), and you can also choose whether to include linked images as separate links or to embed them and include them inside the SVG file. An option appears in the SVG Options dialog box (which opens when you click Save after choosing SVG from the Save as type dropdown list [popup menu]), as shown in Figure 19.20, to Preserve Illustrator Editing Capabilities. Clicking this check box allows you to convert the file back into Illustrator without losing any native information. Because the option adds data into the file that only Illustrator can use, it increases the file size, so deselect this option if you don't need to edit the file later. Of course, saving a copy of the file as a regular file is always a good idea so that you don't lose any work.

In the SVG Options dialog box, you also find a More/Less Options button, which allows you to specify even more details about your SVG files. You can specify CSS Properties settings, choose how precisely vectors are calculated (Decimal Places), and choose text-encoding formats. Optimize for Adobe SVG Viewer, which installs along with Illustrator, allows you to take advantage of certain features that only the Adobe SVG Viewer plug-in can offer. (This is currently the standard, so using it is a safe choice.) Include Slicing Data does exactly what it says: It includes Web-slice data in the file. (Web slicing is covered later in this chapter.)

FIGURE 19.20

Use the SVG Options dialog box to specify settings for SVG files.

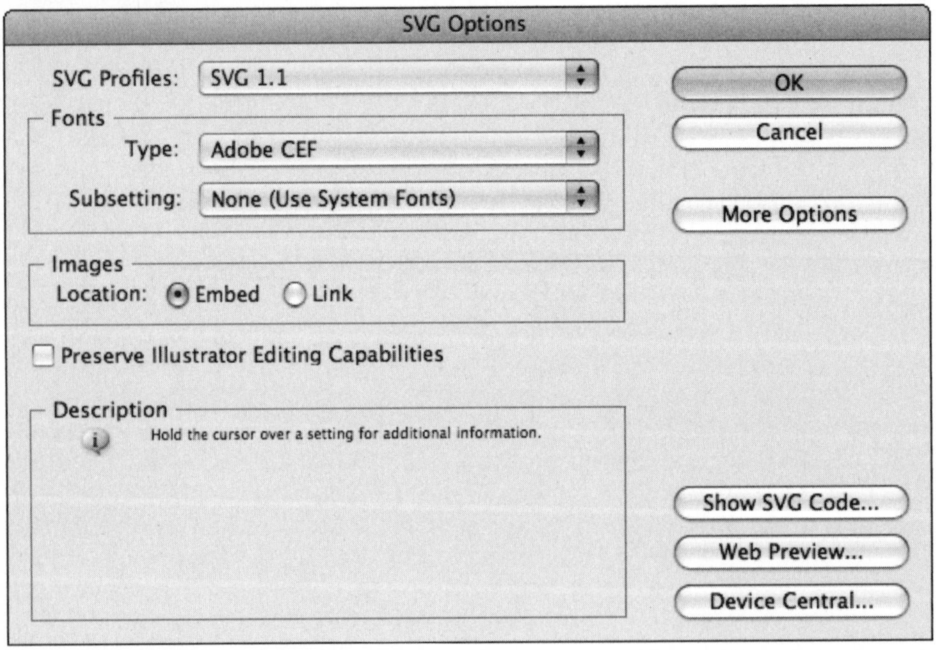

Applying SVG effects

SVG effects are cool because they're attributes you can apply to your art in real time as they display in a Web browser. If you apply a drop shadow to text as an SVG effect, that text is still live and editable in your Web browser (you can select, copy, and paste it, and a search engine can see the text), yet it has a drop shadow applied to it when it displays on the Web page. Because you can zoom in on vector graphics in a Web browser, you can enlarge the SVG text as much as you want, and the drop shadow renders each time, ensuring a smooth drop shadow. (You won't get the jaggies.)

Applying an SVG effect is similar to applying any other effect. Figure 19.21 shows the SVG Filters submenu. Make your selection, choose Effect ➪ SVG Filters, and then choose one. You can't preview some of these effects in the Illustrator window, so previewing the file in your browser is a good idea. After you apply an effect, you can see it listed in the Appearance panel, as shown in Figure 19.22, for that object or selection. Therefore, to edit or remove the effect, you use the Appearance panel.

FIGURE 19.21

Use SVG filters to apply an SVG effect to an object.

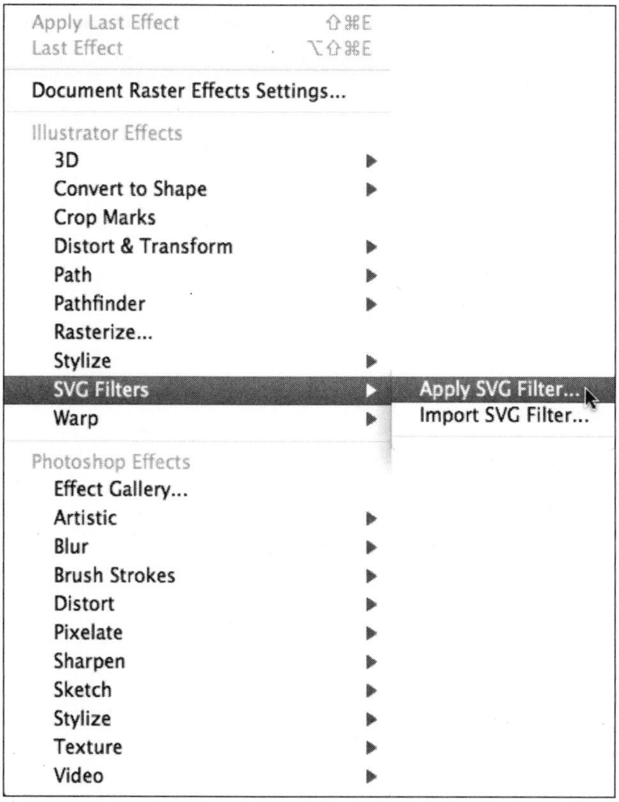

Apply Last Effect	⇧⌘E
Last Effect	⌥⇧⌘E
Document Raster Effects Settings...	
Illustrator Effects	
3D	▶
Convert to Shape	▶
Crop Marks	
Distort & Transform	▶
Path	▶
Pathfinder	▶
Rasterize...	
Stylize	▶
SVG Filters	▶ → **Apply SVG Filter...**
Warp	▶ → **Import SVG Filter...**
Photoshop Effects	
Effect Gallery...	
Artistic	▶
Blur	▶
Brush Strokes	▶
Distort	▶
Pixelate	▶
Sharpen	▶
Sketch	▶
Stylize	▶
Texture	▶
Video	▶

FIGURE 19.22

This shows an SVG effect as it appears in the Appearance panel after it's applied.

CROSS-REF For more on effects, see Chapter 15.

Illustrator comes with several SVG effects. However, if you know SVG, you can also create your own effects by choosing Effect ➪ SVG Filters ➪ Apply SVG Filter and then clicking the New SVG Filter button. Figure 19.23 shows an existing effect being modified. You can also import SVG effects from other Illustrator files by choosing Effect ➪ SVG Filters ➪ Import SVG Filter.

The SVG Interactivity panel

In reality, SVG is JavaScript-driven XML code. Illustrator allows you to add interactive options to graphics that you can save as SVG via the SVG Interactivity panel. Doing so requires the knowledge of JavaScript because you must select an object, choose an event from the dropdown list (popup menu) shown in Figure 19.24, and write or reference a JavaScript to perform a specific function (change color, animate, resize, etc.).

NOTE The SVG format supports many levels of interactivity and animation. Although Illustrator can't create or preview these effects directly, you can use a text editor to add these functions after you create the graphics. For more on using SVG, check out the SVG Zone on the Web at www.adobe.com/svg.

FIGURE 19.23

Create your own SVG effect by modifying an existing SVG effect.

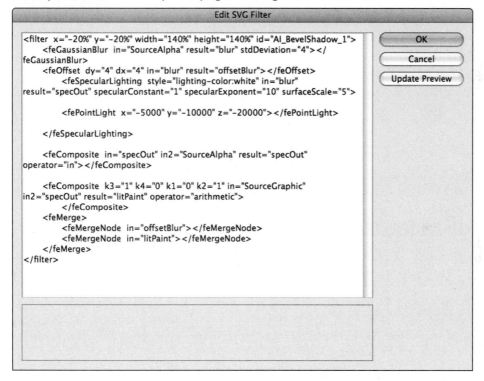

641

FIGURE 19.24

Applying a JavaScript event via the SVG Interactivity panel

Understanding Web Slicing

Throughout this chapter, the term slicing comes up. It refers to the process of cutting up Web graphics into smaller pieces to achieve several goals:

- Rather than waiting for one large graphic to load in a Web page, loading several different smaller pieces makes the graphic load faster.

- You don't have to force a graphic with several different parts or styles to use just one file format or compression setting. For example, if you have a graphic that has some text or a logo on one side and a photo or gradation of color on another side, rather than force the entire graphic to a larger size to ensure the gradient looks good, you can split the image into pieces and optimize the text and gradient differently, saving on overall file size.

- You can assign links to a slice. By creating different slices, you can allow users to click different parts of a graphic, which link to different locations or pages on the Internet.

■ You can assign rollovers to a slice. Rollovers are actually created outside of Illustrator, but you can still assign the slices right in Illustrator to save time in the workflow process. A rollover swaps one graphic for another when a user performs an action, such as moving the mouse over the slice. For example, you can make a graphic of a button look lit up when the user rolls the mouse over the button.

What the slicing process really does is divide your image into different pieces, which are described in HTML as a table. Figure 19.25 shows an example of such a table. Each cell of the table contains a different image, optimized as you specify with or without a link. Because a cell must be rectangular, you must also make all slices rectangular. When the table is rendered in a Web browser, the image looks like a complete graphic.

FIGURE 19.25

This shows a Web graphic sliced into an HTML table.

Object-Based Web Slicing

Illustrator has two ways of applying slices. The traditional way is to choose the Slice tool from the Tools panel and then draw slices over your graphics. Figure 19.26 shows what a graphic might look like sliced. Numbered slices appear on your screen as you create the slices, and auto slices are also created. (*User slices* are those that you create; *auto slices* are those that are automatically created to fill the rest of the table.) Slices don't print — they just indicate how the slice table is going to be created. The downside of using this method is that if you ever want to edit your art, you may also need to update or redraw the slices.

Illustrator includes a second way to create slices called *object-based slicing*. By applying slices as an attribute to an object rather than just drawing a separate shape, Illustrator creates a dynamic slice that moves and resizes itself based on the shape or selection to which it's assigned. You do this by first making a selection and then choosing Object ➪ Slice ➪ Make. Figure 19.27 shows the Slice submenu. A slice appears, but now when you edit that object, the slice grows or shrinks to fit the updated object.

FIGURE 19.26

You can draw a slice with the Slice tool, as shown here.

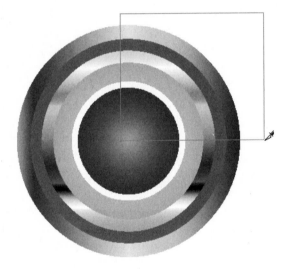

FIGURE 19.27

You can also create a dynamic object-based slice by choosing Object ⇨ Slice ⇨ Make.

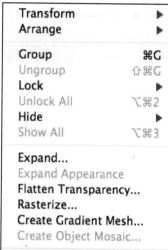

Working with slices

Object-based slices don't need modifying — they're basically maintenance-free slices. But if you draw slices with the Slice tool, you can edit those slices using the Slice Selection tool, which allows you to move the slices as well as to resize them. The Slice Selection tool also allows you to select slices so that you can apply settings to them. You find the Slice Selection tool behind the Slice tool. Selecting a slice and then choosing Object ➪ Slice ➪ Slice Options opens the Slice Options dialog box, as shown in Figure 19.28, where you can specify the slice name, a URL link, Alt text (for alternative text display in Web browsers), and more.

FIGURE 19.28

The Slice Options dialog box allows you to set parameters for a selected slice.

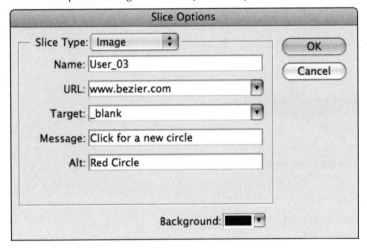

The dropdown list (popup menu) at the bottom of the dialog box allows you to specify a background for that slice — each slice can have its own background color or image — and there's a Slice Type dropdown list (popup menu) that lets you specify the slice in one of three states:

- **Image:** The contents of the slice, or table cell, are an image — GIF, JPEG, etc. — that you specify.

- **No Image:** The content of the table cell is an HTML statement, which you can specify directly in the dialog box. This is useful if the graphic you have is just a placeholder for something else, such as a QuickTime video clip or a script that loads a graphic.

■ **HTML Text:** If the contents of the slice are displayed as text, this option becomes available, and Illustrator basically codes the HTML to display text rather than an image in the table cell.

> **TIP** Specifying slice options in Illustrator can save you time down the road if you're also using Photoshop, as the options that you specify in Illustrator are stored and recognized there.

Other functions from the Object ⇨ Slice submenu let you release an object-based slice, divide a single slice into multiple slices of equal size, create slices from either guides or selections (these won't be object-based slices), and combine multiple slices into a single slice. There's also an option called Clip to Artboard that uses the Artboard size as the table boundaries rather than the size of the art on your Artboard. This is a great feature if you need to create a table of a specific size. By setting the document Artboard size to the correct dimensions, you've one less thing to worry about.

After you create all your slices, you can open the Save for Web & Devices dialog box and then use the Slice Select tool to choose individual optimization settings. You can press Shift+click to select multiple slices. If you're exporting HTML directly from Illustrator, click Save.

Understanding CSS layers

In HTML, you can describe only one layer, which means that text and images can't overlap each other. You can't overlap images either. When CSS layers were added to the HTML specifications, Web designers finally had the ability to specify layers of information in a single HTML page. CSS gives designers and developers the ability to lay out elements of a page with pixel-by-pixel accuracy. It allows images and text to overlap each other.

The catch is that Web browsers don't always support CSS layers in the same way, so use this feature with caution and lots of testing. Basically, Illustrator allows all top-level layers to be described as CSS layers. You can turn this option on in the Layers panel of the Save for Web & Devices dialog box, as shown in Figure 19.29. You can then choose what state you want each layer to assume (Visible, Hidden, or Do Not Export).

Choosing to export CSS layers from the Save for Web & Devices dialog box

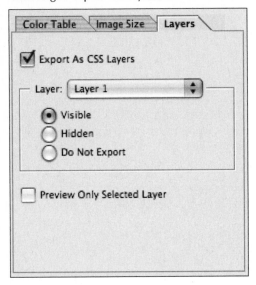

Getting Interactive

As mentioned earlier in this chapter, adding interactivity to a Web site is a great way for designers to add interest to sites as well as to add a functional element. Be it a cool animation or a navigation bar, Illustrator can help turn a static Web site into something that adds flair and value. Although Illustrator isn't Flash, it can still hold its own when creating these kinds of elements.

Specifying an image map

Some Web sites feature a graphic that links to different pages or places depending on what part of the graphic you click. An *image map* is basically a set of coordinates (sometimes called *hotspots*) that you can apply to a Web graphic — with each coordinate taking the user to a link of your choice. Setting up an image map is really easy in Illustrator if you follow these steps:

1. **Select an object and then open the Attributes panel.** For more on selecting an object, see Chapter 6. To open the Attributes panel, choose Window ➪ Attributes.

2. **From the Image dropdown list (popup menu), choose Rectangle or Polygon.** You want to choose the latter for nonuniform shapes.

3. **Type the full link in the URL text field, as shown in Figure 19.30.** Illustrator stores each URL you use in a single file so you don't have to repeatedly type the URL if you're using it again.

4. **Click Browser.** The Browser button that appears in the Attributes panel lets you quickly test your URL to ensure that it works.

FIGURE 19.30

Selecting an image map and specifying a URL

> **NOTE** Image maps are used less these days because slicing can achieve the same functionality and also add fancy effects, such as rollovers. However, there are still times when image maps are useful, such as when creating nonrectangular links. (Remember that slices are always rectangular.)

Image maps are written in several ways, and you should speak to a Web developer or a technical contact at your Web-hosting company to find out which image map is best to use for your particular needs and configurations. *Client-side* image maps reside inside the HTML code itself; *server-side* image maps reside in a separate file that links to the HTML file.

Creating animations

Creating animations for the Web in Illustrator can be fun and is actually easy too! Creating *animations* basically involves creating multiple images and playing them consecutively to give the appearance of motion. Each image in an animation is called a *frame*. In Illustrator, you animate by using each layer in your file as a frame. You can then export your file as an SWF file and choose the AI Layers to SWF Frames option at export time to create your animation.

You can create unique and interesting animations when you combine blends along with effects, such as 3-D and Scribble. Animating blends is easy because Illustrator has a feature called Release to Layers that automatically places each step of a blend onto its own layer — ready for exporting as an animated SWF.

The Release to Layers commands are found in the Layers panel menu, and you can choose between sequence and build. A sequence is much like traditional animation in that each frame contains a single image that moves from frame to frame. A build allows you to keep art in multiple frames and is useful for animating text, where you want letters to stay on the screen while others appear. For example, the animated word "Hello" would contain "H" in the first frame, "He" in the second frame, "Hel" in the third, etc. When you blend effects, Illustrator actually calculates each step of the blend individually, allowing you to create some spectacular effects, such as this one with the Scribble effect:

1. **Type the letter A.** Scale it so that it's good and big (there's no need for you to squint at the screen).

2. **Choose Type ⇨ Create Outlines to convert the text to a path.**

3. **Choose Effect ⇨ Stylize ⇨ Scribble.**

4. **Choose Sketch from the Settings dropdown list (popup menu).**

5. **Click OK to apply the effect shown in Figure 19.31.**

6. **Choose a color for the letter A.**

7. **Copy it by pressing Ctrl+C (⌘+C).**

8. **Paste in Front by pressing Ctrl+F (⌘+F).** This makes a copy of the A right on top of the original one.

9. **With the new A still selected, give it a different fill color.**

10. **Use the Selection tool to select both letters.** For more on the Selection tool, see Chapter 6.

FIGURE 19.31

Applying a Scribble effect to an A

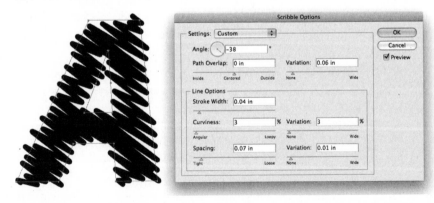

11. Choose Object ⇨ Blend ⇨ Make.

12. With the blended object still selected, choose Object ⇨ Blend ⇨ Blend Options to display the Blend Options dialog box.

13. Change the selection in the Spacing dropdown list (popup menu) to Specified Steps and then choose 10 for the number of steps, as shown in Figure 19.32.

FIGURE 19.32

Specifying the number of blend steps

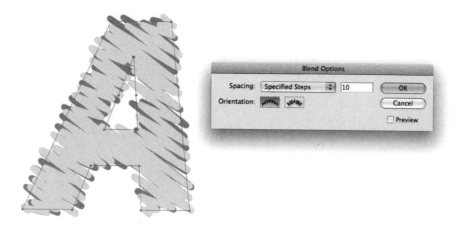

14. Now that you've created your blend, head over to the Layers panel and then click the little triangle to expose the contents of Layer 1.

15. Select the Blend layer and then choose Release to Layers (Sequence) from the Layers panel's popup menu, as shown in Figure 19.33. The Layers panel now lists many more layers — and each layer now contains one step of the blend that you created in step 13, as shown in Figure 19.34.

16. Choose File ⇨ Save for Web & Devices and then choose SWF for the image format. You should now see only the first frame of the animation in your Preview pane (switch to 1-up so you can view it more easily).

17. Choose Layers to SWF Frames in the Type of export dropdown list (popup menu).

18. To see what the animation looks like, click the Preview in Browser button. If you're happy with the results, as shown in Figure 19.35, go back to the Save for Web & Devices dialog box and then click Save.

FIGURE 19.33

Choosing the Release to Layers (Sequence) option

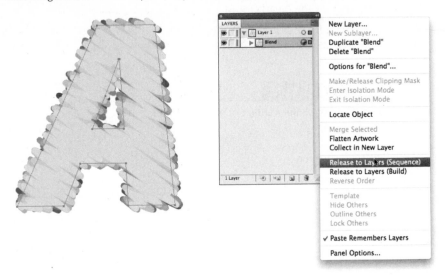

FIGURE 19.34

The Layers panel with all the new layers displayed

FIGURE 19.35

Viewing the animation in your Web browser

Using Data-Driven Graphics to Streamline Design Work

Designing a business card can be fun. It's challenging to come up with a cool and clean design that gets the message across in a readable and usable format. What isn't fun is copying that card over and over and typing different information for each employee in the company. Wouldn't it be great if you could do all the fun stuff yourself and then let the computer do all the tedious, boring stuff?

That's where data-driven graphics come into play. Sure, it's a mouthful to say, but it can save lots of time. You start off by creating a regular Illustrator file, which you use as a base file, or template. Figure 19.36 shows a business card template. This template contains your design, but you tag the content as *variables*. You then have a *script* fetch data from an external file, such as a text file or any ODBC-compliant database, and the script automatically generates customized files for you while you search for a cold beverage to enjoy. Now that you know the basic steps for creating data-driven graphics, the rest of the sections in this chapter walk you through how to perform those steps.

FIGURE 19.36

A sample data-driven graphics template adds data from another file.

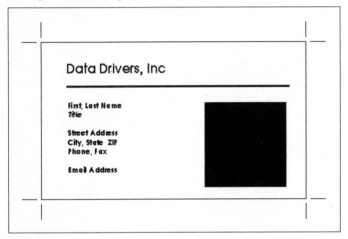

TIP The data-driven graphics feature was originally created for Web graphics because that medium demands instant updates and graphics that are generated on the fly. However, it can also prove very beneficial to print workflows.

Understanding variables

A variable is something that changes. In Illustrator, defining something as a variable means that "this will change." For example, when you type the name Joe Smith on a business card and then define it as a variable called Name, running the appropriate script replaces the words Joe Smith with whatever you have in the Name text field of your database.

You can set four kinds of variables in Illustrator:

- **Text:** A text variable is simply a string of text, either point text or area text, that's replaced with new text. The font and style applied to that text remains. Only the characters themselves change — as in the example of the names on business cards.

- **Visibility:** You can apply visibility to any kind of object in Illustrator and control whether that object is shown or hidden. For example, you can show a starburst graphic in certain cases but not others.

- **Linked image:** This kind of variable is specific to replacing linked images (any format). For example, if your business card design contains a picture of the employee, setting the image as a variable allows you to create business cards with each employee's photo on his or her card by replacing the value of the variable with the correct link.

- **Graph data:** Creating a graph in Illustrator is easy enough (see Chapter 5), and by defining a graph as a variable, you can replace the data of that graph to generate customized graphs automatically. For example, you can automatically generate a weather chart by retrieving the latest weather forecasts from the Internet.

Using the Variables panel

You define Variables in Illustrator via the Variables panel (accessed by choosing Window⇨Variables), as shown in Figure 19.37. The panel allows you to keep tabs of all your variables in a single location and allows you to also define *data sets*. A data set is very much like a record in a database and stores information for a specific range of variables.

The Variables panel shows all four kinds of variables defined.

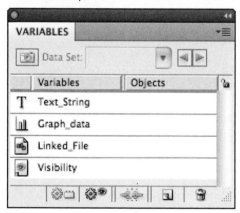

You define a visibility variable by making a selection and then clicking the Make Visibility Dynamic button (it looks like a gear/eyeball). Likewise, you define other variables by making a selection and then clicking the Make Dynamic button. These are context-sensitive, so if you select text, the button is labeled Make Text Dynamic, and if you select a graph, the button is labeled Make Graph Dynamic.

Clicking the little camera icon in the upper left of the panel allows you to capture a data set. Data sets are stored in Illustrator as XML data, and you can both import and export variables and data sets from the Variables panel menu. Because XML is a standard format, Illustrator can very easily integrate into complex workflows and back-end systems.

Understanding scripting

A script is a list of commands that are contained in a single file. When you run a script, your computer follows the commands that are contained within the script. In reality, a script is much like computer-programming code, except that it's what's called a high-level language in that it controls existing programs rather than actually being a program itself. A script tells applications what to do. In fact, most scripting languages read almost like English — making them easier to learn and use.

Illustrator supports three scripting languages:

- **AppleScript:** Created by Apple, this language works only on the Macintosh platform.
- **Visual Basic:** Created by Microsoft, this language only works on the Windows platform.
- **JavaScript:** Originally developed by Netscape, this language is cross-platform.

Scripting versus actions

If you've been paying attention, you remember a discussion about something called actions back in Chapter 17. Because you're a smart person, you're probably wondering why you need scripting if you already have actions.

There are several big differences between actions and scripts:

- An action is simply a recorded sequence of events that you can play over and over, performing exactly the same way each time. A script can contain logic and therefore perform different steps depending on the situation.
- An action is a task that can be completely performed only within Illustrator. A script can involve multiple applications, not just Illustrator.
- An action is easy to create right in Illustrator. A script requires the knowledge of at least one of the scripting languages (AppleScript, VBScript, or JavaScript). So, although scripts are far more powerful, they're also far more difficult to create.

For example, you can write a script to automatically create a forecast graphic by going to a weather site on the Internet, retrieving temperature information for a particular city, and drawing a graphic. You can code the graphic so that temperatures below 32° are colored blue, temperatures over 90°

are colored red, and temperatures between 75° and 85° have a smiley face with sunglasses. The script brings that information into Illustrator from another application (your Web browser) and then makes decisions within Illustrator based on that data. Actions are cool but nowhere near as cool as scripts.

It takes much more work to write a script than it does to record an action, but a script can do much more and is more powerful than an action is.

NOTE Not everything in Illustrator is actionable, and not everything in Illustrator is scriptable. There are even some things that you can do with AppleScript or VBScript that you can't do with JavaScript. With each new version of Illustrator, you can record more and more features and commands of the application as actions or scripts.

Don't let all this talk about scripting scare you. Just because a script is a necessary step in the data-driven graphics process, it doesn't mean that you (the designer) have to do it. Some companies have developers on staff who know how to script, and you can have them write the required scripts for you. You can also hire a developer or consultant on a freelance basis to write your scripts. Because of the potential time savings you gain when you utilize a script, this method can also prove very economical.

Setting up a data-driven graphics template

It's beyond the scope of this book to learn how to write a script to automatically fill a template, but it's easy to set up a template and create some sample data sets, which allow you to preview what your files will look like when they're filled with data:

1. **Using the Text tool, click an empty part of the Artboard to create some point text.** The example uses the words Bezier Games. Be creative and choose a good font and even a drop shadow if you want.

2. **Click the Selection tool and then choose the type you just created.** For more on the Selection tool, see Chapter 6.

3. **Choose Window ➪ Variables to open the Variables panel.**

4. **Click the Make Text Dynamic button at the bottom of the panel, as shown in Figure 19.38.** Alternatively, you can choose the Make Text Dynamic option from the Variables panel's popup menu. A variable called Variable1 is thus created.

5. **Double-click the Variable1 item in the Variables panel to open the Variable Options dialog box.**

You define a Text variable by using the Variables panel.

6. **Type a name for the variable.** Change the name of the variable so that you (or a script) can readily identify it. In the example, the name is changed to Company_Name, as shown in Figure 19.39.

Changing the name of the variable to something more descriptive makes it easier to remember.

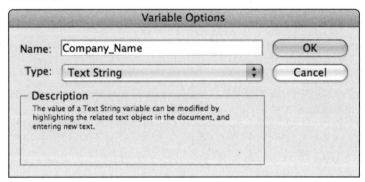

7. Click OK.

8. Click the little camera button (this is the Capture Data Set button in the upper left of the Variables panel) to create Data Set 1.

9. Using the Text tool, edit the text on your Artboard to have it read something else.

10. Click the Capture Data Set button. This creates Data Set 2.

11. Edit the text on your Artboard to change it again. The example was changed to Alspach Inc.

12. Click the Capture Data Set button again, as shown in Figure 19.40. You now have three data sets in your Illustrator file.

FIGURE 19.40

Capturing a third data set

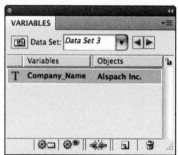

13. Using the left and right arrows in the Variables panel, click to step through all three of the data sets. As you switch among data sets, the text on your screen changes. This is extremely helpful when you create templates because it allows you, as a designer, to create a design that works well with different data. For example, a long word or name takes up more space than a short word does. Setting up several different data sets in your file allows you to preview how your design looks with different sets of data.

Taking advantage of data-driven graphics with Adobe GoLive

Adobe GoLive has support for working with dynamically generated content, while Dreamweaver doesn't (yet). You can also use the variable feature in Illustrator to create those graphics in GoLive yourself — and it's really easy! Follow these steps:

1. **Start by creating a template in Illustrator.** Design your art and then assign some variables.
2. **Choose File ⇨ Save As.** This opens the Save As dialog box.
3. **Choose SVG for the format, as shown in Figure 19.41.** The SVG Options dialog box opens. The reason for choosing this format is that SVG can contain variable content.

FIGURE 19.41

Save the file as SVG for use in GoLive.

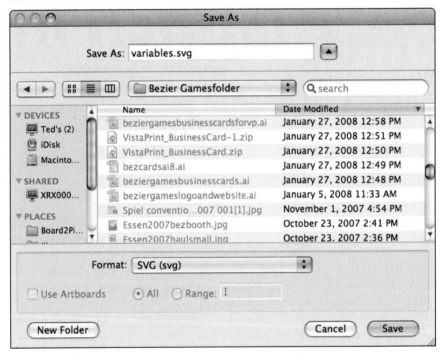

4. **Click Save As to display the SVG Options dialog box.**

5. **Click the Preserve Illustrator Editing Capabilities check box.** This allows you to reopen the SVG file in Illustrator later.

6. **Click More Options to display the advanced options section of the dialog box.**

7. **Ensure to click the Include Adobe Graphics Server data check box, as shown in Figure 19.42.**

FIGURE 19.42

Clicking the Include Adobe Graphics Server data check box in the SVG Options dialog box includes the variables and data sets.

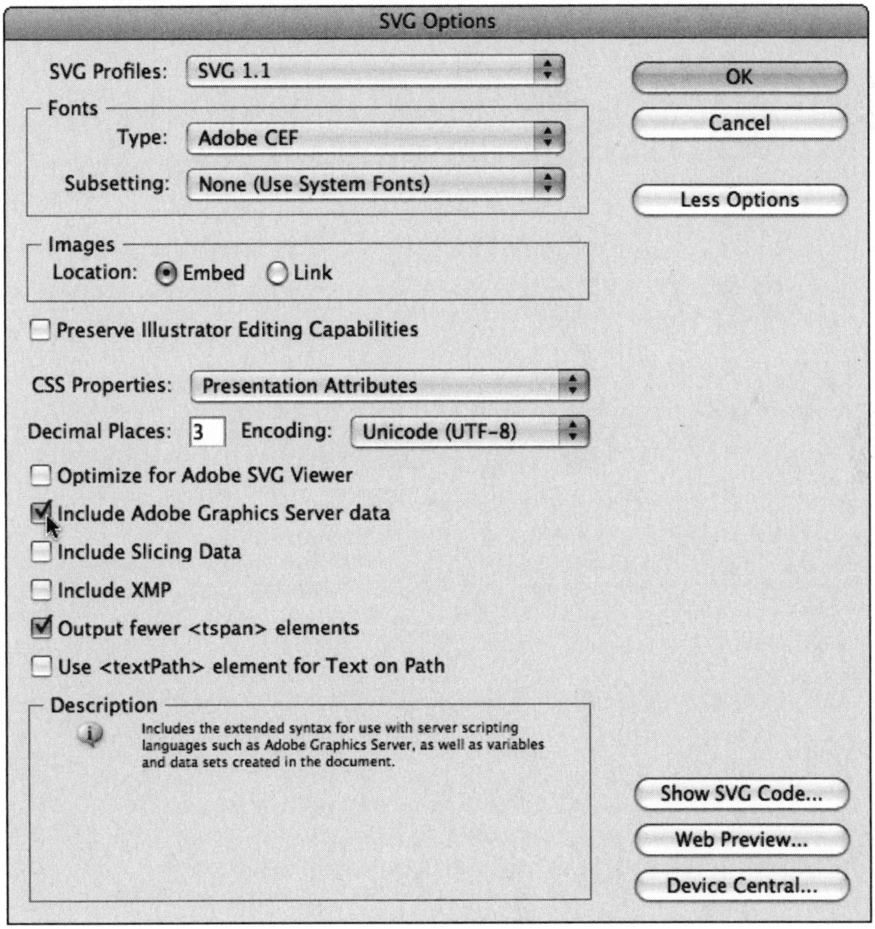

8. Click OK.

9. In GoLive, open or create an HTML file.

10. From the Object panel in GoLive, drag an Illustrator Smart Object (from the GoLive Tools panel) onto your page.

    Using the point-and-shoot icon (drag from the Illustrator Smart Object to the SVG graphic directly), load the SVG graphic that you created in Illustrator. Because GoLive sees the variable content in the Illustrator SVG file, GoLive prompts you with a dialog box listing all the variables. Here, you can choose to replace text or change attributes of your variables.

You can change these variables at any time in GoLive by clicking the Variables button in the GoLive Inspector panel. It's a powerful way to quickly update your graphics without even launching Illustrator!

Summary

In this chapter, you learned the following:

■ Pixel Preview mode displays graphics as they would appear in a Web browser.

■ The Save for Web & Devices dialog box lets you optimize graphics in one easy step.

■ You can both open and save SVG files in Illustrator.

■ Illustrator can export animated SWF files.

■ Data-driven graphics can streamline repetitive tasks and help save time.

■ Illustrator can define four kinds of variables in the Variables panel.

■ Many variables are stored in XML.

■ Illustrator supports AppleScript (Mac), VBScript (Windows), and JavaScript.

■ Scripting is far more powerful than actions.

Chapter 20

Illustrator Workflow

Throughout this book, you've learned pretty much everything there is to know about Illustrator. So, what's left? Putting it all together, of course! In this chapter, I walk you through a project that uses all sorts of Illustrator functions and explain how and why I used Illustrator's capabilities throughout the process.

Everyone uses Illustrator a little differently, and even as I wrote this, I realized that I could have done a few things differently in order to be more efficient. Each project that you work on in Illustrator results in a different set of tools and processes, and even if you do very similar things again and again, you find your workflows evolving over time.

Project Background

The goal of this project was to create the box for a brand-new edition of a game I published more than a year ago: *Ultimate Werewolf*. This would be the second box I created at this size with this particular printer, so I already had some experience in terms of the production parameters. Figure 20.1 shows the final box.

However, I made some mistakes the first time around, such as not including enough bleed (printed area that extends beyond the expected cuts) and fold space for the corners. While the bleed issue was an oversight on my part, the fold space was something totally new to me.

Boxes with printed covers are created by gluing a printed sheet onto flat cardboard, then folding the cardboard sides down to form the shape of the box. The printed paper is what holds the box together at the corners.

Because the cardboard is fairly thick, when the sides are folded down, the printed paper on top slides up a bit to make its way around the corner. This has to be compensated for in the original design or the sides of the box will appear too close to the top of the box compared to the original location they were designed for. Once you understand this concept, adding a few millimeters in between the center (top) of the box and the sides is easy.

TIP

This project was printed overseas, where the standard forms of measurement are millimeters, not inches, so I did all my work in the metric system. Working in the measurement system of the printer is always a good idea, especially if there are changes to the files during the process. You don't want to be doing the conversions either inside Illustrator or out, as that introduces some significant risk into the project.

FIGURE 20.1

This is a photograph of the finished box; this chapter walks you through the process of creating it.

The box was to be printed using the four-color process (see Chapter 18 for more on printing and four-color separations). 95% of the work I do is now four-color process, as the savings from using just two or three spot colors tend to be miniscule. The other 5% tends to be black ink only, and that's for items like score sheets or rules inserts — and the cost to produce those is still only marginally cheaper than using four colors!

Building the Documents

Despite using Illustrator for the last 20 years, I don't consider myself an artist. In fact, if you take away Illustrator and stick me with a pad and pencil, the doodles that I would generate would embarrass a first-grade art teacher. So, I don't sketch out anything first. Ever. Instead, I tend to bring all the elements of a project together and start working on it right away in Illustrator. The advantage to doing this is that I have a single file to work on that will eventually be the one that's used for printing.

The box consists of two pieces, and therefore, I need two files for it: the box cover and the box bottom. I created a new document (CMYK, of course, because this would be printed) for the box cover first. In order to help me organize the files, I created layers for each of the components I anticipated needing: Guides, Background, Sides, Frames and Edges, UW logo, Front characters, tagline, flags, game info, Bézier logo, and peeps (how I refer to the people illustrations on the sides of the box).

I worked with a very talented illustrator — a person, not another program — who created a whole series of characters for the cards in the game as well as the cover illustration. The resulting images were Photoshop files with transparent backgrounds, allowing me a lot of flexibility in how I used them.

Setting up the document

The first step after the basic document was created was to get the guides in place. Because I had done a box previously, I could copy the guides directly from the existing file to the new one. In order to do this, I locked all the layers except my guide layer in my previous file, then did a select all and copy there. In my new document, I checked the Layers panel's popup menu to be sure that Paste Remembers Layers was selected (to ensure that all pasted items go onto layers with the same names as where they were copied from) and then chose Edit ➪ Paste In Front. Paste In Front keeps the location of the guides consistent between documents.

Creating the front cover

The first item I placed was the background image, as shown in Figure 20.2.

FIGURE 20.2

The initial document with the background image in place. Note that all the layers are already created, but only the background image layer has any objects on it.

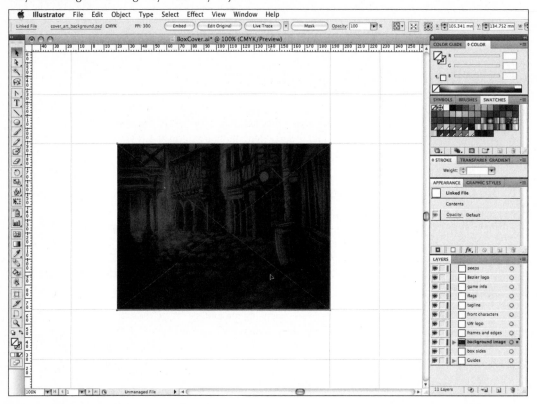

Next, I placed the logo. The *Ultimate Werewolf* logo, as shown in Figure 20.3, was created in Illustrator (although it uses a pixel-based image for the texture for the letters), but instead of copying and pasting the logo from the original file, I placed it as a linked file. The reason I chose this method was twofold:

- I was still tweaking the logo, and this way, any changes to the logo would be reflected in the artwork automatically (Illustrator automatically updates linked placed files).

- I used effects with x and y coordinates, such as a drop shadow. The location of the shadow is based on x and y coordinates in the effect itself. These values always move in the same direction, so a drop shadow that's set to the lower right of the artwork would be in the lower right of that art even if the artwork is rotated (when you look at the rotated art right-side up, the shadow would not be in the lower right anymore). When artwork is placed, those settings are relative to the original artwork, not the position/rotation of the artwork on the page.

> **TIP** Whenever I'm combining different elements together in a project, I always place-link files as opposed to embedding or copy/pasting from other Illustrator documents. This is primarily so that changes made to the components are reflected in the final document. All elements I placed in this document were place-linked.

I then placed the Bézier Games logo, the flags (this game includes components for both English and German), and the front characters. I didn't place the peeps for the box sides yet, as I was focusing on the front cover first.

I then typed the tagline, applying a drop shadow to it by choosing Effect ⇨ Stylize ⇨ Drop Shadow. I used the settings shown in Figure 20.4 to make the shadow small, as my main goal was to make the tagline as readable as possible.

FIGURE 20.3

The *Ultimate Werewolf* logo file

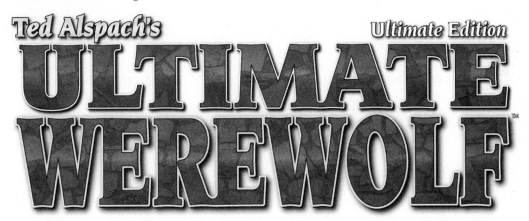

The Drop Shadow settings for the tagline text

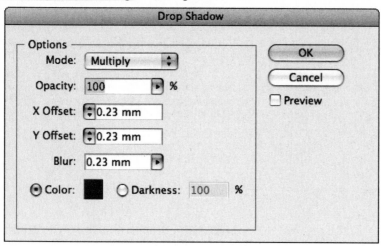

I duplicated the tagline text by dragging it down while pressing Alt (Option) and Shift, ensuring that it didn't move horizontally when I dragged. I then double-clicked on the new type object to change it to text-editing mode, pressed Ctrl+A (⌘+A) to select all the text, and pasted the translated German text (copied from a Word document supplied by my translator). I colored the German text a light blue (I do the same thing for the German text on the back of the box).

The last step on the front cover was to position the front characters (including the werewolf). I placed them on a different layer than the background image so that the werewolf would appear in front of the logo and then the other front characters would be in front of the werewolf. When working with my artist, I specified that the characters and their backgrounds should be on separate layers to ensure I would have this sort of flexibility. Figure 20.5 shows the finalized front cover.

Creating the box sides

The bottom/top box sides and left/right box sides are virtually duplicates of each other (just the peeps are different), so I knew that I could just do one of each, then rotate/duplicate each to create the opposite version. I started at the bottom first, since it was right-side up on my screen.

FIGURE 20.5

The box top of the box cover is complete.

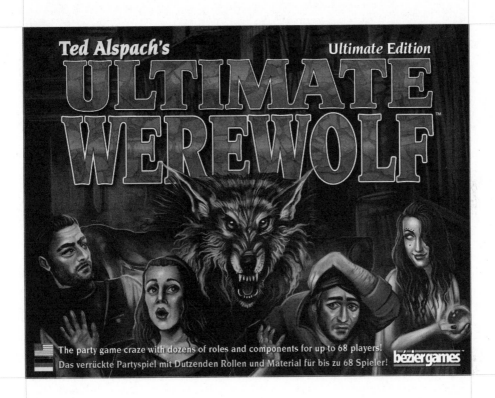

For the background image for the sides, I jumped into Photoshop and created two smaller versions of the background I used for the front. I place-linked the longer of the two for the bottom side on the background image layer. Figure 20.6 shows the placed image. Note that it extends beyond the guides. This isn't just bleed; it's also *wrap*. Wrap is the printed portion of the paper that goes around the bottom edges and corners of the box (look at any box that has a cover like this, and you see the wrap there, which is usually about $1/2$-inch wide).

The bottom box side has a background image in place.

Next, I Alt+dragged (Option+dragged) the *Ultimate Werewolf* logo down and used the Scale tool to scale it so that it fit better on the side. When I scale in Illustrator, I find it's best to keep the Bounding Box off (it only shows up with the Selection tool, and I use the Direct Selection tool more anyway) and just press S to quickly access the Scale tool. After scaling, I press A to return to the Direct Selection tool.

I copied the Bézier Games logo down and scaled it up because it needs to be bigger on the box sides. I also added the URL info below it here (having it on the front cover would have added too much busyness, but having it on the sides doesn't have that same negative impact). Finally, I copied the game information graphic (number of players, playing time, suggested age range) from another file. I didn't place-link this graphic because the values are specific to this game, and there isn't any place where this information appears on the product except the box cover.

Finally, I placed two peeps and sized and positioned them appropriately. Figure 20.7 shows the bottom edge with everything in place. Note that the peeps are just slightly overlapping the *Ultimate Werewolf* logo; this was done to add an element of depth to the graphics.

The bottom side with all elements in place

To create the top side of the box, I selected all the elements on the bottom side and rotate-duplicated them 180°. Normally, when duplicating a bunch of items that I want to move, rotate, or scale, I group them first. However, this wasn't an option here because that would have moved all the objects to the topmost layer, and I wanted to keep all items on the same layers that they were on originally. Instead, I clicked with the Rotate tool in the middle of the cover portion (I just estimated this), then pressed Alt+Shift (Option+Shift) and dragged from the bottom side to the top, which snapped a copy of the selected artwork up almost exactly in place. To vertically adjust the art into the correct position, I used the up and down arrow keys, which moved the art 1 point per keystroke.

To swap out the characters with new ones, I selected each of them, chose File ⇨ Place, picked a different character, and clicked the Replace check box. Replace automatically applies any transformations to the new image that were applied to the previously placed image. In this case, that included scaling and rotating. Using this technique meant that I only had to do slight tweaking to the placed images on the top side of the box.

For the left and right sides, I first created the left side by rotate-duplicating just the logo and characters from the bottom 90°. I just replaced the characters and added the smaller background side image. Then, I selected the four elements (background image, logo, and two characters) and rotate-duplicated them 180° to create the right side. After replacing the characters on the right side, the box cover was complete, as shown in Figure 20.8. Time to work on the box bottom!

Creating the box bottom

The box bottom essentially started as the box top. After saving the box top again, I chose File ⇨ Save As and gave the file a different name for the box bottom. For the bottom, I worked a little differently. First, I deleted items I knew I wouldn't need: The front characters went first, followed by the logos on the box sides. I kept the right-side up game information graphic because I needed that for the box bottom.

FIGURE 20.8

The box cover in its finished state

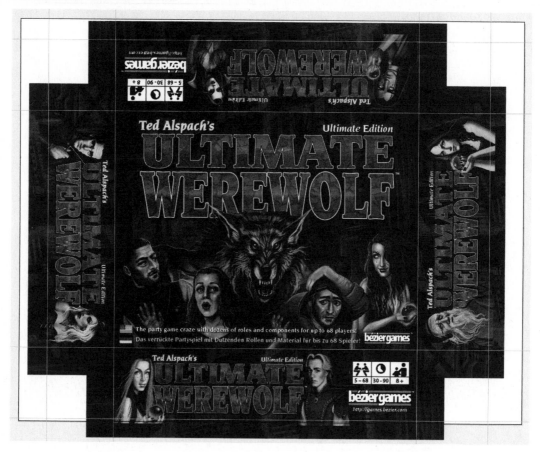

Then, I started working backward from what I did for the cover: I swapped the top and bottom side graphics because they would appear upside down if I used them on the box bottom illustration. I added two additional characters to the top and bottom sides and then replaced all the characters with new ones. Figure 20.9 shows the box bottom at this time.

Next, I scaled the *Ultimate Werewolf* logo down and moved it into the upper left. I moved the Bézier Games logo to the upper right and added the location information below it. I placed three different card images below the Bézier Games logo and positioned them to fill up the space. These three cards are the only place on the box you see any components from the game directly (even though the characters are on all the cards), so it was critical that they be clearly defined as such. I gave them substantial drop shadows to ensure that they looked like individual cards.

Next, I placed the bar code graphic, the Panda Manufacturing information, the printing location, and added the rules (in English and German) as well as the copyright information.

Finally, I created a text box for the English text and pasted the text there that I copied from a Word document. Then, I duplicated the text box by Alt+dragging (Option+dragging) it to the right and pasted in the German translation of the text. I colored the German text light blue to match the German tagline from the front of the box. Figure 20.10 shows the final box bottom artwork.

FIGURE 20.9

The box bottom after the sides have been completed

FIGURE 20.10

The box bottom with all elements in place

Preparing for production

I saved both files as PDF files. Saving as PDF files allows you to deliver a single file, even if you have a lot of place-linked files and use all sorts of unusual fonts. Even so, I always click the Preserve Illustrator Editing Capabilities check box in the PDF Options dialog box when saving, so if there are changes after submission, I can make them to the PDF version of the file instead of opening up the original Illustrator file and then resaving it as a PDF.

I usually use the High Quality Print preset, but I often tweak a few other settings too, such as clicking the All Printer's Marks check box in the Marks and Bleeds section (shown in Figure 20.11) and typing a manual bleed of at least 18 points (I used 15 mm, or about 42 points) in the same section.

FIGURE 20.11

The Marks and Bleeds section of the Save Adobe PDF dialog box with the settings I used for these project files

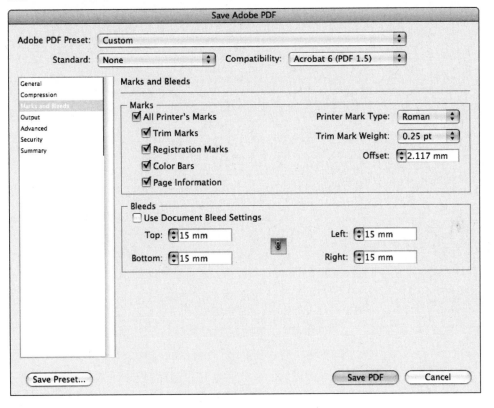

Summary

While each project is different, you can use Illustrator effectively by following these guidelines:

- Figure out the components in the project first and then set up layers for each of them as appropriate.

- Place-link elements when possible so that your document uses the most recent version of those elements.

- Work with your printer prior to creating your files so you don't have to make changes later — when it's much harder to do.

- Save your final file as a PDF, using the High Quality Print preset as your base setting.

Appendix

Shortcuts in Illustrator CS4

I llustrator has more keyboard commands, functions, and shortcuts than ever before. The tables in this appendix give you a quick reference to the commands, functions, and shortcuts for both Windows and Mac.

CAUTION Mac users should check to make sure that their function keys aren't assigned to complete any system tasks. In the Mac's Keyboard & Mouse System Preferences pane's Keyboard Shortcuts tab, you can assign or reassign keyboard shortcuts that are in conflict.

IN THIS APPENDIX

Learning commands for almost every situation

Using functions

Saving time with shortcuts

Menu Commands

TABLE A-1

The File Menu

Command	Shortcut
New	Ctrl (⌘)+N
New from Template	Ctrl (⌘)+Shift+N
Open	Ctrl (⌘)+O
Browse	Ctrl (⌘)+Alt (Option)+O
Close	Ctrl (⌘)+W
Save	Ctrl (⌘)+S
Save As	Ctrl (⌘)+Shift+S
Save a Copy	Ctrl (⌘)+Alt (Option)+S
Save for Web	Ctrl (⌘)+Shift+Alt (Option)+S
Revert	F12*
Document Setup	Ctrl (⌘)+Alt (Option)+P
File Info	Ctrl (⌘)+Shift+Alt (Option)+I
Print	Ctrl (⌘)+P
Exit (Quit)	Ctrl (⌘)+Q (under the Illustrator menu for Mac OS X)

* In Mac OS X 10.4 (Tiger), reassign this in the Exposé & Dashboard System Preferences pane, and in Mac OS X 10.5 (Leopard), reassign this in the Exposé & Spaces System Preferences pane.

TABLE A-2

The Edit Menu

Command	Shortcut
Undo	Ctrl (⌘)+Z
Redo	Ctrl (⌘)+Shift+Z
Cut	Ctrl (⌘)+X
Copy	Ctrl (⌘)+C
Paste	Ctrl (⌘)+V
Paste in Front	Ctrl (⌘)+F
Paste in Back	Ctrl (⌘)+B
Check Spelling	Ctrl (⌘)+I

Command	Shortcut
Color Settings	Ctrl (⌘)+Shift+K
Keyboard Shortcuts	Ctrl (⌘)+Shift+Alt (Option)+K
General Preferences	Ctrl (⌘)+K (under the Illustrator menu for Mac OS X)

TABLE A-3

The Object Menu

Command	Shortcut
Transform ⇨ Transform Again	Ctrl (⌘)+D
Transform ⇨ Move	Ctrl (⌘)+Shift+M
Transform ⇨ Transform Each	Ctrl (⌘)+Shift+Alt (Option)+D
Arrange ⇨ Bring to Front	Ctrl (⌘)+Shift+]
Arrange ⇨ Bring Forward	Ctrl (⌘)+]
Arrange ⇨ Send Backward	Ctrl (⌘)+[
Arrange ⇨ Send to Back	Ctrl (⌘)+Shift+[
Group	Ctrl (⌘)+G
Ungroup	Ctrl (⌘)+Shift+G
Lock ⇨ Selection	Ctrl (⌘)+2
Unlock All	Ctrl (⌘)+Alt (Option)+2
Hide ⇨ Selection	Ctrl (⌘)+3
Show All	Ctrl (⌘)+Alt (Option)+3
Path ⇨ Join	Ctrl (⌘)+J
Path ⇨ Average	Ctrl (⌘)+Alt (Option)+J
Blend ⇨ Make	Ctrl (⌘)+Alt (Option)+B
Blend ⇨ Release	Ctrl (⌘)+Alt (Option)+Shift+B
Envelope Distort ⇨ Make with Warp	Ctrl (⌘)+Alt (Option)+Shift+W
Envelope Distort ⇨ Make with Mesh	Ctrl (⌘)+Alt (Option)+M
Envelope Distort ⇨ Make with Top Object	Ctrl (⌘)+Alt (Option)+C
Envelope Distort ⇨ Edit Contents	Ctrl (⌘)+Shift+V
Live Paint ⇨ Make	Ctrl (⌘)+Alt (Option)+X
Clipping Mask ⇨ Make	Ctrl (⌘)+7
Clipping Mask ⇨ Release	Ctrl (⌘)+Alt (Option)+7
Compound Path ⇨ Make	Ctrl (⌘)+8
Compound Path ⇨ Release	Ctrl (⌘)+Alt (Option)+8

TABLE A-4

The Type Menu

Command	Shortcut
Create Outlines	Ctrl (⌘)+Shift+O
Show Hidden Characters	Ctrl (⌘)+Alt (Option)+I

TABLE A-5

The Select Menu

Command	Shortcut
Select All	Ctrl (⌘)+A
Deselect All	Ctrl (⌘)+Shift+A
Reselect	Ctrl (⌘)+6
Next Object Above	Ctrl (⌘)+Alt (Option)+]
Next Object Below	Ctrl (⌘)+Alt (Option)+[

TABLE A-6

The Effect Menu

Command	Shortcut
Apply Last Effect	Ctrl (⌘)+Shift+E
Last Effect dialog box	Ctrl (⌘)+Shift+Alt (Option)+E

TABLE A-7

The View Menu

Command	Shortcut
Outline/Preview	Ctrl (⌘)+Y (toggle)
Overprint Preview	Ctrl (⌘)+Shift+Alt (Option)+Y
Pixel Preview	Ctrl (⌘)+Alt (Option)+Y
Zoom In	Ctrl (⌘)++ (plus sign)
Zoom Out	Ctrl (⌘)+− (minus sign)

Command	Shortcut
Fit in Window	Ctrl (⌘)+0 (zero)
	Double-click the Hand tool
Actual Size (100%)	Ctrl (⌘)+1
	Double-click the Zoom tool
Hide Edges	Ctrl (⌘)+H (toggle)
Hide Template	Ctrl (⌘)+Shift+W (toggle)
Show/Hide Rulers	Ctrl (⌘)+R (toggle)
Show/Hide Bounding Box	Ctrl (⌘)+Shift+B (toggle)
Show/Hide Transparency Grid	Ctrl (⌘)+Shift+D (toggle)
Show/Hide Text Threads	Ctrl (⌘)+Shift+Y (toggle)
Guides ⇨ Show/Hide Guides	Ctrl (⌘)+; (toggle)
Guides ⇨ Lock Guides	Ctrl (⌘)+Alt (Option)+;
Guides ⇨ Make Guides	Ctrl (⌘)+5
Guides ⇨ Release Guides	Ctrl (⌘)+Alt (Option)+5
Smart Guides	Ctrl (⌘)+U
Show/Hide Grid	Ctrl (⌘)+" (toggle)
Snap to Grid (Pixel)	Ctrl (⌘)+Shift+"
Snap to Point	Ctrl (⌘)+Alt (Option)+"

CAUTION Mac users should check to make sure that their function keys aren't assigned to complete any system tasks. In the Mac's Keyboard & Mouse System Preferences pane's Keyboard Shortcuts tab, you can assign or reassign keyboard shortcuts that are in conflict.

TABLE A-8

The Window Menu

Command	Shortcut
Align	Shift+F7 (toggle)
Appearance	Shift+F6 (toggle)
Attributes	Ctrl (⌘)+F11 (toggle)
Brushes	F5 (toggle)
Color	F6 (toggle)
Gradient	Ctrl (⌘)+F9 (toggle)

continued

TABLE A-8 *(continued)*

Command	Shortcut
Styles	Shift+F5 (toggle)
Info	F8 (toggle)
Layers	F7 (toggle)
Pathfinder	Ctrl (⌘)+Shift+F9 (toggle)
Stroke	Ctrl (⌘)+F10 (toggle)
Symbols	Ctrl (⌘)+Shift+F11 (toggle)
Transform	Shift+F8 (toggle)
Transparency	Ctrl (⌘)+Shift+F10 (toggle)
Type ➪ Character	Ctrl (⌘)+T (toggle)
Type ➪ OpenType	Ctrl (⌘)+Shift+Alt (Option)+T
Type ➪ Paragraph	Ctrl (⌘)+Alt (Option)+T
Type ➪ Tabs	Ctrl (⌘)+Shift+T

TABLE A-9

The Help Menu

Command	Shortcut
Illustrator Help	F1 (Windows)
	Help key or Cmd+? (Mac)

Toolbox Commands

TABLE A-10

Tool Selection

Function	Shortcut
Select the next popup tool	Drag to the right and then release on the desired tool
	Alt (Option)+click on a tool
Open a tool's dialog box	Double-click on the tool
Hide the Tools panel and other panels	Tab
Hide the panels (except the Tools panel)	Shift+Tab

TABLE A-11

Selection Tools

Tool	Shortcut
Selection tool	V
	Ctrl+Tab with the Direct Selection tool and then hold Ctrl (⌘)
	Ctrl (⌘) with all other tools if the Selection tool was the last tool used
Direct Selection tool	A
	Ctrl+Tab with the Selection tool and then hold Ctrl (⌘)+Alt (Option) with the Group Selection tool
	Ctrl (⌘) with all other tools if the Direct Selection tool was the last tool used
Group Selection tool	Alt (Option) with the Direct Selection tool
	Ctrl (⌘)+Alt (Option) with all other tools if the Direct Selection tool was the last tool used
Magic Wand tool	Y
Direct Select Lasso tool	Q

Function	Procedure
Select one point	Click with the Direct Selection tool
Select one segment	Click with the Direct Selection tool
Select one path	Click with the Group Selection tool
Select the next group up	Click the selected path again with the Group Selection tool
Select the top-level group	Click with the Selection tool
Select additional points/paths/objects	Shift+click additional points/paths/objects
Select specific points	Drag with the Direct Selection tool
Select specific paths	Drag with the Selection tool
Deselect selected points/paths/objects	Shift+click selected points/paths/objects
Move a selection	Drag
Duplicate a selection	Alt (Option)+drag
Constrain to a 45-degree movement	Shift+drag
Duplicate and constrain	Alt (Option)+Shift+drag
Proportionately resize an object	Shift+drag bounding box handle
Resize from the center	Alt (Option)+drag bounding box handle
Resize proportionately from the center	Alt (Option)+Shift+drag bounding box handle
Select all	Ctrl (⌘)+A
Deselect all	Ctrl (⌘)+Shift+A

continued

TABLE A-11 *(continued)*

Tool	Shortcut
Select all objects with a similar fill, stroke, opacity, and/or blending mode	Click with the Magic Wand tool
Add similar colored and stroked objects to the current selection	Shift+Magic Wand tool
Subtract similar colored and stroked objects from the current selection	Alt (Option)+Magic Wand tool
Set the Magic Wand options	Double-click on the Magic Wand tool to open the Magic Wand panel

TABLE A-12

Path Tools

Tool	Shortcut
Pen tool	P
Add Anchor Point tool	=
	Alt (Option)+Delete Anchor Point tool
	Alt (Option)+Scissors tool
Delete Anchor Point tool	–
	Alt (Option)+Add Anchor Point tool
Convert Anchor Point tool	Shift+C
	Alt (Option)+Pen tool
Pencil tool	N
Smooth tool	Alt (Option)+Pencil tool
	Alt (Option)+Erase tool
	Alt (Option)+Paintbrush tool
Paintbrush tool	B
Scissors tool	C
Function	Procedure
Create a straight corner point	Click with the Pen tool
Create a smooth point	Drag with the Pen tool
Continue an existing open path	Click+drag with the Pen tool on an endpoint of an existing path
Close an open path	While drawing, click+drag with the Pen tool on the initial endpoint
	Click+drag with the Pen tool on each endpoint in succession
	Select the path and then join it (Ctrl (⌘)+J)

Tool	Shortcut
Constrain a new point to 45 degrees from the last point	Shift+drag with the Pen tool
Constrain control handles to 45 degrees	Shift while dragging a handle with the Pen tool
Create a path	Click+drag a succession of points with the Pen tool
Add anchor points to an existing path	Click with the Pen tool on a path
Delete anchor points from an existing path	Shift+click with the Pen tool on an anchor point
Convert an anchor point to a smooth point	Drag with the Convert Direction Point tool on an existing point
Convert a smooth point to a corner point	Click with the Convert Direction Point tool on a smooth point
Convert a smooth corner to a combination corner	Drag one handle with the Direct Selection tool back into the anchor point
Convert a smooth corner to a curved corner	Drag one handle with the Convert Direction Point tool
Draw freestyle paths	Drag with the Pencil tool
View the Paintbrush options	Double-click the Paintbrush tool in the Tools panel
Reshape a path	Select the points with the Direct Selection tool and then drag with the Reshape tool
Split a path	Click with the Scissors tool
Slice multiple paths	Drag with the Knife tool
Constrain a Knife slice to straight lines	Option (Alt)+drag with the Knife tool
Constrain a Knife slice to 45 degrees	Shift+Option (Alt)+drag with the Knife tool

TABLE A-13

Type Tools

Tool	Shortcut
Type tool	T
	Shift+Vertical Type tool
Area Type tool	Alt (Option)+Path Type tool
	Shift+Vertical Area Type tool
	Alt (Option)+Shift Vertical Path Type tool
Path Type tool	Alt (Option)+Area Type tool
	Shift+Vertical Path Type tool
	Alt (Option)+Shift+Vertical Area Type tool

continued

TABLE A-13 *(continued)*

Tool	Shortcut
Vertical Type tool	Shift+Type tool
Vertical Area Type tool	Alt (Option)+Vertical Path Type tool
	Shift+Area Type tool
	Alt (Option)+Shift+Area Type tool
Vertical Path Type tool	Alt (Option)+Vertical Area Type tool
	Shift+Path Type tool
	Alt (Option)+Shift+Area Type tool
Function	Procedure
Create individual type	Click with the Type tool
Create a type container	Drag with the Type tool
Place path type on a closed path	Click the path with the Path Type tool
	Alt (Option)+click the path with the Type tool
	Alt (Option)+click the path with the Area Type tool
Place path type on an open path	Click the path with the Path Type tool
	Click the path with the Type tool
	Alt (Option)+click the path with the Area Type tool
Place area type on a closed path	Click the path with the Area Type tool
	Click the path with the Type tool
	Option (Alt)+click the path with the Path Type tool
Place area type on an open path	Click the path with the Area Type tool
	Alt (Option)+click the path with the Type tool
	Alt (Option)+click the path with the Path Type tool
Change vertical type to horizontal type	Choose Type ➪ Type Orientation ➪ Horizontal
Change horizontal type to vertical type	Choose Type ➪ Type Orientation ➪ Vertical
Select an entire text block	Highlight the text block with the Selection tool
Select one character	Drag across a character with any Type tool
Select one word	Double-click a word with any Type tool
Select one paragraph	Triple-click a paragraph with any Type tool
Select all text in a text block	Click in text block with any Type tool and then press Ctrl (⌘)+A
Flip type on a path	Double-click the I-bar with any selection tool or just drag it to the opposite side

TABLE A-14

Line Tools

Tool	Shortcut
Line Segment tool	\
Function	Procedure
Create line segments using numbers	Click with the Line Segment tool
Draw a line segment	Drag with the Line Segment tool
Constrain line segments to 45 degrees	Shift+drag with the Line Segment tool
Create a line segment from the center using numbers	Alt (Option)+click with the Line Segment tool
Draw a line segment from the center	Alt (Option)+drag with the Line Segment tool
Move a line segment while drawing	Spacebar+drag with the Line Segment tool
Create multiple line segments	~+drag with the Line Segment tool
Create arc segments using numbers	Click with the Arc tool
Draw an arc segment	Drag with the Arc tool
Constrain arc segments to circular sections	Shift+drag with the Arc tool
Create an arc segment from the center	Alt (Option)+click with the Arc tool
Draw an arc segment from the center	Alt (Option)+drag with the Arc tool
Move an arc segment while drawing	Spacebar+drag with the Arc tool
Create multiple arc segments	~+drag with the Arc tool
Toggle an arc between concave and convex	X+drag with the Arc tool
Toggle between open and closed arcs	C+drag with the Arc tool
Flip an arc	F+drag with the Arc tool
Increase an arc's slope	↑+drag with the Arc tool
Decrease an arc's slope	↓+drag with the Arc tool
Create a spiral using numbers	Click with the Spiral tool
Draw a spiral	Drag with the Spiral tool
Constrain a spiral's angle	Shift+drag with the Spiral tool
Move a spiral while drawing	Spacebar+drag with the Spiral tool
Create multiple spirals	~+drag with the Spiral tool
Decrease a spiral decay	Ctrl (⌘)+drag with the Spiral tool
Increase a spiral's length and size	Alt (Option)+drag with the Spiral tool (toggle)
Increase a spiral's length	↑+drag with the Spiral tool

continued

TABLE A-14 *(continued)*

Tool	Shortcut
Decrease a spiral's length	↓+drag with the Spiral tool
Create a rectangular grid using numbers	Click with the Rectangular Grid tool
Draw a rectangular grid	Drag with the Rectangular Grid tool
Constrain a rectangular grid to a square	Shift+drag with the Rectangular Grid tool
Create a square rectangular grid	Alt (Option)+click with the Rectangular Grid tool
Draw a rectangular grid from the center	Alt (Option)+drag with the Rectangular Grid tool
Move a rectangular grid while drawing	Spacebar+drag with the Rectangular Grid tool
Create a multiple rectangular grid	~+drag with the Rectangular Grid tool
Skew horizontal dividers to the left	X+drag with the Rectangular Grid tool
Skew horizontal dividers to the right	C+drag with the Rectangular Grid tool
Skew vertical dividers to the top of the rectangular grid	F+drag with the Rectangular Grid tool
Skew vertical dividers to the bottom of the rectangular grid	V+drag with the Rectangular Grid tool
Increase vertical dividers	↑+drag with the Rectangular Grid tool
Decrease vertical dividers	↓+drag with the Rectangular Grid tool
Increase horizontal dividers	→+drag with the Rectangular Grid tool
Decrease horizontal dividers	←+drag with the Rectangular Grid tool
Create a polar grid using numbers	Click with the Polar Grid tool
Draw a polar grid	Drag with the Polar Grid tool
Constrain a polar grid to a circle	Shift+drag with the Polar Grid tool
Create a circular polar grid	Alt (Option)+click with the Polar Grid tool
Draw a polar grid from the center	Alt (Option)+drag with the Polar Grid tool
Move a polar grid while drawing	Spacebar+drag with the Polar Grid tool
Create a multiple polar grid	~+drag with the Polar Grid tool
Skew concentric dividers inward	X+drag with the Polar Grid tool
Skew concentric dividers outward	C+drag with the Polar Grid tool
Skew radial dividers counterclockwise	F+drag with the Polar Grid tool
Skew radial dividers clockwise	V+drag with the Polar Grid tool
Increase concentric dividers	↑+drag with the Polar Grid tool
Decrease concentric dividers	↓+drag with the Polar Grid tool
Increase radial dividers	→+drag with the Polar Grid tool
Decrease radial dividers	←+drag with the Polar Grid tool

TABLE A-15

Shape Tools

Tool	Shortcut
Rectangle tool	M
Ellipse tool	L
Function	Procedure
Create a rectangle using numbers	Click with the Rectangle tool or the Rounded Rectangle tool
Draw a rectangle	Drag with the Rectangle tool
Draw a square	Shift+drag with the Rectangle tool
Create a centered rectangle using numbers	Alt (Option)+click with the Rectangle tool
Draw a centered rectangle	Alt (Option)+drag with the Rectangle tool
Draw a square from the center	Alt (Option)+Shift+drag with the Rectangle tool
Move a rectangle while drawing	Spacebar+drag with the Rectangle tool
Create multiple rectangles	~+drag with the Rectangle tool
Create a rounded rectangle using numbers	Click with the Rounded Rectangle tool
Draw a rounded rectangle	Drag with the Rounded Rectangle tool
Draw a square with rounded corners	Shift+drag with the Rounded Rectangle tool
Create a centered rounded rectangle	Alt (Option)+click with the Rounded Rectangle tool
Draw a centered rounded rectangle	Alt (Option)+drag with the Rounded Rectangle tool
Draw a square with rounded corners from the center	Alt (Option)+Shift+drag with the Rounded Rectangle tool
Move a rounded rectangle while drawing	Spacebar+drag with the Rounded Rectangle tool
Create multiple rounded rectangles	~+drag with the Rounded Rectangle tool
Create an ellipse using numbers	Click with the Ellipse tool
Draw an ellipse	Drag with the Ellipse tool
Draw a circle	Shift+drag with the Ellipse tool
Create a centered ellipse using numbers	Alt (Option)+click with the Ellipse tool
Draw a centered ellipse	Alt (Option)+drag with the Ellipse tool
Move an ellipse while drawing	Spacebar+drag with the Ellipse tool
Create multiple ellipses	~+drag with the Ellipse tool
Create a polygon using numbers	Click with the Polygon tool
Draw a polygon	Drag with the Polygon tool
Constrain a polygon's angle	Shift+drag with the Polygon tool
Create a centered polygon using numbers	Alt (Option)+click with the Polygon tool

continued

TABLE A-15 *(continued)*

Tool	Shortcut
Draw a centered polygon	Alt (Option)+drag with the Polygon tool
Increase a polygon's sides	↑+drag with the Polygon tool
Decrease a polygon's sides	↓+drag with the Polygon tool
Move a polygon while drawing	Spacebar+drag with the Polygon tool
Create multiple polygons	~+drag with the Polygon tool
Create a star using numbers	Click with the Star tool
Draw a star	Drag with the Star tool
Constrain a star's angle	Shift+drag with the Star tool
Draw an even-shouldered star	Alt (Option)+drag with the Star tool
Move outer points only	Ctrl (⌘)+drag with the Star tool
Increase a star's points	↑+drag with the Star tool
Decrease a star's points	↓+drag with the Star tool
Move a star while drawing	Spacebar+drag with the Star tool
Create multiple stars	~+drag with the Star tool

TABLE A-16

Transformation Tools

Tool	Shortcut
Rotate tool	R
Reflect tool	O
Scale tool	S
Free Transform tool	E

Function	Procedure
Moving objects	Drag with the Selection or Free Transform tool
Constrain movements along a 45-degree axis	Shift+drag with the Selection or Free Transform tool
Rotate using numbers	Alt (Option)+click with the Rotate tool
Rotate from the center of a selection with numbers	Double-click with the Rotate tool
Free rotate (live)	Click with the Rotate tool to set the origin and then drag with the Rotate tool
Free rotate around a selection's center	Drag with the Rotate tool
Constrain a rotation to 45 degrees	Shift+drag with the Rotate tool

Function	Procedure
Rotate a copy	Alt (Option)+drag with the Rotate tool
Rotate a pattern only	~+drag with the Rotate tool
Scale using numbers	Alt (Option)+click with the Scale tool
Scale from the center of a selection with numbers	Double-click with the Scale tool
Free scale (live)	Click with the Scale tool to set the origin and then drag with the Scale tool
Free scale around a selection's center	Drag with the Scale tool
Constrain scaling to 45 degrees	Shift+drag with the Scale tool
Scale a copy	Alt (Option)+drag with the Scale tool
Scale a pattern only	~+drag with the Scale tool
Reflect using numbers	Alt (Option)+click with the Reflect tool
Reflect from the center of a selection with numbers	Double-click with the Reflect tool
Free reflect (live)	Click with the Reflect tool to set the origin and then drag with the Reflect tool
Free reflect around a selection's center	Drag with the Reflect tool
Constrain a reflecting angle to 45 degrees	Shift+drag with the Reflect tool
Reflect a copy	Alt (Option)+drag with the Reflect tool
Reflect a pattern only	~+drag with the Reflect tool
Shear using numbers	Alt (Option)+click with the Shear tool
Shear from the center of a selection with numbers	Double-click with the Shear tool
Free shear (live)	Click with the Shear tool to set the origin and then drag with the Shear tool
Free shear around a selection's center	Drag with the Shear tool
Constrain a shearing to 45 degrees	Shift+drag with the Shear tool
Shear a copy	Alt (Option)+drag with the Shear tool
Shear a pattern only	~+drag with the Shear tool

TABLE A-17

Distortion Tools

Tool	Shortcut
Warp tool	Shift+R
Function	Procedure
Twirl using numbers	Alt (Option)+click with the Rotate tool

continued

TABLE A-17	*(continued)*
Tool	**Shortcut**
Free twirl (live)	Drag with the Twirl tool
Reshape a distortion brush	Alt (Option)+drag with the Warp, Twirl, Pucker, Bloat, Scallop, Crystallize, or Wrinkle tool
Constrain a brush to horizontal or vertical movements	Shift+drag with the Warp, Twirl, Pucker, Bloat, Scallop, Crystallize, or Wrinkle tool
Set the distortion options	Double-click on the selected distortion tool

TABLE A-18

Symbol Tools

Tool	**Shortcut**
Symbol Sprayer tool	Shift+S
Function	Procedure
Add a single symbol	Click+Symbol Sprayer tool
Add multiple symbols	Drag+Symbol Sprayer tool
Remove symbols from set	Alt (Option)+Symbol Sprayer tool
Move symbols in a set	Drag with the Symbol Shifter tool
Change the stacking order of the symbols	Alt (Option)+Symbol Shifter tool
Scrunch the symbols closer together	Drag with the Symbol Scruncher tool
Move the symbols farther apart	Alt (Option)+Symbol Scruncher tool
Increase a symbol's size	Drag with the Symbol Sizer tool
Decrease a symbol's size	Alt (Option)+Symbol Sizer tool
Rotate the symbols	Drag with the Symbol Spinner tool
Increase a symbol's transparency	Drag with the Symbol Screener tool
Decrease a symbol's transparency	Alt (Option)+Symbol Screener tool
Change a symbol's color	Drag with the Symbol Stainer tool
Restore a symbol's original color	Alt (Option)+Symbol Stainer tool
Apply a style to a symbol	Drag with the Symbol Styler tool
Remove a style from a symbol	Alt (Option)+Symbol Styler tool

TABLE A-19

Graph Tools

Tool	Shortcut
Column Graph tool	J
Function	Procedure
Create a graph sized by numbers	Click with any Graph tool
Create a graph sized by dragging	Drag with any Graph tool
Create a square or circular graph	Shift+drag with any Graph tool
Create a graph from the center	Alt (Option)+drag with any Graph tool

TABLE A-20

Paint Tools

Tool	Shortcut
Gradient tool	G
Gradient Mesh tool	U
Live Paint Bucket tool	K
	Option (Alt)+Eyedropper tool
Eyedropper tool	I
	Alt (Option)+Paint Bucket tool
Function	Procedure
Change the linear gradient direction and/or length	Drag with the Gradient tool
Constrain the gradient direction to a 45-degree angle	Shift+drag with the Gradient tool
Change the radial gradient size and/or location	Drag with the Gradient tool
Change the radial gradient's origin point	Click with the Gradient tool
Add the sample color to the Color panel	Click with the Eyedropper tool
Add the sample screen color to the Color panel	Shift+click with the Eyedropper tool
Change the paint style of selected objects	Double-click with the Eyedropper tool on an object with the desired style
Measure a distance	Click the start and end locations with the Measure tool
Measure a distance by 45-degree angles	Shift+click the start and end locations with the Measure tool

TABLE A-21

Blend, Auto Trace, Artboard, and Slice Tools

Tool	Shortcut
Blend tool	W
Slice tool	Shift+K
Artboard tool	Shift+O

Function	Procedure
Blend two paths	Click corresponding selected points on each path with the Blend tool
Set the blend options	Double-click on the Blend tool
Auto-trace images	Click area to be traced with the Auto Trace tool
Divide artwork into slices	Drag+Slice tool
Constrain a slice to a square	Alt (Option)+drag with the Slice tool
Slice selected objects	Drag+Slice Selected tool

TABLE A-22

Viewing Tools

Tool	Shortcut
Hand tool	H
	Spacebar (when not typing text)
Zoom tool	Z
	Ctrl (⌘)+spacebar
Zoom Out tool	Ctrl (⌘)+Option (Alt)+spacebar
	Alt (Option)+Zoom tool

Function	Procedure
Reposition the page	Drag with the Hand tool
Fit the page within the document window	Double-click on the Hand tool
Moving page boundaries	Drag with the Page tool
Reset page boundaries	Double-click on the Page tool
Zoom in	Click with the Zoom tool
	Ctrl (⌘)++ (plus sign)
Zoom out	Alt (Option)+click with the Zoom tool
	Ctrl (⌘)+- (hyphen)
Zoom in to a specific area	Drag with the Zoom tool
Move the zoom marquee while drawing	Spacebar while dragging with the Zoom tool
Draw the zoom marquee from its center	Ctrl+drag with the Zoom tool

Type Commands

Type Shortcuts

Action	Shortcut
Copy type on a path	Alt (Option)+drag the I-bar using any selection tool
Flip type on a path	Double-click the I-bar with any selection tool or just drag it to the opposite side of the path
Move the insertion point to the next character	→ (right arrow)
Move the insertion point to the previous character	← (left arrow)
Move the insertion point to the next line	↓ (down arrow)
Move the insertion point to the previous line	↑ (up arrow)
Move the insertion point to the next word	Ctrl (⌘)+→
Move the insertion point to the previous word	Ctrl (⌘)+←
Move the insertion point to the next paragraph	Ctrl (⌘)+↓
Move the insertion point to the previous paragraph	Ctrl (⌘)+↑
Select (by highlighting) all type in a story	Ctrl (⌘)+A when the insertion point is in the story
Select all type in a document	Ctrl (⌘)+A when any tool but the Type tool is selected
Select the next character	Shift+→
Select the previous character	Shift+←
Select the next line	Shift+↓
Select the previous line	Shift+↑
Select the next word	Ctrl (⌘)+Shift+→
Select the previous word	Ctrl (⌘)+Shift+←
Select the next paragraph	Ctrl (⌘)+Shift+↓
Select the previous paragraph	Ctrl (⌘)+Shift+↑
Select the word	Double-click the word
Select the paragraph	Triple-click the paragraph
Deselect all type	Ctrl (⌘)+Shift+A

continued

TABLE A-23   *(continued)*

Action	Shortcut
Duplicate the column outline and flow text	Alt (Option)+drag the column outline with the Direct Selection tool
Insert a discretionary hyphen (one that only appears if the word has to break)	Ctrl (⌘)+Shift+- (hyphen)
Insert a line break	Press Enter (Return)

TABLE A-24

Paragraph Formatting

Action	Shortcut
Display the Paragraph panel	Ctrl (⌘)+Shift+M
Align a paragraph flush left	Ctrl (⌘)+Shift+L
Align a paragraph flush right	Ctrl (⌘)+Shift+R
Align a paragraph flush center	Ctrl (⌘)+Shift+C
Align a paragraph justified	Ctrl (⌘)+Shift+J
Align a paragraph force justified	Ctrl (⌘)+Shift+F
Display the Tab Ruler panel	Ctrl (⌘)+Shift+T
Align the Tab panel to a selected paragraph	Click the Tab panel size box
Cycle through tab stops	Alt (Option)+click tab stop
Move multiple tab stops	Shift+drag tab stops

TABLE A-25

Character Formatting

Action	Shortcut
Display the Character panel	Ctrl (⌘)+T
Highlight a font	Crtrl (⌘)+Alt (Option)+Shift+M
Increase the type size	Ctrl (⌘)+Shift+>
Decrease the type size	Ctrl (⌘)+Shift+<
Increase the type to the next size on the menu	Ctrl (⌘)+Alt (Option)+>
Decrease the type to the next size on the menu	Ctrl (⌘)+Alt (Option)+<
Set the leading to solid (same as point size)	Double-click the Leading symbol in the Character panel

Action	Shortcut
Increase the baseline shift (raise)*	Alt (Option)+Shift+↑
Decrease the baseline shift (lower)*	Alt (Option)+Shift+↓
Increase the baseline shift (raise) × 5*	Ctrl (⌘)+Alt (Option)+Shift+↑
Decrease the baseline shift (lower) × 5*	Ctrl (⌘)+Alt (Option)+Shift+↓
Kern/track closer*	Alt (Option)+←
Kern/track apart*	Alt (Option)+→
Kern/track closer × 5*	Ctrl (⌘)+Alt (Option)+←
Kern/track apart × 5*	Ctrl (⌘)+Alt (Option)+→
Reset the kerning/tracking to 0	Ctrl (⌘)+Shift+Q
Highlight the kerning/tracking	Ctrl (⌘)+Alt (Option)+K
Reset the horizontal scale to 100%	Ctrl (⌘)+Shift+X

* Set this value/amount in Preferences.

Color Commands

Color Panel

Action	Shortcut
Show/hide the Color panel	F6 (toggle)
	Ctrl (⌘)+I (toggle)
Revert to default colors	D (White fill; Black stroke)
Toggle the focus between the fill and the stroke	X
Choose the current color in the Color panel	, (comma)
Change the paint style to None	/
Apply to inactive fill/stroke (fill when stroke is active; stroke when fill is active)	Alt (Option)+click in the color ramp on the Color panel
Apply a color to an unselected object	Drag the color swatch from the Color panel to the object
Apply a color to a selected object	Click the swatch in the Color panel
Copy the paint style to unselected objects	Click unselected objects with the Paint Bucket tool
Copy the paint style from any (source) object to all selected objects	Click the source object with the Eyedropper tool
Tint a process color	Shift+drag any Color panel slider
Cycle through the color modes	Shift+click the color ramp (Grayscale, CMYK, RGB)

TABLE A-27

Swatches Panel

Action	Shortcut
Show/hide the Swatches panel	None
Toggle focus between the fill and the stroke	X
Add a swatch	Click the New Swatch icon
	Drag the swatch from the Color or Gradient panel into the Swatches panel
Replace a swatch	Alt (Option)+drag the swatch from the Color or Gradient panel into the Swatches panel
Duplicate a swatch	Alt (Option)+drag the swatch onto the New Swatch icon in the Swatches panel
Delete a swatch	Drag the swatch to the trash icon in the Swatches panel
	Click the trash icon with the swatches selected
Select contiguous swatches	Shift+click the first and last swatches
Select noncontiguous swatches	Ctrl (⌘)+click each swatch
Switch the keyboard focus to the Swatches panel (for selecting swatches by name as they are typed)	Ctrl (⌘)+Alt (Option)+click in the Swatches panel
Apply a color to an unselected object	Drag the color swatch from the Swatches panel to the object
Apply a color to a selected object	Click the swatch in the Swatches panel

TABLE A-28

Gradient Panel

Action	Shortcut
Choose the current gradient in the Gradient panel	. (period)
Show/hide the Gradient panel	Ctrl (⌘)+F9 (toggle)
Apply a swatch to the selected color stop (triangle) in the Gradient panel	Alt (Option)+click the swatch
Add a new color stop	Click below the gradient ramp
Duplicate a color stop	Alt (Option)+drag the color stop
Swap color stops	Option (Alt)+drag the color stop on top of another color stop
Suck color for a color stop with the Eyedropper tool	Shift+click with the Eyedropper tool
Reset a gradient to the default color	Ctrl (⌘)+click in the Gradient swatch

Action	Shortcut
Apply a color to an unselected object	Drag a color swatch from the Gradient panel to the object
Apply a color to a selected object	Click the swatch in the Gradient panel

TABLE A-29

Stroke Panel

Action	Shortcut
Show/hide the Stroke panel	Ctrl (⌘)+F10 (toggle)
Increase/decrease a stroke's weight	Highlight the Stroke field, use the up or down arrows, and then press Enter (Return) when finished
Increase/decrease the miter amount	Highlight the Miter field, use the up or down arrows, and then press Enter (Return) when finished

Other Panels

TABLE A-30

Miscellaneous Panel Commands

Action	Shortcut
Collapse/display a panel	Click the box in the upper-right corner
Cycle through panel views	Double-click the panel tab
Apply the settings	Enter (Return)
Apply the settings while keeping the last text field highlighted	Shift+ Enter (Return)
Highlight the next text field	Tab
Highlight the previous text field	Shift+Tab
Highlight any text field	Click the label or double-click the current value
Increase a value by the base increment	Highlight field, ↑
Decrease a value by the base increment	Highlight field, ↓
Increase a value by a large increment	Highlight field, Shift+↑
Decrease a value by a large increment	Highlight field, Shift+↓
Combine panels	Drag the panel tab within another panel
Dock a panel	Drag the panel tab to the bottom of another panel
Separate a panel	Drag the panel tab from the current panel

TABLE A-31

Transform Panel

Action	Shortcut
Show/hide the Transform panel	Shift+F8
Copy an object while transforming	Alt (Option)+Enter (Return)
Scale proportionately	Ctrl (⌘)+Enter (Return)
Copy an object while scaling proportionately	Ctrl (⌘)+Alt (Option)+Enter (Return)

TABLE A-32

Layers Panel

Action	Shortcut
Show/hide the Layers panel	F7
Add a new layer	Click the New Layer icon
Add a new layer with the Options dialog box	Alt (Option)+click the New Layer icon
Add a new layer above the active layer	Ctrl (⌘)+Alt (Option)+click the New Layer icon
Add a new layer below the active layer	Ctrl (⌘)+click the New Layer icon
Duplicate layer(s)	Drag layer(s) to the New Layer icon
Change the layer order	Drag layers up or down within the Layer list
Select all objects on a layer	Alt (Option)+click that layer
Select all objects on several layers	Shift+Alt (Option)+click each layer
Select contiguous layers	Shift+click the layers
Select noncontiguous layers	Ctrl (⌘)+click the layers
Move objects to a different layer	Drag the colored square to a different layer
Copy objects to a different layer	Alt (Option)+drag the color square to a different layer
Hide/show a layer	Click the Eyeball icon
View a layer while hiding others	Alt (Option)+click the Eyeball icon
View a layer in Outline mode	Ctrl (⌘)+click the Eyeball icon
View a layer in Preview mode while others are Outline mode	Ctrl (⌘)+Alt (Option)+click the Eyeball icon
Lock/unlock a layer	Click the Pencil icon
Unlock a layer while locking others	Alt (Option)+click the Pencil icon
Delete a layer	Drag the layer to the trash icon
	Select the layer and then click the trash icon
Delete a layer without warning	Alt (Option)+drag the layer to the trash icon
	Select the layer and then Alt (Option)+click the trash icon

Miscellaneous Commands

Viewing Shortcuts

Action	Shortcut
Fit a document in the window	Ctrl (⌘)+0
	Double-click Hand tool
Outline/Preview mode	Ctrl (⌘)+Y (toggle)
Show/hide edges	Ctrl (⌘)+H (toggle)
Show/hide guides	Ctrl (⌘)+;
Show/hide a grid	Ctrl (⌘)+"
Show/hide rulers	Ctrl (⌘)+R
Hide selected objects	Ctrl (⌘)+3
Show all hidden objects	Ctrl (⌘)+Alt (Option)+3
Window mode (normal)	F (when in Full Screen mode)
Full Screen mode with menu	F (when in Window mode)
Full Screen mode (no menus)	F (when in Full Screen mode with menus)

Miscellaneous Commands

Action	Shortcut
Nudge selection*	Arrow keys
See the special Status Line categories	Click the status bar (lower-left corner)
Display the context-sensitive menus	Ctrl+click (right-click)
Highlight the last active text field	Ctrl (⌘)+~ (tilde)

* Set this value/amount in Preferences.

Generic Dialog Box Commands

TABLE A-35

Generic Dialog Box Commands

Action	Shortcut
Cancel	Esc
OK (or dark-bordered button)	Enter (Return)
Highlight the next text field	Tab
Highlight the previous text field	Shift+Tab
Highlight any text field	Click the label or double-click the current value

Index

H

N